Come with us to the French-speaking world!

Allez, viens!

—a fully integrated French program—makes it possible for you to accomplish all your teaching objectives as never before! *Allez, viens!* ensures development of language proficiency in French and builds students' language skills, so they can communicate effectively and express themselves with confidence.

- The FOUR LANGUAGE SKILLS—listening, speaking, reading, and writing—plus CULTURE, are all interwoven throughout the program.

- Strong GRAMMAR support lays an invaluable foundation for proficiency.

- All three levels of *Allez, viens!* are PACED so that you can finish each text within the year. And because the first two chapters of the Levels 2 and 3 *Pupil's Editions* are review, the program provides an easy transition from level to level.

- Designed for LEARNERS OF ALL TYPES, *Allez, viens!* is the program of choice for every one of your students.

- VIDEO CORRELATIONS and ON-PAGE BARCODES let you easily integrate video and videodisc segments into your instruction.

- A COMPLETE AUDIO PROGRAM—available on audiocassettes or compact discs—reinforces the text material and gives students another learning option.

- Constant SPIRALING and RE-ENTRY of material from earlier chapters provide consistent reinforcement and review.

See and hear native speakers in authentic locations around the francophone world!

Allez, viens
à Québec

Québec

Where Will We Go?

Each Location Opener introduces your students to the diversity of French-speaking countries. The *Video Program*, *Expanded Video Program*, and *Videodisc Program* target the same locations so your students see, hear, understand—and use— the language and culture.

How Will We Get There?

Chapter Openers serve as advance organizers, identifying learner outcomes and stimulating interest.

CHAPITRE **5**

On va au café?

① On va au café?

124 cent vingt-quatre

Where are your favorite places to meet and relax with your friends? In France, people of all ages meet at cafés to talk, have a snack, or just watch the people go by!

In this chapter you will learn
- to make suggestions; to make excuses; to make a recommendation
- to get someone's attention; to order food and beverages
- to inquire about and express likes and dislikes; to pay the check

And you will
- listen to people ordering in a café
- read a café menu
- write about your food and drink preferences
- find out about French cafés

② L'addition, s'il vous plaît.

cent vingt-**cinq** 125

Mise en train

Un petit service

Do you ever run errands for your family? What kinds of things do you have to do? Look at the pictures below and see if you can figure out what Lucien's mother, father, and sister are asking him to do.

Lucien   Lisette   La mère

Le père   Une voisine

CHAPITRE 12   En ville

MISE EN TRAIN

Authentic Locations & Language

Mise en train features introduce the functions, vocabulary, and grammar targeted in the chapter and are reproduced in both the video and audio programs.

Your Building Blocks to Proficiency

The function, grammar, and vocabulary features in each chapter of *Allez, viens!* are linked to give your students the building blocks they need to develop complete language proficiency.

The *Grammaire* presentation provides strong grammar support for the function-driven base of *Allez, viens!*, the perfect combination to help your students develop their French proficiency.

The *Vocabulaire* found in each chapter relates to the theme and language function, and is presented visually whenever possible.

In this function-driven program, each *Comment dit-on?* presentation equips your students for specific language tasks appropriate to the chapter theme.

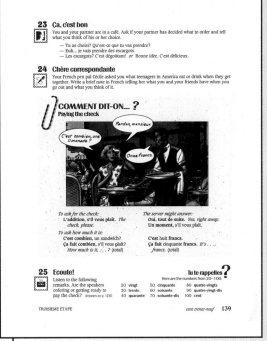

An Abundance of Activities

Throughout *Allez, viens!*, activities flow from controlled and structured through transitional to open-ended, communicative activities. Plenty of activities are contained within the program to build competency in each of the four language skills. Types of activities included in each chapter are:

- Contextualized listening activities
- Pair and group work
- Journal writing activities (can be used as portfolio assessment activities)
- Reading, writing, and role-playing activities
- Discovery questions and discussions of culture topics

Critical Thinking Through Multicultural Awareness

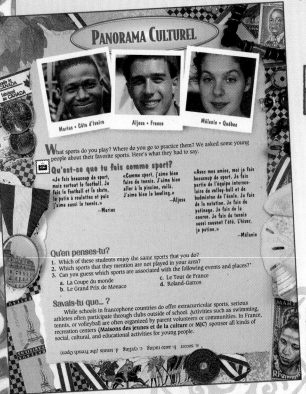

The *Panorama Culturel* is designed to give your students a chance to meet people from around the French-speaking world who share their views, opinions, and thoughts on a variety of topics that are thematically related to the chapters in *Allez, viens!*. Filmed on location, authentic interviews with native speakers can be found in the text, on the *Video Program*, the *Expanded Video Program*, the *Audio Program*, and the *Videodisc Program*. The result: total video, audio, and text integration for complete language development. The *Panorama Culturel* also contains critical-thinking activities that expand upon what students learn from the interviews.

An Encounter of Cultures

Do you ever wonder how you can make your students "walk in someone else's shoes?" With *Allez, viens!*'s *Rencontre Culturelle*, you can do just that! This unique presentation introduces your students to customs in French-speaking cultures that may be unfamiliar to them, but are a way of life in those cultures. They'll also learn what people in the target cultures may find unfamiliar about Americans, and follow up what they've learned with critical-thinking questions. This expands your students' horizons beyond their own backyard. They'll realize that diverse viewpoints and different ways of doing similar things enrich our global community.

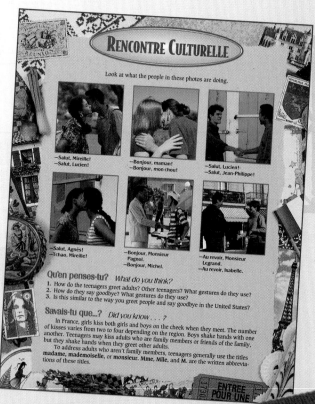

Allez, viens!

Holt French

Level 1

ANNOTATED
TEACHER'S EDITION

HOLT, RINEHART AND WINSTON

Harcourt Brace & Company

Austin • New York • Orlando • Atlanta • San Francisco • Boston • Dallas • Toronto • London

In the *Annotated Teacher's Edition:*

Photography Credits
Abbreviations used: (t) top, (c) center, (b) bottom, (l) left, (r) right.
Front Matter: Page T26(b), HRW Photo/Marty Granger/Edge Productions; T30(br), HRW Photo/Marty Granger/Edge Productions; T37(b), HRW Photo/Marty Granger/Edge Productions; T43(bl), HRW Photo/Lance Shriner; T43(br), HRW Photo/Helen Kolda. **Preliminary Chapter:** Page T58(bc), Reuters/Bettmann; T58(br) J. M. Jimenez/Shooting Star; T58(bl), Gastaud/Sipa Press. **Chapter Three:** Page 65D (all), HRW Photo/Sam Dudgeon. **Chapter Four:** Page 93D(t), HRW Photo/Marty Granger/Edge Productions; 93D(b), Bill Bachmann/PhotoEdit. **Chapter Five:** Page 123F (both), HRW Photo/Marty Granger/Edge Productions. **Chapter Six:** Page 147D(l), Robert Fried/Stock Boston; 147D(r) Jean Paul, Nacivet/Leo de Wys; 147D(cl), HRW Photo/Marty Granger/Edge Productions; 147D(cr), Tabuteau/The Image Works. **Chapter Eight:** Page 201C (both), HRW Photo; 201E, HRW Photo; 201F (bl) HRW Photo/Eric Beggs; 201F(br), HRW Photo/Sam Dudgeon. **Chapter Ten:** Page 255E(br), HRW Photo/Sam Dudgeon. **Chapter Twelve:** Page 309F(tl), (bc), HRW Photo; 309 (all remaining), HRW Photo/Sam Dudgeon.

Illustration Credits
Front Matter: Page T45(b), Pascal Garnier. **Preliminary Chapter:** T58 (all), Bruce Roberts; T61(br), Guy Maestracci. **Chapter One:** Page 15E (all), Yves Larvor; 15F(b), Joycelyn Bouchard. **Chapter Two:** Page 41F(bl), Janet Brooks; 41F(rt, rc, rb), Pascal Garnier. **Chapter Three:** Page 65E(b), Michel Loppé; 65F(b), Michel Loppé. **Chapter Four:** Page 93F(br), Janet Brooks. **Chapter Five:** Page 123D(b), Andrew Bylo; 123F (all), Leslie Kell. **Chapter Six:** Page 147F (all), Guy Maestracci. **Chapter Seven:** Page 173D (all), Vincent Rio; 173F(br), Guy Maestracci. **Chapter Nine:** Page 231F(b), Michel Loppé. **Chapter Ten:** Page 255F(b), Michel Loppé. **Chapter Eleven:** Page 281E(b), Michel Loppé; 281F(b), Brian Stevens. **Chapter Twelve:** Page 309C (all), Brian Stevens; 309D(b), Anne de Masson; 309E(b), Anne Stanley.

For permission to reprint copyrighted material, grateful acknowledgment is made to the following sources:
Editions Estel Blois France: front and back of postcard, "Arènes d'Arles," no. 10033 Z.
France Miniature: Illustration, photograph, and excerpt from *Le Pays France Miniature.*
Parc Astérix S. A.: Cover of *Parc Astérix,* 1992 edition.

In the *Pupil's Edition:*
Air Afrique: Adaptation of "Menu" from Air Afrique.
Air France: Front of a boarding pass, "Carte d'accès à bord."
A. Leconte, Éditeur: Cover of *Paris Monumental.*
Bayard Presse International: Title and illustrations from pages 51–53 from "Sondage : les lycéens ont-ils le moral?" from *Phosphore,* September 1989. Copyright ©1989 by Bayard Presse International.
Cacharel: Four photographs from *RENTREE TRES CLASSE A PRIX PETITS:* Nouvelles Galeries Lafayette.
Canal B: Logo for Canal B, 94 MHz (Bruz).
Casino France: Advertisement, "Nouvelle Collection Claude Saint Genest," from *Femme Actuelle,* no. 496, page 29, March 28–April 3, 1994.
Cathédrale d'images: Advertisement, "Cathédrale d'images" from *Évasion Plus.*
Château Musée de l'Empéri: Advertisement, "Château Musée de l'Empéri," from *Évasion Plus.*
Clip FM: Logo, "Clip FM, 88.7 MHz" (Chalon/Saone.) Created by Christian Bernard.
Comité Français d'Education pour la Santé, 2 rue Auguste Comte 92170 Vanves: "Les Groupes d'Aliments" from *Comment équilibrer votre alimentation.*
C'Rock Radio: Logo from C'Rock Radio, 89.5 MHz (Vienne).
Editions Estel Blois France: Front and back of postcard, "Arènes d'Arles," no. 10033 Z.

ACKNOWLEDGMENTS continued on page 374, which is an extension of the copyright page.

Annotated Teacher's Edition

Contributing Writers

Jennie Bowser Chao
Consultant
East Lansing, MI

Ms. Chao was the principal writer of the Level 1 *Annotated Teacher's Edition.*

Jayne Abrate
The University of Missouri
Rolla Campus
Rolla, MO

Dr. Abrate contributed teaching suggestions, notes, and background information for the Location Openers of the Level 1 *Annotated Teacher's Edition.*

Margaret Sellstrom
Consultant
Austin, TX

Ms. Sellstrom contributed answers to activities of the Level 1 *Annotated Teacher's Edition.*

Field Test Participants

Marie Allison
New Hanover High School
Wilmington, NC

Gabrielle Applequist
Capital High School
Boise, ID

Jana Brinton
Bingham High School
Riverton, UT

Nancy J. Cook
Sam Houston High School
Lake Charles, LA

Rachael Gray
Williams High School
Plano, TX

Priscilla Koch
Troxell Junior High School
Allentown, PA

Katherine Kohler
Nathan Hale Middle School
Norwalk, CT

Nancy Mirsky
Museum Junior High School
Yonkers, NY

Myrna S. Nie
Whetstone High School
Columbus, OH

Jacqueline Reid
Union High School
Tulsa, OK

Judith Ryser
San Marcos High School
San Marcos, TX

Erin Hahn Sass
Lincoln Southeast High School
Lincoln, NE

Linda Sherwin
Sandy Creek High School
Tyrone, GA

Norma Joplin Sivers
Arlington Heights High School
Fort Worth, TX

Lorabeth Stroup
Lovejoy High School
Lovejoy, GA

Robert Vizena
W.W. Lewis Middle School
Sulphur, LA

Gladys Wade
New Hanover High School
Wilmington, NC

Kathy White
Grimsley High School
Greensboro, NC

Reviewers

Jane Canales
Dripping Springs High School
Dripping Springs, TX

Jennifer Jones
U.S. Peace Corps volunteer
Côte d'Ivoire 1991–1993
Austin, TX

Kristin Kajer-Cline
Consultant
Kirkland, WA

Jo Anne S. Wilson
Consultant
Glen Arbor, MI

Professional Essays

Standards for Foreign Language Education
Robert LaBouve
Board of National Standards in Foreign Language Education
Austin, TX

Teaching Culture
Nancy A. Humbach
The Miami University
Oxford, OH

Dorothea Brushke
Parkway School District
Chesterfield, MO

Learning Styles and Multi-Modality Teaching
Mary B. McGehee
Louisiana State University
Baton Rouge, LA

Higher-Order Thinking Skills
Audrey L. Heining-Boynton
The University of North Carolina
Chapel Hill, NC

Using Portfolios in the Foreign Language Classroom
Jo Anne S. Wilson
J. Wilson Associates
Glen Arbor, MI

Pupil's Edition

AUTHORS

Emmanuel Rongiéras d'Usseau
Le Kremlin-Bicêtre, France

Mr. Rongiéras d'Usseau contributed to the development of the scope and sequence for the chapters, created the basic material and listening scripts, selected realia, and wrote activities.

John DeMado
Washington, CT

Mr. DeMado helped form the general philosophy of the French program and wrote activities to practice basic material, functions, grammar, and vocabulary.

CONTRIBUTING WRITERS

Jayne Abrate
The University of Missouri
Rolla Campus
Rolla, MO

Sally Adamson Taylor
Publishers Weekly
San Francisco, CA

Linda Bistodeau
Saint Mary's University
Halifax, Nova Scotia

Betty Peltier
Consultant
Batz-sur-Mer, France

REVIEWERS

Dominique Bach
Rio Linda Senior High School
Rio Linda, CA

Jeannette Caviness
Mount Tabor High School
Winston-Salem, NC

Jennie Bowser Chao
Consultant
East Lansing, MI

Pierre F. Cintas
Penn State University
Ogontz Campus
Abington, PA

Donna Clementi
Appleton West High School
Appleton, WI

Cathy Cramer
Homewood High School
Birmingham, AL

Jennifer Jones
U.S. Peace Corps volunteer
Côte d'Ivoire 1991–1993
Austin, TX

Joan H. Manley
The University of Texas at El Paso
El Paso, TX

Jill Markert
Pflugerville High School
Pflugerville, TX

Inge McCoy
Southwest Texas State University
San Marcos, TX

Gail Montgomery
Foreign Language Program
Administrator
Greenwich, CT Public Schools

Agathe Norman
Consultant
Austin, TX

Audrey O'Keefe
David Starr Jordan High School
Los Angeles, CA

Sherry Parker
Selvidge Middle School
Ballwin, MO

Sherron N. Porter
Robert E. Lee High School
Baton Rouge, LA

Marc Prévost
Austin Community College
Austin, TX

Norbert Rouquet
Consultant
La Roche-sur-Yon, France

Michèle Shockey
Gunn High School
Palo Alto, CA

Ashley Shumaker
Central High School West
Tuscaloosa, AL

Antonia Stergiades
Washington High School
Massillon, OH

Frederic L. Toner
Texas Christian University
Fort Worth, TX

Jeannine Waters
Harrisonburg High School
Harrisonburg, VA

Jo Anne S. Wilson
Consultant
Glen Arbor, MI

FIELD TEST PARTICIPANTS

Marie Allison
New Hanover High School
Wilmington, NC

Gabrielle Applequist
Capital High School
Boise, ID

Jana Brinton
Bingham High School
Riverton, UT

Nancy J. Cook
Sam Houston High School
Lake Charles, LA

Rachael Gray
Williams High School
Plano, TX

Priscilla Koch
Troxell Junior High School
Allentown, PA

Katherine Kohler
Nathan Hale Middle School
Norwalk, CT

Nancy Mirsky
Museum Junior High School
Yonkers, NY

Myrna S. Nie
Whetstone High School
Columbus, OH

Jacqueline Reid
Union High School
Tulsa, OK

Judith Ryser
San Marcos High School
San Marcos, TX

Erin Hahn Sass
Lincoln Southeast High School
Lincoln, NE

Linda Sherwin
Sandy Creek High School
Tyrone, GA

Norma Joplin Sivers
Arlington Heights High School
Fort Worth, TX

Lorabeth Stroup
Lovejoy High School
Lovejoy, GA

Robert Vizena
W.W. Lewis Middle School
Sulphur, LA

Gladys Wade
New Hanover High School
Wilmington, NC

Kathy White
Grimsley High School
Greensboro, NC

To the Student

*Some people have the opportunity to learn a new language by living in another country.
Most of us, however, begin learning another language and getting acquainted with a foreign
culture in a classroom with the help of a teacher, classmates, and a book.
To use your book effectively, you need to know how it works.*

Allez, viens! *(Come along!)* takes you to six different French-speaking locations. Each location is introduced with photos and information on four special pages called Location Openers.

There are twelve chapters in the book, and each one follows the same pattern.

The two Chapter Opener pages announce the chapter theme and list the objectives. These objectives set goals that you can achieve by the end of the chapter.

Mise en train *(Getting started)* The next part of the chapter is an illustrated story that shows you French-speaking people in real-life situations, using the language you'll be learning in the chapter. You'll also have fun watching this story on video.

Première, Deuxième, Troisième Etape *(First, Second, Third Part)* Following the opening story, the chapter is divided into three parts, called **étapes**. At the beginning of each **étape** there's a reminder of the objective(s) you'll be aiming for in this part. In order to communicate, you'll need the French expressions listed in boxes called **Comment dit-on... ?** *(How do you say . . . ?)*. You'll also need vocabulary; look for new words under the heading **Vocabulaire**. You won't have trouble finding grammar, for you're sure to recognize the headings **Grammaire** and **Note de Grammaire**. Now all you need is plenty of practice. In each **étape** there are listening, speaking, reading, and writing activities for you to do individually, with a partner, or in groups. By the end of the **étape**, you'll have achieved your objective(s).

This book will also help you get to know the cultures of the people who speak French.

Panorama Culturel *(Cultural Panorama)* On this page of the chapter you'll read interviews with French-speaking people around the world. They'll talk about themselves and their lives, and you can compare their culture to yours. You'll watch these interviews on video or listen to them on audiocassette or CD.

Note Culturelle *(Culture Note)* These notes provide a lot of interesting cultural information.

Rencontre Culturelle *(Cultural Encounter)* This page in six of the chapters offers a firsthand encounter with French-speaking cultures.

Lisons! *(Let's read!)* After the three **étapes**, one or more reading selections related to the chapter theme will help you develop your reading skills.

Mise en pratique *(Putting into practice)* A variety of activities gives you opportunities to put into practice what you've learned in the chapter in new situations. You'll improve your listening skills and practice communicating with others orally and in writing.

Que sais-je? *(What do I know?)* On this page at the end of the chapter, a series of questions and short activities will help you decide how well you've done.

Vocabulaire *(Vocabulary)* On the last page of the chapter, you'll find a French-English vocabulary list. The words are grouped by **étape** and listed under the objectives they support. You'll need to know these words and expressions for the Chapter Test.

Throughout the book, you'll get a lot of help.

De bons conseils *(Good advice)* Check out the helpful study hints in these boxes.

Tu te rappelles? *(Do you remember?)* Along the way, these notes will remind you of things you might have forgotten.

A la française *(The French way)* Be on the lookout for these boxes, too. They'll give you additional language tips to help you sound more like a native speaker.

Vocabulaire à la carte *(Your choice of vocabulary)* From these lists, you'll be able to choose extra words and expressions you might want to use when you talk about yourself and your interests.

At the end of your book, you'll find more helpful material, including a list of the communicative expressions you'll need, a summary of the grammar you've studied, supplementary vocabulary, and French-English, English-French vocabulary lists with the words you'll need to know in bold type.

Allez, viens! Come along on an exciting trip to a new culture and a new language.

Bon voyage!

iv

ANNOTATED TEACHER'S EDITION

Contents

Allez, viens! Contents

Come along—to a world of new experiences!

Allez, viens! offers you the opportunity to learn the language spoken by millions of people in countries in Europe, Africa, Asia, and around the world. Let's find out what those countries are.

CHAPITRE PRELIMINAIRE

Allez, viens! 1

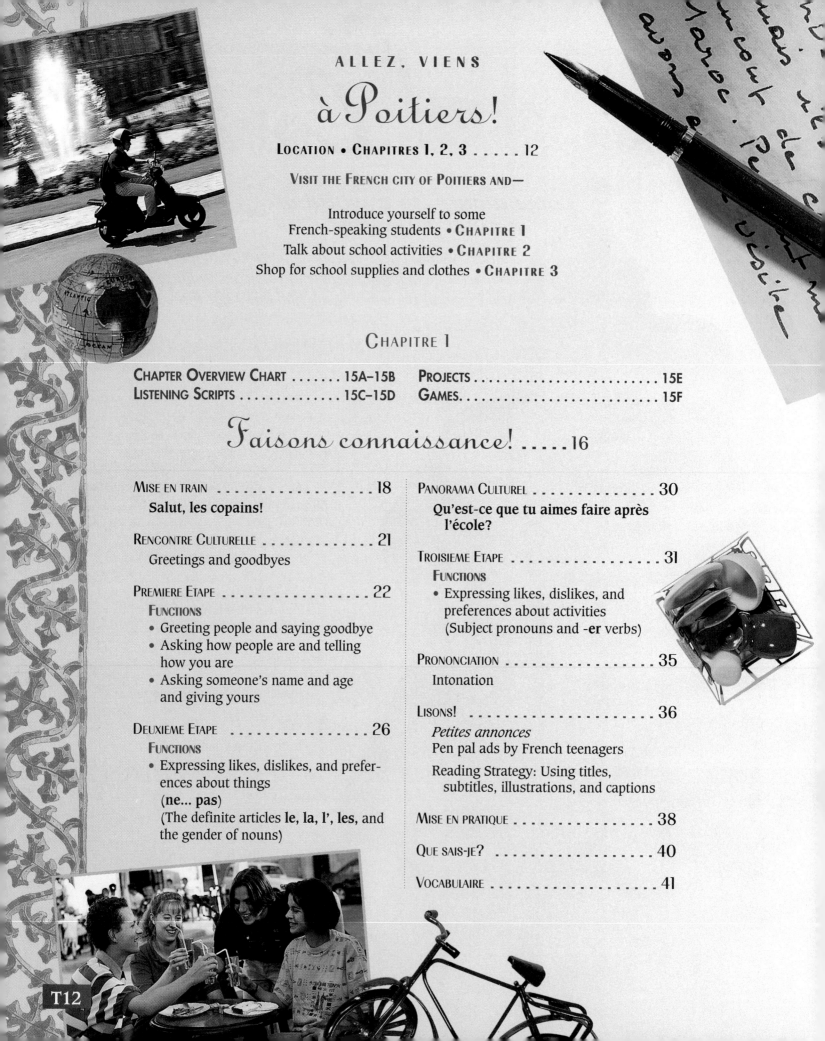

ALLEZ, VIENS

à Poitiers!

VISIT THE FRENCH CITY OF POITIERS AND—

Introduce yourself to some
French-speaking students • CHAPITRE 1
Talk about school activities • CHAPITRE 2
Shop for school supplies and clothes • CHAPITRE 3

CHAPITRE 1

Faisons connaissance! 16

CHAPITRE 2

Vive l'école! 42

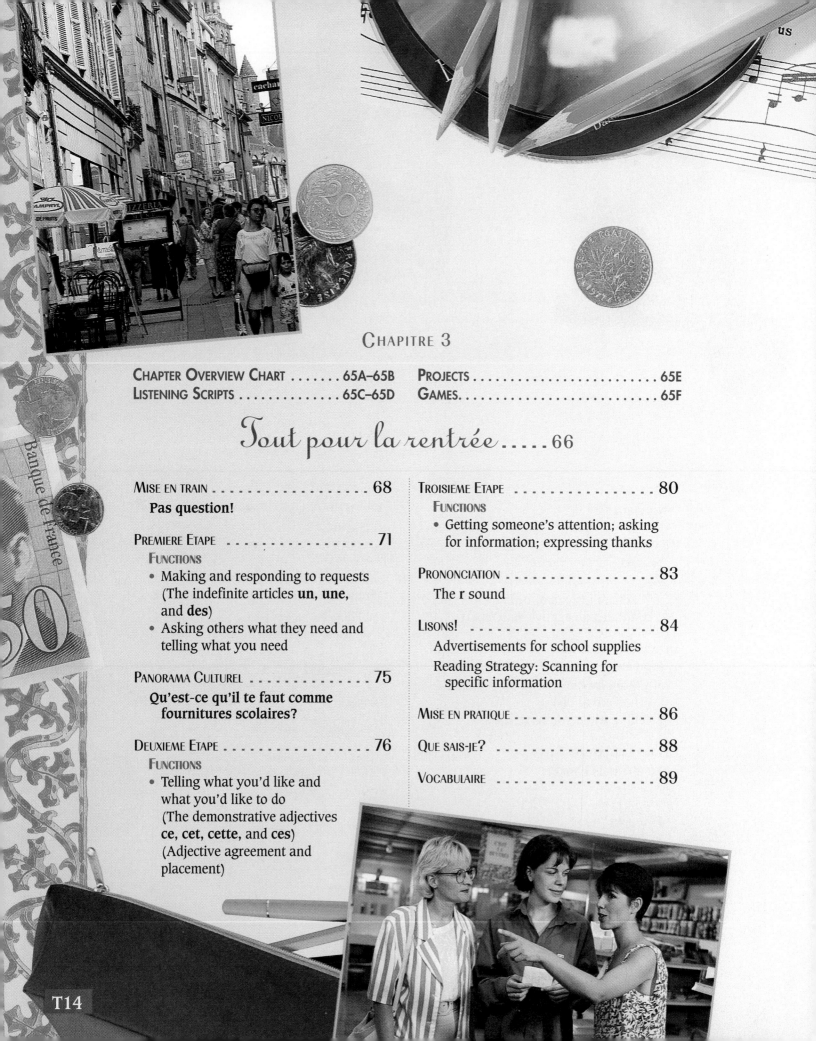

CHAPITRE 3

Tout pour la rentrée 66

ALLEZ, VIENS

à Québec!

VISIT THE CANADIAN CITY OF QUEBEC AND—

Find out about sports and hobbies in francophone countries • CHAPITRE 4

CHAPITRE 4

Sports et passe-temps 94

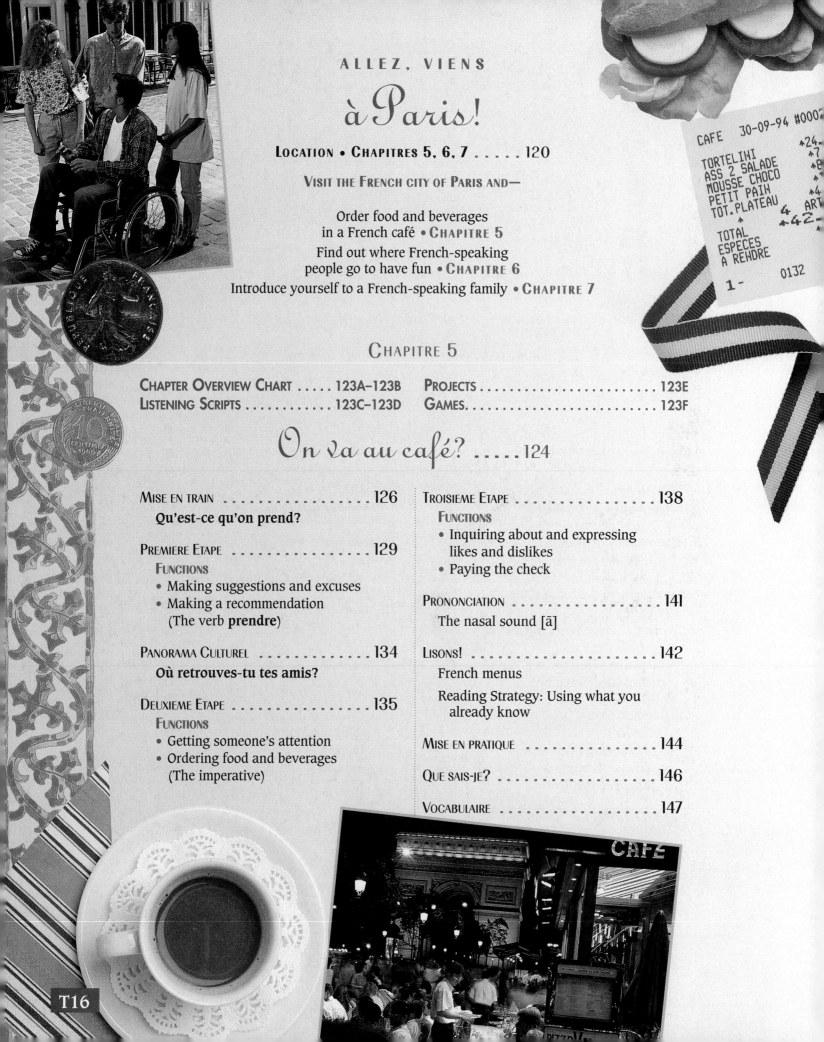

ALLEZ, VIENS

à Paris!

VISIT THE FRENCH CITY OF PARIS AND—

Order food and beverages
in a French café • **CHAPITRE 5**
Find out where French-speaking
people go to have fun • **CHAPITRE 6**
Introduce yourself to a French-speaking family • **CHAPITRE 7**

CHAPITRE 5

On va au café? 124

CHAPITRE 6

Amusons-nous! 148

CHAPITRE 7

La famille 174

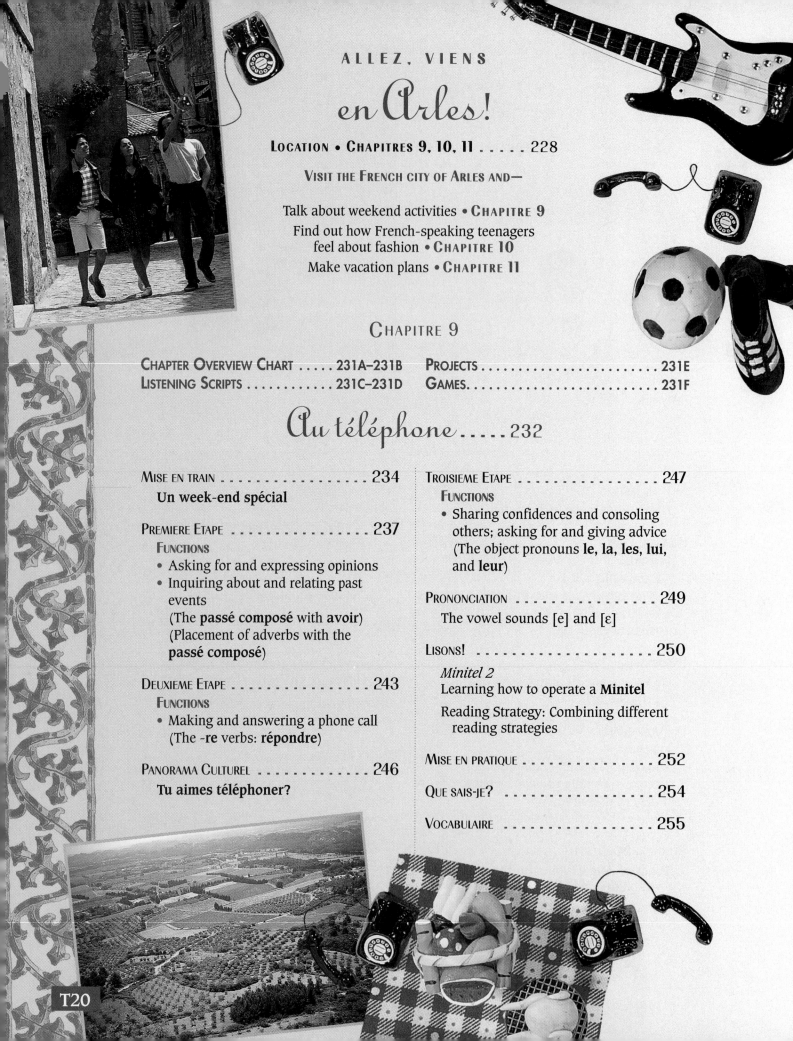

ALLEZ, VIENS

en Arles!

VISIT THE FRENCH CITY OF ARLES AND—

Talk about weekend activities • CHAPITRE 9
Find out how French-speaking teenagers
feel about fashion • CHAPITRE 10
Make vacation plans • CHAPITRE 11

CHAPITRE 9

Au téléphone 232

CHAPITRE 10

Dans un magasin de vêtements 256

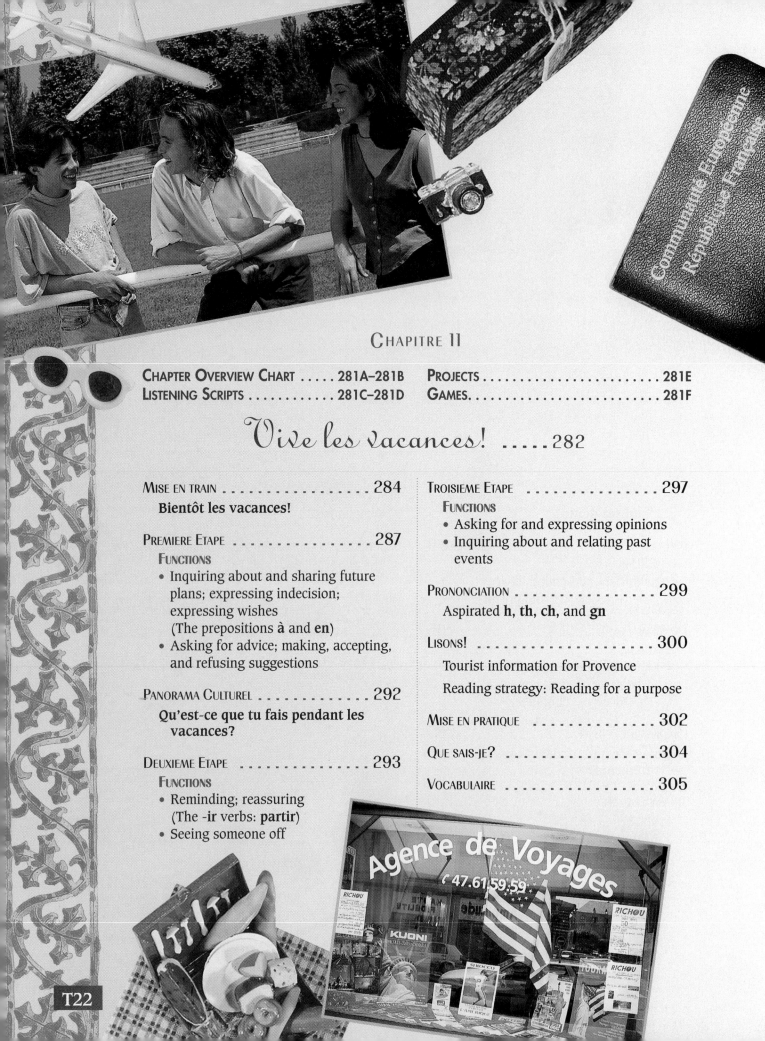

CHAPITRE 11

Vive les vacances! 282

ALLEZ, VIENS
à Fort-de-France!

LOCATION • CHAPITRE 12 306

VISIT THE CAPITAL OF MARTINIQUE AND—

Ask directions
around town • CHAPITRE 12

CHAPITRE 12

En ville 310

REFERENCE SECTION

Cultural References

La France

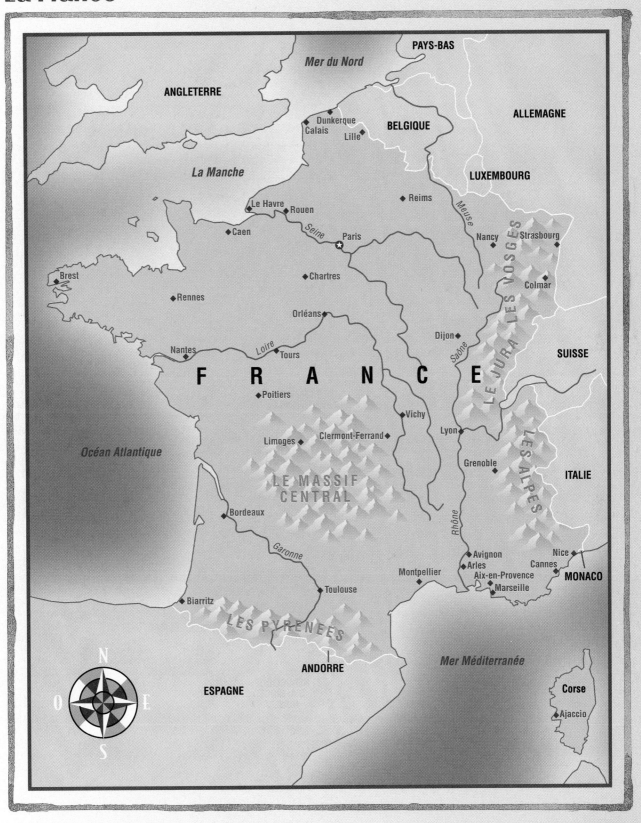

PAYS-BAS

Mer du Nord

ANGLETERRE

Dunkerque
Calais
Lille

BELGIQUE

ALLEMAGNE

La Manche

LUXEMBOURG

Reims

Meuse

Le Havre
Rouen

Nancy

Strasbourg

LES VOSGES

Caen

Seine

Paris

Brest

Chartres

Colmar

Rennes

Orléans

Dijon

Saône

SUISSE

Nantes

Loire

Tours

LE JURA

F R A N C E

Poitiers

Vichy

Lyon

Océan Atlantique

Limoges

Clermont-Ferrand

Grenoble

LES ALPES

ITALIE

LE MASSIF
CENTRAL

Rhône

Bordeaux

Garonne

Avignon
Arles

Nice
Cannes

Montpellier

Aix-en-Provence

MONACO

Toulouse

Marseille

Biarritz

LES PYRÉNÉES

Mer Méditerranée

ANDORRE

N

O   E

S

ESPAGNE

Corse

Ajaccio

L'Afrique francophone

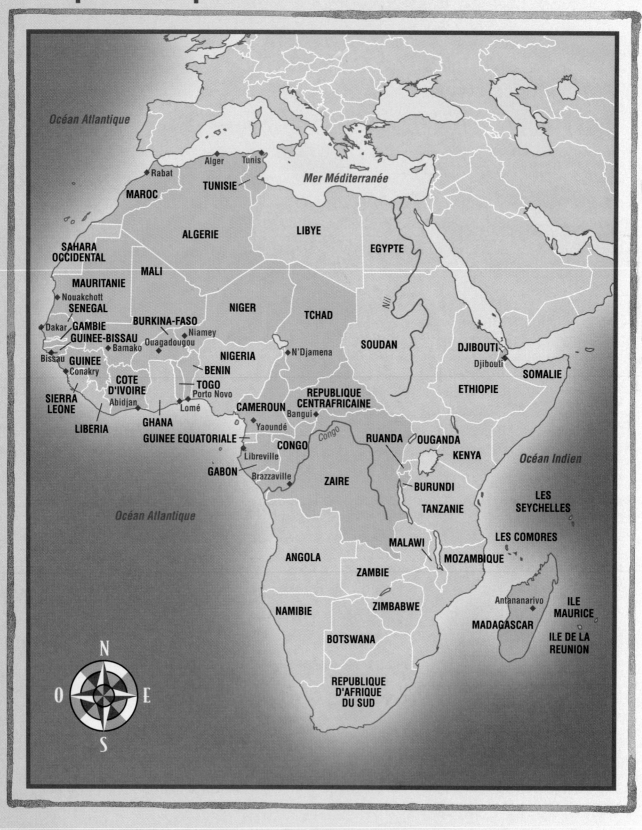

Océan Atlantique

Mer Méditerranée

Alger   Tunis

Rabat

TUNISIE

MAROC

ALGERIE

LIBYE

EGYPTE

SAHARA OCCIDENTAL

MALI

MAURITANIE

Nouakchott

SENEGAL

NIGER

TCHAD

Dakar

GAMBIE

BURKINA-FASO

GUINEE-BISSAU

Niamey

Bamako   Ouagadougou

N'Djamena

SOUDAN

DJIBOUTI

Djibouti

Bissau

GUINEE

NIGERIA

Conakry

BENIN

SOMALIE

COTE D'IVOIRE

TOGO

ETHIOPIE

SIERRA LEONE

Porto Novo

Abidjan

Lomé

CAMEROUN

REPUBLIQUE CENTRAFRICAINE

LIBERIA

GHANA

Bangui

GUINEE EQUATORIALE

Yaoundé

RUANDA

OUGANDA

Congo

CONGO

KENYA

Océan Indien

Librenville

GABON

Brazzaville

ZAIRE

BURUNDI

LES SEYCHELLES

TANZANIE

Océan Atlantique

LES COMORES

MALAWI

ANGOLA

MOZAMBIQUE

ZAMBIE

Antananarivo

ILE MAURICE

NAMIBIE

ZIMBABWE

MADAGASCAR

ILE DE LA REUNION

BOTSWANA

N   O   E   S

REPUBLIQUE D'AFRIQUE DU SUD

Nil

L'Amérique francophone

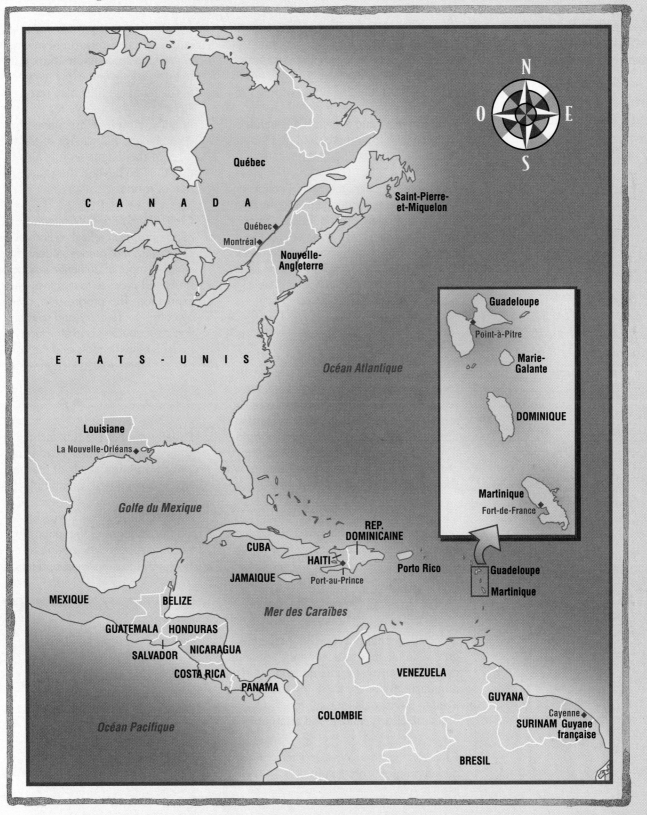

*S*ince the early eighties, we have seen significant advances in modern foreign language curriculum practices:

(1) a redefinition of the objectives of foreign language study involving a commitment to the development of proficiency in the four skills and in cultural awareness;

(2) a recognition of the need for longer sequences of study;

(3) a new student-centered approach that redefines the role of the teacher as facilitator and encourages students to take a more active role in their learning;

(4) the inclusion of students of all learning abilities.

The new Holt, Rinehart and Winston foreign language programs take into account not only these advances in the field of foreign language education, but also the input of teachers and students around the country. ◆

PRINCIPLES AND PRACTICES

As nations become increasingly interdependent, the need for effective communication and sensitivity to other cultures becomes more important. Today's youth must be culturally and linguistically prepared to participate in a global society. At Holt, Rinehart and Winston, we believe that proficiency in more than one language is essential to meeting this need.

The primary goal of the Holt, Rinehart and Winston foreign language programs is to help students develop linguistic proficiency and cultural sensitivity. By interweaving language and culture, our programs seek to broaden students' communication skills while at the same time deepening their appreciation of other cultures.

◆◆

We believe that all students can benefit from foreign language instruction. We recognize that not everyone learns at the same rate or in the same way; nevertheless, we believe that all students should have the opportunity to acquire language proficiency to a degree commensurate with their individual abilities.

Holt, Rinehart and Winston's foreign language programs are designed to accommodate all students by appealing to a variety of learning styles.

◆◆

We believe that effective language programs should motivate students. Students deserve an answer to the question they often ask: "Why are we doing this?" They need to have goals that are interesting, practical, clearly stated, and attainable.

Holt, Rinehart and Winston's foreign language programs promote success. They present relevant content in manageable increments that encourage students to attain achievable functional objectives.

We believe that proficiency in a foreign language is best nurtured by programs that encourage students to think critically and to take risks when expressing themselves in the language. We also recognize that students should strive for accuracy in communication. While it is imperative that students have a knowledge of the basic structures of the language, it is also important that they go beyond the simple manipulation of forms.

Holt, Rinehart and Winston's foreign language program reflects a careful progression of activities that guides students from comprehensible input of authentic language through structured practice to creative, personalized expression. This progression, accompanied by consistent re-entry and spiraling of functions, vocabulary, and structures, provides students with the tools and the confidence to express themselves in their new language.

◆◆

Finally, we believe that a complete program of language instruction should take into account the needs of teachers in today's increasingly demanding classrooms.

At Holt, Rinehart and Winston, we have designed programs that offer practical teacher support and provide resources to meet individual learning and teaching styles.

Using the Pupil's Edition of *Allez, viens!*

Allez, viens! *offers an integrated approach to language learning. Presentation and practice of functional expressions, vocabulary, and grammar structures are interwoven with cultural information, language learning tips, and realia to facilitate both learning and teaching. The technology, audiovisual materials, and additional print resources integrated throughout each chapter allow instruction to be adapted to a variety of teaching and learning styles.* ◆

*A*LLEZ, *VIENS!* LEVEL 1

Allez, viens! Level 1 consists of a preliminary chapter that introduces students to French and the French-speaking world followed by twelve instructional chapters. To ensure successful completion of the book and to facilitate articulation from one level to the next, Chapter 11 introduces minimal new material and Chapter 12 is a review chapter.

Following is a description of the various features in *Allez, viens!* and suggestions on how to use them in the classroom.

While it is not crucial for students to cover all material and do all activities to achieve the goals listed at the beginning of each chapter, the material within each chapter has been carefully sequenced to enable students to progress steadily at a realistic pace to the ultimate goal of linguistic and cultural proficiency. You, the teacher, as presenter, facilitator, and guide, will determine the precise depth of coverage, taking into account the individual needs of each class and the amount and type of alternative instructional material to be used from the *Allez, viens!* program.

*S*TARTING OUT...

In *Allez, viens!,* chapters are arranged by location. Each new location is introduced by a **Location Opener,** four pages of colorful photos and background information that can be used to introduce the region and help motivate students.

The two-page **Chapter Opener** is intended to pique students' interest and focus their attention on the task at hand. It is a visual introduction to the theme of the chapter and includes a brief description of the topic and situations students will encounter, as well as a list of objectives they will be expected to achieve.

*S*ETTING THE SCENE...

Language instruction begins with the **Mise en train,** the comprehensible input that models language in a culturally authentic setting. Whether presented on video or as a reading accompanied by the audiocassette or compact disc recording, the highly visual presentation—frequently in **roman-photo** format in the textbook—ensures success as students practice their receptive skills and begin to recognize some of the new functions and vocabulary they will encounter in the chapter. Following the **Mise en train** is a series of activities that can be used to help guide students through the story and check comprehension.

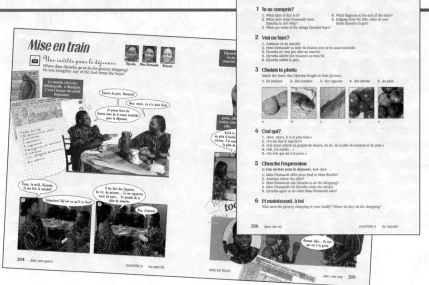

BUILDING PROFICIENCY STEP BY STEP...

Première, Deuxième, and **Troisième étape** are the three core instructional sections where the greater part of language acquisition will take place. The communicative goals in each chapter center on the functional expressions presented in **Comment dit-on... ?** boxes. These expressions are supported and expanded by material in the **Vocabulaire, Grammaire,** and **Note de grammaire** sections. Activities immediately following the above features are designed to practice recognition or to provide closed-ended practice with the new material. Activities then progress from controlled to open-ended practice where students are able to express themselves in meaningful communication. Depending on class size, general ability level, and class dynamics, you may wish to proceed sequentially through all activities in a chapter, supplementing presentation or practice at various points with additional materials from *Allez, viens!*, or to proceed more quickly to open-ended pair and group work.

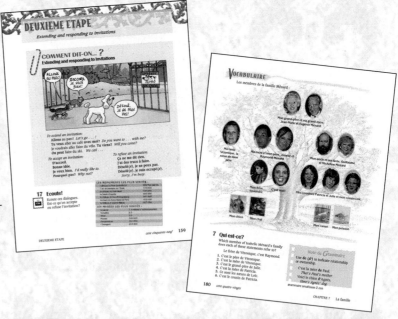

DISCOVERING THE PEOPLE AND THE CULTURE...

Cultural information has been incorporated into activities wherever possible. There are also two major cultural features to help students develop an appreciation and understanding of the cultures of French-speaking countries.

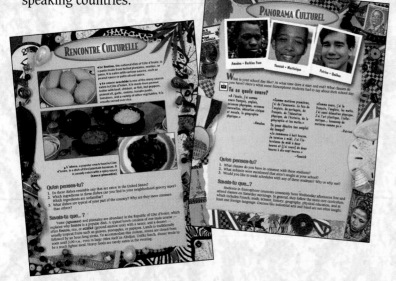

Panorama Culturel presents spontaneous interviews conducted in various countries in the French-speaking world on a topic related to the chapter theme. The interviews may be presented on video or done as a reading supplemented by the audiocassette or compact disc recording. Culminating activities on this page may be used to verify comprehension and encourage students to think critically about the target culture as well as their own.

Rencontre Culturelle presents a cultural encounter that invites students to compare and contrast the foreign culture with their own.

Note Culturelle provides tidbits of both "big C" and "little c" culture that can be used to enrich and enliven activities and presentations at various places throughout each chapter.

UNDERSTANDING AUTHENTIC DOCUMENTS...

Lisons! presents reading strategies that help students understand authentic French documents. The reading selections vary from advertisements to letters to short stories in order to accommodate different interests and familiarize students with different styles and formats. The accompanying activities progress from prereading to reading to postreading tasks and are designed to develop students' overall reading skills and challenge their critical thinking abilities.

TARGETING STUDENTS' NEEDS

In each **étape** several special features may be used to enhance language learning and cultural appreciation.

De bons conseils suggests effective ways for students to learn a foreign language.

A la française provides students with tips for speaking more natural-sounding French.

Vocabulaire à la carte presents optional vocabulary related to the chapter theme. These words are provided to help students personalize activities; students will not be required to produce this vocabulary on the Chapter Quizzes and Test.

Tu te rappelles? is a re-entry feature that lists and briefly explains previously-learned vocabulary, functions, and grammar that students might need to review at the moment.

Si tu as oublié... is a handy page reference to either an earlier chapter where material was presented or to a reference section in the back of the book that includes such aids as the Summary of Functions and the Grammar Summary.

PRONONCIATION

At the end of each **Troisième étape** is **Prononciation,** a pronunciation feature where certain sounds and spelling rules are explained. Pronunciation is practiced using vocabulary words that contain the targeted sounds. In a dictation exercise that follows, students hear and write sentences using the targeted sounds and letters.

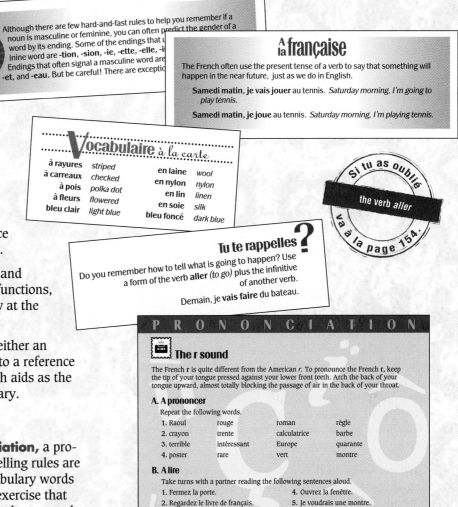

De bons conseils

Although there are few hard-and-fast rules to help you remember if a noun is masculine or feminine, you can often predict the gender of a word by its ending. Some of the endings that signal a feminine word are **-tion, -sion, -ie, -ette, -elle, -**... Endings that often signal a masculine word are **-et,** and **-eau.** But be careful! There are exceptions.

A la française

The French often use the present tense of a verb to say that something will happen in the near future, just as we do in English.

Samedi matin, je vais jouer au tennis. *Saturday morning, I'm going to play tennis.*

Samedi matin, je joue au tennis. *Saturday morning, I'm playing tennis.*

Vocabulaire à la carte

à rayures	striped	en laine	wool
à carreaux	checked	en nylon	nylon
à pois	polka dot	en lin	linen
à fleurs	flowered	en soie	silk
bleu clair	light blue	bleu foncé	dark blue

Tu te rappelles?

Do you remember how to tell what is going to happen? Use a form of the verb **aller** (*to go*) plus the infinitive of another verb.

Demain, je **vais faire** du bateau.

Si tu as oublié... the verb aller va à la page 154.

PRONONCIATION

The r sound

The French **r** is quite different from the American *r*. To pronounce the French **r**, keep the tip of your tongue pressed against your lower front teeth. Arch the back of your tongue upward, almost totally blocking the passage of air in the back of your throat.

A. A prononcer

Repeat the following words.

1. Raoul	rouge	roman	règle
2. crayon	trente	calculatrice	barbe
3. terrible	intéressant	Europe	quarante
4. poster	rare	vert	montre

B. A lire

Take turns with a partner reading the following sentences aloud.

1. Fermez la porte.
2. Regardez le livre de français.
3. Prenez un crayon.
4. Ouvrez la fenêtre.
5. Je voudrais une montre.
6. Je regrette. Je n'ai pas de règle.

C. A écrire

You're going to hear a short dialogue. Write down what you hear.

WRAPPING IT ALL UP...

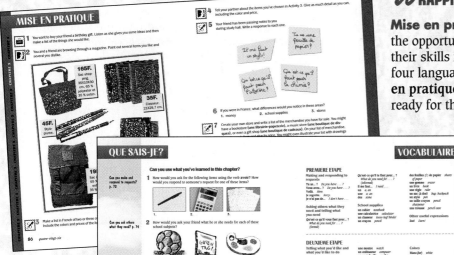

Mise en pratique, at the end of each chapter, gives students the opportunity to review what they have learned and to apply their skills in new communicative contexts. Focusing on all four language skills as well as cultural awareness, the **Mise en pratique** can help you determine whether students are ready for the Chapter Test.

Que sais-je? follows the **Mise en pratique** and is a checklist that students can use on their own to see if they have achieved the goals stated on the Chapter Opener. Each communicative function is paired with one or more activities for students to use as a self-check. Page references are given for students who need to return to the chapter for review.

Vocabulaire presents the chapter vocabulary grouped by **étape** and arranged according to communicative function or theme. This list represents the active words and expressions that students will be expected to know for the Chapter Quizzes and Test.

Allez, viens! *Video*

Allez, viens! *Video Program and* Allez, viens! *Expanded Video Program bring the textbook to life and introduce your students to people they will encounter in every chapter of the* Pupil's Edition. *Filmed entirely on location in French-speaking countries around the world, these video programs feature native speakers of French in realistic, interesting situations.*

Video is an ideal medium for providing authentic input needed to increase proficiency in French. Both informative and entertaining, the episodes of the **Video Program** *and* **Expanded Video Program** *provide rich visual clues to aid comprehension and motivate students to learn more.* ◆

A LLEZ, VIENS! VIDEO PROGRAM

The video program is fully integrated and correlates directly with the *Allez, viens! Pupil's Edition:*

MISE EN TRAIN The introductory dialogue or story in each chapter is a videotaped dramatic episode based on the chapter theme. It introduces the targeted functions, vocabulary, and grammar of the chapter, in addition to re-entering material from previous chapters in new contexts. Since this video episode corresponds directly with the **Mise en train** and the chapter, it can be used as a general introduction to the chapter, as a chapter review, and as a visual support for presenting the elements of the lesson.

PANORAMA CULTUREL Authentic interviews with native speakers of French bring the French-speaking world to life as real people talk about themselves, their country, and their way of life. Each interview topic is thematically related to the chapter.

A LLEZ, VIENS! EXPANDED VIDEO PROGRAM

The **Expanded Video Program** includes all of the material provided in the **Video Program,** plus additional materials designed to extend and enrich students' learning experience through additional authentic input. Included in the **Expanded Video Program** are the following:

LOCATION OPENER A narrated collage of images from regions of French-speaking countries expands students' acquaintance with the geography and people of the places presented in each Location Opener.

MISE EN TRAIN (see **Video Program**)

MISE EN TRAIN (SUITE) These continuations of the dramatic episodes provide high-interest input that helps motivate students and offers additional opportunities to expand on what they've learned. The **Mise en train (suite)** continues the story and resolves the dramatic conflict that was created in the **Mise en train.** Designed to facilitate proficiency by providing additional comprehensible input, this episode

offers an extended presentation of the chapter material as well as re-entering functions, vocabulary, and structures from previous chapters.

PANORAMA CULTUREL Additional authentic interviews are offered in the **Expanded Video Program.** They feature a wide variety of native speakers from around the world and introduce students to regional variations in speech, cultural diversity, and varying points of view. This assortment of interviews from around the French-speaking world enriches students' appreciation of French-speaking cultures and helps them better understand their own.

VIDÉOCLIPS Students will enjoy the authentic footage from French television: music videos, commercials, and more. These short segments of video give students confidence as they realize that they can understand and enjoy material that was produced for native speakers of French!

A LLEZ, VIENS! VIDEO GUIDE

Allez, viens! **Video Guide** provides background information together with suggestions for presentation and pre- and post-viewing activities for all portions of the **Video Program** and the **Expanded Video Program.** In addition, the **Video Guide** contains a transcript and synopsis of each episode, supplementary vocabulary lists, and reproducible student activity sheets.

A LLEZ, VIENS! VIDEODISC PROGRAM AND GUIDE

Allez, viens! **Videodisc Program** presents in videodisc format all the authentic footage, interviews, and dramatic episodes presented in the **Expanded Video Program,** plus additional cultural and geographic material to further enrich your students' experience. Bar codes provide instant access to all material and facilitate efficient integration of video resources into each lesson. Key bar codes are provided in the *Annotated Teacher's Edition.* Teaching suggestions, activity masters, and a complete bar-code directory are provided in the **Videodisc Guide.**

Allez, viens! *Ancillaries*

The **Allez, viens!** *French program offers a state-of-the-art ancillary package that addresses the concerns of today's teachers. Because foreign language teachers are working with all types of students, the activities in our ancillaries accommodate all learning styles. The activities provided in the* **Allez, viens!** *ancillary materials are both innovative and relevant to students' experiences.* ◆

TEACHING RESOURCES WITH PROFESSIONAL ORGANIZER

Holt, Rinehart and Winston has taken an innovative approach to organizing our teaching resources. The *Allez, viens!* ancillaries are conveniently packaged in time-saving **Chapter Teaching Resources** booklets with a tri-fold **Professional Organizer**. Each **Chapter Teaching Resources** booklet puts a wealth of resources at your fingertips!

CHAPTER TEACHING RESOURCES, BOOKS 1-3

Oral communication is the language skill that is most challenging to develop and test. The *Allez, viens!* **Situation Cards** and **Communicative Activities** help students develop their speaking skills and give them opportunities to communicate in a variety of situations.

Additional Listening Activities, in combination with the **Audiocassette** and **Audio CD Program,** provide students with a unique opportunity to actively develop their listening skills in a variety of authentic contexts.

The *Allez, viens!* **Realia** reproduce real documents to provide your students with additional reading and language practice using culturally authentic material. Included with the **Realia** are teacher suggestions and student activities.

The **Student Response Forms** are provided for your convenience. These copying masters can be reproduced and used as answer forms for all the textbook listening activities.

The **Assessment Program** responds to your requests for a method of evaluation that is fair to all students and that encourages students to work towards realistic, communicative goals. The

Assessment Program includes the following components:

- Three **Quizzes** per chapter (one per **étape**)
- One **Chapter Test** per chapter; each **Chapter Test** includes listening, reading, writing, and culture sections and a score sheet for easy grading. Part of each test can be corrected on ScanTron®.
- **Speaking tests,** provided in the **Assessment Guide.**

Also included in the **Chapter Teaching Resources:**

- **Answer Key** for the **Practice and Activity Book**
- **Teaching Transparency Masters** and suggestions for use in a variety of activities
- **Listening Scripts** and **Answers** for the **Additional Listening Activities, Quizzes,** and **Chapter Tests.**

ASSESSMENT GUIDE

The **Assessment Guide** describes various testing and scoring methods. This guide also includes:

- **Portfolio Assessment** suggestions and rubrics
- **Speaking Tests** to be used separately or as part of the **Chapter Test**
- A cumulative **Midterm Exam** with scripts and answers
- A comprehensive **Final Exam** with scripts and answers.

PROFESSIONAL ORGANIZER

A tri-fold binder helps you organize the ancillaries for each chapter.

TEACHING TRANSPARENCIES

The **Teaching Transparencies** benefit all students, and the visual learner in particular. These colorful transparencies add variety and focus to your daily lesson plans. Suggestions for using the transparencies can be found in the **Chapter Teaching Resources** books.

AUDIO PROGRAM

All recorded material is available in either the **Audiocassette Program** or the **Audio CD Program.** The listening activities, pronunciation activities, interviews, and dialogues help students further develop their listening and pronunciation skills by providing opportunities to hear native speakers of French in a variety of authentic situations.

PRACTICE AND ACTIVITY BOOK

The **Practice and Activity Book** is filled with a variety of activities that provide further practice with the functions, grammar, and vocabulary presented in each **étape**. Additional reading, culture, and journal activities for each chapter give students the opportunity to apply the reading and writing strategies they've learned in relevant, personalized contexts.

TEST GENERATOR

The **Test Generator** is a user-friendly software program that enables you to create customized worksheets, quizzes, and tests for each chapter in *Allez, viens!* The **Test Generator** is available for IBM® PC and Compatibles and Macintosh® computers.

The Annotated Teacher's Edition

The **Allez, viens!** Annotated Teacher's Edition *is designed to help you meet the increasingly varied needs of today's students by providing an abundance of suggestions and strategies. The* Annotated Teacher's Edition *includes the reduced pages of the* Pupil's Edition *with teacher annotations, wrap-around teacher text with video references and bar codes, notes, suggestions, answers, and additional activities, as well as interleafed pages of scripts, projects, and games before each chapter.* ◆

USING THE LOCATION OPENER

Each reduced student page is wrapped with background information for you about the photographs and settings. In addition, teaching suggestions help you motivate students to learn more about the history, geography, and culture of French-speaking countries.

USING THE CHAPTER INTERLEAF

The chapter interleaf includes a chapter overview correlation chart for teaching resources, *Pupil's Edition* listening scripts, and suggestions for projects and games.

The **Chapter Overview** chart outlines at a glance the functions, grammar, culture, and re-entry items featured in each **étape**. A list of corresponding print and audiovisual resource materials for each section of the chapter is provided to help integrate video and ancillaries into your lessons. The pronunciation, reading, and review features for each chapter are also referenced, as well as a variety of assessment and portfolio options.

Textbook Listening Activities Scripts provide the scripts of the chapter listening activities for reference or for use in class. The answers to each activity are provided below each script for easy reference.

Projects propose extended four-skills activities based on the chapter theme and content. **Projects** suggestions are provided to give students the opportunity to personalize the information they've learned in the chapter. Individual projects offer students the chance to explore topics related to the chapter theme that are of personal interest to them. Group and cooperative learning projects encourage students to work together to apply what they've learned in the chapter by creating a poster, brochure, or report, often accompanied by an oral presentation.

Games provide students with informal, entertaining activities in which they can apply and reinforce the functions, structures, vocabulary, and culture of the chapter. **Games** appeal to a variety of learners and encourage teamwork and cooperation among students of different levels and learning styles.

USING THE WRAP-AROUND TEACHER TEXT

Wrap-around teacher text gives point-of-use suggestions and information to help you make the most of class time. The wrap-around style of the *Annotated Teacher's Edition* conveniently presents bar codes, video references, teacher notes, suggestions, and activity answers together on the same page with the reduced *Pupil's Edition* page.

TEACHING CYCLE

For each **étape**, a logical instructional sequence includes the following steps to enable you to:
• **Jump Start!** your students with an individual writing activity that focuses their attention on previously-learned material while they wait for class to begin.
• **Motivate** students by introducing the topic in a personalized and contextualized way.
• **Teach** the functions, vocabulary, structures, and culture with a variety of approaches.
• **Close** each **étape** with activities that review and confirm the communicative goals.
• **Assess** students' progress with a quiz and/or performance assessment activity. **Performance Assessment** suggestions provide an alternative to pen and paper tests and give you the option of evaluating students' progress by

having them perform communicative, competency-based tasks. These may include teacher-student interviews, conversations, dialogues, or skits that students perform for the entire class. These tasks can also be recorded or videotaped for evaluation at a later time.

Portfolio icons signal activities that are appropriate for students' oral or written portfolios. They may include lists, posters, letters, journal entries, or taped conversations or skits. A variety of suggestions are provided within each chapter so that you can work with your students to select the activities that would best document their strengths and progress in the language. Portfolio information, including checklists and suggestions for evaluation, is provided in the *Assessment Guide,* pages 2–13. On pages 14–25 of the *Assessment Guide,* there are suggestions for the expansion of the two designated portfolio activities from the *Pupil's Edition.* In each chapter overview, these two activities (one written and one oral) are listed under "Portfolio Assessment." The portfolio suggestions will help students to further develop their oral and written language skills, often in the context of real-life situations. For a discussion of portfolio creation and use, see *Using Portfolios in the Foreign Language Classroom,* page T48.

FOR INDIVIDUAL NEEDS

Suggestions under the following categories provide alternate approaches to help you address students' diverse learning styles.
• **Visual, Auditory, Tactile, and Kinesthetic Learners** benefit from activities that accommodate their unique learning styles.
• **Slower Pace** provides ideas for presenting material in smaller steps to facilitate comprehension.

- **Challenge** extends activities into more challenging tasks that encourage students to expand their communicative skills.

Making Connections

To help students appreciate their membership in a global society, suggestions for linking French with other disciplines, their community, and other cultures appear under the following categories:

- **Math...Geography...Health...Science ...History...Language Arts Links** relate the chapter topic to other subject areas, making French relevant to the students' overall academic experience.
- **Multicultural Links** provide students the opportunity to compare and contrast their language and culture with those of French-speaking countries and other parts of the world.
- **Community...Family Links** encourage students to seek opportunities for learning outside of the classroom by interacting with neighbors and family members. These suggestions also call on students to share their learning with their family and community.

Developing Thinking Skills

Thinking Critically helps students develop their higher-order thinking skills.

Drawing Inferences, Comparing and Contrasting, Analyzing, Observing, and Synthesizing offer suggestions to extend activities beyond an informational level. They increase comprehension of language and culture, and they help students exercise and develop higher-order thinking skills.

Establishing Collaborative Learning

Cooperative Learning allows students to work together in small groups to attain common goals by sharing responsibilities. Students are accountable for setting the group objectives, completing the assignment, and ensuring that all group members master the material. Working together in cooperative groups allows students to take an active role in the classroom, to develop more self-esteem as they contribute to the success of the group, and to experience less anxiety by working in small groups. Cooperative learning enables students to improve interpersonal communication skills by encouraging them to listen to and respect other opinions, and to share their own.

Total Physical Response (TPR) techniques visually and kinesthetically reinforce structures and vocabulary. They are active learning exercises that encourage students to focus on class interaction while learning French.

Teaching Lisons!

Teacher's notes and suggestions in **Lisons!** offer prereading, reading, and postreading activities to help students develop reading skills. Background information and useful terms related to the reading are provided as well.

Chapter 5 Sample Lesson Plan

*T*he following lesson plan suggests how the material in Chapter 5 may be distributed over twelve days. You may choose to prepare similar plans to guide you through the other chapters of **Allez, viens!**, adjusting the daily schedule and selecting appropriate activities and ancillary materials that best suit your individual needs and those of your students. (Page numbers set in **boldface** type refer to activities in the Annotated Teacher's Edition.) ◆

CHAPITRE 5 : ON VA AU CAFE?

DAILY PLANS	RESOURCES
DAY 1 **OBJECTIVE: To find out what French-speaking teenagers might say in a café**	

Chapter Opener, pp. 124–125
   Motivating Activity, **p. 124**
   Focusing on Outcomes, **p. 125**
Mise en train, pp. 126-128
   Presentation: **Qu'est-ce qu'on prend?, p. 127**
   Activities 1, 2, 4, p. 128
Close: Activity 5, p. 128
Assignment: Activity 3, p. 128; Activity 1, *Practice and Activity Book,* p. 49
	Textbook Audiocassette 3A/Audio CD 5
	Practice and Activity Book, p. 49
	Video Program OR Expanded Video Program,
	   Videocassette 2
	Videodisc Program, Videodisc 3A

DAY 2 **OBJECTIVE: To make suggestions; to make excuses**	

Review Assignment from Day 1
Première étape, p. 129
   Jump Start!, **p. 129**
   Motivate, **p. 129**
   Presentation: **Comment dit-on... ?, p. 129**
   Activity 6, p. 129
   Activity 7, p. 130
   Option: Building on Previous Skills, **p. 130**
Close: Activity 5, *Practice and Activity Book,* p. 50
Assignment: Activity 8, p. 130; Activities 3–5, *Practice and Activity Book,* pp. 50–51
	Textbook Audiocassette 3A/Audio CD 5
	Practice and Activity Book, pp. 50–52
	Chapter Teaching Resources, Book 2
	   Teaching Transparency 5-1, pp. 7, 10
	Videodisc Program, Videodisc 3A

DAY 3 **OBJECTIVE: To make recommendations about what to order in a café**	

Review Assignment from Day 2
   Presentation: **Vocabulaire, p. 131**
   Activities 9-10, p. 132
   Option: Cooperative Learning, **p. 131**
   Presentation: **Comment dit-on... ?, p. 132**
   Presentation: **Grammaire, p. 133**
   Activity 12, p. 133
Close: **p. 133**
Assignment: Activity 11, p. 132; Activities 6–7, *Practice and Activity Book,* p. 51
	Textbook Audiocassette 3A/Audio CD 5
	Practice and Activity Book, pp. 50–52
	Chapter Teaching Resources, Book 2
	   Teaching Transparency 5-1, pp. 7, 10
	Videodisc Program, Videodisc 3A

DAY 4 **OBJECTIVE: To find out about cafés in France**	

Review Assignment from Day 3
   Activity 13, p. 133
   Option: Activities 2, 9, *Practice and Activity Book,* pp. 50, 52
   Teaching Transparency 5-1
Quiz 5-1
Assessment: Performance Assessment, **p. 133**
Panorama Culturel, p. 134
   Presentation: **Panorama Culturel, p. 134**
   Questions, p. 134
   Savais-tu que... ?, p. 134
Close: Thinking Critically, **p. 134**
Assignment: Activity 27, *Practice and Activity Book,* p. 60
	Practice and Activity Book, pp. 50–52
	Chapter Teaching Resources, Book 2
	   Teaching Transparency 5-1, pp. 7, 10
	   Quiz 5-1, pp. 23-24
	Assessment Items
	   Audiocassette 7B/Audio CD 5
	Video Program OR Expanded Video Program,
	   Videocassette 2
	Videodisc Program, Videodisc 3A

DAY 5 **OBJECTIVE: To get someone's attention; to order food and beverages**	

Review assignment from Day 4
Deuxième étape, p. 135
   Jump Start!, **p. 135**
   Motivate, **p. 135**
   Presentation: **Comment dit-on... ?, p. 135**
   Activities 14–15, p. 135
   Activity 16, p. 136
Close: Activity 10, *Practice and Activity Book,* p. 53
Assignment: Activities 15, 16, *Practice and Activity Book,* pp. 54–55
	Textbook Audiocassette 3A/Audio CD 5
	Practice and Activity Book, pp. 53–55
	Chapter Teaching Resources, Book 2
	   Teaching Transparency 5-2, pp. 8, 10
	Videodisc Program, Videodisc 3A

DAY 6	**OBJECTIVE:** To use commands to order food and beverages	

	Review Assignment from Day 5
	  Presentation: **Grammaire, p. 136**
	  TPR, p. 136
	  Activity 17, p. 136
	  Activity 18, p. 137
	  Note Culturelle, p. 137
	  Option: Activity 19, p. 137
	Close: Close, **p. 137**
	Assignment: Activity 20, p. 137; Activities 12–13, *Practice and Activity Book,* pp. 53–54
		Textbook Audiocassette 3A/Audio CD 5
		Practice and Activity Book, pp. 53–55
		Chapter Teaching Resources, Book 2
		  Teaching Transparency 5-2, pp. 8, 10
		Videodisc Program, Videodisc 3A

DAY 7	**OBJECTIVE:** To inquire about and express likes and dislikes	

	Review Assignment from Day 6
	  Activity 17, *Practice and Activity Book,* p. 55
	  Teaching Transparency 5-2
	Quiz 5-2
	Assessment: Performance Assessment, **p. 137**
	Troisième étape, p. 138
	  Jump Start!, **p. 138**
	  Motivate, **p. 138**
	  Presentation: **Comment dit-on... ?, p. 138**
	  Activity 21, p. 138
	Close: For Individual Needs, **p. 138**
	Assignment: Activity 22, p. 138; Activities 19, 20, 21, *Practice and Activity Book,* pp. 56–57
		Textbook Audiocassette 3A/Audio CD 5
		Practice and Activity Book, pp. 53–58
		Chapter Teaching Resources, Book 2
		  Teaching Transparency 5-2, pp. 8, 10
		  Quiz 5-2, pp. 25–26
		Assessment Items
		  Audiocassette 7B/Audio CD 5

DAY 8	**OBJECTIVE:** To pay the check	

	Review Assignment from Day 7
	  Activity 23, p. 139
	  Presentation: **Comment dit-on... ?, p. 139**
	  Activity 25, p. 139
	  Activity 26, p. 140
	Note Culturelle, p. 140
	Close: Additional Practice, **p. 140**
	Assignment: Activity 27, p. 140; Activities 23–24, *Practice and Activity Book,* pp. 57–58
		Textbook Audiocassette 3A/Audio CD 5
		Practice and Activity Book, pp. 56–58
		Chapter Teaching Resources, Book 2
		  Teaching Transparency 5-3, pp. 9, 10
		Videodisc Program, Videodisc 3A

DAY 9	**OBJECTIVE:** To order in a café, comment on the meal, and pay the check	

	Review Assignment from Day 8
	  Activity 28, p. 140
	  Prononciation, Activities A–C, p. 141
	Close: **p. 141**
	  Teaching Transparency 5-3
	Quiz 5-3
	Assessment: Performance Assessment, **p. 141**
	Assignment: Activity 24, p. 139; Activities 1–12, **Que sais-je?,** p. 146
		Textbook Audiocassette 3A/Audio CD 5
		Practice and Activity Book, pp. 56–58
		Chapter Teaching Resources, Book 2
		  Teaching Transparency 5-3, pp. 9, 10
		Videodisc Program, Videodisc 3A

DAY 10	**OBJECTIVE:** To read French café menus	

	Lisons!, pp. 142–143
	  Motivating Activity, **p. 142**
	  Activities A, B, p. 142
	  Activities C–G, p. 143
	Close: Activity H, p. 143
	Assignment: Activity I, p. 143; Activity 25, *Practice and Activity Book,* p. 58
		Textbook Audiocassette 3A/Audio CD 5
		Practice and Activity Book, p. 59
		Chapter Teaching Resources, Book 2

DAY 11	**OBJECTIVE:** To use what you have learned; to prepare for Chapter Test	

	Review Assignments from Days 9 and 10
	Mise en pratique, pp. 144–145
	  Activities 1–2, p. 144
	  Activities 3, 5, p. 145
	  Option: Activity 6, p. 145
	  Jeu de rôle, p. 145
	  Options: Games, **p. 123F**
	         Projects, **p. 123E**
	Assignment: Activity 4, p. 145; **Mon journal,** *Practice and Activity Book,* p. 149
		Textbook Audiocassette 3A/Audio CD 5
		Practice and Activity Book, p. 149
		Chapter Teaching Resources, Book 2
		Video Program OR *Expanded Video Program,*
		  Videocassette 2
		Videodisc Program, Videodisc 3A

DAY 12	**OBJECTIVE:** To assess progress	

	Chapitre 5 Chapter Test	*Chapter Teaching Resources, Book 2,* pp. 29–34
		Assessment Guide
		  Speaking Test, p. 30
		  Portfolio Assessment, pp. 10–13, 18
		Assessment Items
		  Audiocassette 7B/Audio CD 5

Standards for Foreign Language Education

BY ROBERT LABOUVE

STANDARDS AND SCHOOL REFORM

In 1989 educational reform in the United States took on an entirely different look when state and national leaders reached consensus on six national educational goals for public schools. In 1994 a new law, *Goals 2000: Educate America Act,* endorsed these six goals and added two more. The most important national goal in the law for foreign language educators is Goal Three, which establishes a core curriculum and places foreign languages in that core. As a result of this consensus on national goals, the Federal government encouraged the development of high standards in the core disciplines. While the Federal government does not have the authority to mandate the implementation of foreign language standards locally, it will encourage their use through leadership and projects funded by the U.S. Department of Education.

We must first define "standards" in order to fully understand the rationale for their development. Content standards ask: What should students know and be able to do? Content standards are currently under development by foreign language professionals. Performance standards ask: How good is good enough? Opportunity-to-learn standards ask: Did the school prepare all students to perform well? There is a growing consensus that states and local districts should address the last two types of standards.

PROGRESS TOWARD FOREIGN LANGUAGE STANDARDS

A task force of foreign language educators began work on the standards in 1993 by establishing specific foreign language goals. They then set content standards for each goal. The task force sought feedback from the foreign language profession through an extensive dissemination program and produced a draft of the standards document for introduction at a number of sites around the United States during the 1994–1995 school year.

The target publication date for a final document is late 1995. The final version will incorporate suggestions from the sites where the standards were introduced and reaction from volunteer reviewers and the field in general. While the standards should be world class, they must also be realistic and attainable by most students. The task force also realizes that the general set of goals and standards will have to be made language specific in a curriculum development process and that continuing staff development will be essential.

PROPOSED FOREIGN LANGUAGE STANDARDS

Goal One	Communicate in languages other than English	**Standard 1.1**	Students engage in conversations, provide and obtain information, express feelings and emotions, and exchange opinions.
		Standard 1.2	Students understand and interpret written and spoken language on a variety of topics.
		Standard 1.3	Students present information, concepts, and ideas to an audience of listeners or readers on a variety of topics.
Goal Two	Gain knowledge and understanding of other cultures	**Standard 2.1**	Students demonstrate knowledge and understanding of the traditions, institutions, ideas and perspectives, the literary and artistic expressions, and other components of the cultures being studied.
Goal Three	Connect with other disciplines and acquire information	**Standard 3.1**	Students reinforce and further their knowledge of other disciplines through the foreign language.
		Standard 3.2	Students gain access to information and perspectives that are only available through the foreign language and within culture.
Goal Four	Develop insight into own language and culture	**Standard 4.1**	Students recognize that different languages use different patterns to express meaning and can apply this knowledge to their own language.
		Standard 4.2	Students recognize that cultures develop different patterns of interaction and can apply this knowledge to their own culture.
Goal Five	Participate in multi-lingual communities and global society	**Standard 5.1**	Students use the language both within and beyond the school setting.
		Standard 5.2	Students use the language for leisure and personal enrichment.

PROPOSED FOREIGN LANGUAGE GOALS AND STANDARDS

The proposed goals and standards in the draft document describe a K–12 foreign language program for *all* students, presenting languages, both modern and classical, as part of the core curriculum for every student, including those whose native language is not English. Broad goals establish the basic framework of the language program. The proposed content standards set for these goals describe what students should know and be able to do in a language. The chart on page T40 shows how the standards are arrayed alongside the goals.

The first two goals in this expanded language program describe today's typical school language program. The last three are often identified by teachers as important, but are not always implemented. The standards-based program moves beyond an emphasis on skills to a redefinition of the content of a language program itself.

Sample benchmark tasks will be provided for Grades 4, 8, and 12 as examples of what students can do to meet the standards and accomplish the goals of the language program. A higher level of performance will be expected as students progress from one benchmark grade to another. For example, Standard 1.1 at Grade 4 suggests that students can "describe various objects and people in their everyday environment at home and in school," but Standard 1.1 at Grade 12 suggests that students can "exchange opinions and individual perspectives on a variety of topics including issues that are of contemporary and historical interest in the foreign culture and in their own."

IMPACT OF THE STANDARDS

While there is an assumption that foreign language goals and standards will have a great impact upon the states and local districts, the standards themselves are voluntary. Clearly, standards will influence instruction and curriculum development in districts that choose to align their language programs with the national standards. Assessment programs will most likely begin to reflect the influence of the standards. The standards will also have an impact on the prepara-tion of future teachers and on staff development for teachers now in the classroom.

A curriculum based on the standards will encourage students to take responsibility for their learning by making the language curriculum coherent and transparent to them. Students will know from the beginning what they should be able to do when they exit the program and they will be able to judge for themselves how they are progressing, especially at established benchmarks, i.e., Grades 4, 8, and 12.

The standards will direct instruction in the classroom by providing curriculum developers and teachers with a broad framework upon which to construct the expanded language program. Standards for each goal will ensure that no goal is treated informally or left to chance. Teachers who use the content standards should play a critical role in their district by deciding how good is good enough for students who exit the program.

The standards will also have a significant impact on the demand for sequential, cross-disciplinary instructional materials for a K–12 language program. Another challenge will be the development of new technologies that increase learning in order to meet high standards.

Probably the greatest benefit that national standards may bring will be in the area of making possible articulation that is horizontal (linking languages to other disciplines) and vertical (grade to grade, school to school, and school to college). Language teachers will join their English and social studies colleagues in helping students become language-competent, literate citizens of the world. A language program that is at once coherent and transparent to students and others will provide all language educators a basis for reaching consensus about their expectations on what students should know and do. To those of us who feel that foreign language education is basic education for all students, the national standards document will become a strong advocate for languages in the curriculum of every school and for the extended sequences of study presented by the goals and standards. The standards document will make it easier for language educators to present a solid rationale for foreign languages in the curriculum.

The standards document is still in draft form and some changes are expected before the official document is published. To receive the most up-to-date version, please contact the project office:

National Standards Project
c/o ACTFL
6 Executive Plaza
Yonkers, NY 10701
(914) 963–8830

Allez, viens!

supports the proposed Foreign Language Goals and Standards in the following ways:

THE PUPIL'S EDITION

- Encourages students to take responsibility for their learning by providing clearly defined objectives at the beginning of each chapter.

- Provides a variety of pair- and group-work activities to give students an opportunity to use the target language in a wide range of settings and contexts.

- Offers culture-related activities and poses questions that develop students' insight and encourage them to develop observational and analytical skills.

THE ANNOTATED TEACHER'S EDITION

- Provides a broad framework for developing a foreign language program and offers specific classroom suggestions for reaching students with various learning styles.

- Offers ideas for multicultural and multidisciplinary projects as well as community and family links that encourage students to gain access to information both at school and in the community.

THE ANCILLARY PROGRAM

- Provides students with on-location video footage of native speakers interacting in their own cultural and geographic context.

- Includes multiple options for practicing and assessing performance, including situation cards, portfolio suggestions, speaking tests, and other alternatives.

- Familiarizes students with the types of tasks they will be expected to perform on exit exams.

Teaching Culture

BY NANCY HUMBACH AND DOROTHEA BRUSCHKE

Ask students what they like best about studying a foreign language. Chances are that learning about culture, the way people live, is one of their favorite aspects. Years after language study has ended, adults remember with fondness the customs of the target culture, even pictures in their language texts. It is this interest in the people and their way of life that is the great motivator and helps us sustain students' interest in language study.

We must integrate culture and language in a way that encourages curiosity, stimulates analysis, and teaches students to hypothesize and seek answers to questions about the people whose language they are studying. Teaching isolated facts about how people in other cultures live is not enough. This information is soon dated and quickly forgotten. We must go a step beyond and teach students that all behavior, values, and traditions exist because of certain aspects of history, geography, and socio-economic conditions.

There are many ways to help students become culturally knowledgeable and to assist them in developing an awareness of differences and similarities between the target culture and their own. Two of these approaches involve critical thinking, that is, trying to find reasons for a certain behavior through observation and analysis, and putting individual observations into larger cultural patterns. ◆

> We must integrate culture and language in a way that encourages curiosity, stimulates analysis, and teaches students to hypothesize.

FIRST APPROACH: QUESTIONING

The first approach involves questioning as the key strategy. At the earliest stages of language learning, students begin to learn ways to greet peers, elders, and strangers, as well as the use of **tu** and **vous**. Students need to consider questions such as: "How do French-speaking people greet each other? Are there different levels of formality? Who initiates a handshake? When is a handshake or kisses on the cheeks **(la bise)** appropriate?" Each of these questions leads students to think about the values that are expressed through word and gesture. They start to "feel" the other culture, and at the same time, understand how much of their own behavior is rooted in their cultural background.

Magazines, newspapers, advertisements, and television commercials are all excellent sources of cultural material. For example, browsing through a French magazine, one finds a number of advertisements for food items and bottled water. Could this indicate a great interest in eating and preparing healthy food? Reading advertisements can be followed up with viewing videos and films, or with interviewing native speakers or people who have lived in French-speaking countries to learn about customs involving food selection and preparation.

Students might want to find answers to questions such as: "How much time do French people spend shopping for and preparing a meal? How long does a typical meal **en famille** last? What types of food and beverages does it involve?" This type of questioning might lead students to discover different attitudes toward food and mealtimes.

An advertisement for a refrigerator or a picture of a French kitchen can provide an insight into practices of shopping for food. Students first need to think about the refrigerator at home, take an inventory of what is kept in it, and consider when and where their family shops. Next, students should look closely at a French refrigerator. What is its size? What could that mean? (Shopping takes place more often, stores are within walking distance, and people eat more fresh foods.)

Food wrappers and containers also provide good clues to cultural insight. For example, since bread is often purchased fresh from a **boulangerie,** it is usually carried in one's hand or tote bag, with no packaging at all. Since most people shop daily and carry their own groceries home, heavier items like sodas often come in bottles no larger than one and one-half litres.

SECOND APPROACH: ASSOCIATING WORDS WITH IMAGES

The second approach for developing cultural understanding involves forming associations of words with the cultural images they suggest. Language and culture are so closely related that one might actually say that language *is* culture. Most words, especially nouns, carry a cultural connotation. Knowing the literal equivalent of a word in another language is of little use to students in understanding this connotation. For example, **ami** cannot be translated simply as *friend*, **pain** as *bread,* or **rue** as *street.* The French word **pain**, for instance, carries with it the image of a small local bakery stocked with twenty or thirty different varieties of freshly-baked bread, all warm from a brick oven. At breakfast, bread is sliced, covered with butter and jam, and eaten as a **tartine;** it is eaten throughout the afternoon and evening meals, in particular as an accompaniment to the cheese course. In French-speaking countries, "bread" is more than a grocery item; it is an essential part of every meal.

When students have acquired some sense of the cultural connotation of words —not only through teachers' explanations but, more importantly, through observation of visual images—they start to discover the larger underlying cultural themes, or what is often called deep culture.

These larger cultural themes serve as organizing categories into which individual cultural phenomena fit to form a pattern. Students might discover, for example, that French speakers, because they live in much more crowded conditions, have a great need for privacy (cultural theme), as reflected in such phenomena as closed doors, fences or walls around property, and sheers on windows. Students might also discover that love of nature and the outdoors is an important cultural theme, as indicated by such phenomena as flower boxes and planters in public places—even on small traffic islands—well-kept public parks in every town, and people going for a walk or going hiking.

As we teach culture, students learn not only to recognize elements of the target culture but also of their American cultural heritage. They see how elements of culture reflect larger themes or patterns. Learning what constitutes American culture and how that information relates to other people throughout the world can be an exciting journey for a young person.

As language teachers, we are able to facilitate that journey into another culture and into our own, to find our similarities as well as our differences from others. We do not encourage value judgments about others and their culture, nor do we recommend adopting other ways. We simply say to students, "Other ways exist. They exist for many reasons, just as our ways exist due to what our ancestors have bequeathed us through history, traditions, values, and geography."

Allez, viens!

develops cultural understanding and awareness in the following ways:

THE PUPIL'S EDITION

- Informs students about francophone countries through photo essays, maps, almanac boxes, and **Notes Culturelles** that invite comparison with the students' own cultural experiences.
- Engages students in analysis and comparison of live, personal interviews with native speakers in the **Panorama Culturel** sections.
- Uses the **Rencontre Culturelle** section to expose students to cross-cultural situations that require observation, analysis, and problem-solving.
- Helps students integrate the language with its cultural connotations through a wealth of authentic documents.

THE ANNOTATED TEACHER'S EDITION

- Provides teachers with additional culture, history, and language notes, background information on photos and almanac boxes, and multicultural links.
- Suggests problem-solving activities and critical thinking questions that allow students to hypothesize, analyze, and discover larger underlying cultural themes.

THE ANCILLARY PROGRAM

- Includes additional realia to develop cultural insight by serving as a catalyst for questioning and direct discovery.
- Offers activities that require students to compare and contrast cultures.
- Provides songs, short readings, and poems, as well as many opportunities for students to experience regional variation and idioms in the video and audio programs.

Learning Styles and Multi-Modality Teaching

BY MARY B. MCGEHEE

The larger and broader population of students who are enrolling in foreign language classes brings a new challenge to foreign language educators, calling forth an evolution in teaching methods to enhance learning for all our students. Educational experts now recognize that every student has a preferred sense for learning and retrieving information: visual, auditory, or kinesthetic. Incorporating a greater variety of activities to accommodate the learning styles of all students can make the difference between struggle and pleasure in the foreign language classroom. ◆

> Incorporating a greater variety of activities to accommodate the learning styles of all students can make the difference between struggle and pleasure in the foreign language classroom.

ACCOMMODATING DIFFERENT LEARNING STYLES

A modified arrangement of the classroom is one way to provide more effective and enjoyable learning for all students. Rows of chairs and desks must give way at times to circles, semicircles, or small clusters. Students may be grouped in fours or in pairs for cooperative work or peer teaching. It is important to find a balance of arrangements, thereby providing the most comfort in varied situations.

Since visual, auditory, and kinesthetic learners will be in the class, and because every student's learning will be enhanced by a multi-sensory approach, lessons must be directed toward all three learning styles. Any language lesson content may be presented visually, aurally, and kinesthetically.

Visual presentations and practice may include the chalkboard, charts, posters, television, overhead projectors, books, magazines, picture diagrams, flashcards, bulletin boards, films, slides, or videos. Visual learners need to see what they are to learn. Lest the teacher think he or she will never have the time to prepare all those visuals, Dickel and Slak (1983) found that visual aids generated by students are more effective than ready-made ones.

Auditory presentations and practice may include stating aloud the requirements of the lesson, oral questions and answers, paired or group work on a progression of oral exercises from repetition to communication, tapes, CDs, dialogues, and role-playing. Jingles, catchy stories, and memory devices using songs and rhymes are good learning aids. Having students record themselves and then listen as they play back the cassette allows them to practice in the auditory mode.

Kinesthetic presentations entail the students' use of manipulatives, chart materials, gestures, signals, typing, songs, games, and role-playing. These lead the students to associate sentence constructions with meaningful movements.

A SAMPLE LESSON USING MULTI-MODALITY TEACHING

A multi-sensory presentation on greetings might proceed as follows.

FOR VISUAL LEARNERS

As the teacher begins oral presentation of greetings and introductions, he or she simultaneously shows the written forms on transparencies, with the formal expressions marked with an adult's hat, and the informal expressions marked with a baseball cap.

The teacher then distributes cards with the hat and cap symbols representing the formal or informal expressions. As the students hear taped mini-dialogues, they hold up the appropriate card to indicate whether the dialogues are formal or informal. On the next listening, the students repeat the sentences they hear.

FOR AUDITORY LEARNERS

A longer taped dialogue follows, allowing the students to hear the new expressions a number of times. They write from dictation several sentences containing the new expressions. They may work in pairs, correcting each other's work as they "test" their own understanding of the lesson at hand. Finally, students respond to simple questions using the appropriate formal and

informal responses cued by the cards they hold.

► FOR KINESTHETIC LEARNERS

For additional kinesthetic input, members of the class come to the front of the room, each holding a hat or cap symbol. As the teacher calls out situations, the students play the roles, using gestures and props appropriate to the age group they are portraying. Non-cued, communicative role-playing with props further enables the students to "feel" the differences between formal and informal expressions.

*H*ELPING STUDENTS LEARN HOW TO USE THEIR PREFERRED MODE

Since we require all students to perform in all language skills, part of the assistance we must render is to help them develop strategies within their preferred learning modes to carry out an assignment in another mode. For example, visual students hear the teacher assign an oral exercise and visualize what they must do. They must see themselves carrying out the assignment, in effect watching themselves as if there were a movie going on in their heads. Only then can they also hear themselves saying the right things. Thus, this assignment will be much easier for the visual learners who have been taught this process, if

they have not already figured it out for themselves. Likewise, true auditory students, confronted with a reading/writing assignment, must talk themselves through it, converting the entire process into sound as they plan and prepare their work. Kinesthetic students presented with a visual or auditory task must first break the assignment into tasks and then work their way through them.

Students who experience difficulty because of a strong preference for one mode of learning are often unaware of the degree of preference. In working with these students, I prefer the simple and direct assessment of learning styles offered by Richard Bandler and John Grinder in their book *Frogs into Princes*, which allows the teacher and student to quickly determine how the student learns. In an interview with the student, I follow the assessment with certain specific recommendations of techniques to make the student's study time more effective.

It is important to note here that teaching students to maximize their study does not require that the teacher give each student an individualized assignment. It does require that each student who needs it be taught how to prepare the assignment using his or her own talents and strengths. This communication between teacher and student, combined with teaching techniques that

reinforce learning in all modes, can only maximize pleasure and success in learning a foreign language.

► REFERENCES

Dickel, M.J. and S. Slak. "Imaging Vividness and Memory for Verbal Material." *Journal of Mental Imagery* 7, i (1983):121–6.

Bandler, Richard, and John Grinder. *Frogs into Princes*. Real People Press, Moab, UT. 1978.

Allez, viens!
accommodates different learning styles in the following ways:

THE PUPIL'S EDITION

- Presents basic material in audio, video, and print formats.
- Includes role-playing activities and a variety of multi-modal activities, including an extensive listening strand and many art-based activities.

THE ANNOTATED TEACHER'S EDITION

- Provides suggested activities for visual, auditory, and kinesthetic learners, as well as suggestions for slower-paced learning and challenge activities.
- Includes Total Physical Response activities.

THE ANCILLARY PROGRAM

- Provides additional reinforcement activites for a variety of learning styles.
- Presents a rich blend of audiovisual input through the video program, audio program, transparencies, and blackline masters.

The following is an example of an art-based activity from *Allez, viens!*

15 Ils ont quels cours?

Some students are day-dreaming about the future. What classes are they taking to prepare for these careers?

Ils ont géométrie, physique et géographie.

1.

2.   3.   4.

Higher-Order Thinking Skills

BY AUDREY L. HEINING-BOYNTON

Our profession loves acronyms! TPR, ALM, OBI, and now the HOTS! HOTS stands for higher-order thinking skills. These thinking skills help our students listen, speak, write, and learn about culture in a creative, meaningful way while providing them with necessary life skills. ◆

Introduce students to the life skills they need to become successful, productive citizens in our society.

WHAT ARE HIGHER-ORDER THINKING SKILLS?

Higher-order thinking skills are not a new phenomenon on the educational scene. In 1956, Benjamin Bloom published a book that listed a taxonomy of educational objectives in the form of a pyramid similar to the one in the following illustration:

Bloom's Taxonomy of Educational Objectives

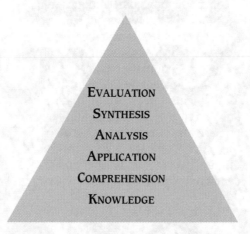

EVALUATION
SYNTHESIS
ANALYSIS
APPLICATION
COMPREHENSION
KNOWLEDGE

Knowledge is the simplest level of educational objectives and is not considered a higher-order thinking skill. It requires the learner to remember information without having to fully understand it. Tasks that students perform to demonstrate knowledge are recalling, identifying, recognizing, citing, labeling, listing, reciting, and stating.

Comprehension is not considered a higher-order thinking skill either. Learners demonstrate comprehension when they paraphrase, describe, summarize, illustrate, restate, or translate.

Foreign language teachers tend to focus the most on knowledge and comprehension. The tasks performed at these levels are important because they provide a solid foundation for the more complex tasks at the higher levels of Bloom's pyramid. However, offering our students the opportunity to perform at still higher cognitive levels provides them with more meaningful contexts in which to use the target language.

When teachers incorporate **application, analysis, synthesis,** and **evaluation** as objectives, they allow students to utilize **higher-order thinking skills.**

- **Application** involves solving, transforming, determining, demonstrating, and preparing.

- **Analysis** includes classifying, comparing, making associations, verifying, seeing cause-and-effect relationships, and determining sequences, patterns, and consequences.

- **Synthesis** requires generalizing, predicting, imagining, creating, making inferences, hypothesizing, making decisions, and drawing conclusions.

- Finally, **evaluation** involves assessing, persuading, determining value, judging, validating, and solving problems.

Most foreign language classes focus little on higher-order thinking skills. Some foreign language educators mistakenly think that all higher-order thinking skills require an advanced level of language ability. Not so! Students can demonstrate these skills by using very simple language available even to beginning students. Also, higher-order thinking tasks about the target culture or language can be conducted in English. The use of some English in the foreign language class in order to utilize higher cognitive skills does not jeopardize progress in the target language.

Higher-order thinking skills prepare our students for more than using a foreign language. They introduce students to the life skills they need to become successful, productive citizens in our society. When we think about it, that *is* the underlying purpose of education.

Why Teach Higher-Order Thinking Skills?

There is already so much to cover and so little time that some teachers may question the worth of adding these types of activities to an already full schedule. Yet we know from experience that simply "covering" the material does not help our students acquire another language. Incorporating higher-order thinking skills in the foreign language classroom can help guide students toward language acquisition by providing meaningful experiences in a setting that can otherwise often feel artificial.

Also, we now know that employing higher-order thinking skills assists all students, including those who are at risk of failing. In the past, we felt that at-risk students were incapable of higher-order thinking, but we have since discovered that we have been denying them the opportunity to experience what they are capable of doing and what they need to do in order to be successful adults.

Sample Activities Employing Higher-Order Thinking Skills

There are no limitations on incorporating higher-order thinking skills in the foreign language classroom. What follows are a few sample activities, some of which you might already be familiar with. Use *your* higher-order thinking skills to develop other possibilities!

▶ LISTENING

HOTS:	Analysis
TASKS:	Patterning and sequencing
VOCABULARY NEEDED:	Three colors
MATERIALS REQUIRED:	Three colored-paper squares for each student

After reviewing the colors, call out a pattern of colors and have the students show their comprehension by arranging their colored pieces of paper from left to right in the order you give. Then have them finish the pattern for you. For example, you say: **rouge, vert, bleu, rouge, vert, bleu...** now what color follows? And then what color?

This is not only a HOTS activity, it also crosses disciplines. It reviews the mathematical concept of patterning and sequencing. You can have the students form patterns and sequences using any type of vocabulary.

▶ READING

HOTS:	Synthesis
TASKS:	Hypothesizing and imagining
VOCABULARY NEEDED:	Determined by level of students
MATERIALS REQUIRED:	Legend or short story

After the students have read the first part of the story, have them imagine how the story would end, based on the values of the target culture.

▶ SPEAKING

HOTS:	Evaluation
TASKS:	Assessing and determining value
VOCABULARY NEEDED:	Numbers 0-25, five objects students would need for school
MATERIALS REQUIRED:	Visuals of five school-related objects with prices beneath them

Tell students that they each have twenty-five dollars to spend on back-to-school supplies. They each need to tell you what they would buy with their money.

▶ WRITING

HOTS:	Analysis
TASKS:	Classifying
VOCABULARY NEEDED:	Leisure activities
MATERIALS REQUIRED:	Drawings of leisure activities on a handout

From the list of activities they have before them, students should write the ones that they like to do on the weekend. Then they should write those that a family member likes to do. Finally, students should write a comparison of the two lists.

Commitment to Higher-Order Thinking Skills

Teaching higher-order thinking skills takes no extra time from classroom instruction since language skills are reinforced during thinking skills activities. What teaching higher-order thinking skills does require of teachers is a commitment to classroom activities that go beyond the objectives of Bloom's knowledge and comprehension levels. Having students name objects and recite verb forms is not enough. Employing HOTS gives students the opportunity to experience a second language as a useful device for meaningful communication.

▶ REFERENCES

Bloom, Benjamin. *Taxonomy of Educational Objectives. Handbook 1: Cognitive Domain.* New York: David McKay Company, 1956.

Allez, viens!

encourages higher-order thinking skills in the following ways:

THE PUPIL'S EDITION

- Develops critical thinking skills through a variety of activities, including interpretation of the visually presented **Mise en train**, journal writing, interviews, **Rencontre Culturelle** presentations, application of reading strategies, and situational role-plays.

THE ANNOTATED TEACHER'S EDITION

- Includes Thinking Critically and Multicultural Links features that provide the teacher with suggestions for activities requiring students to draw inferences, compare and contrast, evaluate, and synthesize.

THE ANCILLARY PROGRAM

- Incorporates higher-order thinking skills in Communicative Activities, Additional Listening Activities, and the chapter-related realia. In the *Practice and Activity Book,* students are guided carefully from structured practice to open-ended tasks that require higher-order thinking.

Using Portfolios in the Foreign Language Classroom

BY JO ANNE S. WILSON

*T*he communicative, whole-language approach of today's foreign language instruction requires assessment methods that parallel the teaching and learning strategies in the proficiency-oriented classroom. We know that language acquisition is a process. Portfolios are designed to assess the steps in that process. ◆

Portfolios offer a more realistic and accurate way to assess the process of language teaching and learning.

WHAT IS A PORTFOLIO?

A portfolio is a purposeful, systematic collection of a student's work. A useful tool in developing a student profile, the portfolio shows the student's efforts, progress, and achievements for a given period of time. It may be used for periodic evaluation, as the basis for overall evaluation, or for placement. It may also be used to enhance or provide alternatives to traditional assessment measures, such as formal tests, quizzes, class participation, and homework.

WHY USE PORTFOLIOS?

Portfolios benefit both students and teachers because they

- **Are ongoing and systematic.** A portfolio reflects the real-world process of production, assessment, revision, and reassessment. It parallels the natural rhythm of learning.

- **Offer an incentive to learn.** Students have a vested interest in creating the portfolios through which they can showcase their ongoing efforts and tangible achievements. Students select the works to be included and have a chance to revise, improve, evaluate, and explain the contents.

- **Are sensitive to individual needs.** Language learners bring varied abilities to the classroom and do not acquire skills in a uniformly neat and orderly fashion. The personalized, individualized assessment offered by portfolios responds to this diversity.

- **Provide documentation of language development.** The material in a portfolio is evidence of student progress in the language learning process. The contents of the portfolio make it easier to discuss student progress with the students as well as with parents and others interested in the student's progress.

- **Offer multiple sources of information.** A portfolio presents a way to collect and analyze information from multiple sources that reflect a student's efforts, progress, and achievements in the language.

PORTFOLIO COMPONENTS

The foreign language portfolio should include both oral and written work, student self-evaluation, and teacher observation, usually in the form of brief, nonevaluative comments about various aspects of the student's performance.

THE ORAL COMPONENT

The oral component of a portfolio might be an audio- or videocassette. It may contain both rehearsed and extemporaneous monologues and conversations. For a rehearsed speaking activity, give a specific communicative task that students can personalize according to their individual interests (for example, ordering a favorite meal in a restaurant). If the speaking activity is extemporaneous, first acquaint students with possible topics for discussion or even the specific task they will be expected to perform. (For example, tell them they will be asked to discuss a picture showing a sports activity or a restaurant scene.)

THE WRITTEN COMPONENT

Portfolios are excellent tools for incorporating process writing strategies into the foreign language classroom. Documentation of various stages of the writing process—brainstorming, multiple drafts, and peer comments—may be included with the finished product.

Involve students in selecting writing tasks for the portfolio. At the beginning levels, the tasks might include some structured writing, such as labeling or listing. As students become more pro-

ficient, journals, letters, and other more complicated writing tasks are valuable ways for them to monitor their progress in using the written language.

STUDENT SELF-EVALUATION

Students should be actively involved in critiquing and evaluating their portfolios and monitoring their own progress. The process and procedure for student self-evaluation should be considered in planning the contents of the portfolio. Students should work with you and their peers to design the exact format. Self-evaluation encourages them to think about what they are learning (content), how they learn (process), why they are learning (purpose), and where they are going in their learning (goals).

TEACHER OBSERVATION

Systematic, regular, and ongoing observations should be placed in the portfolio after they have been discussed with the student. These observations provide feedback on the student's progress in the language learning process.

Teacher observations should be based on an established set of criteria that has been developed earlier with input from the student. Observation techniques may include the following:

- Jotting notes in a journal to be discussed with the student and then placed in the portfolio
- Using a checklist of observable behaviors, such as the willingness to take risks when using the target language or staying on task during the lesson
- Making observations on adhesive notes that can be placed in folders
- Recording anecdotal comments, during or after class, using a cassette recorder.

Knowledge of the criteria you use in your observations gives students a framework for their performance.

HOW ARE PORTFOLIOS EVALUATED?

The portfolio should reflect the process of student learning over a specific period of time. At the beginning of that time period, determine the criteria by which you will assess the final product and convey them to the students. Make this evaluation a collaborative effort by seeking students' input as you formulate these criteria and your instructional goals.

Students need to understand that evaluation based on a predetermined standard is but one phase of the assessment process; demonstrated effort and growth are just as important. As you consider correctness and accuracy in both oral and written work, also consider the organization, creativity, and improvement revealed by the student's portfolio over the time period. The portfolio provides a way to monitor the growth of a student's knowledge, skills, and attitudes, and shows the student's efforts, progress, and achievements.

HOW TO IMPLEMENT PORTFOLIOS

Teacher-teacher collaboration is as important to the implementation of portfolios as teacher-student collaboration. Confer with your colleagues to determine, for example, what kinds of information you want to see in the student portfolio, how the information will be presented, the purpose of the portfolio, the intended purposes (grading, placement, or a combination of the two), and criteria for evaluating the portfolio. Conferring among colleagues helps foster a departmental cohesiveness and consistency that will ultimately benefit the students.

THE PROMISE OF PORTFOLIOS

The high degree of student involvement in developing portfolios and deciding how they will be used generally results in renewed student enthusiasm for learning and improved achievement. As students compare portfolio pieces done early in the year with work produced later, they can take pride in the progress as well as reassess their motivation and work habits.

Portfolios also provide a framework for periodic assessment of teaching strategies, programs, and instruction. They offer schools a tool to help solve the problem of vertical articulation and accurate student placement. The more realistic and accurate assessment of the language learning process that is provided by portfolios is congruent with the strategies that should be used in the proficiency-oriented classroom.

Allez, viens!

supports the use of portfolios in the following ways:

THE PUPIL'S EDITION

- Includes numerous oral and written activities that can be easily adapted for student portfolios, such as **Mon journal** and the more global review activities in the **Mise en pratique.**

THE ANNOTATED TEACHER'S EDITION

- Suggests activities in the Portfolio Assessment feature that may serve as portfolio items.

THE ANCILLARY PROGRAM

- Includes criteria in the *Assessment Guide* for evaluating portfolios, as well as Speaking Tests for each chapter that can be adapted for use as portfolio assessment items.

Professional References

This section provides information about several resources that can enrich your French class. Included are addresses of government offices of francophone countries, pen pal organizations, subscription agencies, and many others. Since addresses change frequently, you may want to verify them before you send your requests. ◆

CULTURAL AGENCIES

For historic and tourist information about France and francophone countries, contact:

French Cultural Services
972 Fifth Ave.
New York, NY 10021
(212) 439-1400

French Cultural Services
540 Buth St.
San Francisco, CA 94108
(415) 397-4330

TOURIST OFFICES

Maison de la France
1007 Slocum St.
Dallas, TX 75027
(214) 742-1222

Délégation du Québec
53 State Street
Exchange Place Bldg., 19th floor
Boston, MA 02109
(617) 723-3366

Caribbean Tourism Association
20 E. 46th St., 4th floor
New York, NY 10017
(212) 682-0435

INTERCULTURAL EXCHANGE

American Field Service
220 East 42nd St.
New York, NY 10017
(212) 949-4242

CIEE Student Travel Services
205 East 42nd St.
New York, NY 10017
(212) 661-1414

PEN PAL ORGANIZATIONS

For the names of pen pal groups other than those listed below, contact your local chapter of AATF. There are fees involved, so be sure to write for information.

Student Letter Exchange (League of Friendship)
630 Third Avenue
New York, NY 10017
(212) 557-3312

World Pen Pals
1694 Como Avenue
St. Paul, MN 55108
(612) 647-0191

PERIODICALS

Subscriptions to the following cultural materials are available directly from the publishers. See also the section on Subscription Services.

- *Phosphore* is a monthly magazine for high school students.
- *Okapi* is a bimonthly environmentally-oriented magazine for younger teenagers in France.
- *Vidéo-Presse* is a monthly magazine, aimed at 9- to 16-year-olds in Quebec schools.
- *Le Monde* is the major daily newspaper in France.
- *Le Figaro* is an important newspaper in France. Daily or Saturday editions are available by subscription.
- *Elle* is a weekly fashion magazine for women.
- *Paris Match* is a general interest weekly magazine.
- *Le Point* is a current events weekly magazine.
- *L'Express* is a current events weekly magazine.

SUBSCRIPTION SERVICES

French-language magazines can be obtained through subscription agencies in the United States. The following companies are among the many that can provide your school with subscriptions.

EBSCO Subscription Services
P. O. Box 1943
Birmingham, AL 35201-1943
(205) 991-6600

Continental Book Company
8000 Cooper Ave., Bldg. 29
Glendale, NY 11385
(718) 326-0572

PROFESSIONAL ORGANIZATIONS

The two major organizations for French teachers at the secondary-school level are:

The American Council on the Teaching of Foreign Languages (ACTFL)
6 Executive Blvd.
Upper Level
Yonkers, NY 10701
(914) 963-8830

The American Association of Teachers of French (AATF)
57 East Armory Ave.
Champaign, IL 61820
(217) 333-2842

A Bibliography for the French Teacher

This bibliography is a compilation of several resources available for professional enrichment. ◆

SELECTED AND ANNOTATED LIST OF READINGS

▶ I. METHODS AND APPROACHES

Cohen, Andrew D. *Assessing Language Ability in the Classroom,* 2/e. Boston, MA: Heinle, 1994.
- Assessment processes, oral interviews, role-playing situations, dictation, and portfolio assessment.

Hadley, Alice Omaggio. *Teaching Language in Context,* 2/e. Boston, MA: Heinle, 1993.
- Language acquisition theories and models and adult second language proficiency.

Krashen, Stephen, and Tracy D. Terrell. *The Natural Approach: Language Acquisition in the Classroom.* New York: Pergamon, 1983.
- Optimal Input Theory: listening, oral communication development, and testing.

Oller, John W., Jr. *Methods That Work: Ideas for Language Teachers,* 2/e. Boston, MA: Heinle, 1993.
- Literacy in multicultural settings, cooperative learning, peer teaching, and CAI.

Shrum, Judith L., and Eileen W. Glisan. *Teacher's Handbook: Contextualized Language Instruction.* Boston, MA: Heinle, 1993.
- Grammar, testing, using video texts, microteaching, case studies, and daily plans.

▶ II. SECOND LANGUAGE THEORY

Krashen, Stephen. *The Power of Reading.* New York: McGraw, 1994.
- Updates Optimal Input Theory by incorporating the reading of authentic texts.

Liskin-Gasparro, Judith. *A Guide to Testing and Teaching for Oral Proficiency.* Boston, MA: Heinle, 1990.
- Oral proficiency through interview techniques and speech samples.

Rubin, Joan, and Irene Thompson. *How To Be a More Successful Language Learner,* 2/e. Boston, MA: Heinle, 1993.
- Psychological, linguistic, and practical matters of second language learning.

▶ III. VIDEO AND CAI

Altmann, Rick. *The Video Connection: Integrating Video into Language Teaching.* Boston, MA: Houghton, 1989.
- Diverse strategies for using video texts to support second language learning.

Dunkel, Patricia A. *Computer-Assisted Language Learning and Testing.* Boston, MA: Heinle, 1992.
- CAI and computer-assisted language learning (CALL) in the foreign language classroom.

Kenning, M. J., and M.M. Kenning. *Computers and Language Learning: Current Theory and Practice.* New York, NY: E. Horwood, 1990.
- Theoretical discussions and practical suggestions for CAI in second language development.

▶ IV. PROFESSIONAL JOURNALS

Calico
(Published by Duke University, Charlotte, N.C.)
- Dedicated to the intersection of modern language learning and high technology. Research articles on videodiscs, using computer-assisted language learning, how-to articles, and courseware reviews.

The Foreign Language Annals
(Published by the American Council on the Teaching of Foreign Languages)
- Consists of research and how-to-teach articles.

The French Review
(Published by the American Association of Teachers of French)
- Articles on French-language literature.

The IALL Journal of Language Learning Technologies
(Published by the International Association for Learning Laboratories)
- Research articles as well as practical discussions pertaining to technology and language instruction.

The Modern Language Journal
- Primarily features research articles.

Scope and Sequence: French Level 1

CHAPITRE PRELIMINAIRE : ALLEZ, VIENS!

Functions
- Introducing yourself
- Spelling
- Counting
- Understanding classroom instructions

Grammar
- French alphabet
- French accent marks

Culture
- The French-speaking world
- Famous French-speaking people
- The importance of learning French
- French gestures for counting

CHAPITRE 1 : FAISONS CONNAISSANCE!
Location: Poitiers

Functions
- Greeting people and saying goodbye
- Asking how people are and telling how you are
- Asking someone's name and age and giving yours
- Expressing likes, dislikes, and preferences about things
- Expressing likes, dislikes, and preferences about activities

Grammar
- ne... pas
- The definite articles le, la, l', and les
- The connectors et and mais
- Subject pronouns
- -er verbs

Culture
- Greetings and goodbyes
- Hand gestures
- Leisure-time activities

Re-entry
- Introductions
- Numbers 0–20
- Expressing likes, dislikes, and preferences about things

CHAPITRE 2 : VIVE L'ECOLE!
Location: Poitiers

Functions
- Agreeing and disagreeing
- Asking for and giving information
- Telling when you have class
- Asking for and expressing opinions

Grammar
- Using si instead of oui to contradict a negative statement
- The verb avoir
- Omission of definite articles with avoir and school subjects

Culture
- The French educational system/le bac
- L'heure officielle
- Curriculum in French schools
- The French grading system

Re-entry
- Greetings
- The verb aimer
- Numbers for telling time

CHAPITRE 3 : TOUT POUR LA RENTREE
Location: Poitiers

Functions
- Making and responding to requests
- Asking others what they need and telling what you need
- Telling what you'd like and what you'd like to do
- Getting someone's attention
- Asking for information
- Expressing thanks

Grammar
- The indefinite articles un, une, and des
- The demonstrative adjectives ce, cet, cette, and ces
- Adjective agreement and placement

Culture
- Bagging your own purchases
- Buying school supplies in French-speaking countries
- French currency

Re-entry
- The verb avoir
- Expressing likes and dislikes
- Numbers

CHAPITRE 4 : SPORTS ET PASSE-TEMPS
Location: Quebec

Functions
- Telling how much you like or dislike something
- Exchanging information
- Making, accepting, and turning down suggestions

Grammar
- Contractions with à and de
- Questions with est-ce que
- de after a negative verb
- The verb faire
- Adverbs of frequency

Culture
- Old and new in Quebec City
- Celsius and Fahrenheit
- Sports in francophone countries
- Maison des jeunes et de la culture

Re-entry
- Expressing likes and dislikes
- The verb aimer; regular -er verbs
- Agreeing and disagreeing

CHAPITRE 5 : ON VA AU CAFE?
Location: Paris

Functions
- Making suggestions and excuses
- Making a recommendation
- Getting somone's attention
- Ordering food and beverages
- Inquiring about and expressing likes and dislikes
- Paying the check

Grammar
- The verb prendre
- The imperative

Culture
- Food served in a café
- Waitpersons as professionals
- La litote
- Tipping

Re-entry
- Accepting and turning down a suggestion
- Expressing likes and dislikes
- Numbers 20–100

CHAPITRE 6 : AMUSONS-NOUS!
Location: Paris

Functions
- Making plans
- Extending and responding to invitations
- Arranging to meet someone

Grammar
- Using le with days of the week
- The verb aller and aller + infinitive
- The verb vouloir
- Information questions

Culture
- Going out
- Dating in France
- Conversational time

Re-entry

- Expressing likes and dislikes
- Contractions with **à**
- Making, accepting, and turning down suggestions
- **L'heure officielle**

CHAPITRE 7 : LA FAMILLE
Location: Paris

Functions

- Identifying people
- Introducing people
- Describing and characterizing people
- Asking for, giving, and refusing permission

Grammar

- Possession with **de**
- Possessive adjectives
- Adjective agreement
- The verb **être**

Culture

- Family life
- Pets in France

Re-entry

- Asking for and giving people's names and ages
- Adjective agreement

CHAPITRE 8 : AU MARCHE
Location: Abidjan

Functions

- Expressing need
- Making, accepting, and declining requests
- Telling someone what to do
- Offering, accepting, or refusing food

Grammar

- The partitive articles **du, de la, de l'**, and **des**
- **avoir besoin de**
- The verb **pouvoir**
- **de** with expressions of quantity
- The pronoun **en**

Culture

- The Ivorian market
- Shopping for groceries in francophone countries
- The metric system
- Foods of Côte d'Ivoire
- Mealtimes in francophone countries

Re-entry

- Food vocabulary
- Activities
- Making purchases

CHAPITRE 9 : AU TELEPHONE
Location: Arles

Functions

- Asking for and expressing opinions
- Inquiring about and relating past events
- Making and answering a telephone call
- Sharing confidences and consoling others
- Asking for and giving advice

Grammar

- The **passé composé** with **avoir**
- Placement of adverbs with the **passé composé**
- The -**re** verbs: **répondre**
- The object pronouns **le, la, les, lui**, and **leur**

Culture

- History of Arles
- The French telephone system
- Telephone habits of French-speaking teenagers

Re-entry

- Chores
- Asking for, giving, and refusing permission
- **aller** + infinitive

CHAPITRE 10 : DANS UN MAGASIN DE VETEMENTS
Location: Arles

Functions

- Asking for and giving advice
- Expressing need; inquiring
- Asking for an opinion; paying a compliment; criticizing
- Hesitating; making a decision

Grammar

- The verb **mettre**
- Adjectives used as nouns
- The -**ir** verbs: **choisir**
- The direct object pronouns **le, la**, and **les**
- **c'est** versus **il/elle est**

Culture

- Clothing sizes
- Fashion in francophone countries
- Responding to compliments

Re-entry

- The future with **aller**
- Colors
- Likes and dislikes

CHAPITRE 11 : VIVE LES VACANCES!
Location: Arles

Functions

- Inquiring about and sharing future plans
- Expressing indecision; expressing wishes
- Asking for advice; making, accepting, and refusing suggestions
- Reminding; reassuring
- Seeing someone off
- Asking for and expressing opinions
- Inquiring about and relating past events

Grammar

- The prepositions **à** and **en**
- The -**ir** verbs: **partir**

Culture

- **Colonies de vacances**
- Vacations

Re-entry

- **aller** + infinitive
- Asking for advice
- Clothing vocabulary
- The imperative
- Weather expressions
- The **passé composé**
- The verb **vouloir**

CHAPITRE 12 : EN VILLE
Location: Fort-de-France
(Review)

Functions

- Pointing out places and things
- Making and responding to requests
- Asking for advice
- Making suggestions
- Asking for and giving directions

Grammar

- The pronoun **y**

Culture

- Store hours in France and Martinique
- Making "small talk" in francophone countries
- Getting a driver's license in francophone countries
- **DOMs** and **TOMs**
- Public areas downtown

Re-entry

- Contractions with **à**
- The partitive
- Contractions with **de**
- Family vocabulary
- Possessive adjectives
- The **passé composé**
- Expressing need
- Making excuses
- Inviting

Scope and Sequence: French Level 2

CHAPITRE 1 : BON SEJOUR!
Location: Paris region (Review)

Functions
- Describing and characterizing yourself and others
- Expressing likes, dislikes, and preferences
- Asking for information
- Asking for and giving advice
- Asking for, making, and responding to suggestions
- Relating a series of events

Grammar
- Adjective agreement
- The imperative
- The future with **aller**

Culture
- Travel documents for foreign countries
- Ethnic restaurants
- Studying abroad

Re-entry
- Adjectives to characterize people
- Pronunciation: **liaison**
- Family vocabulary
- Clothing and colors
- Weather expressions and seasons
- Telling time

CHAPITRE 2 : BIENVENUE A CHARTRES!
Location: Paris region (Review)

Functions
- Welcoming someone and responding to someone's welcome
- Asking about how someone is feeling and telling how you're feeling
- Pointing out where things are
- Paying and responding to compliments
- Asking for and giving directions

Grammar
- Irregular adjectives
- Contractions with **à**

Culture
- Paying and receiving compliments
- Teens' bedrooms in France
- **Notre-Dame-de-Chartres**
- Houses in francophone countries

Re-entry
- Use of **tu** vs. **vous**

- Pronunciation: intonation
- Prepositions of location
- Contractions with **de**
- Making suggestions

CHAPITRE 3 : UN REPAS A LA FRANÇAISE
Location: Paris region

Functions
- Making purchases
- Asking for, offering, accepting, and refusing food
- Paying and responding to compliments
- Asking for and giving advice
- Extending good wishes

Grammar
- The object pronoun **en**
- The partitive articles
- The indirect object pronouns **lui** and **leur**

Culture
- Neighborhood stores
- Typical meals in the francophone world
- Courses of a meal
- Polite behavior for a guest
- Special occasions

Re-entry
- Giving prices
- Expressions of quantity
- Food vocabulary

CHAPITRE 4 : SOUS LES TROPIQUES
Location: Martinique

Functions
- Asking for information and describing a place
- Asking for and making suggestions
- Emphasizing likes and dislikes
- Relating a series of events

Grammar
- The use of **de** before a plural adjective and noun
- Recognizing reflexive verbs
- The reflexive verbs **se coucher** and **se lever**
- The present tense of reflexive verbs

Culture
- **La ville de Saint-Pierre**
- Places to visit in different regions
- **Yoles rondes**
- The **créole** language
- **Carnaval**
- Music and dance in Martinique

Re-entry
- Connectors for sequencing events
- Adverbs of frequency
- Pronunciation: **e muet**
- Sports vocabulary

CHAPITRE 5 : QUELLE JOURNEE!
Location: Touraine

Functions
- Expressing concern for someone
- Inquiring; expressing satisfaction and frustration
- Sympathizing with and consoling someone
- Giving reasons and making excuses
- Congratulating and reprimanding someone

Grammar
- The **passé composé** with **avoir**
- Introduction to verbs that use **être** in the **passé composé**

Culture
- **Carnet de correspondance**
- Meals at school
- French grades and report cards
- School life in francophone countries

Re-entry
- Connector words
- Sports and leisure activities
- Pronunciation: the nasal sound [$\tilde{\varepsilon}$]
- Question words
- Reflexive verbs

CHAPITRE 6 : A NOUS, LES CHATEAUX!
Location: Touraine

Functions
- Asking for opinions; expressing enthusiasm, indifference, and dissatisfaction
- Expressing disbelief and doubt
- Asking for and giving information

Grammar
- The phrase **c'était**
- The **passé composé** with **être**
- Formal and informal phrasing of questions
- The verb **ouvrir**

Culture
- Types of châteaux in France
- Buses and trains in France
- Historical figures of Chenonceau
- Studying historical figures in school

Re-entry
- Pronunciation: [y] versus [u]
- The **passé composé** with **avoir**
- Expressing satisfaction and frustration
- Telling time

CHAPITRE 7 : EN PLEINE FORME
Location: Touraine

Functions
- Expressing concern for someone and complaining
- Giving advice; accepting and rejecting advice
- Expressing discouragement and offering encouragement
- Justifying your recommendations; advising against something

Grammar
- Reflexive verbs in the **passé composé**
- The pronoun **en** with activities
- The verb **se nourrir**

Culture
- Pharmacies in France
- Figures of speech
- Teenagers' exercise habits
- Staying healthy
- Mineral water

Re-entry
- Expressing doubt
- Telling how often you do something
- Pronunciation: the [r] sound
- Sports activities

CHAPITRE 8 : C'ETAIT COMME ÇA
Location: Côte d'Ivoire

Functions
- Telling what or whom you miss; reassuring someone
- Asking and telling what things were like
- Reminiscing
- Making and responding to suggestions

Grammar
- Introduction to the **imparfait**
- Formation of the **imparfait**
- **si on** + the **imparfait**

Culture
- Village life in Côte d'Ivoire
- Ethnic groups in West Africa
- High school in Côte d'Ivoire
- Félix Houphouët-Boigny
- Abidjan
- City versus country living

Re-entry
- Pronunciation: the [ɛ] sound

- Adjectives of physical traits and personality
- Chores
- Places in a city

CHAPITRE 9 : TU CONNAIS LA NOUVELLE?
Location: Provence

Functions
- Wondering what happened; offering possible explanations
- Accepting and rejecting explanations
- Breaking some news; showing interest
- Beginning, continuing, and ending a story

Grammar
- **avoir l'air** + adjective
- The **passé composé** vs. the **imparfait**
- The **passé composé** and the **imparfait** with interrupted actions
- **être en train de**

Culture
- The **Cours Mirabeau**, Aix-en-Provence
- **Histoires marseillaises**
- Friendship

Re-entry
- School-related mishaps
- The **passé composé** of reflexive verbs
- Accidents and injuries
- Explanations and apologies

CHAPITRE 10 : JE PEUX TE PARLER?
Location: Provence

Functions
- Sharing a confidence
- Asking for and giving advice
- Asking for and granting a favor; making excuses
- Apologizing and accepting an apology; reproaching someone

Grammar
- Object pronouns and their placement
- Direct object pronouns with the **passé composé**
- Object pronouns before an infinitive

Culture
- Paul Cézanne
- Roman ruins in Aix-en-Provence
- Provençale cuisine
- Talking about personal problems

Re-entry
- Accepting and refusing advice
- Personal happenings
- Pronunciation: the nasal sound [ã]
- Making excuses

CHAPITRE 11 : CHACUN SES GOUTS
Location: Provence

Functions
- Identifying people and things
- Asking for and giving information
- Giving opinions
- Summarizing

Grammar
- The verb **connaître**
- **c'est** versus **il/elle est**
- The relative pronouns **qui** and **que**

Culture
- **La Fête de la Musique**
- Musical tastes
- Movie theaters in France
- The **Minitel**

Re-entry
- Emphasizing likes and dislikes
- Making and responding to suggestions

CHAPITRE 12 : A LA BELLE ETOILE
Location: Quebec
(Review)

Functions
- Asking for and giving information; giving directions
- Complaining; expressing discouragement and offering encouragement
- Asking for and giving advice
- Relating a series of events; describing people and places

Grammar
- The verb **emporter**
- The **passé composé** and the **imparfait**

Culture
- **Le parc de la Jacques-Cartier**
- Ecology in Canada
- Endangered animals
- French-Canadian expressions

Re-entry
- Sports and activities
- Clothing vocabulary
- Making and responding to suggestions

CHAPITRE 1 : FRANCE, LES REGIONS
Location: France
(Review)

Functions
- Renewing old acquaintances
- Inquiring; expressing enthusiasm and dissatisfaction
- Exchanging information
- Expressing indecision
- Making recommendations
- Ordering and asking for details

Grammar
- The passé composé

Culture
- Traditional regional clothing
- Regional specialties
- Eating out in France
- Regional foods

Re-entry
- Food vocabulary
- Question formation

CHAPITRE 2 : BELGIQUE, NOUS VOILA!
Location: Belgium
(Review)

Functions
- Asking for and giving directions
- Expressing impatience
- Reassuring someone
- Expressing enthusiasm and boredom
- Asking and telling where things are

Grammar
- The verb conduire

Culture
- Languages in Belgium
- Favorite comic book characters
- Overview of Belgium

Re-entry
- Extending invitations
- The imperative
- Direct and indirect object pronouns
- The forms of the imperfect
- Making, accepting, and refusing suggestions

CHAPITRE 3 : SOYONS RESPONSABLES!
Location: Switzerland

Functions
- Asking for permission
- Granting and refusing permission
- Expressing obligation
- Forbidding
- Reproaching

- Justifying your actions and rejecting others' excuses

Grammar
- The verb devoir
- The subjunctive
- ne... pas + infinitive

Culture
- Swiss work ethic
- Switzerland's neutrality
- Overview of Switzerland
- Environmental issues
- La minuterie

Re-entry
- Complaining
- Chores

CHAPITRE 4 : DES GOUTS ET DES COULEURS
Location: France

Functions
- Asking for and giving opinions
- Asking which one(s)
- Pointing out and identifying people and things
- Paying and responding to compliments
- Reassuring someone

Grammar
- The interrogative and demonstrative pronouns
- The causative faire

Culture
- French clothing stores
- Fashion and personal style
- The French sense of fashion

Re-entry
- Clothing vocabulary
- Adjectives referring to clothing
- Family vocabulary
- Chores

CHAPITRE 5 : C'EST NOTRE AVENIR
Location: Senegal

Functions
- Asking about and expressing intentions
- Expressing conditions and possibilities
- Asking about future plans
- Expressing wishes
- Expressing indecision
- Giving advice
- Requesting information
- Writing a formal letter

Grammar
- The future

- The conditional

Culture
- Careers and education in Senegal
- Overview of Senegal
- Planning for a career
- The apprenticeship system

Re-entry
- The subjunctive
- Giving advice

CHAPITRE 6 : MA FAMILLE, MES COPAINS ET MOI
Location: Morocco

Functions
- Making, accepting, and refusing suggestions
- Making arrangements
- Making and accepting apologies
- Showing and responding to hospitality
- Expressing and responding to thanks
- Quarreling

Grammar
- Reciprocal verbs
- The past infinitive

Culture
- Bargaining in North Africa
- Values of francophone teenagers
- Overview of Morocco
- Hospitality in Morocco

Re-entry
- Reflexive verbs
- Family vocabulary

CHAPITRE 7 : UN SAFARI-PHOTO
Location: Central African Republic

Functions
- Making suppositions
- Expressing doubt and certainty
- Asking for and giving advice
- Expressing astonishment
- Cautioning someone
- Expressing fear
- Reassuring someone
- Expressing relief

Grammar
- Structures that take the subjunctive
- Using the subjunctive
- Irregular subjunctive forms

Culture
- Overview of the Central African Republic
- Animal conservation in the Central African Republic

- Stereotypical impressions of francophone regions

Re-entry
- The subjunctive
- The conditional

CHAPITRE 8 : LA TUNISIE, PAYS DE CONTRASTES
Location: Tunisia

Functions
- Asking someone to convey good wishes
- Closing a letter
- Expressing hopes or wishes
- Giving advice
- Complaining
- Expressing annoyance
- Making comparisons

Grammar
- **si** clauses
- The comparative

Culture
- Overview of Tunisia
- Traditional and modern life in Tunisia
- Carthage
- Modernization in francophone countries
- Traditional and modern styles of dress in Tunisia

Re-entry
- The imperfect
- Formation of the conditional
- Making requests

CHAPITRE 9 : C'EST L'FUN!
Location: Canada

Functions
- Agreeing and disagreeing
- Expressing indifference
- Making requests
- Asking for and making judgments
- Asking for and making recommendations
- Asking about and summarizing a story

Grammar
- Negative expressions
- The relative pronouns **qui, que,** and **dont**

Culture
- Multilingual broadcasting in Canada
- Overview of Montreal
- Favorite types of movies
- The Canadian film industry

Re-entry
- Expressing opinions

- Quarreling
- Types of films

CHAPITRE 10 : RENCONTRES AU SOLEIL
Location: Guadeloupe

Functions
- Bragging
- Flattering
- Teasing
- Breaking some news
- Showing interest
- Expressing disbelief
- Telling a joke

Grammar
- The superlative
- The past perfect

Culture
- Climate and natural assets of Guadeloupe
- Overview of Guadeloupe
- **La fête des cuisinières**
- Daily routines of francophone teenagers
- Greetings in Guadeloupe

Re-entry
- Forms of the comparative
- The **passé composé**

CHAPITRE 11 : LAISSEZ LES BONS TEMPS ROULER!
Location: Louisiana

Functions
- Asking for confirmation
- Asking for and giving opinions
- Agreeing and disagreeing
- Asking for explanations
- Making observations
- Giving impressions

Grammar
- The relative pronouns **ce qui** and **ce que**

Culture
- **Mardi Gras** and festivals in Louisiana
- Cajun French
- Cajun music
- History of Louisiana
- Parties and celebrations in francophone countries

Re-entry
- Renewing old acquaintances
- Food vocabulary
- Making suggestions

CHAPITRE 12 : ECHANGES SPORTIFS ET CULTURELS
Location: Worldwide (Review)

Functions
- Expressing anticipation

- Making suppositions
- Expressing certainty and doubt
- Inquiring
- Expressing excitement and disappointment

Grammar
- The future after **quand** and **dès que**

Culture
- International sporting events in francophone countries
- Stereotypes of people in francophone countries

Re-entry
- Sports vocabulary
- Prepositions with countries
- Adjectives of nationality

Chapitre Préliminaire, pp. T58–11
Chapter Overview

RESOURCES FOR CHAPITRE PRELIMINAIRE

Map Transparency 4
Textbook Audiocassette 1A/Audio CD 1
Practice and Activity Book, pp. 1–2
Video Guide
Video Program
Expanded Video Program, Videocassette 1
Videodisc Guide
Videodisc Program, Videodisc 1A

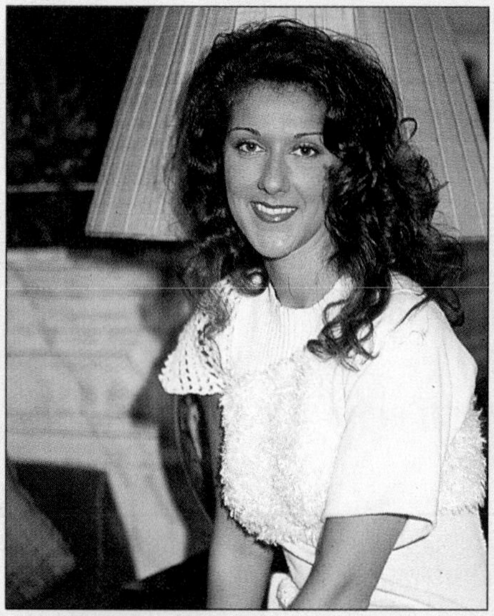

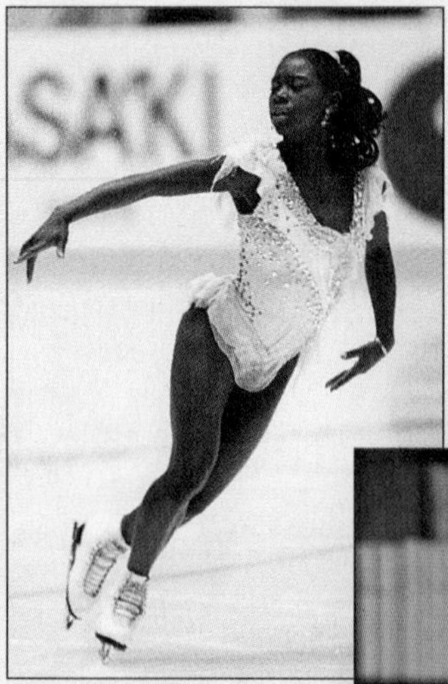

1 un

2 deux

3 trois

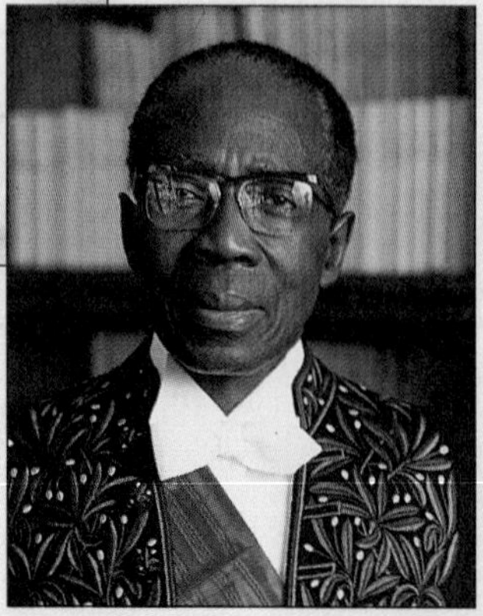

A artiste

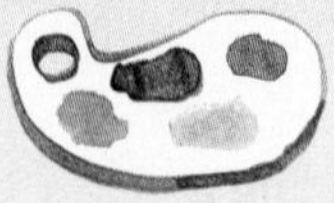

B banane

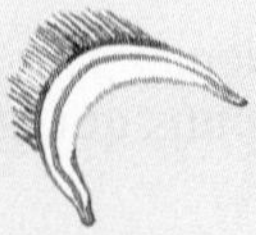

C cinéma

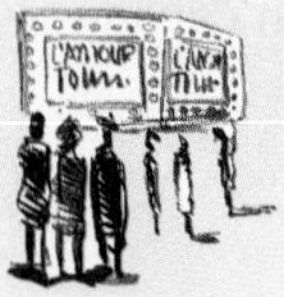

Textbook Listening Activities Scripts

*N*oms de filles/Noms de garçons

For this script, see *Pupil's Edition,* p. 5.

*L'*alphabet

For this script, see *Pupil's Edition,* p. 6.

3 Ecoute! p. 7

1. k–a–n–g–o–u–r–o–u
2. s–e–r–p–e–n–t
3. p–i–n–g–o–u–i–n
4. c–r–a–b–e
5. s–i–n–g–e
6. t–i–g–r–e

Answers to Activity 3
1. f   2. e   3. b   4. a   5. d   6. c

*L*es accents

For this script, see *Pupil's Edition,* p. 8.

5 Ecoute! p. 8

1. p–o–è–m–e
2. h–ô–p–i–t–a–l
3. a–m–é–r–i–c–a–i–n
4. c–a–n–o–ë
5. f–r–a–n–ç–a–i–s
6. s–é–v–è–r–e

*L*es chiffres de 0 à 20

For this script, see *Pupil's Edition,* p. 9.

6 Ecoute! p. 10

1. Moi, mon numéro de téléphone, c'est le vingt, quatorze, huit, douze.
2. Téléphone-moi au vingt, seize, cinq, dix-sept.
3. Mon numéro, c'est le vingt, dix-huit, onze, dix-neuf.
4. Voilà le numéro: vingt, quinze, quatre, treize.

Answers to Activity 6
1. e   2. a   3. b   4. d

A l'école

For this script, see *Pupil's Edition,* p. 11.

9 Ecoute! p. 11

1. Allez au tableau!
2. Fermez la porte!
3. Regardez la carte!
4. Levez la main!
5. Ouvrez le livre!
6. Sortez une feuille de papier!
7. Levez-vous!

Answers to Activity 9
1. Lynn   5. Paul
2. Emilio   6. Dena
3. Brian   7. Evelyne
4. Alison

Pourquoi apprendre le français?
(Individual Project)

ASSIGNMENT

In this project, students will consider their reasons (motivation) for studying French and set personal objectives and goals. Students will share their ideas with the class through oral presentations, using creative posters that might also be displayed in the classroom to provide motivation later in the term. This project is meant to be done in English.

MATERIALS

✂ **Students may need**
- Posterboard
- Construction paper
- Scissors
- Glue or tape
- Magazines
- Catalogues
- Travel brochures (some in French, if possible)

PLANNING

Students should address the following areas in planning their posters:

Motivation What are two or three major reasons why you are studying French?

Objectives What are two or three realistic objectives you would like to achieve in this class this term?

Long-Term Goals What are your long-range goals in your study of French?

SUGGESTED SEQUENCE

1. Talk with students about the importance of being motivated and setting objectives and goals for language learning. Mention that initial motivation, objectives, and goals are likely to change throughout the learning process. You may want to share your own story with students, explaining the reasons why you began to learn French and describing how your motivation, objectives, and goals may have changed.

2. Describe the project and assign a date for the oral presentations. Write the three planning considerations on the board or on a project assignment sheet. Be sure to set a time limit for the presentations.

3. Go over each of the planning considerations and elicit a few responses from the class to serve as examples. If no one has any ideas at first, you might want to give a few of the examples listed here. Stress that students should be honest with themselves, even if their motivation, objectives, and goals are not what others think they should be.

Motivation
- I need credit to graduate.
- I need foreign language for college or future career.
- I have French-speaking relatives.
- I like French food.
- I want to learn about the culture and people in francophone countries.

Objectives
- I want to be able to carry on a simple conversation in French.
- I want to be able to write a letter to a French-speaking pen pal.
- I want to get a good grade in this class.

Long-Term Goals
- I would like to test out of the foreign language requirement in college.
- I would like to speak fluently enough to order a meal in a French restaurant.
- I would like to travel in francophone countries.
- I would like to study at a French university.

4. Give students some time in class for introspection and organizing their thoughts.

5. Have students create posters based on their personal motivation, objectives, and goals. This might be done in class or as homework. Encourage students to be as creative as possible, using words, photos, and drawings to express themselves.

6. Have students make their presentations to the class, showing their posters and explaining their motivation, objectives, and long-term goals.

GRADING THE PROJECT

The purpose of this project is to encourage students to examine their reasons for learning French and the various outcomes they expect for themselves. Because of the personal nature of the project, it would be counterproductive to assign a grade to the subjective content of the project. Instead, the project might be designated as a component of the students' portfolios. Students might review it later in the term or at the end of the term to assess their progress, or to note any changes in their motivation or goals and examine the reasons for the changes. If, however, you feel a grade is necessary, it might be based on completion of all aspects of the assignment, presentation, and creativity.

Suggested point distribution (total = 100 points):

Completion of assignment . . . . 40 points

Poster and presentation . . . . 40 points

Creativity . . . . 20 points

Chapitre Préliminaire: Allez, viens!

Games

TEACHER NOTE

Simulations and games can provide effective learning experiences that lower student anxiety and promote language acquisition. Games often improve group dynamics, particularly when they require students to cooperate rather than compete. Here are some points to consider when you think of incorporating games in your lesson plans.

1. Games should be played in French. However, ground rules might be explained in English.

2. Games should be simple so that precious class time is not taken up explaining the rules.

3. Games should have a pedagogical objective. Is the game for language recognition only? For language production? To recycle previously presented material? To practice a particular skill? To develop higher-order thinking skills?

4. There should be a time limit for every game. If you consistently enforce announced time limits, students will help one another to stay on task.

5. When you find that a game is effective and that your students enjoy it, recycle it throughout the year in new contexts with different content.

MINI-LOTO

This game will give students practice in recognizing and saying numbers in French.

Students make a grid with four squares across and four down. They fill in all the squares randomly with numbers 20 and below, using each number once. To begin, call out numbers at random or have a student do it. Students cross off those numbers that appear on their grids. Students win by crossing off four numbers in a row horizontally, vertically, or diagonally, but they must be able to correctly read aloud the winning row of numbers!

Variation This game can also be played using letters of the alphabet or the names or pictures of objects in this chapter.

9	4	1	3
12	8	19	17
5	6	14	20
2	11	13	18

JE PEUX LAISSER UN MESSAGE?

In this game, students will practice letters of the alphabet and numbers in French.

Have students write down fictitious French names and phone numbers on slips of paper. You can refer them to page 10 for some examples of French phone numbers. Collect the papers, and tell students to imagine they're exchange students in France taking phone messages for their host families. As you read and spell the names and read the phone numbers, have students write down the messages — names and numbers. Then, ask individual students to read aloud what they have written. As an extra challenge, students might read their own messages to one another.

GEOGRAPHY CONTEST

This game will test students' knowledge of the location of francophone countries.

Cover up any maps visible in the classroom and have students close their books. Form teams of three or four players. Name an area of the world such as Africa, Europe, or the Caribbean. For each area you name, teams must think of a francophone country or department in that area and write their answer correctly on the board or on a transparency. After each item, ask the teams to hold up their answers. Each team with a correct answer wins a point. For more challenge or to break a tie, ask teams to name cities in addition to the countries or departments, or ask them to name additional countries or departments in each area.

VIDEO PROGRAM
OR EXPANDED VIDEO
PROGRAM,
Videocassette 1
00:34–05:39

OR *VIDEODISC PROGRAM*,
Videodisc 1A

Search 1, Play To 7725

The video for the Preliminary Chapter will introduce your students to some of the people they will see in the rest of *Allez, viens!* Some are actors in the **romans-photos** found in the **Mise en train** sections, and others are people interviewed for the **Panorama Culturel.** You may wish to play the video to preview the program and to give your students an introduction to the French language.

Motivating Activity

Before students open their books, ask them to answer the following questions. What comes to mind when you think of the French-speaking countries of the world? Besides France, do you know any other countries where French is spoken? Can you think of any cities in the United States with French names? (Des Moines, Iowa; Beaumont, Texas; Pierre, South Dakota; Baton Rouge, Louisiana; Detroit, Michigan; St. Louis, Missouri; La Crosse, Wisconsin)

Teaching Suggestion

You might want to use *Map Transparency 4* (**Le Monde francophone**) as you introduce students to the countries where French is spoken.

CHAPITRE PRELIMINAIRE
Allez, viens!

Language Note

The title of this French program, *Allez, viens!,* is a popular idiomatic expression meaning *Come along!, Come on!,* or *Let's go! Allez, viens!* is particularly appropriate as the title of this program because it is an invitation to each student of French to *Come along!* on an exciting trip to a new culture and a new language.

History Link

Ask students if they know anything about the French exploration of the Western Hemisphere. They may have heard of the French explorers Marquette, Joliet, and La Salle. Marquette and Joliet explored the Wisconsin, Mississippi, and Illinois rivers, and La Salle explored the Ohio River, the Great Lakes, and the Mississippi River. Cartier and de Champlain were explorers of Canada.

Bienvenue
dans le monde francophone!

Welcome to the French-speaking world!

You know, of course, that French is spoken in France, but did you know that French is spoken by many people in North America? About one-third of Canadians speak French, mostly in Quebec province (**le Québec**). In the United States, about 400,000 people in New England (**la Nouvelle Angleterre**), whose ancestors immigrated from Canada, speak or understand French. French is also an official language in the state of Louisiana (**la Louisiane**).

French is the official language of France's overseas possessions. These include the islands of Martinique (**la Martinique**) and Guadeloupe (**la Guadeloupe**) in the Caribbean Sea, French Guiana (**la Guyane française**) in South America, the island of Réunion (**la Réunion**) in the Indian Ocean, and several islands in the Pacific Ocean. French is also spoken in Haiti (**Haïti**).

Did you know that French is also widely used in Africa? Over twenty African countries have retained French as an official language. Many people in West and Central African countries, such as Senegal (**le Sénégal**), the Republic of Côte d'Ivoire (**la République de Côte d'Ivoire**), Mali (**le Mali**), Niger (**le Niger**), and Chad (**le Tchad**), speak French. In North Africa, French has played an important role in Algeria (**l'Algérie**), Tunisia (**la Tunisie**), and Morocco (**le Maroc**). Although Arabic is the official language of these North African countries, French is used in many schools across North Africa and in parts of the Middle East.

Take a minute to find France on the map. Several of the countries bordering France use French as an official language. It's the first or second language of many people in Belgium (**la Belgique**), Switzerland (**la Suisse**), Luxembourg (**le Luxembourg**), and Andorra (**l'Andorre**), as well as in the principality of Monaco (**Monaco**).

As you look at the map, what other places can you find where French is spoken? Can you imagine how French came to be spoken in these places?

un 1

Teacher Note
The scripts for the listening activities for the Preliminary Chapter are on page T59, on *Textbook Audiocassette 1A,* and on *Audio CD 1.*

Motivating Activity
If they are available, show photos, slides, or short videos of the places mentioned. You might also start a discussion by asking students if they have any travel stories to share, if they would like to live or travel overseas, and if they have preconceived impressions of people in these places. Point out that even different regions of the United States can feel like foreign countries at times!

Presentation
Ask students to look at the map of the French-speaking world on the opposite page. Ask them where French is spoken and what ethnic groups are represented in these areas. Call out the names of some francophone countries and have students locate them on the map. Circulate to help students find the different countries or ask individual students to point to the places you mention on *Map Transparency 4* or on a large wall map.

Multicultural Link
Numerous authors from francophone regions are quite popular in France: Maryse Condé from Guadeloupe, Tahar Ben Jelloun from Morocco, and Albert Camus, who was born in Algeria. You might have students research various francophone authors and report their findings to the class.

Culture Note
There are numerous mosques in France because of its large African Muslim population. Because Martinique and Guadeloupe are departments (**départements**) of France, the people of these islands are French citizens and have French passports. They speak both French and Creole. Creole is also spoken in Haiti, an independent country that shares the island of Hispaniola with the Dominican Republic in the Caribbean Sea.

History Link
France had overseas colonies until the 1960s and still maintains close ties with many of the countries. Algeria was the last to gain its independence, in 1962.

Background Information

1. **Léopold Senghor** served in the French parliament from 1946 to 1960, when he was elected president of Senegal. He founded the magazine *L'étudiant noir* with Aimé Césaire. In the magazine's first issue in 1934, they presented the principles of **Négritude,** a literary movement that emphasized the black experience. Senghor was a prisoner during World War II, and after his release in 1942, he became a member of the French Resistance.

2. **Isabelle Adjani** started a theater troupe with some friends at age 12, and at 15, she began her acting career at the Comédie-Française, a historic theater in Paris. While playing Agnès in Molière's *L'école des femmes,* she continued to study for the **baccalauréat.** Her film portrayals have won her four Césars, the French equivalent of the Oscars.

3. **Victor Hugo,** noted at an early age for his poetry, won a prize from Louis XVIII at age 19. His first volume of poetry was published in 1822, the same year he was awarded a royal pension. Hugo was a royalist during his youth, but he became more and more liberal and was elected to the National Assembly in 1849. He was exiled in 1851 for speaking out against Napoleon III. Hugo's exile, spent mostly in the Channel Islands, lasted 19 years, during which time he continued to write. Because of his popularity during his lifetime, his 80th birthday was celebrated like a national holiday. His principal works include eight novels *(Les Misérables),* nine plays *(Hernani),* and 22 volumes of poetry *(Les feuilles d'automne).*

TU LES CONNAIS? *Do you know them?*

In science, politics, technology, and the arts, French-speaking people have made important contributions. How many of these pictures can you match with their descriptions?

1. **Léopold Senghor** (b. 1906)
A key advocate of **Négritude,** which asserts the values and the spirit of black African civilization, Senghor is a man of many talents. He was the first black African high school teacher in France. He was President of Senegal from 1960 to 1980. He won the **Grand Prix International de Poésie** for *Nocturnes,* a book of poetry.

2. **Isabelle Adjani** (b. 1955)
A talented actress and producer, Isabelle Yasmine Adjani is well known for her award-winning roles in French films. In the 1980s, Adjani publicly acknowledged her Algerian heritage and began a personal campaign to raise consciousness about racism in France.

3. **Victor Hugo** (1802–1885)
Novelist, poet, and political activist, Hugo led the Romantic Movement in French literature. In his most famous works, *Notre-Dame de Paris (The Hunchback of Notre Dame)* and *Les Misérables,* he sympathizes with the victims of poverty and condemns a corrupt political system.

4. **Surya Bonaly** (b. 1974)
Surya Bonaly is a four-time gold-medal winner in the European Figure-Skating Championships and a silver medalist in the 1993 and 1994 World Championships.

4. **Surya Bonaly** won fourth place in figure skating at the 1994 Olympics and fifth place at the 1992 Olympics. Her biological parents are from the island of Réunion, but she was adopted as a baby by a couple from France. Originally a gymnast, she is an accomplished skater.

5. **Jacques-Yves Cousteau** has won over 20 film awards and has produced numerous TV series and specials. His interest in inventing and ocean exploration mani- fested itself early, and at age 11, he made a patentable improvement on a marine crane. During World War II, he worked for the resistance movement. His voyages in his vessel *Calypso* began in 1951, and in 1959, he helped invent a mini-submarine that holds two people and photography equipment. He founded the Cousteau Society in 1973 to alert the public about pollution in the oceans.

5. **Jacques Cousteau** (b. 1910)

Jacques-Yves Cousteau first gained worldwide attention for his undersea expeditions as the commander of the *Calypso* and for inventing the aqualung. In order to record his explorations, he invented a process for filming underwater.

6. **Céline Dion** (b. 1968)

A native of Quebec, Dion is a bilingual singer. After recording nine albums in French, she began to learn English and has since produced several albums in English. She performed the award-winning title song for the movie *Beauty and the Beast.*

7. **Gérard Depardieu** (b. 1948)

Gérard Depardieu is a popular actor, director, and producer, who has appeared in over 70 films. His performance in the 1990 movie *Green Card,* which won him a Golden Globe award, marked his American film debut.

8. **Marie Curie** (1867-1934)

Along with her husband Pierre, Marie Curie won a Nobel prize in physics for her study of radioactivity. Several years later, she also won an individual Nobel prize for chemistry. Marie Curie was the first woman to teach at the Sorbonne in Paris.

1e 2a 3h 4b 5g 6f 7d 8c

trois **3**

7. **Gérard Depardieu,** one of six children of an illiterate sheetmetal worker, had a rough childhood, which included arrests for petty theft and truancy. By his late teens, he was in jail and had become mute. A prison official sent him to a speech therapist who helped him discover acting. When he started his career, he had difficulty reading scripts, but was quickly noticed for his talent in an extremely wide range of roles. His films include *My Father the Hero, Danton* (about the French Revolution), *Jean de Florette, Le retour de Martin Guerre* (remade in the United States as *Sommersby*), *Cyrano de Bergerac,* and *Tous les matins du monde,* which also starred his son Guillaume.

8. **Marie Curie,** famous for giving radioactivity its name, was born in Poland and moved to Paris where she attended the Sorbonne. After discovering several radioactive elements, she and her husband finally isolated radium in 1902. She drove an ambulance in World War I and provided X-ray services to hospitals during World War II. She is the only person to win two Nobel prizes in science, but she was denied entrance into the French Academy by one vote because of her gender. She died of leukemia.

For Individual Needs

Challenge Ask students if they know of other famous French-speaking people. You might have students prepare oral reports on them.

6. **Céline Dion** was Canada's Entertainer of the Year in 1993, the same year she hosted the Juno awards, which are similar to the American Grammy Awards. At the awards ceremony, she won four Junos. Some of her hit songs include *Les mots qui sonnent,* "If You Asked Me To," and "Love Can Move Mountains." She is from Charlemagne, a town 20 kilometers east of Montreal.

POURQUOI APPRENDRE LE FRANÇAIS?

Why learn French?

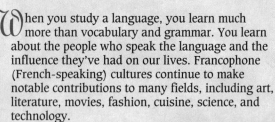

When you study a language, you learn much more than vocabulary and grammar. You learn about the people who speak the language and the influence they've had on our lives. Francophone (French-speaking) cultures continue to make notable contributions to many fields, including art, literature, movies, fashion, cuisine, science, and technology.

Someday you may live, travel, or be an exchange student in one of the more than 30 countries all over the world where French is spoken. You can imagine how much more meaningful your experience will be if you can talk to people in their own language.

Being able to communicate in another language can be an advantage when you're looking for employment in almost any field. As a journalist, sportscaster, hotel receptionist, tour guide, travel agent, buyer for a large company, lawyer, engineer, economist, financial expert, flight attendant, diplomat, translator, teacher, writer, interpreter, publisher, or librarian, you may have the opportunity to use French in your work. Did you know that over 600 American companies have offices in France?

Perhaps the best reason for studying French is for the fun of it. Studying another language is a challenge to your mind, and you'll get a great feeling of accomplishment the first time you have a conversation in French.

Teaching Suggestion

Have students work in pairs or small groups to identify the careers shown in some of the photos and think of products and brand names from francophone countries. Examples include Perrier® and Evian® mineral water, Le Lion (Food Lion®) supermarkets, Air France®, Peugeot® cars, Cartier® jewelry, and Yves Saint-Laurent® fashions. You might also ask students to bring in products from home that were made in francophone countries and have French directions. Some examples are food, shampoo, clothes, and perfume.

Thinking Critically

Analyzing Ask students to discuss why French is necessary in business, travel, and other areas if "everyone speaks English." Ask them why it is different to read something in the language in which it was written rather than in translation. Ask if any of the professions listed on this page interest them and why. In addition, have students find classified ads for employment that either require or prefer knowledge of a foreign language. You might bring in a variety of ads from different newspapers for this activity.

QUI SUIS-JE? *Who am I?*

Here's how you introduce yourself to young people who speak French.

To ask someone's name:
Tu t'appelles comment?

To give your name:
Je m'appelle...

Here's a list of some popular French names for girls and boys. Can you find your name, or a name similar to yours?

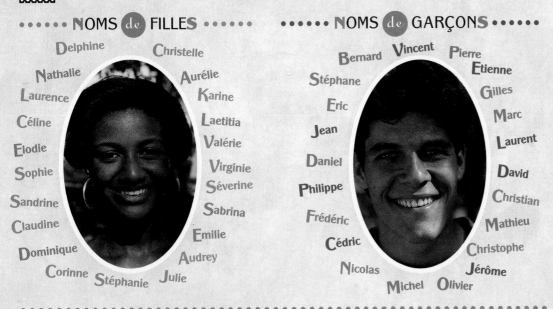

•••••• NOMS de FILLES ••••••

Delphine
Christelle
Nathalie
Aurélie
Laurence
Karine
Céline
Laetitia
Elodie
Valérie
Sophie
Virginie
Sandrine
Séverine
Claudine
Sabrina
Dominique
Emilie
Corinne
Audrey
Stéphanie
Julie

•••••• NOMS de GARÇONS ••••••

Bernard Vincent Pierre
Stéphane Etienne
Eric Gilles
Jean Marc
Daniel Laurent
Philippe David
Frédéric Christian
Cédric Mathieu
Nicolas Christophe
Michel Olivier Jérôme

1 Présente-toi! *Introduce yourself!*

If you like, choose a French name for yourself. Introduce yourself to two or three students in the class, using your own name or your new French name. Ask them their names, too.

Culture Note

For Catholics in francophone countries, each day of the year commemorates a saint. French-speaking Catholics choose a personal saint when they are confirmed as members of the Church. They also celebrate their saint's day **(la fête)** with a cake and cards as they do their own birthdays. People in France sometimes refer to well-known saints' days instead of saying the date; for example, **On se verra avant la Sainte Catherine.** *(We'll see each other before November 25th.)* Ask students to try to guess which saint is commemorated on February 14. The answer is **saint Valentin!** Another example is St. Patrick's Day on March 17.

Teaching Suggestion

Ask students if the English language ever had an informal or intimate way of saying *you.* (The pronouns *thou* and *thee,* which are still used by groups such as the Quakers, were used to address close friends and family.)

Presentation

You might want to have students make name cards for their desks; this will help you learn their names. They might want to choose a French name.

For videodisc application, see *Videodisc Guide.*

Teacher Notes

• Other French boys' names are Antoine, Emmanuel, François, Guillaume, and Julien.
• Additional French girls' names are Anne, Béatrice, Charlotte, Claire, Françoise, Hélène, Jeanne, Nicole, and Véronique.
• Some French African boys' names (from Côte d'Ivoire) are Koffi, Kouassi, Yapo, Séka, Alidou, Moussa, Kouamé, and Daba.
• Some French African girls' names (from Côte d'Ivoire) are Amenan, Aya, Awa, Ami, Fatoumata, Adjoua, Assika, Aminata, Djeneba, and Ahou.

Language Note

Some French names have a masculine and feminine form, which sometimes sound the same; for example, Michel/ Michèle, René(e), and Frédéric/Frédérique. Still other names are used for both boys and girls: Claude and Dominique.

Motivating Activity

Ask students to suggest situations in which you use the alphabet. These situations might include taking or leaving phone messages, making reservations, understanding acronyms (FBI, FDA), and distinguishing between homonyms, such as **mère** *(mother)* and **maire** *(mayor)*. You might use the "Alphabet Song" to help students learn the pronunciation of the letters.

Additional Practice

- Ask students to spell their names or the names of the famous people mentioned on pages 2 and 3. You might also spell other names aloud — Jean-Claude, Eliane, Maryse, Hélène, Blondine — and have students write them on the board and try to pronounce them. You might also ask students to spell classroom objects that you have labeled.
- To practice letters, write a short run-on message, interspersing extra letters throughout. Distribute copies. Then, dictate only the letters of your message. Students circle each letter as they hear it. The circled letters should spell out your message. For example, you would dictate the boldfaced letters in the following series to spell out the message **J'adore le français.**

```
v y j n a w m p c d y l h o
r c u e b x l t e q g f z v y r
a m b n w ç h a g u i p s k
```

For videodisc application, see *Videodisc Guide.*

L'ALPHABET

The French alphabet looks the same as the English alphabet. The difference is in pronunciation. Look at the letters and words below as your teacher pronounces them or as you listen to the audio recording. Which letters sound similar in English and French? Which ones have a different sound?

A artiste

B banane

C cinéma

D dessert

E Europe

F fantôme

G géométrie

H hélicoptère

I igloo

J jardin

K kangourou

L lion

M monstre

N Noël

O orange

P parachute

Q question

R rose

S serpent

T trompette

U uniforme

V voyage

W western

X xylophone

Y yo-yo

Z zèbre

6 *six*

CHAPITRE PRELIMINAIRE   Allez, viens!

Language Note

You might want to tell students that learning to pronounce the alphabet, especially the vowels, can help with their French pronunciation.

Have you noticed that many French words look like English words? Words in different languages that look alike are called *cognates.* Although they're pronounced differently, cognates often have the same meaning in French and English. You may not realize it, but you already know hundreds of French words.

Can you figure out what these words mean?

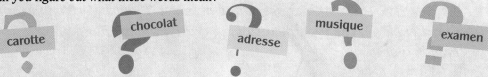

carotte   chocolat   adresse   musique   examen

2 Le dictionnaire

Scan the French-English vocabulary list in the back of your book to see if you can find ten cognates.

3 Ecoute! *Listen!* 1. f 2. e 3. b 4. a 5. d 6. c

Write down the words as you hear them spelled. Then, match the words you've written with the pictures. Be careful! One of the words isn't a cognate.

a.   crabe

b.   pingouin

c.   tigre

d.   singe

e.   serpent

f.   kangourou

4 Tu t'appelles comment?

Can you spell your name, pronouncing the letters in French?

Language Note
2 Explain one of the sources of cognates. Both French and English have words with Latin roots; for example, unitas (Latin), **unité** (French), *unity* (English). You may also want to warn students about false cognates **(faux amis):** words in two languages that look alike but have different meanings. **Librairie** and *library* look alike, but **librairie** is the French word for *bookstore.* The French word for *library* is **bibliothèque.** Other examples are the French word **pain,** which means *bread,* not *pain;* **raisin,** which means *grape,* not *raisin;* and **sympathique,** which means *nice,* not *sympathetic.*

Group Work
2 This activity might be done in groups, with one student in each group responsible for compiling the list. Set a time limit within which each group must find and write down ten cognates.

Teaching Suggestion
3 Ask students to repeat the letters or have them try to pronounce the animals' names.

◆ For Individual Needs
4 Challenge If students have made name cards, you might collect them and redistribute them to different individuals. Each student should spell the name on the card and point out that particular student. As a variation, the student who hears his or her name spelled might say **C'est moi.**

LES ACCENTS *Accent marks*

Have you noticed the marks over some of the letters in French words? These marks are called accents. They're very important to the spelling, the pronunciation, and even the meaning of French words.

- The **accent aigu** (´) tells you to pronounce an *e* similar to the *a* in the English word *date:*

  éléphant   **Sénégal**

- The **accent grave** (`) tells you to pronounce an *e* like the *e* in the English word *jet:*

  zèbre   **chèque**

  However, an **accent grave** over an *a* or *u* doesn't change the sound of these letters:

  à   **où**

- The **accent circonflexe** (ˆ) can appear over any vowel, and it doesn't change the sound of the letter:

  pâté   forêt   île   hôtel   flûte

- The **cédille** (¸) under a *c* tells you to pronounce the *c* like an *s:*

  français   **ça**

- When two vowels appear next to each other, a **tréma** (¨) over the second one tells you to pronounce each vowel separately:

  Noël   **Haïti**

- You usually will not see accents on capital letters.

  île   Ile   état   Etats-Unis

- When you spell a word aloud, be sure to say the accents, as well as the letters.

5 Ecoute!

Write down the words as you hear them spelled.

1. poème	3. américain	5. français
2. hôpital	4. canoë	6. sévère

LES CHIFFRES DE 0 A 20
Numbers from 0 to 20

 How many times a day do you use numbers? Giving someone a phone number, checking grades, and getting change at the store all involve numbers. Here are the French numbers from 0 to 20.

0	1	2	3
zéro	un	deux	trois

4	5	6	7
quatre	cinq	six	sept

8	9	10	11
huit	neuf	dix	onze

12	13	14	15
douze	treize	quatorze	quinze

16	17	18	19
seize	dix-sept	dix-huit	dix-neuf

20
vingt

NOTE CULTURELLE

When you count on your fingers, which finger do you start with? The French way is to start counting with your thumb as number *one,* your index finger as *two,* and so on. How would you show *four* the French way? And *eight?*

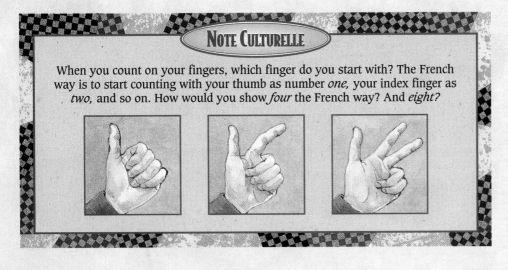

CHAPITRE PRELIMINAIRE

neuf **9**

Motivating Activity
Ask students to suggest why numbers are important. They might list flight numbers, time, temperature, phone numbers, train platform numbers, prices, dates, ages, TV channels, radio stations, and money changing. Point out that the spelling of numbers is also important for writing checks and other banking transactions.

Presentation
You might teach numbers using only numerals before students see the words. Call out the numbers that correspond to the age range of your students and ask them to raise their hands when they hear their age.

For Individual Needs

Slower Pace Students may learn numbers more easily if they group them in short sequences; for example, 1–3, 4–6, 7–9, and then 1–9.

 For videodisc application, see *Videodisc Guide.*

Teacher Note

6 You might tell students that phone numbers in France consist of four sets of two-digit numbers.

Teaching Suggestion

6 After this listening activity, have students pair off to practice reading the phone numbers aloud. They might also practice saying their own phone numbers in French.

 **For Individual Needs**

Auditory Learners Read pairs of numbers aloud and tell the students to write down the smaller (or larger) number.

Challenge Have students count backwards from 20 or count forward by twos or threes.

6 **Ecoute!**

Listen as Nicole, Paul, Vincent, and Corinne tell you their phone numbers. Then, match the numbers with their names.

a. 20. 16. 05. 17   d. 20. 15. 04. 13

b. 20. 18. 11. 19   e. 20. 14. 08. 12

c. 20. 17. 07. 18

1. Nicole e
2. Paul a
3. Vincent b
4. Corinne d

7 **Devine!**   *Guess!*

Think of a number between one and twenty. Your partner will try to guess your number. Help out by saying **plus** *(higher)* or **moins** *(lower)* as your partner guesses. Take turns.

8 **Plaques d'immatriculation**   *License plates*

Look at the license plates pictured below. Take turns with a partner reading aloud the numbers and letters you see.

1.

2.

3.

4.

5.

6.

A L'ECOLE *At school*

You should familiarize yourself with these common French instructions. You'll hear your teacher using them in class.

Ecoutez! *Listen!*	**Fermez la porte!** *Close the door!*
Répétez! *Repeat!*	**Sortez une feuille de papier!**
Levez-vous! *Stand up!*	*Take out a sheet of paper!*
Levez la main! *Raise your hand!*	**Allez au tableau!**
Asseyez-vous! *Sit down!*	*Go to the blackboard!*
Ouvrez vos livres à la page... !	**Regardez la carte!** *Look at the map!*
Open your books to page . . . !	

9 Ecoute!

Listen to the teacher in this French class tell his students what to do. Then, decide which student is following each instruction.

1. Lynn
2. Emilio
3. Brian
4. Alison
5. Paul
6. Dena
7. Evelyne

Presentation
First, demonstrate the commands without English by using gestures and actions. Point out to students that many of the commands are also useful in settings other than the classroom.

TPR Have students carry out the commands as you say them aloud. Students might then practice giving and following the commands in pairs or small groups.

Additional Practice

9 Have students look at the classroom illustration and tell whether the following statements are true or false.
1. **Alison lève la main.**
2. **Emilio ouvre la porte.**
3. **Evelyne se lève.**
4. **Amy ferme la porte.**
5. **Lynn est au tableau.**
6. **Brian regarde le professeur.**
7. **Mike répète le vocabulaire.**
8. **Dena prend une feuille de papier.**
9. **Paul ouvre un livre.**

Allez, viens à Poitiers! pp. 12–89

Motivating Activity

Have students tell what they know about France: the people, culture, food, cities, tourist attractions, and so on. Then, have them compare their impressions with the photos of Poitiers on pages 12–15.

Background Information

Poitiers, often called **Ville d'art et d'histoire** and **Ville de tous les âges,** is an ancient city. It is the capital of Poitou-Charentes, one of the 22 regions into which France is now divided. In 56 B.C., the town came under Roman control, which lasted for several centuries. A famous battle occurred near Poitiers in 732 when Charles Martel, grandfather of Charlemagne, defeated the invading Saracens, Muslims who had crossed from North Africa into Spain and settled there. In the twelfth century, Poitiers was the city from which Aliénor d'Aquitaine, and later her son Richard I the Lionhearted (**Richard Cœur de Lion**), ruled the provinces of Aquitaine and Poitou.

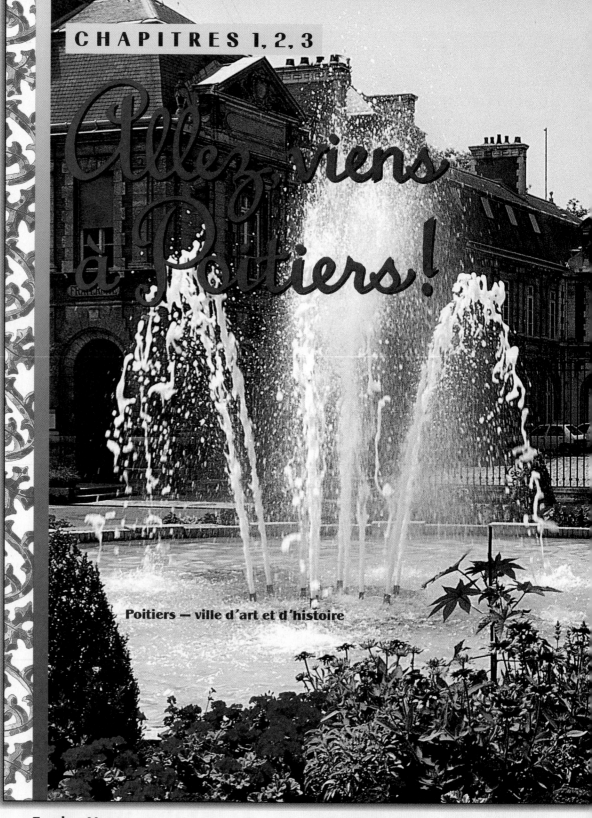

CHAPITRES 1, 2, 3

Allez, viens à Poitiers!

Poitiers — ville d'art et d'histoire

Teacher Note

La place Aristide Bruant The beautiful square shown on pages 12 and 13 was named after Aristide Bruant, a popular singer-songwriter (**chansonnier**), who sang his own songs in various cafés near Montmartre in Paris. He lived from 1851 to 1925.

Language Note

The earliest inhabitants of the region were the **Pictaves,** or **Pictons,** a Gallic tribe of sailors and tradesmen. Their name is a possible origin of the name of the region, Poitou, and the city, Poitiers.

History Link

The town of Poitiers was held by the English from 1152 until 1204.

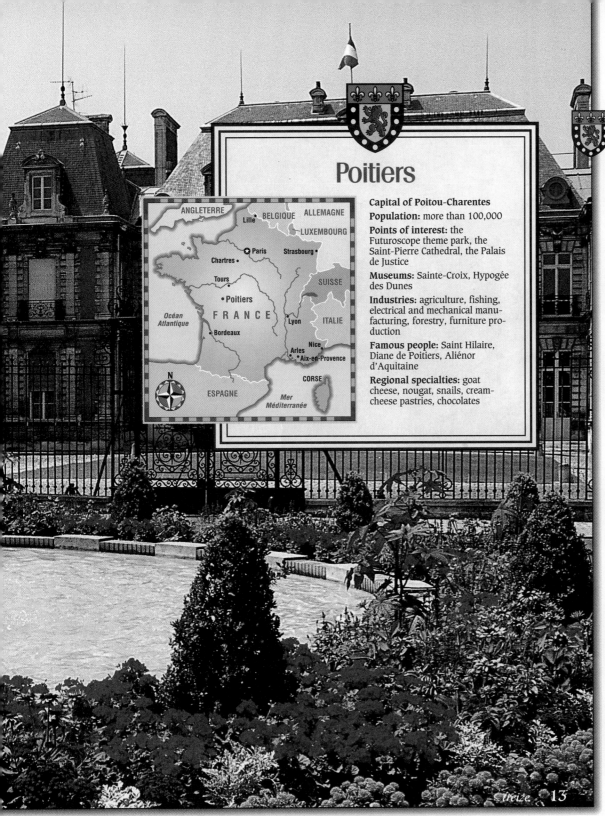

Poitiers

Capital of Poitou-Charentes

Population: more than 100,000

Points of interest: the Futuroscope theme park, the Saint-Pierre Cathedral, the Palais de Justice

Museums: Sainte-Croix, Hypogée des Dunes

Industries: agriculture, fishing, electrical and mechanical manufacturing, forestry, furniture production

Famous people: Saint Hilaire, Diane de Poitiers, Aliénor d'Aquitaine

Regional specialties: goat cheese, nougat, snails, cream-cheese pastries, chocolates

treize 13

Using the Almanac and Map

Terms in the Almanac

- **Le Palais de Justice** is a courthouse built in the nineteenth century around the remains of the palais des Ducs d'Aquitaine.
- **Le musée Sainte-Croix,** located on the site of the Abbaye Sainte-Croix, houses a fine arts collection and an archeological museum.
- **L'Hypogée des Dunes,** an underground chapel from the seventh century, is built over an ancient Roman cemetery.
- **Saint Hilaire** was the first bishop of Poitiers.
- **Aliénor d'Aquitaine** (1122–1204) was Duchess of Aquitaine. Among her nine children with Henry II of England were Richard the Lionhearted and John Lackland, the English king who was forced to sign the Magna Carta in 1215.

Teaching Suggestion

Have students report on the many fascinating historical figures from this region, such as Aliénor d'Aquitaine, Henri II, Richard the Lionhearted, and others. Have them make a timeline of the events of the eleventh and twelfth centuries that occurred in Aquitaine and Poitou.

Language Note

You might give students the French equivalents of the regional specialties listed in the almanac: *goat cheese* (**chabichou**), *nougat* (**nougâtines**), *snails* (**escargots**), *cream-cheese pastries* (**tourteau fromager**), and *chocolates* (**marguerites**).

Using the Map

1. Have students name the bodies of water and the countries surrounding France.
2. Ask students if they can name the four major rivers shown on the map (**la Garonne**—southwest; **la Loire**—central; **la Seine**—north; **le Rhône**—southwest).
3. Have students locate the island of Corsica (**Corse**) in the Mediterranean Sea. Corsica is part of France and is located about 115 miles east-southeast of the city of Nice.

History/Literature Link

Henry II of England, the husband of Aliénor d'Aquitaine, was responsible for the assassination of Sir Thomas Becket, Archbishop of Canterbury. Their story was the basis for T. S. Eliot's play *Murder in the Cathedral* and Jean Anouilh's play *Becket.*

Using the Photo Essay

① Two other impressive attractions of **le Futuroscope** are the "Showscan," which produces an incredibly realistic image at 60 frames per second, and the "Dynamic Simulator," which has moving seats that are synchronized with the action on the screen.

② **Le centre-ville** Because Poitiers is an ancient city, the oldest streets are very narrow and unsuitable for automobile traffic. Some have been converted to pedestrian shopping areas where traffic is not allowed.

Thinking Critically

② **Observing** Ask students if there are any particular features they notice about the buildings in this photo. Ask what the green cross on the right stands for (a pharmacy).

③ **Le marché aux fleurs** The French are generally very fond of flowers and gardening, and flower markets are a common sight throughout France. French gardens (**les jardins à la française**) are defined by their sculpted shrubs and plants laid out in intricate, symmetrical designs.

Thinking Critically

Observing Call students' attention to the flowers and gardens in the photographs on pages 12–15. Would they find similar decorations around American buildings or towns?

③ **Drawing Inferences** Ask students for the name of the café at the end of the street in this photo. Tell them that **la gargouille** means *gargoyle* and ask why this name was chosen for the café and where they think this area might be located (possibly near a church or cathedral — see Art Link). Finally, ask students what they think a **glacier** is (*ice cream shop*).

Poitiers

Poitiers is famous for its art and history. It was here in 732 A.D. that Charles Martel defeated the Saracens in the Battle of Poitiers. Home to an important university and attractions such as a futuristic park devoted to cinematic technology, Poitiers is also a very modern city.

① People of all ages enjoy **le Futuroscope**, a popular futuristic theme park filled with cinematic exhibits. Of particular interest are the 360-degree theater, and the **Kinémax** with its 600-square-meter screen.

② The heart of French cities and towns is called **le centre-ville**. In Poitiers, it is the bustling center of town where people gather in cafés and frequent the many shops.

③ At least once a week, French towns usually have an outdoor market such as this **marché aux fleurs**.

Culture Note

② Since most train stations in France are located in the **centre**-ville, train travel is very convenient, and people generally do not need their cars for travel outside the metropolitan area or even within the city itself.

Art Link

③ **Les gargouilles**, or *gargoyles*, are decorative sculptures on cathedrals and churches. They serve to drain off rainwater and are often carved in the form of grotesque animals and monsters.

④ **La Pierre Levée** is a dolmen, a prehistoric monument constructed of upright stones supporting a horizontal stone. Found especially in Britain and France, dolmens are believed to be tombs. This one dates from about 3000 B.C.

⑤ Contruction on the **cathédrale Saint-Pierre** was begun towards the end of the twelfth century. It is a cathedral of impressive proportions. Built in the gothic style, its facade has three gabled portals and a rose window.

⑥ In most French cities you will find the **Hôtel de ville**, which houses the government administration offices.

Culture Note

④ Dolmens are enormous stone structures, somewhat like tables, with a large stone placed horizontally on other stones standing vertically. About 150 are found in the Poitou region. Menhirs are tall, free-standing stones. Both dolmens and menhirs date from between 5000 and 2000 B.C.

History Link

⑥ The French flag flying over the **Hôtel de ville** is known as **le tricolore** because of its three colors: blue, white, and red **(bleu, blanc et rouge)**. The tricolor flag first appeared shortly after the French Revolution in 1789. Ask students if they know the nickname of the flag of the United States (the star-spangled banner).

LOCATION OPENER
CHAPTERS 1, 2, 3

④ **La Pierre Levée** This monument was a popular gathering place for students in the sixteenth century when the author François Rabelais was a frequent visitor to Poitiers.

Multicultural Link

④ Ask students if they know of other huge stone structures in the world that were built in ancient times (the pyramids in Egypt, Mexico, and South America, and the stone structures on Easter Island and at Stonehenge in England). Ask students to imagine how these structures were built without modern machinery.

Culture Note

⑤ Ask students if they can determine what the sculptor has depicted over the door **(le portail)** of the **cathédrale Saint-Pierre.** (On most cathedrals, the sculptures over the central door depict the Last Judgment. God is surrounded by St. Peter, Mary, angels, or other holy figures. Below are the souls condemned to Purgatory, and at the very bottom are those in Hell. The figures in the four arches over the door include apostles, prophets, and saints.)

Architecture Link

⑤ The **gothique angevin** style of the **cathédrale Saint-Pierre** marked a transition from Roman to Gothic architecture. Roman architecture was characterized by rounded arches, heavy, solid walls, few windows, and dark interiors. In contrast, the development of **arcs boutants** *(flying buttresses)*, which supported the weight of the roof, permitted higher walls and large numbers of **vitraux** *(stained-glass windows)*. Gothic architecture was characterized by the pointed **arc brisé** *(Gothic arch)*.

Chapitre 1 : Faisons connaissance!
Chapter Overview

Mise en train pp. 18–20	Salut, les copains!		Practice and Activity Book, p. 3		Video Guide OR Videodisc Guide

	FUNCTIONS	GRAMMAR	CULTURE	RE-ENTRY
Première étape pp. 21–25	• Greeting people and saying goodbye, p. 22 • Asking how people are and telling how you are, p. 23 • Asking someone's name and giving yours, p. 24 • Asking someone's age and giving yours, p. 25		• **Rencontre Culturelle,** Greetings and goodbyes, p. 21 • **Note Culturelle,** Hand gestures, p. 23	• Introductions • Numbers 0–20
Deuxième étape pp. 26–30	Expressing likes, dislikes, and preferences about things, p. 26	• **ne... pas,** p. 26 • The definite articles **le, la, l', les,** and the gender of nouns, p. 28	• Realia: French movie ad for *Casablanca*, p. 26 • **Panorama Culturel,** Leisure-time activities, p. 30	
Troisième étape pp. 31–35	Expressing likes, dislikes, and preferences about activities, p. 32	Subject pronouns and **-er** verbs, p. 33		Expressing likes, dislikes, and preferences about things

Prononciation p. 35	Intonation		**Dictation:** *Textbook Audiocassette 1A/Audio CD 1*

Lisons! pp. 36–37	**Petites annonces**		**Reading Strategy:** Using titles, subtitles, illustrations, and captions

Review pp. 38–41	Mise en pratique, pp. 38–39	Que sais-je? p. 40	Vocabulaire, p. 41

Assessment Options	**Etape Quizzes**
	• *Chapter Teaching Resources, Book 1*
	  Première étape, Quiz 1-1, pp. 23–24
	  Deuxième étape, Quiz 1-2, pp. 25–26
	  Troisième étape, Quiz 1-3, pp. 27–28
	• *Assessment Items, Audiocassette 7A/Audio CD 1*
		Chapter Test
		• *Chapter Teaching Resources, Book 1,* pp. 29–34
		• *Assessment Guide,* Speaking Test, p. 28
		• *Assessment Items, Audiocassette 7A/Audio CD 1*
		
		Test Generator, Chapter 1

Video Program OR *Expanded Video Program, Videocassette 1* OR *Videodisc Program, Videodisc 1A*

Textbook Audiocassette 1A/Audio CD 1

RESOURCES: Print	RESOURCES: Audiovisual

Textbook Audiocassette 1A/Audio CD 1

Practice and Activity Book, pp. 4–6
Chapter Teaching Resources, Book 1
• Teaching Transparency Master 1-1, pp. 7, 10 . . . . *Teaching Transparency 1-1*
• Additional Listening Activities 1-1, 1-2, p. 11 . . . . *Additional Listening Activities, Audiocassette 9A/Audio CD 1*
• Realia 1-1, pp. 15, 17
• Situation Cards 1-1, pp. 18–19
• Student Response Forms, pp. 20–22
• Quiz 1-1, pp. 23–24 . . . . *Assessment Items, Audiocassette 7A/Audio CD 1*
Videodisc Guide . . . . *Videodisc Program, Videodisc 1A*

Textbook Audiocassette 1A/Audio CD 1

Practice and Activity Book, pp. 7–8
Chapter Teaching Resources, Book 1
• Communicative Activity 1-1, pp. 3–4
• Teaching Transparency Master 1-2, pp. 8, 10 . . . . *Teaching Transparency 1-2*
• Additional Listening Activities 1-3, 1-4, p. 12 . . . . *Additional Listening Activities, Audiocassette 9A/Audio CD 1*
• Realia 1-2, pp. 16, 17
• Situation Cards 1-2, pp. 18–19
• Student Response Forms, pp. 20–22
• Quiz 1-2, pp. 25–26 . . . . *Assessment Items, Audiocassette 7A/Audio CD 1*
Video Guide . . . . *Video Program* OR *Expanded Video Program, Videocassette 1*
Videodisc Guide . . . . *Videodisc Program, Videodisc 1A*

Textbook Audiocassette 1A/Audio CD 1

Practice and Activity Book, pp. 9–10
Chapter Teaching Resources, Book 1
• Communicative Activity 1-2, pp. 5–6
• Teaching Transparency Master 1-3, pp. 9, 10 . . . . *Teaching Transparency 1-3*
• Additional Listening Activities 1-5, 1-6, p. 13 . . . . *Additional Listening Activities, Audiocassette 9A/Audio CD 1*
• Realia 1-2, pp. 16, 17
• Situation Cards 1-3, pp. 18–19
• Student Response Forms, pp. 20–22
• Quiz 1-3, pp. 27–28 . . . . *Assessment Items, Audiocassette 7A/Audio CD 1*
Videodisc Guide . . . . *Videodisc Program, Videodisc 1A*

Practice and Activity Book, p. 11

Video Guide . . . . *Video Program* OR *Expanded Video Program, Videocassette 1*
Videodisc Guide . . . . *Videodisc Program, Videodisc 1A*

Alternative Assessment
• Performance Assessment
  Première étape, p. 25
  Deuxième étape, p. 29
  Troisième étape, p. 35
• Portfolio Assessment
  Written: **Mise en pratique,** Activity 5, *Pupil's Edition,* p. 39
    Assessment Guide, p. 14
  Oral: **Mise en pratique,** Activity 3, *Pupil's Edition,* p. 38
    Assessment Guide, p. 14

For Student Response Forms, see *Chapter Teaching Resources, Book 1,* pp. 20–22.

Première étape

6 Ecoute! p. 22

1. — Bonjour, Philippe!
   — Bonjour, Elodie!
2. — Au revoir, Mlle Latour!
   — Au revoir, Paul!
3. — Salut, Julien.
   — Salut. Au revoir.
4. — Tchao, Sophie!
   — A tout à l'heure, Christelle!
5. — Salut, Gilles.
   — Bonjour, M. Dupont.

Answers to Activity 6
1. hello   2. goodbye   3. goodbye   4. goodbye   5. hello

9 Ecoute! p. 23

1. — Alors, Valérie, ça va?
   — Super!
2. — Tiens, salut, Jean-Michel. Comment ça va?
   — Oh, ça va.
3. — Et toi, Anne?
   — Moi, ça va très bien!
4. — Bonjour, Marie. Ça va?
   — Pas terrible!
5. — Et toi, Karim?
   — Pas mal.

Answers to Activity 9
1. good   2. fair   3. good   4. bad   5. fair

12 Ecoute! p. 24

1. Il s'appelle Mathieu.
2. Elle s'appelle Corinne.
3. Elle, elle s'appelle Danielle.
4. Il s'appelle Michel.
5. Lui, il s'appelle Stéphane.
6. Elle s'appelle Laurence.

Answers to Activity 12
1. garçon   2. fille   3. fille   4. garçon   5. garçon   6. fille

13 Ecoute! p. 25

Il s'appelle comment?
Comment s'appelle-t-il?
Il aime les concerts!
Il s'appelle Robert.
Elle s'appelle comment?
Comment s'appelle-t-elle?
Elle est très sympa!
Elle s'appelle Linda.
Comment s'appelle-t-il?
Il s'appelle comment?
Le garçon blond là-bas.
Il s'appelle Thomas!
Comment s'appelle-t-elle?
Elle s'appelle comment?
Elle aime faire du ski.
Elle s'appelle Julie!
Comment t'appelles-tu?
Tu t'appelles comment?
Moi, je m'appelle Jean.
Voilà! J'me présente!

Answers to Activity 13
Robert, Linda, Thomas, Julie, Jean

15 Ecoute! p. 25

1. Salut! Je m'appelle Bruno. J'ai quinze ans.
2. Bonjour! Je m'appelle Véronique. J'ai dix-sept ans.
3. Salut! Ça va? Je m'appelle Laurent. J'ai seize ans.
4. Salut! Je m'appelle Céline. J'ai treize ans.

Answers to Activity 15
Bruno–15   Véronique–17   Laurent–16   Céline–13

Deuxième étape

18 Ecoute! p. 26

PAUL   Claude, c'est bien pour un garçon, mais je n'aime pas ça pour une fille. Claudette ou Claudine ou...

SOPHIE   Oh, je n'aime pas Claudette!

PAUL   OK, OK. Pour une fille, j'adore Sandrine.

SOPHIE   Oui, Sandrine, c'est adorable. J'aime bien Sandrine aussi, mais j'aime mieux Laetitia. C'est original, non?

PAUL   Laetitia Dubois? Hum? Possible, mais j'aime mieux Sandrine.

Answers to Activity 18a
Paul prefers Sandrine.
Sophie prefers Laetitia.

20 Ecoute! p. 28

1. C'est Pierre. Moi, j'adore le ski.
2. Salut. C'est Monique. Moi, j'aime les hamburgers.
3. C'est Robert. Moi, j'aime les concerts.
4. Bonjour! C'est Suzanne. Moi, je n'aime pas la glace.
5. C'est Paul. J'aime la plage.
6. C'est Emilie. Moi, j'aime les amis.

Answers to Activity 20
a. Paul   b. Suzanne   c. Emilie   d. Monique   e. Robert   f. Pierre

Troisième étape

24 Ecoute! p. 32

1. J'aime parler au téléphone.
2. J'aime étudier.
3. J'aime danser.
4. J'aime faire le ménage.
5. J'aime dormir.
6. J'aime regarder la télé.

Answers to Activity 24
1. Nicolas   2. Danielle   3. Solange   4. Hervé   5. Olivier   6. Stéphanie

Prononciation, p. 35

For the script for Part A, see p. 35.

B. A écouter

1. Tu t'appelles Nicole? question
2. Moi, je m'appelle Marie. statement
3. Elle aime les maths. statement
4. Nous aimons les escargots et les frites. statement
5. Ça va? question

C. A écrire

(Dictation)

1. — Pierre, tu aimes regarder la télé?
   — Oui, mais j'aime mieux sortir avec les copains.
2. — Salut, Sylvie. Ça va?
   — Très bien. Et toi?
   — Ça va.

Mise en pratique

2 p. 38

Bonjour, c'est Sandrine Dupont à l'appareil de l'O.I.C. J'ai des détails sur votre correspondant. C'est un garçon, Robert Perrault. Il a quinze ans et il est parisien. Il aime faire du sport, écouter de la musique et sortir avec les copains. Par contre, il n'aime pas danser. Voilà, j'espère que ça va. Pour plus de détails, téléphonez au dix-sept, treize, quinze, zéro neuf.

Answers to Mise en pratique Activity 2
Name–Robert Perrault
Age–15
Phone number–17.13.15.09
Likes–sports, listening to music, and going out with friends
Dislikes–dancing

Chapitre 1 : Faisons connaissance!
Projects

Moi!
(Individual Project)

ASSIGNMENT

Students make a collage, like those in the **Mise en train,** showing their favorite and least favorite activities.

MATERIALS

✂ **Students may need**
- Magazines
- Scissors
- Glue or tape
- Colored pens, pencils, and markers
- Construction paper or posterboard

SUGGESTED SEQUENCE

1. Working individually, students start by making a list of activities they know in French that they like and don't like to do.

2. Students plan how to present their likes and dislikes visually.

3. Students find pictures in magazines or make their own drawings that illustrate their likes and dislikes and start writing what they want to say in French. Students should mount their illustrations around the text on a large sheet of construction paper or posterboard, using paper clips or small pieces of removable tape to hold the illustrations and text in place until they decide on the final layout.

4. Students write their text on a sheet of paper, double-checking it before they ask you or another student to edit it.

5. Students edit a partner's text, checking for comprehensibility, spelling, and language use.

6. Finally, students write the final version of the text and arrange the final placement of the illustrations.

Students might show their projects to a family member or a friend who is not taking French to see if they have made themselves understood.

GRADING THE PROJECT

As students present their projects to the class, have them cover the French text on their project and tell their classmates in French about their likes and dislikes as they show their pictures.

To evaluate the written content of the projects, you might collect the projects and grade them, or you might display them all around the classroom, giving you time to evaluate and grade each one.

Instead of grading these projects, or after grading them, you might suggest that students place them in their portfolios. If the projects are destined for the portfolio, tell students to include the notes they made in French as well as the initial and final drafts of the French texts.

Suggested Point Distribution: (total = 100 points)

Content . . . . 20 points
Oral presentation . . . . 20 points
Presentation/appearance . . . . 20 points
Language use . . . . 20 points
Creativity . . . . 20 points

 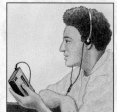   

INTRODUCTIONS

In this game, students will practice giving their names and ages.

Before you begin the game, you might want to put the following incomplete sentences on the board or on a transparency. Explain that you use **Il/Elle a...** to give another person's age.

> **Je m'appelle...**
> **J'ai... ans.**
> **Il/Elle s'appelle...**
> **Il/Elle a... ans.**

This game can be played by the whole class or by two or three large groups. Student A begins by giving his or her name and age in French. Student B must repeat A's name and age and then give his or her own name and age. Student C must repeat A's and B's names and ages and then give his or her own name and age, and so on. The game continues until a student makes a mistake. At this point, the game can start over, beginning with the student who made the mistake or with the following student.

EXAMPLE:

ÉLÈVE 1   Je m'appelle Louise. J'ai quinze ans.

ÉLÈVE 2   Elle s'appelle Louise. Elle a quinze ans. Moi, je m'appelle Todd. J'ai quatorze ans.

ÉLÈVE 3   Elle s'appelle Louise. Elle a quinze ans. Il s'appelle Todd. Il a quatorze ans. Moi, je m'appelle Keesha. J'ai quatorze ans.

JACQUES A DIT

In this game, students will practice giving commands.

As you begin the game, tell students that they must carry out the commands that are preceded by **Jacques a dit...** If you don't say **Jacques a dit...** , students who carry out the command are eliminated from the game. Before you start, you may want to demonstrate gestures students might use to carry out the commands: cupping a hand behind the ear in response to **Ecoutez!** or pretending to carry bags or pay for purchases in response to **Faites les magasins!** Students who are eliminated from the game can stay involved by acting as monitors or by writing down the commands that are used.

Here are some commands you might use:

Dansez!	**Faites le ménage!**
Parlez au téléphone!	**Dormez!**
Lisez!	**Regardez la télévision!**
Voyagez!	**Etudiez!**
Ecoutez de la musique!	**Faites du sport!**
Faites les magasins!	**Faites du vélo!**
Nagez!	

In addition to the above-mentioned commands, you might use the following commands from the Preliminary Chapter: **Répétez! Levez-vous! Asseyez-vous!**

Chapitre 1 Faisons connaissance!

pp. 16–41

*U*sing the Chapter Opener

Motivating Activity

Ask students the following questions. What do you say to someone you've just met? What differences would there be between meeting someone your own age and introducing yourself to an adult? Why?

Teacher Notes

- You might want to point out to your students that fountain pens, or **stylo-plumes**, are still quite common in France and other francophone countries. There is no need for an inkwell, as the ink is contained in disposable cartridges (**cartouches**) that are easily replaced when the ink runs out.

- The passport shown on this page is a European passport, which is available to citizens of most countries in Europe. It allows the bearer to travel more freely among the countries of Europe and avoid long lines at borders.

CHAPITRE

1 Faisons connaissance!

① Bonjour!

16 *seize*

When you meet new people, it's fun to find out what you have in common with them—and even what you don't!

In this chapter you will learn

- to greet people and say goodbye; to ask how people are and tell how you are; to ask someone's name and age and give yours
- to express likes, dislikes, and preferences about things
- to express likes, dislikes, and preferences about activities

And you will

- listen to French-speaking students tell what they like to do
- read about French-speaking teenagers who are looking for pen pals
- write a letter of introduction to a pen pal
- find out how French-speaking people greet one another

② Ça va?

③ J'aime les pâtisseries!

Focusing on Outcomes

- Have students suggest as many English expressions as possible to say hello and goodbye. When would they use each expression? What gestures (if any) do they use with these greetings (a handshake, a kiss, a hug)?
- Have students brainstorm what they would write about if they were introducing themselves in a letter to a pen pal.
- Ask students to match the photos with the appropriate outcomes.

NOTE: You may want to use the video to support the objectives. The self-check activities in **Que sais-je?** on page 40 help students assess their achievement of the objectives.

Photo Flash!

③ This **pâtisserie** window display shows several popular French pastries. The **baba** on the left is a soft cake pastry; the round **amandine** in the middle is a type of almond tart; the **ganache** on the right is a chocolate tart filled with chocolate cream; the **reli-gieuses** in the back row are made up of two cream puffs filled with pastry cream and topped with chocolate. Pastries may also be in the form of different animals, such as the pink raspberry-filled pigs **(cochons à la framboise)** seen here.

VIDEO PROGRAM OR EXPANDED VIDEO PROGRAM, Videocassette 1 07:46–12:52

OR VIDEODISC PROGRAM, Videodisc 1A

Search 11575, Play To 20690

Video Synopsis

In this segment of the video, Claire introduces herself and welcomes us to the town of Poitiers. Next, teenagers from around the French-speaking world say hello and introduce themselves. They each talk about the things they like and what they like to do. We then return to Claire, who is joined by some of her friends in Poitiers. They also introduce themselves.

Motivating Activity

To focus students' attention on making introductions, ask the following questions:
• When was the last time you introduced yourself? What information did you give?
• Why is it a good idea to practice introducing yourself and others in French? (Imagine being an exchange student or hosting one.)
• What could happen if you didn't understand someone's introduction? (You might call the person by the wrong name or talk about an activity the person doesn't like.)

Mise en train

Salut, les copains!

What can you tell about these teenagers just by looking at their photos?

Claire

Bonjour! Ça va? Je m'appelle Claire. J'ai 15 ans. Je suis française, de Poitiers. J'adore le cinéma. Mais j'aime aussi danser, lire, voyager et écouter de la musique.

Djeneba

Salut! Je m'appelle Djeneba. J'ai 16 ans. Je suis ivoirienne. J'aime étudier, mais j'aime mieux faire du sport. C'est super cool!

Ahmed

Salut! Je m'appelle Ahmed. Je suis marocain. J'aime tous les sports, surtout le football. J'aime aussi faire du vélo.

Thuy

Salut! Ça va? Je m'appelle Thuy. J'ai 14 ans. Je suis vietnamienne. J'aime faire les magasins. En général, je n'aime pas la télévision. J'aime mieux aller au cinéma.

18 *dix-huit*   CHAPITRE 1   Faisons connaissance!

RESOURCES FOR **MISE EN TRAIN**
Textbook Audiocassette 1A/Audio CD 1
Practice and Activity Book, p. 3
Video Guide
Video Program
Expanded Video Program, Videocassette 1
Videodisc Guide
Videodisc Program, Videodisc 1A

Didier

Salut! Je m'appelle Didier. J'ai 13 ans. Je suis belge. J'aime écouter de la musique. J'aime aussi les vacances. J'aime surtout voyager!

Stéphane

Bonjour! Je m'appelle Stéphane. J'ai 15 ans et je suis martiniquais. J'aime la plage, la mer, le soleil, la musique et j'aime aussi nager. J'aime surtout danser.

André

Tiens, bonjour! Comment ça va? Je m'appelle André. J'ai 17 ans et je suis suisse. Je parle français et allemand. J'aime beaucoup la télévision. J'aime aussi parler au téléphone avec mes copains.

Emilie

Bonjour! Je m'appelle Emilie. J'ai 16 ans. Je suis québécoise. J'adore faire du sport, surtout du ski et du patin. J'aime bien aussi faire de l'équitation.

MISE EN TRAIN

dix-neuf **19**

Presentation

Have students look at the questions in Activity 1 on page 20 before you play the video so that they will have an idea of what they will see and hear. Then, show *Map Transparency 4* (**Le Monde francophone**) on the overhead projector, or use a wall map if you have one. Ask students to locate on the map the places the teenagers mention.

Video Integration

- **EXPANDED VIDEO PROGRAM,** *Videocassette 1, 12:53–16:13*
- **VIDEODISC PROGRAM,** *Videodisc 1A*

Search 20690, Play To 26765

You may choose to continue with **Salut, les copains! (suite)** at this time or wait until later in the chapter. At this point in the story, Marc arrives at school on his bicycle and sees M. Balland, the math teacher. They greet each other and ask how things are going. Then, Claire arrives and introduces Ann, an American exchange student. M. Balland leaves, and Jérôme arrives on his moped, which breaks down. Later that day, Claire, Ann, Marc, and Jérôme go to a café. Marc, Jérôme, and Claire pay for Ann's part of the check to welcome her to Poitiers.

For Individual Needs

2 Slower Pace Have students find the cognates in the activity and write them down. Have them find the name of the person in each sentence in **Salut, les copains!** They should then find the name(s) of the activity(-ies) in that person's remarks and decide whether the information in both the true-false statement and the basic text are the same.

2 Challenge Have students work individually or in pairs to write three or four additional true-false statements based on **Salut, les copains!** Students might exchange papers and mark their answers, or you might call on individuals to read one of their statements and have other students respond.

Teaching Suggestion

3 Play the video of **Salut, les copains!** Have students call out when they identify each of these functions. Then, stop the video and have students repeat the French expressions.

For videodisc application, see *Videodisc Guide.*

---

1 Tu as compris? *Did you understand?*

Answer the following questions about the teenagers you've just met. Look back at **Salut, les copains!** if you have to. Don't be afraid to guess. See answers below.

1. What are these teenagers talking about?
2. What information do they give you in the first few lines of their introductions?
3. What are some of the things they like?
4. Which of them have interests in common?

2 Vrai ou faux? *True or false?*

According to **Salut, les copains!**, are the following statements true **(vrai)** or false **(faux)**?

1. André aime parler au téléphone. vrai
2. Ahmed n'aime pas le sport. faux
3. Stéphane aime écouter de la musique. vrai
4. Claire aime voyager et danser. vrai
5. Didier n'aime pas voyager. faux
6. Emilie aime faire de l'équitation. vrai
7. Thuy aime la télévision. faux
8. Djeneba n'aime pas faire du sport. faux

3 Cherche les expressions *Look for the expressions*

Look back at **Salut, les copains!** How do the teenagers . . .

1. say hello? Bonjour/Salut
2. give their name? Je m'appelle...
3. give their age? J'ai... ans.
4. say they like something? J'aime...

4 Qui est-ce? *Who is it?*

Can you identify the teenagers in **Salut, les copains!** from these descriptions?

1. Elle est québécoise. Emilie
2. Il parle allemand. André
3. Il a quinze ans. Stéphane
4. Il aime voyager. Didier
5. Elle adore le ski. Emilie
6. Elle n'aime pas la télévision. Thuy
7. Il adore le football. Ahmed
8. Elle aime étudier. Djeneba

5 Et maintenant, à toi *And now, it's your turn*

Which of the students in **Salut, les copains!** would you most like to meet? Why? Jot down your thoughts and share them with a classmate.

Possible answers

1 1. names, ages, interests, and nationalities
2. name, age, nationality, what they like to do
3. music, dancing, sports, movies, reading, traveling, shopping, television
4. Claire and Thuy — movies; Djeneba, Ahmed, and Emilie — sports; Claire, Didier, and Stéphane — music; Claire and Didier — traveling.

RENCONTRE CULTURELLE

Look at what the people in these photos are doing.

—Salut, Mireille!
—Salut, Lucien!

—Bonjour, maman!
—Bonjour, mon chou!

—Salut, Lucien!
—Salut, Jean-Philippe!

—Salut, Agnès!
—Tchao, Mireille!

—Bonjour, Monsieur
  Balland.
—Bonjour, Marc.

—Au revoir, Monsieur
  Legrand.
—Au revoir, Isabelle.

Qu'en penses-tu? *What do you think?* See answers below.

1. How do the teenagers greet adults? Other teenagers? What gestures do they use?
2. How do they say goodbye? What gestures do they use?
3. Is this similar to the way you greet people and say goodbye in the United States?

Savais-tu que...? *Did you know . . . ?*

   In France, girls kiss both girls and boys on the cheek when they meet. The number of kisses varies from two to four depending on the region. Boys shake hands with one another. Teenagers may kiss adults who are family members or friends of the family, but they shake hands when they greet other adults.
   To address adults who aren't family members, teenagers generally use the titles **madame, mademoiselle,** or **monsieur. Mme, Mlle,** and **M.** are the written abbreviations of these titles.

Answers
1. Adults: Bonjour, maman! Bonjour, Monsieur
   Balland.
   Teenagers: Salut!
   Gestures—adults: kiss (relatives); handshake
   Gestures—teenagers: kiss; handshake
2. Adults: Au revoir, Monsieur Legrand.
   Teenagers: Salut! Tchao!
   Gestures—adults: handshake
   Gestures—teenagers: kiss

Culture Notes

• In France, people say **Bonjour** only the first time they see someone on a given day. If they see that person again during the same day, they might just say **Ça va?**
• In Djoula, the market language of Côte d'Ivoire, greeting one another is truly an art form. There are separate greetings for men, women, a person who is working, a person you haven't seen in a long time, and a person who is going to the market.

Jump Start!

Write several numbers between 0 and 20 at random on the board. Have students write the words for these numbers. Then, have them correct their papers by turning to page 9 in the Preliminary Chapter.

MOTIVATE

Ask students to identify as many situations as they can in which people are required to give their name and age.

TEACH

Presentation

Comment dit-on... ? Say these expressions, using appropriate gestures. Have students repeat after you and imitate your gestures.

For Individual Needs

Kinesthetic Learners Have students practice saying the expressions while making the corresponding gestures.

Teaching Suggestions

• Encourage students to copy the functional expressions into their notebooks to aid retention.

6 Students might respond by raising their right hand to signal *hello* and their left hand to signal *goodbye*.

8 Have students draw or cut out pictures of people greeting each other or saying goodbye. Have them add captions or speech bubbles in French.

PREMIERE ETAPE

Greeting people and saying goodbye; asking how people are and telling how you are; asking someone's name and age and giving yours

COMMENT DIT-ON... ?
Greeting people and saying goodbye

To anyone:	**Bonjour.** *Hello.*	**Au revoir.** *Goodbye.*
		A tout à l'heure. *See you later.*
		A bientôt. *See you soon.*
		A demain. *See you tomorrow.*
To someone your own age or younger:	**Salut.** *Hi.*	**Salut.** *Bye.*
		Tchao. *Bye.*

6 Ecoute! Answers on p. 15C.

Imagine you overhear the following short conversations on the street in Poitiers. Listen carefully and decide whether the speakers are saying hello or goodbye.

7 Comment le dire? *How should you say it?*

How would you say hello to these people in French?

Mme Leblanc	**M. Diab**	**Nadia**	**Eric**	**Mme Desrochers**
Bonjour!	Bonjour!	Salut!	Salut!	Bonjour!

8 Comment répondre? *How should you answer?* 3. A tout à l'heure! A bientôt! Salut! Tchao!

How would you respond to the greeting from each of the following people?

1. Bonjour!
2. Au revoir! A tout à l'heure! A bientôt! A demain!
3.
4. Salut!

22 *vingt-deux* CHAPITRE 1 Faisons connaissance!

RESOURCES FOR PREMIERE ETAPE

Textbook Audiocassette 1A/Audio CD 1
Practice and Activity Book, pp. 4–6
Videodisc Guide
  Videodisc Program, Videodisc 1A

Chapter Teaching Resources, Book 1
• Teaching Transparency Master 1-1, pp. 7, 10
  Teaching Transparency 1-1
• Additional Listening Activities 1-1, 1-2, p. 11
  Audiocassette 9A/Audio CD 1
• Realia 1-1, pp. 15, 17
• Situation Cards 1-1, pp. 18–19
• Student Response Forms, pp. 20–22
• Quiz 1-1, pp. 23–24
  Audiocassette 7A/Audio CD 1

COMMENT DIT-ON... ?
Asking how people are and telling how you are

To ask how your friend is: **Comment ça va?** *or* **Ça va?**

To tell how you are:

Super! *Great!*
Très bien. *Very well.*

Ça va. *Fine.*
Comme ci, comme ça.
So-so.
Pas mal. *Not bad.*
Bof! *(expression of indifference)*

Pas terrible. *Not so great.*

To keep a conversation going: **Et toi?** *And you?*

9 Ecoute!

You're going to hear a student ask Valérie, Jean-Michel, Anne, Marie, and Karim how they're feeling. Are they feeling good, fair, or bad?   Answers on p. 15C.

NOTE CULTURELLE

Gestures are an important part of communication. They often speak louder than words. Can you match the gestures with these expressions?

a. Super!
b. Comme ci, comme ça.
c. Pas terrible!

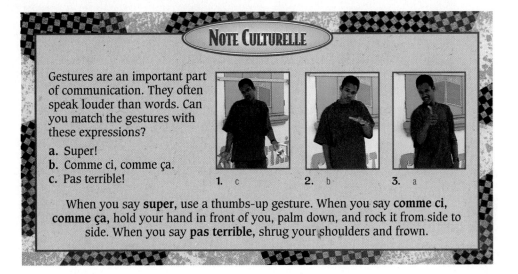

1. c   2. b   3. a

When you say **super**, use a thumbs-up gesture. When you say **comme ci, comme ça**, hold your hand in front of you, palm down, and rock it from side to side. When you say **pas terrible**, shrug your shoulders and frown.

Presentation

Comment dit-on... ? Draw the three faces in **Comment dit-on... ?** on a transparency and number them. Say the expressions in the box aloud in random order and ask students to call out or write down the number of the face that corresponds to the expression. Then, have students pair off and practice the expressions, using the appropriate gestures. One student gives an expression, and his or her partner makes the appropriate gesture.

 For videodisc application, see *Videodisc Guide.*

For Individual Needs

Visual Learners Have students add the functional expressions to their notebooks. You might want to illustrate the intonation pattern by drawing on the board or on a transparency lines that curve upward above **Et toi?** and **Ça va?**

Group Work

9 Ask students to make the face that shows how they feel at the moment. Then, they should form a group with others who feel the same. The members of each group create an illustration of how they feel on a large piece of paper and write the appropriate expression next to it.

Culture Note

The gesture for **comme ci, comme ça** can also show uncertainty. For example, if someone says that the bus will arrive at eight o'clock while making this gesture, then it means that the bus will arrive around eight, more or less.

Presentation

Comment dit-on... ? Give your name and ask several individuals theirs. Students should recall these expressions using **je** and **tu** from the Preliminary Chapter. Have students practice in pairs asking and giving their names. Then, point to boys and girls in the class, naming them. Occasionally, give a wrong name and encourage students to correct you, saying **Non, il/elle s'appelle...**

For Individual Needs

12 Slower Pace Before doing this listening activity, ask students to say **il** or **elle** as you point to different students. Or you might say **Il/Elle s'appelle...** as you point to individuals, having students complete the sentence with the person's name. Then, hold up pictures of people, asking **C'est un garçon?** or **C'est une fille?** Remind students that some French girls' and boys' names sound the same, such as Dominique, Michel/Michèle, and Claude.

10 **Méli-mélo!** *Mishmash!*

Work with a classmate to rewrite this conversation in the correct order, using your own names. Then, act it out with your partner. Remember to use the appropriate gestures. See answers below.

> Très bien. Super! Et toi?
> Tchao. Salut,... ! Ça va?
> Bon. Alors, à tout à l'heure! Bonjour,... !

11 **Et ton voisin (ta voisine)?** *And your neighbor?*

Create a conversation with a partner. Be sure to greet your partner, ask how he or she is feeling, respond to any questions your partner asks you, and say goodbye. Don't forget to include the gestures you learned in the **Note Culturelle** on page 23.

COMMENT DIT-ON... ?
Asking someone's name and giving yours

—Tu t'appelles comment?
—Je m'appelle Magali.

To ask someone his or her name:
Tu t'appelles comment?

To ask someone else's name:
Il/Elle s'appelle comment? *What is his/her name?*

To give your name:
Je m'appelle...

To give someone else's name:
Il/Elle s'appelle... *His/Her name is . . .*

12 **Ecoute!**

Listen as some French teenagers tell you about their friends. Are they talking about a boy (**un garçon**) or a girl (**une fille**)? Answers on p. 15C.

Answers
10 Bonjour,... !
Salut,... ! Ça va?
Super! Et toi?
Très bien.
Bon. Alors, à tout à l'heure!
Tchao.

13 Ecoute!

You're going to hear a song called **S'appeler rap.** Which of the following names are mentioned in the song? *Answers on p. 15C.*

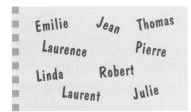

Emilie   Jean   Thomas

Laurence   Pierre

Linda   Robert

Laurent   Julie

14 Je te présente... *Let me introduce . . .*

Select a French name for yourself from the list of names on page 5, or ask your teacher to suggest others. Then, say hello to a classmate, introduce yourself, and ask his or her name. Now, introduce your partner to the rest of the class, using **il s'appelle** or **elle s'appelle.**

COMMENT DIT-ON... ?
Asking someone's age and giving yours

To find out someone's age:
Tu as quel âge?

To give your age:
J'ai douze **ans.**
treize
quatorze
quinze
seize
dix-sept
dix-huit

---

15 Ecoute!

Listen as Bruno, Véronique, Laurent, and Céline introduce themselves to you. Write down each student's age. *Answers on p. 15C.*

16 Faisons connaissance! *Let's get to know one another!*

Create a conversation with two other classmates. Introduce yourself, ask your partners' names and ages, and ask how they are.

17 Mon journal *My journal*

A good way to learn French is to use it to express your own thoughts and feelings. From time to time, you'll be asked to write about yourself in French in a journal. As your first journal entry, identify yourself—give your name, your age, and anything else important to you that you've learned how to say in French.

Building on Previous Skills

14 Review the alphabet in the Preliminary Chapter. Have partners practice spelling their names after introducing each other.

Presentation

Comment dit-on... ?
Review the numbers 1–20. Then, write **âge** on the board and ask the students what they think it means. Now, write **14 ans** and ask what they think **ans** means. Tell the students we get the words *annual* and *anniversary* from the same root. Next, have students pair off and practice the question and response several times.

CLOSE

Group Work
Teams of 3–5 students create short dialogues like the one in Activity 10 on page 24 and write lines on separate strips of paper. Teams mix up their strips of paper and exchange them. Team members work together to arrange the slips of paper in the correct order. Then, teams line up in the order of the dialogue, each member holding a line of dialogue on a slip of paper. Each team reads its dialogue aloud in order, one student at a time.

ASSESS

Quiz 1-1, *Chapter Teaching Resources, Book 1,* pp. 23–24

Assessment Items, Audiocassette 7A/Audio CD 1

Performance Assessment
Have students act out their conversations from Activity 16, using appropriate gestures.

Culture Note
Next to Activity 13 is a photo of the popular French rapper known as MC Solaar. A native of Senegal, Claude M'Barali created his stage name from the English abbreviation for *Master of Ceremonies* and the French word for sun, **le soleil.** In his music, which is a combination of jazz, funk, and soul, Solaar advocates peace and tries to serve as a means of communication for young people. Solaar has created many tongue twisters to describe his philosophy; one example is **Ma tactique attaque tous tes tics avec tact** *(My tactics attack all your tics with tact).* Among his most popular albums are *Qui sème le vent récolte le tempo* ("He Who Sows the Wind Reaps the Tempo") and *Prose combat.*

Language Note
You might want to tell your students that in everyday speech, one might give a short answer for one's age: **Quatorze ans.**

COMMENT DIT-ON... ?
Expressing likes, dislikes, and preferences about things

To ask if someone likes something:
Tu aimes les hamburgers?

To say that you like something:
J'adore le chocolat.
J'aime bien le sport.
J'aime les hamburgers.

To say that you dislike something:
Je n'aime pas les hamburgers.

To say that you prefer something:
J'aime mieux le chocolat.
Je préfère le français.

Note de *Grammaire*

Look at the sentences in the illustrations to the left. Can you figure out when to use **ne (n')... pas**?

You put **ne (n')... pas** around the verb **aime** to make the sentence negative. Notice the contraction **n'** before the vowel.

J'aime le sport.
Je **n'aime pas** le sport.

18 ### Ecoute!

a. Listen to Paul and Sophie Dubois discuss names for their baby girl. Which of the names does Paul prefer? And Sophie? Answers on p. 15C.

Claude   Sandrine   Claudette
Laetitia   Claudine

b. Do you agree with Paul and Sophie's choices? With a partner, discuss whether you like or dislike the names Paul and Sophie mention. What's your favorite French girl's name? And your favorite French boy's name? You might refer to the list of names on page 5.

— Tu aimes... ?
— Non. J'aime mieux...

19 ### Quel film?   *Which movie?*

With two of your classmates, decide on a movie you all like.

— J'aime *Aliens*®! Et toi?
— Moi, je n'aime pas *Aliens*®. Tu aimes *Star Trek*®?
— Oui, j'aime *Star Trek*®, mais j'aime mieux *Casablanca!*

CASABLANCA RE
1942. 1h40. Film d'aventures américain en noir et blanc de Michael Curtiz avec Humphrey Bogart, Ingrid Bergman, Paul Henreid, Conrad Veidt, Claude Rains. *Casablanca à l'heure de Vichy. Un réfugié américain retrouve une femme follement aimée et fuit la persécution nazie. Une distribution étincelante et une mise en scène efficace.*
• V.O. Saint Lambert 96

26   **DEUXIEME ETAPE**

Jump Start!

Have students write the answers to the following questions: Ça va? Tu t'appelles comment? Tu as quel âge?

MOTIVATE

Ask students what they ask about, besides name and age, when they meet someone. Tell students that finding out what others like and dislike is a good way to get to know people.

TEACH

Presentation

Comment dit-on... ?
Gather pictures of various things you like and dislike; some may be in **Comment dit-on... ?** Tell the class in French which ones you like, which you really like, which you prefer, and which you dislike, using the expressions in **Comment dit-on... ?** Then, ask students in French if they like or dislike the same things. They might just answer **Oui** or **Non** at first.

For videodisc application, see *Videodisc Guide.*

Teaching Suggestions

• Students might draw smiling, neutral, and unhappy faces and write sentences about what they like and dislike under the appropriate faces.

19 Students might also discuss music groups or sports teams, in addition to movies.

RESOURCES FOR **DEUXIEME ETAPE**

Textbook Audiocassette 1A/Audio CD 1
Practice and Activity Book, pp. 7–8
Video Guide
  Video Program
  Expanded Video Program, Videocassette 1
Videodisc Guide
  Videodisc Program, Videodisc 1A

Chapter Teaching Resources, Book 1
• Communicative Activity 1-1, pp. 3–4
• Teaching Transparency Master 1-2, pp. 8, 10
  Teaching Transparency 1-2
• Additional Listening Activities 1-3, 1-4, p. 12
  Audiocassette 9A/Audio CD 1
• Realia 1-2, pp. 16, 17
• Situation Cards 1-2, pp. 18–19
• Student Response Forms, pp. 20–22
• Quiz 1-2, pp. 25–26
  Audiocassette 7A/Audio CD 1

VOCABULAIRE

les amis (m.)

le cinéma

le ski

le football

le magasin

la plage

le vélo

la glace

l'école (f.)

le français

les frites (f.)

le chocolat

l'anglais (m.)

les examens (m.)

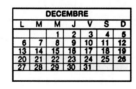

les vacances (f.)

les escargots (m.)

You can probably guess what these words mean:

les concerts (m.)   les hamburgers (m.)   les maths (f.)   la pizza   le sport

---

Presentation

Vocabulaire Have students scan the vocabulary for cognates (**cinéma, ski, examens, vacances, chocolat**). Make sure they are also aware of the **faux amis** (**magasins, football, glace**). Have students make flashcards of this vocabulary with the French on one side and drawings or magazine pictures on the other.

For Individual Needs

Visual Learners Bring in magazine illustrations of the vocabulary items. Ask students **Qu'est-ce que c'est?** as you hold up each illustration. Ask individual students whether they like the item, using **Tu aimes... ?** Then, have partners practice asking each other.

Culture Note

As students learn the words **plage** and **vélo,** they may be interested in learning about the beaches of the Riviera (**la Côte d'Azur**), or about the Tour de France, the famous bicycle race that covers more than 1,500 miles.

Language Note

Explain that **le football** means *soccer.* Tell students they must say **le football américain** if they mean *football.* Also, point out that the word for *vacation* is always plural in French: **les vacances.**

20 Slower Pace Before they hear the recording, students might look back at the **Vocabulaire** on page 27 to find the words for the things shown in the pictures and practice them orally with a partner. After correcting their answers, students might write the letters of the pictures in the order of their own preference and compare their list with a partner's.

20 Challenge Ask students to check their answers with a partner by telling what each teenager likes or dislikes.

Presentation

Grammaire Tell students that many languages have several ways of saying *the*. For example, German has **der**, **die**, and **das**. Explain that French has three different articles that depend on the type of noun they're used with (masculine, feminine, and plural). Have students repeat the articles and nouns after you. You might hold up vocabulary flashcards and have students identify the item, using the correct article.

20 Ecoute!

Listen as several French teenagers call in to a radio talk-show poll of their likes and dislikes. Match their names with the pictures that illustrate the activities they like or dislike. Answers on p. 15D.

Paul Monique Pierre Suzanne Robert Emilie

a.

b.

c.

d.

e.

f.

---

*G*rammaire The definite articles le, la, l', and les

There are four ways to say *the* in French: **le**, **la**, **l'**, and **les**. These words are called *definite articles*. Look at the articles and nouns below. Can you tell when to use **les**? When to use **l'**?

le français	la glace	l'école	les escargots
le football	la pizza	l'anglais	les magasins

- As you may have guessed, you always use **les** before plural nouns.
- Before a singular noun, you use **l'** if the noun begins with a vowel sound, **le** if the noun is masculine, or **la** if the noun is feminine. How do you know which nouns are masculine and which are feminine? One general rule to follow is that normally, nouns that refer to males are masculine (**le garçon** *the boy*) and those that refer to females are feminine (**la fille** *the girl*). There are no hard-and-fast rules for nouns that refer to neither males nor females; you'll just have to learn the definite article **le**, **la**, **l'**, or **les** that goes with each one.

28 *vingt-huit*   CHAPITRE 1   Faisons connaissance!

Teaching Suggestion

Read aloud some sentences that contain nouns and articles from the **Vocabulaire** on page 27, some singular, some plural. Have students hold up one hand if the noun they hear is singular and both hands if it's plural. For example, if you say **J'aime la pizza**, they would raise one hand; if you say **J'aime les magasins**, they would raise both hands.

21 Et toi, qu'est-ce que tu aimes?

Lucie and Gilbert are talking about the things they like. With a partner, complete their conversation according to the pictures.

la plage

LUCIE   Moi, j'aime bien _____ . Et toi?

les copains

CINEMA

le cinéma

GILBERT   Moi, j'aime mieux _____ . J'aime bien aussi sortir avec _____ .

J'adore le sport aussi. Et toi, tu aimes le sport?

le vélo

le ski

LUCIE   Oui, j'adore _____ et j'aime bien _____ aussi.

De bons conseils

How can you remember if a noun is masculine or feminine? Here are a few hints. Choose the one that works best for you.

• Practice saying each noun aloud with **le** or **la** in front of it. (NOTE: This won't help with nouns that begin with vowels!)

• Write the feminine nouns in one column and the masculine nouns in another. You might even write the feminine nouns in one color and the masculine nouns in a second color.

• Make flash cards of the nouns, writing the feminine and masculine nouns in different colors.

22 Tu aimes...?   *Do you like . . . ?*

Choose six things from the vocabulary on page 27. Next, write down which of those things you like and which you dislike. Then, with a partner, try to guess each other's likes and dislikes by asking **Tu aimes... ?**

À la française

Two common words you can use to connect your ideas are **et** *(and)* and **mais** *(but)*. Here's how you can use them to combine sentences.

J'aime les hamburgers. J'aime le chocolat.
J'aime les hamburgers **et** le chocolat.

J'aime le français. Je n'aime pas les maths.
J'aime le français, **mais** je n'aime pas les maths.

23 Mon journal

In your journal, write down some of your likes and dislikes. Use **et** and **mais** to connect your sentences. You might want to illustrate your journal entry.

DEUXIEME ETAPE

vingt-neuf **29**

Mon journal

23 For an additional journal entry suggestion for Chapter 1, see *Practice and Activity Book,* page 145.

Teaching Suggestion
22 Introduce **Il/Elle aime...** so that students can describe their partner's likes and dislikes to the class.

For Individual Needs

Visual/Auditory Learners
To review vocabulary, put pictures or drawings of the vocabulary on the board or on a transparency and number them. Then, say the French words for the pictures at random. Students should call out the numbers of the corresponding pictures in French. Finally, call out the numbers of the pictures and have students say the corresponding French words.

CLOSE

To close this **étape,** have pairs of students use the **Vocabulaire** on page 27 to describe orally the young people shown in the pictures: **Il aime les amis. Elle aime le football.** Then, referring to the pictures, students should tell what they themselves like and dislike. You might have them do this as a written activity.

ASSESS

Quiz 1-2, *Chapter Teaching Resources, Book 1,* pp. 25–26

Assessment Items, Audiocassette 7A/Audio CD 1

Performance Assessment
Have students make a collage of things they like and dislike. See page 15E for a full description of this project. You might refer students to the Supplementary Vocabulary, which begins on page 341, for additional likes and dislikes. Have students present their collage to the class, telling whether they like or dislike the objects pictured.

VIDEO PROGRAM OR EXPANDED VIDEO PROGRAM, Videocassette 1
16:14–18:15

OR VIDEODISC PROGRAM, Videodisc 1A

Search 26765, Play To 28245

Teacher Notes

- See *Video Guide, Videodisc Guide,* and *Practice and Activity Book* for activities related to the **Panorama Culturel.**
- Remind students that cultural material may be included in the Chapter Quizzes and Test.
- The interviewees' language represents informal, unrehearsed speech. Occasionally, edits have been made for clarification.

Motivating Activity

Have students name several activities they enjoy. Ask them if there are certain activities that are particularly popular in their city or region.

Presentation

First, have students view the video. Next, ask easy yes-no questions based on the video or have students tell in English what they have understood about these people. Then, ask them the **Questions** below and have them answer the questions in **Qu'en penses-tu?** This might be done in small groups or as a writing assignment.

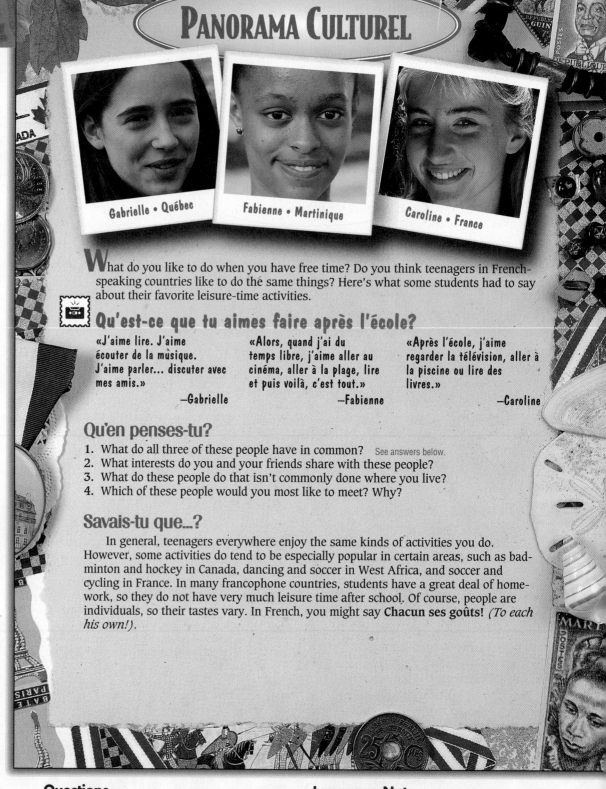

PANORAMA CULTUREL

Gabrielle • Québec

Fabienne • Martinique

Caroline • France

What do you like to do when you have free time? Do you think teenagers in French-speaking countries like to do the same things? Here's what some students had to say about their favorite leisure-time activities.

Qu'est-ce que tu aimes faire après l'école?

«J'aime lire. J'aime écouter de la musique. J'aime parler... discuter avec mes amis.»

—Gabrielle

«Alors, quand j'ai du temps libre, j'aime aller au cinéma, aller à la plage, lire et puis voilà, c'est tout.»

—Fabienne

«Après l'école, j'aime regarder la télévision, aller à la piscine ou lire des livres.»

—Caroline

Qu'en penses-tu?

1. What do all three of these people have in common? See answers below.
2. What interests do you and your friends share with these people?
3. What do these people do that isn't commonly done where you live?
4. Which of these people would you most like to meet? Why?

Savais-tu que...?

In general, teenagers everywhere enjoy the same kinds of activities you do. However, some activities do tend to be especially popular in certain areas, such as badminton and hockey in Canada, dancing and soccer in West Africa, and soccer and cycling in France. In many francophone countries, students have a great deal of homework, so they do not have very much leisure time after school. Of course, people are individuals, so their tastes vary. In French, you might say **Chacun ses goûts!** *(To each his own!).*

Questions

1. Qu'est-ce que Gabrielle aime faire? (Elle aime lire, écouter de la musique, parler et discuter avec des amis.)
2. Est-ce que Fabienne aime la plage? Où est-ce qu'elle aime aussi aller? (Oui; Elle aime aussi aller au cinéma.)
3. Qu'est-ce que Caroline aime faire après l'école? (Elle aime regarder la télévision, aller à la piscine ou lire des livres.)

Language Note

You might want to define the following terms for students: **du temps libre** *(free time),* **la piscine** *(swimming pool).*

Answers
1. They all like to read.

TROISIEME ETAPE

Expressing likes, dislikes, and preferences about activities

VOCABULAIRE

Stéphanie adore **regarder la télé.**

Etienne aime **sortir avec les copains.**

Nicolas aime **parler au téléphone.**

Olivier aime **dormir.**

Danielle aime **étudier.**

Sylvie aime bien **faire du sport.**

Michèle aime **faire les magasins.**

Hervé aime **faire le ménage.**

Raymond aime **faire de l'équitation.**

Serge aime **voyager.**

Eric aime **écouter de la musique.**

Laurence aime bien **nager.**

Solange adore **danser.**

Annie aime **lire.**

Jump Start!

Ask students to write sentences telling two things they like and two things they dislike.

MOTIVATE

Ask students to tell in English what activities they like to do. Make a list of the activities they mention on the board or on a transparency. Have students vote for their favorite activity by a show of hands. If their most popular activities are not represented in the **Vocabulaire,** have them check the Supplementary Vocabulary on page 343, or write the French equivalents for the students.

TEACH

Presentation

Vocabulaire To present this vocabulary, you might want to show pictures of the activities or mime the activities yourself, while saying aloud what you like to do. **(J'aime écouter de la musique.)** After students have repeated the expressions, have volunteers tell what they like to do. Then, ask other students in the class to tell what their classmates like to do. **(Jennifer adore danser.)** Finally, have students work in small groups, with each student miming an activity while the others try to guess what it is.

(TPR) Give commands using the activities in the **Vocabulaire: Regarde(z) la télé! Fais/Faites de l'équitation! Nage(z)!** Have students mime the activities to show that they understand.

Presentation

Comment dit-on... ?
Review briefly the expressions of liking and disliking from page 26. Then, tell the students that they can use the same expressions, substituting activities for things, to tell what they like to do. Next, as you act out the activities or refer to the pictures in the **Vocabulaire** on page 31, ask **Qui aime... ?** completing the question with the activity. Have individuals raise their hands and answer **Moi, et j'aime aussi...** if they want to add another activity that they like. Point out that the verbs following the forms of **aimer** are in the infinitive form.

Group Work

25 Have students number a piece of paper from 1–6 and write down one response for each category. Then, have them ask other students if they like these same items: **Tu aimes... ?** If another student agrees (**Oui, j'aime...**), he or she signs the interviewer's paper next to the appropriate item. Students must get six different signatures to complete the activity. To practice the **nous** form of **aimer**, students might report their findings to the class, saying **Patrick et moi, nous aimons surtout les frites.**

24 **Ecoute!**   Answers on p. 15D.

You're going to hear six students tell you what they like or don't like to do. For each statement you hear, decide which of the students pictured on page 31 is speaking.

COMMENT DIT-ON... ?

Expressing likes, dislikes, and preferences about activities

To ask if someone likes an activity:
Tu aimes voyager?

To tell what you like to do:
J'aime voyager.
J'adore danser.
J'aime bien dormir.

To tell what you don't like to do:
Je n'aime pas aller aux concerts.

To tell what you prefer to do:
J'aime mieux regarder la télévision.

25 **Sondage**   *Poll*

a. Complete the following poll.

1. J'aime...
 a. faire de l'équitation.
 b. sortir avec les copains.
 c. parler français.
 d. dormir.
 e. écouter le professeur.
 f. faire du sport.

2. Chez moi, j'aime...
 a. regarder la télévision.
 b. écouter de la musique.
 c. dormir.
 d. parler au téléphone.

3. Avec mes copains, j'aime mieux...
 a. faire du sport.
 b. manger au restaurant.
 c. faire les magasins.
 d. danser.
 e. nager.
 f. aller au cinéma.

4. J'aime surtout...
 a. le chocolat.
 b. les hamburgers.
 c. la salade.
 d. les frites.
 e. la pizza.

5. J'aime aussi...
 a. le ski.
 b. le vélo.
 c. le volley.
 d. le basket-ball.

6. Je n'aime pas...
 a. les escargots.
 b. la pollution.
 c. l'école.
 d. la violence.
 e. les dentistes.
 f. les examens.

b. Compare your responses to the poll with those of a classmate. Which interests do you have in common?

32   *trente-deux*   CHAPITRE 1   Faisons connaissance!

Language Note

You might explain to your students that the *infinitive* is the *to* form of a verb and that -**er**, -**re**, and -**ir** are typical infinitive endings for French verbs.

Grammaire   Subject pronouns and -er verbs

The verb **aimer** has different forms. In French, the verb forms change according to the subjects just as they do in English: *I like, you like,* but *he* or *she likes.*

Look at the chart below. Most **-er** verbs, that is, verbs whose infinitive ends in **-er**, follow this pattern.

aimer *(to like)*

J'aime	⎫	Nous aim**ons**	⎫
Tu aim**es**	⎬ les vacances.	Vous aim**ez**	⎬ les vacances.
Il/Elle aime	⎭	Ils/Elles aim**ent**	⎭

- The forms **aime, aimes,** and **aiment** sound the same.
- The subject pronouns in French are **je** *(I)*, **tu** *(you)*, **il** *(he or it)*, **elle** *(she or it)*, **nous** *(we)*, **vous** *(you)*, **ils** *(they)*, and **elles** *(they)*.
- Notice that there are two pronouns for *they.* Use **elles** to refer to a group of females. Use **ils** to refer to a group of males or a group of males and females.
- **Tu** and **vous** both mean *you.* Use **vous** when you talk to more than one person or to an adult who is not a family member. Use **tu** when you talk to a friend, family member, or someone your own age.
- Noun subjects take the same verb forms as their pronouns.

Philippe aime la salade.	**Sophie et Julie aiment** faire du sport.
Il aime la salade.	**Elles aiment** faire du sport.

26 «Tu» ou «vous»?

During your trip to France, you meet the following people. Would you use **tu** or **vous** to greet them? How would you ask them if they like a certain thing or activity?

M. et Mme Roland
Vous aimez... ?

Mlle Normand
Vous aimez... ?

Flore et Loïc
Vous aimez... ?

Lucie
Tu aimes... ?

TROISIEME ETAPE

trente-trois 33

Presentation

Grammaire Introduce this section by asking students to recall any subject pronouns they have learned in French. Supply the ones they don't know, without using English, by pointing to individuals and groups as you say the pronouns in French: **nous, ils, elles...** Then, have students look at the **Grammaire** and repeat the pronouns and verb forms after you. You might want to discuss **liaison** and **élision** at this time. See **Prononciation** on page 59.

Teaching Suggestions

Grammaire This would be a good time for students to play a variation of the game "Introductions" on page 15F, using the verb **aimer.** Student A might start by saying **J'aime sortir avec mes copains.** Student B repeats that and then adds his or her own preferred activity. The game continues until a student makes a mistake, at which point the game could start all over again with the student who made the mistake, or with the following student.

26 To extend this activity, have students pair off. Call out two names of people pictured here: Lucie and Mlle Normand. Partners should assume the identity of these people and create a brief dialogue between them, using **tu** or **vous** appropriately.

Additional Practice

26 You might want to hold up pictures of people of various ages, asking **tu ou vous?**

Teaching Suggestions

27 Students might pair off and ask and tell each other whether they like or dislike the activities shown. Remind them to use the connectors **et** and **mais**.

28 You might want to refer students to the famous French-speaking people described in **Tu les connais?** on pages 2 and 3 of the Preliminary Chapter.

 **For Individual Needs**

Challenge Have students write a short description of a friend, family member, or famous personality, naming that person's favorite activities.

Additional Practice

Show *Teaching Transparency 1-3* and have students tell what the people in each room like to do.

 For videodisc application, see *Videodisc Guide*.

27 Qu'est-ce qu'ils aiment faire?

Your French pen pal wants to know what your friends like to do. Use the following photographs as cues.

Julio
Il aime lire.

Robert
Il aime voyager.

Mark, David et Thomas
Ils aiment nager.

Pam
Elle aime faire les magasins.

Marie
Elle aime faire de l'équitation.

Eric
Il aime parler au téléphone.

Karen
Elle aime écouter de la musique.

Blair
Elle aime dormir.

Emily et Raymond
Ils aiment danser.

28 Les vedettes! *Celebrities!*

a. Make a list of three public figures you admire (movie stars, musicians, athletes, . . .). Write down one or two things you think each person might like to do.

Shaquille O'Neal aime faire du sport, surtout du basket-ball!

b. Now, get together with a classmate. Tell your partner what one of the celebrities you've chosen likes to do. Use **il** or **elle** instead of the person's name. Your partner will try to identify the celebrity. Take turns.

34   *trente-quatre*   CHAPITRE 1   Faisons connaissance!

Culture Note

27 You might want to point out the train in the second photo. Train travel is very common in France, owing to an efficient and inexpensive railway system.

29 Enquête *Survey*

Get together with three classmates. Ask questions to find out who shares your likes and dislikes. After you've discovered what you have in common, report your findings to the rest of the class.

> Paul et moi, nous aimons le français et l'anglais, mais nous n'aimons pas le sport.

30 Mon journal

Expand upon your previous journal entry. Write about the activities you like and dislike. Tell which activities you and your friends like to do together. Find or draw pictures to illustrate the activities.

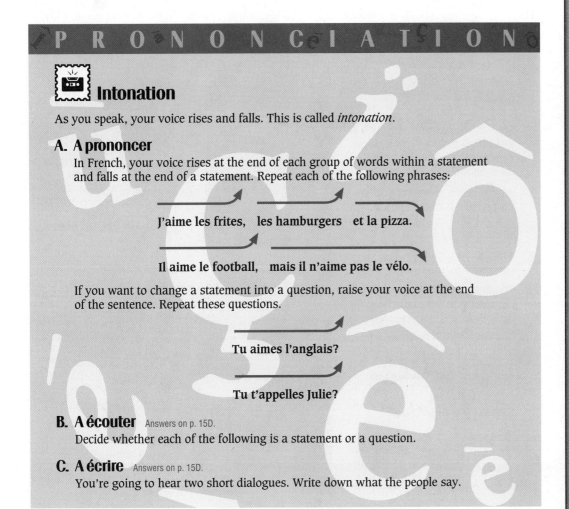

P R O N O N C I A T I O N

Intonation

As you speak, your voice rises and falls. This is called *intonation*.

A. A prononcer

In French, your voice rises at the end of each group of words within a statement and falls at the end of a statement. Repeat each of the following phrases:

J'aime les frites,   les hamburgers   et la pizza.

Il aime le football,   mais il n'aime pas le vélo.

If you want to change a statement into a question, raise your voice at the end of the sentence. Repeat these questions.

Tu aimes l'anglais?

Tu t'appelles Julie?

B. A écouter   Answers on p. 15D.

Decide whether each of the following is a statement or a question.

C. A écrire   Answers on p. 15D.

You're going to hear two short dialogues. Write down what the people say.

Mon journal

30 For an additional journal entry suggestion for Chapter 1, see *Practice and Activity Book,* page 145.

Language Note

Prononciation You might tell students that the rising intonation indicates a yes-no question, rather than a question that seeks information.

Teaching Suggestion

Have students read the **Mise en train** again, silently or aloud in small groups. They might copy some of the text into their notebooks, underlining functional expressions, circling activities or things, and highlighting **ne... pas** or other structures. This will help them to review functions, vocabulary, and grammar.

CLOSE

To close this **étape**, have students tell, either orally or in writing, what activities they like to do, both on their own and with friends. You might have volunteers speak at the beginning or end of class over several days. You might also want to play **Jacques a dit...** on page 15F at this point.

ASSESS

Quiz 1-3, *Chapter Teaching Resources, Book 1,* pp. 27–28

Assessment Items, Audiocassette 7A/Audio CD 1

Performance Assessment

When students have finished Activity 28 on page 34, have them pair off and take turns interviewing the celebrities they have chosen to be. The interviewer might use a dummy microphone, and the celebrity might dress in an identifying costume. If possible, have students videotape their interviews.

Teaching Suggestion

Prononciation After students have finished the activities, you might have them make up their own statements and questions about likes and dislikes and have them practice in pairs or small groups. Pairs or groups could then volunteer to recite their statements and questions in front of the class, using the proper intonation.

Teacher Note

For an additional reading, see *Practice and Activity Book*, page 11.

PREREADING
Activities A–C

Motivating Activity

Ask students if they have pen pals or friends they write to, why people want pen pals, and when writing is better than phoning. You might pass around postcards from abroad, or any ads for pen pals you may have found. Let students know that many students abroad want pen pals and that a number of organizations exist that match up young people who want to correspond. See page T50 for addresses. Point out that exchanging letters often leads to exchanging visits.

READING
Activities D–F

Thinking Critically

Analyzing Ask students to group the pen pals by interest. Then, ask them to choose the pen pal(s) they would most like to correspond with.

Teaching Suggestion

To check for understanding, ask simple questions about the pen pals. **(Il/Elle s'appelle comment? Qui aime la musique?)**

LISONS!

When you look through French magazines, you'll often find a section called **Petites annonces** where people place personal or business ads.

DE BONS CONSEILS

You can often figure out what a reading selection is about simply by looking at the titles, subtitles, illustrations, and captions.

A. Look at the pictures and titles of this article from a French magazine. What do you think the article is about? pen pals

B. Do you remember what you've learned about cognates? Can you find at least five cognates in this article? See answers below.

C. What do you think **Petites annonces** means? · Classified ads

D. Which of the pen pals would you choose if you were searching for the following? See answers below.

Quelqu'un qui *(someone who)*…

aime faire les boutiques

aime les animaux

parle français et espagnol

aime la musique et le cinéma

aime le rap et la techno

COPAINS ★ COPINES ★ COPAINS

PETITES

Christiane Saulnier
Marseille

Si vous aimez la télévision, les animaux et les vacances, qu'est-ce que vous attendez pour m'écrire et m'envoyer votre photo! Je voudrais correspondre avec des filles ou des garçons de 13 à 16 ans. J'attends votre réponse avec impatience!

Karim Marzouk
Tunis, Tunisie

J'adorerais recevoir des lettres de personnes habitant le monde entier; j'adore voyager, écouter de la musique, aller au concert et lire sur la plage. J'aime bien les langues et je parle aussi l'arabe et l'espagnol. A bientôt.

Mireille Lacombe
Nantes

J'ai 15 ans et je voudrais bien correspondre avec des filles et des garçons de 13 à 17 ans. J'aime le rap et surtout la techno. Je fais aussi de l'équitation. Ecrivez-moi vite et je promets de vous répondre (photos S.V.P.)!

Didier Kouassi
Abidjan, Côte d'Ivoire

La techno me fait délirer et je suis aussi très sportif. Je cherche des correspondants filles ou garçons entre 15 et 17 ans. N'hésitez pas à m'écrire!

Answers

B *Possible answers*
correspondre, réponse, lettres, musique, science-fiction, fan, âge, adresse, photo d'identité

D Aime faire les boutiques—Hugues Vallet
Aime les animaux—Christiane Saulnier
Parle français et espagnol—Karim Marzouk
Aime la musique et le cinéma—Amélie Perrin
Aime le rap et la techno—Mireille Lacombe

PINES ★ COPAINS ★ COPINES

ANNONCES

Laurence Simon
La Marin, Martinique

J'ai 16 ans, je suis dingue de sport, j'aime les soirs de fête entre copains. Le week-end, j'aime faire les magasins. Alors, si vous me ressemblez, dépêchez-vous de m'écrire. Réponse assurée à 100%!

Etienne Hubert
Poitiers

Je suis blond aux yeux bleus, assez grand, timide mais très sympa. J'aime sortir et j'aime lire la science-fiction. Je cherche des amis entre 14 et 16 ans. Répondez vite!

Hugues Vallet
la Rochelle

Je voudrais correspondre avec des filles et des garçons de 16 à 18 ans. J'aime sortir, délirer et faire les boutiques. Je suis fan de Vanessa Paradis et de Julia Roberts. Alors, j'attends vos lettres!

Amélie Perrin
Périgord

Je voudrais correspondre avec des jeunes de 14 à 17 ans qui aiment faire la fête, écouter de la musique et aller au cinéma. Moi, j'étudie la danse et la photographie. Ecrivez-moi et je me ferai une joie de vous répondre.

Vous voulez correspondre avec des gens sympa? Écrivez votre petite annonce en précisant vos nom, prénom, âge et adresse, et en y joignant une photo d'identité.

E. Several of your friends are looking for pen pals. Based on their wishes, find a good match for each of them in **Petites annonces.**

Didier Kouassi, Laurence Simon
> My pen pal should like sports.

Etienne Hubert, Hugues Vallet
> I'd like to hear from someone who likes going out.

Amélie Perrin
> I'm looking for a pen pal who likes to go to the movies.

Laurence Simon, Hugues Vallet
> It would be great to have a pen pal who enjoys shopping.

Karim Marzouk, Didier Kouassi
> I'd like to hear from someone from Africa.

Karim Marzouk
> I'd like a pen pal who likes to travel.

F. If you want to place an ad for a pen pal, what should you do?
See answers below.

G. Jot down a few things you might like to include in your own letter requesting a pen pal. Using your notes, write your own request for a pen pal like the ones you read in **Petites Annonces.**

trente-sept **37**

POSTREADING
Activity G

Teaching Suggestion

French exchange students in your area or advanced students of French are possible pen pals. You might have classes exchange letters. It might be fun for students to assume a pen name (**nom de plume**) so that they are corresponding with a mystery pen pal. Later in the year, you can arrange a party where the correspondents finally meet.

Thinking Critically

Analyzing Ask students the following: What can be gained from corresponding with someone from another culture? Are you already familiar with other cultures? Is there any culture in particular that interests you? Have you traveled to other regions in the United States? What, if anything, seemed strange or different to you? If your region has several ethnic groups, how do they interact? Are there any students from other cultures at your school? Students might interview them to find out what was difficult for them when they came to this country (being careful, of course, to respect their privacy). You might discuss with students appropriate ways to begin their interviews with foreign students.

Answers
F Send your name, age, photo, and address to the magazine.

MISE EN PRATIQUE

The **Mise en pratique** reviews and integrates all four skills and culture in preparation for the Chapter Test.

1 Do the following photos represent French culture, American culture, or both?

1. French   2. both   3. French

4. American   5. French

 2 **L'Organisation internationale de correspondants** (l'O.I.C.), a pen pal organization you wrote to, has left a phone message on your answering machine. Listen carefully to the message and write down your pen pal's name, age, phone number, likes, and dislikes.

Answers on p. 15D

 3 Tell a classmate in French about your new pen pal.

Name:

Age:

Likes:

Dislikes:

38   *trente-huit*   CHAPITRE 1   Faisons connaissance!

Robert Perrault
25, Boulevard Saint
92700 TANNAY
FRANCE

Bonjour.

Je suis bien content d'être ton correspondant. J'ai quinze ans. J'aime bien sortir avec les copains et écouter de la musique aussi, mais j'aime pas danser. J'adore la pizza et la glace au chocolat. Et toi? Le week-end, j'adore faire du sport. J'aime bien le vélo, mais pendant les vacances, j'aime mieux nager; c'est super! Tu aimes nager aussi? J'espère que oui. Écris-moi.

A bientôt,
Robert

4 You've received your first letter from Robert Perrault. Read it twice— the first time for general understanding, the second time for details. Then, answer the questions below in English.

1. How old is Robert? 15

2. What sports does he like? biking, swimming

3. What foods does he like? pizza, chocolate ice cream

4. What doesn't he like to do? dance

5 Now, answer Robert's letter. Begin your reply with **Cher Robert.** Be sure to . . .

- introduce yourself.
- ask how he's doing.
- tell about your likes and dislikes.
- ask him about other likes and dislikes he might have.
- answer his questions to you.
- say goodbye.

6

JEU DE ROLE

A French exchange student has just arrived at your school. How would you find out his or her name? Age? Likes and dislikes? Act out the scene with a partner. Take turns playing the role of the French student.

Teaching Suggestion

5 Remind students to use Robert's letter as a model for their own.

📁 **Portfolio**

5 Written You may want to ask students to write their letters on stationery and keep them in their portfolios. Students might also record their letter as if they were going to send an audiocassette to Robert. They might want to include their favorite song or get members of their family to say **Bonjour!** Have students write a script for the recording. For portfolio suggestions, see *Assessment Guide,* page 14.

 **Video Wrap-Up**

- *VIDEO PROGRAM*
- *EXPANDED VIDEO PROGRAM,* **Videocassette 1, 07:46–19:46**
- *VIDEODISC PROGRAM,* **Videodisc 1A**

At this time, you might want to use the video resources for additional review and enrichment. See *Video Guide* or *Videodisc Guide* for suggestions regarding the following:

- **Salut, les copains!** (Dramatic episode)
- **Panorama Culturel** (Interviews)
- **Vidéoclips** (Authentic footage)

This page is intended to help students prepare for the test. It is a brief checklist of the major points covered in the chapter. The students should be reminded that this is only a checklist and does not necessarily include everything that will appear on the test.

Teaching Suggestions

This section can be used as a written review assignment, as an oral review in class, or as the basis for a review game. One possible game is tic-tac-toe. Divide the class into two teams, one representing X, the other O. Contestants choose a square, and you ask them a question from **Que sais-je?** If they answer correctly, they win the square they chose. If their answer is incorrect, the other team may choose the same or another square. The team that wins three squares in a row wins the game.

7 To review the **vous** form, have students ask pairs of students if they like what is pictured here.

QUE SAIS-JE?

Can you use what you've learned in this chapter?

Can you greet people and say goodbye? p. 22

1 How would you say hello and goodbye to the following people? What gestures would you use?   See answers below.
1. a classmate
2. your French teacher

Can you ask how people are and tell how you are? p. 23

2 Can you ask how someone is?   Ça va? Comment ça va?

3 If someone asks you how you are, what do you say if . . .
1. you feel great?   2. you feel OK?   3. you don't feel well?
   Super!   Pas mal.   Pas terrible.

4 How would you . . .
1. ask someone's name?   2. tell someone your name?
   Tu t'appelles comment?   Je m'appelle...

Can you ask someone's name and age and give yours? pp. 24–25

5 How would you . . .
1. find out someone's age?   2. tell someone how old you are?
   Tu as quel âge?   J'ai... ans.

Can you express likes, dislikes, and preferences? pp. 26, 32

6 Can you tell what you like and dislike, using the verb **aimer**?
                                                                See answers below.
1. horseback riding   4. shopping
2. soccer   5. the movies
3. going out with friends

7 Can you ask a friend in French if he or she likes . . .   See answers below.

a.

b.

c.

d.

e.

8 Can you tell in French what these people like, dislike, or prefer?
1. Robert never studies.   Robert n'aime pas étudier.
2. Emilie thinks reading is the greatest.   Emilie adore lire.
3. Hervé prefers pizza.   Hervé préfère la pizza.
4. Nathalie never goes to the beach.   Nathalie n'aime pas la plage.
5. Nicole is always cycling or playing soccer.   Nicole aime le vélo et le football.

40   *quarante*   CHAPITRE 1   Faisons connaissance!

Answers
1 1. Hello—bonjour, salut; Goodbye—au revoir, salut, tchao, à bientôt, à tout à l'heure; boys shake hands with other boys and use the **bise** with girls, and girls use the **bise** with both boys and girls
   2. Hello—bonjour; Goodbye—au revoir, à demain, à bientôt, à tout à l'heure; hand wave/no specific gesture

6 *Possible answers*
   1. J'aime faire de l'équitation.
   2. Je n'aime pas le football.
   3. J'aime mieux sortir avec des copains.
   4. Je n'aime pas faire les magasins.
   5. J'aime le cinéma.
7 1. Tu aimes étudier?
   2. Tu aimes regarder la télévision?
   3. Tu aimes danser?
   4. Tu aimes faire du sport?
   5. Tu aimes l'école?

PREMIERE ETAPE

Greeting people and saying goodbye

Bonjour!   *Hello!*
Salut!   *Hi! or Goodbye!*
Au revoir!   *Goodbye!*
A tout à l'heure!   *See you later!*
A bientôt.   *See you soon.*
A demain.   *See you tomorrow.*
Tchao!   *Bye!*
madame (Mme)   *ma'am; Mrs.*
mademoiselle (Mlle)   *miss; Miss*
monsieur (M.)   *sir; Mr.*

Asking how people are and telling how you are

(Comment) ça va?   *How's it going?*

Ça va.   *Fine.*
Super!   *Great!*
Très bien.   *Very well.*
Comme ci, comme ça.   *So-so.*
Bof!   *(expression of indifference)*
Pas mal.   *Not bad.*
Pas terrible.   *Not so great.*
Et toi?   *And you?*

Asking someone's name and giving yours

Tu t'appelles comment?   *What's your name?*
Je m'appelle...   *My name is . . .*
Il/Elle s'appelle comment?   *What's his/her name?*

Il/Elle s'appelle...   *His/Her name is . . .*

Asking someone's age and giving yours

Tu as quel âge?   *How old are you?*
J'ai... ans.   *I am . . . years old.*
douze   *twelve*
treize   *thirteen*
quatorze   *fourteen*
quinze   *fifteen*
seize   *sixteen*
dix-sept   *seventeen*
dix-huit   *eighteen*

DEUXIEME ETAPE

Expressing likes, dislikes, and preferences about things

Moi, j'aime (bien)...   *I (really) like . . .*
Je n'aime pas...   *I don't like . . .*
J'aime mieux...   *I prefer . . .*
Je préfère...   *I prefer . . .*
J'adore...   *I adore . . .*
Tu aimes... ?   *Do you like . . . ?*
les amis (m.)   *friends*
l'anglais (m.)   *English*
le chocolat   *chocolate*

le cinéma   *the movies*
les concerts (m.)   *concerts*
l'école (f.)   *school*
les escargots (m.)   *snails*
les examens (m.)   *tests*
le football   *soccer*
le français   *French*
les frites (f.)   *French fries*
la glace   *ice cream*
les hamburgers (m.)   *hamburgers*
les magasins (m.)   *stores*
les maths (f.)   *math*
la pizza   *pizza*

la plage   *beach*
le ski   *skiing*
le sport   *sports*
les vacances (f.)   *vacation*
le vélo   *biking*

Other useful expressions

et   *and*
mais   *but*
non   *no*
oui   *yes*

TROISIEME ETAPE

Expressing likes, dislikes, and preferences about activities

aimer   *to like*
danser   *to dance*
dormir   *to sleep*
écouter de la musique   *to listen to music*
étudier   *to study*

faire de l'équitation   *to go horseback riding*
faire les magasins   *to go shopping*
faire le ménage   *to do housework*
faire du sport   *to play sports*
lire   *to read*
nager   *to swim*
parler au téléphone   *to talk on the phone*

regarder la télé   *to watch TV*
sortir avec les copains   *to go out with friends*
voyager   *to travel*

Other useful expressions

aussi   *also*
surtout   *especially*

For subject pronouns, see page 33.

VOCABULAIRE   *quarante et un*   **41**

Teaching Suggestion

You might want to use *Teaching Transparencies 1-1, 1-2,* and *1-3* to review functional expressions and vocabulary.

CHAPTER 1 ASSESSMENT

CHAPTER TEST

- *Chapter Teaching Resources, Book 1,* pp. 29–34
- *Assessment Guide,* Speaking Test, p. 28
- *Assessment Items, Audiocassette 7A Audio CD 1*

TEST GENERATOR, CHAPTER 1

ALTERNATIVE ASSESSMENT

Performance Assessment

You might want to use the **Jeu de rôle** (p. 39) as a cumulative performance assessment activity.

📁 **Portfolio Assessment**

- **Written: Mise en pratique,** Activity 5, *Pupil's Edition,* p. 39
  Assessment Guide, p. 14
- **Oral: Mise en pratique,** Activity 3, *Pupil's Edition,* p. 38
  Assessment Guide, p. 14

♖ **Game**

DESSINER, C'EST GAGNER Divide the class into two or more teams. A volunteer from the first team goes to the board. Show the student a vocabulary word or expression by pointing it out in the book or by using a flashcard. The student has 30 seconds to illustrate the word for his or her team, who must say the correct French word or expression within the time limit. Teams alternate turns.

Chapitre 2 : Vive l'école!
Chapter Overview

Mise en train pp. 44–46	La rentrée		Practice and Activity Book, p. 13		Video Guide OR Videodisc Guide

	FUNCTIONS	GRAMMAR	CULTURE	RE-ENTRY
Première étape pp. 47–50	Agreeing and disagreeing, p. 50	Using **si** instead of **oui** to contradict a negative statement, p. 50	• **Note Culturelle,** The French educational system/**Le bac,** p. 49 • Realia: *Bac 1991,* p. 49	• Greetings • The verb **aimer**
Deuxième étape pp. 51–56	• Asking for and giving information, p. 51 • Telling when you have class, p. 54	The verb **avoir,** p. 51	• Realia: French class schedules, p. 52 • **Note Culturelle,** 24-hour time, p. 54 • **Panorama Culturel,** Curriculum in French schools, p. 56	Numbers for telling time
Troisième étape pp. 57–59	Asking for and expressing opinions, p. 57		**Note Culturelle,** The French grading system, p. 57	

Prononciation p. 59	Liaison	**Dictation:** *Textbook Audiocassette 1B/Audio CD 2*

Lisons! pp. 60–61	Les lycéens ont-ils le moral?	**Reading Strategy:** Using visual clues to determine meaning

Review pp. 62–65	Mise en pratique, pp. 62–63	Que sais-je? p. 64	Vocabulaire, p. 65

Assessment Options

Etape Quizzes
• *Chapter Teaching Resources, Book 1*
  Première étape, Quiz 2-1, pp. 79–80
  Deuxième étape, Quiz 2-2, pp. 81–82
  Troisième étape, Quiz 2-3, pp. 83–84
• *Assessment Items, Audiocassette 7A/Audio CD 2*

Chapter Test
• *Chapter Teaching Resources, Book 1,* pp. 85–90
• *Assessment Guide,* Speaking Test, p. 28
• *Assessment Items, Audiocassette 7A/Audio CD 2*

Test Generator, Chapter 2

Video Program OR Expanded Video Program, Videocassette 1
OR Videodisc Program, Videodisc 1B

Textbook Audiocassette 1B/Audio CD 2

RESOURCES: Print	RESOURCES: Audiovisual

Textbook Audiocassette 1B/Audio CD 2

Practice and Activity Book, pp. 14–16
Chapter Teaching Resources, Book 1
- Teaching Transparency Master 2-1, pp. 63, 66 . . . . *Teaching Transparency 2-1*
- Additional Listening Activities 2-1, 2-2, p. 67 . . . . *Additional Listening Activities, Audiocassette 9A/Audio CD 2*
- Realia 2-1, pp. 71, 73
- Situation Cards 2-1, pp. 74–75
- Student Response Forms, pp. 76–78
- Quiz 2-1, pp. 79–80 . . . . *Assessment Items, Audiocassette 7A/Audio CD 2*
Videodisc Guide . . . . *Videodisc Program, Videodisc 1B*

Textbook Audiocassette 1B/Audio CD 2

Practice and Activity Book, pp. 17–19
Chapter Teaching Resources, Book 1
- Communicative Activity 2-1, pp. 59–60
- Teaching Transparency Master 2-2, pp. 64, 66 . . . . *Teaching Transparency 2-2*
- Additional Listening Activities 2-3, 2-4, p. 68 . . . . *Additional Listening Activities, Audiocassette 9A/Audio CD 2*
- Realia 2-2, pp. 72, 73
- Situation Cards 2-2, pp. 74–75
- Student Response Forms, pp. 76–78
- Quiz 2-2, pp. 81–82 . . . . *Assessment Items, Audiocassette 7A/Audio CD 2*
Video Guide . . . . *Video Program OR Expanded Video Program, Videocassette 1*
Videodisc Guide . . . . *Videodisc Program, Videodisc 1B*

Textbook Audiocassette 1B/Audio CD 2

Practice and Activity Book, pp. 20–22
Chapter Teaching Resources, Book 1
- Communicative Activity 2-2, pp. 61–62
- Teaching Transparency Master 2-3, pp. 65, 66 . . . . *Teaching Transparency 2-3*
- Additional Listening Activities 2-5, 2-6, p. 69 . . . . *Additional Listening Activities, Audiocassette 9A/Audio CD 2*
- Realia 2-2, pp. 72, 73
- Situation Cards 2-3, pp. 74–75
- Student Response Forms, pp. 76–78
- Quiz 2-3, pp. 83–84 . . . . *Assessment Items, Audiocassette 7A/Audio CD 2*
Videodisc Guide . . . . *Videodisc Program, Videodisc 1B*

Practice and Activity Book, p. 23

Video Guide . . . . *Video Program OR Expanded Video Program, Videocassette 1*
Videodisc Guide . . . . *Videodisc Program, Videodisc 1B*

Alternative Assessment
- Performance Assessment
  Première étape, p. 50
  Deuxième étape, p. 55
  Troisième étape, p. 59
- Portfolio Assessment
  Written: Activity 27, *Pupil's Edition,* p. 58
    Assessment Guide, p. 15
  Oral: **Mise en pratique, Jeu de rôle,** *Pupil's Edition,* p. 63
    Assessment Guide, p. 15

Chapitre 2 : Vive l'école!
Textbook Listening Activities Scripts

For Student Response Forms, see *Chapter Teaching Resources, Book 1,* pp. 76–78.

Première étape

7 Ecoute! p. 48

CELINE   Mais non! C'est de l'espagnol!

AURELIE   Zut!

AURELIE   Alors, qu'est-ce que c'est?

CELINE   C'est un cours d'arts plastiques.
C'est ici, le français?

AURELIE   Non. C'est la salle d'informatique.

AURELIE   Voilà! Enfin. C'est le français.

CELINE   Mais non! C'est de l'histoire!
Oh là là! Ce n'est pas ici non plus.

AURELIE   Et là, qu'est-ce que c'est?

CELINE   C'est la salle de travaux pratiques de chimie.

Answers to Activity 7
L'espagnol — 122
Les arts plastiques — 123
L'informatique — 224
L'histoire — 222
Les travaux pratiques de chimie — 221

11 Ecoute! p. 50

HELENE   Salut, Gérard. Tu as physique maintenant?

GERARD   Euh, oui.

HELENE   Tu aimes ça?

GERARD   Non, pas trop.

HELENE   Moi, si! J'aime bien la physique!

GERARD   Et toi, tu as quoi maintenant?

HELENE   J'ai géométrie. J'adore!

GERARD   Moi aussi! C'est super intéressant, mais j'aime mieux l'informatique.

Answers to Activity 11
Agree — la géométrie
Disagree — la physique

Deuxième étape

18 Ecoute! p. 53

1. Salut, Stéphanie. C'est Frédéric. Tu as quoi le lundi matin? Moi, le lundi, j'ai allemand, français, sport et sciences nat.
2. Salut, Stéphanie. C'est Nadine. Tu as quoi le jeudi? Le matin, j'ai maths, sciences nat et allemand. L'après-midi, j'ai français, géographie et musique. Et toi?
3. Salut! Ça va? Ici Georges. Tu as quoi le mercredi? Moi, j'ai maths, anglais, français et histoire/géo.

Answers to Activity 18
Frédéric — same
Nadine — different
Georges — same

20 Ecoute! p. 54

ANNE   Salut, Jérôme. Tu as quoi maintenant?

JEROME   C'est huit heures? Alors, j'ai anglais!

ANNE   Et tu as espagnol à quelle heure?

JEROME   Euh... à quatorze heures quinze.

ANNE   Moi, j'ai histoire à quatorze heures quinze. Et toi, tu as histoire à quelle heure?

JEROME   J'ai histoire à neuf heures et après, j'ai maths à dix heures vingt. La récré, c'est à dix heures. J'aime ça!

Answers to Activity 20
Anglais — 8:00
Espagnol — 14:15
Histoire — 9:00
Maths — 10:20

𝒯roisième étape

24 Ecoute! p. 57

ERIC   Dis, tu as sciences nat avec moi ce matin?

AURELIE   Oui. Comment tu trouves ça, les sciences nat?

ERIC   C'est génial!

AURELIE   Et on a aussi géographie cet aprèm, n'est-ce pas? Ça te plaît, la géo?

ERIC   Oui. C'est super! Tu n'aimes pas, toi?

AURELIE   Non, pas trop. Mais j'adore l'allemand. C'est cool.

ERIC   L'allemand? Mais c'est nul, l'allemand! J'aime mieux l'anglais. C'est plus intéressant.

AURELIE   Mais c'est plus difficile.

Answers to Activity 24
Eric likes les sciences nat, la géographie et l'anglais.
Eric dislikes l'allemand.
Aurélie likes l'allemand.
Aurélie dislikes la géographie.

𝒫rononciation, p. 59

For the scripts for Parts A and B, see p. 59.

C. A écrire

(Dictation)

1. — Nous aimons l'informatique. C'est cool.
   — Moi, j'aime mieux les arts plastiques.

2. — Ils ont quoi mardi?
   — Ils ont anglais et physique.

𝑀ise en pratique

1 p. 62

Le lycée aux Etats-Unis, c'est bizarre! On a chimie tous les matins à neuf heures cinq! Et on a sport, mais à quatorze heures quarante-six! Pourquoi «quarante-six»? On a latin à onze heures trente, ça, c'est normal. Mais on a informatique l'après-midi à treize heures cinquante-deux! Je ne comprends pas l'emploi du temps américain!

Answers to Mise en pratique Activity 1
André thinks that his schedule is strange because some classes don't start exactly on the hour or half hour.
Chimie — 9:05
Sport — 14:46 (2:46 P.M.)
Latin — 11:30
Informatique — 13:52 (1:52 P.M.)

Projects

Notre école
(Group Project)

ASSIGNMENT

Have small groups create a school map to help exchange students find their way around. If your school consists of more than one building, assign each group part of the school. Individual group maps may be combined to show the whole school.

MATERIALS

✂ **Students may need**

- Large pieces of paper or posterboard
- Pens and pencils
- Correction fluid
- Glue
- Markers or colored pencils

PREPARATION

Each group should make a list of the subjects taught in their assigned part of the school. They might need to see existing school maps and teacher rosters.

SUGGESTED SEQUENCE

First Sketch   Groups should begin sketching their part of the school in pencil on a large piece of paper or posterboard. For the final drawing, students can retrace their work in pen, crayon, or marker. You might assign a different color to each section of the school. Then, referring to the lists they wrote, groups should label each room in French with the teacher's name, room number, and subject(s) taught in that room. You might want to give students the words for *hallway* (**le couloir**), *lockers* (**les casiers**), *ground floor* (**le rez-de-chausée**), *second floor* (**le premier étage**), *lunchroom* (**la cantine**), *teachers' lounge* (**la salle des professeurs**), and so on.

Peer Editing   Groups should review one another's work to check for accuracy of content and spelling.

Final Drawing   Encourage students to make their maps decorative as well as informative. They might add small drawings or photos to illustrate their maps. The maps can then be joined together to show the entire school. You might display them in the classroom or hallway.

Mon avenir
(Individual Project)

ASSIGNMENT

Students will make posters that show pictures of themselves and illustrate their career goals and the steps toward these goals. See the **Teacher Note** and **Group Work** for Activity 15 on page 52 for French names of professions.

MATERIALS

✂ **Students may need**

- Large pieces of plain or construction paper
- Scissors
- Pens or crayons
- Glue
- Magazines

PREPARATION

Students make a short list in French or English of several careers that interest them. They then add the names of several school subjects that are helpful for each career.

SUGGESTED SEQUENCE

First Draft   Students pick their top career choice, which they will represent in a dream bubble above their picture. Next, to illustrate themselves, their goals, and the steps toward their goals, students might draw or cut out pictures from magazines. They might want to sketch a layout before they assemble the final poster.

Final Draft   Students paste their illustrations on the poster and then label the pictures of their career choice with the names of the subjects necessary to prepare for that career. The posters might be displayed in the classroom.

GRADING THE PROJECT

You might base students' grades on timely completion of the assignment, presentation, and creativity.

Suggested Point Distribution (total = 100 points)

    Completion of assignment . . . . 40 points

    Presentation (spelling, neatness,
    organization) . . . . 40 points

    Creativity . . . . 20 points

TEACHER NOTE

The posters might be included in students' portfolios along with the notes they made about career possibilities and the subjects required for each.

LOTO

In this game, students will practice telling time using the 24-hour system.

Have students make a grid, five squares across and five squares down. They should write **libre** in the center square. Have them fill in the squares by drawing clocks that show times on the hour, quarter past the hour, quarter to the hour, or half past the hour. Call out various times, using the 24-hour system. Students should make a small pencil mark in the corner of the appropriate square when their clock shows the time called. A student who marks a complete row of clocks horizontally, vertically, or diagonally wins, provided that he or she is able to say the times in each square correctly. After erasing the pencil marks, students are ready for another game.

Variation   Instead of clocks, students fill in their **Loto** grids with numbers from 20–59. Call out numbers or easy addition or subtraction problems. Students make a small pencil mark in the corner of the appropriate square when their number is called or the solution to the problem is given. Ask students who win to write additional problems while the rest of the class continues to play. They might then call out the problems they've written.

DESSIN ANIME

In this game, students will practice the names of school subjects in French.

Form two or more teams and have one player from one team go to the board. Whisper to the player the name of a subject in French. In 60 seconds or less, the student must make a drawing to represent that subject; letters and symbols are not allowed. The first team to correctly guess the French word for the subject wins a point. The turn then passes to another team. This game might also be played in small groups with individuals competing against one another. In this situation, students can choose subjects from the vocabulary list at the end of the chapter and draw them on paper or on transparencies.

Variation   You might want to have students act out the subjects instead of drawing them.

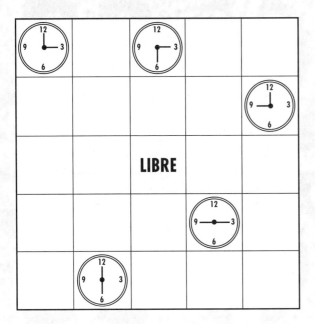

Chapitre 2
Vive l'école!

pp. 42–65

Using the Chapter Opener

Motivating Activity

Ask students what subjects they are taking and which ones are required of all students. Ask them if they like their schedules and their classes. Find out how much homework they have.

Teaching Suggestion

Have students look at the photos and identify the subjects depicted. Then, as you say the French name of each subject, ask students to raise their hand if they are currently taking the subject. Ask them if they like that particular subject. Next, ask students to look at the chapter objectives on the top of page 43 and try to match each photo with one of these objectives. (Photo 1: agreeing; Photo 2: telling time and giving information; Photo 3: expressing opinions)

Photo Flash!

① These teenagers are playing volleyball at a recreation center. In France, the **MJC** (**Maison des jeunes et de la culture**) offers numerous recreational activities, such as sports classes, art and drama classes, musical performances, and movies. Physical education (**EPS**) is just one of the courses students will discuss in this chapter.

CHAPITRE

2
Vive l'école!

① — J'adore le sport!
  — Moi aussi!

42   *quarante-deux*

Language Note

You might tell students that **plastique** is not only a material, but it also means *capable of being shaped or formed,* and can be used to describe clay.

When school starts, new schedules are the main topic of conversation, at least for a while. What classes do you have? How do you feel about them?

In this chapter you will learn

- to agree and disagree
- to ask for and give information
- to ask for and express opinions

And you will

- listen to French-speaking students talk about their classes
- read a French student's class schedule
- write about your own classes
- compare schools in francophone countries with schools in the United States

② J'ai latin à dix heures quinze.

③ Les arts plastiques, c'est génial!

quarante-trois **43**

Focusing on Outcomes

Call students' attention to the chapter objectives. Ask small groups to brainstorm expressions in English they might use to accomplish the chapter objectives. For example, to express opinions, they might list *boring, fun, OK,* and *interesting.* NOTE: You may want to use the video to support the objectives. The self-check activities in **Que sais-je?** on page 64 help students assess their achievement of the objectives.

Teacher Note

In this chapter, students will ask about time (**à quelle heure?**), days of the week (**quel(s) jour(s)?**), school subjects (**quel(s) cours?**), and opinions (**comment?**). Other interrogative expressions will be presented later.

Photo Flash!

③ The students in this photo are busy in an art class. **Les arts plastiques** is a class that includes painting and sculpture as well as art history.

Video Synopsis

In this segment of the video, Claire and Ann meet Delphine on the way to school. They talk about their classes and whether or not they like them. Delphine is worried that she will be late, so she leaves. As Claire and Ann approach the school, they meet Marc and Jérôme. The four of them compare their schedules and express opinions about their classes. They discover they all have gym at the same time. Jérôme realizes he forgot his sneakers.

Motivating Activity

Before presenting the material, ask students to scan the photos and text to find the names of subjects they may be taking. Ask them if they can find any cognates other than class names (**super, courage, cool**).

Presentation

Before playing the video, have students answer the questions at the top of this page. Then, have them suggest a one- or two-sentence summary of what **La rentrée** might be about. After students view the video, ask the questions in Activity 1 on page 46 to check comprehension.

Mise en train

La rentrée

Where do you think these teenagers are?
What do you think they're talking about?
How do you know?

Les jeunes de Poitiers : Claire Delphine Marc
et du Texas : Jérôme Ann

C'est la première semaine de cours...

Tu as quel cours maintenant?

Allemand. J'adore. Et toi, tu as quoi?

Sciences nat.

Ecoutez. Je ne veux pas être en retard. Bon courage!

Pourquoi?

C'est difficile, les sciences nat.

Mais non, c'est passionnant. Et le prof est sympa.

Alors, les garçons, ça boume?

Super.

Bof. Pas terrible.

Qu'est-ce qu'il y a?

Oh rien. J'ai maths.

Tu n'aimes pas les maths?

Non, c'est nul.

44 *quarante-quatre*

CHAPITRE 2 Vive l'école!

RESOURCES FOR **MISE EN TRAIN**
Textbook Audiocassette 1B/Audio CD 2
Practice and Activity Book, p. 13
Video Guide
Video Program
Expanded Video Program, Videocassette 1
Videodisc Guide
Videodisc Program, Videodisc 1B

quarante-cinq 45

Thinking Critically

Comparing and Contrasting
Ask students to examine the photos for similarities and differences between their school experience and the school in the photos. Students might consider the subjects offered, how students arrive at school, and how students dress.

Synthesizing Ask students if they think they could fit in easily at this school and to explain why or why not.

Teaching Suggestion

You might explain the following abbreviations:
nat = naturelles
maths = mathématiques
baskets = chaussures de basket-ball
aprèm = après-midi
Ask students to list as many examples as they can of abbreviations of school subjects used in English. Some examples are *PE* or *phys ed* (physical education), *poly sci* (political science), *math* (mathematics), *psych* (psychology), *home ec* (home economics), *trig* (trigonometry), *ag* (agriculture), and *bio* (biology).

Culture Note

French students entering the **collège (en sixième)** must take a foreign language. Most **baccalauréat** exams require two foreign languages. Ask students why there might be more emphasis on foreign languages in French schools than in American schools. (Geographical location, greater need to communicate with other countries, and trade among countries in the European Union are some of the reasons students might give.)

Video Integration

- *EXPANDED VIDEO PROGRAM,*
  Videocassette 1, 23:35–27:17
- *VIDEODISC PROGRAM,*
  Videodisc 1B

Search 6820, Play To 13490

You may choose to continue with **La rentrée (suite)** at this time or wait until later in the chapter. The story continues later in the school day. Marc meets Jérôme after the last class of the morning. Marc tells him how he likes his math class. Jérôme is preoccupied about his sneakers and decides to go home during lunch to get them. He rides through the streets of Poitiers, rushing to get back to school in time. He returns, shoes in hand, only to find that gym class has been canceled! The teacher is sick, and they have study hall. Jérôme can't believe he went to all that trouble for nothing.

For Individual Needs

2 Challenge Have students correct the false statements. You might also have them write three or four additional true–false questions and exchange papers with a partner.

For videodisc application, see *Videodisc Guide*.

Building on Previous Skills

4 Have students answer each item in French, either orally or in writing, using the expressions they learned in Chapter 1 to express likes and dislikes. (**Il/Elle aime les maths. Il/Elle n'aime pas les sciences nat.**) Then, have them give their own opinions of each subject.

Teaching Suggestion

5 Have students identify the numbers of the frames in the **Mise en train** that support their answers.

---

1 Tu as compris?

Answer the following questions about **La rentrée**.

1. What are the students discussing?   their schedules
2. What do you think **La rentrée** means?   back to school
3. What class do they all have together?   gym class
4. Why are they in a hurry at the end of the conversation?   They are late for class.
5. What is Jérôme worried about?   He forgot his shoes for P.E.

2 Vrai ou faux?

1. Ann est américaine.   vrai
2. Jérôme n'aime pas l'espagnol.   faux
3. Ann et Marc n'aiment pas les maths.   faux
4. Jérôme a allemand.   vrai
5. Marc n'a pas sport cet aprèm.   faux

3 Cherche les expressions

In **La rentrée**, what do the students say to . . .

1. ask what class someone has?   Tu as quoi? Tu as quel cours?
2. tell why they like a class?   C'est passionnant. Le prof est sympa. C'est super intéressant. C'est plus cool.
3. tell why they don't like a class?   C'est difficile. C'est nul.
4. tell which class they prefer?   J'aime mieux... ; J'aime encore mieux...
5. ask what time it is?   Il est quelle heure?

4 Ils aiment ou pas?

Do these students like or dislike the subjects or teachers they're talking about?

1. «Les sciences nat, c'est passionnant.»   like
2. «Les maths, c'est nul.»   dislike
3. «C'est super intéressant, les maths.»   like
4. «Le prof est sympa.»   like

5 Qu'est-ce qui manque?   *What's missing?*

Choose the correct words from the box to complete these sentences based on **La rentrée**.

1. Après maths, Marc a _____.   géographie
2. Jérôme a _____.   allemand
3. Jérôme aime mieux _____ que l'allemand.   l'espagnol
4. On a tous sport à _____ heures.   quatorze
5. On est en retard! Il est _____ heures.   huit

> géographie   allemand   quatorze   huit   l'espagnol

6 Et maintenant, à toi

Which students in **La rentrée** share your own likes or dislikes about school subjects?

PREMIERE ETAPE
Agreeing and disagreeing

VOCABULAIRE

l'algèbre (f.)	*algebra*	la chorale	*choir*	la musique	*music*
la biologie	*biology*	le cours de développement		le cours	*course, school subject*
la chimie	*chemistry*	personnel et social (DPS)	*health*	les devoirs (m.)	*homework*
la géométrie	*geometry*	la danse	*dance*	l'élève (m./f.)	*student*
la physique	*physics*	le latin	*Latin*	le professeur	*teacher*

*You can abbreviate **Education Physique et Sportive** as **EPS**. In conversation, students often say **le sport** instead of **EPS**.

𝒥ump Start!
Have students write sentences telling three things they like to do and three things they don't like to do.

MOTIVATE
Re-enter **l'anglais, les maths,** and **le français** from Chapter 1 by asking students how they feel about each of these classes. (**Tu aimes mieux l'anglais ou les maths?**)

TEACH

Presentation
Vocabulaire Survey your students to determine the most popular subjects. Begin by asking **Qui aime la biologie?** Students who raise their hands might say simply **Moi** or **Moi, j'aime la biologie.** Record the number of responses on the board or on a transparency. Continue asking about other subjects. Have students categorize the vocabulary. Categories might include **les sciences, les langues, l'éducation civique** *(government)*, **les maths, les cours facultatifs** *(electives)*, and **les cours obligatoires** *(required courses)*. Write these categories on the board or on a transparency. Then, give the name of a subject and ask **Quelle catégorie?** Write the subject under the proper category on the board. As you proceed, have students copy the information in their notebooks.

RESOURCES FOR **PREMIERE ETAPE**	

Textbook Audiocassette 1B/Audio CD 2
Practice and Activity Book, pp. 14–16
Videodisc Guide
   Videodisc Program, Videodisc 1B
	Chapter Teaching Resources, Book 1
	• Teaching Transparency Master 2-1, pp. 63, 66
	  Teaching Transparency 2-1
	• Additional Listening Activities 2-1, 2-2, p. 67
	  Audiocassette 9A/Audio CD 2
	• Realia 2-1, pp. 71, 73
	• Situation Cards 2-1, pp. 74–75
	• Student Response Forms, pp. 76–78
	• Quiz 2-1, pp. 79–80
	  Audiocassette 7A/Audio CD 2

Teaching Suggestions

7 Before students hear the recording, have them locate and give the numbers of each classroom.

8 Students might pair off and ask each other questions based on the pictures: **Qui aime le français?**

For Individual Needs

8 Slower Pace Before doing this activity, ask students to imagine what they think the interests of the two students might be.

8 Challenge You might have students draw their own pictures illustrating their interests. Then, have partners exchange papers and tell what subjects their partner likes.

Additional Practice

9 Give various items (a compass, a Spanish dictionary) to different students. Have students use facial expressions to indicate whether they like or dislike the subject associated with the item. Have the class tell what each student likes and dislikes. (**Joel aime les maths. Jennifer n'aime pas l'espagnol.**)

7 Ecoute!

On the first day of school, Céline and Aurélie are looking for their French class. As you listen to their conversation, look at the drawing of the school on page 47 and write the numbers of the classrooms they're looking into. Answers on p. 41C.

8 Ils aiment quels cours? *What subjects do they like?*

Name three subjects Nicole and Gérard probably like, according to their interests.

Nicole
l'algèbre, la chimie, les mathématiques

Gérard
la géographie, l'histoire, le français

9 C'est qui? *Who is it?*

Tell your partner what subject one of these students likes, without naming the person. Your partner will try to guess the person's name. Take turns until you've identified all of the students.

— Il aime le français.
— C'est Michel.

Michel

Julien
Il aime le sport.

Nathalie
Elle aime la chorale.

Virginie
Elle aime la danse.

Guillaume
Il aime la géographie.

Franck
Il aime l'anglais.

Karine
Elle aime la chimie.

48 *quarante-huit*

CHAPITRE 2   Vive l'école!

Study at regular intervals. It's best to learn language in small chunks and to review frequently. Cramming will not usually work for French. Study at least a little bit every day, whether you have an assignment or not. The more often you review words and structures, the easier it will be for you to understand and participate in class.

NOTE CULTURELLE

In France and other countries that follow the French educational system, the grade levels are numbered in descending order. When students begin junior high (**le collège**) at about 10 or 11 years of age, the grade they are in is called **sixième**. Then they go into **cinquième, quatrième,** and **troisième**. The grade levels at the high school (**le lycée**) are called **seconde, première,** and **terminale**.

Le baccalauréat, or **le bac,** is a national exam taken at the end of study at a **lycée**. Not all students take the **bac,** but those who plan to go on to a university must pass it. It's an extremely difficult oral and written test that covers all major subjects. Students spend the final year of the **lycée, la terminale,** preparing for this exam. There are several kinds of **baccalauréat** exams, each appropriate to a major field of study. For example, students who specialize in literature and languages take **le bac A2,** students of math and physical science take **le bac C.**

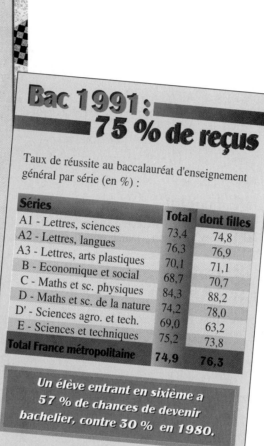

Bac 1991: 75 % de reçus

Taux de réussite au baccalauréat d'enseignement général par série (en %) :

Séries	Total	dont filles
A1 - Lettres, sciences	73,4	74,8
A2 - Lettres, langues	76,3	76,9
A3 - Lettres, arts plastiques	70,1	71,1
B - Economique et social	68,7	70,7
C - Maths et sc. physiques	84,3	88,2
D - Maths et sc. de la nature	74,2	78,0
D' - Sciences agro. et tech.	69,0	63,2
E - Sciences et techniques	75,2	73,8
Total France métropolitaine	**74,9**	**76,3**

Un élève entrant en sixième a 57 % de chances de devenir bachelier, contre 30 % en 1980.

10 Mon journal

Make a list of your favorite school subjects in your journal. If you were taking these subjects in France, which **bac** do you think you would take?

> **Je ferais le bac...** *(I would take* **bac** *. . .)*

PREMIERE ETAPE

History Link

The wreath of laurel leaves that the ancient Romans used to crown their heroes gave us the word *baccalaureate,* from **baccalaureatus,** the Latin word for *laurel berry.* The English expression "to rest on one's laurels" reflects this ancient custom.

Culture Note

Children may enter **l'école maternelle** as early as two years of age. These schools are subsidized by the government and are strictly monitored. Some families have in-home child care, which is also licensed and monitored by the government.

Teacher Note

There are many types of **bac-calauréat** exams. Each one tests students on a number of subjects which are weighted differently according to the student's major. For example, a student who is majoring in literature needs to score higher in literature, philosophy, and languages than in math in order to pass. Students who don't score high enough must try to get a better grade by taking oral exams. If students fail, they must repeat their last year at the **lycée (terminale)** before retaking the **baccalauréat**. Students who don't have their **baccalauréat** need to pass a college entrance exam called **l'ESEU (Examen spécial d'entrée à l'université)** in order to be admitted to college.

Thinking Critically
Comparing and Contrasting
Have students compare passing the **baccalauréat** with graduating from high school in the United States. How does the Scholastic Assessment Test (SAT) or the American College Test (ACT) compare with the **baccalauréat?**

Mon journal
10 You might ask students to write about their most difficult subjects and their favorite ones. Give them these sentence starters: **Pour moi, les cours les plus difficiles sont...** and **Mes cours préférés sont...** For an additional journal entry suggestion for Chapter 2, see *Practice and Activity Book,* page 146.

Additional Practice
10 Have students work in pairs and write sentences in their journals about the subjects their partner likes. (**Les cours préférés de... sont...**)

Presentation

Comment dit-on... ? Read the text of the illustrations to students, using appropriate intonation and facial gestures. Ask them to guess whether each character likes or dislikes the subjects. Have students tell you what subjects they like. Agree with some and disagree with others. Then, tell them what you like and elicit their responses. You might have students form groups of three and role-play the minidialogues in the illustrations, changing the names of the subjects to reflect their own feelings.

For videodisc application, see *Videodisc Guide.*

For Individual Needs

11 Slower Pace Distribute a list of school subjects. Have students listen to the dialogue and circle the subjects they hear mentioned. After you give the correct subjects, tell students to listen again to decide whether Hélène and Gérard like or dislike these courses.

13 Challenge Ask the group reporter to differentiate among the students when giving the final report: **Pierre et moi, nous aimons la glace, mais Marie n'aime pas ça. Elle aime mieux la pizza.**

CLOSE

Ask students to draw cartoons with speech bubbles to show several students' opinions about different subjects. You might have students add them to their portfolios or use them as part of **"Mon avenir,"** one of the chapter projects on page 41E.

COMMENT DIT-ON... ?
Agreeing and disagreeing

To agree:

Oui, beaucoup. *Yes, very much.*
Moi aussi. *Me too.*
Moi non plus. *Neither do I.*

To disagree:

Moi, non. *I don't.*
Non, pas trop. *No, not too much.*
Moi, si. *I do.*
Pas moi. *Not me.*

11 **Ecoute!**

Listen as Hélène and Gérard talk about the subjects they like and dislike. Which one do they agree on? Which one do they disagree on? Answers on p. 41C.

12 **Parlons!** *Let's talk!*

Ask your partner's opinion about several subjects and then agree or disagree. Take turns.

— Tu aimes les arts plastiques?
— Non, pas trop.
— Moi, si.

13 **Ça te plaît?** *Do you like it?*

Get together with two classmates. Find at least two things or activities that you all like. Then, tell the rest of the class what you agree on.

ELEVE 1 — J'aime les hamburgers. Et toi?
ELEVE 2 — Oui, beaucoup.
ELEVE 3 — Moi aussi.
ELEVE 1 — Nous aimons tous *(all)* les hamburgers.

> **Note de Grammaire**
>
> Use **si** instead of **oui** to contradict a negative statement or question.
>
> — Tu **n'**aimes **pas** la biologie?
> — Mais **si!** J'adore la bio!

> le cinéma le foot les concerts
> la pizza faire du sport
> écouter de la musique
> la glace faire les magasins le ski

ASSESS

Quiz 2-1, *Chapter Teaching Resources, Book 1,* pp. 79–80

Assessment Items, Audiocassette 7A Audio CD 2

Performance Assessment

Have partners prepare and act out a conversation between a student and a school counselor in which they discuss the student's interests and the subjects he or she likes and dislikes.

DEUXIEME ETAPE

Asking for and giving information

COMMENT DIT-ON...?
Asking for and giving information

To ask about someone's classes:	*To tell what classes you have:*
Tu as quels cours aujourd'hui?	**J'ai** arts plastiques et physique.
What classes do you have . . . ?	
Tu as quoi le matin?	**J'ai** algèbre, DPS et sport.
What do you have . . . ?	
Vous avez espagnol l'après-midi?	Oui, **nous avons** aussi espagnol et géo.
Do you have . . . ?	

14 **On a quoi?** *What do we have?*

a. Find out what subjects your partner has in the morning and in the afternoon.

— Tu as quoi le matin
(l'après-midi)?
— Bio, algèbre et chorale.
Et toi?
— Moi, j'ai algèbre, chimie,
chorale et DPS.

b. Now, tell the rest of the class
which subjects you and your
partner have in common.

Marc et moi, nous avons
algèbre et chorale.

VOCABULAIRE

le matin	*in the morning*
l'après-midi	*in the afternoon*
aujourd'hui	*today*
demain	*tomorrow*
maintenant	*now*

Grammaire   The verb avoir

Avoir is an irregular verb. That means it doesn't follow the pattern of the **-er**
verbs you learned in Chapter 1.

avoir *(to have)*

J' **ai**	Nous **avons**
Tu **as** } chimie maintenant.	Vous **avez** } chimie maintenant.
Il/Elle/On **a**	Ils/Elles **ont**

As you saw in Chapter 1, you often use an article (**le, la, l'**, or **les**)before a
noun. When you're telling which school subjects you have, however, you don't
use an article.

DEUXIEME ETAPE

cinquante et un **51**

Jump Start!

Write on the board or on a
transparency: **Tu aimes
l'algèbre? Tu aimes l'histoire?** and **J'aime l'anglais.
Je n'aime pas les sciences
naturelles.** Have students
write answers to the questions
and responses to the statements, agreeing or disagreeing
with each one.

MOTIVATE

Ask students in English
whether they prefer their
morning or afternoon class
schedule and why.

TEACH

Presentation

**Comment dit-on... ?/
Vocabulaire** Teach **le matin,
l'après-midi,** and **aujourd'hui**
by drawing pictures and using
a clock or calendar. Play the
role of a student and tell which
subjects you have today, in the
morning and in the afternoon.
Then, as you ask students the
questions, have them respond.
Next, have students pair off
and practice.

Grammaire Write the
paradigm of **avoir** on the
board or on a transparency.
Say the forms aloud and have
students repeat after you.
Then, erase them at random
and have students say them
aloud from memory. Have
students tell what class they
have first period. (**J'ai maths.**)
Then, have them tell what
their classmates have then.
(**Jamie et Tom ont histoire.**)

For videodisc
application, see
Videodisc Guide.

52 **DEUXIEME ETAPE** **CHAPITRE 2**

Teacher Note

15 Professions will be presented later, but students might want to know the names of the professions pictured here: **le pilote, le/la vétérinaire, l'archéologue, la femme (l'homme) d'affaires, le danseur (la danseuse).**

Group Work

15 Students might do this activity in groups, with each person naming a subject suggested by each illustration. Each student might then name another profession, in English or French, and ask group members to name appropriate subjects. You might want to give students the French names for other professions: **un(e) journaliste, un(e) météorologiste, un acteur (une actrice), un instituteur (une institutrice), un ingénieur, un(e) avocat(e), un médecin (une femme médecin), un homme (une femme) politique.**

Presentation

Vocabulaire Start by presenting the days of the week. Ask students **Quel jour est-ce aujourd'hui?** Practice the days of the week by naming one and having students name the following day or the preceding day. To elicit quick responses, you might point forward for the following day and backwards for the preceding day. Next, call out a certain day and time (**le mardi matin, à 10h15**) and have students call out the class that Stéphanie has then. You might also say the name of a subject and have students tell the day(s) that Stéphanie has that subject.

15 Ils ont quels cours?

Some students are day-dreaming about the future. What classes are they taking to prepare for these careers?

> Ils ont géométrie, physique et géographie.

Possible answers:

1. Elle a chimie et biologie.

2. Il a histoire et géographie.

3. Ils ont informatique et espagnol.

4. Il a danse et musique.

VOCABULAIRE

Voilà l'emploi du temps de Stéphanie Lambert.

EMPLOI DU TEMPS				**NOM:** Stéphanie Lambert			**CLASSE:** 3e	
		LUNDI	**MARDI**	**MERCREDI**	**JEUDI**	**VENDREDI**	**SAMEDI**	**DIMANCHE**
MATIN	8h00	Allemand	Arts plastiques	Mathématiques	Mathématiques	Français		
	9h00	Français	Arts plastiques	Anglais	Sciences nat	Français	Anglais	
	10h00	**Récréation**	**Récréation**	**Récréation**	**Récréation**	**Récréation**	TP physique	L
	10h15	EPS	Allemand	Français	EPS	Sciences nat	TP physique	I
	11h15	Sciences nat	**Etude**	Histoire/Géo	**Etude**	Arts plastiques	[Sortie]	B
	12h15	Déjeuner	Déjeuner	[Sortie]	Déjeuner	Déjeuner	APRES-MIDI	R
APRES-MIDI	14h00	Histoire/Géo	Mathématiques	**APRES-MIDI**	Histoire/Géo	Allemand	LIBRE	E
	15h00	Anglais	Physique/Chimie	**LIBRE**	Physique/Chimie	Mathématiques		
	16h00	**Récréation**	[Sortie]		**Récréation**	[Sortie]		
	16h15	Mathématiques			Arts plastiques			
	17h15	[Sortie]			[Sortie]			

Thinking Critically

Analyzing Ask students what they think are the advantages and disadvantages of the French schedule.

Culture Note

In France and many other countries, the first day of the week is Monday, not Sunday, as it is in the United States.

16 Tu comprends?

1. lundi, mardi, mercredi, jeudi, vendredi, samedi, dimanche
2. lunch and break

Answer the following questions about Stéphanie Lambert's schedule on page 52.

1. Can you find and copy the words in the schedule that refer to days of the week?
2. **Déjeuner** and **Récréation** don't refer to school subjects. What do you think they mean?
3. What do you think **14h00** means?   2:00 P.M.
4. If **étudier** means *to study,* what do you think **Etude** means?*   study hall
5. You know that **sortir** means *to go out.* What do you think **Sortie** means?
6. Can you list two differences between Stéphanie's schedule and yours?

5. school is out (literally: exit)
6. She goes to school on Saturdays and gets out early on Wednesdays.

17 Vrai ou faux?

Decide whether the following statements are true (**vrai**) or false (**faux**) according to Stéphanie's schedule. Correct the false statements.

1. Le lundi et le jeudi, elle a histoire.   vrai
2. Stéphanie a arts plastiques le lundi.
3. Le vendredi, elle a allemand.   vrai
4. Stéphanie a sport le lundi et le jeudi.   vrai
5. Elle a étude le mercredi.   faux; Elle a étude le mardi et le jeudi.
6. Elle n'a pas cours le samedi.

2. faux; Elle a arts plastiques le mardi, le jeudi et le vendredi.
6. faux; Elle a cours le samedi.

18 Ecoute!

Look at Stéphanie's schedule as you listen to three of her friends call her on the phone. They're going to tell her what subjects they have on a certain day of the week. Do they have the same subjects as Stéphanie on that day?   Answers on p. 41C.

VOCABULAIRE

You've already learned the numbers 0–20. Here are the numbers 21–59 in French.

21	22	23	24	25
vingt et un	vingt-deux	vingt-trois	vingt-quatre	vingt-cinq

26	27	28	29	30
vingt-six	vingt-sept	vingt-huit	vingt-neuf	trente

31	32	40	41	42
trente et un	trente-deux	quarante	quarante et un	quarante-deux

50	51	52	59
cinquante	cinquante et un	cinquante-deux	cinquante-neuf

* In casual conversation, students use **perm** to say *study hall.*

DEUXIEME ETAPE   *cinquante-trois* **53**

Math Link

Divide the class into two or more teams. Ask each student to write an addition or subtraction problem on a piece of paper, making sure that neither the numbers used in the problem nor the answers are more than 59. Collect the papers and ask a contestant from each team to go to the board. For the first round, read aloud one of the problems. The first contestant to write the correct answer in numerals wins a point for his or her team. For the second round, contestants must write out the numbers in words in order to win a point. You will need to teach the words **et** *(plus),* **moins** *(minus),* and **font** *(equals).* (**Deux et deux font quatre. Quatre moins deux font deux.**)

Teaching Suggestion

16 Ask how many times a week Stéphanie has various classes, how many different classes she has, and what **TP de physique** means (travaux pratiques de physique, *physics lab*).

For Individual Needs

18 Slower Pace Have students form small groups. Play the recording, stopping it after each speaker. Have students in each group write down the subjects each student has that day.

Teaching Suggestion

18 After students have done this activity, you might want to type a copy of the script for the first, second, or third schedule and give it to small groups of students. Then, have them write sentences using **aussi** and the connectors **et** and **mais** to compare and contrast each schedule with Stéphanie's. (**Le mercredi, Georges a maths, et Stéphanie a maths aussi. Le jeudi, Nadine a musique, mais Stéphanie n'a pas musique.**)

Presentation

Vocabulaire Review the numbers 1–20. Then, before students open their books, start with the number **vingt** and have students count after you from 20–29. Point out that 21 is different from 22 through 29. Teach the word **trente** and ask students to count from 31–39 based on what they have just learned about the 20s. Repeat this process with **quarante** and **cinquante.**

19 Quels sont les nombres?

1. Say these numbers in French.

   a. 25   b. 37   c. 46   d. 53

2. Write the numerals for these numbers.

   a. vingt-huit   b. trente-quatre   c. quarante et un   d. cinquante-cinq
      28   34   41   55

1. a. vingt-cinq
   b. trente-sept
   c. quarante-six
   d. cinquante-trois

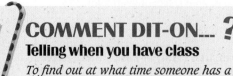

COMMENT DIT-ON... ?
Telling when you have class

To find out at what time someone has a certain class:
   Tu as maths **à quelle heure**?

To tell at what time you have a certain class:
   J'ai maths **à neuf heures.**

huit heures   **dix heures quinze**   **sept heures vingt**   **quinze heures trente**   **seize heures quarante-cinq**

20 Ecoute! Answers on p. 41C.

Listen as Jérôme answers Ann's questions about his schedule. At what time does he have these classes: **anglais, espagnol, histoire,** and **maths?**

À la française

In casual conversation, you might try using the abbreviated forms of words just as French teenagers do. For example, **la récréation** can be abbreviated to **la récré**. Do you recall the abbreviated forms of the words listed below? If not, look for them in **La rentrée** or in Stéphanie's schedule.

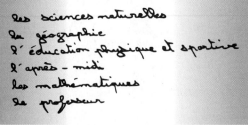

les sciences naturelles
la géographie
l'éducation physique et sportive
l'après-midi
les mathématiques
le professeur

NOTE CULTURELLE

Although in familiar conversation people may use the 12-hour system to give the time, they use the 24-hour system (**l'heure officielle**) to give schedules for transportation, schools, stores, and movies. For example, the school day generally begins at 8h00 (**huit heures**) and continues until 17h00 (**dix-sept heures**) or 18h00 (**dix-huit heures**) with a break from 12h00 (**douze heures**) to 14h00 (**quatorze heures**). You will learn about the 12-hour system in Chapter 6.

54   *cinquante-quatre*   CHAPITRE 2   Vive l'école!

21 Une journée chargée

A busy day

Claudine is busy today. What does she have at each of the times listed? See answers below.

A huit heures, elle a géographie.

1. 8h00

2. 9h35

3. 11h50

4. 14h05

5. 16h20

22 Nos emplois du temps *Our schedules*

a. You and your partner prepare schedules showing only the times classes meet at your school. Take turns asking at what time you each have the classes listed here. Fill in each other's schedule, writing the subjects next to the appropriate times.

— Tu as histoire à quelle heure?
— A onze heures trente.

français   histoire   sport
maths   sciences   anglais

b. Now complete the schedules by asking what subjects you each have at the remaining times.

— Tu as quoi à treize heures?

23 Mon journal

In your journal, make a list of your classes. Include the days and times you have them, and the names of your teachers.

Answers
21 2. A neuf heures trente-cinq, elle a maths.
   3. A onze heures cinquante, elle a récréation.
   4. A quatorze heures cinq, elle a espagnol.
   5. A seize heures vingt, elle a biologie/sciences naturelles.

DEUXIEME ETAPE
CHAPITRE 2

Teaching Suggestion

21 You might have students add what they are doing at the times shown in the pictures, according to their own schedules.

📖 **Mon journal**

23 For an additional journal entry suggestion for Chapter 2, see *Practice and Activity Book,* page 146.

CLOSE

To close this **étape,** have pairs of students describe their schedules to each other, including days and times. You might also play the variation of **"Loto"** as described on page 41F.

ASSESS

Quiz 2-2, *Chapter Teaching Resources, Book 1,* pp. 81–82

Assessment Items, Audiocassette 7A/Audio CD 2

Performance Assessment

Have students write their schedules entirely in French, including days, classes, and times according to the 24-hour clock. Then, have students pair off, ask each other what classes they have and when, and tell which subjects they like and dislike.

VIDEO PROGRAM OR EXPANDED VIDEO PROGRAM, Videocassette 1
27:18–31:00

OR VIDEODISC PROGRAM, Videodisc 1B

Search 13500, Play To 16170

Teacher Notes

- See *Video Guide, Videodisc Guide,* and *Practice and Activity Book* for activities related to the **Panorama Culturel.**
- Remind students that cultural material may be included in the Chapter Quizzes and Test.
- The interviewees' language represents informal, unrehearsed speech. Occasionally, edits have been made for clarification.

Presentation

Ask students what courses they are required to take, and what courses they think French-speaking students might be required to take. Play the video, and then ask if there were any unfamiliar courses mentioned. You might use the **Questions** below to check comprehension.

Thinking Critically

Analyzing Have students compare the subjects they are taking with those the interviewees are taking and make lists of the ones they don't have in common. Have them give advantages and disadvantages of the courses that the interviewees are taking, such as Portuguese or Geography, as well as American courses, such as Band and Home Economics.

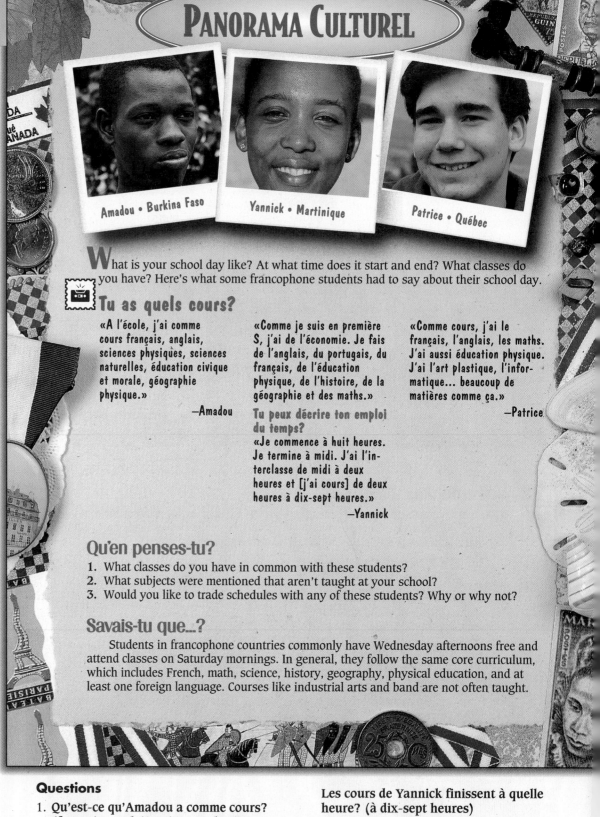

PANORAMA CULTUREL

Amadou • Burkina Faso   Yannick • Martinique   Patrice • Québec

What is your school day like? At what time does it start and end? What classes do you have? Here's what some francophone students had to say about their school day.

Tu as quels cours?

«A l'école, j'ai comme cours français, anglais, sciences physiques, sciences naturelles, éducation civique et morale, géographie physique.»
—Amadou

«Comme je suis en première S, j'ai de l'économie. Je fais de l'anglais, du portugais, du français, de l'éducation physique, de l'histoire, de la géographie et des maths.»

Tu peux décrire ton emploi du temps?
«Je commence à huit heures. Je termine à midi. J'ai l'interclasse de midi à deux heures et [j'ai cours] de deux heures à dix-sept heures.»
—Yannick

«Comme cours, j'ai le français, l'anglais, les maths. J'ai aussi éducation physique. J'ai l'art plastique, l'informatique... beaucoup de matières comme ça.»
—Patrice

Qu'en penses-tu?

1. What classes do you have in common with these students?
2. What subjects were mentioned that aren't taught at your school?
3. Would you like to trade schedules with any of these students? Why or why not?

Savais-tu que...?

Students in francophone countries commonly have Wednesday afternoons free and attend classes on Saturday mornings. In general, they follow the same core curriculum, which includes French, math, science, history, geography, physical education, and at least one foreign language. Courses like industrial arts and band are not often taught.

Questions

1. Qu'est-ce qu'Amadou a comme cours? (français, anglais, sciences physiques, sciences naturelles, éducation civique et morale, géographie physique)
2. Qu'est-ce que Yannick étudie comme matières premières? (économie)
3. Quelles langues est-ce que Yannick étudie? (anglais, portugais, français)
4. Entre quelles heures est-ce que Yannick a l'interclasse? (de midi à deux heures)

Les cours de Yannick finissent à quelle heure? (à dix-sept heures)
5. Qu'est-ce que Patrice a comme cours? (français, anglais, maths, éducation physique, art plastique, informatique)

Multicultural Link

Have students research the educational systems in francophone countries, such as Canada and Côte d'Ivoire.

TROISIEME ETAPE

Asking for and expressing opinions

COMMENT DIT-ON... ?

Asking for and expressing opinions

To ask someone's opinion:
  Comment tu trouves ça?
  Comment tu trouves le cours de biologie?

To express a favorable opinion:	*To express indifference:*	*To express an unfavorable opinion:*
C'est... *It's . . .*	**C'est pas mal.** *It's not bad.*	**C'est...** *It's . . .*
facile. *easy.*	**Ça va.**	**difficile.** *hard.*
génial. *great.*		**pas terrible.** *not so great.*
super. *super.*		**pas super.** *not so hot.*
cool. *cool.*		**zéro.** *a waste of time.*
intéressant. *interesting.*		**nul.** *useless.*
passionnant. *fascinating.*		**barbant.** *boring.*

À la française

In informal conversation, French speakers will often leave out the **ne** in a negative sentence.

  J'aime pas les hamburgers, moi.
  C'est pas super, la géo.

In writing, you should include the **ne** in negative sentences.

24 Ecoute! Answers on p. 41D.

Listen as Aurélie and Eric talk about their subjects. Which ones does Eric like? Which doesn't he like? And Aurélie?

les sciences nat   la géo
l'anglais   l'allemand
    l'espagnol
l'histoire   les maths

NOTE CULTURELLE

The French system of grading is based on a scale of 0–20. A score of less than 10 isn't a passing grade. Students are usually pleased with a score of 10 or higher. They must work very hard to receive a 17 or an 18, and it's very rare to earn a 19 or a 20.

RESOURCES FOR TROISIEME ETAPE

Textbook Audiocassette 1B/Audio CD 2
Practice and Activity Book, pp. 20–22
Videodisc Guide
  Videodisc Program, Videodisc 1B

Chapter Teaching Resources, Book 1
• Communicative Activity 2-2, pp. 61–62
• Teaching Transparency Master 2-3, pp. 65, 66
  Teaching Transparency 2-3
• Additional Listening Activities 2-5, 2-6, p. 69
  Audiocassette 9A/Audio CD 2
• Realia 2-2, pp. 72, 73
• Situation Cards 2-3, pp. 74–75
• Student Response Forms, pp. 76–78
• Quiz 2-3, pp. 83–84
  Audiocassette 7A/Audio CD 2

---

*J*ump Start!

Ask students to write down their daily class schedules, showing official times and the subjects in French.

MOTIVATE

Have students rate each of their classes on a scale of 1–10. Ask them what makes a class fun or boring.

TEACH

Presentation

Comment dit-on... ? Use appropriate facial expressions and gestures as you present the new vocabulary. Have students repeat the words after you. Then, make the facial expressions and gestures and have students try to recall the appropriate words.

 For videodisc application, see *Videodisc Guide.*

Teaching Suggestion

Call out the words **cinéma, télévision, concert,** and **école,** having students react to each word with an appropriate French expression of opinion.

For Individual Needs

24 Slower Pace Distribute a list of the subjects mentioned in the script. Tell students to listen for the subjects the speakers don't like and circle them. Play the recording again. This time, students are to identify the speakers who don't like the subjects they have circled and write the initials of the speakers' names next to the subjects.

25 Qu'est-ce qu'on se dit? *What are they saying to themselves?*

What do you think these students are saying to themselves? *Possible answers:*

1. **L'histoire, c'est...**
   nul.

2. **La géométrie, c'est...**
   pas terrible.

3. **L'algèbre, c'est...**
   facile.

4. **La biologie, c'est...**
   intéressant.

5. **L'espagnol, c'est...**
   difficile.

6. **Les arts plastiques, c'est...**
   génial.

26 Comment tu trouves?

With your partner, discuss how you feel about your classes.
— Tu as maths?
— Oui, à neuf heures.
— Comment tu trouves ça?
— C'est super!

27 La vie scolaire *School life*

Read this letter that your new pen pal Laurent wrote to you after his first day of class. Then, write your reply.

- Cher/Chère ...,

Ça va au lycée? Tu aimes tes cours? Moi, mes cours sont super! J'adore les maths, c'est facile. Mais la physique, c'est turbant. Et la bio, c'est difficile. Et toi? Tu aimes les sciences? Pas moi. J'aime mieux les langues. C'est génial, et c'est plus intéressant. J'ai sport l'après-midi. J'aime bien; c'est cool. Et toi? Tu as sport aussi? Ça te plaît?

A bientôt,
Laurent

28 Un sondage

What is your favorite in each of the following categories? Ask three of your classmates how they like your favorites.

— Comment tu trouves *Jurassic Park*®?
— C'est pas terrible.

> les groupes
> (musical groups)
>
> les films
>
> les cours
>
> les bandes dessinées
> (comic strips)

PRONONCIATION

Liaison

In French you don't usually pronounce consonants at the end of a word, such as the **s** in **les** and the **t** in **c'est**. But you do pronounce some final consonants if the following word begins with a vowel sound. This linking of the final consonant of one word with the beginning vowel of the next word is called **liaison**.

les examens	C'est intéressant.	vous avez	deux élèves
z	t	z	z

A. A prononcer

Repeat the following phrases and sentences.

les maths / les escargots
nous n'aimons pas / nous aimons
C'est super./ C'est intéressant.
les profs / les élèves

B. A lire

Take turns with a partner reading the following sentences aloud. Make all necessary liaisons.

1. Ils ont maths.
2. Elles ont histoire.
3. Elles aiment l'espagnol.
4. Elle a deux examens lundi.
5. Vous avez cours le samedi?
6. Nous aimons les arts plastiques.

C. A écrire Answers on p. 41D.

You're going to hear two short dialogues. Write down what you hear.

Teaching Suggestion

28 Have students write down their classmates' reactions next to each of their favorites. Collect the papers and have volunteers make a list of the top two or three choices in each category.

Presentation

Prononciation Ask students to think of examples of liaison they've already learned (between **ils/elles** and the forms of **aimer, écouter,** and **avoir** that follow). Then, draw the liaison links between each set of words and have students repeat. Have them deduce the rule for using liaison.

Teaching Suggestion

Prononciation When students have completed the dictation in Part C, have them indicate where liaison occurs by linking the appropriate words with a pencil mark.

CLOSE

To close this **étape,** have students list subjects they like and those they dislike. Next to each subject, have them write when the class meets and give their opinion of it.

ASSESS

Quiz 2-3, *Chapter Teaching Resources, Book 1,* pp. 83–84

Assessment Items, Audiocassette 7A/Audio CD 2

Language Note

Make sure students make a *z* sound, not an *s* sound, when making liaison.

Performance Assessment

Have students work in pairs to create a conversation between a French student and an American student, comparing and contrasting their school schedules and times. They should express opinions and agreement or disagreement.

READING STRATEGY

Using visual clues to determine meaning

Teacher Note

For an additional reading, see *Practice and Activity Book*, page 23.

PREREADING
Activities A–C

Motivating Activity

Bring in newspapers or textbooks that contain graphs and ask what information they convey. Discuss the advantages of graphs over written explanations.

Teaching Suggestion

A., B. You might want to ask students to support the choices they made in these activities.

READING
Activities D–G

Teaching Suggestions

• Have students read the title boxes and pick out the cognates. Next, have them determine what information is displayed in each graph and in what way. They might do this in small groups.
• Have students read the graphs carefully and then do Activities D through G.

LISONS!

How do most American students feel about their classes and their teachers? Do you think French students feel the same way?

DE BONS CONSEILS
You'll find photos, drawings, charts, and other visual clues when you read newspapers, magazines, and even your textbooks! These illustrations will usually give you an idea of what you're going to read before you begin.

A. First, look at the illustrations. Based on what you see, do you think you're going to read . . .
   1. price lists?
   2. math exercises?
   3. results from a survey?
   4. ads from a sales catalogue?

B. Now, scan the titles and texts. Based on the titles and the drawings, do you think these articles are about . . .
   1. teenagers' favorite pastimes?
   2. grades given to students on exams?
   3. students' attitudes toward school?
   4. prices at several stores?

C. Here are some cognates from the graph entitled **Profs.** What do you think these words mean in English? See answers below.

> distants   respectueux
> compétents   absents

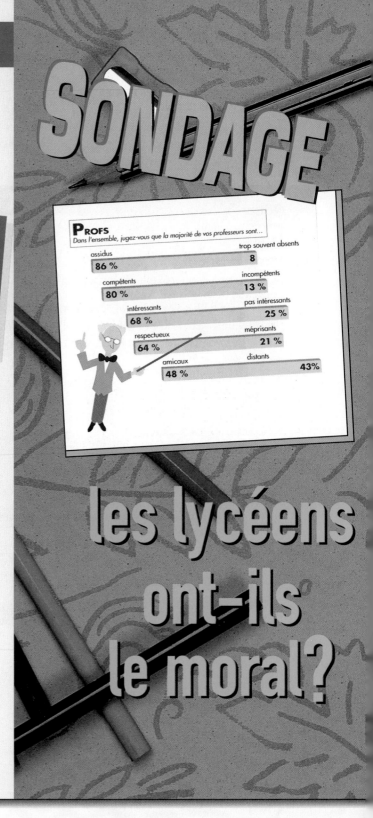

SONDAGE

PROFS
Dans l'ensemble, jugez-vous que la majorité de vos professeurs sont...

assidus	trop souvent absents
86 %	8
compétents	incompétents
80 %	13 %
intéressants	pas intéressants
68 %	25 %
respectueux	méprisants
64 %	21 %
amicaux	distants
48 %	43%

les lycéens ont-ils le moral?

Answers
C Distants – *distant, aloof*
Respectueux – *respectful, considerate*
Compétents – *competent*
Absents – *absent*

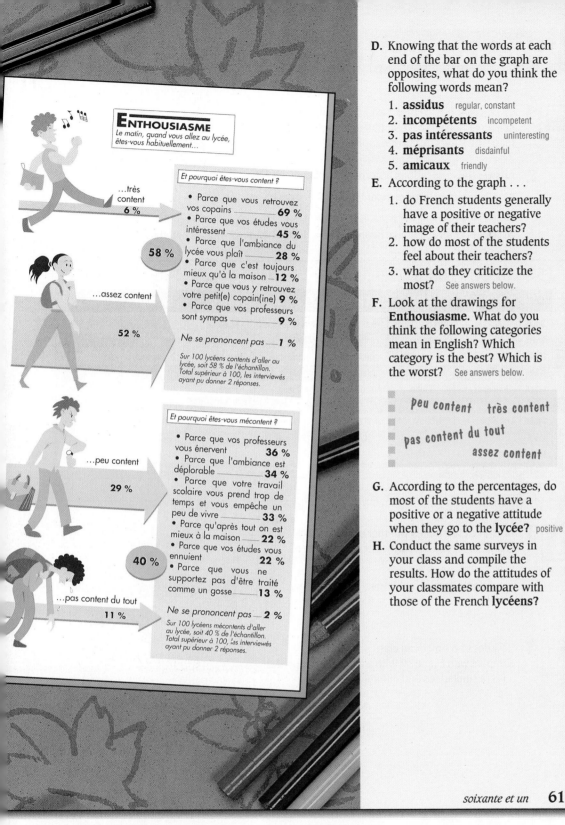

ENTHOUSIASME

Le matin, quand vous allez au lycée, êtes-vous habituellement...

...très content **6 %**

...assez content **52 %** | **58 %**

Et pourquoi êtes-vous content ?

- Parce que vous retrouvez vos copains _____ **69 %**
- Parce que vos études vous intéressent _____ **45 %**
- Parce que l'ambiance du lycée vous plaît _____ **28 %**
- Parce que c'est toujours mieux qu'à la maison _____ **12 %**
- Parce que vous y retrouvez votre petit(e) copain(ine) **9 %**
- Parce que vos professeurs sont sympas _____ **9 %**

Ne se prononcent pas _____ **1 %**

Sur 100 lycéens contents d'aller au lycée, soit 58 % de l'échantillon. Total supérieur à 100, les interviewés ayant pu donner 2 réponses.

...peu content **29 %** | **40 %**

Et pourquoi êtes-vous mécontent ?

- Parce que vos professeurs vous énervent _____ **36 %**
- Parce que l'ambiance est déplorable _____ **34 %**
- Parce que votre travail scolaire vous prend trop de temps et vous empêche un peu de vivre _____ **33 %**
- Parce qu'après tout on est mieux à la maison _____ **22 %**
- Parce que vos études vous ennuient _____ **22 %**
- Parce que vous ne supportez pas d'être traité comme un gosse _____ **13 %**

Ne se prononcent pas _____ **2 %**

...pas content du tout **11 %**

Sur 100 lycéens mécontents d'aller au lycée, soit 40 % de l'échantillon. Total supérieur à 100, les interviewés ayant pu donner 2 réponses.

D. Knowing that the words at each end of the bar on the graph are opposites, what do you think the following words mean?

1. **assidus** regular, constant
2. **incompétents** incompetent
3. **pas intéressants** uninteresting
4. **méprisants** disdainful
5. **amicaux** friendly

E. According to the graph . . .

1. do French students generally have a positive or negative image of their teachers?
2. how do most of the students feel about their teachers?
3. what do they criticize the most? See answers below.

F. Look at the drawings for **Enthousiasme.** What do you think the following categories mean in English? Which category is the best? Which is the worst? See answers below.

> peu content   très content
>
> pas content du tout
>
> assez content

G. According to the percentages, do most of the students have a positive or a negative attitude when they go to the **lycée**? positive

H. Conduct the same surveys in your class and compile the results. How do the attitudes of your classmates compare with those of the French **lycéens**?

LISONS!
CHAPITRE 2

Teaching Suggestion

Ask students for examples of student and teacher behavior that would illustrate the different categories.

POSTREADING
Activity H

Teaching Suggestion

H. You might have students present the results of their survey in a colorful graph.

Thinking Critically

Analyzing Discuss the results of the class survey. Ask students for suggestions on improving student and teacher attitudes and behavior. After comparing the results with those in **Lisons!**, have students suggest reasons why the results of the two surveys are similar or different.

Answers

E 1. positive
   2. They think they are diligent, competent, interesting, respectful, and friendly.
   3. They criticize them for being distant.

F Très content – *very happy (best)*
   Assez content – *somewhat happy*
   Peu content – *not very happy*
   Pas content du tout – *not happy at all (worst)*

MISE EN PRATIQUE

MISE EN PRATIQUE

The Mise en pratique reviews and integrates all four skills and culture in preparation for the Chapter Test.

For Individual Needs

1 **Visual Learners**
Students might benefit from seeing the typed script after hearing it once.

Group Work

3 Have students work in groups of four. One student in each group might be selected to report the number of votes for and against Eliane's schedule and to explain why the group feels the way it does.

Teaching Suggestion

4 This activity might be extended to include comparisons of the grading systems in the **bac** versus the SAT.

1 Listen as André, a French exchange student, tells you how he feels about his American schedule. What is his reaction to his schedule in general? At what times does he have the following subjects: **chimie, sport, latin, informatique**? Answers on page 41D.

2 Answer these questions according to Eliane's schedule. See answers below.

1. Eliane a quoi le lundi matin?
2. Elle a quels cours le jeudi après-midi?
3. Quels jours et à quelle heure est-ce qu'elle a histoire? Anglais? Maths?

EMPLOI DU TEMPS   NOM: Eliane Soulard   CLASSE: 3ᵉ

		LUNDI	MARDI	MERCREDI	JEUDI	VENDREDI	SAMEDI	DIMANCHE
MATIN	8h00	Anglais	Arts plastiques	Histoire/Géo	Mathématiques	Musique		
	9h00	Français	Musique	Anglais	Sciences nat	Arts plastiques	Anglais	L
	10h00	Récréation	Récréation	Récréation	Récréation	Récréation	TP physique	I
	10h15	EPS	Mathématiques	Sciences nat	EPS	Sciences nat	TP physique	B
	11h15	Sciences nat	Etude	Arts plastiques	Etude	Français	[Sortie]	R
	12h15	Déjeuner	Déjeuner	[Sortie]	Déjeuner	Déjeuner	APRES-MIDI	E
APRES-MIDI	14h00	Arts plastiques	Mathématiques	**APRES-MIDI**	Histoire/Géo	Physique	LIBRE	
	15h00	Musique	Physique	**LIBRE**	Physique	Anglais		
	16h00	Récréation	[Sortie]		Récréation	[Sortie]		
	16h15	Mathématiques			Français			
	17h15	[Sortie]			[Sortie]			

3 Tell three classmates whether or not you like Eliane's schedule and why. Then, ask them if they like it.

> J'aime l'emploi du temps d'Eliane. Elle a étude et arts plastiques. C'est cool! Et vous?

4 How does an American class schedule compare with Eliane's? With a partner, make a list of similarities and differences.

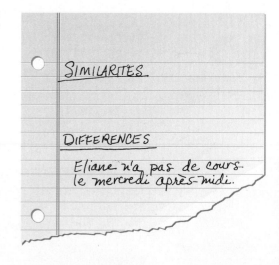

SIMILARITES

DIFFERENCES
Eliane n'a pas de cours le mercredi après-midi.

Answers
2 1. anglais, français, EPS et sciences nat
2. histoire/géographie, physique et français
3. Histoire – mercredi à 8h00, jeudi à 14h00
Anglais – lundi à 8h00, mercredi à 9h00, vendredi à 15h00, samedi à 9h00
Maths – lundi à 16h15, mardi à 10h15 et à 14h00, jeudi à 8h00

5 Answer these questions according to Eliane's report card.   See answers below.

1. What are Eliane's best subjects?

2. What would she probably say about French class? Music class? Science class?

BULLETIN TRIMESTRIEL

Année scolaire : 19 95 - 19 96

NOM et Prénom: _Soulard Eliane_   Classe de: 3ᵉ

MATIERES D'ENSEIGNEMENT	Moyenne de l'élève	OBSERVATIONS
Français	5	Montre peu l'enthousiasme
Anglais	8	Assez mauvais travail!
Mathématiques	18	Très bonne élève!
Histoire-Géographie	11	Travail moyen
Sciences naturelles	17	Élève sérieuse
Education physique	12	Un peu paresseuse
Physique-Chimie	18	Très douée pour la physique
Arts plastiques	14	Bon travail.
Musique	13	Fait des efforts.

Ce bulletin doit être conservé précieusement par les parents.
Il n'en sera pas délivré de duplicata.

---

6 Create your ideal schedule showing subjects, days, and times. Write it down in the form of a French **emploi du temps.** Then, compare your ideal schedule with a partner's.

7

JEU DE ROLE

Create a conversation with two classmates. Talk about . . .

a. the subjects you like best and your opinion of them.

b. the subjects you don't like and your opinion of them.

c. whether or not you agree with your classmates' likes and dislikes.

Answers

5 1. mathématiques, physique-chimie, sciences naturelles

2. *Possible answers:* Le français, c'est barbant/c'est difficile/c'est nul/c'est zéro.
La musique, c'est pas mal/c'est pas super/c'est pas terrible.
Les sciences nat, c'est cool/c'est facile/c'est génial/c'est intéressant/c'est passionnant.

Teaching Suggestion

5 Have students make their own French report card. They should give themselves the grades they think they deserve in each subject and write the French comments they think their teachers would make.

◆ For Individual Needs

6 **Auditory Learners**
Have partners dictate their ideal schedules to each other and write down the classes and times as they hear them. Then, have them exchange the schedules to check each other's work.

📁 Portfolio

7 **Oral**   Students might want to include this conversation in their oral portfolios. For portfolio suggestions, see *Assessment Guide,* page 15.

 Video Wrap-Up

- **VIDEO PROGRAM**
- **EXPANDED VIDEO PROGRAM,** Videocassette 1, 19:47–37:11
- **VIDEODISC PROGRAM,** Videodisc 1B

At this time, you might want to use the video resources for additional review and enrichment. See *Video Guide* or *Videodisc Guide* for suggestions regarding the following:

- **La rentrée** (Dramatic episode)
- **Panorama Culturel** (Interviews)
- **Vidéoclips** (Authentic footage)

This page is intended to help students prepare for the test. It is a brief checklist of the major points covered in the chapter. The students should be reminded that this is only a checklist and does not necessarily include everything that will appear on the test.

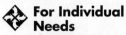 **For Individual Needs**

6 Challenge Encourage students to come up with as many phrases as possible to express each reaction to the geography class.

QUE SAIS-JE?

Can you use what you've learned in this chapter?

Can you agree and disagree? p. 50

1 How would you agree if your friend said the following? How would you disagree with your friend?

1. J'adore l'histoire! *agree* — Moi aussi! *disagree* — Moi, non.
2. J'aime les sciences nat. Et toi? *agree* — Oui, beaucoup! *disagree* — Non, pas trop.
3. Je n'aime pas le français. *agree* — Moi non plus. *disagree* — Moi, si!

Can you ask for and give information? pp. 51, 54

2 How would you ask . . .

1. what subjects your friend has in the morning? Tu as quoi le matin?
2. what subjects your friend has in the afternoon? Tu as quoi l'après-midi?
3. what subjects your friend has on Tuesdays? Tu as quoi le mardi?
4. if your friend has music class? Tu as musique?
5. if your friend has English today? Tu as anglais aujourd'hui?

3 How would you say in French that the following students have these classes, using the verb **avoir**? See answers below.

1. you / French and choir
2. Paul / physics
3. we / gym
4. Francine and Séverine / Spanish

4 How would you ask your friend at what time he or she has these classes? See answers below.

1.   2.   3.

Can you tell when you have class? p. 54

5 How would you tell your friend that you have the following classes at the times given? See answers below.

1. 9h15   2. 11h45   3. 15h50

Can you ask for and express opinions? p. 57

6 How would you tell your friend that your geography class is . . . See answers below.

1. fascinating?   2. not so great?   3. boring?

64 *soixante-quatre*   CHAPITRE 2   Vive l'école!

Answers

3 1. Tu as français et chorale.
   2. Paul a physique.
   3. Nous avons sport.
   4. Francine et Séverine ont espagnol.

4 1. Tu as géométrie à quelle heure?
   2. Tu as informatique à quelle heure?
   3. Tu as arts plastiques à quelle heure?

5 1. J'ai sport à neuf heures quinze.
   2. J'ai allemand à onze heures quarante-cinq.
   3. J'ai DPS à quinze heures cinquante.

6 1. C'est passionnant!
   2. C'est pas terrible.
   3. C'est barbant.

PREMIERE ETAPE

School subjects

l'algèbre (f.) *algebra*
l'allemand (m.) *German*
les arts (m.) plastiques *art class*
la biologie *biology*
la chimie *chemistry*
la chorale *choir*
le cours de développement
  personnel et social (DPS)
  health
la danse *dance*
l'éducation (f.) physique et
  sportive (EPS) *physical
  education*

l'espagnol (m.) *Spanish*
la géographie *geography*
la géométrie *geometry*
l'histoire (f.) *history*
l'informatique (f.) *computer
  science*
le latin *Latin*
la musique *music*
la physique *physics*
les sciences (f.) naturelles
  natural science
le sport *gym*
les travaux (m.) pratiques *lab*

School-related words

le cours *course*
les devoirs (m.) *homework*
l'élève (m./f.) *student*
le professeur (le prof) *teacher*

Agreeing and disagreeing

Oui, beaucoup. *Yes, very much.*
Moi aussi. *Me too.*
Moi, non. *I don't.*
Non, pas trop. *No, not too much.*
Moi non plus. *Neither do I.*
Moi, si. *I do.*
Pas moi. *Not me.*

DEUXIEME ETAPE

Asking for and giving information

Tu as quels cours... ? *What
  classes do you have . . . ?*
Tu as quoi... ? *What do you
  have . . . ?*
J'ai... *I have . . .*
Vous avez... ? *Do you have . . . ?*
Nous avons... *We have . . .*
avoir *to have*

Telling when you have class

Tu as... à quelle heure? *At what
  time do you have . . . ?*
à... heures *at . . . o'clock*
à... heures quinze *at . . . fifteen*

à... heures trente *at . . . thirty*
à... heures quarante-cinq *at . . .
  forty-five*
aujourd'hui *today*
demain *tomorrow*
maintenant *now*
le matin *in the morning*
l'après-midi *in the afternoon*
le lundi *on Mondays*
le mardi *on Tuesdays*
le mercredi *on Wednesdays*
le jeudi *on Thursdays*
le vendredi *on Fridays*
le samedi *on Saturdays*
le dimanche *on Sundays*

Parts of the school day

la récréation *break*
l'étude *study hall*
le déjeuner *lunch*
la sortie *dismissal*
l'après-midi libre *afternoon off*

Numbers

See p. 53 for the numbers 21
  through 59.

TROISIEME ETAPE

Asking for and expressing opinions

Comment tu trouves... ? *What do
  you think of . . . ?*
Comment tu trouves ça? *What
  do you think of that/it?*
Ça va. *It's OK.*

C'est... *It's . . .*
  super *super*
  cool *cool*
  facile *easy*
  génial *great*
  intéressant *interesting*
  passionnant *fascinating*

pas mal *not bad*
barbant *boring*
difficile *difficult*
nul *useless*
pas super *not so hot*
pas terrible *not so great*
zéro *a waste of time*

Teaching Suggestion

You might want to have students list the feminine nouns together and the masculine nouns together in their notebooks. Ask them also to note any similarities within each group. For example, many of the feminine nouns end in -**ie**.

CHAPTER 2 ASSESSMENT

CHAPTER TEST

- *Chapter Teaching Resources, Book 1,* pp. 85–90
- *Assessment Guide,* Speaking Test, p. 28
- *Assessment Items, Audiocassette 7A Audio CD 2*

TEST GENERATOR, CHAPTER 2

ALTERNATIVE ASSESSMENT

Performance Assessment

You might want to use the **Jeu de rôle** (p. 63) as a cumulative performance assessment activity.

Portfolio Assessment

- **Written:** Activity 27, *Pupil's Edition,* p. 58
  Assessment Guide, p. 15
- **Oral:** Mise en pratique, Jeu de rôle, *Pupil's Edition,* p. 63
  Assessment Guide, p. 15

Game

TIC-TAC-TOE Divide the class into two teams and draw a grid on the board or on a transparency. In each square, write one of the chapter functions or vocabulary categories in English: agreeing, disagreeing, telling time, school subjects, expressing positive and negative opinions, the numbers 20–59, days of the week, and so on. Call out a French expression or sentence. If the contestant chooses the correct functional objective your remark represents, the team symbol goes in the square. If not, a player from the other team may try. You can also reverse the procedure by supplying French expressions in the grid and calling out the functional objectives in English.

Chapitre 3 : Tout pour la rentrée
Chapter Overview

Mise en train pp. 68–70	Pas question!	Practice and Activity Book, p. 25		Video Guide OR Videodisc Guide

	FUNCTIONS	GRAMMAR	CULTURE	RE-ENTRY
Première étape pp. 71–75	• Making and responding to requests, p. 72 • Asking others what they need, p. 74 • Telling what you need, p. 74	The indefinite articles **un, une,** and **des,** p. 73	• **Note Culturelle,** Bagging your own purchases, p. 72 • **Panorama Culturel,** Buying school supplies in French-speaking countries, p. 75	The verb **avoir**
Deuxième étape pp. 76–79	• Telling what you'd like, p. 77 • Telling what you'd like to do, p. 77	• The demonstrative adjectives **ce, cet, cette,** and **ces,** p. 77 • Adjective agreement and placement, p. 79		Expressing likes and dislikes
Troisième étape pp. 80–83	• Getting someone's attention, p. 82 • Asking for information, p. 82 • Expressing thanks, p. 82		• **Note Culturelle,** French currency, p. 80 • Realia: Radio station logos, p. 80 • Realia: French money, p. 80	Numbers

Prononciation p. 83	The r sound	**Dictation:** Textbook Audiocassette 2A/Audio CD 3

Lisons! pp. 84–85	Advertisements for school supplies	**Reading Strategy:** Scanning for specific information

Review pp. 86–89	**Mise en pratique,** pp. 86–87	**Que sais-je?** p. 88	**Vocabulaire,** p. 89

Assessment Options

Etape Quizzes
• *Chapter Teaching Resources, Book 1*
  Première étape, Quiz 3-1, pp. 135–136
  Deuxième étape, Quiz 3-2, pp. 137–138
  Troisième étape, Quiz 3-3, pp. 139–140
• *Assessment Items, Audiocassette 7A/Audio CD 3*

Chapter Test
• *Chapter Teaching Resources, Book 1,* pp. 141–146
• *Assessment Guide,* Speaking Test, p. 29
• *Assessment Items, Audiocassette 7A/Audio CD 3*

Test Generator, Chapter 3

Video Program OR *Expanded Video Program, Videocassette 1* OR *Videodisc Program, Videodisc 2A*

Textbook Audiocassette 2A/Audio CD 3

RESOURCES: Print	RESOURCES: Audiovisual

Textbook Audiocassette 2A/Audio CD 3

Practice and Activity Book, pp. 26–28
Chapter Teaching Resources, Book 1
- Teaching Transparency Master 3-1, pp. 119, 122 . . . . *Teaching Transparency 3-1*
- Additional Listening Activities 3-1, 3-2, p. 123 . . . . *Additional Listening Activities, Audiocassette 9A/Audio CD 3*
- Realia 3-1, pp. 127, 129
- Situation Cards 3-1, pp. 130–131
- Student Response Forms, pp. 132–134
- Quiz 3-1, pp. 135–136 . . . . *Assessment Items, Audiocassette 7A/Audio CD 3*
Video Guide . . . . *Video Program* OR *Expanded Video Program, Videocassette 1*
Videodisc Guide. . . . . *Videodisc Program, Videodisc 2A*

Textbook Audiocassette 2A/Audio CD 3

Practice and Activity Book, pp. 29–31
Chapter Teaching Resources, Book 1
- Communicative Activity 3-1, pp. 115–116
- Teaching Transparency Master 3-2, pp. 120, 122 . . . . *Teaching Transparency 3-2*
- Additional Listening Activities 3-3, 3-4, p. 124 . . . . *Additional Listening Activities, Audiocassette 9A/Audio CD 3*
- Realia 3-2, pp. 128, 129
- Situation Cards 3-2, pp. 130–131
- Student Response Forms, pp. 132–134
- Quiz 3-2, pp. 137–138 . . . . *Assessment Items, Audiocassette 7A/Audio CD 3*
Videodisc Guide. . . . . *Videodisc Program, Videodisc 2A*

Textbook Audiocassette 2A/Audio CD 3

Practice and Activity Book, pp. 32–34
Chapter Teaching Resources, Book 1
- Communicative Activity 3-2, pp. 117–118
- Teaching Transparency Master 3-3, pp. 121, 122 . . . . *Teaching Transparency 3-3*
- Additional Listening Activities 3-5, 3-6, p. 125 . . . . *Additional Listening Activities, Audiocassette 9A/Audio CD 3*
- Realia 3-2, pp. 128, 129
- Situation Cards 3-3, pp. 130–131
- Student Response Forms, pp. 132–134
- Quiz 3-3, pp. 139–140 . . . . *Assessment Items, Audiocassette 7A/Audio CD 3*
Videodisc Guide. . . . . *Videodisc Program, Videodisc 2A*

Practice and Activity Book, p. 35

Video Guide. . . . . *Video Program* OR *Expanded Video Program, Videocassette 1*
Videodisc Guide. . . . . *Videodisc Program, Videodisc 2A*

Alternative Assessment
- Performance Assessment
  Première étape, p. 74
  Deuxième étape, p. 79
  Troisième étape, p. 83
- Portfolio Assessment
  Written: **Mise en pratique,** Activity 7, *Pupil's Edition,* p. 87
  Assessment Guide, p. 16
  Oral: **Mise en pratique, Jeu de rôle,** *Pupil's Edition,* p. 87
  Assessment Guide, p. 16

Chapitre 3 : Tout pour la rentrée
Textbook Listening Activities Scripts

For Student Response Forms, see *Chapter Teaching Resources, Book 1,* pp. 132–134.

Première étape

6 Ecoute! p. 71

HAFAÏDH   Qu'est-ce qu'il y a dans mon sac? Voilà le cahier de français. J'ai aussi des stylos et des crayons dans ma trousse, et une gomme.

KARINE   Bon, qu'est-ce qu'il y a dans mon sac? Je ne peux rien trouver! Tiens, voilà le cahier de français. Il y a, bien sûr, des feuilles de papier et ma trousse, avec un crayon et des stylos dedans. Ah, voilà la règle pour les maths.

Answers to Activity 6
a. Neither   b. Karine   c. Hafaïdh

9 Ecoute! p. 73

1. — Jacqueline, tu as une feuille de papier?
 — Ben, oui. Voilà.

2. — Ali, tu as un crayon?
 — Non, mais j'ai un stylo.

3. — Paul, tu as un crayon?
 — Oui. Le voilà.

4. — Xavier, tu as une calculatrice?
 — Je regrette. Je n'ai pas de calculatrice.

Answers to Activity 9
1. c   2. a   3. b   4. e

Deuxième étape

14 Ecoute! p. 76

1. Je voudrais un jean.
2. Moi, j'aime faire du sport. Je voudrais des baskets.
3. Je voudrais acheter un portefeuille.
4. J'aime beaucoup la musique. Je voudrais un disque compact.
5. J'adore lire. Je voudrais acheter un roman.

Answers to Activity 14
1. Dorothée   4. Stéphane
2. Odile   5. Denis
3. M. Prévost

15 Ecoute! p. 77

Euh, il me faut des cahiers pour le français, les maths, la biologie et l'histoire. Je voudrais donc quatre cahiers. Il me faut aussi un compas pour les maths. Et, je n'ai pas de règle non plus. Il me faut des classeurs pour l'informatique et les travaux pratiques de chimie. Alors, euh, je voudrais quatre cahiers, un compas, une règle et deux classeurs.

Answers to Activity 15
quatre cahiers, un compas, une règle et deux classeurs

Troisième étape

23 Ecoute! p. 80

1. Vous écoutez quatre-vingt-dix-neuf FM, le rock des Lillois!

2. Génial, phénoménal et amical, c'est canal B sur quatre-vingt-quatorze megahertz de plaisir.

3. Quatre-vingt-neuf virgule cinq pour swinger dans les chaumières.

4. Qui m'aime? Moi, FM cent deux virgule trois. La station des copains.

Answers to Activity 23
1. b   2. e   3. a   4. d

27 Ecoute! p. 82

1. — Bonjour. C'est combien, ce classeur?
   — Vingt-cinq francs.
   — Merci beaucoup.

2. — C'est cinquante-neuf francs, cette calculatrice?
   — Oui.
   — Merci.
   — A votre service.

3. — Pardon, madame. C'est combien, ce cahier?
   — Quatorze francs.
   — Merci, madame.

4. — Une règle, c'est combien?
   — Onze francs.
   — Merci.
   — A votre service.

5. — Pardon, madame.
   — Oui.
   — Vous avez des trousses?
   — Oui. Ces trousses-là font trente-deux francs.
   — Eh bien, ce n'est pas cher.

6. — C'est combien, ce livre?
   — Quarante-huit francs.
   — Merci, madame.

Answers to Activity 27
1. classeur — 25 F
2. calculatrice — 59 F
3. cahier — 14 F
4. règle — 11 F
5. trousse — 32 F
6. livre — 48 F

Prononciation, p. 83

For the scripts for Parts A and B, see p. 83.

C. A écrire, p. 83

(Dictation)
— Pardon, monsieur.
— Oui?
— Je voudrais un crayon rouge et une trousse rose.
— Trente-trois francs, s'il vous plaît.

Mise en pratique

1 p. 86

J'aime beaucoup faire du sport. Il me faut des baskets. J'adore écouter de la musique. Je voudrais des cassettes. Je n'ai pas de dictionnaire pour le cours d'espagnol. Je voudrais une calculatrice pour le cours d'algèbre.

Answers to Mise en pratique Activity 1
des baskets, des cassettes, un dictionnaire et une calculatrice

La publicité
(Individual or Group Project)

ASSIGNMENT

Students will create advertisements for their own stores, either by creating an illustrated catalogue or by preparing and performing a television or radio commercial. This project can be done individually, in pairs, or in groups.

MATERIALS

✂ **Students may need**
• Paper
• Magazines
• Scissors
• Colored pens and pencils
• Glue or tape

PREPARATION

Have students determine the type of store or the products they want to advertise. They should make a list of their products, looking up any words they might need, and assign a price to each item. (See **Mise en pratique**, Activity 7, page 87.)

SUGGESTED SEQUENCE

First Draft   Have students choose the format for their advertisement, either a catalogue or a commercial.

If they choose to make a catalogue, they will need to find or create illustrations for their products and design an attractive layout. They should arrange their text and illustrations before finally gluing or taping them.

If students choose to create a commercial, they should start writing the script. They can treat their products seriously or make outrageous claims. Students will probably need some guidance; encourage them to find visual aids to get their message across. You may choose to have them memorize their scripts.

Peer Editing   Those students who create commercials should now rehearse them to determine if their commercials are convincing and easy to understand. The catalogue producers might serve as an audience.

Those students doing catalogues should ask for feedback from the commercial writers regarding the descriptions and prices of the items as well as the layout.

Final Draft   Students doing commercials should correct any mistakes pointed out in peer editing, gather all their visual aids, and present the commercial to the class.

Students making catalogues should revise their projects according to the feedback from their classmates and display them around the classroom.

GRADING THE PROJECT

You might assign grades for this project based on completion of the assignment, language use, presentation, and content.

Suggested Point Distribution (total = 100 points)

Completion of assignment . . . . 20 points
Language use. 20 points
Presentation. . . . . 30 points
Content . . . . 30 points

GO FISH

In this game, students will practice vocabulary for school supplies.

Procedure   This game should be prepared ahead of time. Draw or glue pictures of school supplies onto index cards. You will need four cards of each item for a complete deck and a complete deck for each pair or group playing the game. Deal each player five cards and place the remaining cards face down on the table. Then, players should remove all matching pairs from their hands and set them aside. The dealer begins by asking a player for a card. **(Stan, tu as un stylo?)** If the player has the card, he or she must give it to the person who asks for it, who then sets the pair aside and takes another turn. If the player doesn't have the card, the person requesting the card must draw one from the pile, and the next player takes a turn. The game ends when one player puts down or gives away the last card. All players count their pairs, and the player with the most pairs wins.

JE VOIS QUELQUE CHOSE (*I SPY*)

This game will help students review colors and classroom vocabulary.

Procedure   Have students think of an item in the classroom. It must be visible, and it should be an item that students can name in French. Ask a volunteer to tell only the color of his or her item. **(Je vois quelque chose de bleu, de blanc...)** Other students then try to guess what the item is. **(C'est un stylo?)** You might want to set a one-minute time limit for each item. You might even limit the number of guesses to keep a fast pace. The student who guesses correctly then tells the color of his or her item. If one student guesses correctly more than once, he or she may choose another student to continue the game. If no one guesses correctly, the student should name the item and choose another student to continue.

Chapitre 3
Tout pour la rentrée
pp. 66–89

𝒰sing the Chapter Opener

Motivating Activity

Ask students if they usually go shopping before the beginning of the school year. If so, ask the following questions. Do you go shopping for school supplies or clothes? Are you taking classes now that require extra or special supplies? Have you ever had to buy a book for a class, either for required reading or to replace a lost textbook? How much do school supplies cost? Are certain items considered better or less acceptable than others? Why?

Photo Flash!

① Claire and her mother are trying to decide whether to buy a **calculatrice** *(calculator)* or a **calculatrice-traductrice** *(calculator-translator),* which is a calculator and an electronic dictionary in one.

Teaching Suggestion

Ask students to name the theme in the photos on pages 66 and 67 (shopping) and what each person is looking for. Ask students to match a chapter objective with each caption (Photo 1: asking for information; Photo 2: telling what you need; Photo 3: telling what you would like). Ask students what vocabulary they think they will learn in this chapter (school supplies, clothing, more numbers).

CHAPITRE 3
Tout pour la rentrée

① C'est combien, cette calculatrice?

66   *soixante-six*

Literature Link

Antoine de Saint-Exupéry, a well-known French aviator and writer, appears on the 50-franc bill, which is partially visible on this page. One of his best known works is *Le petit prince (The Little Prince),* a story that emphasizes love and friendship rather than wealth and material possessions.

At the start of a new school year, French students have to buy supplies, including their textbooks, at the store. They may also buy things that are less essential for school, like compact discs and clothes.

In this chapter you will learn

- to make and respond to requests; to ask others what they need and tell what you need
- to tell what you'd like and what you'd like to do
- to get someone's attention; to ask for information; to express thanks

And you will

- listen to teenagers talk about what they need for school
- read a page from a French catalogue
- write a list of supplies you need for your classes
- find out about the school supplies French teenagers buy

② Il me faut un sac.

③ Je voudrais ce tee-shirt.

Focusing on Outcomes

Call students' attention to the chapter objectives. Ask small groups to brainstorm expressions in English they might use to accomplish the chapter objectives. For example, to express what they'd like to do, they might suggest *I'd like to . . . , I feel like . . . , I want to . . .* , and so on. NOTE: You may want to use the video to support the objectives. The self-check activities in **Que sais-je?** on page 88 help students assess their achievement of the objectives.

Teacher Note

Students will learn **je voudrais** in this chapter; the other forms of **vouloir** are presented later.

Photo Flash!

② Claire is shopping for a schoolbag in Poitiers. There are usually no lockers in French schools, so students must have a sturdy bookbag in which to carry their supplies from class to class.

**VIDEO PROGRAM
OR EXPANDED VIDEO
PROGRAM,
Videocassette 1
37:12–41:45**

OR *VIDEODISC PROGRAM,*
Videodisc 2A

Search 1, Play To 8145

Video Synopsis

In this segment of the video, Claire and her mother, Mme Millet, are shopping for school supplies. Claire's mother asks her what she needs and asks a saleswoman for help. They pick out pencils, notebooks, a pencil case, and other supplies. Claire sees a schoolbag that she really likes, but her mother tells her it's too expensive. Mme Millet wants to buy a less expensive bag. Claire says she would rather go without a bag than have one she doesn't like.

Motivating Activity

Ask students if they shop with friends, a family member, or alone. Have them think of possible difficulties that might arise while shopping with a parent.

Presentation

Before playing the video, have students read the questions in Activity 1 on page 70. Tell them to look for the answers as they view the episode. You might also ask them to guess the moods of Claire and her mother and what the problem might be.

Mise en train

Pas question!

Where are Claire and Mme Millet?
What do you think they are shopping for?

Claire · Mme Millet · La vendeuse

Alors, qu'est-ce qu'il te faut?

Eh bien, des crayons, des stylos, une gomme, une calculatrice, un pot de colle...

Pardon, mademoiselle, vous avez des trousses, s'il vous plaît?

Bien sûr. Là, à côté des cahiers.

Merci.

C'est combien, ces cahiers-ci?

12 F.

Oh, regarde, maman, une calculatrice-traductrice.

C'est pour les maths ou pour l'anglais?

Euh, il me faut une calculatrice pour les maths... Mais une calculatrice-traductrice, c'est pratique pour l'anglais.

68 *soixante-huit*

CHAPITRE 3   Tout pour la rentrée

RESOURCES FOR MISE EN TRAIN

Textbook Audiocassette 2A/Audio CD 3
Practice and Activity Book, p. 25
Video Guide
  Video Program
  Expanded Video Program, Videocassette 1
Videodisc Guide
  Videodisc Program, Videodisc 2A

Teacher Note

The monetary exchange rate has remained fairly steady since the mid-1980s: between five and six francs to the dollar. In the early 80s, the rate went as high as ten francs per dollar.

Language Note

You might point out the connection between the word **colle** *(glue)* and the French word **collage**, which is also used in English (illustrations glued together to make a picture).

 **Cooperative Learning**

Have students calculate in dollars the prices of the items in the story. Form groups of four: a recorder, a reader to call out prices in francs, a money-changer to calculate the dollar price, and a checker to review the calculations. Students will need a copy of the latest money exchange rates, which can be found in the newspaper.

MISE EN TRAIN *soixante-neuf* **69**

 Video Integration

- *EXPANDED VIDEO PROGRAM,*
  Videocassette 1, 41:46–46:19
- *VIDEODISC PROGRAM,*
  Videodisc 2A

Search 8145, Play To 16400

You may choose to continue with **Pas question! (suite)** at this time or wait until later in the chapter. The story continues the next day as Claire and Ann are leaving for school. Claire is carrying her supplies in her arms and drops everything. Her mother shows her a bag in a catalogue. Claire tries to order it through Minitel, but it is out of stock. She goes back to the store she went to with her mother and finds the same 70 F bag in a different color. Claire buys the bag as well as two T-shirts, one for herself and one as a gift for her mother. Mme Millet is surprised to see that Claire bought the inexpensive bag after all.

For videodisc
application, see
Videodisc Guide.

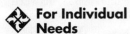 **For Individual
Needs**

2 Slower Pace Students
might work in pairs to find
the answers. To check their
answers, you might have students repeat each sentence,
replacing **elle** with either Claire
or Mme Millet.

3 Slower Pace You might
write the French expressions
for each of these functions in
random order on a trans-
parency. Have students match
the functions and the expressions. Then, play the video
and have students raise their
hands when they hear these
expressions.

Teaching Suggestion

5 You might suggest several
possible endings to the story:
a) **Claire va à l'école sans
sac.**
b) **Mme Millet achète le sac à
215 F.**
c) **Mme Millet achète le sac à
70 F.**
You might write these on a
transparency and have the
class vote on an ending for the
story.

1 Tu as compris?

Answer the following questions based on **Pas question!**

1. What is the relationship between Claire and Mme Millet? How do you know?   daughter and mother; Claire calls her **maman.**
2. Where are they?   at a store
3. What are they doing there?   buying school supplies
4. Why does Claire need a calculator?   for math class
5. What is Mme Millet's main concern?   saving money
6. What do you think of Claire's decision at the end of **Pas question!**?

2 Claire ou sa mère?

Does **elle** in each of the following sentences refer to Claire or Mme Millet?

1. Elle aime la calculatrice à 590 F.   Claire
2. Elle voudrait une calculatrice-traductrice.   Claire
3. Elle aime mieux le sac à 70 F.   Mme Millet
4. Elle aime mieux le sac vert.   Claire
5. Elle va aller à l'école sans sac.   Claire
6. Elle n'achète pas un sac à 215 F.   Mme Millet

3 Cherche les expressions

Can you find an expression in **Pas question!** to . . .

1. ask what someone needs?   Qu'est-ce qu'il te faut?
2. tell what you need?   Il me faut...
3. get a salesperson's attention?   Pardon, mademoiselle...
4. ask the price of something?   C'est combien?
5. say you like something?   Il est super! J'aime mieux...
6. say you don't like something?   Il est horrible!

4 Mets en ordre

Put these sentences about **Pas question!** in chronological order.

1. Mme Millet asks the price of a calculator.   4
2. Mme Millet asks a salesperson if she has any pencil cases.   2
3. Claire says she will go to school without a bag.   6
4. Mme Millet asks Claire what she needs for school.   1
5. Mme Millet asks the price of the notebooks.   3
6. Claire points out a bag she likes.   5

5 Et maintenant, à toi

What do you think will happen next in the story? Discuss your ideas with a partner.

PREMIERE ETAPE

Making and responding to requests; asking others what they need and telling what you need

VOCABULAIRE

un stylo

un crayon

une gomme

une règle

un sac (à dos)

un taille-crayon

un livre

une trousse

un classeur

une calculatrice

des feuilles (f.) de papier

un cahier

Make flashcards to learn new words. On one side of a card, write the French word you want to learn. (If the word is a noun, include an article to help you remember the gender.) On the other side, paste or draw a picture to illustrate the meaning of the word. Then, ask a classmate to show you the picture while you try to name the object, or use the cards to test yourself.

6 Ecoute!

Listen as Hafaïdh and Karine check the contents of their bookbags. Then, look at the pictures and decide which bag belongs to each of them. *Answers on p. 65C.*

a.

b.

c.

*J*ump Start!

Have students list all the classes they have this semester.

MOTIVATE

Have students pair off. Give them one minute to write down in English as many school supplies as they can. Call time and check the lists. You might give a prize to the pair who listed the most items.

TEACH

Presentation

Vocabulaire Before students see the French words, gather the objects pictured. Hold them up as you say the French words, having students repeat after you. Then, have students try to identify the items in French. As you hold them up, ask **Qu'est-ce que c'est?** Have individual students respond and have the whole class repeat the answer. You might want to circulate among the students, picking up an object from a student's desk and having the class identify it.

For Individual Needs

Auditory/Kinesthetic Learners After presenting all the words, ask **Qui a un(e)... ?** Have students hold up the object you named and say **Moi, j'ai un(e)...**

6 Slower Pace Before playing the recording, have students identify the items in each bookbag.

6 Auditory Learners Describe the contents of the three bookbags and have students give the letter of each corresponding photo.

Thinking Critically

Drawing Inferences — Note Culturelle Have students consider these questions. What are the advantages and disadvantages of having to bag your own purchases? Of having shoppers bring their own bags? Do American stores encourage shoppers to bring their own bags? Why or why not?

Teaching Suggestion

8 Have partners make a list of 3–4 items and ask each other if they have these items. Then, have individuals tell which items their partners have and don't have.

Presentation

Comment dit-on... ?
Circulate among the students asking for certain items. (**Tu as une règle?**) Prompt the responses **Voilà** and **Non, je regrette.** Then, have students practice in pairs. Next, have students ask you for certain things, saying **Vous avez... ?** Have them ask a partner for two things they need.

Thinking Critically

Drawing Inferences Ask students whether they should use **tu** or **vous** with a classmate and with a salesperson in a store (classmate — **tu;** salesperson — **vous**). Ask students what they think the reaction would be if they used the wrong pronoun (anger, confusion, feeling mocked or offended).

---

7 Objets trouvés
Lost and found

When Paulette gets home from the store, she realizes that she forgot to put some of her school supplies into her bag. Look at the receipt showing what she bought and make a list, in French, of the missing items. *See answers below.*

Elle n'a pas le...

```
VEN 13-05-94              3004
047CA BELLIOT Stephanie

GOMME CAOUTCH           3.30
CRAYONS GRAH.           5.15
REGLE GRADUEE           5.20
CAH. BROUILLON          1.90
COPIES DBLES PF GC      4.25
CLASSEUR 17X22         16.15
TROUSSE                28.10
SOUS/TOTAL             64.05

TOTAL                  64.05

REÇU                  100.00
RENDU                  35.95

00617    7 ARTC       16:36TM
```

NOTE CULTURELLE

In large stores in France, customers are expected to place their items on the conveyer belt and then remove and bag them as well. Most stores provide small plastic sacks, but many shoppers bring their own basket (**un panier**) or net bag (**un filet**). Although bar-code scanners were a French invention, they first caught on in the United States. Now they're becoming more common in France, especially in larger stores.

8 Devine!

Write down the name of one of the objects from the **Vocabulaire** on page 71. Don't let the other members of your group know what you've chosen. They will then take turns guessing which object you chose.

—C'est un taille-crayon?
—Oui, c'est ça. *or* Non, ce n'est pas ça.

—Tu as une calculatrice, Paul?
—J'ai un stylo, un crayon, une règle et des feuilles de papier, mais je n'ai pas de calculatrice!

COMMENT DIT-ON... ?
Making and responding to requests

To ask someone for something:
Tu as un stylo?
Vous avez un crayon?

To respond:
Oui. **Voilà.** *Here.*
Non. **Je regrette. Je n'ai pas de** crayons. *Sorry. I don't have . . .*

Multicultural Link

You might want to have students make a list of school supplies and other items they need for school. Then, have them choose a country and find out what high school students there usually need for school by interviewing someone from that country.

Answers
7 Elle n'a pas le classeur. Elle n'a pas le cahier. Elle n'a pas la gomme. Elle n'a pas la règle. Elle n'a pas les copies.

Grammaire The indefinite articles **un, une,** and **des**

The articles **un** and **une** both mean *a* or *an*. Use **un** with masculine nouns and **une** with feminine nouns. Use **des** *(some)* with plural nouns. Notice that **un, une,** and **des** change to **de** after **ne... pas.**

J'ai **un** crayon, mais je n'ai pas **de** papier.

9 Ecoute!

Listen as Nadine asks her friends for some school supplies. Match her friends' responses to the appropriate pictures. Answers on p. 65C.

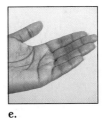

a.   b.   c.   d.   e.

10 Tu as ça, toi?

With a partner, take turns pointing out the differences you notice between Christophe's desk and Annick's.

Regarde! Christophe a une gomme, mais Annick n'a pas de gomme.

PREMIERE ETAPE   *soixante-treize* **73**

Presentation

Grammaire Hold up a masculine object such as a pencil and have students tell what you're holding. (**Vous avez un crayon.**) Repeat with a feminine object (**Vous avez une gomme.**) and with several other objects. (**Vous avez des crayons et des gommes.**) Put the items away, display your empty hands, and have students tell you that you don't have these objects. (**Vous n'avez pas de...**) Then, have students make a chart in their notebooks with two columns and four rows. Down the left-hand side of the chart, they should write *masculine, feminine,* and *plural.* They should label the columns *Definite articles* and *Indefinite articles.* Have students fill in the chart with **le, la, les, un, une,** and **des,** and keep it for later use.

Teacher Note

Demonstrative adjectives can be added to the chart when they are presented later in this chapter.

Teaching Suggestion

10 As a variation, form small groups or teams for a competition. Set a time limit within which groups must write down all of the items they see on one of the desks in the illustration.

Culture Note

French notebook paper is usually graph paper rather than lined. It is sold either as **copies simples** *(single-page sheets)* or **copies doubles,** which are two-page sheets used for **rédactions** or **interros écrites.**

Presentation

Comment dit-on... ? Have pairs of students role-play the short dialogue in the illustration, substituting other courses and objects. Students might want to know the negative **Il ne me faut pas de...**

For videodisc application, see *Videodisc Guide.*

Thinking Critically

Synthesizing Ask students to imagine situations other than shopping for school supplies when they might use the expressions in **Comment dit-on... ?** (at a pharmacy, library, or post office, and when cooking).

CLOSE

To close this **étape**, display ten school supplies on a tray or table and allow students one minute to look at them. Then, cover the objects and have students write down as many objects as they can remember. You might give a prize or extra credit to the student who remembers the most objects and give credit for completion to the others.

ASSESS

Quiz 3-1, *Chapter Teaching Resources, Book 1,* pp. 135–136

Assessment Items, Audiocassette 7A/Audio CD 3

Performance Assessment

Show *Teaching Transparency 3-1.* Have students assume the identity of one of the shoppers and tell what they need for school.

COMMENT DIT-ON... ?
Asking others what they need and telling what you need

To ask what someone needs:

Qu'est-ce qu'il te faut pour la bio?
What do you need for . . . ? (informal)

Qu'est-ce qu'il vous faut pour la géo?
What do you need for . . . ? (formal)

To tell what you need:

Il me faut un stylo et un classeur.

Alors, qu'est-ce qu'il te faut pour l'anglais?

Euh, il me faut un classeur et un sac aussi.

11 Qu'est-ce qu'il te faut?

Make a list of your school subjects. Exchange lists with a partner. Then take turns asking each other what you need for various classes.

— Qu'est-ce qu'il te faut pour les maths?
— Il me faut une calculatrice et un crayon.

12 Aide-mémoire

Write a note to remind yourself of the school supplies you need to buy for two or three of your classes.

13 Un petit service

Vou're late for class, and you've forgotten your supplies. Ask a friend if he or she has what you need. Your friend should respond appropriately. Then, change roles.

— Oh là là! J'ai histoire! Il me faut un stylo et un cahier. Tu as un stylo?
— Non, je regrette.
— Zut! *(Darn!)*

Vocabulaire à la carte

Here are some additional words you can use to talk about your school supplies.

un compas	*a compass*
des crayons (m.) **de couleur**	*some colored pencils*
un feutre	*a marker*
du liquide correcteur	*some correction fluid*
du ruban adhésif (m.)	*some transparent tape*
une tenue de gymnastique	*a gym suit*

Pour le français il me faut...

Language Notes

Vocabulaire à la carte Make sure students don't pronounce the **s** at the end of **compas. Feutre** also means *felt,* as in felt-tip pen.

• After presenting the **Vocabulaire à la carte,** you might want to give students the names of other items they might like to know in French: **un surligneur** *(highlighter);* **la craie** *(chalk);* and **un agenda** *(memo book or personal calendar).*

PANORAMA CULTUREL

Séverine • Martinique

Onélia • France

Marius • Côte d'Ivoire

We asked some francophone students what supplies they bought for the opening of school, **la rentrée.** Here's what they had to say.

Qu'est-ce qu'il te faut comme fournitures scolaires?

«Alors, donc pour l'école j'ai acheté un nouveau sac à dos, des livres pour étudier, des vêtements, entre autres des jeans, des chaussures, bien sûr et puis bon, des tee-shirts, des jupes, des robes.»
—Séverine

«Il faut des classeurs, des cahiers, des crayons, des règles, des instruments de géométrie, [une] calculatrice pour les mathématiques, des feuilles... C'est tout.»
—Onélia

«Pour l'école, il faut des règles, des bics, des stylos, des cahiers, des livres et la tenue.»
—Marius

Qu'en penses-tu?

1. What school supplies did you have to purchase for the school year?
2. What did these students buy that is usually provided by schools in the United States?
3. What are the advantages and disadvantages of each system?
4. What other items do you usually buy at the beginning of a school year?

textbooks

Savais-tu que...?

In French-speaking countries, students usually buy their own textbooks and even maintain their own grade book, **un livret scolaire.** Some schools require students to purchase school uniforms. A store that specializes in school supplies, textbooks, and paper products is called **une librairie-papeterie.**

VIDEO PROGRAM OR EXPANDED VIDEO PROGRAM, Videocassette 1 46:20–48:26

OR **VIDEODISC PROGRAM,** Videodisc 2A

Search 16400, Play To 18510

Teacher Notes
• See *Video Guide, Videodisc Guide,* and *Practice and Activity Book* for activities related to the **Panorama Culturel.**
• Remind students that cultural material may be included in the Chapter Quizzes and Test.
• The interviewees' language represents informal, unrehearsed speech. Occasionally, edits have been made for clarification.

Presentation

As students view the video or listen to the recording, have them jot down the items mentioned by the interviewees. Then, in pairs or in small groups, have them take turns reading the interviews aloud. Next, ask students the **Questions** to check comprehension. Finally, have them discuss the questions in **Qu'en penses-tu?** in small groups or as a class.

Culture Note
You might tell students that Ivorian students wear school uniforms. In high school, the boys wear khaki shirts and pants, while the girls wear blue skirts and white blouses.

Questions

1. **Qu'est-ce que Séverine a acheté comme vêtements pour l'école?** (des jeans, des chaussures, des tee-shirts, des jupes et des robes)
2. **Onélia a besoin de quelles fournitures scolaires?** (des classeurs, des cahiers, des crayons, des règles, des instruments de géométrie, une calculatrice et des feuilles) **Pour quel cours?** (les maths, la géometrie)
3. **Qu'est-ce que Marius a acheté pour l'école?** (des règles, des bics, des stylos, des cahiers, des livres et la tenue)

Language Note

Some new terms are **une tenue** *(a school uniform)* and **des bics** *(ballpoint pens).* See *Video Guide* for additional vocabulary.

DEUXIEME ETAPE
Telling what you'd like and what you'd like to do

Jump Start!

Have students make a list of five things they have with them for class and anything they did not bring. They might begin with **Aujourd'hui, j'ai...** and **Je n'ai pas de...**

MOTIVATE

Have students mention one item they would most like to have in each of these categories: clothes, gifts, and reading material. Next, have them discuss what they most like to do during their free time.

TEACH

Presentation

Vocabulaire Say the cognates at the bottom of the **Vocabulaire** and have students guess their English equivalents. Then, present the other words (**baskets, ordinateur, montre, portefeuille,** and **roman**), using the actual items, drawing them on the board, or showing pictures of them.

◆ For Individual Needs

Tactile/Kinesthetic Learners
Name an item in the classroom and have students point to it or pick it up from among items you have displayed on a table.

14 Challenge Have students write down the item each person would like to buy as well as the person's name.

DEUXIEME ETAPE

Telling what you'd like and what you'd like to do

VOCABULAIRE

Qu'est-ce qu'on va acheter?

Hervé regarde **un short.**

Odile regarde **des baskets.**

Denis regarde **un roman.**

Stéphane regarde **un disque compact/un CD.**

Dorothée regarde **un jean.**

Mme Roussel regarde **un ordinateur.**

M. Beauvois regarde **une montre.**

M. Prévost regarde **un portefeuille.**

You can probably figure out what these words mean:

un bracelet	un magazine	une radio	une télévision
une cassette	un poster	un sweat-shirt	une vidéocassette
un dictionnaire	un pull-over	un tee-shirt	

14 Ecoute!

Several shoppers in the **Vocabulaire** are going to tell you what they would like to buy. As you listen to each speaker, look at the illustrations above and identify the person. Write down his or her name. Answers on p. 65C.

76 *soixante-seize*

CHAPITRE 3 Tout pour la rentrée

RESOURCES FOR DEUXIEME ETAPE

Textbook Audiocassette 2A/Audio CD 3
Practice and Activity Book, pp. 29–31
Video Guide
  Video Program
  Expanded Video Program, Videocassette 1
Videodisc Guide
  Videodisc Program, Videodisc 2A

Chapter Teaching Resources, Book 1
• Communicative Activity 3-1, pp. 115–116
• Teaching Transparency Master 3-2, pp. 120, 122
  Teaching Transparency 3-2
• Additional Listening Activities 3-3, 3-4, p. 124
  Audiocassette 9A/Audio CD 3
• Realia 3-2, pp. 128, 129
• Situation Cards 3-2, pp. 130–131
• Student Response Forms, pp. 132–134
• Quiz 3-2, pp. 137–138
  Audiocassette 7A/Audio CD 3

COMMENT DIT-ON... ?

Telling what you'd like and what you'd like to do

Je voudrais un sac. *I'd like . . .*
Je voudrais acheter un tee-shirt. *I'd like to buy . . .*

---

15 **Ecoute!**

Since Georges doesn't have time to go shopping for school supplies, you've offered to get them. Listen as Georges tells you what he needs and write down what you have to buy at the store. *Answers on p. 65C.*

16 **Vive le week-end!**

What would you like to do this weekend? Find three classmates who want to do the same thing.

—Je voudrais sortir avec des copains.
 Et toi?
—Moi aussi. *or* Moi, je voudrais faire
 du sport.

faire les magasins   dormir
danser   écouter de la musique
parler au téléphone
   étudier
regarder la télévision
nager   sortir avec des copains
faire le ménage   faire du sport

17 **Un cadeau**   *A gift*

Make a list of what you would like to buy for . . .

1. a friend who likes horror movies and books.
2. a friend who loves sports.
3. someone who's always late for class.
4. a friend who loves music.
5. someone who loves French.
6. your best friend.

18 **Mon journal**

You earned 100 dollars this summer. Write down three or four items you'd like to buy for yourself.

Grammaire   The demonstrative adjectives **ce, cet, cette, and ces**

Ce, cet, and **cette** mean *this* or *that.* **Ces** means *these* or *those.*

	Singular	Plural
Masculine before a consonant sound	**ce** stylo	**ces** stylos
Masculine before a vowel sound	**cet** examen	**ces** examens
Feminine	**cette** école	**ces** écoles

When you want to specify *that* as opposed to *this*, add **-là** *(there)* to the end of the noun.

—J'aime **ce sac.**
—Moi, j'aime mieux **ce sac-là.**

Presentation

Comment dit-on... ?   After modeling the function, hold up various items or illustrations of items or activities and have individual students say what they would like or what they would like to do.

Teaching Suggestion

17   After students complete this activity, name gifts you are buying for imaginary friends (**un poster de Paris pour Pierre**). Ask students to imagine why you are buying that gift for the person. (**Pierre aime voyager.**)

Presentation

Grammaire   Show students two of the same item and ask them which one they would choose. For example, hold up two different pens and ask **Tu aimes mieux quel stylo?** Students should answer **Ce stylo-là** as they point to the one they choose. Tell students that forms of *this* and *that* are called demonstrative adjectives because they point out or demonstrate one or more things among many.

   For videodisc application, see *Videodisc Guide.*

Teaching Suggestion

Grammaire   Review definite and indefinite articles. If you had students make the suggested chart of articles (see **Presentation** on page 73), you might have them add **ce, cet, cette,** and **ces** to it now.

Language Notes

- French teenagers often use the abbreviation **CD** for **disque compact.**
- Tell students that the infinitive, the *to* form of a verb *(to go, to have, to buy)*, is used after **Je voudrais.** You might also tell them that this is a polite way to express a desire.

19 Slower Pace You might have students determine the gender and number of the noun in each sentence before they choose the correct article or adjective.

Presentation

Vocabulaire Say each color as you point out items of that color. Then, name three colors in a row and challenge a volunteer to point to items of those colors in the order in which the colors were mentioned. Ask students if they see any similarities or associations with English. Then, ask students to give the colors of the sky, a Valentine, fall, Halloween, and the French flag.

Additional Practice

You might want to hold up various items and ask about the color: **C'est bleu ou rouge?** Have individuals or the entire class respond. For more of a challenge, ask **C'est de quelle couleur?**

---

19 Le cadeau parfait   *The perfect gift*

Claire is shopping for a gift for her mother. The salesperson is making suggestions. Choose the correct articles to complete their conversation.

LE VENDEUR   Vous aimez (**ce**/**cette**) montre, mademoiselle?
CLAIRE   Oui, mais ma mère a déjà (**un**/**une**) montre.
LE VENDEUR   Euh, (**ces**/**ce**) roman, il vous plaît?
CLAIRE   Non, elle n'aime pas lire.
LE VENDEUR   Elle aime (**la** /**l'**) musique?
CLAIRE   Oui. Elle adore le jazz.
LE VENDEUR   (**Cet**/**Cette**) cassette de Wynton Marsalis, peut-être?
CLAIRE   C'est une bonne idée.

20 Qu'est-ce que tu aimes mieux?

Take turns with a partner asking and answering questions about the items below.

— Tu aimes ce sac?
— Non. J'aime mieux ce sac-là!

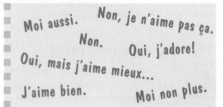

Moi aussi.   Non, je n'aime pas ça.
Non.   Oui, j'adore!
Oui, mais j'aime mieux...
J'aime bien.   Moi non plus.

1.   2.   3.   4.

Vocabulaire

J'aime le sac...   Moi, j'adore la trousse...   J'aime le sac...   Moi, j'adore la trousse...

ROUGE   ROUGE   ROSE   ROSE
ORANGE   ORANGE   BLANC   BLANCHE
JAUNE   JAUNE   GRIS   GRISE
VERT   VERTE   NOIR   NOIRE
BLEU   BLEUE   MARRON   MARRON
VIOLET   VIOLETTE

21 Vrai ou Faux?

Read the statements below and tell whether they're true (**vrai**) or false (**faux**) according to the picture. Correct the false statements.

1. Claire a un sac jaune.   vrai
2. Claire et Thierry ont des tee-shirts bleus.
3. Claire a un short marron.   faux; un short vert
4. Thierry a des baskets bleues.
5. Thierry a un classeur rouge.   vrai
6. Claire et Thierry ont des shorts noirs.

    2. faux; Claire—un tee-shirt blanc
    4. faux; des baskets grises
    6. faux; Claire—un short vert/Thierry—un short blanc

---

*G*rammaire   Adjective agreement and placement

Did you notice in the **Vocabulaire** on page 78 that the spelling of the colors changes according to the nouns they describe?

	Singular	Plural
Masculine	le classeur vert	les classeurs vert**s**
Feminine	la gomme vert**e**	les gommes vert**es**

- Usually, you add an **e** to make an adjective feminine; however, when an adjective ends in an unaccented **e**, you don't have to add another **e**: **le classeur rouge, la gomme rouge.**
- Some adjectives have irregular feminine forms: **blanc, blanche; violet, violette.**
- Usually, you add an **s** to make an adjective plural; however, when an adjective ends in an **s**, you don't have to add another **s**: **les crayons gris.**
- Some adjectives don't change form. Two examples are **orange** and **marron.**
- What do you notice about where the adjectives are placed in relation to the nouns they describe?*

---

22 Chasse au trésor   *Scavenger hunt*

Copy the list of items below. Ask your classmates if they have the items on your list. When you find someone who does, write his or her name next to the item.

> un tee-shirt violet   une montre blanche   un poster de France
>
> des baskets bleues   un roman de science-fiction   un short rose
>
> une trousse violette   un stylo rouge
>
> une cassette de musique classique   un portefeuille gris

* Colors and many other adjectives are placed **after** the nouns they describe.

DEUXIEME ETAPE   *soixante-dix-neuf*   **79**

Presentation

Grammaire Have students deduce how the feminine forms of colors are formed by observing the **Vocabulaire** on page 78. Then, ask students how they think the spelling of the colors would change if they described several things. Show various combinations of school supplies in certain colors (two red binders, one green pencil, three white rulers) and have volunteers write the French equivalents on the board (**les classeurs rouges, le crayon vert, les règles blanches**).

For Individual Needs

21 Visual Learners First, ask students to identify in French the clothes in the illustration.

22 Slower Pace Review the colors in French before starting this activity. You might say **Cette personne a des baskets noires** and have students call out the name of the person in class wearing those sneakers.

CLOSE

Game
Play the game "**Je vois quelque chose**" on page 65F to practice vocabulary and colors. Extend it to refer to people: **Je vois quelqu'un qui a des baskets blanches.** You might also re-enter earlier vocabulary: **Je vois quelqu'un qui a une calculatrice noire.**

ASSESS

Quiz 3-2, *Chapter Teaching Resources, Book 1,* pp. 137–138

Assessment Items, Audiocassette 7A/Audio CD 3

Performance Assessment
Have students form groups, gather ten of their own school supplies, and make a list of the objects. Have one student show what the group has, saying **Nous avons ces stylos verts, cette calculatrice blanche...**

Getting someone's attention; asking for information; expressing thanks

*J*ump Start!

Have students make a list of three things they would like or would like to do.

MOTIVATE

Ask students to count in English from 0–50 by tens and then by fives. Ask what patterns they see.

TEACH

Presentation

Vocabulaire After students have done the motivating activity, write the word **soi-xante** on the board, pointing out the similarity with **six**. Ask students to count aloud from 60–69. Next, write **soi-xante-dix** on the board, asking students what number it represents. After establishing that it is 70, ask students to guess how to count from 71–79. Next, write **quatre-vingts** on the board and ask students how to continue; do the same with **quatre-vingt-dix**. Finally, write **cent** and ask students to suggest English words that have the same root *(century, cent, centennial)*. Make sure students understand that **quatre-vingts** and **deux cents** end in -s only if no other numbers follow. Have students count by hundreds from 200–900. You might want to refer students to the list of numbers on page 351.

Teaching Suggestion

23 After this activity, ask students to say the frequency and call letters of their favorite radio stations. (**Moi, j'écoute KKMJ 95,5 FM.**) You might take a poll to see which three stations are the most popular.

VOCABULAIRE

60 soixante	**70** soixante-dix	**71** soixante et onze	**72** soixante-douze
80 quatre-vingts	**81** quatre-vingt-un	**90** quatre-vingt-dix	
100 quatre-vingt-onze	**101** cent	**200** cent un	
200 deux cents	**201** deux cent un		

23 Ecoute!

Listen to four French disc jockeys announce the dial frequencies of their radio stations. Then, match the frequency to the station logo. Answers on p. 65D.

RADIOS ROCK

a C'ROCK
89.5 MHZ (VIENNE)

d OUÏ FM
102.3 MHZ (PARIS)

b RCV
99 MHZ (LILLE)

e CANAL B

c CLIP FM
88.7 MHZ (CHALON/SAONE)

94 MHz

NOTE CULTURELLE

If you ask about prices in French stores, they will be given in **francs**, the French monetary unit. In addition to French francs, there are Swiss francs, Belgian francs, Luxembourg francs, and C.F.A. (**Communauté financière africaine**) francs in many African countries. There are 100 **centimes** in one French franc. Coins are available in denominations of 5, 10, and 20 centimes, 1/2 franc, 1 franc, and 2, 5, 10, and 20 francs. Bills come in denominations of 20, 50, 100, 200, and 500 francs. The size of the bill varies according to the amount—the larger the bill, the more it's worth—and each bill carries the picture of a French author, artist, or philosopher.

Prices can be said and written in two ways, either **quarante-cinq francs, cinquante** (45F50) or **quarante-cinq, cinquante** (45,50). Notice that a comma is used instead of a decimal point.

80 *quatre-vingts* CHAPITRE 3 Tout pour la rentrée

RESOURCES FOR TROISIEME ETAPE

Textbook Audiocassette 2A/Audio CD 3
Practice and Activity Book, pp. 32–34
Videodisc Guide
  Videodisc Program, Videodisc 2A

Chapter Teaching Resources, Book 1
• Communicative Activity 3-2, pp. 117–118
• Teaching Transparency Master 3-3, pp. 121, 122
  Teaching Transparency 3-3
• Additional Listening Activities 3-5, 3-6, p. 125
  Audiocassette 9A/Audio CD 3
• Realia 3-2, pp. 128, 129
• Situation Cards 3-3, pp. 130–131
• Student Response Forms, pp. 132–134
• Quiz 3-3, pp. 139–140
  Audiocassette 7A/Audio CD 3

24 Ça fait combien? *How much is it?*

How much money is shown in each illustration? Give the totals in French.

1. quatre-vingt-sept francs

2. soixante-trois francs

25 C'est combien?

Look at the drawing of the store display below. How much money does each of these customers spend in **Papier Plume?**

1. Alain achète deux stylos et une trousse.   20F70
2. Geneviève achète un classeur, un dictionnaire et un cahier.   127F45
3. Paul achète six crayons et un taille-crayon.   2F95
4. Marcel achète une règle, une gomme et un stylo.   5F80
5. Sarah achète deux cahiers et un dictionnaire.   125F20
6. Cécile achète une règle et une calculatrice.   123F20

TROISIEME ETAPE

quatre-vingt-un **81**

Culture Note

The name of the monetary unit to be used in the European Union is the **ECU**, for *European Currency Unit*. The écu is also the name of an old French coin no longer in use.

Reteaching

25 School supplies, numbers Write on the board the prices of several items in francs:

> un crayon = 2F30
> un cahier = 14F80
> une trousse = 39F50
> six stylos = 75 F

Say the names of several items and their prices and have students repeat. Then, write several more items on the board and have individual students suggest prices for them. Next, have students work in pairs, with one student naming items and prices at random, and the other student calculating the total cost and the change due from a 100 F bill.

Teaching Suggestion

25 For listening comprehension, ask some true–false statements as students look at the illustration. (**La trousse coûte 20 F. Les règles coûtent 3F20.**)

Language Notes

- Ask students to suggest slang terms we use in English to refer to money (dough, bucks). You might give them some slang terms in French for money. Money in general is **le fric. Les sous** is used for **francs** in slang expressions like **Je n'ai pas un sou** or **Il est sans le sou.**
- Some idiomatic expressions with numbers include **couper les cheveux en quatre** *(to split hairs),* **voir trente-six chandelles** *(to see stars),* **faire les cent pas** *(to pace up and down).*
- Francophone Swiss and Belgians say **septante** and **nonante** for 70 and 90. For 80, the Belgians say **quatre-vingts,** while the Swiss say **octante.**

Mon journal

26 For an additional journal entry suggestion for Chapter 3, see *Practice and Activity Book*, page 147. You might also refer students to additional school supplies listed in the Supplementary Vocabulary on page 343.

Motivating Activity

Ask students what else they will need to know besides numbers in order to buy something at a store. Ask them how they get the clerk's attention and how they ask for help.

Presentation

Comment dit-on... ? Ask students to look only at the illustrations and infer which functions the girl is expressing in each (1st: asking how much something costs; 2nd: expressing thanks). After introducing the expressions, have students role-play the dialogues, changing the item and price.

Teaching Suggestion

28 You might want to have students use their own school supplies as props for their dialogues.

---

26 **Mon journal**

Do you budget your money? Make a list of the items you've bought in the last month and the approximate price of each in francs. To convert American prices to francs, look up the current exchange rate in the newspaper.

COMMENT DIT-ON... ?
Getting someone's attention; asking for information; expressing thanks

To get someone's attention:
Pardon, monsieur/madame/
mademoiselle.
Excusez-moi, monsieur/madame/
mademoiselle.

To ask how much something costs:
C'est combien?

To express thanks:
Merci.

27 **Ecoute!**

In a department store in France, you overhear shoppers asking salespeople for the prices of various items. As you listen to the conversations, write down the items mentioned and their prices. Answers on p. 65D.

28 **Jeu de rôle**

You're in a French **librairie-papeterie** buying school supplies. For each item you want, get the salesperson's attention and ask how much the item costs. The salesperson will give you the price. Act out this scene with a partner. Then, change roles.

82   *quatre-vingt-deux*   CHAPITRE 3   Tout pour la rentrée

29 Les magazines

You've decided to subscribe to a French magazine. Take turns with a partner playing the roles of a customer and a salesperson. Use the advertisement to discuss the prices of several magazines.

Abonnez-vous à :

FEMME A LA MODE	(12 numéros) France 210 FF
DECOUVERTE SCIENTIFIQUE	(22 numéros) France 499 FF
L'AFRIQUE DE NOS JOURS	(12 numéros) France 250 FF, Europe 250 FF, Dom-Tom 250 FF, Afrique 265 FF
TÉLÉ-TUBE	(52 numéros) France et Dom-Tom 580 FF, USA $140, Canada $180, Autres pays 855 FF
LA VOIX DU MONDE	(52 numéros) France 728 FF
LES GRANDS MOUVEMENTS DE L'ECONOMIE	(12 numéros) France 170 FF
LA VIE SPORTIVE	(12 numéros) France 215 FF

PRONONCIATION

The r sound

The French **r** is quite different from the American *r*. To pronounce the French **r**, keep the tip of your tongue pressed against your lower front teeth. Arch the back of your tongue upward, almost totally blocking the passage of air in the back of your throat.

A. A prononcer

Repeat the following words.

1. Raoul	rouge	roman	règle
2. crayon	trente	calculatrice	barbe
3. terrible	intéressant	Europe	quarante
4. poster	rare	vert	montre

B. A lire

Take turns with a partner reading the following sentences aloud.

1. Fermez la porte.
2. Regardez le livre de français.
3. Prenez un crayon.
4. Ouvrez la fenêtre.
5. Je voudrais une montre.
6. Je regrette. Je n'ai pas de règle.

C. A écrire

You're going to hear a short dialogue. Write down what you hear. *Answers on p. 65D.*

For Individual Needs

29 Slower Pace Ask individuals to name the different magazines and the prices shown. Ask them what kinds of magazines they think these are.

Teaching Suggestion

Prononciation To make the French **r** sound, have students practice the correct position of the tongue by pronouncing the French word **garage**. At first, they may simply say **gara**, since the two consonants are produced in the same place in the back of the throat. Then, have them say the whole word **garage**.

CLOSE

Read aloud some addition and subtraction problems for students to solve. You might have students work individually, in pairs, or in small groups. You will need to teach the words **et** *(plus)* and **moins** *(minus)*. Sample problems: $83 + 156$; $92 - 16$; $64 + 71$; $48 + 27$; $212 - 13$ (Answers: 239, 76, 135, 75, 199). Ask volunteers to write the problems and answers on the board and read them aloud.

ASSESS

Quiz 3-3, *Chapter Teaching Resources, Book 1,* pp. 139–140

Assessment Items, Audiocassette 7A/Audio CD 3

Performance Assessment

Have partners make lists of what they have and what they need for their courses. Then, have them role-play a scene in a store where they purchase the items they need.

Teacher Note

For subscription information and descriptions of French language periodicals, see page T50.

READING STRATEGY

Scanning for specific information

Teacher Note

For an additional reading, see *Practice and Activity Book*, page 35.

PREREADING
Activities A–B

Motivating Activity

Ask students where they go shopping for school supplies and why they go there. Next, ask students to imagine they are going to school in another country. Ask them how they would find the supplies and clothes they want.

Teaching Suggestion

Have students identify the type of reading they are faced with so that they will know what type of information to look for. Ask them for examples of words or phrases that give clues as to what the ad is about.

Teacher Note

There are several large discount store chains in France, including **Monoprix** and **Prisunic** for general items, and **Tati** for clothes.

READING
Activities C–J

 For Individual Needs

Visual/Auditory Learners
You might want to read the selection aloud or have students read it to each other in pairs.

LISONS!

$\mathcal{L}$ook at the information presented on this page. Where would you expect to find a text like this? Would you normally use information like this for a specific purpose? What would it be?

DE BONS CONSEILS

When you read material like this, you are generally looking for specific information—prices, colors, or sizes, for example. When that is your purpose, you don't have to read or understand every word. You can simply scan the material until you find what you are looking for.

A. At what time of year would you expect to see an advertisement like this? fall

B. When you buy school supplies, what is most important to you? Color? Price? Brand name?

C. Working with a partner, scan the ad for information about price, size, and quantity. Make a list of the words you find in the text that fit each of these categories.

D. What do you think **les 3** means?

E. The word **écolier** is used to describe the notebook. Do you recognize a word you've learned before in this word? What do you think **écolier** means?

F. What is the most expensive item? The least expensive?
See answers below.

C. See answers below.
D. See answer below.
E. See answers below.

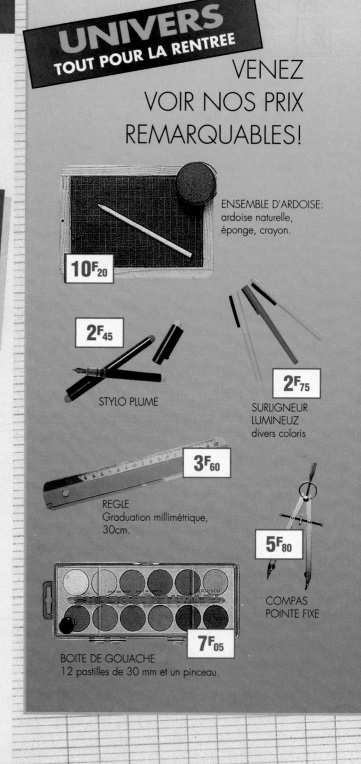

UNIVERS TOUT POUR LA RENTREE

VENEZ VOIR NOS PRIX REMARQUABLES!

ENSEMBLE D'ARDOISE: ardoise naturelle, éponge, crayon. **10F20**

2F45 STYLO PLUME

2F75 SURLIGNEUR LUMINEUZ divers coloris

3F60 REGLE Graduation millimétrique, 30cm.

5F80 COMPAS POINTE FIXE

BOITE DE GOUACHE 12 pastilles de 30 mm et un pinceau. **7F05**

Answers

C *Price:* 10F20, 2F45, 2F75, 3F60, 5F80, 7F05, 5F90, 14F, 4F20, 1F75, 8F45, 7F40, 1F70

Size: 30 cm., 30 mm., 19 mm. × 33 m., 24 × 32 cm., 0,50 × 2 m.

Quantity: 12 pastilles, 8 chiffres, 4 opérations

D for three

E école; *for school use*

F *Most expensive*—calculatrice
Least expensive—rouleau protège livres

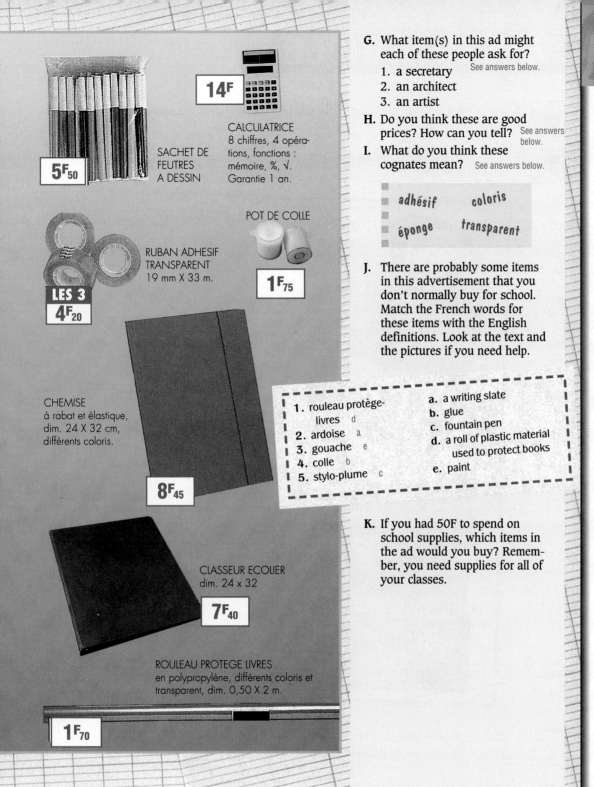

G. What item(s) in this ad might each of these people ask for? See answers below.
1. a secretary
2. an architect
3. an artist

H. Do you think these are good prices? How can you tell? See answers below.

I. What do you think these cognates mean? See answers below.

> adhésif   coloris
>
> éponge   transparent

J. There are probably some items in this advertisement that you don't normally buy for school. Match the French words for these items with the English definitions. Look at the text and the pictures if you need help.

1. rouleau protège-livres d
2. ardoise a
3. gouache e
4. colle b
5. stylo-plume c

a. a writing slate
b. glue
c. fountain pen
d. a roll of plastic material used to protect books
e. paint

K. If you had 50F to spend on school supplies, which items in the ad would you buy? Remember, you need supplies for all of your classes.

quatre-vingt-cinq **85**

Language Note

In addition to the school supplies presented in Activity J, students might be interested in the following items:
- **chemise:** folder with flaps that fold in to hold papers and elastic bands to keep the folder shut
- **stylo plume:** fountain or ink pen that can be refilled
- **ensemble d'ardoise:** small chalkboard used instead of scratch paper

POSTREADING
Activity K

Thinking Critically

Analyzing Have students examine the ad and determine why they think it is effective or ineffective.

Comparing and Contrasting Have students compare the items in the selection to the one(s) they usually see. Do the items shown seem similar to those used by American students? How do they differ in price or appearance?

Answers

G *Possible answers*
1. *Secretary:* stylo plume, surligneur
2. *Architect:* feutres à dessin, compas, règle
3. *Artist:* gouache, feutres à dessin

H Our prices are impressive/competitive.

I adhésif: *adhesive*
éponge: *sponge*
coloris: *colors*
transparent: *transparent*

The **Mise en pratique** reviews and integrates all four skills and culture in preparation for the Chapter Test.

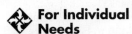
For Individual Needs

1 Challenge Have students listen to the recording again. This time they should note the reasons why the speaker would like each gift.

Teaching Suggestions

2 Encourage students to use the expressions of agreement and disagreement they learned in Chapter 2: **Moi aussi, Moi non plus, Moi si,** and so forth.

3 This activity might be used as a journal or portfolio entry.

MISE EN PRATIQUE

 1 You want to buy your friend a birthday gift. Listen as she gives you some ideas and then make a list of the things she would like. Answers on p. 65D.

 2 You and a friend are browsing through a magazine. Point out several items you like and several you dislike.

165F. Sac shopping, 35X10X30 cm, 65 % polyester et 35 % coton.

35F. Classeur, 21X29,7 cm.

45F. Stylo-plume.

22,50F. Chemise 3 rabats élastique, 24X32 cm.

195F. Sac à dos, 65 % polyester et 35 % coton.

59,50F. Portefeuille, 65 % polyester et 35 % coton.

 3 Make a list in French of two or three of the items pictured above that you'd like to buy. Include the colors and prices of the items you choose.

86 *quatre-vingt-six*

CHAPITRE 3   Tout pour la rentrée

4 Tell your partner about the items you've chosen in Activity 3. Give as much detail as you can, including the color and price.

5 Your friend has been passing notes to you during study hall. Write a response to each one.

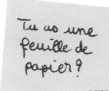

Tu as une feuille de papier?

Il me faut un stylo!

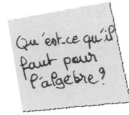

Qu'est-ce qu'il faut pour l'algèbre?

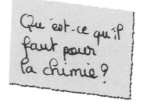

Qu'est-ce qu'il faut pour la chimie?

6 If you were in France, what differences would you notice in these areas? See answers below.

1. money   2. school supplies   3. stores

7 Create your own store and write a list of the merchandise you have for sale. You might have a bookstore **(une librairie-papeterie)**, a music store **(une boutique de disques)**, or even a gift shop **(une boutique de cadeaux)**. On your list of merchandise, describe each item and give its price. You might even illustrate your list with drawings or clippings from a newspaper or magazine.

8

JEU DE ROLE

Visit the "store" your partner created and decide on something you'd like to buy. Your partner will play the role of the salesperson. Get the salesperson's attention, tell what you want, ask the price(s), pay for your purchases, thank the salesperson, and say goodbye. Your partner should respond appropriately. Then change roles. Remember to use **madame, monsieur,** or **mademoiselle,** and **vous.**

Possible answers
6 1. The larger the denomination, the larger the bill.
2. Notebook paper looks like graph paper.
3. One is expected to bag one's own purchases.

MISE EN PRATIQUE
CHAPITRE 3

Teaching Suggestion

5 Extend this activity by asking students to write notes of their own to one another, exchange them, and write replies.

📁 **Portfolio**

7 Written You might ask students to add this to their written portfolios. It might also be used as part of the chapter project (see page 65E).

8 Oral Students might record their conversations as an oral entry in their portfolios. You might also assign this activity to small groups, with two or three students acting as customers. For portfolio suggestions, see *Assessment Guide,* page 16.

 Video Wrap-Up

VIDEO PROGRAM
• **EXPANDED VIDEO PROGRAM,** Videocassette 1, 37:12–50:26
• **VIDEODISC PROGRAM,** Videodisc 2A

At this time, you might want to use the video resources for additional review and enrichment. See *Video Guide* or *Videodisc Guide* for suggestions regarding the following:
• **Pas question!** (Dramatic episode)
• **Panorama Culturel** (Interviews)
• **Vidéoclips** (Authentic footage)

This page is intended to help students prepare for the test. It is a brief checklist of the major points covered in the chapter. The students should be reminded that this is only a checklist and does not necessarily include everything that will appear on the test.

Teaching Suggestion

In pairs, have students ask and respond to each of the questions in Activities 1–5.

QUE SAIS-JE?

Can you use what you've learned in this chapter?

Can you make and respond to requests? p. 72

1 How would you ask for the following items using the verb **avoir**? How would you respond to someone's request for one of these items? See answers below.

1.   2.   3.

Can you ask others what they need? p. 74

2 How would you ask your friend what he or she needs for each of these school subjects? See answers below.

1.   2.   3.

Can you tell what you need? p. 74

3 How would you tell a friend that you need . . . See answers below.

1. a calculator and an eraser for math?
2. a binder and some sheets of paper for Spanish class?
3. some pens and a notebook for English?
4. a pencil and a ruler for geometry?
5. a backpack and a book for history?

Can you tell what you'd like and what you'd like to do? p. 77

4 How would you tell your friend that you'd like . . . See answers below.

1. those white sneakers?
2. this blue bag?
3. that purple and black pencil case?
4. to listen to music and talk on the phone?
5. to go shopping?

Can you get someone's attention, ask for information, and express thanks? p. 82

5 What would you say in a store to . . .

1. get a salesperson's attention? Pardon, madame/mademoiselle/monsieur...
2. politely ask the price of something? C'est combien, s'il vous plaît?
3. thank a clerk for helping you? Merci.

Answers

1 *Questions*
1. Vous avez/Tu as un stylo, s'il vous/te plaît?
2. Vous avez/Tu as une calculatrice?
3. Vous avez/Tu as des feuilles de papier?
Possible responses
Non, je regrette; Non, je n'ai pas de... ; Oui, voilà.

2 1. Qu'est-ce qu'il te faut pour le sport?
2. Qu'est-ce qu'il te faut pour l'allemand?
3. Qu'est-ce qu'il te faut pour les arts plastiques?

3 1. Il me faut une calculatrice et une gomme pour les maths.
2. Il me faut un classeur et des feuilles pour l'espagnol.
3. Il me faut des stylos et un cahier pour l'anglais.
4. Il me faut un crayon et une règle pour la géométrie.
5. Il me faut un sac et un livre pour l'histoire.

4 1. Je voudrais ces baskets blanches.
2. Je voudrais ce sac bleu.
3. Je voudrais cette trousse violette et noire.
4. Je voudrais écouter de la musique et parler au téléphone.
5. Je voudrais faire les magasins.

PREMIERE ETAPE

Making and responding to requests

Tu as... ?   *Do you have . . . ?*
Vous avez... ?   *Do you have . . . ?*
Voilà.   *Here.*
Je regrette.   *Sorry.*
Je n'ai pas de...   *I don't have . . .*

Asking others what they need and telling what you need

Qu'est-ce qu'il vous faut pour... ?
   What do you need for . . . ?
   (formal)

Qu'est-ce qu'il te faut pour... ?
   What do you need for . . . ?
   (informal)
Il me faut...   *I need . . .*
un   *a; an*
une   *a; an*
des   *some*

School supplies

un cahier   *notebook*
une calculatrice   *calculator*
un classeur   *loose-leaf binder*
un crayon   *pencil*

des feuilles (f.) de papier   *sheets of paper*
une gomme   *eraser*
un livre   *book*
une règle   *ruler*
un sac (à dos)   *bag; backpack*
un stylo   *pen*
un taille-crayon   *pencil sharpener*
une trousse   *pencil case*

Other useful expressions

Zut!   *Darn!*

DEUXIEME ETAPE

Telling what you'd like and what you'd like to do

Je voudrais...   *I'd like . . .*
Je voudrais acheter...   *I'd like to buy . . .*

For school and fun

des baskets (f.)   *sneakers*
un bracelet   *a bracelet*
une cassette   *cassette tape*
un dictionnaire   *dictionary*
un disque compact/un CD   *compact disc/CD*
un jean   *(a pair of) jeans*
un magazine   *magazine*

une montre   *watch*
un ordinateur   *computer*
un portefeuille   *wallet*
un poster   *poster*
un pull-over   *a pullover*
une radio   *a radio*
un roman   *novel*
un short   *(a pair of) shorts*
un sweat-shirt   *a sweatshirt*
un tee-shirt   *T-shirt*
une télévision   *a television*
une vidéocassette   *a videotape*
ce, cet, cette   *this; that*
ces   *these; those*
-là   *there (noun suffix)*

Colors

blanc(he)   *white*
bleu(e)   *blue*
gris(e)   *grey*
jaune   *yellow*
marron   *brown*
noir(e)   *black*
orange   *orange*
rose   *pink*
rouge   *red*
vert(e)   *green*
violet(te)   *purple*

TROISIEME ETAPE

Getting someone's attention; asking for information; expressing thanks

Pardon.   *Pardon me.*
Excusez-moi.   *Excuse me.*
C'est combien?   *How much is it?*
Merci.   *Thank you.*

A votre service.   *At your service; You're welcome.*
s'il vous/te plaît   *please*
franc   *(the French monetary unit)*
soixante   *sixty*
soixante-dix   *seventy*
quatre-vingts   *eighty*

quatre-vingt-dix   *ninety*
cent   *one hundred*
deux cents   *two hundred*

Other useful expressions

Bien sûr.   *Of course.*

Teaching Suggestions

• Encourage students to try to remember words by association. For example, **un porte-feuille** carries **(porte)** little pieces of paper **(feuilles)**, such as franc notes.
• Have students group the vocabulary by categories, such as *things you write with, things you wear, things you listen to,* and *things you use to organize.*

CHAPTER 3 ASSESSMENT

CHAPTER TEST

• *Chapter Teaching Resources, Book 1*, pp. 141–146
• *Assessment Guide,* Speaking Test, p. 29
• *Assessment Items, Audiocassette 7A Audio CD 3*

TEST GENERATOR, CHAPTER 3

ALTERNATIVE ASSESSMENT

Performance Assessment

You might want to use the **Jeu de rôle** (p. 87) as a cumulative performance assessment activity.

Portfolio Assessment

• **Written: Mise en pratique,** Activity 7, *Pupil's Edition,* p. 87
   Assessment Guide, p. 16
• **Oral: Mise en pratique, Jeu de rôle,** *Pupil's Edition,* p. 87
   Assessment Guide, p. 16

Science Link

Have students arrange the colors according to the spectrum they learned about in science or art class.

Allez, viens à Québec! pp. 90–119

EXPANDED VIDEO
PROGRAM,
Videocassette 2
01:22–03:33

OR *VIDEODISC PROGRAM,*
Videodisc 2B

Search 1, Play To 3945

Motivating Activity

Have students recall what they already know about Canada and Quebec concerning history, climate, food, culture, relationship with the United States, historical sites, tourist attractions, and other aspects. Then, have them look at the photos on pages 90–93. Ask them to find features that seem French and others that seem American.

Background Information

La Nouvelle-France, founded by the explorer Jacques Cartier in 1534, was ceded to the British by the Treaty of Paris in 1763 at the end of the Seven Years' War (known in North America as the French and Indian War). Quebec City, one of the oldest cities in North America, was founded in 1608 by Samuel de Champlain. It is known for its old-world charm, narrow streets, beautiful parks, and numerous cafés. The name **Québec** comes from the Indian word **Kébec,** meaning *narrowing of the river* (referring to its strategic location where the St. Lawrence River narrows). With a current population of more than half a million, Quebec City has been the capital of the province of Quebec since 1867.

CHAPITRE 4

Allez, viens à Québec!

Le château Frontenac

Geography Link

Given its northern location, it is not surprising that the region around Quebec City receives approximately 130 inches of snow each winter and has average temperatures of -16 to -7 degrees Celsius (3 to 19 degrees Fahrenheit) in January, and 13 to 25 degrees Celsius (55 to 77 degrees Fahrenheit) in July. As they say in Quebec, there are two seasons: winter and July.

Québec

Capitale de la province du Québec

Population : plus de 574.400

Points d'intérêt : le château Frontenac, l'université de Laval, la terrasse Dufferin, le musée du Québec, les fortifications de Québec, les chutes Montmorency, le mont Sainte-Anne, Québec Expérience

Québécois célèbres : Samuel de Champlain, François de Montmorency-Laval, le marquis de Montcalm

Ressources et industries : dérivés du bois, du cuir et de l'érable; tourisme

Spécialités : ragoût de boulettes, tourtière, cretons, soupe aux pois, tarte au sucre, tarte à la ferlouche

quatre-vingt-onze **91**

Using the Almanac and Map

Terms in the Almanac

- **Le château Frontenac,** named for the comte de Frontenac, governor of la Nouvelle-France in the late seventeenth century, was built on the site of the former administrative headquarters for the colony. The building is now a luxury hotel.
- **L'université de Laval,** founded in 1852, is the oldest French-language university in North America.
- **Les chutes Montmorency** This impressive waterfall is 1.5 times the height of Niagara Falls.
- **Le mont Sainte-Anne,** located 40 kilometers east of Quebec City, is famous for its ski slopes.
- **Québec Expérience** is a multimedia presentation of the history of Quebec City.
- **Le marquis de Montcalm** commanded the French troops during the French and Indian War.
- **dérivés de l'érable:** Canada is known for its maple products. A favorite treat of children, **tire,** is formed by pouring maple syrup on snow where it congeals to form a sort of caramel.
- **ragoût de boulettes:** pork stew with meatballs, eaten on special occasions.
- **tourtière:** a meat pie usually eaten at Christmastime.
- **cretons:** similar to **pâté,** made from ground pork.
- **tarte au sucre:** a sugar pie made with brown sugar or sometimes maple syrup.
- **tarte à la ferlouche:** a pie made with molasses or maple syrup and raisins.

Language Notes

- Because the owners of the logging companies in Quebec were generally English speakers, much of the lumberjack's language contained anglicisms. For example, the men who floated the lumber downriver were called **draveurs** *(drivers),* they used a **bécosse** *(backhouse* or *outhouse),* and they ate in the **cookerie.**
- After the passage of **la Loi 101,** which required all advertising and documentation to be in French, the **Office de la Langue Française** was created to help develop appropriate French terminology.

Using the Map

You might tell students that the vast majority of place names in Quebec are derived from geographic features, Amerindian words, or saints' names.

Using the Photo Essay

① **Typical houses in Vieux-Québec** The narrow streets and stone structures of the older parts of Quebec City are reminiscent of European cities, but many buildings also represent the long, low, one-story construction typical of French-Canadian houses.

② **Les chutes Montmorency** Overlooking these impressive falls is the Manoir Montmorency, built in 1780 for Edward, Duke of Kent, then governor-general of the colony and future father of Queen Victoria. Today it is a restaurant and conference center.

③ **Street performers** For years, **Québécois** families and friends have gathered for **veillées** where people sing, dance, and tell stories. This tradition lives on in the street performers often seen in Quebec City or Montreal. Each July, the **Festival d'été international** brings francophone musicians and performers from all over the world to play their music in Quebec City.

④ **Le quartier Petit-Champlain** The cobblestone pedestrian street in this photo dates from 1680. It is linked with the upper part of the city by a cable car (**le funiculaire**). Recent restoration efforts have transformed the district into an animated gathering place with cafés, restaurants, and shops.

Thinking Critically

④ **Observing** Ask students to identify the most striking feature of the buildings here. The proliferation of plants and flowers is typically **québécois,** but at the same time, very reminiscent of the French love of flowers and gardens.

Québec

Quebec City, one of the oldest cities in North America, is the capital of **La Nouvelle-France**, as the French-speaking part of Canada used to be called. The **Québécois** people are fiercely proud of their heritage and traditions, and they work hard to maintain their language and culture. The narrow streets and quaint cafés of **Vieux-Québec** have an old-world feeling, but Quebec is also a dynamic, modern city — as exciting as any you'll find in North America!

① Typical houses in **Vieux-Québec.**

② The spectacular **chutes Montmorency** are just outside of the city.

③ Musicians, jugglers, and other entertainers perform frequently in the streets of **Vieux-Québec.**

④ **Le quartier Petit-Champlain** is a picturesque shopping district filled with boutiques and cafés.

92   *quatre-vingt-douze*

Culture Note

① Following several disastrous fires in Quebec City, new regulations require structures to be made of stone with slate roofs and to have high fire walls between buildings.

History Link

The early inhabitants of Quebec included settlers (**habitants**), fur trappers, and **voyageurs** who traveled by canoe to the interior to trade with the Indians. The French generally cooperated with their Indian neighbors.

Geography Link

② The Canadian Shield (**le bouclier canadien**), a range of mountains and peaks, reaches down toward the Great Lakes. Many of the rivers that empty into the St. Lawrence River "fall off" the edge of this shield in impressive waterfalls.

(5) **La rue du Trésor** is where local artists sell their work. This street in the heart of the old section of town is very popular among tourists.

(5) **La rue du Trésor** is a tiny pedestrian street (**rue piétonne**) where local artists sell their paintings, watercolors, drawings, and engravings.

Teacher Note

Although many Americans, French, and English-speaking Canadians visit Quebec, a large percentage of tourists are **Québécois** from other regions of Quebec who come to visit the capital.

(6) **Les plaines d'Abraham,** located in le parc des Champs de Bataille, are named after Abraham Martin, a seventeenth-century settler.

Thinking Critically

(6) **Drawing inferences**
Ask students to suggest other activities that people might do in the park. (Cycling, jogging, and walking are common pastimes. In the winter, one might find sledders or cross-country skiers.)

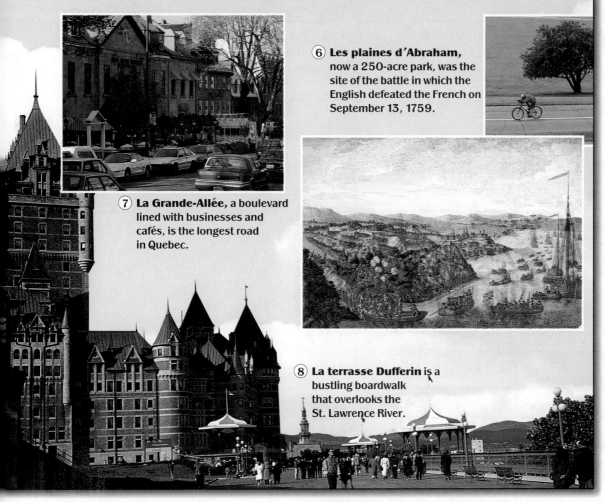

(6) **Les plaines d'Abraham,** now a 250-acre park, was the site of the battle in which the English defeated the French on September 13, 1759.

(7) **La Grande-Allée,** a boulevard lined with businesses and cafés, is the longest road in Quebec.

(8) **La terrasse Dufferin** is a bustling boardwalk that overlooks the St. Lawrence River.

(7) **La Grande-Allée** This boulevard holds the same place in **Québécois** hearts as the Champs-Elysées does in the hearts of Parisians. It was originally an Indian trail used to transport furs to sell to the French. In the seventeenth century, it was only a country lane separating two properties, and in later centuries, the address of several luxurious residences. Today, it is a busy street lined with many restaurants, cafés, shops, and offices.

(8) **La terrasse Dufferin**
This 671-meter walkway overlooks the lower town and the river. The part facing the château Frontenac was built over the remains of the château Saint-Louis (the governorgeneral's residence), which burned down in 1834.

History Links

(6) During the famous battle in 1759, the British forces under General Wolfe scaled the cliff to attack and defeat the outnumbered French forces under General Montcalm.

(7) It was from the balcony of the Hôtel du Parlement, located on **la Grande-Allée,** that Charles de Gaulle gave his famous and controversial **"Vive le Québec libre!"** speech.

Chapitre 4 : Sports et passe-temps
Chapter Overview

Mise en train pp. 96–98	**Nouvelles de Québec**	*Practice and Activity Book, p. 37*	*Video Guide* OR *Videodisc Guide*

	FUNCTIONS	**GRAMMAR**	**CULTURE**	**RE-ENTRY**
Première étape pp. 99–103	Telling how much you like or dislike something, p. 102	• Contractions with **à** and **de**, p. 101 • Questions with **est-ce que**, p. 103	**Rencontre Culturelle**, Old and new in Quebec City, p. 99	Expressing likes and dislikes
Deuxième étape pp. 104–109	Exchanging information, p. 104	• **de** after a negative verb, p. 104 • The verb **faire**, p. 104	• **Note Culturelle**, Celsius and Fahrenheit, p. 107 • **Panorama Culturel**, Sports in francophone countries, p. 109	• The verb **jouer**, regular **-er** verbs • Agreeing and disagreeing
Troisième étape pp. 110–113	Making, accepting, and turning down suggestions, p. 110	Adverbs of frequency, p. 110		Seasons and activities

Prononciation p. 113	The sounds [u] and [y]	**Dictation:** *Textbook Audiocassette 2B/Audio CD 4*

Lisons! pp. 114–115	**Les jeunes au micro**	**Reading Strategy:** The five "W" questions

Review pp. 116–119	**Mise en pratique**, pp. 116–117	**Que sais-je?** p. 118	**Vocabulaire**, p. 119

Assessment Options	**Etape Quizzes**
	• *Chapter Teaching Resources, Book 1*
	  Première étape, Quiz 4-1, pp. 191–192
	  Deuxième étape, Quiz 4-2, pp. 193–194
	  Troisième étape, Quiz 4-3, pp. 195–196
	• *Assessment Items, Audiocassette 7B/Audio CD 4*
		Chapter Test
		• *Chapter Teaching Resources, Book 1*, pp. 197–202
		• *Assessment Guide*, Speaking Test, p. 29
		• *Assessment Items, Audiocassette 7B/Audio CD 4*
		
		Test Generator, Chapter 4

Video Program OR *Expanded Video Program, Videocassette 2* OR *Videodisc Program, Videodisc 2B*   *Textbook Audiocassette 2B/Audio CD 4*

RESOURCES: Print	RESOURCES: Audiovisual

Textbook Audiocassette 2B/Audio CD 4

Practice and Activity Book, pp. 38–40
Chapter Teaching Resources, Book 1
- Teaching Transparency Master 4-1, pp. 175, 178 . . . . *Teaching Transparency 4-1*
- Additional Listening Activities 4-1, 4-2, p. 179 . . . . *Additional Listening Activities, Audiocassette 9B/Audio CD 4*
- Realia 4-1, pp. 183, 185
- Situation Cards 4-1, pp. 186–187
- Student Response Forms, pp. 188–190
- Quiz 4-1, pp. 191–192 . . . . *Assessment Items, Audiocassette 7B/Audio CD 4*
Videodisc Guide . . . . *Videodisc Program, Videodisc 2B*

Textbook Audiocassette 2B/Audio CD 4

Practice and Activity Book, pp. 41–43
Chapter Teaching Resources, Book 1
- Communicative Activity 4-1, pp. 171–172
- Teaching Transparency Master 4-2, pp. 176, 178 . . . . *Teaching Transparency 4-2*
- Additional Listening Activities 4-3, 4-4, p. 180 . . . . *Additional Listening Activities, Audiocassette 9B/Audio CD 4*
- Realia 4-2, pp. 184, 185
- Situation Cards 4-2, pp. 186–187
- Student Response Forms, pp. 188–190
- Quiz 4-2, pp. 193–194 . . . . *Assessment Items, Audiocassette 7B/Audio CD 4*
Video Guide . . . . *Video Program* OR *Expanded Video Program, Videocassette 2*
Videodisc Guide . . . . *Videodisc Program, Videodisc 2B*

Textbook Audiocassette 2B/Audio CD 4

Practice and Activity Book, pp. 44–46
Chapter Teaching Resources, Book 1
- Communicative Activity 4-2, pp. 173–174
- Teaching Transparency Master 4-3, pp. 177, 178 . . . . *Teaching Transparency 4-3*
- Additional Listening Activities 4-5, 4-6, p. 181 . . . . *Additional Listening Activities, Audiocassette 9B/Audio CD 4*
- Realia 4-2, pp. 184, 185
- Situation Cards 4-3, pp. 186–187
- Student Response Forms, pp. 188–190
- Quiz 4-3, pp. 195–196 . . . . *Assessment Items, Audiocassette 7B/Audio CD 4*
Videodisc Guide . . . . *Videodisc Program, Videodisc 2B*

Practice and Activity Book, p. 47

Video Guide . . . . *Video Program* OR *Expanded Video Program, Videocassette 2*
Videodisc Guide . . . . *Videodisc Program, Videodisc 2B*

Alternative Assessment
- Performance Assessment
  Première étape, p. 103
  Deuxième étape, p. 108
  Troisième étape, p. 113
- Portfolio Assessment
  Written: **Mise en pratique**, Activity 4, *Pupil's Edition*, p. 117
    Assessment Guide, p. 17
  Oral: **Mise en pratique, Jeu de rôle**, *Pupil's Edition*, p. 117
    Assessment Guide, p. 17

For Student Response Forms, See *Chapter Teaching Resources, Book 1,* pp. 188–190.

Première étape

6 Ecoute! p. 100

PHILIPPE Eh, salut, Pascal! Tu vas en vacances à la montagne! Quelle chance! Tu vas faire des photos?

PASCAL Des photos? Non, je ne fais jamais de photos.

PHILIPPE Tu vas faire du ski?

PASCAL Non, pas moi. Je n'aime pas le ski.

PHILIPPE Qu'est-ce que tu aimes faire, alors?

PASCAL Mais des tas de choses. J'aime faire de la natation. Et puis, le champion du patin à glace, c'est moi. J'adore ça. J'aime aussi beaucoup faire de la vidéo. A la rentrée, on va regarder une vidéo formidable de mes vacances.

Answers to Activity 6
Likes: swimming, ice-skating, making videos
Dislikes: taking pictures, skiing

9 Ecoute! p. 102

— Tu aimes faire du sport?

— Le sport, j'adore ça, surtout le roller en ligne et le hockey. Par contre, je n'aime pas beaucoup le volley. Et toi, tu aimes faire du sport?

— Le volley, pas du tout. Le roller en ligne, pas tellement. Je n'aime pas les sports d'équipe. J'aime bien faire du ski, et je fais du jogging tous les matins à sept heures.

Answers to Activity 9
Canadian student likes: in-line skating, hockey
Canadian student dislikes: volleyball
Your classmate likes: skiing, jogging
Your classmate dislikes: volleyball, in-line skating, team sports

Deuxième étape

21 Ecoute! p. 107

JOURNALISTE Bonjour, Paul. Qu'est-ce que tu aimes faire en hiver?

PAUL J'écoute de la musique, et je regarde la télévision.

JOURNALISTE Tu ne fais pas de sport?

PAUL Si. Je fais du ski, et je joue au hockey.

JOURNALISTE Est-ce que tu fais du sport, Anne?

ANNE De temps en temps, mais j'aime mieux aller au cinéma. Je regarde souvent la télé aussi.

JOURNALISTE Et toi, Julie, tu regardes la télévision?

JULIE Jamais. Je fais du sport. J'adore faire du ski et du patin.

JOURNALISTE Tu es sportive! Est-ce que tu écoutes de la musique aussi?

JULIE Oui, très souvent.

JOURNALISTE Et toi, Anne, tu aimes la musique?

ANNE Oui, beaucoup. Et j'aime aussi danser.

Answers to Activity 21
1. Julie
2. Paul, Julie, Anne
3. Paul
4. Anne
5. Anne

*T*roisième étape

26 Ecoute! p. 110

1. — Allô?
   — Allô, Lise? C'est Germain. Tiens, vendredi après-midi, on joue au volley-ball?
   — Vendredi après-midi? D'accord. Bonne idée.

2. — Allô, oui?
   — Salut, Renaud! Dis, tu fais quoi vendredi après-midi?
   — Eh ben, rien. Pourquoi?
   — On joue au volley-ball?
   — Le volley... euh, ça ne me dit rien, le volley. C'est barbant.

3. — Allô?
   — Salut, Philippe. C'est Germain. Qu'est-ce que tu fais ce week-end?
   — Je ne sais pas. Et toi?
   — J'ai une idée. On joue au volley-ball?
   — Bonne idée! Le volley, c'est le fun!

4. — Allô?
   — Allô, Monique? C'est Germain. On joue au volley?
   — Je n'aime pas tellement le volley.

Answers to Activity 26
1. Lise: accepts
2. Renaud: turns down
3. Philippe: accepts
4. Monique: turns down

28 Ecoute! p. 111

1. EMILE   Thierry, tu fais souvent du sport?
    THIERRY   Oui, je fais du jogging une fois par semaine.

2. EMILE   Salut, Odile. Dis-moi, tu fais du sport?
    ODILE   Non, jamais. Je déteste le sport.

3. EMILE   Et toi, Martine?
    MARTINE   Oh, de temps en temps. J'aime bien jouer au basket-ball.

4. EMILE   Dis, François, tu fais souvent du sport?
    FRANÇOIS   Euh, pas vraiment. Quelquefois, je joue au tennis ou au base-ball.

5. EMILE   Et toi, Vincent?
    VINCENT   Oui, je fais de l'aérobic deux fois par semaine.

Answers to Activity 28
1. Thierry: once a week
2. Odile: never
3. Martine: from time to time
4. François: sometimes
5. Vincent: twice a week

*P*rononciation, p. 113

For the scripts for Parts A and B, see p. 113.

C. A écrire

(Dictation)
— Salut! On joue au foot?
— Non. J'ai musique.
— Tu aimes la musique?
— Oui, bien sûr. C'est super.

*M*ise en pratique

1 p. 116

Vous aimez le ski, le patin, le hockey? Venez au Village des Sports. C'est le fun en hiver! Au printemps aussi, c'est le fun. Faites de l'athlétisme ou du roller en ligne. Vous venez en été? Eh bien, c'est aussi le fun quand il fait chaud. Jouez au base-ball et faites du ski nautique. Et l'automne au Village des Sports, c'est super! Avec du volley et du football, Le Village des Sports, c'est le fun des quatre saisons!

Answers to Mise en pratique Activity 1
Winter: skiing, skating, hockey
Spring: track and field, in-line skating
Summer: baseball, water-skiing
Fall: volleyball, soccer

Projects

Mon calendrier
(Individual Project)

ASSIGNMENT

Students will make a calendar showing a month and the activities they participate in each day.

MATERIALS

✄ **Students may need**
- Large sheets of paper
- Magazines
- Scissors
- Colored pens and pencils
- Glue or tape

SUGGESTED SEQUENCE

Prewriting   After students choose a month, have them make a list of the activities they participate in (or would like to participate in) during that month.

Students might want to add illustrations to their calendars, so they should begin to look for photos or make drawings of the activities they want to depict.

First Draft   Have students draw a calendar of the month they chose and write their activities in the appropriate squares. Then, have them write at least four sentences describing their activities, telling how much they like the activities and how often they participate in each one.

Peer Editing   Have students exchange their lists of activities and sentences with at least one other student. Students should check each other's work for comprehensibility and accuracy (spelling, verb forms, and word order).

Final Draft   Have students rewrite their lists and sentences, making any necessary corrections. Then, have them write their information around the calendar and glue or tape their photos or illustrations to the calendar days. Finally, have students display and describe their calendars to the class.

Le sport
(Individual Project)

ASSIGNMENT

Students will make a poster or collage presenting their favorite sport or team.

MATERIALS

✄ **Students may need**
- Large sheets of paper or posterboard
- Magazines
- Scissors
- Colored pens and pencils
- Glue or tape

SUGGESTED SEQUENCE

Prewriting   Have students choose and research their favorite sport or team. They might want to look through the **Vocabulaire** pages of Chapters 1–4 to find useful vocabulary. You might also refer them to the Supplementary Vocabulary on page 343.

First Draft   Have students write at least four sentences describing their poster topic and choose photos or drawings to illustrate their posters. They should also begin to organize the information for their poster and plan where they will write the information and position their photos and drawings.

Peer Editing   Have students exchange their sentences with at least one other student. Have them check each other's work for comprehensibility and accuracy (spelling, verb forms, and word order). Have them also comment on the poster layout and choice of illustrations.

Final Draft   Have students rewrite their lists and sentences, making any necessary corrections. Then, have them copy their information onto the poster and glue or tape their photos or illustrations to it. Have students display their posters in the classroom and describe them to the class.

GRADING THE PROJECTS

You might assign grades for both projects based on the completeness of the assignment, presentation, language use, and content.

Suggested Point Distribution (total = 100 points)

Completeness of assignment . . . . 20 points

Presentation . . . . 30 points

Language use . . . . 20 points

Content . . . . 30 points

Chapitre 4: Sports et passe-temps
♜ *Games*

CHARADES

In this game, students will review the verbs they've learned so far.

Have teams of three or four students recall the verbs they've learned in Chapters 1-4. Distribute index cards and have each group write a different verb on each one. Collect the cards, decide which team will start, and give the first player from that team one of the cards. The player has thirty seconds to mime the action and have his or her team call out the correct French verb. If the player succeeds, the team wins a point. In order to give all team members a chance to guess, no team member may make consecutive guesses. If the first team is unable to guess correctly, allow the other teams to try. Repeat the process with the other teams. After you have gone through all the verbs, use any that weren't guessed as tie-breakers.

MEMOIRE

This game provides an entertaining way for students to practice and review vocabulary.

Have students make two cards for each vocabulary word from this chapter. On one card, they should write the French word; on the other, they should illustrate the word or write the English equivalent. Mix the cards and number them on the blank side. You will need to write the number so that the vocabulary or illustration is right-side up when the card is flipped up. Tape the cards to the board so that the numbers show. Each player says two numbers in French. Turn up the two cards bearing those numbers to reveal the vocabulary or illustration on the reverse side. The object is to find the two cards that match. Each student or team wins a point for each correct match. If the two cards do not match, be sure to turn the cards back to the number side so that they will remain in play.

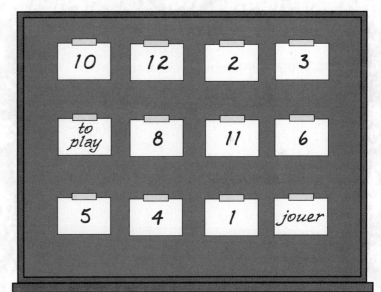

Chapitre 4
Sports et passe-temps

pp. 94–119

*U*sing the Chapter Opener

Motivating Activity

Ask students what activities are represented by the pictures and objects on pages 94 and 95. Have them tell what activities they would like to learn to say in French. Write their suggestions on a transparency. You might want to show this transparency at the end of the chapter and have students give the French for the activities listed.

Teaching Suggestion

Have students look at the photos and try to guess the meanings of the captions.

Photo Flash!

These photos were taken in Quebec City and the surrounding area.

① The young people in this photo are rehearsing a play during a drama class at a recreation center. See the Culture Note on page 109 for more information about the **Maisons des jeunes et de la culture.**

CHAPITRE

4
Sports et passe-temps

① On aime faire du théâtre!

94   *quatre-vingt-quatorze*

Teacher Note

In this chapter, students will discuss their participation in various activities and the weather. Students will also learn to use **on** to make suggestions.

Teenagers in French-speaking countries find plenty of time for hobbies. They play sports, watch television, listen to music, take photos, and go out with friends. Many of their spare-time activities are similar to yours.

In this chapter you will learn

- to tell how much you like or dislike something
- to exchange information
- to make, accept, and turn down suggestions

And you will

- listen to French-speaking students talk about what they do for fun
- read about a sports camp in Canada
- write about your hobbies and what you do to have fun
- find out about sports and hobbies in francophone countries

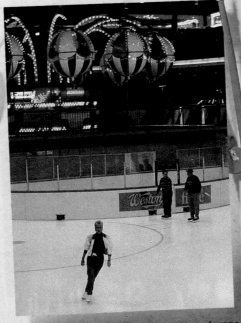

② On fait du patin à glace de temps en temps.

③ En automne, on fait du vélo.

quatre-vingt-quinze 95

Focusing on Outcomes

Have students read the three functional objectives listed on this page. Ask them which objectives correspond to the photos on pages 94 and 95. You might also ask students if they like the activities pictured. NOTE: You may want to use the video to support the objectives. The self-check activities in **Que sais-je?** on page 118 help students assess their achievement of the objectives.

Teaching Suggestion

Ask students what they would say in English to make a suggestion.

Photo Flash!

② Ice-skating has long been a popular activity in Quebec City. In 1856, the city acquired the first covered skating rink in North America in order to accommodate its famous hockey team, **les Nordiques.** When a second skating arena **(Le Colisée)** was built in 1949, it was the most modern of all covered rinks. Skating is not exclusively an indoor sport for the **Québécois,** however. When the Saint Charles River freezes in the winter, people go there to skate **en plein air.**

③ This cyclist is riding a mountain bike in the **parc du mont Sainte-Anne** near Quebec City. In the fall and spring, mountain biking and hiking are popular activities in the thirty-square-mile park. In the winter, the park is even more popular as the largest ski resort in Quebec. With the latest in timing technology, the park has hosted famous ski races such as the World Cup.

Community Link

Have students research one of the sports in this chapter and any famous events or athletes associated with that sport in francophone countries. Then, have them find a club for that sport and offer to share what they have learned about francophone events and athletes.

VIDEO PROGRAM
OR EXPANDED VIDEO
PROGRAM,
Videocassette 2
03:34–08:41

OR VIDEODISC PROGRAM,
Videodisc 2B

Search 3945, Play To 13170

Video Synopsis

In this segment of the video, Emilie is making a video for Leticia, her pen pal in San Diego, to tell her about Quebec City and the sports and hobbies she likes. Emilie introduces her friends Michel, François, and Marie. Emilie and her friends talk about the sports and hobbies they like, the weather, and the different things you can do in each season in Quebec. We see scenes of Emilie, her friends, and other people participating in these activities.

Motivating Activity

Ask students what they would include in a videotape to a French pen pal. Would they show their city, their friends, or what they like to do?

Presentation

Since the letter is not read on the video, you might first read the letter aloud to students and have them listen with their books closed. Have them tell what they understood, or have them answer the questions in Activity 1 on page 98. Then, tell students they're going to see the video Emilie made for Leticia. Play the video and then have students open their books and read the letter and photo captions.

Mise en train

Nouvelles de Québec

Emilie is eager to get to know her American pen pal Leticia. What kind of information do you think Emilie might include in a letter to her new pen pal?

Salut, Leticia!

Comment ça va? Juste une petite lettre pour accompagner ces photos, une brochure sur le mont Sainte-Anne, une montagne près de Québec et aussi une cassette vidéo sur Québec... et sur moi! Comme ça, tu as une idée des activités ici... C'est l'automne à Québec et il fait déjà froid! Heureusement, il y a du soleil, mais il y a du vent. Quel temps est-ce qu'il fait à San Diego? Est-ce qu'il fait froid aussi? J'aime beaucoup Québec. C'est très sympa. Il y a beaucoup de choses à faire. En automne, je fais du patin et de la natation. J'adore le sport. En été, je fais du deltaplane et de la voile. Au printemps, je fais de l'équitation et je joue au tennis. Et en hiver, bien sûr, je fais du ski. C'est super ici pour le ski. Il neige de novembre à avril! Tu imagines? Est-ce qu'il neige à San Diego? Qu'est-ce qu'on fait comme sport? Du ski? Du base-ball? Quand il fait trop froid, je regarde la télévision et j'écoute de la musique. J'adore le rock et la musique québécoise. Et toi? Qu'est-ce que tu écoutes comme musique? Qu'est-ce qu'on fait à San Diego les fins de semaine? J'ai aussi une autre passion : de temps en temps, je fais des films avec un caméscope. C'est le fun! Tu sais, c'est super, Québec. Et la Californie, c'est comment? C'est le fun ou pas?

À très bientôt

Emilie

96 *quatre-vingt-seize*   CHAPITRE 4   Sports et passe-temps

RESOURCES FOR MISE EN TRAIN

Textbook Audiocassette 2B/Audio CD 4
Practice and Activity Book, p. 37
Video Guide
   Video Program
   Expanded Video Program, Videocassette 2
Videodisc Guide
   Videodisc Program, Videodisc 2B

Language Note

You might explain that the expression **C'est le fun** is Canadian slang; it is often contracted as **l'fun.**

① Ça, c'est notre café préféré.

② La musique, c'est super!
Tu fais de la musique, toi?

③ Au printemps, on joue
au tennis. J'adore!

④ C'est mon copain Michel.
En été, on fait du vélo.

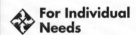
PARC DU MONT-SAINTE-ANNE

⑤ En automne, on fait
de l'équitation.

⑥ C'est moi! En hiver,
on fait du patin.

Thinking Critically

Drawing Inferences　Have students try to guess the seasons, climate, and activities shown on page 97. Ask if they can think of an English word that looks like **hiver** and has to do with winter? (Some animals *hibernate* in winter, living off their stored energy sources.)

Teaching Suggestion

Have students find examples of the chapter objectives and activities in the letter and in the photo captions. (Examples include talking about how much someone likes an activity, asking someone about his or her pastimes, talking about hobbies and sports, and sharing information about Canada.)

For Individual Needs

Kinesthetic Learners　Have students or pairs of students come to the front of the class and mime the action in one of the photos. The first person to call out the number of the corresponding photo takes the next turn. As a challenge, you might also have students find the sentence in Emilie's letter where she talks about the activity being mimed.

Video Integration

- **EXPANDED VIDEO PROGRAM,** Videocassette 2, 08:42–18:38
- **VIDEODISC PROGRAM,** Videodisc 2B

Search 13170, Play To 31080

You may choose to continue with **Nouvelles de Québec (suite)** at this time or wait until later in the chapter. The story continues with Michel filming Emilie as she talks about Quebec City. We see scenes of different parts of the city as Emilie goes window-shopping, and Michel goes to a hockey match. Next, Emilie and some friends go to **mont Sainte-Anne,** where they hike and ride mountain bikes. Finally, Emilie and Michel go to a skating rink. They interview a man who talks about sports. Emilie and Michel say goodbye to Leticia and suggest that she make a video for them about San Diego.

Teaching Suggestion

2 This activity can be used as a listening comprehension exercise. Read the sentences aloud and have students write **Oui** or **Non** on their papers. After students have determined what Emilie would and wouldn't say, ask them to change the sentences to reflect their own opinions.

For videodisc application, see *Videodisc Guide.*

◆ For Individual Needs

3 Slower Pace Make a list of the French expressions corresponding to each of these functions and distribute copies to the students. Then, read aloud the English functions and have students write the number of the English function you read next to the corresponding French expression on their paper.

4 Slower Pace Go over the list of sports with students to make sure they understand them before completing the activity. You might mime the sports to avoid using English.

Language Note

4 You might point out that seasons are preceded by **en**, except for **printemps**, which is preceded by **au.**

1 Tu as compris?

Answer the following questions about Emilie's letter to Leticia. Don't be afraid to guess.

See answers below.

1. What is Emilie sending to Leticia along with her letter?
2. What are some of Emilie's hobbies and pastimes?
3. What would she like to know about Leticia and San Diego?
4. What does Emilie tell Leticia about the city of Quebec?
5. What else have you learned about Emilie from her letter?

2 C'est Emilie?

Tell whether Emilie would be likely or unlikely to say each of the statements below.

1. «J'adore faire du sport.»   likely
2. «Le ski? Ici on n'aime pas beaucoup ça.»   unlikely
3. «Pour moi, Québec, c'est barbant en hiver.»   unlikely
4. «Faire des films avec un caméscope, pour moi, c'est passionnant.»   likely
5. «Je regarde la télé en hiver quand il fait trop froid.»   likely
6. «La musique? Bof! Je n'aime pas beaucoup ça.»   unlikely

3 Cherche les expressions

In **Nouvelles de Québec**, what does Emilie say to . . .

1. greet Leticia?   Salut!
2. ask how Leticia is?   Comment ça va?
3. ask about the weather?   Quel temps est-ce qu'il fait?
4. tell what she likes?   J'aime... ; J'adore...
5. express her opinion about something?   C'est super. C'est le fun. C'est très sympa.
6. inquire about California?   Et la Californie, c'est comment?
7. say goodbye?   A très bientôt.

4 Les saisons et les sports

D'après la lettre d'Emilie, quels sports est-ce qu'elle fait? En quelle saison? Choisis des sports pour compléter ces phrases.

de l'équitation   du ski
du deltaplane   de la voile
du patin   de la natation

1. Au printemps, Emilie fait...   de l'équitation
2. En hiver, elle fait...   du ski
3. En automne, elle fait...   du patin et de la natation
4. En été, elle fait...   du deltaplane et de la voile

5 Et maintenant, à toi

Emilie fait beaucoup de choses! Tu fais les mêmes choses? Pour chaque activité, réponds **Moi aussi** ou **Pas moi.**

1. Emilie fait du ski.
2. Elle écoute de la musique.
3. Emilie fait des films avec un caméscope.
4. Elle fait de l'équitation.
5. Quand il fait trop froid pour sortir, Emilie regarde la télé.
6. Emilie joue au tennis.

98   *quatre-vingt-dix-huit*   CHAPITRE 4   Sports et passe-temps

Answers

1 1. photographs, a brochure, and a videocassette
2. ice-skating, swimming, hang gliding, sailing, horseback riding, tennis, skiing, watching TV, listening to music, and making video films
3. her favorite hobbies and pastimes, what the weather is like, what music she listens to, what California is like
4. It's already cold in autumn. It's sunny, but windy. There are a lot of fun things to do there. It snows from November to April.
5. *Possible answers:* She's athletic, active, friendly, and extroverted.

RENCONTRE CULTURELLE

What do you know about Quebec? What impressions do you get of Quebec when you look at these photos?

Qu'en penses-tu? See answers below.

1. What things do you see that are typically American?
2. What do you see in these photos that you wouldn't see in the United States?

Savais-tu que... ?

One of the first things you'll notice about Quebec City is its fascinating blend of styles—old and new, European and North American. Old Quebec (**Vieux-Québec**) is filled with quaint neighborhood cafés and shops that maintain the old-world flavor of Europe. And yet, it is surrounded by a vibrant, modern city with high-rise hotels, office buildings, and a complex network of freeways. All of these elements together give the city its unique character.

Geography Link

Have students find Quebec on a map of Canada. You might have them calculate the distance between their city and Quebec. Have them look at a globe or world map to find out what other cities are on the same latitude as Quebec.

History Link

Have students look up information about the founding of Quebec, the exploration of the region, and the important people involved. You might also have them turn to the Location Opener on pages 90–93.

Motivating Activity

Ask students what they already know about Quebec. Based on the Location Opener and Emilie's letter, what are their impressions?

Presentation

Have students describe the photos orally, and then answer the questions in **Qu'en penses-tu?** Ask them if they would like to visit or study in Quebec and have them explain why or why not.

Thinking Critically

Comparing and Contrasting

In English, have students compare their city with Quebec, writing or naming several similarities and differences. You might have them consult an encyclopedia to obtain more information about Quebec.

Teaching Suggestion

Have students choose one of the pictures of Quebec and write a short note as if they were sending it as a postcard.

Multicultural Link

Have students research cities in the United States where there is evidence of more than one major culture. They might choose New Orleans (French), Miami (Hispanic/Cuban), or any city with a large Asian population. Have students research how these cultures have enriched the city and what contributions citizens of these cultures have made to their city and state.

Possible answers

1. freeways, freeway signs, skyscrapers, and other modern buildings
2. cobblestone streets, European-style cafés and shops, French signs

PREMIERE ETAPE

Telling how much you like or dislike something

VOCABULAIRE

Qu'est-ce que tu aimes faire après l'école?

jouer au foot(ball)

jouer au football américain

faire de la vidéo

faire du roller en ligne

faire du patin à glace

faire du théâtre

faire de l'athlétisme

faire du vélo

faire de la natation *

You can probably guess what these activities are:

faire de l'aérobic	faire du ski	jouer au basket(-ball)	jouer à des jeux vidéo
faire du jogging	faire du ski nautique	jouer au golf	jouer au tennis
faire des photos	jouer au base-ball	jouer au hockey	jouer au volley(-ball)

6 Ecoute!

Listen to this conversation between Philippe and Pascal. List at least two activities Pascal likes and two he doesn't like. Answers on p. 93C.

* Remember that **nager** also means *to swim*.

CHAPITRE 4   Sports et passe-temps

*G*rammaire Contractions with **à** and **de**

You use **faire** *(to make, to do)* followed by the preposition **de** with activities, including sports.

- When the sport is a masculine noun, **de** becomes **du**.

  faire **du** ski   faire **du** patin

- If the activity is plural, **de** becomes **des**.

  faire **des** photos

- The preposition **de** doesn't change before **la** or **l'**.

  faire **de la** natation   faire **de l'**aérobic

You use **jouer** *(to play)* with games, and sports that you play. It is followed by the preposition **à**.

- When the game or sport is a masculine noun, **à** becomes **au**.

  jouer **au** football

- The preposition **à** doesn't change before **la, l'** or **des**.

Presentation

Grammaire Play "Jeter et attraper" (see page 123F) with activities. First, have students look back at the **Vocabulaire** on page 100, noticing which activities use **faire** and which ones use **jouer**. Then, have them close their books. Call out an activity (**ski**) and toss a ball to a student, who catches it and calls out the full expression (**faire du ski**).

For videodisc application, see *Videodisc Guide.*

Language Note

Some other activities using **faire** that students might like to know are: **faire de la planche à roulette** *(to skateboard)*, **faire de la gymnastique** *(to do gymnastics, to exercise in general)*, **faire de la boxe** *(to box)*, and **faire de l'alpinisme** *(to hike or climb)*.

Teacher Note

7 Remind students that they will need to fill in the verb as well as the name of the activity.

For Individual Needs

7 Challenge After students have completed the activity, have them pair off and rewrite the dialogue to express their own preferences.

Thinking Critically

8 Comparing and Contrasting Have students look at the TV sports schedule and tell what information is given. Then, have them compare this schedule with TV schedules they use.

7 Qu'est-ce que tu aimes faire?

Ariane and Serge are telling each other about the activities they like to do after school. Complete their conversation by substituting the activities suggested by the pictures.

ARIANE   Qu'est-ce que tu aimes faire après l'école?

SERGE   Moi, j'aime avec mes copains. Et toi?
jouer au football

ARIANE   Moi, j'aime   et j'adore .
faire du roller en ligne   faire des photos

SERGE   Tu aimes ? On va jouer à la plage demain. Tu viens?
jouer au volley-ball

ARIANE   Non, merci. J'aime mieux avec des copains.
faire du ski nautique

8 Télé 7 jours

While you're staying with a friend, you both decide to watch sports on TV. Take turns checking the days and times of the sports you'd like to watch.

— Le tennis de table, c'est quel jour?
— Samedi.
— A quelle heure?
— A vingt heures trente.

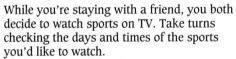

La semaine en direct

GOLF Open de Belgique	Samedi à 14.00 — *TV Sport*	
BASKET-BALL Levallois/Villeurbanne	Samedi à 20.25 — *TV Sport*	
TENNIS DE TABLE G.P. de Paris	Sam. à 20.30 — *Paris Première*	
FOOTBALL Botafogo/Corinthians	Samedi à 0.00 — *TV Sport*	
ATHLÉTISME Finale Coupe du monde	Sam. à 22.00 — *Eurosport*	
TENNIS Tournoi indoor féminin à Tokyo	Mer. à 18.00 — *TV Sport*	
FOOT AMÉRICAIN Kansas City/Los Angeles	Mar. à 19.30 — *TV Sport*	

PREMIERE ETAPE   *cent un* **101**

Culture Notes

8 The title of this activity, **Télé 7 jours,** is the name of one French equivalent of *TV Guide.* Students might want to know that France has both national and private channels, just as the United States. **Canal +** (Canal Plus), **TV Sport, Paris Première,** and **Eurosport** are private channels. **TF1, FR2, FR3, Arte,** and **M6** are national channels.

8 There are four major TV stations in Canada. **CBC** has one English and one French network and is the largest and most far-reaching station. **CTV,** a private national station, reaches most of the English-speaking population. **Global Television** is another English-language station. **TVA** is a French-language network that covers most of Quebec and parts of New Brunswick.

Motivating Activity

Ask students if they always answer questions in complete sentences. Have them suggest short answers they might give in English if someone asked whether they liked or disliked something. Have them compare their short answers to those in **Comment dit-on... ?**

Presentation

Comment dit-on... ? Have a volunteer ask you if you like soccer. Then, give all of the short answers listed here, delivering each with exaggerated facial expressions and gestures to get the meaning across. Ask students which activities they like. (**Tu aimes nager?**) To prompt certain responses, you might use the thumbs-up gesture, the **comme-ci, comme ça** gesture, or the thumbs-down gesture.

Additional Practice

Give each student a card with a smiling face, a face with a straight line for a mouth, or a frowning face drawn on it. Then, have partners ask each other about certain activities and respond according to the card they have.

For Individual Needs

9 Slower Pace Play the recording twice. The first time, tell students to listen only for those activities the speakers say they like. The second time, have students listen for those activities the speakers dislike.

COMMENT DIT-ON... ?
Telling how much you like or dislike something

To tell how much you like something:
  J'aime **beaucoup** le sport. *I like . . . a lot!*
  J'aime **surtout** faire du ski. *I especially like . . .*

To tell how much you dislike something:
  Je n'aime **pas tellement** le football. *I don't like . . . too much.*
  Je n'aime **pas beaucoup** le volley-ball. *I don't like . . . very much.*
  Je n'aime **pas du tout** la natation. *I don't like . . . at all.*

You can use the expressions in bold type alone as short answers:
  — Tu aimes faire du sport?
  — Oui, **beaucoup!** *or*
    Non, **pas tellement.**

9 Ecoute!

On a school trip to Quebec, you listen to your classmate talk to a Canadian student. Write down at least one sport or game each speaker likes and one each speaker dislikes.
Answers on p. 93C.

10 Pas d'accord!

You and a Canadian exchange student want to watch sports on TV, but you can't agree on what to watch. Each time one of you finds something you like, the other doesn't like it and changes the channel. Act this out with a partner.

  — Oh, voilà le football. J'aime bien le football. Et toi, tu aimes?
  — Pas beaucoup. Regarde, un match de tennis. Tu aimes le tennis?

Teaching Suggestion

10 Remind students of the expression **Moi, si** and practice it briefly in contradictory responses.
—**Tu aimes le hockey?**
—**Non, pas beaucoup.**
—**Moi, si!**

11 Qu'est-ce que je lui achète?

What should I buy him/her?

Your visit to Canada is about over. You'd like to buy gifts for several of the students you've met, so you ask a Canadian classmate about their interests. Create a conversation with a partner.

—Qu'est-ce que Marc aime faire?
—Il aime beaucoup le football.
—Il aime le tennis?
—Non, pas tellement.

faire des photos
faire de la vidéo
jouer au golf
jouer au hockey
faire du ski   lire
jouer à des jeux vidéo

 **Marc**    **Isabelle**    **Jean-Paul**    **Antoine**    **Anne-Marie**

Grammaire   Question formation

You've already learned to make a yes-or-no question by raising the pitch of your voice at the end of a sentence. Another way to ask a yes-or-no question is to say **est-ce que** before a statement and raise your voice at the very end.

Est-ce que tu aimes faire du vélo?

12 Et toi?

With a partner, discuss the sports and hobbies you both like to do. Take turns asking and answering questions. Be sure to vary the kinds of questions you ask.

— Est-ce que tu aimes jouer au football américain?
— Non! J'aime mieux faire de l'aérobic, du théâtre et du roller en ligne.

Vocabulaire à la carte

faire un pique-nique	*to have a picnic*
faire de la randonnée	*to go hiking*
faire des haltères	*to lift weights*
faire de la gymnastique	*to do gymnastics*
faire du surf	*to surf*
faire de la voile	*to go sailing*

13 Enquête

Poll five of your classmates about the sports and hobbies they like to do. Which activity is the most popular? Which is the least popular?

PREMIERE ETAPE   *cent trois* **103**

Presentation

Grammaire Before students look at the explanation, write the sentence *You like to go bike riding* on the board or on a transparency. Ask students to turn it into a question in as many different ways as they can. (They might just use a rising intonation, place *Do* at the beginning of the sentence, or put *don't you?* at the end.) Next, have them look at the expressions in the box and repeat them after you. Write the following sentences on the board or on a transparency and have students use **est-ce que** to turn them into questions:

1. **Tu aimes faire du roller en ligne.**
2. **Tu aimes faire de la natation.**
3. **Tu aimes étudier.**
4. **Tu aimes faire le ménage.**

Then, write the questions they form on the transparency and have pairs of students ask and answer them.

Teacher Note

Grammaire You might tell students that a third, more formal way to form questions in French is by using *inversion,* reversing the order of the subject pronoun and the verb (**Aimez-vous. . .? Aimes-tu. . .?**) You might also tell students that a -t- is inserted after a third person singular verb that ends with a vowel. (**Aime-t-il faire du vélo?**) As an example of inversion, piont out the **Comment dit-on. . .?** box on page 102 and ask **Comment dit-on** I like to *swim* en français?

CLOSE

Have students give all appropriate responses to the following questions and statements:
1. **Tu aimes le sport? (Oui, beaucoup! Non, pas trop.**

Oui, un peu. Pas tellement. Pas du tout.)
2. **Moi, j'aime le volley-ball. (Moi aussi! Moi, non.)**
3. **Je n'aime pas le ski. (Moi, si! Moi non plus.)**

ASSESS

Quiz 4-1, *Chapter Teaching Resources, Book 1,* pp. 191–192

Assessment Items, Audiocassette 7B Audio CD 4

Performance Assessment

Have pairs of students interview each other to find out their most and least favorite activities. You might have them act out their interviews for the class or record them to be included in their oral portfolios.

*J*ump Start!

Have students draw pictures of three activities from the previous étape. Then, have them exchange drawings and write captions identifying the activities in French.

MOTIVATE

Ask students what they would like to find out about someone they've just met.

TEACH

Presentation

Comment dit-on... ? Write **est-ce que** on the board and ask students how it is used. Next, add **qu'** to the beginning of the expression to make **qu'est-ce que**. Explain that it means *what* and is used to begin an information question. Next, have students find examples of **qu'est-ce que** in Emilie's letter on page 96. Then, hold a toy microphone out to "interview" various students, asking **Qu'est-ce que tu fais comme sport?** You might call students' attention to the **Note de grammaire,** which explains the use of **de** in a negative sentence.

Grammaire Write the forms of **faire** on a transparency and have students repeat the forms after you. Then, form four teams. Have each team make a set of flashcards showing the forms of **faire.** Call out a subject pronoun and have teams hold up the card that shows the appropriate verb form. The first team to hold up the correct card gets the chance to win a bonus point by saying a sentence using that form of **faire.**

For videodisc application, see *Videodisc Guide.*

DEUXIEME ETAPE

Exchanging information

COMMENT DIT-ON... ?
Exchanging information

To find out a friend's interests:

Qu'est-ce que tu fais comme sport? *What sports do you play?*
Qu'est-ce que tu fais pour t'amuser? *What do you do to have fun?*

To tell about your interests:

Je fais de l'athlétisme. *I do . . .*
Je joue au volley-ball. *I play . . .*
Je ne fais pas de ski. *I don't . . .*
Je ne joue pas au foot. *I don't play . . .*

> ### Note de *G*rammaire
>
> **Du, de la,** and **de l'** usually become **de** (or **d'**) in a negative sentence.
>
> Je ne fais pas **de** jogging.
> Je ne fais pas **d'**athlétisme.

14   Qu'est-ce que tu fais pour t'amuser?

With a partner, take turns asking each other about your sports and hobbies.

— Qu'est-ce que tu fais pour t'amuser?
— Je fais du jogging et du ski. Et toi?
— Moi, je...

*G*rammaire   The verb **faire**

The irregular verb **faire** is used in many different expressions.

faire(*to do, to play,* or *to make*)

Je **fais**		Nous **faisons**	
Tu **fais**	du sport.	Vous **faites**	du sport.
Il/Elle/On **fait**		Ils/Elles **font**	

- The subject pronoun **on** is used with the **il/elle** form of the verb. In conversational French, **on** usually means *we.*
  Le samedi, **on** fait du sport. *On Saturdays, we play sports.*

- In some situations, **on** can mean *people in general, they,* or *you.*
  En France, **on** parle français.

- You will have to use context, the surrounding words and phrases, to tell how a speaker is using **on.**

RESOURCES FOR DEUXIEME ETAPE

Textbook Audiocassette 2B/Audio CD 4
Practice and Activity Book, pp. 41–43
Video Guide
  Video Program
  Expanded Video Program, Videocassette 2
Videodisc Guide
  Videodisc Program, Videodisc 2B

Chapter Teaching Resources, Book 1
- Communicative Activity 4-1, pp. 171–172
- Teaching Transparency Master 4-2, pp. 176, 178
  Teaching Transparency 4-2
- Additional Listening Activities 4-3, 4-4, p. 180
  Audiocassette 9B/Audio CD 4
- Realia 4-2, pp. 184, 185
- Situation Cards 4-2, pp. 186–187
- Student Response Forms, pp. 188–190
- Quiz 4-2, pp. 193–194
  Audiocassette 7B/Audio CD 4

15 Quels sports?

Complete the following conversation with the correct forms of the verb **faire**.

— Tu __1__ quels sports? *fais*
— Moi, je __2__ surtout du ski et du patin. *fais*
— Et tes copains, qu'est-ce qu'ils __3__ comme sport? *font*
— Michel __4__ de la natation et Hélène __5__ du roller en ligne. *fait, fait*
— Hélène et toi, est-ce que vous __6__ du sport ensemble? *faites*
— Oui, nous __7__ souvent du vélo. *faisons*

16 Au cercle français *At the French Club*

Based on the activities shown in the photos, talk about some of the activities you do or don't do with your friends.

Mes copains et moi, on fait...

1. 2. 3. 4. 5.

17 Jean et Luc

Jean and Luc are identical twins. They even enjoy the same activities. Tell what activities they do, based on what you see in their room. See answers below.

Teaching Suggestion

15 You might have students pair off and read this dialogue aloud, supplying the missing verb forms and writing them down as they proceed.

Building on Previous Skills

15 If this activity is done orally, correct it by having a different student read each line of the conversation aloud and spell the verb form in French.

Teaching Suggestions

16 Students might work in pairs to do this activity, asking their partner **Et toi?** after each activity they identify.

17 Have pairs of students ask and answer questions about what Jean and Luc like to do, based on the illustration. Remind them to use **Est-ce que.** (Est-ce qu'ils aiment faire du ski? Est-ce qu'ils aiment jouer au hockey?)

Possible answers
17 Ils font du ski, du patin à glace, des photos, du théâtre. Ils jouent au football, au hockey.

Presentation

Vocabulaire Present the weather expressions by talking about the weather conditions that prevail on the day of your presentation. Present other weather conditions by miming, drawing on the board, or showing pictures or props, such as an umbrella, mittens, and suntan lotion. Then, have students repeat the expressions after you as they read along in their books. Have several students answer the question **Qu'est-ce que tu fais quand... ?**

Teaching Suggestion

18 If students find the conditions pleasant, have them change the conditions to make them unpleasant and vice-versa.

For Individual Needs

18 Visual/Auditory Learners You might hold up a magazine picture or drawing of each type of weather (a rainy day) and say an activity (**jouer au football américain**). Have students respond with a thumbs-up gesture if they find it pleasant (**agréable**) and a thumbs-down gesture if they think it's unpleasant (**désagréable**).

Portfolio

19 Written This activity is appropriate for students' written portfolios. For portfolio information, see *Assessment Guide,* pages 2–13.

VOCABULAIRE

Qu'est-ce que tu fais quand...

il fait beau?

il fait chaud?

il fait froid?

il fait frais?

il pleut?

il neige?

18 C'est agréable ou désagréable?

Tell a partner if these activities are pleasant (**agréable**) or unpleasant (**désagréable**).

1. faire du vélo quand il fait froid
2. faire de la natation quand il fait chaud
3. regarder la télé quand il neige
4. faire du jogging quand il fait frais
5. jouer au football américain quand il pleut

19 Et toi?

Qu'est-ce que tu aimes faire quand...

1. il fait froid?
2. il pleut?
3. il fait beau?
4. il neige?

106 *cent six*   CHAPITRE 4   Sports et passe-temps

Additional Practice

Have the class keep a local weather chart for a week, with one student responsible for recording the weather conditions each day. After the data has been recorded each day, ask students about the weather.

NOTE CULTURELLE

Francophone countries, like most other countries of the world, use the metric system, so temperature is measured in degrees centigrade or Celsius rather than Fahrenheit. This means that the freezing point of water is 0°C, and its boiling point is 100°C. A comfortable temperature would be 25°C (77°F). If the temperature were more than 35°C, it would be very hot. If the temperature were 18°C (64.4°F), you would probably need a jacket.

Printemps :	mi-mars à mi-mai
Eté :	mi-mai à mi-septembre
Automne :	mi-septembre à mi-novembre
Hiver :	mi-novembre à mi-mars

QUEBEC

	Température moyenne		moyenne ensoleillement (h)
	Minimale °C	Maximale °C	
Janvier	-14	-6	97
Février	-13	-5	113
Mars	-8	0	140
Avril	0	8	172
Mai	6	16	220
Juin	12	21	224
Juillet	14	24	248
Août	13	23	219
Septembre	9	18	153
Octobre	3	11	116
Novembre	-2	3	74
Décembre	-12	-5	76

20 Il fait quel temps?

In these months, what is the weather usually like where you live?

1. en mai
2. en février
3. en juillet
4. en octobre
5. en avril
6. en décembre

Il fait froid. Il pleut.
Il neige. Il fait frais.
Il fait beau. Il fait chaud.

Tu te rappelles?

Do you remember the endings that you learned to use with the verb **aimer** in Chapter 1? Those endings are exactly the same for all regular **-er** verbs, which include many French verbs. Here's how the verb **jouer** fits the pattern.

jouer (to play)

Je **joue**
Tu **joues** } au tennis.
Il/Elle/On **joue**

Nous **jouons**
Vous **jouez** } au tennis.
Ils/Elles **jouent**

21 Ecoute!

Listen as a newspaper reporter asks three Canadian teenagers, Paul, Anne, and Julie, about their hobbies and pastimes. Then, answer the questions below. Answers on p. 93C.

1. Which teenagers don't watch TV?
2. Which ones like to listen to music?
3. Which ones play hockey?
4. Which ones like to dance?
5. Which teenagers like to go to the movies?

22 Prisonnier des neiges

Imagine that you've been snowed in during a winter storm. Write a note to a friend telling him or her about the weather, what you're doing to pass the time, and how you feel about the situation.

Math Link

Note Culturelle To convert Fahrenheit to Celsius, subtract 32 and then multiply by 5/9. To convert Celsius to Fahrenheit, multiply by 9/5 and then add 32. Ask students if they know what the freezing and boiling temperatures are for water in degrees Fahrenheit (Answer: 32° and 212°). Students might want to practice converting some of the temperatures shown on the chart.

For Individual Needs

20 Challenge Have students answer in complete sentences, either orally or in writing. Then, have them give at least one activity they do for each weather situation and/or for each month. (**En juillet, j'aime nager. En mai, je fais du vélo. Quand il neige, je fais du ski.**)

Building on Previous Skills

22 You might orally review some activities students learned in Chapter 1 (**regarder la télévision, écouter de la musique, étudier, parler au téléphone, danser**).

Teaching Suggestion

22 If students have difficulty writing about a winter storm, they might write about a heatwave (**une vague de chaleur**) instead.

Portfolio

22 Written This activity could be a portfolio entry or a writing assessment activity. For portfolio information, see *Assessment Guide*, pages 2–13.

Game

VERB BEE Play this game to review **-er** verbs. Divide the class into two teams and have one player from each team go to the board. Call out an infinitive (**jouer**) and a subject (**vous**). Award a point to the team of the first player to write the correct verb form.

Presentation

Vocabulaire Show or draw pictures of the four seasons. Write the French words for the seasons on the board next to the pictures. Say aloud a sentence describing an activity. (**On fait du patin à glace.**) Have students add an appropriate season. (**On fait du patin à glace en hiver.**) Re-enter some activities from previous chapters: **danser, faire de l'équitation, nager, sortir avec des copains,** and **voyager.** Present **le matin, l'après-midi,** and **le soir** by drawing the route of the sun from sunrise to sunset on the board. Give various times in the 24-hour system (**13h30, 8h50, 23h15**) and have students tell whether it's **le matin, l'après-midi,** or **le soir.** Teach the phrase **en vacances** by referring to the calendar as you talk about school vacations.

Teaching Suggestion

23 Have students give their choice of activity if they choose **fais autre chose.**

◆ For Individual Needs

25 Slower Pace Before students write their letters, have them think of activities a Canadian pen pal might enjoy.

CLOSE

To close this **étape,** show *Teaching Transparency 4-2.* Have students describe the activities and weather conditions shown. You might prompt students with **Quand il... , ils...**

VOCABULAIRE

Qu'est-ce que tu fais...

en vacances?

le soir?

le week-end?

en automne?

en hiver?

au printemps?

en été?

23 Un questionnaire

To help pair up campers for activities, a camp counselor has sent out the survey you see on the right. Give one answer in each category.

24 Et toi?

Tell other students in your class what activities you do in each season and ask what they do. Try to find someone who does at least two of the same things that you do.

— En hiver, je fais du patin à glace. Et toi?
— Moi non! Quand il fait froid, j'écoute de la musique.

25 Une lettre

In preparation for a visit to Canada, you've decided to write to your French-Canadian pen pal. Write a brief paragraph, asking about your pen pal's sports and hobbies and telling which ones you do and don't do.

1. En automne, je...
a. fais du patin à glace.
b. joue au hockey.
c. écoute de la musique.
d. fais du ski.
e. fais autre chose.

2. En hiver, je...
a. joue au football américain.
b. joue au foot.
c. fais du théâtre.
d. joue au volley.
e. fais autre chose.

3. Au printemps, je...
a. joue au base-ball.
b. fais de l'athlétisme.
c. fais du vélo.
d. fais de la vidéo.
e. fais autre chose.

4. En été, je...
a. fais de la natation.
b. fais du roller en ligne.
c. regarde la télé.
d. fais du ski nautique.
e. fais autre chose.

108 *cent huit*   CHAPITRE 4   Sports et passe-temps

PANORAMA CULTUREL

Marius • Côte d'Ivoire

Aljosa • France

Mélanie • Québec

What sports do you play? Where do you go to practice them? We asked some young people about their favorite sports. Here's what they had to say.

Qu'est-ce que tu fais comme sport?

«Je fais beaucoup de sport, mais surtout le football. Je fais le football et le skate, le patin à roulettes et puis j'aime aussi le tennis.»
—Marius

«Comme sport, j'aime bien faire le tennis. J'aime bien aller à la piscine, voilà. J'aime bien [le] bowling.»
—Aljosa

«Avec mes amies, moi je fais beaucoup de sport. Je fais partie de l'équipe interscolaire de volley-ball et de badminton de l'école. Je fais de la natation. Je fais du patinage. Je fais de la course. Je fais du tennis aussi souvent l'été. L'hiver, je patine.»
—Mélanie

Qu'en penses-tu?

1. Which of these students enjoy the same sports that you do?
2. Which sports that they mention are not played in your area?
3. Can you guess which sports are associated with the following events and places?*

   a. La Coupe du monde
   b. Le Grand Prix de Monaco
   c. Le Tour de France
   d. Roland-Garros

Savais-tu que... ?

While schools in francophone countries do offer extracurricular sports, serious athletes often participate through clubs outside of school. Activities such as swimming, tennis, or volleyball are often organized by parent volunteers or communities. In France, recreation centers **(Maisons des jeunes et de la culture** or **MJC)** sponsor all kinds of social, cultural, and educational activities for young people.

*a. soccer   b. auto racing   c. cycling   d. tennis (the French Open)

Teacher Notes

- See *Video Guide, Videodisc Guide,* and *Practice and Activity Book* for activities related to the **Panorama Culturel.**
- Remind students that cultural material may be included in the Chapter Quizzes and Test.
- The interviewees' language represents informal, unrehearsed speech. Occasionally, edits have been made for clarification.

Presentation

Tell students to listen for the sports that each person mentions. Play the video, and then hold up pictures of various activities, asking **Qui fait ça?** Students call out the name of the person who mentioned that activity.

Thinking Critically

Analyzing   Have students give advantages and disadvantages of having school sports teams (football, cheerleaders, drill team).

Teaching Suggestion

Have students prepare short reports in English on francophone sporting events. They might look up in *The World Almanac* the most recent winners of the events listed in question 3.

Culture Note

Savais-tu que... ?   **Maisons des jeunes et de la culture** provide a variety of sports, movies, and other activities such as music, dance, computer science, photography, and arts and crafts. Annual dues are charged based on the number of activities in which a person participates.

Questions

1. Qu'est-ce que Marius fait comme sport? (du football, du skate, du patin à roulettes, du tennis)
2. Est-ce qu'Aljosa aime le bowling? (Oui)
3. Est-ce que Mélanie fait du sport à l'école? (Oui)
4. Qu'est-ce qu'elle fait en été? (du tennis) En hiver? (Elle patine.)

*J*ump Start!

Have students write six sentences using a different form of **faire** and a different activity in each.

MOTIVATE

Make suggestions to students in English (Let's go eat lunch! How about a pop quiz?) and write their English responses on the board.

TEACH

Presentation

Comment dit-on... ? Make several suggestions using **On... ?** (On fait du jogging?) Ask students to guess what you are doing (making suggestions). Then, name a sport or hold up a picture of it and ask a student to suggest doing that sport using the new expression. Respond by accepting or turning down the suggestion. (**D'accord. Ça ne me dit rien.**) Next, suggest various activities and have students accept or reject your suggestions, using the appropriate expressions.

Grammaire Ask students how often they participate in various sports and activities. Then, draw a timeline on the board with **souvent** and **d'habitude** at one end, **quelquefois** and **de temps en temps** in the middle, and **jamais** at the other end. Name several pastimes (**le vélo**) and have individual students indicate on the timeline how often they do each activity. Then, say the complete sentence and have students repeat. (**Je ne fais jamais de vélo.**)

For videodisc application, see **Videodisc Guide.**

TROISIEME ETAPE

Making, accepting, and turning down suggestions

COMMENT DIT-ON... ?

Making, accepting, and turning down suggestions

To make a suggestion:
On fait du patin?
   How about . . . ?
On joue au foot?
   How about . . . ?

To accept a suggestion:
D'accord. *OK.*
Bonne idée. *Good idea.*
Oui, c'est génial!
Allons-y! *Let's go!*

To turn down a suggestion:
Désolé(e), mais je ne peux pas.
   Sorry, but I can't.
Ça ne me dit rien.
   That doesn't interest me.
Non, c'est barbant!

26 Ecoute!

Listen as Germain calls his friends Lise, Renaud, Philippe, and Monique to suggest activities for the weekend. Do his friends accept or turn down his suggestions?
Answers on p. 93D.

27 Qu'est-ce qu'on fait?

Write down one or two things that you'd like to do this weekend. Then, find three classmates who'd like to join you.

— On fait du jogging ce week-end?
— Le jogging, c'est barbant! *or* D'accord. C'est génial, le jogging.

*G*rammaire   Adverbs of frequency

- To tell how often you do something, use **quelquefois** (*sometimes*), **de temps en temps** (*from time to time*), **une fois par semaine** (*once a week*), **souvent** (*often*), **d'habitude** (*usually*), and **ne... jamais** (*never*).

- Short adverbs usually come after the verb. Longer adverbs can be placed at the beginning or the end of a sentence. Put **d'habitude** at the beginning of a sentence and **une fois par semaine** at the end. Put **ne... jamais** around the verb, as you do with **ne... pas.**

   Je fais **souvent** du ski.
   D'habitude, je fais du ski au printemps.
   Je fais du ski **une fois par semaine.**
   Je **ne** fais **jamais** de ski.

110   *cent dix*   CHAPITRE 4   Sports et passe-temps

RESOURCES FOR TROISIEME ETAPE

Textbook Audiocassette 2B/Audio CD 4
Practice and Activity Book, pp. 44–46
Videodisc Guide
  Videodisc Program, Videodisc 2B

Chapter Teaching Resources, Book 1
- Communicative Activity 4-2, pp. 173–174
- Teaching Transparency Master 4-3, pp. 177, 178
  Teaching Transparency 4-3
- Additional Listening Activities 4-5, 4-6, p. 181
  Audiocassette 9B/Audio CD 4
- Realia 4-2, pp. 184, 185
- Situation Cards 4-3, pp. 186–187
- Student Response Forms, pp. 188–190
- Quiz 4-3, pp. 195–196
  Audiocassette 7B/Audio CD 4

28 Ecoute!

Listen as Emile, a reporter for the school newspaper in Quebec City, interviews his classmates about sports. How often does each person practice sports? Answers on p. 93D.

29 L'agenda de Pauline *Pauline's planner*

Pauline is an active, French-Canadian teenager. Based on her calendar, take turns with a partner asking about her activities and how often she does them.

> — Est-ce qu'elle fait de l'aérobic?
> — Oui, de temps en temps.

NOVEMBRE						
DIMANCHE	LUNDI	MARDI	MERCREDI	JEUDI	VENDREDI	SAMEDI
		1 jogging	**2** photo	**3** jogging	**4** théâtre	**5** patin à glace
6 aérobic	**7** jogging	**8** photo	**9**	**10** jogging	**11**	**12** jogging
13 photo	**14** jogging	**15**	**16** aérobic	**17** jogging	**18** théâtre	**19**
20 patin à glace	**21** jogging	**22** jogging	**23** photo	**24** ski	**25**	**26** aérobic
27 jogging	**28**	**29** jogging	**30** photo			

30 Moi, je fais souvent....

With a partner, discuss your favorite pastimes and how often you do them. Ask questions to keep the conversation going.

> — Qu'est-ce que tu fais pour t'amuser?
> — En été, je fais souvent du ski nautique. Et toi?
> — Je fais du vélo. Et toi? Tu fais du vélo... ?

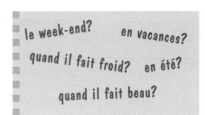

le week-end? en vacances?
quand il fait froid? en été?
quand il fait beau?

Teaching Suggestion

28 Stop the recording after each interview and have students write the adverb of frequency. You may prefer to have individuals volunteer the answer orally.

For Individual Needs

28 Challenge Have students give the sport that each person practices as well as how often he or she does the activity.

29 Slower Pace You might want to go over Pauline's schedule orally before students pair off to discuss it. You might also call out the activity and have students give the days and times when Pauline does that activity, and vice-versa.

29 Challenge Have students make two calendars of their own, one blank and one with their activities filled in like Pauline's. Have them give the blank calendar to a partner, who asks questions about the other's activities and fills in the blank calendar appropriately. They should compare the calendar to the original, and then reverse roles.

30 Kinesthetic Learners You might have students create interview skits based on this activity.

Culture Note

Tell students that calendars in France begin on Monday, but those in Canada begin on Sunday, as in the United States.

Language Note

You might point out that students can replace the number in **une fois par semaine** to fit their situation (**deux fois... , trois fois...**).

Teaching Suggestion

31 You might give students examples of questions for this activity (**Tu aimes... ? Comment tu trouves... ? Est-ce que tu fais/joues... ?**). You might also have students recall ways to express their opinion of activities. (**C'est super, génial, nul, barbant.**)

◆ For Individual Needs

32 Auditory Learners
Students might read the letter aloud in small groups, or you might read it aloud to the class.

Teaching Suggestion

33 Type copies of Lucien's letter, deleting all the activities and the opinion words. Have students fill in the blanks according to their own circumstances.

📁 Portfolio

33 Written This activity might be added to students' portfolios or used at the end of this **étape** as an assessment activity. For portfolio information, see *Assessment Guide*, pages 2–13.

---

31   **Sondage**

a. Make a chart like the one shown here. In the left-hand column, list the activities you enjoy. In the middle column, tell when you do them, and in the right-hand column, tell how often.

ACTIVITE	SAISON	FREQUENCE
Je fais du ski. Je fais...	en hiver	de temps en temps

b. Now, share this information with three other classmates. Ask questions to find out what you have in common and what you don't.

— Je fais du ski de temps en temps.
— Pas moi! Je ne fais jamais de ski.

32 **Le sportif**

Your French pen pal Lucien is coming to visit soon. Read his letter and tell whether he would answer **D'accord** or **Ça ne me dit rien** if you were to suggest the following activities.

1. On fait de la vidéo ce week-end?   D'accord.
2. On fait du ski nautique?   Ça ne me dit rien.
3. On joue au foot?   D'accord.
4. On fait de la natation ce soir?   D'accord.
5. On joue au football américain ce week-end?   Ça ne me dit rien.

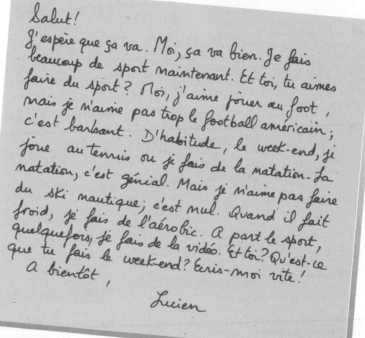

Salut!
J'espère que ça va. Moi, ça va bien. Je fais beaucoup de sport maintenant. Et toi, tu aimes faire du sport? Moi, j'aime jouer au foot, mais je n'aime pas trop le football américain; c'est barbant. D'habitude, le week-end, je joue au tennis ou je fais de la natation. La natation, c'est génial. Mais je n'aime pas faire du ski nautique; c'est nul. Quand il fait froid, je fais de l'aérobic. A part le sport, quelquefois, je fais de la vidéo. Et toi? Qu'est-ce que tu fais le week-end? Écris-moi vite!
A bientôt,
Lucien

33 **Cher Lucien, ...**

Now, answer Lucien's letter. Be sure to . . .

- tell him what activities you like and why you like them;
- tell him when and how often you do each activity;
- tell him what you don't like to do and why not;
- suggest one or two things you might do together and when.

112   *cent douze*   CHAPITRE 4   Sports et passe-temps

34 Une interview

a. You are a guest at a French-Canadian school and you'll soon be interviewed on local television. You've received a list of questions you'll be asked. Write down your answers.

1. Tu fais souvent du sport?
2. Qu'est-ce que tu fais comme sport en hiver?
3. Tu regardes souvent la télé?
4. Qu'est-ce que tu fais le week-end?
5. Qu'est-ce que tu fais en vacances?
6. Tu fais quoi le soir?
7. Tu écoutes souvent de la musique? (Du rock? Du jazz? De la musique classique?)
8. Qu'est-ce que tu fais quand il fait froid?

b. With a partner, take turns asking and answering the questions.

35 Mon journal

Using the information in the chart you made for Activity 31, tell about your favorite weekend and after-school activities, and how often you do them. Give your opinions of the activities, too.

PRONONCIATION

The sounds [u] and [y]

The sound [u] occurs in such English words as *Sue, shoe,* and *too.* The French [u] is shorter, tenser, and more rounded than the vowel sound in English. Listen to these French words: **tout, nous, vous.** The sound [u] is usually represented by the letter combination **ou.**

The sound [y] is represented in the words **salut, super,** and **musique.** This sound does not exist in English. To pronounce [y], start by saying [i], as in the English word *me.* Then, round your lips as if you were going to say the English word *moon,* keeping your tongue pressed behind your lower front teeth.

A. A prononcer

Now, practice first the sound [u] and then [y]. Repeat these words.

1. vous
2. nous
3. douze
4. rouge
5. cours
6. joue
7. tu
8. musique
9. nul
10. étude
11. une
12. du

B. A lire

Take turns with a partner reading the following sentences aloud.

1. Salut! Tu t'appelles Louis?
2. J'ai cours aujourd'hui.
3. Tu aimes la trousse rouge?
4. Elle n'aime pas du tout faire du ski.
5. Nous aimons écouter de la musique.
6. Vous jouez souvent au foot?

C. A écrire

You're going to hear a short dialogue. Write down what you hear. Answers on p. 93D.

Mon journal

35 For an additional journal entry suggestion for Chapter 4, see *Practice and Activity Book,* page 148.

Teaching Suggestion

Prononciation Tell students that when they see the letter *u* by itself, it always represents the sound /y/. Have them make their own lists of words containing the sounds /u/ and /y/. Read aloud words from the students' lists and ask them to raise their left hand to signal /u/ and their right hand to signal /y/. You might also read the list of words from Part A.

For Individual Needs

Slower Pace Have students copy the sentences from **Prononciation** Part B into their notebooks as you write them on the board or on a transparency. Have students circle all the /u/ sounds. As they read the words aloud that contain this sound, circle the correct words in your sentences so students can correct their papers. Then, have students pair off to practice reading the sentences aloud. Do the same for the sound /y/.

CLOSE

TPR To close this **étape,** tell students in French to do a certain activity and have them respond by miming the activity.

ASSESS

Quiz 4-3, *Chapter Teaching Resources, Book 1,* pp. 195–196

Assessment Items, Audiocassette 7B/Audio CD 4

Performance Assessment

Meet with students individually and ask one or two of the questions in Activity 34 to be answered orally, or read several of the questions to the class and have them write appropriate answers.

READING STRATEGY

The five "W" questions

Teacher Note

For an additional reading, see *Practice and Activity Book,* page 47.

PREREADING
Activities A–C

Motivating Activity

Ask students about their favorite pastimes, movies, sports, TV shows, rock stars, and reading materials.

Teaching Suggestion

A.–C. Ask a student to read the introduction or give students a few moments to read it silently. Do Activities A, B, and C with the entire class. Once students have answered B and C, have them read the rest of the selection thoroughly in groups, pairs, or individually.

READING
Activities D–M

Teaching Suggestion

Ask students how the different sections of the reading are related. Point out that polls 2, 3, and 4 examine the top three pastimes that are listed in poll 1.

Teacher Note

The comic strips referred to are not in the newspapers, but in bound book form. **Astérix** relates the adventures of several Gauls in a small village during the Roman occupation. **Lucky Luke** is an American cowboy seen through French eyes. Cartoons on TV are called **dessins animés.**

LISONS!

$\mathcal{W}$hat are your favorite free-time activities? In this reading you will get some additional information about the hobbies enjoyed by francophone students.

DE BONS CONSEILS

If you can find the answers to the questions *Who? What? When? Where? Why?* and *How?,* you can get an idea of what a reading is about. Often, the answers to these questions can be found in the first paragraph of a reading. Not all of these questions will be answered in every reading.

A. How many of the *W* questions are answered in the introduction of this reading? See answers below.

 1. *What* subjects do these surveys cover?
 2. *Who* organized the surveys? *Who* responded to the surveys?
 3. *Where* were the surveys conducted? In which areas of the country?

B. Now, look at the illustrations to see if you can figure out the topics that will be covered in each poll. See answers below.

C. Which poll is the most general? What three topics are covered in detail? Why do you think these topics were chosen?

See answers below.

LES JEUNES

Sondage exclusif

Pour fêter son 20e anniversaire, *Vidéo-Presse* te présente une étude exclusive portant sur les habitudes et les goûts des jeunes.
Plus de 500 jeunes de diverses régions du Québec ainsi que du reste du Canada ont répondu aux questions.

LOISIRS
Quels sont tes loisirs préférés? 1

83% Sports Ça bouge!

51% Lecture Et dire qu'on pense que les jeunes ne lisent pas!

27% Musique Surtout chez les jeunes de 14 ans.

24% Télévision Surprise! nous ne sommes pas toujours devant la télé.

18% Bricolage Surtout chez les 12 ans et moins.

15% Ordinateur À surveiller! Qu'en sera-t-il dans deux ans?

6% Jeux de société

3% Collections

Julie marque un toucher.

SPORTS
Es-tu un vrai sportif? 2

«Moi, j'aime la gymnastique artistique, la natation et le ski» *(école Saint-Clément, Ville Mont-Royal).*
Le ski et la natation sont les activités préférées autant chez les garçons que chez les filles et à tous les groupes d'âge. Les garçons regardent plus d'émissions sportives et lisent plus d'articles sur le sport que les filles.

Savais-tu que... ?
• 6 répondants sur 10 font plus de trois heures d'activités sportives par semaine.
• Sur un total de 10 joueurs de hockey, 2 sont des filles.
• Les filles jouent plus au tennis et au basketball que les garçons.
• 9 garçons sur 10 jouent au baseball.
• 7 garçons sur 10 pratiquent le judo, le karaté, le tae kwon do.

Language Note

Ask students what the second most popular pastime is **(lecture).** Then, have them look at poll 3 and ask if they know the relationship between **livres, lire, lecteurs,** and **lectrices.**

Answers

A 1. the habits and tastes of young people
 2. *Vidéo-Presse;* more than 500 young people
 3. Canada; Ontario, Quebec, Manitoba
B 1. favorite pastimes
 2. sports
 3. reading
 4. music
C *Most general poll:* pastimes
 Topics covered in detail: sports, books, music
 These areas are of great interest to young people.

AU MICRO

LIVRES

Qu'est-ce que tu aimes lire? 3

LECTURES PRÉFÉRÉES

FILLES
1 — Romans
2 — Bandes dessinées
3 — Revues
4 — Poésie

GARÇONS
1 — Bandes dessinées
2 — Revues
3 — Romans
4 — Documentaires
5 — Poésie

BD
Astérix
Archie
Boule et Bill
Garfield
Gaston La Gaffe
Lucky Luke

ROMANS
Alerte au lac des loups
Anne la maison
aux pignons verts
Agathe Christie
Annie-Croche
Le dernier des raisins
Les filles de Caleb

LECTEURS ET LECTRICES AYANT PARTICIPÉ À L'ENQUÊTE

Garçons 530
Filles 640

MUSIQUE

Les lauréats du Gala Vidéo-Presse 4

Les lecteurs de Vidéo-Presse sont branchés. Des mordus de la musique!

1. New kids on the block
2. Roch Voisine
3. Metalica
4. Michael Jackson
5. Rock et belles oreilles
6. Samantha Fox
7. Bon Jovi
8. Michel Rivard
9. Paula Abdoul
10. Def Leppard
11. Prince
12. Beatles, Elvis...

Les abonnés de *Vidéo-Presse* ne font pas qu'écouter de la musique, ils en jouent (54%). La flûte, le piano et la guitare sont les trois instruments les plus joués.

ORIGINE DES RÉPONSES

Ontario 4 %
Québec 37 %
Manitoba 59 %

Quels sont tes loisirs préférés?

D. What are the two most popular pastimes? Which pastimes have the fewest supporters? *See answers below.*

E. Which activity do the fourteen-year-olds prefer? The twelve-year-olds? *See answers below.*

F. Are you surprised by these results? Why or why not?

Es-tu un vrai sportif?

G. Which sports do both boys and girls like? *See answers below.*

H. Which sports do girls play more often than boys? Which do boys play more often than girls? *See answers below.*

I. Do more boys than girls watch sports on TV? Who reads more about sports? *See answers below.*

Qu'est-ce que tu aimes lire?

J. Look at the entries under the heading **BD.** Do you remember what **roman** means? Can you figure out what **BD (bande dessinée)** means? *See answers below.*

K. Do boys and girls have the same taste in their choice of reading? What are the similarities and differences? *No. Girls prefer novels, while boys prefer comics. Neither likes poetry.*

Les lauréats du Gala

L. Do you recognize some of these names? Which ones?

M. What information is contained in the paragraph below the survey results? *See answers below.*

N. Now, conduct a poll of your classmates on one of the topics covered in this survey. Are your results similar to the ones you read here?

Terms in Lisons!

Students might want to know the following words: **bricolage** *(do-it-yourself projects)*; **revues** *(magazines)*; **abonnés** *(subscribers)*; and **branchés** *("in")*.

POSTREADING
Activity N

Teaching Suggestion

N. After students have answered the questions for all the reading sections, have them imagine what the results of this survey might be in the United States. Then, have students conduct the survey as described in this activity.

Thinking Critically

Comparing and Contrasting
How do the results of the class survey differ from the results of the Canadian poll? Are there activities that are more popular with one nationality? Are there activities that the class chose that are not mentioned on the Canadian survey?

Analyzing What are some reasons for any differences or similarities in the results of the surveys? What aspects of life in the United States or Canada could account for the differences?

Teaching Suggestion

Ask students if this reading selection changed their views of Canadian youth at all. You might have them write a short journal entry summarizing the responses to the survey.

Answers

D *Most popular pastimes:* sports, reading
Fewest supporters: board games, collecting things

E *Fourteen-year-olds prefer:* music
Twelve-year-olds prefer: **bricolage** (tinkering at home — repairing a radio, building a model plane or boat)

G Skiing, swimming, hockey, tennis, basketball

H Girls play more tennis and basketball than boys. Boys play more hockey than girls.

I Boys watch more sports on TV than girls. Boys read more about sports than girls.

J Roman: *novel*
Bande dessinée: *comic strip*

M Subscribers to *Vidéo-Presse* not only listen to music, but play music as well. Flute, piano, and guitar are the most popular instruments.

The **Mise en pratique** reviews and integrates all four skills and culture in preparation for the Chapter Test.

For Individual Needs

1 Slower Pace Before students listen to the recording, have them recall the names of the seasons. Write them on the board. Then, ask students to imagine what activities might be appropriate in each season. Write a couple of them under each season.

1 Challenge Have students list more than one activity mentioned for each season. You might give a small prize to the student who lists the most activities mentioned on the recording.

Teaching Suggestion

2 Have students choose one activity that they like from the choices listed under each season in the ad and tell why they like that particular activity. Ask them if there are any other activities that they participate in during each of the four seasons.

MISE EN PRATIQUE

1 Listen to this radio commercial for the **Village des Sports,** a resort in Quebec. List at least one activity offered in each season. Answers on p. 93D.

2 You've decided to spend part of your vacation at the **Village des Sports.** Read the information you've received about the resort. Then, complete the application form on the next page.

Village des Sports

c'est l'fun fun fun!

en hiver comme en été

Le plus grand centre du sport au Canada offre du plaisir pour toute la famille.
Services d'accueil, de restauration et de location sur place.

EN ETE
- le tennis
- le volley
- l'athlétisme
- le base-ball
- le roller en ligne
- le ski nautique
- la natation
- l'équitation
- la voile

EN AUTOMNE
- le football
- l'équitation
- la randonnée
- le volley

EN HIVER
- le hockey
- le ski
- le patin à glace
- la luge

AU PRINTEMPS
- le base-ball
- la randonnée
- le roller en ligne
- le tennis

Village des Sports
1860, boul. Vlaicartier
(418) 844-3725
à 24 km du centre-ville de Québec via
la route 371 Nord

116   *cent seize*   CHAPITRE 4   Sports et passe-temps

Culture Note

You might point out to students that Canadian phone numbers follow the American rather than the French pattern, with a three-digit area code and numbers of three and four digits separated by a dash. To call long-distance, Canadians dial 1 before the area code and number, just as in the United States.

Vos activités préférées

Nom _____   J'aime surtout _____

Prénom _____   _____

Né(e) le _____   De temps en temps, j'aime _____

Domicile _____   _____

_____   Je n'aime pas tellement _____

_____   _____

Village des Sports

3   a. You've arrived at the **Village des Sports.** You meet your three roommates, get to know them, and ask them about the activities they enjoy.

b. You and your roommates decide to participate in an activity together. Each of you suggests an activity until you all agree on one.

4   Write to your French class back home to tell all about your activities at the **Village des Sports.** Mention the activities you're doing, what you like, what you don't like, and what the weather is like there. You might also tell something about your roommates.

5   What differences are there between the way students in your area and students in Quebec spend their free time?

6

JEU DE ROLE

You're a famous Canadian athlete. Your partner, a reporter for the local television station, will interview you about your busy training routine. Tell the interviewer what you do at different times of the year, in various weather conditions, and how often. Then, take the role of the reporter and interview your partner, who will assume the identity of a different Canadian athlete.

Teaching Suggestion

3   Either of these activities could be used in addition to or in place of one of the chapter projects. Have students write and practice these skits and then perform them in front of the class. Students might record them as an oral portfolio entry.

📁 Portfolio

4   **Written**   Have students exchange their papers and write a response to their classmate's letter. This activity is appropriate for students' written portfolios.

6   **Oral**   This activity is appropriate as an oral portfolio entry. For portfolio suggestions, see *Assessment Guide,* page 17.

 Video Wrap-Up

- *VIDEO PROGRAM*
- *EXPANDED VIDEO PROGRAM,* Videocassette 2, 03:34–22:38
- *VIDEODISC PROGRAM,* Videodisc 2B

At this time, you might want to use the video resources for additional review and enrichment. See *Video Guide* or *Videodisc Guide* for suggestions regarding the following:
- **Nouvelles de Québec** (Dramatic episode)
- **Panorama Culturel** (Interviews)
- **Vidéoclips** (Authentic footage)

This page is intended to help students prepare for the test. It is a brief checklist of the major points covered in the chapter. The students should be reminded that this is only a checklist and does not necessarily include everything that will appear on the test.

Teaching Suggestions

1,4 To review the months and seasons of the year, have students tell in which month(s) and/or season(s) the people in the illustrations are doing the activities.

5,6 For further practice, students might use the illustrations on this page to make, accept, and turn down suggestions.

7 You might have students tell how frequently they do each activity, using appropriate adverbs.

QUE SAIS-JE?

Can you use what you've learned in this chapter?

Can you tell how much you like or dislike something? p.102

1 Can you tell someone how much you like or dislike these activities?
See answers below.

1.   2.   3.   4.   5.

2 Can you tell someone which sports and activities you enjoy a lot? Which ones you don't enjoy at all? See answers below.

3 How would you tell someone about a few of your sports and hobbies, using the verbs **jouer** and **faire**? See answers below.

Can you exchange information? p.104

4 How would you find out if someone plays these games? See answers below.

1.   2.   3.

Can you make, accept, and turn down suggestions? p.110

5 How would you suggest that . . .
1. you and a friend go waterskiing? On fait du ski nautique?
2. you and your friends play baseball? On joue au base-ball?

6 If a friend asked you to go jogging, how would you accept the suggestion? How would you turn it down? See answers below.

7 How would you tell someone in French . . . See answers below.
1. what you do in a certain season?
2. what you like to do in a certain month?
3. what you do in certain weather?
4. what you like to do at a certain time of day?

118 *cent dix-huit*   CHAPITRE 4   Sports et passe-temps

Answers

1 *Like:* J'aime beaucoup... ; J'aime surtout...
Dislike: Je n'aime pas tellement... ; Je n'aime pas beaucoup... ; Je n'aime pas du tout...
1. jouer au golf.
2. faire de la natation.
3. jouer au tennis.
4. faire des photos.
5. faire du roller en ligne.
2 *Enjoy:* J'aime beaucoup... ; J'aime surtout...
Don't enjoy: Je n'aime pas tellement... ; Je n'aime pas beaucoup... ; Je n'aime pas du tout...
3 Je joue... ; Je fais...
4 1. Tu joues au football?/Est-ce que tu joues au football?
2. Tu joues au hockey?/Est-ce que tu joues au hockey?
3. Tu joues au volley-ball?/Est-ce que tu joues au volley-ball?
6 Accept: D'accord. Bonne idée. Oui, c'est génial. Oui, c'est super! Allons-y!
Turn down: Désolé(e), mais je ne peux pas. Ça ne me dit rien. Non, c'est barbant. Non, c'est nul!
7 1. Au printemps/En été/En automne/En hiver, je...
2. En janvier/février/mars/avril/mai/juin/juillet/août/septembre/octobre/novembre/décembre, j'aime...
3. Quand il fait froid/il fait frais/il fait beau/il fait chaud/il pleut/il neige, je...
4. Le matin/L'après-midi/Le soir, j'aime...

PREMIERE ETAPE

Telling how much you like or dislike something

Beaucoup. *A lot.*
surtout *especially*
Pas tellement. *Not too much.*
Pas beaucoup. *Not very much.*
Pas du tout. *Not at all.*

Sports and hobbies

faire de l'aérobic *to do aerobics*
 de l'athlétisme *to do track and field*
 du jogging *to jog*
 de la natation *to swim*

du patin à glace *to ice-skate*
des photos *to take pictures*
du roller en ligne *to in-line skate*
du ski *to ski*
du ski nautique *to water-ski*
du théâtre *to do drama*
du vélo *to bike*
de la vidéo *to make videos*
jouer au base-ball *to play baseball*
 au basket(-ball) *to play basketball*
 au foot(ball) *to play soccer*

au football américain *to play football*
au golf *to play golf*
au hockey *to play hockey*
à des jeux vidéo *to play video games*
au tennis *to play tennis*
au volley(-ball) *to play volleyball*

Other useful expressions

Est-ce que *(Introduces a yes-or-no question)*

DEUXIEME ETAPE

Exchanging information

Qu'est-ce que tu fais comme sport? *What sports do you play?*
Qu'est-ce que tu fais pour t'amuser? *What do you do to have fun?*
Je fais... *I play/do . . .*
Je joue... *I play . . .*
Je ne fais pas de... *I don't play/do . . .*
Je ne joue pas... *I don't play . . .*
faire *to do, to play, to make*
jouer *to play*

Weather

Qu'est-ce que tu fais quand... *What do you do when . . .*

il fait beau? *it's nice weather?*
il fait chaud? *it's hot?*
il fait frais? *it's cool?*
il fait froid? *it's cold?*
il pleut? *it's raining?*
il neige? *it's snowing?*

Seasons, months and times

Qu'est-ce que tu fais... *What do you do . . .*
 le week-end? *on weekends?*
 le soir? *in the evening?*
 en vacances? *on vacation?*
 au printemps? *in the spring?*
 en été? *in the summer?*
 en automne? *in the fall?*

en hiver? *in the winter?*
en janvier?
en février?
en mars?
en avril?
en mai?
en juin?
en juillet?
en août?
en septembre?
en octobre?
en novembre?
en décembre?

Other useful expressions

on *we, people in general, they, you*

TROISIEME ETAPE

Making, accepting, and turning down suggestions

On... ? *How about . . . ?*
D'accord. *OK.*
Bonne idée. *Good idea.*
Allons-y! *Let's go!*
Oui, c'est... *Yes, it's . . .*

Désolé(e), mais je ne peux pas. *Sorry, but I can't.*
Ça ne me dit rien. *That doesn't interest me.*
Non, c'est... *No, it's . . .*

Other useful expressions

quelquefois *sometimes*

une fois par semaine *once a week*
de temps en temps *from time to time*
souvent *often*
ne... jamais *never*
d'habitude *usually*

Allez, viens à Paris! pp. 120–197

EXPANDED VIDEO
PROGRAM,
Videocassette 2
22:39–25:14

OR *VIDEODISC PROGRAM,*
Videodisc 3A

Search 1, Play To 4660

Motivating Activity

Ask students if they can name any well-known monuments or places in Paris. Ask if they know how people live, how they get around, where they work, and so on. Then, have them look at the photos on pages 120–123, focusing on such things as signs, activities, and people's clothing, and make inferences about Paris.

Background Information

The earliest known inhabitants of Paris were the **Parisii,** who settled on the Ile de la Cité in the third century B.C. Paris has often played a central role in the political and cultural evolution of France. In 250 A.D., Saint Denis, the patron saint of France, was martyred there. In 451, Sainte Geneviève, the patron saint of Paris, caused Attila and his Huns to retreat from Paris when a large statue fell on them. The major political events of the French Revolution occurred in Paris in 1789. Today, Paris is an important university center. The **quartier Latin** has been home to many students since the Middle Ages. In the late nineteenth century, Baron Haussmann, working under Emperor Napoléon III, razed many areas of the city and created **les grands boulevards.**

Allez, viens à Paris!

L'avenue des Champs-Elysées et l'Arc de Triomphe

Architecture Link

L'avenue des Champs-Elysées extends from the place de la Concorde to the place Charles-de-Gaulle. In the courtyard of the Louvre museum is the Arc de Triomphe du Carrousel; in the center of the place de la Concorde is the obélisque de Louxor, a stone pillar brought back from Egypt by Napoléon I; at the end of the avenue is the famous Arc de Triomphe. These monuments are all perfectly aligned.

History Link

L'Arc de Triomphe, situated in the middle of the place Charles-de-Gaulle (the former place de l'Etoile) where twelve avenues intersect, was constructed on the orders of Napoléon I. Underneath the Arc is the tomb of the French Unknown Soldier, placed there after World War I.

Paris

Capitale de la France

Population : plus de 2.150.000; région parisienne : plus de 10.000.000

Points d'intérêt : la tour Eiffel, l'Arc de Triomphe, la cathédrale de Notre-Dame, le centre Georges Pompidou, la basilique du Sacré-Cœur

Musées : l'Orangerie, le musée du Louvre, le musée d'Orsay, le musée de l'Homme, le musée Rodin

Parcs et jardins : le jardin du Luxembourg, le Champ-de-Mars, le jardin des Tuileries

Parisiens célèbres : Charles Baudelaire, Colette, Victor Hugo, Edith Piaf, Auguste Rodin, Jean-Paul Sartre

Industries : haute couture, finance, technologie, transport, tourisme

cent vingt et un **121**

𝒰sing the Almanac and Map

Terms in the Almanac

- **La tour Eiffel,** built by Gustave Eiffel for the Exposition Universelle of 1889, was the tallest structure in the world at the time.
- **La cathédrale de Notre-Dame** was begun in 1163.
- **Le centre Georges Pompidou,** finished in 1977, is also known as **Beaubourg.** It contains the Museum of Modern Art of Paris.
- **La basilique du Sacré-Cœur,** built between 1876 and 1914, is located on Montmartre, the highest point in Paris.
- **Le musée du Louvre,** the largest museum in the world, houses such works as the *Mona Lisa* (**La Joconde**) and the *Venus de Milo.*
- **Le musée d'Orsay,** formerly a train station, was turned into a museum in 1986, and is devoted to sculpture, painting, and architecture of the nineteenth century.
- **Le musée Rodin** houses many of Rodin's most famous sculptures, including *Le penseur* and *Les bourgeois de Calais.*
- **Le jardin du Luxembourg** is a famous Parisian park.
- **Le jardin des Tuileries** is a park **à l'italienne** with fountains and sculptures.
- **Charles Baudelaire** (1821–1867), a poet in the romantic tradition, was also an art critic. His most famous work was *Les fleurs du mal.*
- **Colette** (1873–1954) was a famous novelist.
- **Victor Hugo** (1802–1885) See page 2 in the Preliminary Chapter.
- **Edith Piaf** (1915–1963) was a singer famous for her heartrending songs.
- **Jean-Paul Sartre** (1905–1980), philosopher, novelist, and playwright, was a proponent of existentialism.

Art Link

Have students research various French artists (David, Monet, Manet, Degas, Rodin, Matisse, Renoir, Chagall) or artists who worked in France (Van Gogh and Picasso).

Using the Map

Have students look at the map and try to determine why Paris was an important crossroads throughout history.

History Link

Even though Paris has long been the center of politics and government, **Notre-Dame** was not the scene of royal coronations or funerals. Kings of France were crowned in the cathedral in Reims where Clovis, the first Christian king of France, was baptized. Many of the French kings are buried in the basilica of Saint-Denis, just north of Paris.

Using the Photo Essay

① **Le centre Georges Pompidou,** a museum named after the second president of the Fifth Republic, offers a splendid view of Paris. The upper floors are reached via escalators encased in glass tubes that allow visitors to look out over Paris as they ascend. The public square in front of the museum is always bustling with all kinds of entertainment, from magicians, to fire eaters, to mimes.

② **Montmartre** is the highest point in Paris. Many of its steep, narrow streets end in staircases. Both Sacré-Cœur and Saint-Pierre-de-Montmartre, one of the earliest Gothic churches, are located in Montmartre. There is some disagreement about how the name **Montmartre** originated. Some speculate that it came from the *mount of Mars,* a Roman temple that stood on top of the hill. Others say it means *mount of martyrs,* referring to the site of the execution of Saint Denis, the first bishop of Paris.

③ Each **bouquiniste** has a green metal box permanently affixed to the stone wall along the Seine. When the **bouquinistes** are not there, their wares are locked inside the box.

Paris

Paris is a city that has no equal. It is the intellectual and cultural capital of the French-speaking world and also the largest city in Europe, if you include the greater Parisian area. Whether you like to visit museums, go to the theater, sit in cafés, or stroll along tree-lined boulevards, there's something for everyone here. Paris is one of the world's most beautiful and exciting cities!

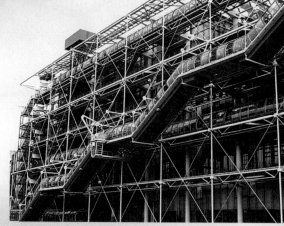

① **Le centre Georges Pompidou** houses a major library and the National Museum of Modern Art. Outside, you can see jugglers, magicians, and all kinds of entertainers. It is one of Paris' most popular tourist attractions.

② Many of the streets in the **Montmartre** district are lined with artists who sell their works and will even paint your portrait.

③ In the shadow of **la cathédrale de Notre-Dame,** booksellers, called **bouquinistes,** sell rare books and posters along the banks of the river Seine.

Architecture Link

① The structure of the **centre Georges Pompidou,** because of its skeletal design of pipes and tubes, has often been the subject of both amusement and controversy for Parisians, who refer to it as "the refinery." In reality, the pipes and tubes are quite functional, as they serve as casing for the heating, air-conditioning, electrical, and telephone conduits.

Culture Note

③ Efforts were made in the past to limit or reduce the number of **bouquinistes** along the Seine. However, the public outcry was so great that the project was abandoned, and these traditional fixtures remain along the banks of the Seine.

④ In Paris, the terrace of a café is a wonderful place to sit and watch the world go by.

⑤ **La tour Eiffel** was erected as a temporary exhibit for the Centennial Exposition in 1889 and has been the object of controversy ever since. It is 320.75 meters tall, including the television antenna added in 1956. To reach the top platform, ride one of the hydraulic elevators or climb the 1,792 stairs!

⑥ The Paris subway, **le métro,** is one of the world's most efficient mass-transit systems.

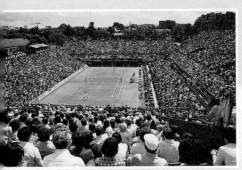

⑦ **Le stade Roland-Garros** is the site of the French Open, one of the grand-slam tennis tournaments.

④ Paris is full of sidewalk cafés, some of which date from the eighteenth century. The most famous, in addition to **Les Deux Magots,** include the nearby **Café Flore** and the **Café Procope,** frequented by Voltaire in the eighteenth century.

⑤ Among the many illuminated monuments in Paris is **la tour Eiffel.** Until 1986, it was illuminated by giant projectors located on the ground. In 1986, lights were installed on the tower itself. These lights give the tower greater depth, making it look like a jewel.

⑥ The Paris **métro** began service with the Vincennes-Maillot line in 1900, several years after both the London and New York subways. Today, there are 13 lines with over 350 stations. Each day the **métro,** run by the **RATP (Réseau Autonome des Transports Parisiens),** carries over 4.5 million passengers. The system extends to the suburbs with four **RER (Réseau Express Régional)** lines. **RER** trains are slightly larger than **métro** trains, and outside the city limits, they travel above ground.

Teaching Suggestion

⑥ Using a map of the Paris **métro,** have students look at the names of the **métro** stations and try to determine which are named after people, which after events, and which after places in Paris. Ask students if they know why the names of so many lines include the word **porte,** such as **Porte de Clignancourt** and **Porte d'Orléans.** (In the Middle Ages, Paris was a walled city whose gates were closed at dusk. Gates **(portes)** were located around the city and named. As the city grew, the wall was extended several times.)

Culture Notes

⑥ French transportation systems are among the best in the world. A network of **autoroutes** crisscrosses the country. The **TGV (Train à Grande Vitesse)** and other trains run by the **SNCF (Société Nationale de Chemins de Fer)** reach every corner of France. In addition, the Paris **métro** is the envy of the world. French firms also have designed and built subways in Cairo and Mexico City.

⑦ **Roland Garros** was a famous French aviator who, in 1913, was the first to successfully cross the Mediterranean.

Chapitre 5 : On va au café?
Chapter Overview

Mise en train pp. 126–128	Qu'est-ce qu'on prend?		Practice and Activity Book, p. 49		Video Guide OR Videodisc Guide

	FUNCTIONS	**GRAMMAR**	**CULTURE**	**RE-ENTRY**
Première étape pp. 129–134	• Making suggestions, p. 129 • Making excuses, p. 129 • Making a recommendation, p. 132	The verb **prendre**, p. 133	**Panorama Culturel**, Food served in a café, p. 134	Accepting and turning down a suggestion
Deuxième étape pp. 135–137	• Getting someone's attention, p. 135 • Ordering food and beverages, p. 135	The imperative, p. 136	• Realia: Menu from **Pomme de Pain**, p. 136 • **Note Culturelle**, Waitpersons as professionals, p. 137 • Realia: Menu from **La Crêperie Normande**, p. 137	Making and turning down a suggestion
Troisième étape pp. 138–141	• Inquiring about and expressing likes and dislikes, p. 138 • Paying the check, p. 139		• **Note Culturelle, La litote**, p. 138 • **Note Culturelle**, Tipping, p. 140 • Realia: Café bill, p. 140 • Realia: Menu from **Café Sport**, p. 140	• Expressing likes and dislikes • Numbers 20–100

Prononciation p. 141	The nasal sound [ɑ̃]		**Dictation:** *Textbook Audiocassette 3A/Audio CD 5*

Lisons! pp. 142–143	French menus		**Reading Strategy:** Using what you already know

Review pp. 144–147	**Mise en pratique**, pp. 144–145	**Que sais-je?** p. 146	**Vocabulaire**, p. 147

Assessment Options

Etape Quizzes
• *Chapter Teaching Resources, Book 2*
  Première étape, Quiz 5-1, pp. 23–24
  Deuxième étape, Quiz 5-2, pp. 25–26
  Troisième étape, Quiz 5-3, pp. 27–28
• *Assessment Items, Audiocassette 7B/Audio CD 5*

Chapter Test
• *Chapter Teaching Resources, Book 2*, pp. 29–34
• *Assessment Guide*, Speaking Test, p. 30
• *Assessment Items, Audiocassette 7B/Audio CD 5*

Test Generator, Chapter 5

Video Program OR Expanded Video Program, Videocassette 2
OR Videodisc Program, Videodisc 3A

Textbook Audiocassette 3A/Audio CD 5

RESOURCES: Print

RESOURCES: Audiovisual

Textbook Audiocassette 3A/Audio CD 5

Practice and Activity Book, pp. 50–52
Chapter Teaching Resources, Book 2
• Teaching Transparency Master 5-1, pp. 7, 10. . . . . Teaching Transparency 5-1
• Additional Listening Activities 5-1, 5-2, p. 11 . . . . Additional Listening Activities, Audiocassette 9B/Audio CD 5
• Realia 5-1, pp. 15, 17
• Situation Cards 5-1, pp. 18–19
• Student Response Forms, pp. 20–22
• Quiz 5-1, pp. 23–24. . . . . Assessment Items, Audiocassette 7B/Audio CD 5
Video Guide. . . . . Video Program OR Expanded Video Program, Videocassette 2
Videodisc Guide. . . . . Videodisc Program, Videodisc 3A

Textbook Audiocassette 3A/Audio CD 5

Practice and Activity Book, pp. 53–55
Chapter Teaching Resources, Book 2
• Communicative Activity 5-1, pp. 3–4
• Teaching Transparency Master 5-2, pp. 8, 10. . . . . Teaching Transparency 5-2
• Additional Listening Activities 5-3, 5-4, p. 12 . . . . Additional Listening Activities Audiocassette 9B/Audio CD 5
• Realia 5-2, pp. 16, 17
• Situation Cards 5-2, pp. 18–19
• Student Response Forms, pp. 20–22
• Quiz 5-2, pp. 25–26. . . . . Assessment Items Audiocassette 7B/Audio CD 5
Videodisc Guide. . . . . Videodisc Program, Videodisc 3A

Textbook Audiocassette 3A/Audio CD 5

Practice and Activity Book, pp. 56–58
Chapter Teaching Resources, Book 2
• Communicative Activity 5-2, pp. 5–6
• Teaching Transparency Master 5-3, pp. 9, 10. . . . . Teaching Transparency 5-3
• Additional Listening Activities 5-5, 5-6, p. 13 . . . . Additional Listening Activities, Audiocassette 9B/Audio CD 5
• Realia 5-2, pp. 16, 17
• Situation Cards 5-3, pp. 18–19
• Student Response Forms, pp. 20–22
• Quiz 5-3, pp. 27–28. . . . . Assessment Items, Audiocassette 7B/Audio CD 5
Videodisc Guide. . . . . Videodisc Program, Videodisc 3A

Practice and Activity Book, p. 59

Video Guide. . . . . Video Program OR Expanded Video Program, Videocassette 2
Videodisc Guide. . . . . Videodisc Program, Videodisc 3A

Alternative Assessment
• Performance Assessment
  Première étape, p. 133
  Deuxième étape, p. 137
  Troisième étape, p. 141
• Portfolio Assessment
  Written: Activity 24, Pupil's Edition, p. 139
    Assessment Guide, p. 18
  Oral: **Mise en pratique,** Activity 2, Pupil's Edition, p. 144
    Assessment Guide, p. 18

Chapitre 5 : On va au café?
Textbook Listening Activities Scripts

For Student Response Forms, see *Chapter Teaching Resources, Book 2,* pp. 20–22.

Première étape

6 Ecoute! p. 129

1. — On va au café?
   — Oui, allons-y!
2. — On fait du jogging?
   — Ça ne me dit rien.
3. — On écoute de la musique?
   — Oui, d'accord. C'est une bonne idée.
4. — On joue au basket?
   — Je ne peux pas. J'ai des devoirs à faire.
5. — On fait des photos?
   — Désolé, mais j'ai des courses à faire.

Answers to Activity 6
1. accepts
2. turns down
3. accepts
4. turns down
5. turns down

9 Ecoute! p. 132

1. Moi, je voudrais une pizza et un coca, s'il vous plaît.
2. Un croque-monsieur, s'il vous plaît.
3. Je voudrais un jus de fruit.
4. Et moi, je vais prendre un steak-frites, s'il vous plaît.
5. Un sandwich au fromage pour moi.

Answers to Activity 9
1. Paul
2. Minh
3. Didier
4. Mamadou
5. Nabil

Deuxième étape

14 Ecoute! p. 135

1. Je vais prendre un steak-frites, s'il vous plaît.
2. Vous avez choisi?
3. Donnez-moi un croque-monsieur, s'il vous plaît.
4. Qu'est-ce que vous avez comme sandwiches?
5. Vous prenez?
6. Apportez-moi un jus de pomme, s'il vous plaît.

Answers to Activity 14
1. customer
2. server
3. customer
4. customer
5. server
6. customer

Troisième étape

21 Ecoute! p. 138

1. Cette pizza, elle n'est pas très bonne.
2. La glace au chocolat, c'est délicieux!
3. Il n'est pas terrible, ce hot-dog.
4. Ne mange pas ça! C'est dégoûtant!
5. Il est bon, ce croque-monsieur.

Answers to Activity 21
1. dislikes
2. likes
3. dislikes
4. dislikes
5. likes

25 Ecoute! p. 139

1. Apportez-moi un coca, s'il vous plaît.
2. L'addition, s'il vous plaît.
3. Je vais prendre un jus de pomme, s'il vous plaît.
4. Ça fait combien, s'il vous plaît?
5. Donnez-moi une limonade, s'il vous plaît.

Answers to Activity 25
1. ordering
2. getting ready to pay the check
3. ordering
4. getting ready to pay the check
5. ordering

Prononciation, p. 141

For the scripts for Parts A and B, see p. 141.

C. A écrire

(Dictation)

— Ça fait combien, un jus d'orange et un sandwich?
— Soixante francs.

Mise en pratique

1 p. 144

1. — Michel, on prend un sandwich?
   — D'accord. Je voudrais un sandwich au jambon et de l'eau minérale.
2. — Je vais prendre une pizza.
   — Moi aussi.
3. — Vous avez choisi?
   — Apportez-moi un steak-frites et un coca, s'il vous plaît.
4. — Je voudrais une coupe melba.
   — Bonne idée.

Answers to Mise en pratique Activity 1
1. Café de la gare
2. Café Américain
3. Café Américain
4. Café de Paris

Chapitre 5 : On va au café?
Projects

Notre café
(Cooperative Learning Project)

ASSIGNMENT
Have groups of three or four students design a menu for a café they will open.

MATERIALS
✂ **Students may need**
- Construction paper
- Markers or colored pencils
- Magazines
- Tape or glue
- Scissors

SUGGESTED SEQUENCE

Prewriting Students should come up with ideas for their café, including the theme or style of the café and the price range. One student should write down the different ideas; the group should then decide which ideas to follow.

First Draft Different tasks should be assigned to individual group members: writing down menu items, designing the menu, editing, and choosing appropriate prices in francs for each item.

Peer Editing Have students check one another's work. Are there enough items for the menu? Do the items have reasonable and consistent prices? Is the spelling correct, and are the items in the correct section of the menu? Is the menu design attractive, and does it reflect the restaurant's style?

Final Draft Students should add their parts to the menu and complete it with any illustrations or graphics according to the design. They should also check for any mistakes before handing it in.

GRADING THE PROJECT
You might base students' grades on the following: content, attractive menu design, accurate spelling and placement of items on the menu, and participation.

Suggested Point Distribution (total = 100 points)

Content	25 points
Menu design	25 points
Spelling/placement of items	25 points
Participation	25 points

TEACHING SUGGESTION
These menus might be displayed in the classroom and/or used in skits or for reading comprehension.

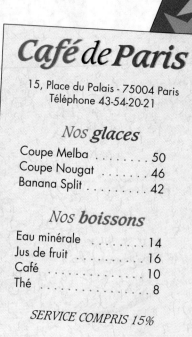

JETER ET ATTRAPER

This game will help students review vocabulary from this chapter and from previous chapters. It is recommended at the end of the first étape.

Procedure   List various categories (food, drink, activities, the infinitive of a particular verb, and so on) on the board or on a transparency. Call out a category and toss a ball or other soft object to a student. The student must catch the ball and name an appropriate item in that category within three seconds. Then, that student will call out a category and toss the ball to another student. The game continues in this manner. You can vary the game by having students conjugate verbs as you call out the subject pronoun and the infinitive, count by threes, and so on. Keep the game moving as quickly as possible. You might choose to start the game with all students standing, having any students who do not respond correctly sit down and monitor the others.

JEU DE CONCOURS

This game will help students review questions in a variety of categories.

Procedure   Draw a game grid on the board, on a transparency, or on a large sheet of paper hanging on the wall. The grid should have six columns, each labeled with a category and five boxes below it containing numbers from 100–500. Divide the class into two or three teams. After deciding the order of play, have one player from the first team choose a category and a numerical value (Ordering, 200). Then, have the player give the French expression appropriate to the category. **(La carte, s'il vous plaît.)** If the player answers correctly, the box is crossed out, and the team receives the given number of points. If the player answers incorrectly, the other team will have the opportunity to answer the question. You might want to have one student keep score and mark off boxes and another student act as an impartial judge in cases where an answer is close or mispronounced. The game grid below can be used or modified for this chapter.

Example:

Suggestions/ Excuses	Menu	Prendre	Ordering	Commands	Potpourri
100 play basketball	100 coffee	100 je	100 get attention	100 watch a film	100 homework
200 go jogging	200 steak & fries	200 elle	200 ask for menu	200 play soccer	200 yummy
300 I have homework	300 hot chocolate	300 nous	300 ask for check	300 do sports	300 how much
400 I have errands to do	400 apple juice	400 vous	400 ask for hot dog	400 have a sandwich	400 gross
500 I have things to do	500 grilled ham & cheese	500 ils	500 ask for types of drinks	500 bring me	500 to be hungry and thirsty

Chapitre 5
On va au café?
pp. 124–147

𝒰sing the Chapter Opener

Motivating Activity

Ask students if they ever eat out with friends, where they go, and what they consider when choosing a place to go. Ask students if they have any preconceptions about French cafés and if they can imagine going there and enjoying themselves.

Photo Flash!

① This photo shows **Les Deux Magots,** a famous café in Paris. In the 1950s, intellectuals such as Simone de Beauvoir and Jean-Paul Sartre frequented this café to discuss current events and philosophy and even to do some of their writing.

Teaching Suggestion

Ask students if there are any restaurants in their town that have both indoor and outdoor seating. Do many people choose to eat outside? Ask students what factors they consider when deciding whether to eat inside or outside. Ask if they have a preference and why.

CHAPITRE

5
On va au café?

① On va au café?

124 *cent vingt-quatre*

Where are your favorite places to meet and relax with your friends? In France, people of all ages meet at cafés to talk, have a snack, or just watch the people go by!

In this chapter you will learn

- to make suggestions; to make excuses; to make a recommendation
- to get someone's attention; to order food and beverages
- to inquire about and express likes and dislikes; to pay the check

And you will

- listen to people ordering in a café
- read a café menu
- write about your food and drink preferences
- find out about French cafés

② Miam, miam! Je vais prendre un croque-monsieur.

③ L'addition, s'il vous plaît.

Focusing on Outcomes

After reading the list of outcomes with students, have them look at the photo captions. Then, have students point out which outcomes are illustrated in the photos. Can students imagine how the functions could be used in a café setting? NOTE: You may want to use the video to support the objectives. The self-check activities in **Que sais-je?** on page 146 help students assess their achievement of the objectives.

Photo Flash!

② A waiter is about to serve a **croque-monsieur,** a grilled cheese and ham sandwich that is often served open-faced. There is also a **croque-madame,** which is a **croque-monsieur** topped with a fried egg. Point out that **Miam, miam!** is an expression that means *Yum-yum.*

VIDEO PROGRAM OR EXPANDED VIDEO PROGRAM, Videocassette 2 25:15–28:30

OR VIDEODISC PROGRAM, Videodisc 3A

Search 4660, Play To 10515

Video Synopsis

In this segment of the video, Simon, Isabelle, Thuy, and Mathieu are together, and Simon suggests that they go to a café. Mathieu is busy and makes an excuse. At the café, they ask for a menu and discuss what they will have. When the waiter arrives, Simon and Thuy order right away. Isabelle has trouble deciding, but finally orders a croque-monsieur. When they've finished their snack, Simon asks for the check. Isabelle discovers that she can't find her wallet. When the waiter brings the check, they don't know what to do.

Motivating Activity

Ask students where the teenagers are and why. You might also ask students where they go for a snack or to people-watch.

Teaching Suggestion

You might have students read the questions in Activity 1 on page 128 to prepare them for viewing the video or reading the story.

Mise en train

 Qu'est-ce qu'on prend?

Where does this story take place? What are the people doing? Why do you think they look upset at the end?

Simon

Thuy

Isabelle

Mathieu

LA CARTE

CAFE	8 F
CHOCOLAT	10 F
JUS DE FRUIT	13 F
COCA	14
LIMONADE	11
SANDWICH	16
HOT-DOG	17
GLACE	12 F

SERVICE ◆ COMPRIS

126 *cent vingt-six*

CHAPITRE 5   On va au café?

RESOURCES FOR MISE EN TRAIN

Textbook Audiocassette 3A/Audio CD 5
Practice and Activity Book, p. 49
Video Guide
    Video Program
    Expanded Video Program, Videocassette 2
Videodisc Guide
    Videodisc Program, Videodisc 3A

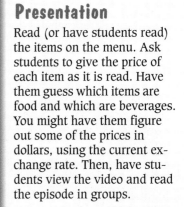

Presentation

Read (or have students read) the items on the menu. Ask students to give the price of each item as it is read. Have them guess which items are food and which are beverages. You might have them figure out some of the prices in dollars, using the current exchange rate. Then, have students view the video and read the episode in groups.

Teaching Suggestions

• Say a line from **Qu'est-ce qu'on prend?**, such as **Parfait. C'est tout?** and have students give the line that follows it. (**Non... une coupe melba aussi pour moi, s'il vous plaît.**) You might have the first person to answer choose the next line to read aloud.

• You might also type and distribute copies of the dialogue with some of the words deleted. Have students work in pairs to complete the dialogue. You might give a small prize to the pair that finishes first.

MISE EN TRAIN *cent vingt-sept* **127**

Video Integration

• ***Expanded Video Program,***
  Videocassette 2, 28:31–32:31
• ***Videodisc Program,***
  Videodisc 3A

Search 10515, Play To 17750

You may choose to continue with **Qu'est-ce qu'on prend? (suite)** or wait until later in the chapter. When the story continues, Simon, Thuy, and Isabelle see that they need six francs more to pay the bill. Then, they learn that they have been given the bill for another table. They need even more money for their own! As they try to figure out what to do, some tourists start a conversation with them. When the tourists learn of the situation, they insist on paying the difference. As Simon, Thuy, and Isabelle are leaving, Isabelle finds her wallet on the ground.

For Individual Needs

2 Slower Pace Have students first look for cognates in the activity title and the sentences in this activity (**en ordre, commande, propose**).

Teaching Suggestions

2 As a variation, make the actual remarks that are paraphrased here (**Apportez-moi une menthe à l'eau, s'il vous plaît.**) and have students choose the correct paraphrase. (**Thuy commande une menthe à l'eau.**)

3 You might choose to have students work in pairs, taking turns asking a question and finding an appropriate response.

For videodisc application, see *Videodisc Guide.*

5 Have students explain the embarrassing situation. Ask them to suggest solutions to the problem. If students can't think of a personal embarrassing situation, they might find one in the comics in the local newspaper to describe.

1 Tu as compris? See answers below.

1. What is the relationship between the teenagers in **Qu'est-ce qu'on prend?**
2. Where are they at the beginning of the story?
3. Where do they decide to go?
4. What does each person order?
5. Who has trouble deciding what to order?
6. What is the problem at the end of the story?

2 Mets en ordre

Mets les phrases suivantes en ordre d'après **Qu'est-ce qu'on prend?**

1. Thuy commande une menthe à l'eau.   2
2. Simon demande l'addition.   4
3. Simon propose à Isabelle, Thuy et Mathieu d'aller au café.   1
4. Isabelle ne retrouve pas son argent.   5
5. Le serveur apporte l'addition.   6
6. Isabelle commande un jus d'orange.   3

3 Les deux font la paire

Choisis la bonne réponse, d'après **Qu'est-ce qu'on prend?**

1. On va au café?   c
2. Qu'est-ce que vous prenez?   b
3. C'est combien, un croque-monsieur?   d
4. Vous avez des pizzas?   e
5. Qu'est-ce que vous avez comme jus de fruit?   a

a. Nous avons du jus d'orange, du jus de pomme...
b. Je vais prendre une menthe à l'eau.
c. Désolé. J'ai des devoirs à faire.
d. Vingt-deux francs.
e. Non, je regrette.

4 Cherche les expressions

Look back at **Qu'est-ce qu'on prend?** What do the students say to . . .

1. suggest that everyone go to the café?   On va au café?
2. give an excuse?   Désolé. J'ai des devoirs à faire.
3. ask what someone's going to order?   Qu'est-ce que vous prenez?
4. order food?   Je vais prendre... ; Apportez-moi...
5. ask what kind of fruit juice the restaurant serves?   Qu'est-ce que vous avez comme jus de fruit?
6. ask how much something costs?   C'est combien,... ?
7. ask for the check?   L'addition, s'il vous plaît.

5 Et maintenant, à toi

Isabelle is in an embarrassing situation. What is she going to do? Have you or has someone you know ever been in a similar situation? Take turns with a partner sharing these experiences.

128 *cent vingt-huit*   CHAPITRE 5   On va au café?

PREMIERE ÉTAPE

Making suggestions; making excuses; making a recommendation

COMMENT DIT-ON... ?
Making suggestions; making excuses

To make suggestions:

On va au café? *How about going to the café?*
On fait du ski?
On joue au base-ball?

To make excuses:

Désolé(e). J'ai des devoirs à faire. *Sorry. I have homework to do.*
J'ai des courses à faire. *I have errands to do.*
J'ai des trucs à faire. *I have some things to do.*
J'ai des tas de choses à faire. *I have lots of things to do.*

6 Écoute!

Listen to the following dialogues. Do the speakers accept or turn down the suggestions?

Answers on p. 123C.

Jump Start!

Have students write whether they like or dislike the following foods: **le chocolat, la glace, les escargots, les hamburgers, les frites, la pizza.**

MOTIVATE

Ask students which French foods they have heard of or eaten. Ask them to suggest French words we use to talk about food (**purée, à la mode, sautée, entrée**).

TEACH

Presentation

Comment dit-on... ?   To begin, have students close their books. Have three students rehearse the first question and the two different responses in the illustration and model them for the class. Ask the others which student is going to the café and which one isn't and why. Ask them how they know. Then, suggest activities to students (**On fait les devoirs?**), prompting various excuses. Write activities on the board or on a transparency, or display pictures of them, and have pairs of students use them to make suggestions and respond with excuses.

For videodisc application, see *Videodisc Guide.*

For Individual Needs

6 Slower Pace   Before students listen to the recording, have them practice distinguishing acceptance from refusal. Say aloud several expressions (**D'accord. Bonne idée. Ça ne me dit rien.**) and tell students to gesture thumbs up if they hear an acceptance and thumbs down if they hear a refusal.

Building on Previous Skills

7 Have students recall or look up expressions for accepting and refusing from previous chapters. (Examples include **C'est le fun! Allons-y! Oui, c'est génial/super/passionnant. Non, c'est barbant/zéro/nul.**)

Teaching Suggestion

8 Have students exchange papers and edit each other's work. They should not make any corrections, but simply underline whatever is incorrect and return the papers. Students should then make their own corrections and rewrite their note.

Portfolio

8 Written This item is appropriate for students' written portfolios. For portfolio information, see *Assessment Guide,* pages 2–13.

Tu te rappelles ?

Do you remember the following ways to accept a suggestion?

D'accord.
Bonne idée.

Do you remember the following ways to turn down a suggestion?

Ça ne me dit rien. J'aime mieux…
Désolé(e), mais je ne peux pas.

7 Qu'est-ce qu'on fait?

Suggest that your friends do these activities with you after class. They will either accept or turn down your suggestions and make excuses. Then, accept or decline their suggestions.

—On… ?
—D'accord,… *or* Désolé(e),…

1. On va au café?

2. On joue au football?

3. On regarde la télévision?

4. On écoute de la musique?

5. On va au concert?

8 Un petit mot

You and your friend have agreed to go to the café on Saturday. You can't make it. Write your friend a note saying that you can't go, make an excuse, and suggest another activity at another time.

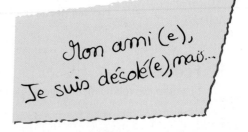

Mon ami(e),
Je suis désolé(e), mais…

130   *cent trente*   CHAPITRE 5   On va au café?

Language Notes

• The term **trucs** (used in **Comment dit-on… ?** on page 129) is slang and very commonly used. Students can use **truc(s)** when they don't know the word for something: **J'aime bien ces trucs.** *(I like these things.)*; **Tu as vu ce truc-là?** *(Did you see that thingama-jig over there?)*. Ask them what they say in English in this situation.

8 Ask students why they think **désolé** is sometimes spelled with an extra **-e**. Tell them that because it is an adjective, the spelling depends on the gender of the speaker. Point out that the pronunciation doesn't change, however.

VOCABULAIRE

Presentation

Vocabulaire If possible, collect containers of the beverages shown in the illustration. If not, draw or paste pictures of the containers on large file cards. Present the terms for the drinks first. Say **J'ai soif** aloud with appropriate gestures to get the meaning across. Then say **Je voudrais...**, showing a container and naming the beverage. Repeat this with the food items, using pictures, drawings, toys, or the real thing. You might also have students review other forms of the verb **avoir** by asking you if you are hungry or thirsty and then asking their classmates.

Cooperative Learning

After students practice the vocabulary orally, you might want to have them work in groups of four or five to role-play a restaurant scene. One student is the server, one is the chef, and the others are the customers. The customers give their orders to the server who writes them down. The server then goes to the chef and reads aloud the orders. The chef draws (or writes down) the items, while repeating the orders aloud. Finally, the server "serves" the customers, restating each person's order. At this point, limit the ordering to the use of **Je voudrais**. Additional means of ordering will be introduced in the **Deuxième étape**.

Language Notes

• If students ask how to say *lemonade,* it is **une citronnade,** not **une limonade.**
• Slang terms for *to eat* and *food* are **bouffer** and **la bouffe.** The slang term for *water* is **la flotte.**
• Make sure students don't pronounce the final **-m** of **faim.** Ask if they can think of an English word related to **faim** *(famished).*

Culture Notes

In France, milk is generally not drunk at meals. Coffee is generally taken black after large meals. At breakfast, people might have **café au lait** in a bowl (**un bol de café**).
• You might want to let students know that most café sandwiches are made on pieces of **baguettes.**

For Individual Needs

9 Slower Pace Have students identify in French the food shown in the thought bubbles. Stop the recording after each person orders and have students write or say the name of the boy who is ordering.

Teaching Suggestion

9 Have students write or say **Il a faim** or **Il a soif,** as appropriate for each of the boys.

For Individual Needs

11 Challenge Students may want to use dictionaries or books on food to help them create a longer list. You might also refer students to the Supplementary Vocabulary on page 342 for additional food-related vocabulary. Students might consult with friends in German, Spanish, and other foreign language classes to learn the names of other cultural dishes to make the fair truly international. They might also learn simple greetings in these languages, and the classes might all participate in a real international fair at school.

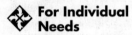

Presentation

Comment dit-on... ? Hold up pictures of various food and drink items and prompt students to recommend them to you. Then, place various food and drink items or pictures of them on a table and recommend them to students. Students should pick up the item or picture you recommend.

---

9 **Ecoute!**

Look at the picture. As the boys tell the waiter what they would like, decide which boy is ordering. *Answers on p. 123C.*

Didier   Minh   Paul   Mamadou   Nabil

10 **Vous désirez?**

Now, take the role of the server in Activity 9. Write down each boy's order. *See answers below.*

11 **La fête internationale**

Your French class is going to participate in an international food fair at school. Make a list of some of the foods and drinks you'd like to serve.

COMMENT DIT-ON... ?
Making a recommendation

To recommend something to eat or drink:
   Prends une limonade. (informal) *Have . . .*
   Prenez un sandwich. (formal) *Have . . .*

132   *cent trente-deux*   CHAPITRE 5   On va au café?

Multicultural Link

11 You might also expand this into a project, with student groups reporting on and even making dishes from different francophone regions. They might present their report to the class in the form of a poster or collage.

Answers
10 Paul: une pizza et un coca
   Minh: un croque-monsieur
   Didier: un jus de fruit
   Mamadou: un steak-frites
   Nabil: un sandwich au fromage

Grammaire The verb **prendre**

Prendre is an irregular verb.

prendre *(to take; to have food or drink)*

Je **prends** ⎫	Nous **prenons** ⎫
Tu **prends** ⎬ des frites.	Vous **prenez** ⎬ un croque-monsieur.
Il/Elle/On **prend** ⎭	Ils/Elles **prennent** ⎭

12 Qu'est-ce qu'ils prennent?

Paul Julie Sandrine Eric Michel Fabienne

Michel : un steak-frites
Paul et Julie : un sandwich
Sandrine et Eric : un hot-dog
Fabienne : une eau minérale

13 Qu'est-ce que je vais prendre?

You and your friends are deciding what to order in a café. Tell one another whether you are hungry or thirsty. Then, recommend something to eat or drink.

—Moi, j'ai très faim.
—Prends un sandwich.
—D'accord! Bonne idée.

or

—Non, je voudrais un croque-monsieur.

De bons conseils

Resist the temptation to match English with French word-for-word. In many cases, it doesn't work. For example, in English you say *I am hungry,* while in French you say **J'ai faim** (literally, *I have hunger*).

PREMIERE ETAPE *cent trente-trois* **133**

PREMIERE ETAPE
CHAPITRE 5

Presentation

Grammaire Introduce the singular forms of **prendre** first, asking students what they notice about the pronunciation (they all sound the same). Then, present the plural forms, making sure students pronounce the **n** sound. Next, say the forms in random order, having students tell whether the form is singular or plural. Finally, give pictures of food (**des frites**) to various students and have the class tell what the students are having (**Ils prennent des frites.**)

Thinking Critically

Synthesizing — De bons conseils Ask students to think of expressions they've learned that can't be matched word for word with an English equivalent. (**Tu t'appelles comment? Tu as quel âge?**)

CLOSE

Have students pair off and take turns recommending five things to eat and telling why.

ASSESS

Quiz 5-1, *Chapter Teaching Resources, Book 2,* pp. 23–24
Assessment Items, Audiocassette 7B/Audio CD 5

Performance Assessment

On a table, display food or beverage items or pictures of these items. Have two students come up to the table. One asks for an item without pointing to it, saying **Je voudrais...** The other student picks up the correct item and hands it to his or her classmate, saying **Voilà.** Have students take turns asking for items.

Teaching Suggestion

You might want to introduce the **Prononciation** section on page 141 at this time and practice the nasal sound [ã].

Language Note

You might want to have students compare the plural forms of **prendre** to the infinitive. Point out that the **d** of the infinitive does not appear in the plural forms. Point out also that the singular forms are pronounced with the nasal vowel [ã], while the plurals have an **n** sound.

VIDEO PROGRAM OR EXPANDED VIDEO PROGRAM, Videocassette 2 32:32–34:54

OR *VIDEODISC PROGRAM, Videodisc 3A*

Search 17750, Play To 19965

Teacher Notes

- See *Video Guide, Videodisc Guide,* and *Practice and Activity Book* for activities related to the **Panorama Culturel.**
- Remind students that cultural material may be included in the Chapter Quizzes and Test.
- The interviewees' language represents informal, unrehearsed speech. Occasionally, edits have been made for clarification.

Presentation

Have students view the video. To check comprehension, ask the **Questions** below. Then, stop the video after each interview and ask questions 1 and 2 of **Qu'en penses-tu?**

Thinking Critically

Comparing and Contrasting
Have students discuss or make a list of similarities and differences between a fast-food restaurant in the United States and a French café. You might pick a specific local establishment in your area or town to use in the comparison.

Teacher Note

Students may want to know the following words: **baby** (-foot) *(Foosball®, table soccer);* **flipper** *(pinball);* **piscine** *(swimming pool).*

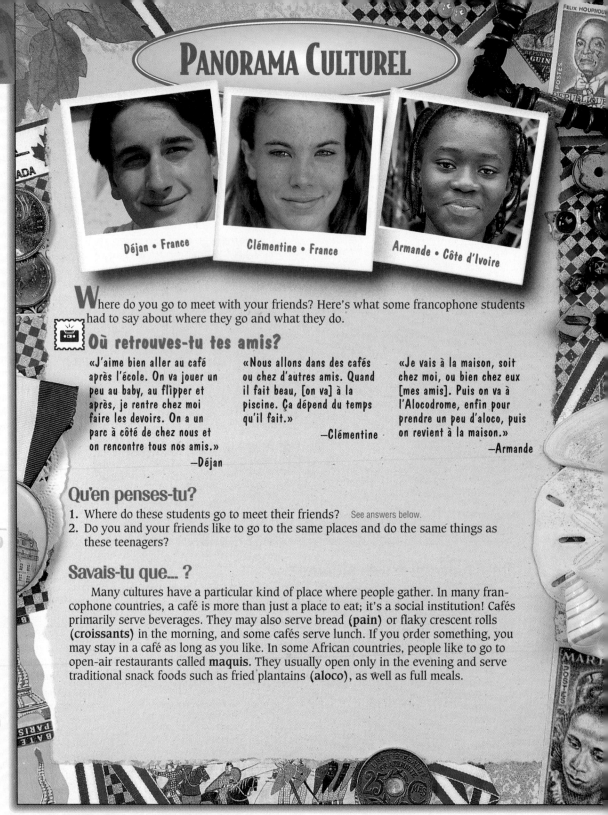

PANORAMA CULTUREL

Déjan • France

Clémentine • France

Armande • Côte d'Ivoire

Where do you go to meet with your friends? Here's what some francophone students had to say about where they go and what they do.

Où retrouves-tu tes amis?

«J'aime bien aller au café après l'école. On va jouer un peu au baby, au flipper et après, je rentre chez moi faire les devoirs. On a un parc à côté de chez nous et on rencontre tous nos amis.»
—Déjan

«Nous allons dans des cafés ou chez d'autres amis. Quand il fait beau, [on va] à la piscine. Ça dépend du temps qu'il fait.»
—Clémentine

«Je vais à la maison, soit chez moi, ou bien chez eux [mes amis]. Puis on va à l'Alocodrome, enfin pour prendre un peu d'aloco, puis on revient à la maison.»
—Armande

Qu'en penses-tu?

1. Where do these students go to meet their friends? See answers below.
2. Do you and your friends like to go to the same places and do the same things as these teenagers?

Savais-tu que... ?

Many cultures have a particular kind of place where people gather. In many francophone countries, a café is more than just a place to eat; it's a social institution! Cafés primarily serve beverages. They may also serve bread **(pain)** or flaky crescent rolls **(croissants)** in the morning, and some cafés serve lunch. If you order something, you may stay in a café as long as you like. In some African countries, people like to go to open-air restaurants called **maquis.** They usually open only in the evening and serve traditional snack foods such as fried plantains **(aloco)**, as well as full meals.

Questions

1. Où est-ce que Déjan va après l'école? (au café) Qu'est-ce qu'il fait là-bas? (jouer au baby et au flipper)
2. Quand est-ce que Clémentine va à la piscine? (quand il fait beau)
3. Qu'est-ce qu'Armande fait à l'Alocodrome? (Elle prend de l'aloco.)

Answers

1. café, park, friends' houses, **Alocodrome**

DEUXIEME ETAPE

Getting someone's attention; ordering food and beverages

COMMENT DIT-ON... ?

Getting someone's attention; ordering food and beverages

To get the server's attention:
Excusez-moi.
Monsieur! Madame! Mademoiselle!
La carte, s'il vous plaît. *The menu, please.*

The server may ask:
Vous avez choisi? *Have you decided/chosen?*
Vous prenez? *What are you having?*

You might want to ask:
Vous avez des jus de fruit?
Qu'est-ce que vous avez comme sandwiches? *What kind of . . . do you have?*
Qu'est-ce que vous avez comme boissons? *What do you have to drink?*

To order:
Je voudrais un hamburger.
Je vais prendre un coca, **s'il vous plaît.** *I'll have . . . , please.*
Un sandwich, **s'il vous plaît.** *. . . , please.*
Donnez-moi un hot-dog, **s'il vous plaît.** *Please give me . . .*
Apportez-moi une limonade, **s'il vous plaît.** *Please bring me . . .*

14 Ecoute!

Listen to these remarks and decide whether the server (**le serveur/la serveuse**) or the customer (**le client/la cliente**) is speaking. *Answers on p. 123C.*

15 Méli-mélo!

Unscramble the following conversation between a server and a customer. Then, act it out with a partner.

—Qu'est-ce que vous avez comme sandwiches? 2
—Bien sûr. 5
—Eh bien, donnez-moi un sandwich au fromage, s'il vous plaît. 4
—Vous avez choisi? 1
—Nous avons des sandwiches au jambon, au saucisson, au fromage... 3

A la française

If you need time to think during a conversation, you can say **Eh bien**... and pause for a moment before you continue speaking.

—Vous prenez, mademoiselle?
—Eh bien... un steak-frites, s'il vous plaît.

At first you'll have to make a conscious effort to do this. The more you practice, the more natural it will become.

DEUXIEME ETAPE

cent trente-cinq **135**

RESOURCES FOR DEUXIEME ETAPE

Textbook Audiocassette 3A/Audio CD 5
Practice and Activity Book, pp. 53–55
Videodisc Guide
  Videodisc Program, Videodisc 3A

Chapter Teaching Resources, Book 2
• Communicative Activity 5-1, pp. 3–4
• Teaching Transparency Master 5-2, pp. 8, 10
  Teaching Transparency 5-2
• Additional Listening Activities 5-3, 5-4, p. 12
  Audiocassette 9B/Audio CD 5
• Realia 5-2, pp. 16, 17
• Situation Cards 5-2, pp. 18–19
• Student Response Forms, pp. 20–22
• Quiz 5-2, pp. 25–26
  Audiocassette 7B/Audio CD 5

On the board or on a transparency, write a list of foods and beverages and several adverbs of frequency. (**quelquefois, souvent, ne... jamais,** and so on). Have students write sentences using the verb **prendre,** telling how often they have each item.

MOTIVATE

Ask students what English words or expressions they might hear in a fast-food restaurant. Ask them what expressions they would need to order something, and what other expressions they might need if they went to a café or restaurant.

TEACH

Presentation

Comment dit-on... ? Have students repeat the expressions after you. Then, play the video or recording of the **Mise en train,** and have students raise their hands whenever they recognize one of the expressions. Play the episode again. This time, have students tell you to stop it when they hear the waiter ask for the order and again when the young people order. Then, take various students' orders by asking **Vous prenez?** You might show a list of food items on a transparency or display vocabulary pictures to prompt students. Finally, have pairs of students practice asking the customer for the order and ordering two different items.

For videodisc application, see *Videodisc Guide.*

16 On prend un sandwich?

You've stopped at a café for lunch. Get the server's attention, look at the menu, and order. Take turns playing the role of the server.

*G*rammaire   The imperative

Did you notice the subject **vous** isn't used in **Donnez-moi...** and **Apportez-moi...** ? When you give a command in French, you leave off the subject pronoun **tu** or **vous,** just as we leave off the subject pronoun *you* in English.

- When you write the **tu** form of an **-er** verb as a command, drop the final **s** of the usual verb ending.

  Tu écoutes... ⟶ **Ecoute!**

  Tu regardes... ⟶ **Regarde!**

- If the verb isn't a regular **-er** verb, the spelling of the command form doesn't change.

  Tu fais... ⟶ **Fais** les devoirs!

  Tu prends... ⟶ **Prends** un hot-dog, Paul!

- Remember to use the **tu** form when you talk with family members and people your own age or younger. Use the **vous** form when you talk with people older than you or with more than one person.

  Prenez un coca, Marc et Eve.

17 Apporte-moi quelque chose!

You and your friends are entertaining a French exchange student at your home. You decide to go out and get something to eat or drink. Ask in French what everyone wants and write down the orders. Read the orders back to verify them.

—Qu'est-ce que tu vas prendre?
—Euh... apporte-moi un hamburger et un coca.   *(later)*
—Tu vas prendre un hamburger, des frites et un coca, c'est ça?
—Oui.

18 Que prendre?

You don't know what to order at the café. The server makes some suggestions for you, but you don't like the suggestions. Take turns playing the server.

—Prenez un sandwich au fromage.
—Non, je n'aime pas le fromage.
—Alors, prenez un sandwich au jambon.
—Non, apportez-moi un hot-dog, s'il vous plaît.

19 A la crêperie

You and some friends get together at a **crêperie** to have some ice cream. Look at the menu and order. Take turns playing the server.

NOTE CULTURELLE

In France, waiters and waitresses are considered professionals. In better restaurants, waiters and waitresses must not only be good servers but they must also be knowledgeable about food and wine. Even in simple restaurants or cafés, servers take great pride in their work. Contrary to what you may have seen in American movies, it is impolite to address a waiter as **Garçon.** It is more polite to say **Monsieur** to a waiter, and **Madame** or **Mademoiselle** to a waitress. It is expected that diners will take time to enjoy their food, so service in French restaurants may seem slow to Americans. It is not uncommon for a meal to last several hours.

La Crêperie Normande

NOS GLACES

Parfait	35
Café ou Chocolat Liégeois	38
Mystère	45
Meringue Royale	55
Meringue - Glace - Chantilly	
Coupe Melba	55
Banana Split	55
Banane - Glace fraise - Noisette - Chantilly	

20 Mon journal

Make a list of the foods and drinks you like to have when you go out with your friends. Then, mention several items you'd try if you were at a café in France.

For Individual Needs

20 Challenge After students make a list, have them give their reactions to some of the items (**J'aime beaucoup...** , **Nous n'aimons pas...** , **Je voudrais...**).

Mon journal

20 For an additional journal entry suggestion for Chapter 5, see *Practice and Activity Book,* page 149.

CLOSE

To close this **étape,** show *Teaching Transparency 5-2* and have students imagine what the people are saying.

ASSESS

Quiz 5-2, *Chapter Teaching Resources, Book 2,* pp. 25–26

Assessment Items, Audiocassette 7B/Audio CD 5

Performance Assessment

Have students form groups of three: two customers and one server. They should enact a scene in a café wherein the customers call the server, ask for the menu, ask the server some questions about the food, and order. The server responds accordingly.

Culture Notes

19 Students may be interested to know that **crêpes** are a specialty of Brittany (**Bretagne**). Traditionally, they are served during **la fête de la chandeleur,** a Christian religious holiday in February celebrating the presentation of Jesus in the temple. **Crêperies** usually serve both dessert and dinner **crêpes** as well as sparkling apple cider.

Note Culturelle Athough the number of cafés is dwindling, the café remains a viable, important institution in French life. In some cafés, you will find pinball machines (**les flippers**), table soccer (**le baby-foot**), and video games (**les jeux vidéo**). Video games may be located in a separate room at the back of the café. Decks of cards and checker games are also available in many cafés.

TROISIEME ETAPE

Inquiring about and expressing likes and dislikes; paying the check

COMMENT DIT-ON... ?
Inquiring about and expressing likes and dislikes

To ask how someone likes the food or drink:
Comment tu trouves ça? *How do you like it?*

To say you like your food/drink:
C'est... *It's . . .*
  bon! *good!*
  excellent! *excellent!*
  délicieux! *delicious!*

To say you don't like your food/drink:
C'est... *It's . . .*
  pas bon. *not very good.*
  pas terrible. *not so great.*
  dégoûtant. *gross.*

21 Ecoute!

Listen to the following remarks. Do the speakers like or dislike the food they've been served? Answers on p. 123D.

NOTE CULTURELLE

French speakers have a tendency to use understatement (**la litote**). For instance, if the food were bad, they might say **C'est pas terrible.** Similarly, rather than saying something is really good, they would say **C'est pas mauvais.**

22 A mon avis...

The school cafeteria is thinking of adding some items to the menu. A poll is being taken among the students. Discuss each of the items below with a partner.

1. 2. 3. 4.

23 Ça, c'est bon

You and your partner are in a café. Ask if your partner has decided what to order and tell what you think of his or her choice.

— Tu as choisi? Qu'est-ce que tu vas prendre?
— Euh... je vais prendre des escargots.
— Les escargots? C'est dégoûtant! *or* Bonne idée. C'est délicieux.

24 Chère correspondante

Your French pen pal Cécile asked you what teenagers in America eat or drink when they get together. Write a brief note in French telling her what you and your friends have when you go out and what you think of it.

COMMENT DIT-ON... ?
Paying the check

Pardon, monsieur.

C'est combien, une limonade?

Onze francs.

To ask for the check:	The server might answer:
L'addition, s'il vous plaît. *The check, please.*	**Oui, tout de suite.** *Yes, right away.*
	Un moment, s'il vous plaît.
To ask how much it is:	
C'est combien, un sandwich?	**C'est** huit **francs.**
Ça fait combien, s'il vous plaît? *How much is it, ... ? (total)*	**Ça fait** cinquante **francs.** *It's ... francs. (total)*

25 Ecoute!

Listen to the following remarks. Are the speakers ordering or getting ready to pay the check? Answers on p. 123D.

Tu te rappelles ?

Here are the numbers from 20–100.

20 **vingt**	50 **cinquante**	80 **quatre-vingts**
30 **trente**	60 **soixante**	90 **quatre-vingt-dix**
40 **quarante**	70 **soixante-dix**	100 **cent**

Culture Note

Most people in France pay for purchases at a café in cash or with personal checks, which are accepted throughout the country. Cafés rarely accept credit cards, but restaurants often take them. It is a good idea to ask before ordering a meal. Many French people pay for their meals at a restaurant with a **Carte Bleue,** a type of debit card that functions much like a bank card.

For videodisc application, see *Videodisc Guide.*

Teaching Suggestion

23 Students will need to practice **Tu as choisi?** before doing this activity. You might have students look at the food items on page 131 or the menus in the **Lisons!** section as they do this activity.

Language Note

24 Remind students that in negative sentences, **de** replaces the indefinite article. (**Nous prenons un sandwich au jambon, mais nous ne prenons jamais de hot-dog.**)

For Individual Needs

24 Slower Pace Before starting this activity, review the food items orally. You might also want to make a list of adverbs of frequency on the board: **souvent, une fois par semaine, quelquefois, ne... jamais.**

Portfolio

24 Written This activity is appropriate for students' written portfolios. You might have students edit one another's note before they write a final draft. For portfolio suggestions, see *Assessment Guide,* page 18.

Presentation

Comment dit-on... ? Ask students to look back at the **Mise en train** or view the video to identify these functions. Then, act out both roles (asking for and paying the check) in front of the class. Act out the dialogue a second time, having students repeat after you. You might have students refer to the menu on page 140 as you ask about the prices of various items. (**C'est combien, un croque-monsieur?**) Finally, have students practice both roles in pairs.

Additional Practice

26 Partners might also use the menu in the **Mise en train** to practice asking and telling each other the price of different items.

Language Note

26 Have students look at the receipt next to Activity 26. Point out that capital letters in French are sometimes printed without accents (**MINERALE, AGREABLE**).

Group Work

27 While students are writing their captions, draw four large columns on the board and number them 1–4. Ask for volunteers to come to the board and write one of their captions in the appropriate column. Then, have students work in small groups to create a story by choosing one caption from each column. See how many logical stories can be told with different captions.

📁 **Portfolio**

28 **Oral** This activity is appropriate for students' oral portfolios. For portfolio information, see *Assessment Guide,* pages 2–13.

NOTE CULTURELLE

In cafés and restaurants, a 15% tip is included in the check if the words **service compris** are posted or written on the menu. If you're not sure, it's acceptable to ask **Le service est compris?** It's customary, however, to leave a little extra if the service is particularly good.

26 **Ça fait combien, chacun?**

You and your friend have just finished eating at a café. Look at the check, tell what you had (**Moi, j'ai pris...**), and figure out how much each of you owes.

—Moi, j'ai pris...
—Ça fait... francs.

27 **Qu'est-ce qu'on dit?**

Write what you think the people in this scene are saying. Then, with a partner, compare what you both have written.

```
        LA GIRAFE
      Port de Cavalaire
      Tél : 94 64 40 31

28-09-96

CROQUE-MONSIEUR  23,00
STEAK-FRITES     29,00
EAU MINERALE      9,00
COCA             14,00

TOTAL            75,00 F

La Direction souhaite
que cet instant de
détente vous ait été
AGREABLE
```

CAFE SPORT

Sandwiches		BOISSONS	
Fromage	15 F	Jus de fruit	13 F
Jambon	19 F	orange, pomme, pamplemousse	
Saucisson	18 F		
Hamburger	22 F	Limonade	11 F
Hot-dog	17 F	Café	8 F
Steak-frites	33 F	Cola	14 F
Croque-monsieur	22 F	Eau minérale	10 F
Pizza	20 F	Chocolat	10 F
Frites	10 F		
Glace	12 F		

28 **Jeu de rôle**

Act out a scene in a café. One student is the server and the others are customers. The customers should get the server's attention, order, comment on the food, and then pay the check.

140   *cent quarante*   CHAPITRE 5   On va au café?

🌐 **Culture Note**

28 Now might be a good time to discuss French table manners: keep both hands above the table (people sometimes rest their wrists on the table edge); keep your fork in your left hand to eat; and avoid eating with your hands (even fries and pizza).

PRONONCIATION

 The nasal sound [ã]

Listen carefully to the vowel sounds in the following words: **ans, en.** These words contain the nasal sound [ã]. It's called a nasal sound because part of the air goes through the back of your mouth and nose when you make the sound. Listen to the English word *sandwich,* and the French **sandwich.** Is the first syllable pronounced the same in the two words? The sound in French is a pure nasal sound, with no trace of the *n* sound in it. In English you say *envy,* but in French you say **envie.** The nasal sound [ã] has four possible spellings: **an, am, en,** and **em.**

These letter combinations don't always represent a nasal sound. If another vowel follows the **n** or the **m,** or if the **n** or **m** is doubled, there may not be a nasal sound. You'll have to learn the pronunciation when you learn the word.

Listen to the following pairs of words and compare the sounds.

Fr*an*ce/*ani*mal pr*en*d/pr*ene*z j*an*b*on*/*ami* *en*vie/*enn*emi

A. A prononcer

Repeat the following words.

en France	attendez	comment	soixante
anglais	dimanche	jambon	temps
orange	tellement	vent	souvent

B. A lire

Take turns with a partner reading the following sentences aloud.

1. Il a cent francs.
2. J'ai un excellent roman allemand.
3. Elle a danse et sciences nat vendredi.
4. Moi, je vais prendre un sandwich au jambon.

C. A écrire

You're going to hear a short dialogue. Write down what you hear. *Answers on p. 123D.*

Teaching Suggestion

Prononciation Write the sentences in Part B on the board or on a transparency. Have students tell you which words contain the nasal sound and circle or underline them. Practice these words first, making sure students pronounce them correctly. Then, have students practice reading the sentences.

CLOSE

To close this **étape,** show *Teaching Transparency 5-3* and have students suggest a dialogue for the first scene, and tell what each person might be saying about his or her food in the second scene.

ASSESS

Quiz 5-3, *Chapter Teaching Resources, Book 2,* pp. 27–28

Assessment Items, Audiocassette 7B/Audio CD 5

Performance Assessment

Have students form groups of three and act out a restaurant scene wherein the customers give opinions about the food and pay the check. The waiter should take and verify their orders and bring their check.

Language Note

Prononciation Have students read the second paragraph above. In French, syllables begin with a consonant. When a consonant has a vowel on each side, the consonant will attach itself to the following vowel, preventing the nasal sound. This can be illustrated by dividing words into syllables: **a-ni-mal, pre-nez.**

Teacher Note

For an additional reading, see *Practice and Activity Book,* page 59.

PREREADING
Activity A

Motivating Activity

You might use the first question of Activity A as an opener to get students thinking about menus and what they reveal about a restaurant. Have students look at the illustrations on the menus. What do they notice?

Thinking Critically

Drawing Inferences Point out the **Champs-Elysées** on a map of Paris. Ask students why they might expect the **Fontaine Elysée** to be more expensive than the other café. Do the cafés in the photos seem very different from small restaurants in the United States?

READING
Activities B–H

Teaching Suggestion

Working in pairs or small groups, have students skim the menus quickly and answer the questions in Activities B, C, and D.

LISONS!

$\mathcal{D}$o you like to go out to eat with your friends? Where do you like to go?

DE BONS CONSEILS

When you're faced with something new to read, look for anything that is familiar, anything that will help you identify the type of reading selection that you're dealing with. For example, a quick glance at these reading selections tells you that they're menus. Since you're familiar with menus, you should have a general idea of the kind of information these will contain, even if you don't know what all the words mean.

A. When you look at menus, what information are you usually looking for? Can you find this type of information on these menus? See answers below.

B. French cuisine is enjoyed the world over. However, you can often find dishes from other cultures at French cafés and restaurants. See answers below.

1. Which items on the menus are American?
2. What French words might you find on American menus?
3. What other French words do you know that are related to food and restaurants?

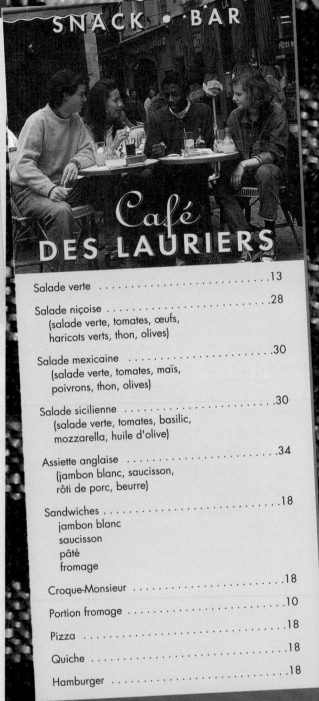

SNACK • BAR

Café
DES LAURIERS

Salade verte	13
Salade niçoise (salade verte, tomates, œufs, haricots verts, thon, olives)	28
Salade mexicaine (salade verte, tomates, maïs, poivrons, thon, olives)	30
Salade sicilienne (salade verte, tomates, basilic, mozzarella, huile d'olive)	30
Assiette anglaise (jambon blanc, saucisson, rôti de porc, beurre)	34
Sandwiches jambon blanc saucisson pâté fromage	18
Croque-Monsieur	18
Portion fromage	10
Pizza	18
Quiche	18
Hamburger	18

142 *cent quarante-deux*

Math Link

Have students calculate how much the most expensive item at each café is in dollars.

Answers
A food choices, prices; Yes
B 1. hamburger, hot-dog, banana split, cola
2. Answers will vary.
3. *Possible answers:* Bon appétit!, bistro, à la mode, soupe du jour, entrée, à la carte, hors d'œuvres, chef, sauté, parfait

Fontaine Elysée

SANDWICHES

Jambon Cru	.30
Jambon de Paris	.24
Pâté	.24
Mixte	.36
Roquefort aux Noix	.28
Croque-Monsieur	.30
Omelette Jambon	.35
Omelette Fromage	.35
Omelette Mixte	.41
Hot-Dog 1 Saucisse	.32
Hot-Dog 2 Saucisses	.57
Escargots (les 6)	.52

BOISSONS FRAICHES

Eau minérale, limonade	.26
Cola	.28
Jus de fruit	.28
raisin, poire, abricot, pamplemousse, ananas	

SPECIALITES

COUPE CHAMPS-ELYSEES :
Chocolat - Pistache - Caramel - Sauce Chocolat - Mandarine Impériale - Chantilly 53

BANANA SPLIT : Glace Vanille - Chocolat - Banane Fruit - Sauce Chocolat - Chantilly 44

COUPE MELBA : Vanille - Pêche Fruit - Chantilly - Sauce Fraise 44

BOISSONS CHAUDES

Café express	.15
Décaféiné	.15
Double express	.30
Double décaféiné	.30
Grand crème ou chocolat	.27
Café ou chocolat viennois	.32
Cappuccino	.33

For Activities C–F, see answers below.

C. Which café lists the beverages served? Do you recognize any of them? What is the difference between **BOISSONS FRAICHES** and **BOISSONS CHAUDES**?

D. How many different cognates can you find on the menus? (You should be able to find at least ten!)

E. Read the following statements about your friends' likes and dislikes. Which café would you recommend to each one?

1. Chantal a soif, mais elle n'a pas faim. Elle aime les jus de fruit.
2. Michel adore la glace.
3. Jean-Paul est végétarien.
4. Mai voudrait des escargots.
5. Alain aime les quiches.

F. Judging from the menus, what are the differences between the two cafés? What is the specialty of each one?

G. If your parents invited you to go out, which café would you choose? Why? Which would you choose if you had to pay?

H. If you had 100 F to spend, what would you order?

I. Now, make your own menu. Plan what you want to serve and how you want the menu to look. Will you have any illustrations? Don't forget to include prices.

cent quarante-trois **143**

Teaching Suggestions

F. Have students pair off to create a conversation in French in which one person asks the other how he or she likes each café:

— **Comment tu trouves le café Fontaine Elysée?**
— **C'est très cher, mais les sandwiches sont très bons.**

G. You might have students work in groups of three to create a conversation in French that might take place in this situation.

POSTREADING
Activity I

Teacher Note

I. For a more detailed explanation of this activity, see page 123E.

Answers

C Fontaine Elysée; boissons fraîches *(cold drinks)*, boissons chaudes *(hot drinks)*

D *Possible answers:* salade, tomates, olives, porc, omelette, vanille, sauce, banane, abricot, caramel, spécialités, sandwiches, mexicaine

E 1. Fontaine Elysée
2. Fontaine Elysée
3. Café des Lauriers
4. Fontaine Elysée
5. Café des Lauriers

F Fontaine Elysée is more expensive and has more choices; Café des Lauriers has no specialty. Fontaine Elysée's specialty is ice cream.

The **Mise en pratique** reviews and integrates all four skills and culture in preparation for the Chapter Test.

For Individual Needs

1 Slower Pace Before doing this activity, go over the menus with students. Ask them to identify as many differences as they can among the cafés, particularly concerning the type of food offered.

1 Challenge Have students write down the items that are ordered in each dialogue.

Portfolio

2 Oral You might want to have students add this to their oral portfolios or use it as an oral assessment tool. For portfolio suggestions, see *Assessment Guide,* page 18.

MISE EN PRATIQUE

 1 In which café would you most likely hear these conversations? Answers on p. 123D.

Café de Paris

15, Place du Palais - 75004 Paris
Téléphone 43-54-20-21

Nos glaces

Coupe Melba	50
Coupe Nougat	46
Banana Split	42

Nos boissons

Eau minérale	14
Jus de fruit	16
Café	10
Thé	8

SERVICE COMPRIS 15%

87, Avenue Victor Hugo - 75017 Paris
Tél. 45-62-52-53

Sandwiches

Croque-monsieur	30
Sandwich au jambon	25
Sandwich au fromage	20
Sandwich au rosbif	25

Boissons

Orangina, Coca	10
Eau minérale	12
Café	8
Jus de fruit	14

Café Américain

135, Boulevard d'Argençon • 75008 Paris • Téléphone 44-15-30-33

★ Pizzas ★

Trois fromages	50
Suprême	65

★ Plats ★

Couscous	50
Steak-frites	45

★ Boissons ★

Coca	12
Limonade	15
Eau minérale	13

SERVICE COMPRIS 15%

 2 You and your partner are hungry. Suggest that you go to a café, decide what you both want to eat, and choose one of the cafés above.

144 *cent quarante-quatre*

CHAPITRE 5 On va au café?

3 Read the following dialogue. Then, answer the questions below.

SERVEUR   Vous avez choisi?

CHANTAL   Je vais prendre un sandwich au fromage.

SERVEUR   Et comme boisson?

CHANTAL   Un jus d'orange, s'il vous plaît.

SERVEUR   Et pour vous, monsieur?

GILLES   Est-ce que vous avez des sandwiches au saucisson?

SERVEUR   Non. Je regrette.

GILLES   Tant pis. Alors, apportez-moi un croque-monsieur et un café, s'il vous plaît.

SERVEUR   Merci.

Café de la Gare

87, Avenue Victor Hugo
75017 Paris
Tél. 45-62-52-53

2 sandwiches au fromage   30
1 jus d'orange   14
2 cafés   16
1 croque-monsieur   22

TOTAL   89F

1. Qu'est-ce que Chantal va prendre?   un sandwich au fromage et un jus d'orange
2. Qu'est-ce que Gilles voudrait *(would like)*?
3. Qu'est-ce que Gilles va prendre?   un sandwich au saucisson / un croque-monsieur et un café
4. Est-ce que l'addition est correcte?   Non. *(There should only be one cheese sandwich and one coffee.)*

4 From what you know about French cafés, are these statements true or false?

1. If you don't see **service compris** on the menu, you should leave a tip.   true
2. To call the waiter, you should say **Garçon!**   false
3. It is acceptable to stay in a French café for a long time, as long as you've ordered something to eat or drink.   true
4. If a French person says **C'est pas mauvais,** he or she doesn't like the food.   false

5 The French Club at your school is going to have a picnic to raise money. Plan the picnic with two classmates. Decide on the time and place, the food, and the activities. Don't forget to talk about how much each item will cost. Jot down all your decisions.

6 Now that you've made your plans for the French Club picnic, create a poster to announce it. Include the food and the activities that you've planned, the price, the date, and the location. Make your poster attractive with drawings or pictures from magazines to illustrate the food and activities.

7

JEU DE ROLE

The day of the French Club picnic has arrived. One person in your group will act as host, the others will be the guests. The host will ask people what they want. Guests will tell what they want and talk about how they like the food and drink. After eating, suggest activities and decide which one you'll participate in.

Teaching Suggestions

3 Some students may find this activity easier if they jot down the items each person orders as they read. They can then compare this list with the check.

5 Have students create a radio announcement for the picnic they're planning. They might record this for their class and other French classes to listen to.

5, 6 Both of these activities could be used as class projects.

 Video Wrap-Up

- *VIDEO PROGRAM*
- *EXPANDED VIDEO PROGRAM,* **Videocassette 2, 25:15–36:26**
- *VIDEODISC PROGRAM,* **Videodisc 3A**

At this time, you might want to use the video resources for additional review and enrichment. See *Video Guide* or *Videodisc Guide* for suggestions regarding the following:

- **Qu'est-ce qu'on prend?** (Dramatic episode)
- **Panorama Culturel** (Interviews)
- **Vidéoclips** (Authentic footage)

This page is intended to help students prepare for the test. It is a brief checklist of the major points covered in the chapter. The students should be reminded that this is only a checklist and does not necessarily include everything that will appear on the test.

Teaching Suggestion

2 Encourage students to give several different responses.

♜ Game

♟ LE BASE-BALL Draw a baseball diamond on the board. Divide the class into two teams. The player up first may try to answer a single question for one base, two questions for a double, and so on. You might want to use the more difficult questions for players trying for extra-base hits.

QUE SAIS-JE?

Can you make suggestions, excuses, and recommendations? p. 129, 132

Can you get someone's attention and order food and beverages? p. 135

Can you inquire about and express likes and dislikes? p. 138

Can you pay the check? p. 139

Can you use what you've learned in this chapter?

1 How would you suggest to a friend that you . . .
  1. go to the café? *On va au café?*
  2. play tennis? *On joue au tennis?*

2 How would you turn down a suggestion and make an excuse? *See answers below.*

3 How would you recommend to a friend something . . . *Possible answers:*
  1. to eat? *Prends un sandwich au jambon.*
  2. to drink? *Prends un coca.*

4 In a café, how would you . . . *See answers below.*
  1. get the server's attention?
  2. ask what kind of sandwiches they serve?
  3. ask what kind of drinks they serve?

5 How would you say that you're . . .
  1. hungry? *J'ai faim.*
  2. thirsty? *J'ai soif.*

6 How would you order . . . *See answers below.*
  1. something to eat?
  2. something to drink?

7 How would you tell what people are having, using the verb **prendre**? *See answers below.*

1. il   2. tu   3. nous   4. ils

8 How would you ask a friend how he or she likes a certain food? *Comment tu trouves ça?*

9 How would you tell someone what you think of these items? *See answers below.*

1.   2.   3.   4.

10 How would you ask how much each item in number 9 costs? *See answers below.*

11 How would you ask for the check? *L'addition, s'il vous plaît.*

12 How would you ask what the total is? *Ça fait combien, s'il vous plaît?*

Answers

2 *Possible answers:* Désolé(e), j'ai des devoirs à faire. J'ai des courses à faire. J'ai des trucs à faire. J'ai des tas de choses à faire.

4 1. Excusez-moi. Monsieur! Madame! Mademoiselle! La carte, s'il vous plaît.
  2. Qu'est-ce que vous avez comme sandwiches?
  3. Qu'est-ce que vous avez comme boissons?

6 *Possible answers*
  1. Je voudrais... ; Je vais prendre... ; Donnez-moi... ; Apportez-moi un steak-frites, s'il vous plaît.
  2. Je voudrais... ; Je vais prendre... ; Donnez-moi... ; Apportez-moi une limonade, s'il vous plaît.

7 1. Il prend un sandwich au jambon.
  2. Tu prends un steak-frites.
  3. Nous prenons un jus d'orange.
  4. Ils prennent une limonade.

9 *Possible answers:* C'est bon! C'est excellent! C'est délicieux! C'est pas bon. C'est pas terrible. C'est dégoûtant.

10 1. C'est combien, un hot-dog?
  2. C'est combien, une pizza?
  3. C'est combien, une glace?
  4. C'est combien, une salade?

PREMIERE ETAPE

Making suggestions; making excuses

On va au café? *How about going to the café?*
On... ? *How about . . . ?*
Désolé(e). J'ai des devoirs à faire. *Sorry. I have homework to do.*
J'ai des courses à faire. *I have errands to do.*
J'ai des trucs à faire. *I have some things to do.*
J'ai des tas de choses à faire. *I have lots of things to do.*

Foods and beverages

un sandwich au jambon *ham sandwich*
  au saucisson *salami sandwich*
  au fromage *cheese sandwich*
un hot-dog *hot dog*
un croque-monsieur *toasted cheese and ham sandwich*
un steak-frites *steak and French fries*
une eau minérale *mineral water*
une limonade *lemon soda*
un coca *cola*
un jus d'orange *orange juice*

un jus de pomme *apple juice*
un café *coffee*
un chocolat *hot chocolate*

Making a recommendation

Prends/Prenez... *Have . . .*
prendre *to take or to have (food or drink)*

Other useful expressions

avoir soif *to be thirsty*
avoir faim *to be hungry*

DEUXIEME ETAPE

Getting someone's attention

Excusez-moi. *Excuse me.*
Monsieur! *Waiter!*
Madame! *Waitress!*
Mademoiselle! *Waitress!*
La carte, s'il vous plaît. *The menu, please.*

Ordering food and beverages

Vous avez choisi? *Have you decided/chosen?*

Vous prenez? *What are you having?*
Vous avez... ? *Do you have . . . ?*
Qu'est-ce que vous avez comme... ? *What kind of . . . do you have?*
Qu'est-ce que vous avez comme boissons? *What do you have to drink?*
Je voudrais... *I'd like . . .*

Je vais prendre... , s'il vous plaît. *I'll have . . . , please.*
... , s'il vous plaît. *. . . , please.*
Donnez-moi..., s'il vous plaît. *Please give me . . .*
Apportez-moi... , s'il vous plaît. *Please bring me . . .*

TROISIEME ETAPE

Inquiring about and expressing likes and dislikes

Comment tu trouves ça? *How do you like it?*
C'est... *It's . . .*
  bon! *good!*
  excellent! *excellent!*
  délicieux! *delicious!*

pas bon. *not very good.*
pas terrible. *not so great.*
dégoûtant. *gross.*

Paying the check

L'addition, s'il vous plaît. *The check, please.*
Oui, tout de suite. *Yes, right away.*

Un moment, s'il vous plaît. *One moment, please.*
C'est combien,... ? *How much is . . . ?*
Ça fait combien, s'il vous plaît? *How much is it, please?*
C'est... francs. *It's . . . francs.*
Ça fait... francs. *It's . . . francs.*

VOCABULAIRE

cent quarante-sept **147**

Teaching Suggestions

• As a comprehensive review of vocabulary, have students write a conversation among two customers and a server in a café using vocabulary from all three **étapes.** Students might do this in pairs.
• Have students write down all of the cognates they can find on this page.

CHAPTER 5 ASSESSMENT

CHAPTER TEST
• *Chapter Teaching Resources, Book 2,* pp. 29–34
• *Assessment Guide,* Speaking Test, p. 30
• *Assessment Items,* Audiocassette 7B Audio CD 5

TEST GENERATOR, CHAPTER 5

ALTERNATIVE ASSESSMENT

Performance Assessment
You might want to use the **Jeu de rôle** (p. 145) as a cumulative performance assessment activity.

Portfolio Assessment
• **Written:** Activity 24, *Pupil's Edition,* p. 139
Assessment Guide, p. 18
• **Oral:** Mise en pratique, Activity 2, *Pupil's Edition,* p. 144
Assessment Guide, p. 18

Chapitre 6 : Amusons-nous!
Chapter Overview

Mise en train pp. 150–152	**Projets de week-end**		*Practice and Activity Book,* p. 61	*Video Guide* OR *Videodisc Guide*
	FUNCTIONS	**GRAMMAR**	**CULTURE**	**RE-ENTRY**
Première étape pp. 153–158	Making plans, p. 153	• Using **le** with days of the week, p. 153 • The verb **aller** and **aller** + infinitive, p. 154	**Panorama Culturel,** Going out with friends, p. 158	• Expressing likes and dislikes • Contractions with **à**
Deuxième étape pp. 159–162	Extending and responding to invitations, p. 159	The verb **vouloir**, p. 160	**Rencontre Culturelle,** Dating in France, p. 162	Making, accepting, and turning down suggestions
Troisième étape pp. 163–167	Arranging to meet someone, p. 163	Information questions, p. 165	• **Note Culturelle,** Conversational time, p. 164 • Realia: Movie schedule, p. 166	Official time

Prononciation p. 167	The vowel sounds [ø] and [œ]		**Dictation:** *Textbook Audiocassette 3B/Audio CD 6*
Lisons! pp. 168–169	Theme-park ads		**Reading Strategy:** Using context to determine meaning
Review pp. 170–173	**Mise en pratique,** pp. 170–171	**Que sais-je?** p. 172	**Vocabulaire,** p. 173

Assessment Options	**Etape Quizzes**
	 • *Chapter Teaching Resources, Book 2*
	   Première étape, Quiz 6-1, pp. 79–80
	   Deuxième étape, Quiz 6-2, pp. 81–82
	   Troisième étape, Quiz 6-3, pp. 83–84
	 • *Assessment Items, Audiocassette 7B/Audio CD 6*
		Chapter Test
		 • *Chapter Teaching Resources, Book 2,* pp. 85–90
		 • *Assessment Guide,* Speaking Test, p. 30
		 • *Assessment Items, Audiocassette 7B/Audio CD 6*
		
		 Test Generator, Chapter 6

Video Program OR *Expanded Video Program, Videocassette 2* OR *Videodisc Program, Videodisc 3B*

Textbook Audiocassette 3B/Audio CD 6

RESOURCES: Print	RESOURCES: Audiovisual

Textbook Audiocassette 3B/Audio CD 6

Practice and Activity Book, pp. 62–64
Chapter Teaching Resources, Book 2
- Teaching Transparency Master 6-1, pp. 63, 66. . . . . *Teaching Transparency 6-1*
- Additional Listening Activities 6-1, 6-2, p. 67 . . . . *Additional Listening Activities, Audiocassette 9B/Audio CD 6*
- Realia 6-1, pp. 71, 73
- Situation Cards 6-1, pp. 74–75
- Student Response Forms, pp. 76–78
- Quiz 6-1, pp. 79–80. . . . . *Assessment Items, Audiocassette 7B/Audio CD 6*
Video Guide. . . . . *Video Program* OR *Expanded Video Program, Videocassette 2*
Videodisc Guide. . . . . *Videodisc Program, Videodisc 3B*

Textbook Audiocassette 3B/Audio CD 6

Practice and Activity Book, pp. 65–67
Chapter Teaching Resources, Book 2
- Communicative Activity 6-1, pp. 59–60
- Teaching Transparency Master 6-2, pp. 64, 66. . . . . *Teaching Transparency 6-2*
- Additional Listening Activities 6-3, 6-4, p. 68 . . . . *Additional Listening Activities, Audiocassette 9B/Audio CD 6*
- Realia 6-2, pp. 72, 73
- Situation Cards 6-2, pp. 74–75
- Student Response Forms, pp. 76–78
- Quiz 6-2, pp. 81–82. . . . . *Assessment Items, Audiocassette 7B/Audio CD 6*
Videodisc Guide. . . . . *Videodisc Program, Videodisc 3B*

Textbook Audiocassette 3B/Audio CD 6

Practice and Activity Book, pp. 68–70
Chapter Teaching Resources, Book 2
- Communicative Activity 6-2, pp. 61–62
- Teaching Transparency Master 6-3, pp. 65, 66. . . . . *Teaching Transparency 6-3*
- Additional Listening Activities 6-5, 6-6, p. 69 . . . . *Additional Listening Activities, Audiocassette 9B/Audio CD 6*
- Realia 6-2, pp. 72, 73
- Situation Cards 6-3, pp. 74–75
- Student Response Forms, pp. 76–78
- Quiz 6-3, pp. 83–84. . . . . *Assessment Items, Audiocassette 7B/Audio CD 6*
Videodisc Guide. . . . . *Videodisc Program, Videodisc 3B*

Practice and Activity Book, p. 71

Video Guide. . . . . *Video Program* OR *Expanded Video Program, Videocassette 2*
Videodisc Guide. . . . . *Videodisc Program, Videodisc 3B*

Alternative Assessment
- Performance Assessment
  Première étape, p. 157
  Deuxième étape, p. 161
  Troisième étape, p. 167
- Portfolio Assessment
  Written: **Mise en pratique,** Activity 5, *Pupil's Edition,* p. 171
  Assessment Guide, p. 19
  Oral: **Mise en pratique, Jeu de rôle,** *Pupil's Edition,* p. 171
  Assessment Guide, p. 19

Midterm Exam
Assessment Guide, pp. 35–42
*Assessment Items,
  Audiocassette 7B
  Audio CD 6*

Chapitre 6 : Amusons-nous!
Textbook Listening Activities Scripts

For Student Response Forms, see *Chapter Teaching Resources, Book 2,* pp. 76–78.

Première étape

7 Ecoute! p. 153

SOPHIE	Alors, qu'est-ce que tu vas faire ce week-end?
THERESE	Ce week-end? Oh là là! Plein de choses! Samedi matin, je vais faire une vidéo à la Maison des jeunes. Samedi après-midi, je vais faire les magasins et le soir, je vais au cinéma avec des copains.
SOPHIE	C'est tout?
THERESE	Non, attends, ce n'est pas fini! Dimanche matin, je vais au café et l'après-midi, je vais aller au Parc Astérix.
SOPHIE	Eh bien, bon week-end!

Possible answers to Activity 7
make a video, go shopping, go to the movies, go to the café, go to Parc Astérix

9 Ecoute! p. 154

1. Samedi après-midi, je vais jouer au football.
2. Michel et moi, nous regardons la télévision.
3. Je prends un sandwich et un coca.
4. Tu vas faire un pique-nique?
5. Nous allons faire une promenade.

Answers to Activity 9

1. going to do	3. doing	5. going to do
2. doing	4. going to do	

Deuxième étape

17 Ecoute! p. 159

1. — Dis, Marc, tu veux aller nager?
   — Désolé, je ne peux pas.
2. — Tu veux bien faire les magasins avec nous, Nathalie?
   — A quelle heure?
   — Vers cinq heures.
   — Pourquoi pas?
3. — On va jouer au foot ce week-end. Tu viens, Malika?
   — Oui, je veux bien.
4. — Stéphane, on va faire un pique-nique. Tu viens?
   — Un pique-nique? Désolé, je suis occupé. J'ai un match de tennis.
5. — Salut, Ferdinand. On va écouter de la musique?
   — Je ne peux pas. J'ai des trucs à faire.
   — Dommage.
6. — Tu veux venir manger un sandwich avec nous, Serge?
   — Oui, je veux bien. A quelle heure?
   — Maintenant.
   — D'accord. J'arrive.

Answers to Activity 17

1. refuse	3. accepte	5. refuse
2. accepte	4. refuse	6. accepte

*T*roisième étape

24 Ecoute! p. 164

Salut, Paul. C'est moi, Sylvie! Ça va?... Demain, je vais au Musée d'Orsay. Tu veux venir avec moi?... Oui, demain... A quelle heure? Bon, vers midi. Tu viens?... Super! Alors, on se retrouve devant le musée... C'est ça. Midi, devant le musée, demain. A demain, Paul...

Answers to Activity 24
1. c   2. a   3. c   4. c

26 Ecoute! p. 164

1. Salut. C'est Laurent. On va au zoo ce week-end avec Nathalie. Est-ce que tu veux venir avec nous? Voilà. On y va samedi après-midi, vers trois heures. On se retrouve devant le zoo à trois heures moins le quart. D'accord? Alors, à demain peut-être.

2. Allô! C'est moi, Patricia. Comment ça va? Je vais au stade dimanche avec Pascal. Tu veux venir avec nous? On va voir un match de foot. On se retrouve à huit heures au métro Saint-Michel. A dimanche. Tchao!

3. Bonjour. Ici Eric. Je vais à la piscine demain matin à dix heures. Est-ce que tu peux venir? Rendez-vous devant la piscine. Au revoir.

Answers to Activity 26
1. Laurent; to the zoo; Saturday afternoon at 2:45; in front of the zoo
2. Patricia, to the stadium; Sunday at 8:00; at the Saint-Michel metro stop
3. Eric; to the swimming pool; tomorrow morning at 10:00; in front of the swimming pool

*P*rononciation, p. 167

For the scripts for Parts A and B, see p. 167.

C. A écrire

(Dictation)
— Tu veux aller à la Maison des jeunes jeudi?
— A quelle heure?
— Vers neuf heures.
— Désolé, je ne peux pas.

*M*ise en pratique

2 p. 170

— Tu viens avec moi visiter la Tour Montparnasse? J'ai un bon de réduction. On a une vue magnifique de la terrasse.
— Bof. Je vais avoir le vertige là-haut.
— Tu veux aller au cinéma ou au musée?
— Non, je voudrais aller écouter les grandes orgues de Notre-Dame. C'est tellement beau.
— D'accord. Tu veux y aller quand?
— Dimanche, si tu veux.
— Pourquoi pas. On se retrouve à quelle heure?
— Le concert est à six heures moins le quart. On peut se donner rendez-vous vers cinq heures et demie.
— Où ça?
— Devant la cathédrale.
— OK. Notre-Dame, dimanche, à cinq heures et demie. Bonne idée. Ça coûte cher?
— Mais non, c'est gratuit.
— Génial! C'est vraiment une excellente idée.

Answers to Mise en pratique Activity 2
Notre-Dame; Sunday at 5:30, in front of the cathedral

Chapitre 6 : Amusons-nous!
Projects

Les vacances parfaites
(Individual or Group Project)

ASSIGNMENT

Students will create a poster or brochure of a vacation spot in the francophone world. This can be done in English or French.

SUGGESTED VACATION SPOTS

Any francophone city is appropriate. You might suggest Chamonix (ski resort near the highest peak in the French Alps), Fort-de-France, Tahiti, Paris, Monte-Carlo, Dakar, Abidjan, Quebec, Casablanca, or Brussels.

MATERIALS

✂ **Students may need**
- Atlases
- Magazines
- Catalogues
- Travel information from newspapers, travel guides, or travel agencies
- Encyclopedias
- Other reference books
- Scissors
- Glue or tape
- Colored pens and pencils
- Construction paper or posterboard

You might want to have photos of some of the places suggested above, or suitcases and tourist gear.

PREPARATION

Have students choose a vacation spot that interests them. Then, have them gather information about the city, using atlases, magazines, catalogues, newspaper articles, and travel brochures.

SUGGESTED SEQUENCE

1. Have students make a list of information tourists might need for their particular destination, including attractions, average weather conditions, local customs, currency, and so on. Have them also draw or photocopy illustrations of the chosen destination.

2. Have students organize their materials and notes and begin planning their posters. If the posters are to be in French, students might also look up unfamiliar words they will need.

3. Have students either show you their organized materials, or have classmates look over their work to check spelling and provide feedback on the appropriateness of the content and arrangement of the layout.

4. Students then finish putting their posters together, adding illustrations, captions, and other written information.

GRADING THE PROJECT

You might want to base students' grades on the appropriateness of the content they provide for their destination, presentation and appearance, correct use of language, and creativity.

Suggested Point Distribution: (total = 100 points)

Content . . . . 30 points
Presentation/appearance . . . . 30 points
Language use (if in French) . . . . 20 points
Creativity . . . . 20 points

DOUBLE HANGMAN

This game will help students review functions and vocabulary from this chapter as well as from preceding chapters.

Procedure   Divide the class into two teams. Draw two scaffolds on the board or on a transparency. Name a category from this chapter (places to go, things to do, excuses) and draw a blank to represent each letter of a word or expression in the category under each scaffold. Each team should have a different word or expression. The first player of the first team suggests a letter. If the letter is found in that team's word or expression, write it in the appropriate blank(s) as many times as it appears. If the letter is not included in the word or expression, draw the noose on that team's scaffold. If the first player's suggestion is correct, the next player on the team may suggest another letter. If the first player's suggestion is incorrect, the turn passes to the opposing team. The rope and body are drawn in the following order: noose, head, torso, each arm, each leg, each hand, each foot, and hair. If teams are tied, or to make the game last longer, additional features (fingers, toes, eyes, mouth) may be drawn.

Teacher Note   To review for the Midterm Exam, you might also use categories from preceding chapters to review vocabulary, functional expressions, and structures.

AROUND THE WORLD

This is a fast vocabulary review game that is easy to set up and fun to play.

Materials   To play this game, you will need flashcards with pictures of vocabulary items.

Teacher Note   Before the game begins, tell students that after the game, they will have to write down as many vocabulary words as they can remember. You may want to have students clear their desks so they won't be tempted to write down the vocabulary as the game proceeds.

Procedure   Arrange students in rows. The first two students in the first row stand next to each other. These are the two players. Hold up a flashcard so that all students can see it. The first player to identify the picture wins and moves to stand beside the next person in the row. The player who loses sits down. The round continues in this manner until each student has had a chance to play. The final winner is the student who has eliminated the most players in the course of the round. Play as many rounds as you like. When the game ends, have students write down as many of the vocabulary words used in the game as they can remember. You might give a prize to the student who recalls the most vocabulary.

Chapitre 6
Amusons-nous!

pp. 148–173

𝒰sing the Chapter Opener

Motivating Activity

After reading the introduction at the top of page 149, ask students to recall what they learned about Paris from the Location Opener on pages 120–123. This would also be a good time to show a travel video or slides of Paris.

Photo Flash!

① The fountain shown in this photo is called *Hommage à Stravinsky* by Niki de Saint Phalle. It is located near the modern Georges Pompidou Center in Beaubourg. The **centre Pompidou,** officially the **Centre National d'Art et de Culture Georges Pompidou,** was named after the second president of the Fifth Republic. For more information on the Pompidou Center, see pages 121–122.

CHAPITRE 6 Amusons-nous!

① On va au centre Pompidou?

148 *cent quarante-huit*

Culture Note

You might ask students if they can identify the monument pictured in the medallion at the top of this page (**la tour Eiffel**). Ask them to recall what they learned about it in the Location Opener on pages 121 and 123. When it was built, **la tour Eiffel** was first declared to be a "monstrosity" although later it was considered to be one of the identifying symbols of Paris. The tower was built on the hundred-year anniversary of the storming of the Bastille and was also the centerpiece of the 1889 International Exhibition of Paris. In addition to being a popular tourist attraction, the tower has been used as a radio and meteorological post since World War I, and in 1985, equipment for France's fifth television channel was installed there.

Teenagers everywhere love to go out with their friends. In Paris there are so many events and activities that it is almost impossible to choose. If you were in Paris, what would you want to do?

In this chapter you will learn

- to make plans
- to extend and respond to invitations
- to arrange to meet someone

And you will

- listen to French teenagers talk about where they go to have fun
- read brochures and advertisements
- write about your plans for the weekend
- find out what French-speaking young people do and where they go to have fun

② On se retrouve au métro Palais-Royal?

③ Je voudrais bien aller au cinéma.

Focusing on Outcomes

Have students look at the chapter outcomes and match them with the three photos. Have them determine which photos show making plans, inviting and responding to invitations, and arranging to meet someone. NOTE: You may want to use the video to support the objectives. The self-check activities in **Que sais-je?** on page 172 help students assess their achievement of the objectives.

Photo Flash!

② The **Palais Royal** was built as a royal residence for Cardinal Richelieu by Lemercier in the seventeenth century. Although most of the building was destroyed during the revolt of 1848, it was rebuilt in the latter part of the nineteenth century and now houses the **Conseil d'Etat,** the supreme administrative court. The **métro** station in the photo is in the Art Nouveau style of the early twentieth century, which is characterized by curvilinear designs and organic forms.

Culture Notes

• You might call students' attention to the metro ticket at the bottom of this page. Remind students that **RATP** stands for **Réseau Autonome des Transports Parisiens.** The large number two at the top of the ticket signifies that the ticket is for a second-class car. Most metro trains have a car or two in the middle of the train reserved for first-class passengers, who pay more for the privilege of riding in a less crowded car.

• You might ask students to identify the cathedral (**Notre-Dame**) pictured in the medallion to the right of the third photo. Ask them to recall what they learned about **Notre-Dame** from the Location Opener on page 122. You might also tell them that during the French Revolution, the cathedral was converted from a Catholic place of worship into a **Temple de la raison,** the name given all churches under the new state religion.

Video Synopsis

In this segment of the video, Mathieu asks Isabelle what she is going to do tomorrow. She tells him about her plans for the day and says she is free in the evening. Mathieu asks her if she would like to go to a concert, but she is not interested. Mathieu suggests they go to the zoo, but Isabelle doesn't like zoos. They each make several more suggestions but cannot agree on anything. During their conversation, we see scenes of their suggested activities. They finally agree to go to the movies, but then can't agree on what film to see!

Motivating Activity

Show *Map Transparency 5* (**Paris**). Call on students to point out the places mentioned in the **Mise en train**. Point out other major places of interest. Ask students if they would like to visit any of these places, and have them explain why or why not.

Mise en train

Projets de week-end

What do you think Mathieu and Isabelle are talking about? Why do you think so?

150 *cent cinquante*   CHAPITRE 6   Amusons-nous!

Culture Note

The Louvre was first used as a defensive structure in 1200 by Philippe II Auguste. Over the years, it has served as a royal residence to several kings, notably Francis I. Now one of the largest museums in the world, the Louvre welcomes visitors through its newly renovated main entrance under the huge glass pyramid designed by I. M. Pei.

5 Qu'est-ce que tu veux faire, alors?

6 S'il fait beau, on peut faire une promenade au palais de Chaillot. On peut même monter au sommet de la tour Eiffel.

Bof.

7 J'ai une idée! Tu ne veux pas aller faire un tour dans un bateau-mouche?

BATEAUX-MOUCHES

Ça, non. C'est pas terrible.

8 On va au Sacré-Cœur?

Non, j'ai pas envie.

On peut tout simplement aller au cinéma. Tu veux?

Oh non, je n'aime pas les films d'horreur. Je préfère aller voir un film comique.

9 D'accord. Je veux bien. Qu'est-ce que tu veux voir comme film?

Moi, je propose *Dracula*. Ça passe à 16h40 et à 18h55.

10 Oh non! Encore un film comique?! Tu sais, c'est bizarre. On n'est jamais d'accord!

MISE EN TRAIN *cent cinquante et un* **151**

For Individual Needs

1 Slower Pace If students have difficulty with this activity, you might indicate the photos where the answers can be found. (1. Photo 1; 2. Photo 1; 3. Photos 3, 4, and 9; 4. Photos 6, 7, and 10; 5. Photos 9 and 10).

Teaching Suggestion

2 If the sentence is true, have students quote the text that verifies it. If it is false, have them correct it.

For Individual Needs

3 Slower Pace Play the video of the **Mise en train.** Ask students to watch and listen carefully for any mention of places and jot them down. Correct the lists with the class and then have pairs or small groups do the activity.

For videodisc application, see *Videodisc Guide.*

Teaching Suggestions

5 You might want to review making excuses from Chapter 5 (see page 129).

6 Students might refer to the activities in Activity 4, or they might reread the story.

For Individual Needs

6 Challenge Have students answer in French. They might begin their answers with **Moi, je voudrais...** , **J'aime bien...** , or **Je préfère...**

1 Tu as compris?

Answer the following questions according to **Projets de week-end.** Don't be afraid to guess. See answers below.

1. What are Isabelle's plans for tomorrow?
2. What day and time of day is it?
3. Can you name three places where Mathieu suggests they go?
4. Can you name three things that Isabelle prefers to do?
5. What do they finally agree to do? What problem remains?

2 Vrai ou faux?

1. Isabelle aime aller au zoo. faux
2. Isabelle a un cours de danse. vrai
3. Mathieu aime la musique de Patrick Bruel. vrai
4. Isabelle aime bien les musées. faux
5. Isabelle veut voir un film d'horreur dimanche après-midi. faux

3 Mets en ordre

Mets les phrases en ordre d'après **Projets de week-end.**

1. Isabelle propose d'aller au palais de Chaillot. 3
2. Mathieu propose d'aller au zoo. 2
3. Isabelle propose d'aller au Sacré-Cœur. 5
4. Mathieu ne veut pas faire de promenade. 4
5. Isabelle refuse d'aller au concert. 1
6. Isabelle accepte d'aller au cinéma. 6

4 Où est-ce qu'on veut aller?

Choisis les activités qu'Isabelle veut faire et les activités que Mathieu préfère. See answers below.

> aller voir un film comique
> aller à un concert aller voir un film d'horreur faire une promenade au palais de Chaillot
> aller au musée
> aller au zoo faire un tour en bateau aller au Sacré-Cœur

5 Invitations et refus

Match Mathieu's suggestions for weekend activities with Isabelle's refusals.

Tu veux...

1. aller au concert de Patrick Bruel? d
2. aller au Louvre? c
3. aller au zoo? a
4. aller voir *Dracula*? b

Désolée, mais...

a. je déteste les zoos.
b. je préfère aller voir un film comique.
c. je n'aime pas trop les musées.
d. je n'ai pas envie.

6 Et maintenant, à toi

How would you react to Mathieu and Isabelle's suggestions for the weekend? Which would you choose to do? Why? Compare your answers with a partner's.

Answers

1. 1. A.M. dance class, P.M. shopping, free evening
   2. Friday afternoon
   3. concert, zoo, museum, movies
   4. take a walk at the palais de Chaillot, go to the top of the Eiffel Tower, take a boat ride, go to Sacré-Cœur
   5. Isabelle and Mathieu decide to go to a movie, but they cannot agree on which one to see.

4. *Isabelle:* aller voir un film comique, faire une promenade au palais de Chaillot, faire un tour en bateau, aller au Sacré-Cœur
   Mathieu: aller à un concert, aller au zoo, aller voir un film d'horreur, aller au musée

PREMIERE ETAPE

Making plans

COMMENT DIT-ON... ?

Making plans

To ask what a friend's planning to do:

Qu'est-ce que tu vas faire demain? *What are you going to do . . . ?*

Tu vas faire quoi ce week-end? *What are you going to do . . . ?*

To tell what you're going to do:

Vendredi, **je vais** faire du vélo. *I'm going to . . .*

Samedi après-midi, **je vais** aller au café.

Dimanche, **je vais** regarder la télé.

Pas grand-chose. *Not much.*

Rien de spécial. *Nothing special.*

7 Ecoute!

Listen as Sophie asks Thérèse about her plans for the weekend. Write down at least three things Thérèse plans to do.   Answers on p. 147C.

8 Qu'est-ce que tu vas faire?

a. Write down three activities you have planned for the weekend.

b. Now, tell your partner what you plan to do and ask about his or her plans.

> Je vais voir un film. Et toi, qu'est-ce que tu vas faire?

VOCABULAIRE

regarder un match	to watch a game (on TV)
manger quelque chose	to eat something
voir un film	to see a movie
voir un match	to see a game (in person)
voir une pièce	to see a play
faire une promenade	to go for a walk
faire les vitrines	to window-shop
faire un pique-nique	to have a picnic
aller à une boum	to go to a party

Note de Grammaire

If you want to say that you do an activity regularly on a certain day of the week, use the article **le** before the day of the week.

> Je fais du patin à glace **le mercredi** *(on Wednesdays).*

To say that you are doing something only on one particular day, use the day of the week without an article before it.

> Je vais faire du patin à glace **mercredi** *(on Wednesday).*

Jump Start!

Have students suggest the following activities in writing: **faire une vidéo, faire une promenade, nager, jouer au basket.**

MOTIVATE

Ask students to write down two or three things they are going to do this weekend.

TEACH

Presentation

Comment dit-on... ?/ Vocabulaire Tell students what you're going to do next weekend, using some of the expressions from the **Vocabulaire.** (Dimanche, je vais voir un film.) Then, ask students about their weekends, real or imaginary. (Qu'est-ce que tu vas faire samedi?) Have pairs practice asking and telling about their plans.

Note de grammaire Ask individual students questions, such as **Tu fais tes devoirs le samedi? Qu'est-ce que tu fais le mardi à 10h?**

 For videodisc application, see *Videodisc Guide.*

For Individual Needs

7 Auditory Learners To check this activity, have students tell aloud what Thérèse plans to do for the weekend.

Language Note

Vocabulaire You might tell students that the verb **faire** is used with a variety of idiomatic expressions and does not always mean *to make* or *to do.*

Grammaire   The verb aller

Aller is an irregular verb.

aller *(to go)*

Je **vais**		Nous **allons**	
Tu **vas**	au café.	Vous **allez**	au café.
Il/Elle/On **va**		Ils/Elles **vont**	

- You can use a form of the verb **aller** plus the infinitive of another verb to say that you're *going to do something* in the future.

  Je vais jouer au base-ball demain.

- To say that you're not going to do something in the near future, put **ne... pas** around the conjugated form of the verb **aller.**

  Je *ne* vais *pas* jouer au base-ball demain.

9 Ecoute!

Listen to the following sentences and decide whether the people are talking about what they're doing or what they're going to do.   Answers on p. 147C.

10 Qu'est-ce qu'ils vont faire?

What are the people in the pictures going to do?

1. Elles vont faire les vitrines.

2. Ils vont manger/aller au café.

3. Il va jouer au football.

4. Elles vont faire un pique-nique.

5. Ils vont voir un film.

6. Elle va faire une promenade.

À la française

The French often use the present tense of a verb to say that something will happen in the near future, just as we do in English.

Samedi matin, je vais jouer au tennis. *Saturday morning, I'm going to play tennis.*

Samedi matin, je joue au tennis. *Saturday morning, I'm playing tennis.*

11 Qu'est-ce qu'il va faire?

Qu'est-ce que Pierre va faire aux Etats-Unis?

1. Il va voir un match.

2. Il va voir un film.

3. Il va aller à la piscine.

4. Il va danser.

5. Il va faire les vitrines.

6. Il va manger au restaurant.

12 Enquête

Ask the members of your group what they're going to do this weekend and tell them what you're planning. Then, tell the class what you're all planning to do.

—Qu'est-ce que tu vas faire ce week-end, Nicole?
—Samedi après-midi, je vais faire du ski nautique. Et toi?
—Moi, je vais voir un match de volley.   *(to the class)*
—Je vais voir un match et Nicole va faire du ski nautique samedi après-midi.

One of the best ways to practice your French is to talk to yourself! You can do this at any time in any place, either quietly under your breath or aloud. For example, if you're learning to say where you're going and what you're going to do, tell yourself in French what you're planning to do. Any time you're in a conversation, think about what you would say in French. In this way you'll learn to apply your French to your life, and you'll become more fluent.

Teaching Suggestion

11 Have students suggest additional activities that Pierre is going to do in the United States. You might also have them draw on their knowledge of French culture to tell what Pierre is *not* going to do in the United States. (**Il ne va pas aller à l'école le samedi matin.**)

For Individual Needs

Kinesthetic Learners Have small groups of students play "Charades." One member of the group acts out an activity he or she plans to do, and the other students try to guess the activity being mimed. The first student to say what the person is going to do (**Tu vas faire du jogging.**) takes the next turn.

11 Challenge Have students look over the Location Opener on pages 120–123 and the **Mise en train** on pages 150–152 and decide what they might want to see and do in Paris. Have each student suggest two activities that he or she is going to do in Paris. Write students' suggestions on a transparency or large sheets of paper for use in later activities.

12 Challenge Have two groups compare their activities and summarize the results. (**Maria, Pam et Damon vont faire du ski nautique samedi, mais Tori va jouer au tennis.**)

Teacher Note

De bons conseils To expand on the study tip given on this page, you might make the following suggestions to students.

• Encourage students to visualize new vocabulary as they study it. To learn the word **la bibliothèque,** for example, they might visualize their local library as they say the French word aloud.

• You might suggest that students create memory devices to learn new material. For example, students might use the first letters (BCCMMPPPRSTZ) of a list of new words (**bibliothèque, centre commercial, cinéma, Maison des jeunes, musée, parc, piscine, plage, restaurant, stade, théâtre, zoo**) to make a sentence. (Bruno Couldn't Cook Mom's Meat Pizza Precisely and Perfectly Round, So he Teased Zelda.)

Presentation

Vocabulaire After introducing the **Vocabulaire**, hold up illustrations (a zebra, a movie star) or props (sunglasses, a shopping bag) to suggest the places, asking **On va où?** Ask students to name local examples of these places. Then, name these local places, and have students call out the French term for the place (for example, *Huntington Beach*—**une plage**; *the Galleria*—**un centre commercial**). Another place students might want to go is *downtown*—**au centre-ville.**

TPR Tell students to go to a place (**Va à la plage!**) and have them mime what they would do there. As a variation, you might whisper the place to a student and have the class try to guess where that student is going as he or she mimes a related activity.

Teaching Suggestion

13 Ask students to suggest other possible completions for these sentences. You might also ask them to prepare similar sentence starters for other locations to be used as a quiz for their classmates.

VOCABULAIRE

Where do you and your friends like to go in your spare time?

au restaurant

au cinéma

au parc

au stade

au zoo

au centre commercial

à la plage

à la piscine

au musée

à la Maison des jeunes

au théâtre

à la bibliothèque

13 Où vas-tu?

Où est-ce que tu vas pour faire ces activités?

1. Je vais faire de la natation... d
2. Je vais faire les vitrines... c
3. Je vais voir un film... a
4. Je vais manger quelque chose... e
5. Je vais voir un match... f
6. Je vais voir une pièce... b

a. au cinéma.
b. au théâtre.
c. au centre commercial.
d. à la piscine.
e. au café.
f. au stade.

156 *cent cinquante-six*   CHAPITRE 6   Amusons-nous!

♜ **Game**

 CONCENTRATION® For each vocabulary word or expression, make two cards. On one card, write the phrase in French (**au théâtre**). On the other, draw a picture or tape a magazine picture of the item. Number the back of each card and tape them to the board with the numbers visible. Divide the class into two teams. Have the first player from the first team call out two numbers. Turn over the cards. If the cards match, the player keeps them and takes another turn. If not, the turn passes to the other team.

14 Projets de week-end

Christine and Alain are talking about where they like to go on weekends. Complete their conversation according to the pictures.

CHRISTINE   Moi, j'adore aller avec mes copains. Après, on va
au cinéma

souvent . Et toi?
au café

ALAIN   Moi, j'aime mieux aller . J'adore le sport. J'aime bien
au stade

aller aussi. On y joue souvent au foot.
au parc

CHRISTINE   Qu'est-ce que tu vas faire ce week-end? On va ? à la piscine/à la plage

ALAIN   Ah, non, je n'aime pas trop nager. Tu veux aller ? au zoo

15 Qu'est-ce que tu aimes faire?

a. Ask your partner if he or she likes to go to the places pictured below. Take turns.

See answers below.

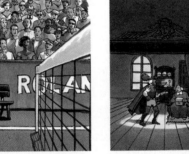

1.   2.   3.   4.

b. Now, take turns suggesting that you go to one of these places. Then, accept or reject each other's suggestions.

—On va... ?
—D'accord. *or*
Non,...

Tu te rappelles ?

The preposition **à** generally means *to* or *at*. It combines with **le** to form **au** and with **les** to form **aux**, but it doesn't combine with **la** or **l'**.
On prend un coca **au** café?
Ils aiment faire du théâtre **à la** Maison des jeunes.

16 Mon journal

Tu as des projets pour le week-end? Qu'est-ce que tu vas faire? Où vas-tu? Quand?

Vendredi après-midi, je vais faire mes devoirs.

PREMIERE ETAPE

cent cinquante-sept **157**

Answers

15a 1. Tu aimes aller à la bibliothèque?
2. Tu aimes aller au stade?
3. Tu aimes aller au théâtre?
4. Tu aimes aller au musée?

Teacher Note
14 Remind students to include **à la** or **au** in their answers.

For Individual Needs
14 Challenge Have partners rewrite the conversation to fit their own interests. This could then be included in their written portfolios. Students could also rewrite their conversations on posterboard, inserting pictures of the places they like to go.

Teaching Suggestion
15 Have students tell the class one place their partners like to go, using **il** or **elle**.

Portfolio
16 Written This activity is appropriate for students' written portfolios. Students might draw and label a calendar of their plans to accompany the entry. For portfolio information, see *Assessment Guide*, pages 2–13.

CLOSE

To close this **étape**, use *Teaching Transparency 6-1* to practice vocabulary. You might call out various activities (**On va lire un livre.**) and have students tell where in town you're going. (**Vous allez à la bibliothèque municipale.**)

ASSESS

Quiz 6-1, *Chapter Teaching Resources, Book 2*, pp. 79–80

Assessment Items,
Audiocassette 7B/Audio CD 6

Performance Assessment

Have students write a letter to a French pen pal who is coming for a visit. Have them suggest what to do during the pen pal's stay, using **on**.

VIDEO PROGRAM
OR EXPANDED VIDEO
PROGRAM,
Videocassette 2
44:09–47:10

OR *VIDEODISC PROGRAM,*
Videodisc 3B

Search 13810, Play To 16015

Teacher Notes

• See *Video Guide, Videodisc Guide,* and *Practice and Activity Book* for activities related to the **Panorama Culturel.**

• Remind students that cultural material may be included in the Chapter Quizzes and Test.

• The interviewees' language represents informal, unrehearsed speech. Occasionally, edits have been made for clarification.

Motivating Activity

Ask students what they do when they go out with friends.

Presentation

Have students view the video and write down the activities that the interviewees mention. To check comprehension, you might ask yes-no questions, such as **Arnaud achète des disques?** as well as the **Questions** below.

Thinking Critically

Comparing and Contrasting
Use questions 1-3 of **Qu'en penses-tu?** to have students compare their favorite activities with those that the interviewees mention.

Teaching Suggestion

Hold up magazine illustrations of the activities and ask **Qui fait ça?**

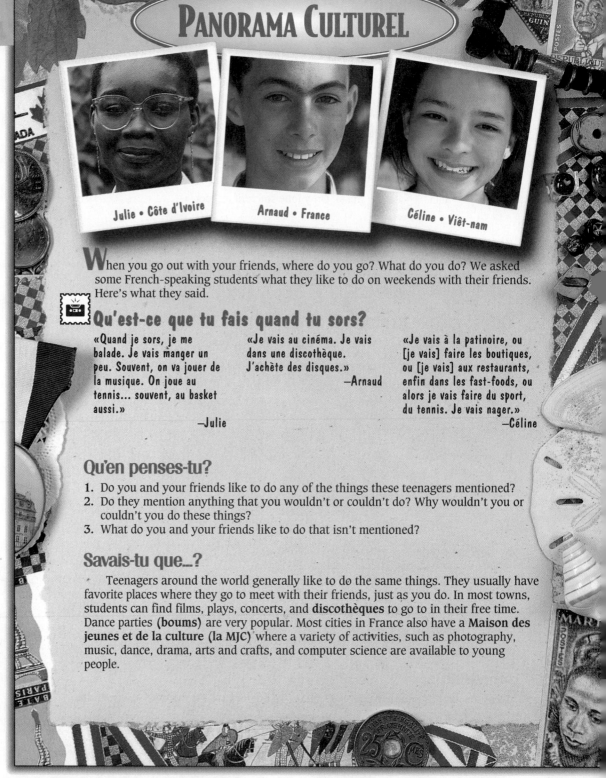

PANORAMA CULTUREL

Julie • Côte d'Ivoire   Arnaud • France   Céline • Viêt-nam

When you go out with your friends, where do you go? What do you do? We asked some French-speaking students what they like to do on weekends with their friends. Here's what they said.

Qu'est-ce que tu fais quand tu sors?

«Quand je sors, je me balade. Je vais manger un peu. Souvent, on va jouer de la musique. On joue au tennis... souvent, au basket aussi.»
—Julie

«Je vais au cinéma. Je vais dans une discothèque. J'achète des disques.»
—Arnaud

«Je vais à la patinoire, ou [je vais] faire les boutiques, ou [je vais] aux restaurants, enfin dans les fast-foods, ou alors je vais faire du sport, du tennis. Je vais nager.»
—Céline

Qu'en penses-tu?

1. Do you and your friends like to do any of the things these teenagers mentioned?
2. Do they mention anything that you wouldn't or couldn't do? Why wouldn't you or couldn't you do these things?
3. What do you and your friends like to do that isn't mentioned?

Savais-tu que...?

Teenagers around the world generally like to do the same things. They usually have favorite places where they go to meet with their friends, just as you do. In most towns, students can find films, plays, concerts, and **discothèques** to go to in their free time. Dance parties (**boums**) are very popular. Most cities in France also have a **Maison des jeunes et de la culture (la MJC)** where a variety of activities, such as photography, music, dance, drama, arts and crafts, and computer science are available to young people.

Culture Notes

• Many French movie theaters and museums have student rates (**tarif réduit**) that are usually available to young tourists with student ID cards or proof of age.

• In Paris, the **métro** trains begin their final runs between midnight and 1:00 A.M. Thus, parties or evenings out usually end in time for everyone to get to the closest subway station in time for the last train.

Questions

1. Julie fait quels sports? (Elle joue au tennis, au basket.)
2. Arnaud va où quand il sort? (au cinéma, dans une discothèque)
3. Où est-ce que Céline va quand elle sort? (à la patinoire, dans les restaurants, dans les fast-foods)
4. Qu'est-ce qu'elle fait comme sport? (du tennis, elle nage.)

DEUXIEME ETAPE

Extending and responding to invitations

COMMENT DIT-ON... ?
Extending and responding to invitations

To extend an invitation:

Allons au parc! *Let's go . . . !*
Tu veux aller au café **avec moi?** *Do you want to . . . with me?*
Je voudrais aller faire du vélo. **Tu viens?** *Will you come?*
On peut faire du ski. *We can . . .*

To accept an invitation:

D'accord.
Bonne idée.
Je veux bien. *I'd really like to.*
Pourquoi pas? *Why not?*

To refuse an invitation:

Ça ne me dit rien.
J'ai des trucs à faire.
Désolé(e), je ne peux pas.
Désolé(e), je suis occupé(e).
Sorry, I'm busy.

17 Ecoute!

Ecoute ces dialogues.
Est-ce qu'on accepte
ou refuse l'invitation?

Answers on p. 147C.

LES MONUMENTS LES PLUS VISITÉS :	
l'abbaye du Mont-Saint-Michel	826 000 entrées
l'arc de triomphe de l'Etoile	775 000
le château de Chambord	730 000
la Sainte-Chapelle	696 000
le château de Haut-Kœnigsbourg	591 000
les tours de Notre-Dame de Paris	452 000
le château d'Azay-le-Rideau	425 000

LES MUSÉES LES PLUS VISITÉS :	
le Louvre	3,4 millions d'entrées payantes
Versailles	2,5
Orsay	2,0
Picasso	340 000
Fontainebleau	291 000
l'Orangerie	254 000

RESOURCES FOR DEUXIEME ETAPE

Textbook Audiocassette 3B/Audio CD 6
Practice and Activity Book, pp. 65–67
Videodisc Guide
  Videodisc Program, Videodisc 3B

Chapter Teaching Resources, Book 2
• Communicative Activity 6-1, pp. 59–60
• Teaching Transparency Master 6-2, pp. 64, 66
  Teaching Transparency 6-2
• Additional Listening Activities 6-3, 6-4, p. 68
  Audiocassette 9B/Audio CD 6
• Realia 6-2, pp. 72, 73
• Situation Cards 6-2, pp. 74–75
• Student Response Forms, pp. 76–78
• Quiz 6-2, pp. 81–82
  Audiocassette 7B/Audio CD 6

Jump Start!

Have students write their
plans for next weekend.

MOTIVATE

Ask students what they say in
English to invite their friends
to do things. Ask them if
they've ever made polite excuses to decline an invitation.
What did they say?

TEACH

Presentation

Comment dit-on... ? Have
students tell which animal in
the cartoon is extending an
invitation, which one is refusing, and which one is accepting. Ask students for expressions they've already learned
for inviting someone and for
accepting and refusing an invitation (see Chapter 5). Then,
extend invitations to individual students. (**Je vais au café.
Tu viens?**) If the student
accepts, have him or her stand
with you and invite the next
student.

Additional Practice

Have two students stand up.
Call out an expression from
Comment dit-on... ? The first
student to call out *invite,
accept,* or *refuse* remains
standing, while the other sits
down, and the next student
stands up. Continue until all
students have had the chance
to respond.

For videodisc
application, see
Videodisc Guide.

**For Individual
Needs**

17 Challenge Have students write down the sug-
gested activity as well as the
type of response.

18 Et toi? Tu veux?

Choisis la bonne réponse.

1. J'ai faim. d
2. Je voudrais faire un pique-nique. a
3. Tu ne viens pas? b
4. Je voudrais voir un match de foot. e
5. Tu veux voir une pièce? c

a. Allons au parc!
b. J'ai des trucs à faire.
c. Pourquoi pas? Allons au théâtre!
d. Tu veux aller au café?
e. Allons au stade!

19 Tu acceptes?

 Your partner will invite you to participate in some of the following activities. Accept or refuse, telling where you're going or what you're going to do instead. Exchange roles.

1. On peut regarder la télévision.

2. Tu veux faire les vitrines?

3. Allons danser!

4. Tu veux jouer au tennis?

5. Je vais voir un film. Tu viens?

6. Tu veux aller à la piscine?

---

*G*rammaire The verb **vouloir**

Vouloir is an irregular verb.

vouloir *(to want)*

Je **veux** ⎤	Nous **voulons** ⎤
Tu **veux** ⎬ aller au café.	Vous **voulez** ⎬ aller au café.
Il/Elle/On **veut** ⎦	Ils/Elles **veulent** ⎦

Je voudrais *(I would like)* is a more polite form of **je veux**.

CHAPITRE 6   Amusons-nous!

Language Note

Grammaire You might point out that all of the singular forms of **vouloir** are pronounced the same, and that the "boot" forms (**je, tu, il/elle,** and **ils/elles**) all contain -**eu**.

20 Qu'est-ce qu'ils veulent faire ce soir? See answers below.

1. Pierre et Marc

2. Alain

3. Robert et Lise

4. Elodie et Guy

5. Mes copains

6. David et Monique

21 Invitations pour le week-end

You're making plans for the upcoming weekend. Take turns with a partner suggesting activities and accepting or politely refusing the suggestions.

23 A la boum!

The French club is having a party. Invite three students. Before they accept or refuse your invitation, they want to know what you're planning to do. Tell them about the activities you're planning. Your friends will either accept or refuse.

> écouter de la musique québécoise
> danser
> voir un film français
> parler français avec des copains
> manger des escargots

22 Vous voulez faire quoi?

You and your friends can't decide what to do this weekend. Each of you makes a suggestion, and the others react to it. See if you can find three things you'd all like to do.

> —Vous voulez faire du vélo?
> —Oui, je veux bien.
> —Moi, je ne veux pas. Je n'aime pas faire du vélo.

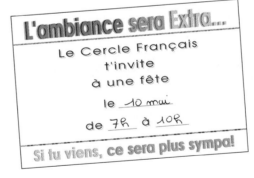

L'ambiance sera Extra...

Le Cercle Français
t'invite
à une fête
le _10 mai_
de _7h_ à _10h_

Si tu viens, ce sera plus sympa!

DEUXIEME ETAPE
CHAPITRE 6

Building on Previous Skills

20 Have students make up reasons why the people shown want to do those activities. For example, one reason for the first activity might be **Ils adorent les animaux.**

Teaching Suggestions

21 Students might want to use the activities in the **Vocabulaire** on page 153.

23 Have students also decide upon a time and place for the party, and then create a colorful invitation to pass out to guests. They might include illustrations or a list of the activities offered to encourage people to come.
• Show *Teaching Transparency 6-2* and assign each person in the illustration to a student or group of students. Provide them with a strip of transparency and a pen and have them create a speech bubble for that person.

Teacher Note

23 Remind students to use **nous** or **on** as the subject of **aller** in their suggestions.

CLOSE

To close this **étape,** have students pair off. Provide one student in each pair with a vocabulary card picturing a place in town (**le musée**) or a sports activity (**jouer au tennis**). Give the other student a card with *accept* or *refuse* written on it. Have students act out a dialogue according to their cards.

ASSESS

Quiz 6-2, *Chapter Teaching Resources, Book 2,* pp. 81–82

Assessment Items, Audiocassette 7B Audio CD 6

Performance Assessment

Have students act out their dialogues from Activity 21.

Motivating Activity

Ask students how they would describe a typical American date to someone from France or another francophone country. They might include who goes out, where they might go, and who pays.

Presentation

Give each photo a number. Then, have students, individually or in pairs, write at least three phrases or sentences in English describing each photo. They might want to tell what the people are doing or wearing, where they are, and any other details they notice. Collect students' papers and read aloud one or two sentences from each. Ask students to identify which photo you are describing by saying **un, deux,** or **trois.**

Teaching Suggestions

• You might have students form small groups to discuss the questions in **Qu'en penses-tu?** Have the group choose a reporter to tell the class their answers. Have students read and discuss **Savais-tu que... ?** while in their group.

• Tell students that their French pen pal has asked some questions about going out in the United States. Ask them what they would take pictures of (a movie theater, the mall, their favorite restaurant) to make an informative photo-collage about going out in their town, similar to the one on this page.

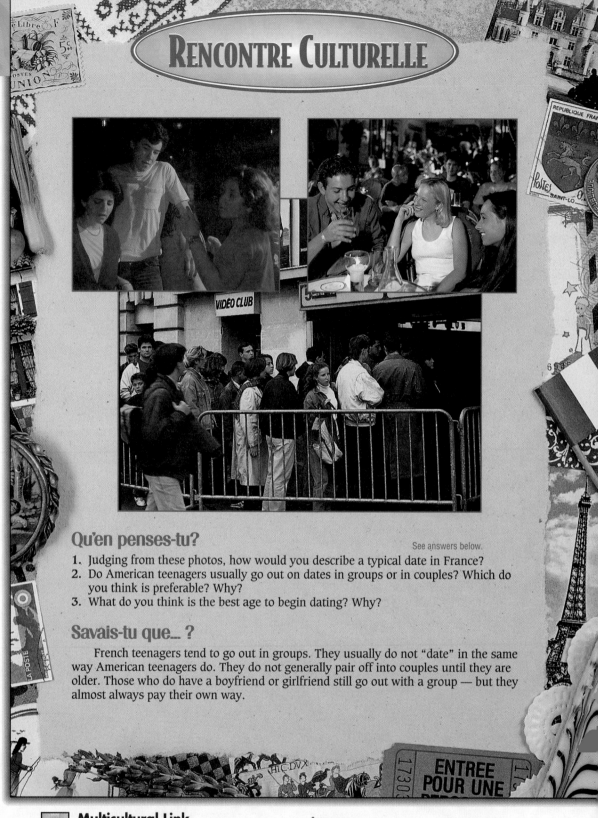

RENCONTRE CULTURELLE

Qu'en penses-tu?

See answers below.

1. Judging from these photos, how would you describe a typical date in France?
2. Do American teenagers usually go out on dates in groups or in couples? Which do you think is preferable? Why?
3. What do you think is the best age to begin dating? Why?

Savais-tu que... ?

French teenagers tend to go out in groups. They usually do not "date" in the same way American teenagers do. They do not generally pair off into couples until they are older. Those who do have a boyfriend or girlfriend still go out with a group — but they almost always pay their own way.

Multicultural Link

Have students research dating habits and customs in other countries. They might interview exchange students or students or community members with different cultural backgrounds to find out the normal age to begin dating, popular places to go on dates, and who pays.

Answers
1. French teenagers go out in groups rather than in couples.

TROISIEME ETAPE

Arranging to meet someone

COMMENT DIT-ON... ?
Arranging to meet someone

To ask when:
Quand?
Quand ça?

To tell when:
Lundi./Demain matin./Ce week-end.
Tout de suite. *Right away.*

To ask where:
Où?

Où ça?

To tell where:
Au café.
Devant le cinéma. *In front of . . .*
Dans le café. *In . . .*
Au métro Saint-Michel. *At the . . . subway stop.*
Chez moi. *At . . . house.*

To ask with whom:
Avec qui?

To tell with whom:
Avec Ahmed et Nathalie.

To ask at what time:
A quelle heure?

To tell at what time:
A dix heures du matin. *At ten in the morning.*
A cinq heures de l'après-midi. *At five in the afternoon.*
A cinq heures et quart. *At quarter past five.*
A cinq heures et demie. *At half past five.*
Vers six heures. *About six o'clock.*

To tell time:
Quelle heure est-il?
What time is it?

Il est six heures. *It's six o'clock.*
Il est six heures moins le quart. *It's quarter to six.*
Il est six heures moins dix. *It's ten to six.*
Il est midi. *It's noon.***/Il est minuit.** *It's midnight.*

To confirm:
Bon, on se retrouve à trois heures. *OK, we'll meet . . .*
Rendez-vous mardi au café. *We'll meet . . .*
Entendu. *OK.*

---

*J*ump Start!

Write three invitations on the board or on a transparency and have students write a different response to each.

MOTIVATE

Ask students what information they need to set up a date or a meeting (when, where, with whom, what time).

TEACH

Presentation

Comment dit-on... ? With a toy phone, act out both sides of a phone conversation wherein you arrange to meet someone. Check comprehension by asking **Où ça? Quand ça?** and so on. Then, pretend to arrange a meeting with the class by asking individual students when, where, and at what time to meet. Have pairs of students practice arranging to meet after school. Introduce conversational time expressions by drawing a clock on the board with the minute hand at 15, 30, and 45 past; label them **et quart, et demie,** and **moins le quart.** Show students various times on a toy clock and have them repeat the time expressions after you. Then, call out various times and have students display them on the clock.

For videodisc application, see *Videodisc Guide.*

Teaching Suggestion

To practice question words, you might give possible answers **(Au stade.)** and have students say the appropriate question word. **(Où?)**

RESOURCES FOR TROISIEME ETAPE

Textbook Audiocassette 3B/Audio CD 6
Practice and Activity Book, pp. 68–70
Videodisc Guide
  Videodisc Program, Videodisc 3B

Chapter Teaching Resources, Book 2
- Communicative Activity 6-2, pp. 61–62
- Teaching Transparency Master 6-3, pp. 65, 66
  Teaching Transparency 6-3
- Additional Listening Activities 6-5, 6-6, p. 69
  Audiocassette 9B/Audio CD 6
- Realia 6-2, pp. 72, 73
- Situation Cards 6-3, pp. 74–75
- Student Response Forms, pp. 76–78
- Quiz 6-3, pp. 83–84
  Audiocassette 7B/Audio CD 6

24 **Ecoute!**

While you're waiting to use a public phone in Paris, you overhear a young woman inviting a friend to go out. Listen to the conversation and then choose the correct answers to these questions.

1. Sylvie parle **avec qui?**
   a. Marc   b. Anna   c. Paul

2. Elle va **où?**
   a. Au musée   b. Au parc   c. Au stade

3. **À quelle heure?**
   a. 1h30   b. 10h15   c. 12h00

4. **Où est-ce qu'ils se retrouvent?**
   a. au métro Solférino   b. dans un café   c. devant le musée

---

NOTE CULTURELLE

You've already learned that train, airline, school, and other official schedules use a 24-hour system called **l'heure officielle.** When you look in an entertainment guide such as *Pariscope,* you may see that a movie starts at 20h00, which is 8:00 P.M. In everyday conversation, however, people use a 12-hour system. For example, for 1:30 P.M., you may hear, **une heure et demie de l'après-midi,** rather than **treize heures trente.** Expressions such as **et demie, et quart,** and **moins le quart** are used only in conversational time, never in official time.

---

25 **A quelle heure?**

Où est-ce que Christian et Noëlle vont aujourd'hui? Qu'est-ce qu'ils vont faire? A quelle heure? See answers below.

1. 9h00   2. 12h00   3. 5h45   4. 8h30

26 **Ecoute!**

Listen to these three messages on your answering machine and write down who they're from and where you're being invited to go. Listen a second time and write down the meeting time and place. Answers on p. 147D.

Language Note

Explain to students that the masculine form **demi** is used after **minuit** and **midi.** The feminine form **demie** is used after **heures,** as in **Il est trois heures et demie.**

Answers

25 1. Ils vont faire du jogging à neuf heures.
   2. Ils vont à la bibliothèque à midi.
   3. Ils vont au zoo à six heures moins le quart.
   4. Ils vont au musée à huit heures et demie.

27 Qu'est-ce que tu vas faire ce soir?

a. Make a list of at least three things that you're going to do tonight. Be sure to include the time and place.

b. Now, ask what your partner is going to do tonight. Then, continue to ask questions about his or her plans.

Grammaire Information questions

There are several ways to ask information questions in French.

- People often ask information questions using only a question word or phrase. They will sometimes add **ça** after it to make it sound less abrupt.

  Où ça?

  Quand ça?

- Another way to ask an information question is to attach the question word or phrase at the end of a statement.

  Tu vas **où?**

  Tu veux faire **quoi?**

  Tu vas au cinéma **à quelle heure?**

  Tu vas au parc **avec qui?**

- Still another way is to begin an information question with the question word or phrase, followed by **est-ce que (qu').**

  Où est-ce que tu vas?

  Qu'est-ce que tu veux faire ce soir?

  Avec qui est-ce que tu vas au cinéma?

  A quelle heure est-ce qu'on se retrouve?

---

28 On va où?

Some friends are inviting you to join them. Ask questions to get more information about their plans. Complete the conversation with the appropriate words or phrases.

— Tu veux aller au cinéma?

— Quand ça?

— Demain soir.

— A quelle heure?

— Vers six heures.

— Où ça?

— Au cinéma Gaumont.

— Avec qui?

— Avec Catherine et Michel.

— D'accord!

— Bon, on se retrouve...

📁 Portfolio

27 Oral Part **b** of this activity might be recorded and included in students' oral portfolios. For portfolio information, see *Assessment Guide,* pages 2–13.

Presentation

Grammaire Ask students to recall all the question words they can (**comment, à quelle heure, combien, qu'est-ce que, quoi, quand, où,** and **avec qui**). Using these words, ask students simple questions and have them give short answers. (**Tu vas où après l'école?**) Next, write on the board these three questions: **Où? Tu vas où? Où est-ce que tu vas?** Then, have students follow these patterns, substituting **quand, avec qui,** and **à quelle heure.**

Additional Practice

Ask a question using the informal pattern with the question word at the end. (**Tu étudies à quelle heure?**) Ask students to restate the question using the formal pattern with **est-ce que.** (**A quelle heure est-ce que tu étudies?**) Then, reverse the procedure.

⟡ For Individual Needs

28 Challenge Have partners supply their own information for the invitation (what, when, where, with whom, what time). You might have several students present their conversations to the class. As the other students listen, have them write down the information they hear. You might want to videotape these conversations and include them in students' oral portfolios.

♜ Game

AROUND THE WORLD Play the game "Around the World" described on page 147F, using questions instead of vocabulary items. Give the first two students an answer to a question, such as **A l'école.** The first student to call out an appropriate question (**Où est-ce que tu vas?**) continues the game.

29 Qu'est-ce qu'on fait chez toi?

You'd like to find out more about what teenagers in France normally do. Write down at least six questions to ask about your pen pal's classes, activities, and hobbies.

 30 Allons au cinéma!

Look at the movie schedule below. Choose a movie you want to see and invite your partner to go with you. When you've agreed on a movie to see, decide at which time you want to go and arrange a time and place to meet.

Le Beaumont   15, Bd des Italiens • 75002 PARIS

○ **Blanche-Neige et les 7 nains,** *v.f. Séances* : 12h, 14h15, 16h30, 18h45, 20h15

○ **Dinosaures,** *v.f. Séances* : 11h55, 13h55, 15h55

○ **Hamlet,** *v.o. Séances* : 13h40, 16h15, 18h55, 21h30

○ **Tous les matins du monde,** *Séances* : 11h30, 14h, 16h30, 19h, 21h30

○ **Fievel au Far West,** *v.o. Séances* : 13h30, 15h, 16h30

○ **Madame Doubtfire,** *v.o. Séances* : 11h05, 13h45, 16h20, 19h, 21h35

○ **Frankenstein junior,** *v.o. Séances* : 21h

○ **Les voyages de Gulliver,** *v.f. Séances* : 13h30, 16h30

○ **Les tortues Ninja II,** *v.f. Séances* : 12h30, 14h, 16h

○ **Casablanca,** *v.o. Séances* : 16h30, 19h

---

 31 Ça te dit?

A friend has written you this note suggesting some things to do this weekend. Write an answer, reacting to each invitation and making suggestions of your own.

> Salut! Ça va? Tu veux faire quoi ce week-end? Moi, je voudrais faire les magasins vendredi soir et jouer au tennis samedi après-midi. On va au ciné samedi soir vers huit heures et demie. Tu viens? Et dimanche matin, tu veux aller au café? Qu'est-ce que tu en penses? Fabienne

Culture Note

30 You might have students guess the English titles of some of the films in this activity and those of other films as well. *(Cendrillon (Cinderella))*. Tell students that the terms **v.o.** and **v.f.** mean **version origi-** **nale** (in the original language) and **version française.** The film *Tous les matins du monde,* mentioned in the listing, stars Gérard Depardieu, Anne Brochet, and Guillaume Depardieu, the son of Gérard, who plays the main character as a young man.

32 Mon journal

What are you and your friends going to do during the next school vacation? Write about your plans. Tell what you're going to do, with whom, when, where, and so on.

P R O N O N C I A T I O N

The vowel sounds [ø] and [œ]

The vowel sound [ø] in **veux** is represented by the letter combination **eu**. It is pronounced with the lips rounded and the tongue pressed against the back of the lower front teeth. To produce this sound, first make the sound **è**, as in **algèbre**, and hold it. Then round the lips slightly to the position for closed **o**, as in **photo**. Repeat these words.

jeudi	veux	peu	deux

The vowel sound [œ] in the word **heure** is similar to the sound in **veux** and is also represented by the letters **eu.** This sound is more open, however, and occurs when these letters are followed by a consonant sound in the same syllable. To produce this sound, first make the sound **è**, as in **algèbre**, and hold it. Then round the lips slightly to the position for open **o**, as in **short.** Repeat these words.

classeur	feuille	heure

A. A prononcer

Repeat the following words.

1. jeudi	déjeuner	peux
2. deux	veut	mieux
3. ordinateur	jeunes	heure
4. feuille	classeur	veulent

B. A lire

Take turns with a partner reading each of the following sentences aloud.

1. Tu as deux ordinateurs? On peut étudier chez toi jeudi?
2. Tu veux manger des escargots? C'est délicieux!
3. On va à la Maison des jeunes? A quelle heure?
4. Tu as une feuille de papier? Je n'ai pas mon classeur.

C. A écrire

You're going to hear a short dialogue. Write down what you hear. Answers on p. 147D.

Mon journal

32 For an additional journal entry suggestion for Chapter 6, see *Practice and Activity Book,* page 150.

Teaching Suggestion

Prononciation Have students use the end-of-chapter **Vocabulaire** lists to find all the words they know that contain the **eu** combination. Then, have them write sentences like the ones in Part B, using as many of these words as possible. Remind them that the sentences must be logical! You might give groups of students a transparency on which to write their sentences, and then, as they read their sentences for the class, project their transparency.

CLOSE

To close this **étape**, have students think about what they're planning to do this weekend: where, when, and with whom. Then, have them write a sentence about their plans, omitting the activity: **Samedi après-midi, à trois heures, je vais ____ à la piscine avec des copains.** Have students read their sentences to a partner, who will try to fill in the blanks.

ASSESS

Quiz 6-3, *Chapter Teaching Resources, Book 2,* pp. 83–84

Assessment Items, Audiocassette 7B/Audio CD 6

Performance Assessment

Tell students that you'd like to join them for the activities they wrote about for Activity 31 on page 166. Have them tell you what they are doing and when and where to meet. Alternatively, you might have students ask you about your weekend plans.

READING STRATEGY

Using context to determine meaning

Teacher Note

For an additional reading, see *Practice and Activity Book*, page 71.

PREREADING
Activity A

Motivating Activity

Bring in brochures or advertisements from amusement parks or tourist attractions. Pass them around and ask students if they have gone to any of these places or would like to visit them. You might offer students a "free vacation" and ask where they would spend it. Ask them what they consider to be an enjoyable vacation.

Language Arts Link

Read aloud (or have students read) **De bons conseils.** Choose a Language Arts reading and delete every seventh word. Have students use the context to suggest words that could complete the passage.

Teaching Suggestion

A. Begin by having students scan the brochures to answer the question in this activity. You might also ask what types of brochures there are and what information students would expect to find in them.

READING
Activities B–D

Teaching Suggestions

• Before doing Activity B, you might have students describe the illustrations.

B. As part of this activity, you might want to show students an **Astérix** book. These books are published in numerous languages and might be available at local bookstores.

LISONS!

Where do you like to go on the weekend? Look at these brochures to see where Parisians go for fun.

DE BONS CONSEILS

When you run across a word you don't know, use context to guess the meaning of the word. You automatically use this strategy in your own language. For example, you may not know the English word *dingo*, but when you see it in a sentence, you can make an intelligent guess about what it means. Read this sentence: He thought that the kangaroos and the koala bears were cute, but that the dingos were mean-looking. You can guess that a *dingo* is a possibly vicious animal found in Australia. It is, in fact, a wild dog.

theme parks and zoo

A. What kinds of places do these brochures describe?

B. Look at the brochure for **Parc Astérix.** Here are some questions you should consider if you were planning a day trip there with your friends.

See answers below.

1. During which months would you not be able to go on this trip?

2. On which days of the week can you take this trip to **Parc Astérix?**

3. If you took the trip in the advertisement, what time would you leave from Paris?

4. What time would you leave the park for the trip back?

5. What do you think **bienvenue** means?

168   *cent soixante-huit*

Bienvenue
Welcome
Welkom

PARC ASTERIX

Bienvenue en Gaule pour une journée mémorable !

Pour passer une journée partagée entre l'émotion et l'aventure. Pour retrouver cette bonne humeur légendaire et communicative. Pour faire un voyage mémorable en Gaule, au pays du bien-vivre et de l'histoire...

Venez au Parc Astérix! Astérix et tous ses amis vous y attendent...

Départ de Paris les mercredi et samedi à 9h, du 10 avril au 2 octobre. Retour sur le site à 18h et arrivée à Paris vers 19h30.

Prix par personne: **340 F**
Enfants de 3 à 11 ans inclus: **260 F**

Le prix inclut l'hébergement.

France Miniature — le Pays

CALENDRIER SAISON 1994 :

Ouverture : 15 mars au 15 novembre.
Tous les jours de 10h à 19h.
(juillet et août)
Le samedi, nocturne jusqu'à 23h.

TARIFS :

Individuels : Adultes : 68 F.
Enfants : 48 F (de 3 à 13 ans).

RESTAURATION

Deux restaurants de 300 places chacun et 2 kiosques proposent des menus de différentes régions de France (un restaurant ouvert le samedi soir). Aire de pique-nique aménagée.

Culture Note

La Gaule, the name for what is now France, was the territory of Celtic tribes who were conquered by the Romans.

Answers

B 1. November through March
2. Wednesdays and Saturdays
3. 9:00 A.M.
4. 6:00 P.M.
5. Welcome.
6. 1.620 francs; Exchange rate will vary.

MUSEUM NATIONAL D'HISTOIRE NATURELLE
PARC ZOOLOGIQUE DE PARIS
BOIS DE VINCENNES
OUVERT TOUS LES JOURS
de 9 h à 17 h ou 17 h 30 l'hiver - de 9 h à 18 h ou 18 h 30 l'été*
TARIF*
Entrée 40 F - Tarif Réduit 20 F - Groupes Scolaires 10 F
ACCES
Métro : Porte Dorée, Saint-Mandé-Tourelle - Bus : 46-86-325-PC
*Sauf modification
53 Av. de Saint-Maurice - 75012 PARIS - Tel. : 44.75.20.10 - Fax : 43.43.54.73
REPAS DES ANIMAUX
PANDA 9h30 - 17h
PELICANS 14h15
MANCHOTS 14h30
FAUVES 15h
PHOQUES ET OTARIES 16h30
FRIANDISES
VENTE DE SOUVENIRS
ANIMAUX DE VERRE
TOILETTES
POSTE DE SECOURS (week-end)
GRAND ROCHER (70 m)
ANIMAUX PRÉHISTORIQUES
PIQUE-NIQUE
RESTAURANT
PORTE DE PARIS
PORTE DE CHARENTON
AVENUE DE SAINT-MAURICE
AVENUE DU LAC
AVENUE DAUMESNIL
Le Pays FRANCE MINIATURE, c'est la France comme vous ne l'avez jamais vue! Sur une immense carte en relief, sont regroupées les plus belles richesses de notre patrimoine : 166 monuments historiques, 15 villages typiques de nos régions, les paysages et les scènes de la vie quotidienne à l'échelle 1/30ème... au cœur d'un environnement naturel extraordinaire.
PLACE DE LA CONCORDE
JARDIN DES TUILERIES
RUE DE SÈVRES

6. If you go with three friends and one of you brings your ten-year-old sister, how much will it cost? How much is it in American money?

C. One of your friends just came back from **France Miniature** and told you about it. Check the brochure to see if what he said was accurate or not.

1. "I saw more than 150 monuments!" accurate
2. "There were twenty villages represented." inaccurate
3. "The size of everything was on a scale of 1/25." inaccurate
4. "It was more expensive than **Parc Astérix.**" inaccurate
5. "We stayed until midnight." inaccurate
6. "We went on my birthday, June 15th." accurate

D. Imagine you and a friend want to go to the **Parc zoologique de Paris.** See answers below.

1. How can you get there? Can you take a bus? The metro? At which metro stop would you get off?
2. How much is it going to cost? Will it make a difference if you're students?
3. How late can you stay in the summer? In the winter?
4. What are some of the animals you'll get to see?
5. At what time do the pelicans eat? The pandas?
6. What are the restrooms near? How many picnic areas are there? What is near the first-aid station? Where can you buy a gift?

E. Which of these places would you like to go to most? Why?

Math Link

France Miniature Make sure students understand the concept of building on a scale of 1/30. How tall would a 60-meter building be on this reduced scale? (2 meters)

Teaching Suggestions

C. Have students correct the inaccurate statements.

D. Students might enjoy planning their visit to the zoo and listing the animals they would like to see. You might refer them to the names of animals in the Preliminary Chapter.

Terms in Lisons!

- Terms that might interest students from the **Parc Astérix** brochure include:
  bien-vivre—*good living, the good life*
  retrouver—*to find again*
- An important expression from **France Miniature** is **aire de pique-nique aménagée**—*equipped picnic area.*
- Students might want to know some of the other expressions from the zoo brochure:
  friandises—*sweets, desserts*
  manchots—*penguins*
  fauves—*wildcats*
  otaries—*sea lions*

POSTREADING
Activity E

Teaching Suggestion

Use Activity E as a closing discussion question. You might also ask students to name the brochures that give them the most and the least information. Students might enjoy creating a brochure in French to advertise a nearby attraction in their own community to French tourists.

Answers

D 1. by bus or metro; metro stop Porte Dorée, Saint-Mandé-Tourelle
2. 40 F or 20 F; student groups: 10 F
3. Summer: 6:00 or 6:30 P.M.; Winter: 5:00 or 5:30 P.M.
4. *Possible answers:* giraffes, tigers, seals
5. Pelicans: 2:15 P.M.; Pandas: 9:30 A.M. and 5:00 P.M.
6. rhinoceros; two picnic areas; birds and mammoths; vente de souvenirs *(souvenir shop)*

Culture Notes

- The photo of model castles on the **France Miniature** brochure shows several châteaux of the Loire Valley, including Chenonceau (foreground) and Chambord (background).
- The three numbers shown after **bus** on the zoo brochure list the bus routes that stop by the zoo. The zip code shows that the zoo is in the twelfth **arrondissement** in Paris, in the southeastern section of the city.

The **Mise en pratique** reviews and integrates all four skills and culture in preparation for the Chapter Test.

Teaching Suggestions

1 You might play this activity as a game. Have students form small groups and give them a time limit to answer as many questions as possible. You might give a prize to the group that correctly answers the most questions.

1 Ask students which place they would prefer to visit and why.

 Portfolio

3 Oral This activity is appropriate for students' oral portfolios. For portfolio information, see *Assessment Guide*, pages 2–13.

MISE EN PRATIQUE

La tour Eiffel est le monument parisien le plus connu au monde. Elle a été édifiée pour l'exposition universelle de 1889 sous l'impulsion de son concepteur de génie Gustave Eiffel. Avec ses 300 m, c'est l'édifice le plus haut du monde. Il s'agit d'un véritable chef-d'œuvre de légèreté et de résistance. Montée par l'ascenseur de 10h à 23h : 16 à 47 F, par les escaliers 8F. Tél.: 45 55 91 11

Une vue exceptionnelle du Musée d'Orsay

Musée d'Orsay

LE PLUS ELEGANT MUSEE DE PARIS L'architecte italienne Gae Aulenti a implanté dans l'ancienne gare d'Orsay une somptueuse scénographie, développée en un jeu de niveaux, magnifique écrin pour l'art français du 19e siècle : impressionniste, art décoratif, dessins, sculptures et photographies.
1, rue de Bellechasse, 7e. Tél. : 40 49 48 84. Tous les jours sauf le lundi de 10h à 17h30. Nocturne le jeudi jusqu'à 21h45.

PARISTORIC : LE FILM

2 000 ans d'émotions sur écran géant
2000 years of emotion on a giant screen

Adulte 70 F
Jeune 40 F

20 F off

réduction à la caisse sur présentation du guide Paris Midnight

■ SEANCE A CHAQUE DEBUT D'HEURE DE 9H A 21H
■ EVERY DAY, EVERY HOUR ON THE HOUR 9 A.M. TO 9 P.M.

Espace Hebertot, métro : Villiers/Rome
78 bis, bd des batignolles, 75017 Paris
Tél. : 42 93 93 46 — Fax : 42 93 93 48

1 Look over the advertisements and answer the questions below.   See answers below.

1. Which places offer a view of Paris?
2. Where can you see a free concert?
3. Where can you hear a movie about the history of Paris?
4. Where can you see nineteenth-century French art?
5. Where can you see ancient art?
6. Which places offer you a discount?
7. Which places list their prices?
8. Which attractions are closed on Mondays?
9. Which attractions are closed on Tuesdays?
10. Which advertisements tell you the name of the nearest subway stop?

 2 Your French friends are discussing which Paris attraction to visit. Listen to their conversation and write down the attraction they decide on. Listen again and tell when and where they agree to meet.   Answers on p. 147D.

 3 Invite your partner to one of the places advertised above. Your partner will either accept or decline your invitation. Take turns.

Answers
1 1. Tour Montparnasse, tour Eiffel, Notre-Dame
2. Notre-Dame de Paris
3. *Paristoric: Le Film*
4. Musée d'Orsay
5. Louvre
6. Tour Montparnasse, *Paristoric: Le Film*
7. Notre-Dame de Paris, tour Eiffel, *Paristoric: Le Film*
8. Musée d'Orsay
9. Louvre
10. Louvre, *Paristoric: Le Film,* Tour Montparnasse

Notre-Dame de Paris, c'est l'un des monuments les plus visités au monde. Ascension en haut de la tour (386 marches) de 10h à 17h : 27F, visite de la crypte de 10h à 16h30 : 23F, visite du trésor de 10h à 18h, dimanche de 14h à 18h : 15F. Concerts gratuits tous les dimanches à 17h45. Visites et ascension fermées les jours fériés.

Architecte : I. M. Pei

LOUVRE

Palais du Louvre
75001 Paris
Tél. (1) 40 20 51 51
Métro : Palais-Royal, Louvre

Antiquités égyptiennes, orientales, grecques, étrusques et romaines. Peintures. Sculptures. Mobilier et objets d'art. Arts graphiques.
Ouvert de 9h à 18h.
Nocturne les lundi et mercredi jusqu'à 21h45.
Fermé le mardi.

LA VUE PARISIENNE

à 209m!

To the top in 38 seconds!

TOUR MONTPARNASSE
Tous les jours, tous les soirs
56e Étage et Terrasse

VISITE PANORAMIQUE
Métro Montparnasse-Bienvenüe
Téléphone 45 38 52 56

20% de réduction sur le prix d'entrée à la visite panoramique, 59ème étage de la Tour Montparnasse. Présentez ce bon au guichet de la Tour. Valable pour 5 personnes maximum.

20% reduction off the admission price to the 59th floor of the Montparnasse Tower. To receive your discount, present this coupon to the Tower ticket booth, (coupon permits 5 persons discount maximum).

S. A. MONTPARNASSE 56 - Tour Montparnasse
33, avenue du Maine - 75015 PARIS - Tél. 45.38.52.56 - Fax 45.38.69.96

4 Using what you've learned about French culture, answer the following questions. See answers below.

1. Where do French young people like to go to have fun?
2. Would a French teenager be surprised at American dating customs? Why?

5
a. You have one day in Paris to do whatever you like. Make a list of where you're going and at what time you plan to go there.
b. Write a note to your French class back home telling everyone what you plan to do during your day in Paris.

6

JEU DE ROLE

Get together with some classmates. Choose one place in Paris you'd all like to visit and decide on a meeting time and place. Make sure that the Paris attraction you choose to visit will be open when you plan to go. Act this out with your group.

Possible answers
4 1. films, plays, concerts, discothèques, dance parties, **Maisons des jeunes**
   2. Yes, because French teenagers tend to go out in groups rather than couples.

📁 **Portfolio**

5 Written You might have students include this in their written portfolios.

6 Oral Students might include this in their oral portfolios. For portfolio suggestions, see *Assessment Guide,* page 19.

Teaching Suggestion

5 If students have problems getting started or would like more options, refer them to the Location Opener on pages 120–123 for sites and activities in Paris.

📺 **Video Wrap-Up**

- **VIDEO PROGRAM**
- **EXPANDED VIDEO PROGRAM,** Videocassette 2, 36:27–48:15
- **VIDEODISC PROGRAM,** Videodisc 3B

At this time, you might want to use the video resources for additional review and enrichment. See *Video Guide* or *Videodisc Guide* for suggestions regarding the following:
- **Projets de week-end** (Dramatic episode)
- **Panorama Culturel** (Interviews)
- **Vidéoclips** (Authentic footage)

This page is intended to help students prepare for the test. It is a brief checklist of the major points covered in the chapter. The students should be reminded that this is only a checklist and does not necessarily include everything that will appear on the test.

Building on Previous Skills

1 Have students add a day and time to their answers. You might have them practice with the **tu, vous, il,** and **elle** forms as well.

Teaching Suggestion

3, 4 Encourage students to vary the ways they express each function.

Additional Practice

5 Suggest other places these or other people might want to visit.

Teaching Suggestion

7 After students have given possible answers, read a short passage and have them answer the questions in this activity based on what you read. (**Salut, c'est Monique! Ecoute, tu veux aller au musée? On y va samedi avec Daniel vers deux heures—il veut y voir une exposition de photos. Alors, tu peux? Rendez-vous devant le musée—à bientôt!**)

QUE SAIS-JE?

Can you use what you've learned in this chapter?

Can you make plans?
p. 153

1 How would you say that these people are going to these places?

1. je vais au match.   **2. nous** allons au centre commercial.   **3. Anne et Etienne** vont au cinéma.

2 How would you tell what you're planning to do this weekend?
Je vais... ce week-end.

3 How would you invite a friend to . . .   See answers below.

1. go window shopping?   3. go see a basketball game?
2. go for a walk?   4. go to the café?

Can you extend and respond to invitations?
p. 159

4 How would you accept the following invitations? How would you refuse them?   See answers below.

1. Je voudrais aller faire du ski. Tu viens?   3. On va au restaurant. Tu viens?
2. Allons à la Maison des jeunes!   4. Tu veux aller au cinéma?

5 How would you say that the following people want to go to these places?   See answers below.

1. Ahmed   **2. Isabelle et Ferdinand**   **3. Mon amie et moi**

Can you arrange to meet someone?
p. 163

6 If someone invited you to go to the movies, what are three questions you might ask to find out more information?
Possible answers: Où ça? Quand ça? A quelle heure? Avec qui?

7 What are some possible answers to the following questions?   See answers below.

1. Où ça?   3. A quelle heure?
2. Avec qui?   4. Quand ça?

Possible answers
3
1. Tu veux faire les vitrines avec moi?
2. Je voudrais faire une promenade. Tu viens?
3. On peut voir un match de basket.
4. Allons au café!

4
Accepting: D'accord. Bonne idée. Je veux bien. Pourquoi pas?
Refusing: Ça ne me dit rien. J'ai des trucs à faire. Désolé(e), je ne peux pas. Je suis occupé(e).

5 1. Ahmed veut aller à la bibliothèque.
2. Isabelle et Ferdinand veulent aller au théâtre.
3. Mon amie et moi, nous voulons aller au musée.

7
1. au cinéma, devant le stade, au café
2. avec Anne, avec mes amis, avec moi
3. vers trois heures, à huit heures et demie, à midi
4. demain, ce soir, lundi après-midi

PREMIERE ETAPE

Making plans

Qu'est-ce que tu vas faire... ?
  What are you going to do . . . ?
Tu vas faire quoi...? *What are
  you going to do . . . ?*
Je vais... *I'm going . . .*
Pas grand-chose. *Not much.*
Rien de spécial. *Nothing special.*

Things to do

aller à une boum *to go to a party*
faire une promenade *to go for a
  walk*
faire un pique-nique *to have a
  picnic*

faire les vitrines *to window-shop*
manger quelque chose *to eat
  something*
regarder un match *to watch a
  game (on TV)*
voir un film *to see a movie*
voir un match *to see a game (in
  person)*
voir une pièce *to see a play*
aller *to go*
au/à la *to, at*

Places to go

la bibliothèque *the library*
le centre commercial *the mall*

le cinéma *the movie theater*
la Maison des jeunes et de la
  culture (MJC) *the recreation
  center*
le musée *the museum*
le parc *the park*
la piscine *the swimming pool*
la plage *the beach*
le restaurant *the restaurant*
le stade *the stadium*
le théâtre *the theater*
le zoo *the zoo*

DEUXIEME ETAPE

Extending invitations

Allons... ! *Let's go . . . !*
Tu veux... avec moi? *Do you
  want . . . with me?*
Tu viens? *Will you come?*
On peut... *We can . . .*

Accepting an invitation

D'accord. *OK.*
Bonne idée. *Good idea.*

Je veux bien. *I'd really like to.*
Pourquoi pas? *Why not?*

Refusing invitations

Ça ne me dit rien. *That doesn't
  interest me.*
J'ai des trucs à faire. *I've got
  things to do.*
Désolé(e), je ne peux pas. *Sorry,
  I can't.*

Désolé(e), je suis occupé(e).
  Sorry, I'm busy.
vouloir *to want*

Other useful expressions

je voudrais... *I'd like . . .*

TROISIEME ETAPE

Arranging to meet someone

Quand (ça)? *When?*
tout de suite *right away*
Où (ça)? *Where?*
dans *in*
devant *in front of*
au métro... *at the . . . metro stop*
chez... *at . . . ('s) house*
Avec qui? *With whom?*
avec... *with . . .*
A quelle heure? *At what time?*

A cinq heures. *At five o'clock.*
  et demie *half past*
  et quart *quarter past*
  moins le quart *quarter to*
  moins cinq *five to*
Quelle heure est-il? *What time is
  it?*
Il est midi. *It's noon.*
Il est minuit. *It's midnight.*
Il est midi (minuit) et demi. *It's
  half past noon (midnight).*
vers *about*

Bon, on se retrouve... *OK, we'll
  meet . . .*
Rendez-vous... *We'll meet . . .*
Entendu. *OK.*

Other useful expressions

ce week-end *this weekend*
demain *tomorrow*
est-ce que *(introduces a yes-no
  question)*

♖ **Game**

♜ **MOTS CROISÉS** Have
groups of students choose five
or six vocabulary words and
design a crossword puzzle
with pictures or fill-in-the-
blank sentences as clues. Have
groups exchange and fill out
the puzzles.

CHAPTER 6 ASSESSMENT

CHAPTER TEST

• *Chapter Teaching Resources,
  Book 2,* pp. 85–90
• *Assessment Guide,* Speaking
  Test, p. 30
• *Assessment Items,*
  Audiocassette 7B
  Audio CD 6

TEST GENERATOR, CHAPTER 6

ALTERNATIVE ASSESSMENT

Performance Assessment

You might want to use the **Jeu
de rôle** (p. 171) as a cumulative performance assessment
activity.

📁 **Portfolio Assessment**

• **Written: Mise en pratique,**
  Activity 5, *Pupil's Edition,*
  p. 171
  Assessment Guide, p. 19
• **Oral: Mise en pratique, Jeu
  de rôle,** *Pupil's Edition,*
  p. 171
  Assessment Guide, p. 19

MIDTERM EXAM

• *Assessment Guide,* pp. 35–42
• *Assessment Items,*
  Audiocassette 7B
  Audio CD 6

Chapitre 7 : La famille
Chapter Overview

Mise en train pp. 176–178	Sympa, la famille!		Practice and Activity Book, p. 73		Video Guide OR Videodisc Guide

	FUNCTIONS	GRAMMAR	CULTURE	RE-ENTRY
Première étape pp. 179–183	• Identifying people, p. 179 • Introducing people, p. 183	• Possession with **de**, p. 180 • Possessive adjectives, p. 181	**Note Culturelle,** Family life, p. 182	Asking for and giving people's names and ages
Deuxième étape pp. 184–188	Describing and characterizing people, p. 185	• Adjective agreement, p. 186 • The verb **être**, p. 187	**Panorama Culturel,** Pets in France, p. 188	
Troisième étape pp. 189–191	Asking for, giving, and refusing permission, p. 189			Family vocabulary

Prononciation p. 191	The nasal sounds [ɔ̃], [ɛ̃], and [œ̃]		**Dictation:** *Textbook Audiocassette 4A/Audio CD 7*

Lisons! pp. 192–193	**En direct des refuges**	**Reading Strategy:** Finding the main idea

Review pp. 194–197	**Mise en pratique,** pp. 194–195	**Que sais-je?** p. 196	**Vocabulaire,** p. 197

Assessment Options	**Etape Quizzes**
	• *Chapter Teaching Resources, Book 2*
	  Première étape, Quiz 7-1, pp. 135–136
	  Deuxième étape, Quiz 7-2, pp. 137–138
	  Troisième étape, Quiz 7-3, pp. 139–140
	• *Assessment Items, Audiocassette 8A/Audio CD 7*
		Chapter Test
		• *Chapter Teaching Resources, Book 2,* pp. 141–146
		• *Assessment Guide,* Speaking Test, p. 31
		• *Assessment Items, Audiocassette 8A/Audio CD 7*
		
		Test Generator, Chapter 7

Video Program OR Expanded Video Program, Videocassette 3
OR Videodisc Program, Videodisc 4A

Textbook Audiocassette 4A/Audio CD 7

RESOURCES: Print	RESOURCES: Audiovisual

Textbook Audiocassette 4A/Audio CD 7

Practice and Activity Book, pp. 74–76
Chapter Teaching Resources, Book 2
- Teaching Transparency Master 7-1, pp. 119, 122 . . . . Teaching Transparency 7-1
- Additional Listening Activities 7-1, 7-2, p. 123 . . . . Additional Listening Activities, Audiocassette 10A/Audio CD 7
- Realia 7-1, pp. 127, 129
- Situation Cards 7-1, pp. 130–131
- Student Response Forms, pp. 132–134
- Quiz 7-1, pp. 135–136 . . . . Assessment Items, Audiocassette 8A/Audio CD 7
Videodisc Guide . . . . Videodisc Program, Videodisc 4A

Textbook Audiocassette 4A/Audio CD 7

Practice and Activity Book, pp. 77–79
Chapter Teaching Resources, Book 2
- Communicative Activity 7-1, pp. 115–116
- Teaching Transparency Master 7-2, pp. 120, 122 . . . . Teaching Transparency 7-2
- Additional Listening Activities 7-3, 7-4, p. 124 . . . . Additional Listening Activities, Audiocassette 10A/Audio CD 7
- Realia 7-2, pp. 128, 129
- Situation Cards 7-2, pp. 130–131
- Student Response Forms, pp. 132–134
- Quiz 7-2, pp. 137–138 . . . . Assessment Items, Audiocassette 8A/Audio CD 7
Video Guide . . . . Video Program OR Expanded Video Program, Videocassette 3
Videodisc Guide . . . . Videodisc Program, Videodisc 4A

Textbook Audiocassette 4A/Audio CD 7

Practice and Activity Book, pp. 80–82
Chapter Teaching Resources, Book 2
- Communicative Activity 7-2, pp. 117–118
- Teaching Transparency Master 7-3, pp. 121, 122 . . . . Teaching Transparency 7-3
- Additional Listening Activities 7-5, 7-6, p. 125 . . . . Additional Listening Activities, Audiocassette 10A/Audio CD 7
- Realia 7-2, pp. 128, 129
- Situation Cards 7-3, pp. 130–131
- Student Response Forms, pp. 132–134
- Quiz 7-3, pp. 139–140 . . . . Assessment Items, Audiocassette 8A/Audio CD 7
Videodisc Guide . . . . Videodisc Program, Videodisc 4A

Practice and Activity Book, p. 83

Video Guide . . . . Video Program OR Expanded Video Program, Videocassette 3
Videodisc Guide . . . . Videodisc Program, Videodisc 4A

Alternative Assessment
- Performance Assessment
  Première étape, p. 183
  Deuxième étape, p. 187
  Troisième étape, p. 191
- Portfolio Assessment
  Written: **Mise en pratique,** Activity 4, Pupil's Edition, p. 195
  Assessment Guide, p. 20
  Oral: **Mise en pratique, Jeu de rôle,** Pupil's Edition, p. 195
  Assessment Guide, p. 20

Chapitre 7 : La famille
Textbook Listening Activities Scripts

For Student Response Forms, see *Chapter Teaching Resources, Book 2*, pp. 132–134.

Première étape

8 Ecoute! p. 181

1. Voilà mon grand-père. Il n'est pas jeune, mais il est toujours actif. Regarde. Là, il fait du vélo.
2. Et voici ma mère et mon père. Là, ils sont en vacances à la Martinique. Qu'est-ce qu'il fait beau, hein?
3. Et ça, c'est ma sœur. Elle adore jouer au volley!
4. Ce sont mes deux frères. Ils jouent souvent au football.
5. Et ça, c'est moi avec mon chien. Il est mignon, n'est-ce pas?

Answers to Activity 8
1. d 2. b 3. a 4. e 5. c

9 Ecoute! p. 181

1. Notre chien s'appelle Chouchou.
2. Nos poissons aiment beaucoup manger.
3. Leurs chats aiment sortir le matin.
4. Son canari est jaune.
5. Votre chien, il a quel âge?
6. Et vos chats, est-ce qu'ils aiment beaucoup dormir?
7. Ses poissons sont noirs ou rouges?

Answers to Activity 9
1. their own; dog
2. their own; fish
3. someone else's; cats
4. someone else's; canary
5. someone else's; dog
6. someone else's; cats
7. someone else's; fish

12 Ecoute! p. 183

1. Salut, Michèle! Je te présente mon amie Anne-Marie.
2. Regarde. Voilà Mademoiselle Simonet.
3. Maman, je te présente Annick.
4. Voilà Isabelle. C'est une amie.
5. Madame Martin, je vous présente Monsieur Poulain.

Answers to Activity 12
1. introducing
2. identifying
3. introducing
4. identifying
5. introducing

Deuxième étape

15 Ecoute! p. 185

1. Elle est grande et blonde.
2. Il est petit, roux et très fort.
3. Il est grand et brun.
4. Elle est petite, mince et brune.
5. Elle est petite et rousse.

Answers to Activity 15
1. Julie
2. Martin
3. Roger
4. Carmen
5. Denise

16 Ecoute! p. 185

1. Dominique est grande, brune et très intelligente.
2. Ça, c'est Andrée. Andrée est mince et blonde. Euh, un peu pénible.
3. Tu vois, là, c'est Joëlle. Joëlle aime bien faire du sport. Petite mais assez forte. Elle est amusante.
4. Ici, c'est Gabriel. Gabriel est mignon et tellement gentil!
5. Et Danielle. Danielle est brune. Toujours embêtante. Pas facile du tout!

Answers to Activity 16
1. Dominique — favorable
2. Andrée — unfavorable
3. Joëlle — favorable
4. Gabriel — favorable
5. Danielle — unfavorable

Troisième étape

23 Ecoute! p. 189

1. — Je voudrais sortir. Tu es d'accord?
   — Non. Je ne suis pas d'accord.

2. — Je peux aller à la plage?
   — Pas question.

3. — Je voudrais aller au restaurant avec mes amis. Tu es d'accord?
   — Oui, si tu fais d'abord tes devoirs.

4. — On va jouer au football. Je peux y aller?
   — Oui, bien sûr.

5. — Est-ce que je peux aller au cinéma?
   — Oui, si tu veux.

Answers to Activity 23

1. refused	3. given	5. given
2. refused	4. given	

24 Ecoute! p. 190

1. — Maman, Stéphanie et Emilie vont au cinéma ce soir. Je peux y aller?
   — Non, tu dois garder ta sœur.

2. — Je voudrais sortir avec Jean-Luc. Je peux?
   — Si tu promènes le chien, c'est d'accord.

3. — Maman, je peux sortir avec Marc ce soir?
   — Si tu passes d'abord l'aspirateur.

4. — On va au parc cet après-midi pour faire un pique-nique. Je voudrais y aller.
   — Mais non. Tu sais bien, tu dois ranger ta chambre!

5. — Je voudrais aller à la piscine avec Elise et Cécile. D'accord?
   — D'accord, si tu fais d'abord tes devoirs.

6. — Je peux aller au centre commercial ce soir avec Arnaud?
   — Oui, si tu fais d'abord la vaisselle.

Answers to Activity 24
1. c   2. e   3. d   4. a   5. f   6. b

Prononciation, p. 191

For the scripts for Parts A and B, see p. 191.

C. A écrire

(Dictation)
— Voilà mon cousin américain.
— Son chien est très mignon.

Mise en pratique

1 p. 194

Je m'appelle Nathalie. Ma famille habite à Paris. J'ai un frère qui s'appelle Jean-Paul. Il a douze ans. Il est très gentil avec moi. J'ai aussi un chat. Il s'appelle Câlin. Il n'est pas vieux, il a deux ans seulement. Et moi, quel âge j'ai? Eh bien, j'ai quinze ans.

Answers to Mise en pratique Activity 1
1. Jean-Paul
2. douze ans
3. un chat
4. Il n'est pas vieux, il a deux ans.

Ma famille
(Individual Project)

ASSIGNMENT

Students will draw their family trees, labeling at least three generations with the names of family members and their relationships to the student. Students who don't want to give their own family background can draw the family tree of a royal family, a famous family, or an imaginary family.

MATERIALS

✂ **Students may need**
- Construction paper or posterboard
- Colored pens, pencils, or markers
- Photos of family members or magazine photos
- Tape or glue

SUGGESTED SEQUENCE

1. Have students list all of their family members for at least three generations. They should begin with one pair of grandparents and add all their children. Then, have them add any descendants from the second generation, and so on. They should do the same for the other pair of grandparents.

2. Have students sketch the tree in pencil on a large piece of paper or posterboard. Then, have them write in the names and relationships in pencil, using their lists. Remind them to leave space for photos or drawings. Have them exchange posters with a classmate to edit.

3. Have students position their photos or drawings on their trees and make any necessary adjustments.

4. Have students give an oral presentation in which they identify each family member in French. You might want to display students' posters around the classroom.

GRADING THE PROJECT

You might base each student's grade on completeness, presentation and appearance, correct use and spelling of vocabulary, and oral presentation.

Suggested Point Distribution (total = 100 points)

Completeness	30 points
Presentation/appearance	30 points
Use/spelling of vocabulary	20 points
Oral presentation	20 points

FAMILY LINK

Encourage students to take their projects home to share with their families.

Mon album de famille
(Individual Project)

ASSIGNMENT

Students will make a family photo album with descriptions of each family member similar to the one on pages 176–177. This project provides more of a challenge and requires more language use than **Ma famille.** Students might describe a cartoon, television, or royal family instead of their own.

MATERIALS

✂ **Students may need**
- Construction paper
- Stapler and staples
- Colored markers or pens
- Family photos or magazine pictures
- Tape or glue

SUGGESTED SEQUENCE

1. Have students choose at least five family members to describe in their photo albums. They should make a list of words and phrases to be used in their descriptions of each member. For each person, have students list his or her age, at least three adjectives, and two things that he or she likes or dislikes.

2. Have students choose photos or draw sketches of the family members they are featuring in their album.

3. Have students write rough drafts of their descriptions. They might give their descriptions to a classmate to edit.

4. Give students some construction paper and have them tape or glue one photo or drawing on each page and copy their final description of that family member underneath it.

5. Have students design and draw a cover for their album and staple it to the other pages.

GRADING THE PROJECT

You might base students' grades on the completion of the assignment, use of vocabulary, presentation and creativity, and accurate language use.

Suggested Point Distribution (total = 100 points)

Completion of assignment	25 points
Vocabulary use	25 points
Presentation/creativity	25 points
Language use	25 points

QUI SUIS-JE?

In this game, students will interact and practice question formation.

Procedure The day before the game, have each student write the name of a well-known person on an index card. Collect the cards and make sure there are no duplicates. You might want to include the principal or other staff members. On the day of the game, tape a card to each student's back, without letting him or her see the card. Have students try to determine their new identity by asking members of their group yes-no questions. **(Je suis grand(e)?)** Circulate to monitor and help out as needed. You might set a time limit for this game and give prizes to the first few students who guess the name affixed to their back.

Variation An alternate way to play this game is to have students write their own names and a brief but detailed description of themselves on an index card. Have them include their likes and dislikes, their hobbies, and so on. Collect and redistribute the cards, taping one to each student's back. Continue with the game as described above.

TREE FILL-IN

In this game, students will practice family vocabulary.

Procedure In this game, students will try to fill in a family tree as they listen to an oral description of the family relationships. To prepare the game, draw different family trees on pieces of paper and write in only first names. Have students pair off or form small groups. Distribute a family tree to one student in each pair or small group. The person in each pair or group who receives the tree will describe it to the other(s). **(Pierre est le père de Marie.)** The other student(s) must draw a family tree according to the description. Those listening may ask for clarification, as long as they do so in French. After students have drawn their trees, they should compare them to the original and make corrections.

POSSESSIFS

In this game, students will practice using possessive adjectives.

Procedure Prepare in advance two sets of flashcards, one set with subject pronouns and the other set with objects from the first seven chapters. Divide the class into two or three teams and appoint a timekeeper. One player from each team will play at a time. Hold up two flashcards, one showing a subject pronoun and the other a noun. The player must say the possessive adjective appropriate to the subject together with the noun within a set amount of time (five seconds should be long enough). For example, if **ils** and **amis** are shown on the two cards, the player should say **leurs amis.** Give points for all correct answers. Make sure all players have a turn and play as many rounds as you choose. By mixing the pronouns and nouns, you can use the same cards over and over.

Variation This game could also be played by breaking into smaller teams so all of the students can play at once. In this case, each team would write their answer on a piece of paper within a specific time limit (perhaps 5–10 seconds). This way, all students and all teams would play each round.

Chapitre 7
La famille
pp. 174–197

𝒰sing the Chapter Opener

Teaching Suggestion

Ask several students to come to the front of the room. Introduce them to the class, using the caption of the first photo and changing **tu** to **vous**. Show two photos of your family members and introduce and describe them as in the caption of Photo 2. Finally, ask students what they think is going on in the third photo.

Culture Notes

• The candies shown on this page are called **dragées**, sugar-coated almonds that are traditionally given out at weddings and baptisms. They might be offered in small net bags or small boxes. Wedding **dragées** are usually white and may be mixed with silver candies. The pink candies shown here are probably for a girl's baptism; blue might be offered if a boy were being baptized.

• French weddings are similar to traditional American weddings. However, some customs that students might be familiar with aren't usually practiced in France. For example, French grooms don't have bachelor parties, the bride does not throw the bouquet, and guests usually do not throw rice or birdseed at the bride and groom.

• However, the traditional French wedding cake (**la pièce montée**) is very distinctive. It is often made up of layers of stacked cream puffs covered with caramel sauce.

CHAPITRE

7
La famille

① Je te présente mon frère Alexandre.

Families provide support and nurturing for their members. Being part of a family also involves duties and responsibilities. Do you think families in francophone cultures are different from families here in the United States?

In this chapter you will learn
- to identify and introduce people
- to describe and characterize people
- to ask for, give, and refuse permission

And you will
- listen to French-speaking teenagers talk about their families
- read magazine articles about pets
- write a description of someone you know
- find out about pets in France

② Ma cousine? Comment est-elle? Elle est très gentille!

③ Je peux aller au cinéma ce soir, s'il te plaît?

cent soixante-quinze 175

CHAPTER OPENER
CHAPTER 7

Focusing on Outcomes
Have students read the chapter outcomes and match them to the photos. Ask them to think of some situations where these functions would be used, such as introducing people at parties or telling stories. NOTE: You may want to use the video to support the objectives. The self-check activities in **Que sais-je?** on page 196 help students assess their achievement of the objectives.

✦ For Individual Needs

Kinesthetic Learners Draw stick-figure representations of the individuals in the photos on a transparency. Write the speech bubbles for each one on strips of transparency. Then, have volunteers come to the projector and match the speech bubbles to the drawings.

Teacher Note
Also included in this chapter are possessive adjectives and vocabulary describing family relationships, as well as household chores.

🌐 Culture Note
In Africa, "family" refers not only to one's immediate family, but to the extended family as well. Members of the extended family often live under the same roof with the nuclear family. It is normal for all family members to be intimately involved in every aspect of one another's lives, including business matters, health care, education, child care, and employment. Even as more Africans move to the cities, they still manage to keep in close touch with family members in town as well as with those still living in the village. It might be noted that marriage is considered a means of acquiring more family, both by gaining in-laws and by having children.

Video Synopsis

In this segment of the video, Thuy arrives at Isabelle's house for a visit. Isabelle introduces Thuy to her father. Thuy notices Isabelle's family photo album and asks if she can look at it. As they look at the photos, Isabelle explains who all the family members are and describes them. Thuy says that she is an only child and asks about Isabelle's brother Alexandre. Isabelle tells her that he can be difficult.

Motivating Activity

You might ask students if they take pictures, of whom or of what, and if they keep photo albums.

Teaching Suggestion

Have students look at the pictures on pages 176–177 and guess how the people are related to Isabelle.

Presentation

Show the video, stopping after each photo Isabelle describes to ask students to name the relative and describe him or her. You might draw the skeleton of Isabelle's family tree without the names and have students fill it in as they view the video. Replay the video, asking students to concentrate on how Isabelle feels about her family.

Mise en train

Sympa, la famille!

Look at the people pictured in the photo album. Can you guess how they're related to Isabelle?

Tiens, j'adore regarder les photos. Je peux les voir?

Bien sûr!

Ce sont mes grands-parents. Ils sont heureux sur cette photo. Ils fêtent leur quarantième anniversaire de mariage.

C'est une photo de papa et maman.

Là, c'est mon oncle et ma tante, le frère de ma mère et sa femme. Et au milieu, ce sont leurs enfants, mes cousins. Ils habitent tous en Bretagne. Ça, c'est Loïc. Il a 18 ans.

Loïc

Et elle, c'est ma cousine Patricia. Elle est très intelligente. En maths, elle a toujours 18 sur 20!

Ma tante

Patricia

Mon oncle

C'est Julie.
Elle a 8 ans.
Elle est
adorable.

Julie

176   cent soixante-seize

CHAPITRE 7   La Famille

Teaching Suggestion

You might have students scan pages 176–177 for adjectives to find out how Isabelle feels about the different people pictured.

Là, c'est moi. Quel amour de bébé, n'est-ce pas? Je suis toute petite... peut-être un an et demi.

C'est mon frère Alexandre. Il a 11 ans. Il est parfois pénible.

C'est ma tante du côté de mon père. Elle s'appelle Véronique. Ça, c'est son chat Musica. Elle adore les animaux. Elle a aussi deux chiens!

Et toi, tu n'as pas de frères ou de sœurs?

Non. Je suis fille unique.

Tu as de la chance.

MISE EN TRAIN · *cent soixante-dix-sept* · **177**

Teaching Suggestion

2 Have students find a quote from the story to confirm the true statements. Have them change the false statements to make them true.

 For videodisc application, see *Videodisc Guide*.

For Individual Needs

4 **Auditory Learners** You might have students view the video or listen to the recording of **Sympa, la famille!** to find these expressions.

Teaching Suggestions

5 If students are reluctant to talk about their own families, they might invent an imaginary family, select a TV or comic book family, or refer to the photo of the family on page 179 to compare to Isabelle's.

5 Students might also sketch their own family tree in their journals and write a comparison in English.

1 Tu as compris?

Answer these questions about **Sympa, la famille!**

1. What are Isabelle and Thuy talking about?   Isabelle's family photos
2. Does Isabelle have brothers or sisters? If so, what are their names?   Yes, a brother; Alexandre
3. Where do her cousins live?   Bretagne
4. Who are some of the other family members she mentions?   grandparents, parents, an uncle, two aunts
5. How does Isabelle feel about her family? How can you tell?   She likes her family; She speaks favorably of them.

2 Vrai ou faux?

1. Julie a huit ans.   vrai
2. Julie est blonde.   faux
3. Les cousins d'Isabelle habitent à Paris.   faux
4. Tante Véronique n'a pas d'animaux.   faux
5. Thuy a un frère.   faux

3 Quelle photo?

De quelle photo est-ce qu'Isabelle parle?

1. Il a onze ans.   b
2. Elle s'appelle Véronique. Ça, c'est son chat, Musica.   c
3. C'est une photo de papa et maman.   f
4. En maths, elle a toujours 18 sur 20.   a
5. J'ai un an et demi, je crois...   d
6. Elle a huit ans.   e

a.

b.

c.

d.

e.

f.

4 Cherche les expressions

In **Sympa, la famille!**, what does Isabelle or Thuy say to . . .   See answers below.

1. ask permission?
2. identify family members?
3. describe someone?
4. pay a compliment?
5. tell someone's age?
6. complain about someone?

5 Et maintenant, à toi

How does Isabelle's family resemble or differ from families you know?

178   *cent soixante-dix-huit*   CHAPITRE 7   La famille

Answers
4 1. Je peux... ?
2. C'est... , Ce sont...
3. *Possible answers:* Ils sont heureux... Elle est adorable. Elle est très intelligente... Quel amour de bébé... Je suis toute petite.
4. *Possible answers:* Elle est adorable. Elle est très intelligente.
5. Il/Elle a... ans.
6. Il est parfois pénible.

PREMIERE ETAPE

Identifying and introducing people

COMMENT DIT-ON... ?
Identifying people

To identify people:

C'est ma tante Véronique.
Ce sont mes cousins Loïc et Julie. *These/those are . . .*
Voici mon frère Alexandre. *Here's . . .*
Voilà Patricia. *There's . . .*

6 C'est qui?

With a partner, take turns creating identities for the people in this picture.

*J*ump Start!

Have students write answers to the following questions: **Tu t'appelles comment? Tu as quel âge? Ça va?**

*M*OTIVATE

Have students describe different types of families. Ask them to evaluate today's TV families. Are they realistic?

*T*EACH

Presentation

Comment dit-on... ? Before students open their books, use the expressions in the box to identify several students in the classroom and some pictures of faculty members or of family members you bring in. After several examples, point to one or more people and ask **C'est qui?** Then, identify students that are close by or far away, using **voici** and **voilà**.

Teaching Suggestion

6 If students need help with French names, refer them to page 5 of the Preliminary Chapter.

Additional Practice

If you made a family tree transparency for the **Mise en train** (See Presentation, page 176), show it again and call on volunteers to identify the various family members. If not, have students turn to pages 176 and 177 and take turns identifying the people in Isabelle's family.

RESOURCES FOR PREMIERE ETAPE

Textbook Audiocassette 4A/Audio CD 7
Practice and Activity Book, pp. 74–76
Videodisc Guide
　Videodisc Program, Videodisc 4A

Chapter Teaching Resources, Book 2
• Teaching Transparency Master 7-1, pp. 119, 122
　Teaching Transparency 7-1
• Additional Listening Activities 7-1, 7-2, p. 123
　Audiocassette 10A/Audio CD 7
• Realia 7-1, pp. 127, 129
• Situation Cards 7-1, pp. 130–131
• Student Response Forms, pp. 132–134
• Quiz 7-1, pp. 135–136
　Audiocassette 8A/Audio CD 7

Presentation

Vocabulaire Draw a transparency of the family tree with no labels. Uncover one generation at a time and identify each family member, writing in the person's relationship to Isabelle (**ma tante Véronique**). Then, create fill-in-the-blank sentences, such as **Véronique est la _____ d'Alexandre (tante)**, and have students complete them.

✦ For Individual Needs

Slower Pace — Note de grammaire Demonstrate this structure by pointing out students' school supplies. For example, pick up a notebook and say **C'est le cahier de Steven**. Then, pick up an object and have a student identify it and tell whose it is.

Additional Practice

7 Say the names of two of the people on the tree (**Julie et Loïc**). Have students say or write the relationship between them. (**Julie est la sœur de Loïc.**) You might also have students write sentences identifying the relationships between two celebrities. (**Michael Jackson est le frère de Janet Jackson.**)

♜ Game

JEOPARDY® Form two teams and have one player from each team come forward. Place a bell in front of them. Then, say a celebrity relationship (**la femme d'Homer Simpson**). The first student to ring the bell answers. To win the point, students must phrase the response in the form of a question. (**Qui est Marge Simpson?**) Continue until one team has ten points.

VOCABULAIRE

Les membres de la famille Ménard

**Ma grand-mère et mon grand-père
Eugénie et Jean-Marie Ménard**

**Ma tante
Véronique, la
sœur de mon
père**

**Mon père et ma mère Raymond
et Josette Ménard**

**Mon oncle et ma tante, Guillaume
et Micheline Ménard**

**Mon frère
Alexandre**   **C'est moi!**   **Mes cousines Patricia et Julie, et mon cousin Loïc**

Mon chien   **Mon chat**   **Mon canari**   **Mon poisson**

7 Qui est-ce? See answers below.

Which member of Isabelle Ménard's family does each of these statements refer to?

Le frère de Véronique, c'est Raymond.

1. C'est le père de Véronique.
2. C'est la mère de Véronique.
3. C'est le grand-père de Julie.
4. C'est la mère de Patricia.
5. Ce sont les sœurs de Loïc.
6. C'est le cousin de Patricia.

Note de Grammaire

Use **de (d')** to indicate relationship or ownership.

C'est la mère **de** Paul.
That's Paul's mother.
Voici le chien **d'**Agnès.
Here's Agnès' dog.
C'est le copain **du** prof.
That's the teacher's friend.

Language Note

Students might want to know the following common expressions: **les gosses, les mômes,** or **les gamins** *(kids, brats);* **tonton** *(uncle,* also used sometimes to refer to former President François Mitterrand); **tata, tatie,** or **tantine** *(aunt);* **mémé** *(grandma);* and **pépé** *(grandpa).*

Answers
7 1. Le père de Véronique, c'est Jean-Marie.
 2. La mère de Véronique, c'est Eugénie.
 3. Le grand-père de Julie, c'est Jean-Marie.
 4. La mère de Patricia, c'est Micheline.
 5. Les sœurs de Loïc, ce sont Patricia et Julie.
 6. Le cousin de Patricia, c'est Alexandre.

8 Ecoute! 1. d 2. b 3. a 4. e 5. c

Alain montre des photos de sa famille à Jay. De quelle photo est-ce qu'il parle?

a.   b.   c.   d.   e.

---

*G*rammaire   Possessive adjectives

	Before a masculine singular noun		Before a feminine singular noun		Before a plural noun	
my	mon		ma		mes	
your	ton		ta		tes	
his/her	son	} frère	sa	} sœur	ses	} frères
our	notre		notre		nos	
your	votre		votre		vos	
their	leur		leur		leurs	

- **Son, sa,** and **ses** may mean either *her* or *his.*

  C'est **son** père.   That's *her* father. *or* That's *his* father.

  C'est **sa** mère.   That's *her* mother. *or* That's *his* mother.

  Ce sont **ses** parents.   Those are *her* parents. *or* Those are *his* parents.

- **Mon, ton,** and **son** are used before all singular nouns that begin with a vowel sound, whether the noun is masculine or feminine.

  C'est **ton amie** Marianne?

  C'est **mon oncle** Xavier.

- Liaison is always made with **mon, ton,** and **son,** and with all the plural forms.

  mon école   **nos amis**

- Can you figure out when to use **ton, ta, tes,** and when to use **votre** and **vos?**[1]

---

9 Ecoute!

Listen to Roland and Odile. Are they talking about their own pets or someone else's? Then, listen again to find out what kind of pets they're talking about.   Answers on p. 173C.

1. Use **ton, ta,** and **tes** with people you would normally address with **tu.** Use **votre** and **vos** with people you would normally address with **vous.**

Teaching Suggestion

8 You might have students describe the pictures before you play the recording. Tell them to listen for key words to get the general meaning and not to try to translate every word.

Presentation

Grammaire Before students see these structures, ask them for the different ways to say *the* (**le, la, l', les**). Ask them how they choose the correct article (gender, number). Then, pick up classroom objects and say they belong to you. (**C'est mon livre.**) You might also ask about ownership by asking **C'est ton livre?** Then, pick up a boy's pencil and say **C'est son crayon.** Do the same with a girl's pencil. Ask students what they notice about this form (it means both *his* and *her*). Finally, pick up items belonging to various students and ask the class **C'est mon stylo?**, prompting the response **Non, c'est son stylo!** You might also pick up an item from your desk to prompt the response **Oui, c'est votre...** or choose a book that two students are sharing to prompt **Non, c'est leur livre!**

For Individual Needs

9 Slower Pace Before starting this activity, you might ask students to determine which of the possessive adjectives they would use to speak about their own pets (**mon, ma, mes, notre, nos**) and which they would use to speak about someone else's (**son, sa, ses, leur, leurs, ton, ta, tes, votre, vos**).

Teacher Note

Grammaire You might choose to work only with the singular forms during one class period, leaving **notre, votre, leur, nos, vos,** and **leurs** for the following day.

Language Note

Point out to students that they should choose among **son, sa,** or **ses** based on the gender and number of the object possessed, <u>not</u> on the gender of the owner. Tell them that **son stylo** means either *his pen* or *her pen,* and that **sa gomme** means *his eraser* or *her eraser.*

Reteaching

10 Adverbs of frequency
Review adverbs of frequency such as **souvent, jamais,** and **une fois par semaine** by giving students a subject and a verb phrase **(ils/jouer au golf),** and asking them to form a sentence. **(Ils jouent souvent au golf.)**

For Individual Needs

10 Slower Pace Have students tell how they think the people in the illustration are related. Then, have them identify the activities the people like to do. You might write these on the board or on a transparency as students suggest them. Finally, have pairs work together to use this information in their questions and answers.

Teaching Suggestion

10 In order to practice **ton, ta,** and **tes,** you might have students reverse this activity by asking questions such as **C'est ta sœur?**

Additional Practice

11 This activity could be extended by asking students to find a picture in a magazine that illustrates a familial relationship. Have students write on a separate piece of paper what they think the relationship between the people might be. Then, tell them to exchange pictures with a partner and write down the relationship they imagine in their partner's picture. Finally, have partners compare their impressions.

NOTE CULTURELLE

Family life plays an important role in French society. Although modern times have brought changes to the family's daily life (more working mothers, less time for family activities, more divorces, and so on), France is working hard to maintain the family unit. To do this, the French government provides subsidies **(allocations familiales)** to all families with two or more children. Other social benefits also encourage larger families in a country with an ever-decreasing birth rate. These benefits include a paid maternity leave of at least 14 weeks, a renewable maternity or paternity leave of one year, free day-care, and a birth allowance **(allocation de naissance)** for every child after the second. Families also receive subsidies for each child attending school or college.

10 Ma famille française

You're showing a classmate a photo of the family you stayed with in France. Take turns with a partner identifying the people and asking questions about them.

—C'est qui, ça?
—C'est ma sœur.
—Elle joue souvent au tennis?
—Oui. Une fois par semaine.

11 Devine! *Guess!*

Identify the teenagers in the photos below and tell how you think the other people in the photos are related to them. Take turns with a partner.

C'est Nadine et son grand-père.

Nadine

Hassan

Thierry

Liliane

Monique et Annie

COMMENT DIT-ON...?

Introducing people

To introduce someone to a friend:
C'est Jean-Michel.
Je te présente mon ami Jean-Michel.
I'd like you to meet . . .

To introduce someone to an adult:
Je vous présente Jean-Michel.

To respond to an introduction:
Salut, Jean-Michel. **Ça va?**
Bonjour.
Très heureux (heureuse). *Pleased to meet you.* (FORMAL)

Mlle Martin, je vous présente mon ami Jean-Michel.

Bonjour, Jean-Michel!

12 Ecoute!

Are the people in these conversations identifying someone or introducing someone? *Answers on p. 173C.*

13 Je te présente...

A new student from France has just arrived at your school and asks you the names and ages of some students in your class. Introduce him or her to those classmates. Act this out in your group, changing roles.

14 Mon journal

Write about your family, giving the names and ages of each person. Tell what each of them likes to do. You may choose to create an imaginary family or you may want to write about a famous family in real life or on TV.

Tu te rappelles ?

Do you remember how to ask for and give people's names and ages?
—Elle s'appelle comment?
—Magali.
—Elle a quel âge?
—Seize ans.

Vocabulaire *à la carte*

Here are some other words you might need to talk about your family.

une femme	*wife*
un mari	*husband*
une fille	*daughter*
un fils	*son*
un(e) enfant	*child*
des petits-enfants	*grandchildren*
un demi-frère	*stepbrother; half-brother*
une demi-sœur	*stepsister; half-sister*
un(e) enfant unique	*an only child*
une belle-mère	*stepmother*
un beau-père	*stepfather*
un petit-fils	*grandson*
une petite-fille	*granddaughter*

Presentation

Comment dit-on... ?
Demonstrate the expressions by introducing students to stuffed animals you bring in, and then introducing one student to another. Next, have a student introduce someone to you. Then, use **Je vous présente...** to introduce one student to the entire class. Have groups of three role-play introductions.

For videodisc application, see *Videodisc Guide.*

Portfolio

13 Oral This activity can be used for oral assessment or can be added to students' oral portfolios. For portfolio information, see *Assessment Guide,* pages 2–13.

Mon journal

14 For additional family vocabulary, refer students to the Supplementary Vocabulary on pages 341–342. Students might want to include a family tree or photos in their journal entry. For an additional journal entry suggestion for Chapter 7, see *Practice and Activity Book,* page 151.

Language Note

Vocabulaire à la carte
Make sure students pronounce the **s**, but not the **l**, in the word **fils**.

Assess

Quiz 7-1, *Chapter Teaching Resources, Book 2,* pp. 135–136

Assessment Items, Audiocassette 8A Audio CD 7

Performance Assessment

Form groups of three. In each group, one person will introduce another to the third member. This person asks questions to get to know the newcomer, who can take on any identity. Have students present these introductions to the class.

Close

To close this **étape,** have students bring in family photos or magazine pictures of an imaginary family. Have partners identify and describe the people. Encourage them to ask questions.

DEUXIEME ETAPE

Describing and characterizing people

VOCABULAIRE

Ils sont comment?

PETITE   GRAND

BRUNE   BLOND   ROUX

JEUNE   AGEE

MINCE   GROS

You can also use these descriptive words:

mignon(mignonne)(s) *cute*   **ne... ni grand(e)(s) ni petit(e)(s)** *. . . neither tall nor short*

You can use these words to characterize people.

amusant(e)(s)	*funny*	**intelligent(e)(s)**	*smart*	**embêtant(e)(s)**	*annoying*
timide(s)	*shy*	**fort(e)(s)**	*strong*	**pénible(s)**	*a pain in the neck*
gentil(le)(s)	*nice*	**sympa(sympathique(s))**	*nice*	**méchant(e)(s)**	*mean*

Organizing vocabulary in various ways can help you remember words. Group words by categories, like foods, sports, numbers, colors, and so forth. Try to associate words with a certain context, such as school (school subjects, classroom objects) or a store (items for sale, salesperson). Try to use associations like opposites, such as **petit— grand** or **gros—mince.**

15 Ecoute!

Match the descriptions you hear with the students' names. Answers on p. 173C.

Roger   Denise   Julie   Martin   Carmen

COMMENT DIT-ON...?

Describing and characterizing people

To ask what someone is like:

Il est comment? *What is he like?*
Elle est comment? *What is she like?*
Ils/Elles sont comment? *What are they like?*

To describe someone:

Il n'est ni grand ni petit.
Elle est brune.
Ils/Elles sont âgé(e)s.

To characterize someone:

Il est pénible.
Elle est timide.
Ils/Elles sont amusant(e)s.

16 Ecoute!

Ariane is telling a friend about her cousins. Does she have a favorable or unfavorable opinion of them? Answers on p. 173C.

17 Des familles bizarres

Comment sont les membres de ces familles?
See answers below.

DEUXIEME ETAPE

cent quatre-vingt-cinq **185**

Answers

17 *Possible answers for first photo:* L'oncle est gros, et la mère est mince. Les enfants sont pénibles. *Possible answers for second photo:* Bart est petit, pénible et jaune. Maggie est mignonne. Lisa est intelligente et gentille. Homer est gros et amusant.

Language Note

17 Tell students that they should not add an -**s** to family names in French: **Ce sont les Simpson. Voilà les Ménard.**

For Individual Needs

15 Slower Pace Before playing the recording, ask students to suggest adjectives they might use to describe each person shown. Write their suggestions on a transparency for them to refer to as they listen to the recording.

Presentation

Comment dit-on...? Begin by asking **Je suis comment? Grand(e)? Petit(e)? Jeune? Agé(e)? Amusant(e)?** Then, hold up pictures of people and ask what they are like. (**Il/Elle est comment? Ils/Elles sont comment?**) Then, name or hold up a photo of a celebrity. Ask the class various questions about the person, such as **Il est petit? Il est fort? Il est brun?** and then ask **Il est comment?** You might also play the **Mise en train** video episode, pausing after each person is described to ask **Il/Elle est comment?**

For videodisc application, see *Videodisc Guide*.

Teaching Suggestion

16 Before students hear the recording, have them suggest what Ariane might say that would be favorable or unfavorable. Remind students that these categories are matters of opinion.

Portfolio

17 Written This activity could be included in students' written portfolios. For portfolio information, see *Assessment Guide*, pages 2–13.

Presentation

Grammaire Draw stick figures of a boy, a girl, two boys, and two girls on the board. Have students suggest sentences for each one, using adjectives they can recall. (**Il est... , Elle est... , Ils/Elles sont...**) Write the adjectives in the correct form under each figure. Have students suggest rules for adjective formation illustrated by the adjectives you have written. Then, point to the appropriate stick figure as you say the sentences in the grammar box. Have students suggest reasons for the differences. Repeat this with adjectives that don't change and ask students what they notice about these adjectives.

Teaching Suggestions

18 This activity could be written or done orally in pairs, with students taking turns identifying similarities and differences.

18 Have students compare themselves to either Frédéric or Denise.

19 This activity could be written and included in students' portfolios or used as a journal entry.

19 Students may prefer to describe fictitious friends.

Additional Practice

Ask students questions about celebrities or mythical figures, such as **Santa Claus est gros ou grosse? Elvis Presley est brun ou brune?** You might also have students supply the adjective. (**Comment est Santa Claus? Et Michael Jordan?**)

---

*G*rammaire   Adjective agreement

As you may remember from Chapter 3, you often change the pronunciation and spelling of adjectives according to the nouns they describe.

- If the adjective describes a feminine noun, you usually add an **e** to the masculine form of the adjective.
- If the adjective describes a plural noun, you usually add an **s** to the singular form, masculine or feminine.
- If an adjective describes both males and females, you always use the masculine plural form.
- Some adjectives have special (irregular) feminine or plural forms. Here are some irregular adjectives that you've seen in this chapter.

Il est **roux**.	Elle est **rousse**.
Ils sont **roux**.	Elles sont **rousses**.
Il est **mignon**.	Elle est **mignonne**.
Ils sont **mignons**.	Elles sont **mignonnes**.
Il est **gentil**.	Elle est **gentille**.
Ils sont **gentils**.	Elles sont **gentilles**.
Il est **gros**.	Elle est **grosse**.
Ils sont **gros**.	Elles sont **grosses**.

- In the masculine forms, the final consonant sound is silent. In the feminine forms, the final consonant sound is pronounced.
- A few adjectives don't ever change. Here are some that you've already seen.

marron   orange   cool   super   sympa

18   On est différents!

Frédéric and Denise are brother and sister. Look at the picture and tell how they're alike and how they're different.   See answers below.

Frédéric est grand, mais Denise est petite.

19   Les meilleurs amis

Take turns with a partner describing your best friends. Tell about your friends' appearance, personality, and interests.

Language Note

Students might want to know that some adjectives, such as **cool** and **super**, are invariable because they come from a foreign language. Others, such as **marron** and **orange**, are invariable because their adjective forms were derived from nouns *(chestnut* and *orange).*

Possible answers

18 Frédéric est blond, grand, un peu gros et gentil, mais Denise est brune, petite, mince et embêtante.

*G*rammaire The verb être

Etre is an irregular verb.

être *(to be)*

Je **suis** intelligent(e).	Nous **sommes** intelligent(e)s.
Tu **es** intelligent(e).	Vous **êtes** intelligent(e)(s).
Il/Elle/On **est** intelligent(e).	Ils/Elles **sont** intelligent(e)s.

20 Devine!

Describe a member of the Louvain family to your partner. He or she will try to figure out who it is. Take turns.

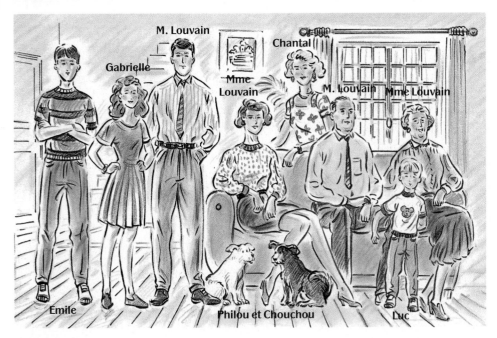

21 Qui suis-je?

Pretend you're a famous person and describe yourself to a partner. Your partner will try to guess who you are. Take turns.

—Je suis très grand et très fort. Je joue au basket-ball. Qui suis-je?
—Tu es Shaquille O'Neal?
—Oui. C'est ça! *or* Non. C'est pas ça.

22 Mon journal

Choose your favorite family member. Write a paragraph describing that person and telling what he or she likes to do and where he or she likes to go. If you prefer, choose a member of your favorite TV family and describe and characterize that person.

Presentation

Grammaire Make two sets of flashcards, one with the forms of **être** and the other with the subject pronouns. Tape the flashcards in random order on the board and have students match the subjects and verbs. Then, leave the subject cards, but remove the verb forms from the board and ask for volunteers to write the verb forms next to the subject cards. Finally, divide the class into two teams. Have the first player from each team come to the board. Give a subject pronoun and an adjective (**elle/ brun**). The first player to write a correct sentence on the board wins a point. (**Elle est brune.**) Continue until all players have had a turn.

Additional Practice

20 Extend this activity by having partners also tell how the person described is related to Gabrielle.

Mon journal

22 As a prewriting activity, you might name a member of a popular TV family and ask students to describe him or her. For an additional journal entry suggestion for Chapter 7, see *Practice and Activity Book,* page 151.

*C*LOSE

To close this **étape,** have students mime adjectives before the whole class or a small group, and they will try to guess the adjective. (**Tu es âgé(e)!**) The mimers might select expressions from a stack of flashcards or mime an adjective of their choice.

*A*SSESS

Quiz 7-2, *Chapter Teaching Resources, Book 2,* pp. 137–138

*Assessment Items, Audiocassette 8A
Audio CD 7*

Performance Assessment

Have students bring in a photo of someone and describe that person to the class, giving a physical description and telling what the person is like. The photo might be of a family member, a relative, a friend, or a famous person. Students might also choose to bring in a picture of a person from a magazine.

VIDEO PROGRAM OR EXPANDED VIDEO PROGRAM, Videocassette 3 09:29–12:06

OR VIDEODISC PROGRAM, Videodisc 4A

Search 14605, Play To 17090

Teacher Notes

- See *Video Guide, Videodisc Guide,* and *Practice and Activity Book* for activities related to the **Panorama Culturel.**
- Remind students that cultural material may be included in the Chapter Quizzes and Test.
- The interviewees' language represents informal, unrehearsed speech. Occasionally, edits have been made for clarification.

Motivating Activity

Before students view the interviews, ask them if they have a pet, and if so, what it is.

Presentation

Ask students for common pet names for dogs, cats, and other pets in the United States. Then, play the video and have them listen for the kind of pet each person has and its name.

Thinking Critically

Analyzing Have students consider the advantages of tatooing pets versus using identification tags. Which system is more effective?

Language Note

Students might want to know the following words: **se promener** *(to go for a walk);* **de garrot** *(at the withers);* **faire des balades** *(to go for walks).*

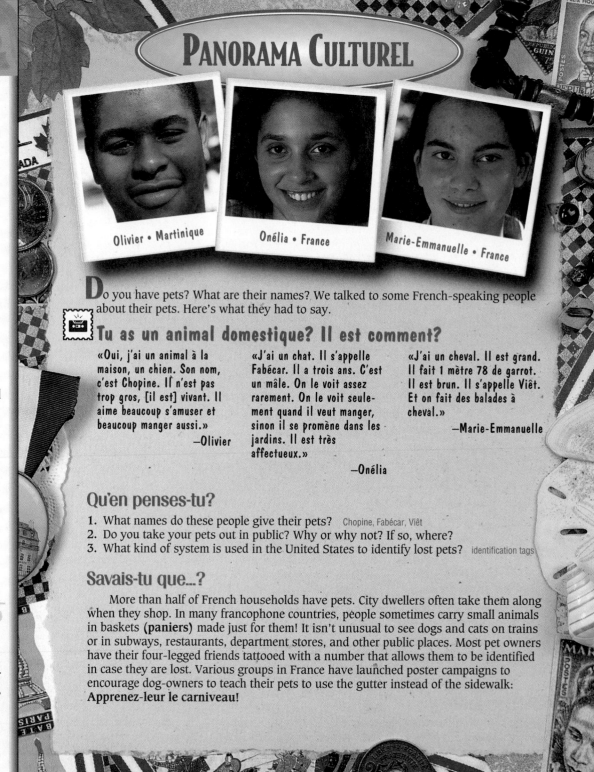

PANORAMA CULTUREL

Olivier • Martinique
Onélia • France
Marie-Emmanuelle • France

Do you have pets? What are their names? We talked to some French-speaking people about their pets. Here's what they had to say.

Tu as un animal domestique? Il est comment?

«Oui, j'ai un animal à la maison, un chien. Son nom, c'est Chopine. Il n'est pas trop gros, [il est] vivant. Il aime beaucoup s'amuser et beaucoup manger aussi.»
—Olivier

«J'ai un chat. Il s'appelle Fabécar. Il a trois ans. C'est un mâle. On le voit assez rarement. On le voit seulement quand il veut manger, sinon il se promène dans les jardins. Il est très affectueux.»
—Onélia

«J'ai un cheval. Il est grand. Il fait 1 mètre 78 de garrot. Il est brun. Il s'appelle Viêt. Et on fait des balades à cheval.»
—Marie-Emmanuelle

Qu'en penses-tu?

1. What names do these people give their pets?   Chopine, Fabécar, Viêt
2. Do you take your pets out in public? Why or why not? If so, where?
3. What kind of system is used in the United States to identify lost pets?   identification tags

Savais-tu que...?

More than half of French households have pets. City dwellers often take them along when they shop. In many francophone countries, people sometimes carry small animals in baskets (**paniers**) made just for them! It isn't unusual to see dogs and cats on trains or in subways, restaurants, department stores, and other public places. Most pet owners have their four-legged friends tattooed with a number that allows them to be identified in case they are lost. Various groups in France have launched poster campaigns to encourage dog-owners to teach their pets to use the gutter instead of the sidewalk: **Apprenez-leur le carniveau!**

Questions

1. Qui est Chopine? Et Fabécar? Et Viêt? (le chien d'Olivier; le chat d'Onélia; le cheval de Marie-Emmanuelle)
2. Comment sont-ils? (Chopine—pas trop gros, vivant; Fabécar—très affectueux; Viêt—brun et grand)
3. Qu'est-ce que Chopine aime faire? (s'amuser, manger)

Language Note

Students might want to know the following animal-related expressions: **minou** *(kitty,* used to call a cat, or as a generic name for a cat); **ouah-ouah** *(bow-wow);* **aboyer** *(to bark);* **miaou** *(meow);* **miauler/faire miaou** *(to mew, whine).*

TROISIEME ETAPE

Asking for, giving, and refusing permission

COMMENT DIT-ON... ?
Asking for, giving, and refusing permission

To ask for permission:
Je voudrais aller au cinéma. **Tu es d'accord?**
  Is that OK with you?
(Est-ce que) je peux sortir? *May I . . .*

To give permission:
Oui, si tu veux. *Yes, if you want to.*
Pourquoi pas?
Oui, bien sûr.
D'accord, si tu fais **d'abord** la vaisselle.
  OK, if you . . . first.

To refuse permission:
Pas question! *Out of the question!*
Non, c'est impossible. *No, that's impossible.*
Non, tu dois faire tes devoirs.
  No, you've got to . . .
Pas ce soir. *Not tonight.*

> PAPA, JE PEUX ALLER AU CAFÉ CE SOIR?

> DEMANDE A TA MERE.

23 Ecoute!

Listen to these people ask for permission. Are they given or refused permission?

Answers on p. 173D.

> Tu peux sortir si tu ranges d'abord ta chambre.

VOCABULAIRE

débarrasser la table	*to clear the table*
faire les courses	*to do the shopping*
faire le ménage	*to clean house*
faire la vaisselle	*to do the dishes*
garder ta petite sœur	*to look after . . .*
laver la voiture	*to wash the car*
passer l'aspirateur	*to vacuum*
promener le chien	*to walk the dog*
ranger ta chambre	*to pick up your room*
sortir la poubelle	*to take out the trash*
tondre le gazon	*to mow the lawn*

RESOURCES FOR TROISIEME ETAPE

Textbook Audiocassette 4A/Audio CD 7
Practice and Activity Book, pp. 80–82
Videodisc Guide
  Videodisc Program, Videodisc 4A

Chapter Teaching Resources, Book 2
• Communicative Activity 7-2, pp. 117–118
• Teaching Transparency Master 7-3, pp. 121, 122
  Teaching Transparency 7-3
• Additional Listening Activities 7-5, 7-6, p. 125
  Audiocassette 10A/Audio CD 7
• Realia 7-2, pp. 128, 129
• Situation Cards 7-3, pp. 130–131
• Student Response Forms, pp. 132–134
• Quiz 7-3, pp. 139–140
  Audiocassette 8A/Audio CD 7

Ask students to write the opposites of **gros, grand, méchant,** and **âgé.**

MOTIVATE

Ask students to suggest activities that require permission.

TEACH

Presentation

Comment dit-on... ? Write *asking for permission, giving permission,* and *refusing permission* on a transparency. Write the new expressions on strips of transparency. Have students select a strip and place it under the appropriate category. Then, have students ask you for permission to do various activities. If you grant permission, they should mime the activity they requested.

For videodisc application, see *Videodisc Guide.*

For Individual Needs

23 Slower Pace To give an example, have a student ask you for permission. Give a positive or negative response and then ask the class if you granted or refused permission.

Presentation

Vocabulaire Bring in props (a leash, trash bag, dishes) and mime the activities, asking **Qu'est-ce que je fais?**

TPR Tell students to do various chores and have them respond by miming the appropriate activity.

Teaching Suggestion

24 You might have students tell or write what is happening in the pictures.

 Portfolio

25 Written This activity could be done as a written exercise, with students telling who does which chores in their homes. Have them list the chores to be done at home with a person's name next to each. Students might exchange rough drafts to read and edit. The first and final drafts might be included in students' written portfolios. For portfolio information, see *Assessment Guide*, pages 2–13.

Group Work

26 After students have written their captions, make four columns on the board, each representing one of the illustrations, and have students write one of their captions in the appropriate column. Then, have small groups make up a story, using one caption from each column.

 For Individual Needs

26 Auditory Learners For additional listening practice, call out two expressions for each illustration and have students choose the correct one. For example, for the second illustration, you might say **Oui, si tu veux** or **Pas question.**

Teaching Suggestions

• Have partners role-play asking for permission to attend a party at a friend's house on a week night.

• Show *Teaching Transparency 7-3* and have groups of four students role-play the situation shown.

---

24 **Ecoute!** 1. c 2. e 3. d 4. a 5. f 6. b

Listen to some French teenagers ask permission to go out with their friends. Which picture represents the outcome of each dialogue?

a.   b.   c.

d.   e.   f.

25 **Qui doit le faire?**

Ask your partner who does various chores at his or her house. Then, change roles.

—Qui promène le chien?
—Mon frère. Et moi aussi quelquefois.

26 **Qu'est-ce qu'ils disent?**

1.   2.   3.   4.

190   *cent quatre-vingt-dix*   CHAPITRE 7   La famille

Language Note

Point out that **aujourd'hui, ce week-end, ce matin,** and **cet après-midi** can be substituted for **ce soir** in the expression **Pas ce soir.**

27 Et toi?

Give or refuse permission in these situations.

1. Your little sister or brother asks to listen to your cassette.
2. Your friend wants to read your novel.
3. Your little sister or brother wants to go to the movies with you and your friend.

28 Jeu de rôle

 Pretend you're a parent. Your partner asks permission to do several activities this weekend. Refuse permission for some, give permission for others, and give reasons. Change roles.

PRONONCIATION

 ### The nasal sounds [õ], [ɛ̃], and [œ̃]

In Chapter 5 you learned about the nasal sound [ã]. Now listen to the other French nasal sounds [õ], [ɛ̃], and [œ̃]. As you repeat the following words, try not to put a trace of the consonant **n** in your nasal sounds.

on   hein   un

How are these nasal sounds represented in writing? The nasal sound [õ] is represented by a combination of **on** or **om**. Several letter combinations can represent the sound [ɛ̃], for example, **in, im, ain, aim, (i)en**. The nasal sound [œ̃] is spelled **un** or **um**. A vowel after these groups of letters or, in some cases, a doubling of the consonants **n** or **m** will result in a non-nasal sound, as in **limonade** and **ennemi**.

A. A prononcer

Repeat the following words.

1. ton   blond   pardon   nombre
2. cousin   impossible   copain   faim
3. un   lundi   brun   humble

B. A lire

Take turns with a partner reading the following sentences aloud.

1. Ils ont très faim. Ils vont prendre des sandwiches au jambon. C'est bon!
2. Allons faire du patin ou bien, allons au concert!
3. Ce garçon est blond et ce garçon-là est brun. Ils sont minces et mignons!
4. Pardon. C'est combien, cette montre? Cent soixante-quinze francs?

C. A écrire

You're going to hear a short dialogue. Write down what you hear. *Answers on p. 173D.*

Portfolio

28 Oral This activity is appropriate for students' oral portfolios. You might have volunteers perform their dialogues for the class. For portfolio information, see *Assessment Guide*, pages 2–13.

Teaching Suggestions

• After presenting the **Prononciation**, have students look through the vocabulary lists for Chapters 1–6 to find words that contain the different nasal sounds.
• For Part B, divide the class into four groups. Have each group identify the nasal sounds in one of the sentences.

CLOSE

To close this **étape**, have students choose one family member (real or fictitious), present and describe this person to the class, and tell what chore(s) the person does or does not do around the house. This might be an oral or written activity.

ASSESS

Quiz 7-3, *Chapter Teaching Resources, Book 2*, pp. 139–140

Assessment Items, Audiocassette 8A/Audio CD 7

Performance Assessment

Have students write three things they would like to do and three chores they must do. Then, tell them to pair off and create a skit in which a student asks a parent for permission to do something and the parent grants or refuses permission. Alternatively, students might create an oral or written monologue in which they complain about all the chores they have to do.

Language Note

Point out that even though the nasal sound [ɛ̃] can be spelled in a variety of ways, the letter **i** is always part of the syllable. Make sure that students pronounce the nasal [õ] with their mouths small and rounded, with most of the sound passing through the nose (**pardon**). For the nasal [ɛ̃], the mouth is wider but still not too open (**jardin**). For the nasal [œ̃] (**lundi**), the jaw should be dropped more than for the [ɛ̃] sound.

Game

CHASSE AU TRÉSOR Provide each student with a list of twenty items, such as **Trouve quelqu'un qui... (1) a deux tantes. (2) a un poisson. (3) ne fait jamais les courses.** Students circulate, asking questions in French to find someone who can answer each question affirmatively. They should have that student sign his or her name next to the item. The first student to complete the list wins.

Teacher Note

For an additional reading, see *Practice and Activity Book*, page 83.

PREREADING
Activities A–B

Motivating Activity

Ask students if they've ever adopted a pet and how they went about finding and choosing one (newspaper, animal shelter, pet shop).

READING
Activities C–G

Teaching Suggestion

You might form small groups and assign each group one of the animals. Students should look for a physical description, personality characteristics, where the pet is located, and how it got to be in the shelter. Have groups share their information with the class. You might also have groups read their information aloud and have the class guess which pet they are describing.

Terms in Lisons!

Write the following terms on the board or on a transparency to help students in their reading:
recueilli *(picked up)*
maître(sse) *(pet owner)*
course *(race)*
courir *(to run)*
s'entendre bien avec *(to get along well with)*

LISONS!

$\mathscr{H}$ave you ever read an article about animals in an American magazine or newspaper? Here are some articles that appeared in the French magazine *Femme Actuelle*.

> ### DE BONS CONSEILS
> When you read something, it's important to separate the main idea from the supporting details. Sometimes the main idea is clearly stated at the beginning, other times it's just implied.

A. Which completion best expresses the main idea of these articles?

These articles are about . . .

1. animals that are missing.
2. animals that have performed heroic rescues.
3. <u>animals that are up for adoption.</u>
4. animals that have won prizes at cat and dog shows.

B. Now that you've decided what the main idea of the reading is, make a list of the kinds of details you expect to find in each of the articles. *See answers below.*

C. How is Mayo different from the other animals? What is the main idea of the article about him? *See answers below.* What other details are given?

D. Each of the articles includes a description of the animal. Look at the articles again and answer these questions.

1. Which animal is the oldest? The youngest? *Camel; Jupiter*
2. Which animals get along well with children? *Camel, Jupiter, Flora*

EN DIRECT DES REFUGES

IL VOUS ATTEND, ADOPTEZ-LE
CAMEL, 5 ANS

Ce sympathique bobtail blanc et gris est arrivé au refuge à la suite du décès accidentel de son maître. Il est vif, joyeux, a bon caractère et s'entend très bien avec les enfants. En échange de son dévouement et de sa fidélité, ce sportif robuste demande un grand espace afin de pouvoir courir et s'ébattre à son aise.

Continuez à nous écrire, et envoyez-nous votre photo avec votre protégé, une surprise vous attend !

Cet animal vous attend au refuge de la Société normande de protection aux animaux, 7 bis, avenue Jacques-Chastellain, Ile Lacroix 76000 Rouen. Tél.: (16) 35.70.20.36. Si Camel a été adopté, pensez à ses voisins de cage.

ELLE VOUS ATTEND, ADOPTEZ-LA
DADY, 2 ANS

Toute blanche, à l'exception de quelques petites taches et des oreilles noires bien dressées, Dady a un petit air de spitz, opulente fourrure en moins. Gentille, enjouée, très attachante, elle a été abandonnée après la séparation de ses maîtres et attend une famille qui accepterait de s'occuper d'elle un peu, beaucoup, passionnément.

Cet animal vous attend au refuge de l'Eden, Rod A'char, 29430 Lanhouarneau. Tél.: (16) 98.61.64.55. Colette Di Faostino tient seule, sans aucune subvention, ce havre exemplaire mais pauvre. Si Dady avait été adoptée, pensez à ses compagnons de malchance !

Mayo a trouvé une famille

Mayo a été adopté à la SPA de Valenciennes par Françoise Robeaux qui rêvait d'un chat gris ! Il a ainsi rejoint l'autre «fils» de la famille, un superbe siamois âgé de 13 ans.

Teacher Note

Remind students that they don't need to know the meaning of every word to understand the reading selections.

ELLE VOUS ATTEND, ADOPTEZ-LA

POUPETTE, 3 ANS

Cette jolie chatte stérilisée au regard tendre et étonné a été recueillie à l'âge de quelques semaines par une vieille dame, dont elle a été la dernière compagne. Sa maîtresse est malheureusement décédée après un long séjour à l'hôpital. Poupette, l'orpheline, ne comprend pas ce qui lui arrive et commence à trouver le temps long ! Elle a hâte de retrouver un foyer «sympa», des bras caressants et une paire de genoux pour ronronner.

Cet animal vous attend avec espoir au refuge Grammont de la SPA 30, av. du Général-de-Gaulle 92230 Gennevilliers. Tél.: (1) 47.98.57.40. Rens. sur Minitel: 36.15 SPA. Si Poupette est déjà partie, pensez aux autres!

IL VOUS ATTEND, ADOPTEZ-LE

JUPITER, 7 MOIS

Cet adorable chaton tigré et blanc vient tout juste d'être castré et est dûment tatoué. Très joueur et affectueux, il a été recueilli au refuge parce que, malheureusement, sa maîtresse a dû être hospitalisée pour un séjour de longue durée. Sociable, il s'entend très bien avec les jeunes enfants et accepterait volontiers un chien pour compagnon.

Cet animal vous attend au refuge de la fondation Assistance aux animaux, 8, rue des Plantes 77410 Villevaudé. Tél.: (1) 60.26.20.48 (l'après-midi seulement).

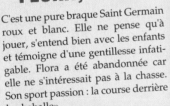

ELLE VOUS ATTEND, ADOPTEZ-LA

FLORA, 3 ANS

C'est une pure braque Saint Germain roux et blanc. Elle ne pense qu'à jouer, s'entend bien avec les enfants et témoigne d'une gentillesse infatigable. Flora a été abandonnée car elle ne s'intéressait pas à la chasse. Son sport passion : la course derrière la «baballe».

Elle vous attend au refuge de l'Eden, Rod A'char, 29430 Lanhouarneau. Tél.: (16) 98.61.64.55. Colette Di Faostino tient seule, sans aucune subvention, ce havre exemplaire mais pauvre. Si Flora est adoptée, pensez à ses compagnons !

Vous avez recueilli un animal par notre intermédiaire ? Envoyez-nous votre photo avec votre protégé, une surprise vous attend!

---

3. Which animal needs a lot of space? **Camel**

4. Which animals love to play? **Jupiter, Flora**

E. Make a list of all the adjectives of physical description that you can find in the articles. Now, list the adjectives that describe the animals' characteristics. **See answers below.**

F. Each article also explains why these animals were sent to the animal shelter. **See answers below.**

1. Which animal wasn't interested in hunting?

2. Whose owner was involved in an accident?

3. Whose owner had to go to the hospital for a long time?

4. Whose family got separated?

G. A third kind of detail tells where you can go to adopt these animals. Can you find the French word for *animal shelter*? **le refuge**

H. Now, write your own classified ad to try to find a home for a lost pet. Remember to give the animal's name and age, tell what the animal looks like, and describe his or her character.

or

Write a letter to the animal shelter telling them what kind of pet you would like to adopt.

1. First, make a list of all of the characteristics you're looking for in a pet. Will you choose to adopt a cat or a dog? What will he or she look like? Act like? Like to do?

2. Write a short letter, including all the important information about your desired pet.

3. Don't forget to give your address and telephone number!

POSTREADING
Activity H

Teaching Suggestions

• Have students write three or four true-false statements about the selections. They should then exchange papers, mark the items either **vrai** or **faux,** and return them to be corrected. You might also have students work in groups to create three or four true-false statements and then include one statement from each group on a short quiz.

H. Have students convert their ads into posters or into a class newspaper with the information neatly displayed and a drawing or photo of the pet, if possible. Display the posters around the room and have each student choose a pet to "adopt." They might write a short paragraph explaining why they chose that particular pet.

📁 Portfolio

H. Written Have students include their initial lists from Activity E in their portfolios. Activity H is appropriate as an entry in students' written portfolios. For portfolio information, see *Assessment Guide,* pages 2–13.

Teaching Suggestion

Ask students to explain which of the animals pictured they might like to adopt and why.

Answers

E *Physical:* blanc et gris, robuste, toute blanche, noires, opulente, gris, jolie, adorable, tigré et blanc, tatoué, pure, roux et blanc
Character: sympathique, vif, joyeux, gentille, enjouée, attachante, tendre, étonné, joueur, affectueux, sociable, infatigable

F 1. Flora
2. Camel's
3. Jupiter's, Poupette's
4. Dady's

The **Mise en pratique** reviews and integrates all four skills and culture in preparation for the Chapter Test.

Teaching Suggestion

1 Have students read the questions to themselves before you play the recording. Tell them they only need to jot down one word or a number to answer each question as they listen.

Group Work

2 Have students form small groups. Assign one of the announcements to each group. Have the groups read the announcement and answer the related questions. Reporters from each group can give the group's answers to the class. Ask groups to share any other details they gleaned from the announcement.

For Individual Needs

2 Tactile Learners Have students make their own birth announcements. Supply stationery or construction paper and markers. You might also have students bring in a baby picture to attach to the announcement. If students don't want to make their own birth announcements, have them create one for a TV or cartoon character.

MISE EN PRATIQUE

1 Ecoute Nathalie qui va te parler de sa famille. Puis, réponds aux questions. Answers on p. 173D.

1. Comment s'appelle le frère de Nathalie?
2. Il a quel âge?
3. Est-ce qu'elle a un chien ou un chat?
4. Comment est son animal?

2 Skim these documents. Then, read them more thoroughly and answer the questions below. See answers below.

1. What kind of document is this? How do you know?
2. Who is Michel Louis Raymond?
3. Who are Denise Morel-Tissot and Raymond Tissot?
4. What happened on May 20, 1994?

Nous avons la joie de vous annoncer la naissance de notre fils

Michel Louis Raymond 20 Mai 1994

Denise Morel-Tissot Raymond Tissot

Christelle et Nicolas

ont le plaisir de vous faire part de leur mariage

qui aura lieu le onze février 1995 à 15 heures, en la Mairie de Saint-Cyr-sur-Loire

M. et Mme Lionel Desombre 305 Rue des Marronniers 37540 Saint-Cyr-sur-Loire

5. What kind of document is this? How do you know?
6. Who are Christelle and Nicolas?
7. What happened on February 11, 1995, at three o'clock?
8. Who do you think M. and Mme Lionel Desombre are?

194 *cent quatre-vingt-quatorze* CHAPITRE 7 La famille

Answers

2 1. birth announcement; *Possible answers:* It is similar to an American birth announcement. The names at the bottom have the same last name.
2. the son of Denise Morel-Tissot and Raymond Tissot
3. the parents

4. Michel Louis Raymond was born.
5. wedding announcement; *Possible answers:* The word **mariage** looks like *marriage.* Christelle and Nicolas are a couple.
6. a couple announcing their wedding plans
7. Christelle and Nicolas got married.
8. Christelle's or Nicolas' parents

3 Take turns with a partner pointing out and describing someone in the picture below. Give the person's name and age and tell a little bit about him or her.

 4 Write a short paragraph describing the family in the picture above. Give French names to all the family members, tell their ages, give a brief physical description, tell something about their personalities, and tell one or two things they like to do.

5 Are the following sentences representative of French culture, American culture, or both?

1. Dogs are not allowed in restaurants or department stores.   *American culture*

2. The government gives money to all families with two or more children.   *French culture*

3. Pets are tattooed with an identification number.   *French culture*

4. Women have a paid maternity leave of 14 weeks.   *French culture*

 **6**

J E U   D E   R O L E

Your friends arrive at your door and suggest that you go out with them. Your parent tells them that you can go out if you finish your chores, so your friends offer to help. As you work around the house, you discuss where to go and what to do. Create a conversation with your classmates. Be prepared to act out the scene, using props.

Teaching Suggestion

 Give each person in the illustration a name (**Adèle, Jean-Paul, Sophie, Laurent, Céline, Danielle, Emile**) and write the names across the board. Have students read their descriptions of one of the people and have the class tell which person is being described.

Group Work

 You might have students work in groups of three or four to do this activity. Each student writes about one or two of the people in the illustration. When all have finished, they should edit one another's work. Then, the group combines all of the contributions into one paragraph. Finally, all members of the group edit the paragraph before handing it in.

📁 **Portfolio**

 Written/ **Oral**   These activities are appropriate for students' portfolios. For portfolio suggestions, see *Assessment Guide,* page 20.

🖥 **Video Wrap-Up**

- *VIDEO PROGRAM*
- *EXPANDED VIDEO PROGRAM,* Videocassette 3, 01:22–13:44
- *VIDEODISC PROGRAM,* Videodisc 4A

At this time, you might want to use the video resources for additional review and enrichment. See *Video Guide* or *Videodisc Guide* for suggestions regarding the following:
- **Sympa, la famille!** (Dramatic episode)
- **Panorama Culturel** (Interviews)
- **Vidéoclips** (Authentic footage)

QUE SAIS-JE?

This page is intended to help students prepare for the test. It is a brief checklist of the major points covered in the chapter. The students should be reminded that this is only a checklist and does not necessarily include everything that will appear on the test.

Teaching Suggestions

1-7 You might assign Activities 2, 3, 4, 5, and 6 to be done in class by small groups or pairs of students. Activities 1 and 7 might be done as homework.

3 Have students write descriptions of the people in the illustrations. Collect the papers, read some of the descriptions at random, and have students write the number of the illustration that fits each description you read.

4 You might expand this activity by having students describe their best friend.

Can you use what you've learned in this chapter?

Can you identify people? p. 179

1 How would you point out and identify Isabelle Ménard's relatives? How would you give their names and approximate ages? See page 180.
1. her grandparents   Ce sont les grand-parents d'Isabelle. Ils s'appellent Jean-Marie et Eugénie Ménard. Ils ont soixante ans.
2. her uncle   C'est l'oncle d'Isabelle. Il s'appelle Guillaume Ménard. Il a quarante ans.
3. her cousin Loïc   C'est le cousin d'Isabelle. Il s'appelle Loïc. Il a dix-huit ans.
4. her brother   C'est le frère d'Isabelle. Il s'appelle Alexandre. Il a onze ans.

Can you introduce people? p. 183

2 How would you introduce your friend to . . .
1. an adult relative?   Je vous présente...
2. a classmate?   C'est... ; Je te présente...

Can you describe and characterize people? p. 185

3 How would you describe these people?   See answers below.

1.

2.

4 How would you . . .
1. tell a friend that he or she is nice?   Tu es gentil(gentille).
2. tell several friends that they're annoying?   Vous êtes embêtant(e)s/pénibles.
3. say that you and your friend are intelligent?   Nous sommes intelligent(e)s.

Can you ask for, give, and refuse permission? p. 189

5 How would you ask permission to . . .   See answers below.
1. go to the movies?
2. go out with your friends?
3. go shopping?
4. go ice-skating?

6 How would you give someone permission to do something? How would you refuse?   See answers below.

7 What are three things your parents might ask you to do before allowing you to go out with your friends?   See answers below.

196   *cent quatre-vingt-seize*   CHAPITRE 7   La famille

Answers

3 *Possible answers*
1. La femme est brune, l'homme est blond et le garçon est roux.
2. Ils sont forts.

5 1. Je peux aller au cinéma? Est-ce que je peux aller au cinéma?
2. Je peux sortir avec des copains? Est-ce que je peux sortir avec des copains?
3. Je peux faire les magasins? Est-ce que je peux faire les magasins?
4. Je peux faire du patin à glace? Est-ce que je peux faire du patin à glace?

6 *Possible answers*
Giving permission: Oui, si tu veux. Pourquoi pas? Oui, bien sûr. D'accord, si tu... d'abord...
Refusing: Pas question! Non, c'est impossible. Non, tu dois... Pas ce soir.

7 *Possible answers:* faire la vaisselle, faire le ménage, ranger ma chambre, promener le chien, garder ma petite sœur, sortir la poubelle, débarrasser la table, laver la voiture, tondre le gazon, passer l'aspirateur

PREMIERE ETAPE

Identifying people

C'est... *This/That is . . .*
Ce sont... *These/those are . . .*
Voici... *Here's . . .*
Voilà... *There's . . .*

Family members

le grand-père *grandfather*
la grand-mère *grandmother*
la mère *mother*
le père *father*
la sœur *sister*
le frère *brother*

l'oncle (m.) *uncle*
la tante *aunt*
la cousine *girl cousin*
le cousin *boy cousin*
le chat *cat*
le chien *dog*
le canari *canary*
le poisson *fish*

Possessive adjectives

mon/ma/mes *my*
ton/ta/tes *your*
son/sa/ses *his, her*

notre/nos *our*
votre/vos *your*
leur/leurs *their*

Introducing people

C'est... *This is . . .*
Je te/vous présente... *I'd like you to meet . . .*
Très heureux (heureuse). *Pleased to meet you.* (FORMAL)

Other useful expressions

de *of (indicates possession)*

Teaching Suggestion

As a comprehensive review of vocabulary, have students write a conversation between two customers in a café, using vocabulary from the first two **étapes**. The customers might identify and comment on the various people who pass by or who come in and leave the café. Students might do this in pairs.

DEUXIEME ETAPE

Describing and characterizing people

Il est comment? *What is he like?*
Elle est comment? *What is she like?*
Ils/Elles sont comment? *What are they like?*
Il est... *He is . . .*
Elle est... *She is . . .*
Ils/Elles sont... *They're . . .*
amusant(e) *funny*
embêtant(e) *annoying*

fort(e) *strong*
gentil (gentille) *nice*
intelligent(e) *smart*
méchant(e) *mean*
pénible *annoying; a pain in the neck*
sympa(thique) *nice*
timide *shy*
âgé(e) *older*
blond(e) *blond*
brun(e) *brunette*

grand(e) *tall*
gros (grosse) *fat*
jeune *young*
mince *slender*
mignon (mignonne) *cute*
ne... ni grand(e) ni petit(e) *neither tall nor short*
petit(e) *short*
roux (rousse) *redheaded*
être *to be*

TROISIEME ETAPE

Asking for, giving, and refusing permission

Tu es d'accord? *Is that OK with you?*
(Est-ce que) je peux...? *May I . . . ?*
Oui, si tu veux. *Yes, if you want to.*
Pourquoi pas? *Why not?*
Oui, bien sûr. *Yes, of course.*
D'accord, si tu... d'abord... *OK, if you . . . first.*
Pas question! *Out of the question!*

Non, c'est impossible. *No, that's impossible.*
Non, tu dois... *No. You've got to . . .*
Pas ce soir. *Not tonight.*

Chores

faire les courses *to do the shopping*
faire la vaisselle *to do the dishes*
faire le ménage *to do housework*
ranger ta chambre *to pick up your room*

passer l'aspirateur *to vacuum*
promener le chien *to walk the dog*
garder... *to look after . . .*
sortir la poubelle *to take out the trash*
débarrasser la table *to clear the table*
laver la voiture *to wash the car*
tondre le gazon *to mow the lawn*

VOCABULAIRE

cent quatre-vingt-dix-sept **197**

CHAPTER 7 ASSESSMENT

CHAPTER TEST

• *Chapter Teaching Resources, Book 2*, pp. 141–146
• *Assessment Guide*, Speaking Test, p. 31
• *Assessment Items*, Audiocassette 8A Audio CD 7

TEST GENERATOR, CHAPTER 7

ALTERNATIVE ASSESSMENT

Performance Assessment
You might want to use the **Jeu de rôle** (p. 195) as a cumulative performance assessment activity.

Portfolio Assessment
• **Written: Mise en pratique,** Activity 4, *Pupil's Edition*, p. 195
Assessment Guide, p. 20
• **Oral: Mise en pratique, Jeu de rôle,** *Pupil's Edition*, p. 195
Assessment Guide, p. 20

Game

JEU D'ASSOCIATION Have students form small groups and arrange their desks in circles. You will need a small ball for each group. Start the game by calling out a word or expression from the **Vocabulaire (le chien)** and tossing the ball to a member of the group, who calls out a related word or expression (**le chat**). Then, that student calls out another word and tosses the ball to another student who must catch the ball and say a related word, and so on. If a student drops the ball or can't think of a word, he or she is out. You might assign an arbiter to monitor each group. The last remaining player wins. As an alternative, you might play for points instead of eliminating players.

Allez, viens à Abidjan! pp. 198-227

EXPANDED VIDEO
PROGRAM,
Videocassette 3
13:45-16:02

OR VIDEODISC PROGRAM,
Videodisc 4B

Search 1, Play To 4085

Motivating Activity

Ask students to share what they know about French-speaking Africa, or Africa in general. Then, have them compare what they know with what they see in the photos of Abidjan on pages 198-201.

Background Information

Abidjan, the largest city of Côte d'Ivoire, is considered to be the economic capital of the country. Abidjan is located on a series of islands and drained lowlands and lies along the Ebrié Lagoon. In 1950, the construction of the Vridi Canal provided an effective passageway between the lagoon and the Gulf of Guinea, part of the Atlantic Ocean. This construction, coinciding with Côte d'Ivoire's independence from France in 1960, allowed the city to expand into one of the busiest seaports and financial centers of francophone West Africa. The name **Abidjan** originated when some French colonial soldiers asked a man where they were, but he misunderstood the question. Thinking they were asking him what he was doing, he answered in Ebrié, one of the lagoon languages, **"T'chan m'bidjan,"** *("I've returned to cut some leaves.")* The soldiers, therefore, reported that they had visited **Abidjan!**

CHAPITRE 8

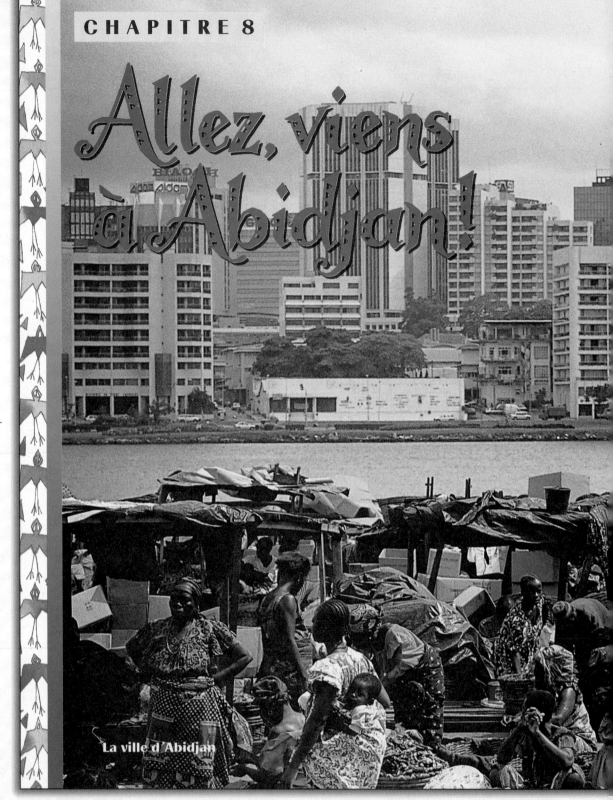

La ville d'Abidjan

Photo Flash

Call students' attention to the skyline of Abidjan on this page and point out the building identified by the letters **BIAO** (directly under the word **Allez**). This is the **Banque Internationale pour l'Afrique Occidentale (BIAO),** one of the largest banks in West Africa. It is located in the **Plateau,** Abidjan's commercial center.

Teacher Note

Even though Abidjan is still the economic capital of Côte d'Ivoire, Yamoussoukro, the home town of former President Houphouët-Boigny, has been the official capital of the country since 1983.

Abidjan

Ville principale de la République de Côte d'Ivoire

Population : plus de 1.850.000

Points d'intérêt : l'Assemblée nationale, le palais du Président, le parc national du Banco, le Musée national

Abidjanais célèbres : Bernard Dadié, Coffi Gadeau, Amon d'Aby, Abdoulaye Traoré

Ressources et industries : café, cacao, bananes, textiles, bois

Spécialités : foutou, aloco, kedjenou, attiéké, sauce arachide, sauce graine, sauce claire

Océan Atlantique

cent quatre-vingt-dix-neuf 199

*U*sing the Almanac and Map

Terms in the Almanac

- **L'Assemblée nationale,** the legislative body whose chamber is located in the Plateau, has 124 representatives, most of whom belong to the ruling political party, the **Parti Démocratique de Côte d'Ivoire (PDCI).**
- **Le palais du Président** is the residence of the Ivorian president. Overlooking the Ebrié Lagoon, the palace has several magnificent gardens.
- **Le parc national du Banco,** a 7,500-acre park outside of Abidjan, is the site of a thriving laundry business. Every morning in the park, hundreds of laundrymen come to the Banco River, pound the clothes on stones to get them clean, and spread them out to dry.
- **Le musée National** gives ample evidence of Côte d'Ivoire's rich cultural heritage. The collection of over 20,000 art objects includes wooden statues and masks, jewelry, pottery, musical instruments, and furniture.
- **foutou:** a dish made from boiled plantains, manioc, or yams, which is served with any one of several sauces.
- **aloco:** a dish of fried plantain bananas.
- **kedjenou:** a traditional main dish made with chicken or meat, vegetables (usually tomatoes and onions), and seasonings.
- **attiéké:** grated manioc, a starchy root, which is served with braised chicken or fish and covered with tomatoes and onions.
- **sauce arachide:** a sauce made from ground peanuts.
- **sauce palme:** a sauce made from palm oil nuts.
- **sauce claire:** a sauce made with eggplant, tomatoes, and other vegetables.

Using the map

As students look at the map, ask them to name the five countries that share a border with Côte d'Ivoire (Liberia, Guinée *(Guinea)*, Mali, Burkina Faso, and Ghana). Ask students if they know the former name of Burkina Faso *(Upper Volta)*. Have students identify the capital city of Côte d'Ivoire (Yamoussoukro).

Culture Notes

- Côte d'Ivoire has consistently been one of the world's leading producers of both coffee and cocoa. In recent years, production has diversified, adding cotton and rubber to the country's list of profitable exports.
- Two other sauces served with various Ivorian dishes are **sauce djoumbre,** made with okra, and **sauce feuille,** made with various leafy green vegetables, such as spinach.

Using the Photo Essay

① The second floor of the Treichville market in Abidjan is the city's best source of a variety of fabrics, such as wax prints, kente cloth, indigo fabric, and woven cloth. Kente cloth is a brightly colored fabric with intricate patterns made by the Ashanti in Ghana.

② Parts of **le parc Banco** serve as coffee and cocoa plantations, managed by villagers who live in the area. Also, there is a small zoo in the center of the park near the lake.

Teaching Suggestion

② Ask students if they have ever visited a national park. Have them brainstorm activities in French that they might do there **(faire du vélo, faire des photos)**. Have them come up with a list of any animals that they might see in a national park. You might refer students to pages 6 and 7 of the Preliminary Chapter for animal names.

③ **Le Plateau** is sometimes known as *little Manhattan* because of its imposing, tall buildings and its dominant position overlooking the water of the lagoon.

Architecture Link

③ **La Pyramide**, the building shown in this photo, is located in the heart of the **Plateau** on avenue Franchet-d'Esperey. Because of its triangular, dissymmetrical structure, **la Pyramide** serves as one of the city's most impressive examples of modern architecture.

Abidjan

*Abidjan is a modern city that lies on the **baie de Cocody** in Côte d'Ivoire. It is a bustling metropolitan area sometimes called the "Paris of Africa." The office buildings and hotels of **Le Plateau** contrast sharply with the lively and colorful district of **Treichville**, the cultural heart of Abidjan.*

① Côte d'Ivoire is famous for its brightly colored fabrics and weavings.

② **Le parc Banco**, a national park since 1953, is a beautiful rain forest reserve.

③ **Le Plateau** is Abidjan's center of commerce and government.

Geography Link

② **Le parc Banco** was established in 1926 outside of Abidjan as a forest reserve and was declared a national park in 1953. The southern part of Côte d'Ivoire, including **le parc Banco**, is dominated by tropical rain forests, which include many varieties of trees, such as palms, fruit trees, ebony, and mahogany. As you move north in the direction of the desert, the land becomes savanna, which is grassland covered with plants that withstand drought and fire. Côte d'Ivoire is fairly flat, except for the hills of Man and Odienné in the western and northwestern parts of the country.

④ The port of **Adjamé** is one of the busiest in West Africa.

⑤ Many different kinds of traditional masks are displayed in the National Museum in Abidjan.

⑥ **Treichville** is the main shopping district of Abidjan. The combination of colors, sounds, and aromas of this lively quarter of town will awaken all the senses.

④ **Adjamé** Many of the workers who built the city of Abidjan originally settled in the **Adjamé** area (a neighborhood north of the **Plateau**) before moving on to Treichville. In the Ebrié language, Adjamé means "place of meeting." The busy port allows Côte d'Ivoire to maintain its trade in cocoa, coffee, and other products, although economic problems have slowed this trade in recent years.

⑤ Several ethnic groups in Côte d'Ivoire are known for their traditional masks. For example, the **Poro** system of life, on which the **Sénoufo** culture is based, follows a complex social code and philosophy. These people use wooden masks to communicate the teachings of their society. Many of these masks are made in artisan villages surrounding Korhogo, in northern Côte d'Ivoire. The ceremonial masks of the **Dan** people, who belong to the larger **Malinké** region surrounding the city of Man in western Côte d'Ivoire, represent the powerful traditions of their group and can be found in museums all over the world.

⑥ **Treichville** is the African hub of Abidjan and is a very lively section of town, day and night. The Treichville market is the largest market in the city and is located across the street from the headquarters of the PDCI, the major political party of the country. This neighborhood is also known for its African restaurants and nightclubs, many of which are situated around the **avenue de la Reine-Pokou,** named for the ancient queen who gave the **Baoulé** people their name (see History Link on this page).

History Link

In the eighteenth century, Queen Abla Pokou, the niece of King Osei Toutou, was leading several families out of Ghana after the king's death when they came upon the Comoë River and could not continue. The high priest asked that a child be given up in exchange for safe passage across the river. Legend has it that Pokou threw her only child into the waters, crying **"Baoulé"** (*"The child is dead"),* and a group of hippos formed a "bridge" on which the families crossed the river. Through this experience, Queen Pokou gave a name to the people who had followed her into what is now central Côte d'Ivoire.

Chapitre 8 : Au marché
Chapter Overview

Mise en train pp. 204–206	Une invitée pour le déjeuner	Practice and Activity Book, p. 85		Video Guide OR Videodisc Guide

	FUNCTIONS	GRAMMAR	CULTURE	RE-ENTRY
Première étape pp. 207–211	Expressing need, p. 210	• The partitive articles **du, de la, de l'**, and **des**, p. 208 • **avoir besoin de**, p. 210	• **Note Culturelle,** The Ivorian market, p. 209 • **Panorama Culturel,** Shopping for groceries in francophone countries, p. 211	Food vocabulary
Deuxième étape pp. 212–216	• Making, accepting, and declining requests, p. 212 • Telling someone what to do, p. 212	• The verb **pouvoir,** p. 213 • **de** with expressions of quantity, p. 214	• **Note Culturelle,** The metric system, p. 214 • **Rencontre Culturelle,** Foods of Côte d'Ivoire, p. 216	• Activities • Making purchases
Troisième étape pp. 217–221	Offering, accepting, or refusing food, p. 219	The pronoun **en,** p. 220	**Note Culturelle,** Mealtimes in francophone countries, p. 218	

Prononciation p. 221	The sounds [o] and [ɔ]		**Dictation:** Textbook Audiocassette 4B/Audio CD 8
Lisons! pp. 222–223	**La cuisine africaine**		**Reading Strategy:** Recognizing false cognates

Review pp. 224–227	**Mise en pratique,** pp. 224–225	**Que sais-je?** p. 226	**Vocabulaire,** p. 227

Assessment Options

Etape Quizzes
• *Chapter Teaching Resources, Book 2*
  Première étape, Quiz 8-1, pp. 191–192
  Deuxième étape, Quiz 8-2, pp. 193–194
  Troisième étape, Quiz 8-3, pp. 195–196
• *Assessment Items, Audiocassette 8A/Audio CD 8*

Chapter Test
• *Chapter Teaching Resources, Book 2,* pp. 197–202
• *Assessment Guide,* Speaking Test, p. 31
• *Assessment Items, Audiocassette 8A/Audio CD 8*

Test Generator, Chapter 8

Video Program OR *Expanded Video Program, Videocassette 3*
OR *Videodisc Program, Videodisc 4B*

Textbook Audiocassette 4B/Audio CD 8

RESOURCES: Print	RESOURCES: Audiovisual

Textbook Audiocassette 4B/Audio CD 8

Practice and Activity Book, pp. 86–88
Chapter Teaching Resources, Book 2
- Teaching Transparency Master 8-1, pp. 175, 178 . . . . *Teaching Transparency 8-1*
- Additional Listening Activities 8-1, 8-2, p. 179 . . . . *Additional Listening Activities, Audiocassette 10A/Audio CD 8*
- Realia 8-1, pp. 183, 185
- Situation Cards 8-1, pp. 186–187
- Student Response Forms, pp. 188–190
- Quiz 8-1, pp. 191–192 . . . . *Assessment Items, Audiocassette 8A/Audio CD 8*
Video Guide . . . . *Video Program* OR *Expanded Video Program, Videocassette 3*
Videodisc Guide . . . . *Videodisc Program, Videodisc 4B*

Textbook Audiocassette 4B/Audio CD 8

Practice and Activity Book, pp. 89–91
Chapter Teaching Resources, Book 2
- Communicative Activity 8-1, pp. 171–172
- Teaching Transparency Master 8-2, pp. 176, 178 . . . . *Teaching Transparency 8-2*
- Additional Listening Activities 8-3, 8-4, p. 180 . . . . *Additional Listening Activities, Audiocassette 10A/Audio CD 8*
- Realia 8-2, pp. 184, 185
- Situation Cards 8-2, pp. 186–187
- Student Response Forms, pp. 188–190
- Quiz 8-2, pp. 193–194 . . . . *Assessment Items, Audiocassette 8A/Audio CD 8*
Videodisc Guide . . . . *Videodisc Program, Videodisc 4B*

Textbook Audiocassette 4B/Audio CD 8

Practice and Activity Book, pp. 92–94
Chapter Teaching Resources, Book 2
- Communicative Activity 8-2, pp. 173–174
- Teaching Transparency Master 8-3, pp. 177, 178 . . . . *Teaching Transparency 8-3*
- Additional Listening Activities 8-5, 8-6, p. 181 . . . . *Additional Listening Activities, Audiocassette 10A/Audio CD 8*
- Realia 8-2, pp. 184, 185
- Situation Cards 8-3, pp. 186–187
- Student Response Forms, pp. 188–190
- Quiz 8-3, pp. 195–196 . . . . *Assessment Items, Audiocassette 8A/Audio CD 8*
Videodisc Guide . . . . *Videodisc Program, Videodisc 4B*

Practice and Activity Book, p. 95

Video Guide . . . . *Video Program* OR *Expanded Video Program, Videocassette 3*
Videodisc Guide . . . . *Videodisc Program, Videodisc 4B*

Alternative Assessment
- Performance Assessment
  Première étape, p. 210
  Deuxième étape, p. 215
  Troisième étape, p. 221
- Portfolio Assessment
  Written: **Mise en pratique,** Activity 3, *Pupil's Edition,* p. 224
    Assessment Guide, p. 21
  Oral: **Mise en pratique, Jeu de rôle,** *Pupil's Edition,* p. 225
    Assessment Guide, p. 21

Chapitre 8 : Au marché
Textbook Listening Activities Scripts

For Student Response Forms, see *Chapter Teaching Resources, Book 2,* pp. 188–190.

*P*remière étape

7 Ecoute! p. 208

1. — Comment sont ces fraises?
   — Bof, elles ne sont pas très mûres.

2. — Tu aimes ce poisson?
   — Ça va. Rien de spécial.

3. — Elle est comment, cette mangue?
   — Elle est délicieuse. Mais moi, j'adore les mangues!

4. — Comment est ce poulet?
   — Pas mauvais.

5. — Alors? Ces haricots? Ils sont bons?
   — Pas terribles.

Answers to Activity 7
1. fruit   4. poultry
2. fish   5. vegetables
3. fruit

*D*euxième étape

14 Ecoute! p. 213

1. — Eh bien, Jean-Luc, tu peux aller faire les courses aujourd'hui?
   — Euh, je regrette, mais je n'ai pas le temps.

2. — Sylvie, tu me rapportes du lait cet après-midi?
   — Bon, d'accord.

3. — Robert! Rapporte-moi du beurre! N'oublie pas!
   — Mais, maman, je ne peux pas maintenant!

4. — Annie, tu peux acheter des fraises pour le dîner?
   — Tout de suite.

5. — Euh, Chantal, achète-moi un paquet de riz cet après-midi!
   — Je veux bien.

Answers to Activity 14
a. 1. making a request
   2. making a request
   3. telling someone what to do
   4. making a request
   5. telling someone what to do
b. 1. declines
   2. accepts
   3. declines
   4. accepts
   5. accepts

17 Ecoute! p. 215

1. — Bonjour, monsieur. Je voudrais douze tranches de jambon, s'il vous plaît.
   — Voilà.
   — C'est combien?
   — Cinquante-trois francs.

2. — Bonjour, madame. Est-ce que vous avez des fraises, s'il vous plaît?
   — Oui, regardez, elles sont mûres!
   — Alors, je vais prendre un kilo de fraises.
   — Voilà. Ça fait vingt-six francs.
   — Tenez.
   — Merci bien. Au revoir.

3. — Bonjour, madame. C'est combien, l'eau minérale, s'il vous plaît?
   — Trois francs soixante-quinze la bouteille.
   — Bien, je vais prendre trois bouteilles.
   — Tenez.
   — Merci. Ça fait combien?
   — Onze francs vingt-cinq.
   — Tenez.
   — Merci.

4. — Je voudrais un morceau de fromage, s'il vous plaît, monsieur.
   — Voilà.
   — Je vais aussi prendre une douzaine d'œufs.
   — C'est tout?
   — Oui.
   — Alors, ça vous fait... vingt-neuf francs.
   — Voilà.
   — Merci.

Answers to Activity 17
1. twelve slices of ham
2. a kilo of strawberries
3. three bottles of mineral water
4. a piece of cheese, a dozen eggs

*T*roisième étape

21 Ecoute! p. 218

1. — Dis, Anne, qu'est-ce que tu prends d'habitude au petit déjeuner?
   — Oh, d'habitude, je prends un chocolat, du pain, du beurre et de la confiture.

2. — Pardon, monsieur. Qu'est-ce que vous prenez en général au petit déjeuner?
   — Je prends un café, un jus d'orange et des fruits.

3. — Bonjour, madame. Qu'est-ce que vous prenez d'habitude au petit déjeuner?
   — J'aime bien prendre du lait avec des céréales, du pain avec du beurre et un jus d'orange.

Answers to Activity 21
1. c   2. a   3. b

25 Ecoute! p. 219

1. Vous prenez de la salade?
2. Merci. Je n'ai plus faim.
3. Oui, avec plaisir.
4. Encore du poisson?
5. Non, merci.

Answers to Activity 25
1. offering   4. offering
2. refusing   5. refusing
3. accepting

*P*rononciation, p. 221

For the scripts for Parts A and B, see p. 221.

C. A écrire

(*Dictation*)
— Tu peux aller faire les courses aujourd'hui?
— D'accord. Qu'est-ce qu'il te faut?
— Il me faut deux kilos de pommes de terre, du fromage et un gâteau.

*M*ise en pratique

1 p. 224

Mesdames, messieurs, aujourd'hui, profitez de nos prix exceptionnels sur l'alimentation! Le kilo de carottes à huit francs, le kilo de pommes de terre à quatre francs et les deux kilos d'oranges, onze francs. Et ce n'est pas fini! Trente-deux francs, le poulet. Quarante-quatre francs, le kilo de jambon. Des prix aussi sur les produits laitiers! Trois francs, le litre de lait, quatre francs vingt, la douzaine d'œufs! Alors, vous hésitez encore? Dépêchez-vous. Remplissez vos placards! Faites de bonnes affaires!

Possible answers to Mise en pratique Activity 1
1 kilo of carrots, 8 francs; 1 kilo of potatoes, 4 francs; 2 kilos of oranges, 11 francs; 1 chicken, 32 francs; 1 kilo of ham, 44 francs; 1 liter of milk, 3 francs; 1 dozen eggs, 4F20

Chapitre 8 : Au marché
Projects

Jour de marché
(Group Project)

ASSIGNMENT

Students will role-play a marketplace scene, acting as vendors and customers.

TEACHER NOTE

You might have students do this project after they complete the **Première étape,** where they will learn about a variety of food items from Côte d'Ivoire.

MATERIALS

✂ **Students may need**
- A variety of foods
- Plates, platters, or bowls
- A small knife for cutting food
- Cardboard or posterboard
- Tape or glue
- Colored markers
- Paper
- Pen or pencil

SUGGESTED SEQUENCE

1. Before market day, ask students to find out if there are any tropical fruits available locally. Have them refer to the **Vocabulaire** on page 207. Then, bring in or have students bring in some of these foods.

2. Ask for five or six volunteers to be the vendors; the others will be the customers. Have the vendors make signs for their stands and set up the marketplace. Several students may work together on one stand. The customers should make CFA francs out of paper and cardboard. (Refer students to pages 203 and 204 for sample CFA bills.)

3. On market day, have the vendors set up their stands and clean and cut the foods into portions so that everyone can "buy" some. All the shopping, bargaining, and purchasing should then be conducted in French.

4. After everyone has shopped and tried some of the foods, have students clean up. Then, have them write about the experience in French, giving their opinions of the foods they tried.

GRADING THE PROJECT

This is an ungraded project, but you might choose to give participation grades or a grade for the writing assignment.

TEACHER NOTE

In the Postreading section of **Lisons!** on page 223, you will find another suggested project that can be graded.

DESSIN ANIME

In this game, students will practice food vocabulary from this chapter.

Procedure   Divide the class into two or more teams. A player from one team goes to the board. Tell him or her the name of a food in French so that the other students cannot hear. The student must draw a picture of that food on the board. Set a time limit of 30 to 60 seconds. The player's team wins a point if they guess the correct French word for the picture. The other team then takes a turn. This game may also be played in small groups. In this case, students choose words from the vocabulary list at the end of the chapter and draw their illustrations on paper.

QUELS INGREDIENTS?

In this game, students will practice expressing need as well as food vocabulary.

Procedure   The game begins with one student naming a particular dish or meal: **un sandwich, une salade, une salade de fruits, une omelette, le déjeuner.** The next student names one ingredient of that particular dish or meal. Subsequent students repeat all the previously mentioned ingredients and add another. For example, the first student might say **un sandwich.** The next student would say **Il faut du pain.** The third student would say **Il faut du pain et du jambon.** When a student is unable to repeat the order correctly, start a new round with a new food item. This can be played either by going in order around the class, or by randomly calling on students, which is more difficult. You might want to have one or two students act as judges, who write down the ingredients mentioned to verify the correct order.

QU'EST-CE QU'ON FAIT?

This game will test students' recognition of the ingredients for various recipes.

Procedure   This game can be played by individuals, partners, or small groups. Read aloud a list of ingredients for a particular dish that students are familiar with. Students will try to guess what dish it is within a given time. You might want to consult a cookbook for recipes, or use the recipes that students create for the **Lisons!** activity on page 223. Students may guess in English if they have not learned the French name of a particular dish.

Examples:
1. **du pain, du fromage, du jambon, du beurre (un croque-monsieur)**
2. **du chocolat, du sucre, du beurre, des œufs, de la farine (un gâteau au chocolat)**
3. **des œufs, des champignons, du fromage, du lait (une omelette)**
4. **de la salade, des tomates, des carottes, des oignons (une salade)**
5. **des bananes, des oranges, des pommes (une salade de fruits)**

Chapitre 8
Au marché

pp. 202–227

𝒰sing the Chapter Opener

Motivating Activity

Have students find the name of a country (Côte d'Ivoire) in the opening spread. Have them locate it on the map of Africa on page xxii or on *Map Transparency 2.* Ask students to share their knowledge, experiences, and/or impressions of Africa. Then, direct students' attention to the photos. Ask them to identify features that are uniquely African.

Thinking Critically

Comparing and Contrasting

Have students compare the Ivorian market they see to outdoor markets they've seen in the United States or photos they've seen of French markets. How are they similar? Different?

Photo Flash!

① The photos on pages 202 and 203 show typical outdoor markets in Côte d'Ivoire. Students might want to know that although there are no set rules as to who sells what, they would generally see women selling fruits, vegetables, and fish, while men would be selling bread and meat. Both men and women sell fabric.

CHAPITRE
8
Au marché

① Le marché en Côte d'Ivoire, c'est un plaisir pour les yeux.

202   *deux cent deux*

Culture Note

Call students' attention to the jewelry shown on pages 202 and 203. There is an abundance of handcrafted jewelry made in Côte d'Ivoire, and the beautiful bracelets, necklaces, rings, and earrings are made out of a variety of raw materials. Jewelry made of bone may be intricately carved like the necklace at the top of this page. Gold, silver, and brass are popular metals used for jewelry. Malachite is a popular dark green stone used for earrings and rings. Leather is used extensively as are cowry shells (see the mask on page 201). Ebony and other kinds of wood may also be used. Beads come in all colors and shapes, and a particularly wide selection can be found in Abidjan's Treichville market.

Imagine shopping for food in the Republic of Côte d'Ivoire—the tropical fruits, lively marketplace, and Ivorian merchants would make it an adventure. You'd also gain experience with the metric system and the currency of francophone Africa, *le franc de la Communauté financière africaine (CFA)*.

In this chapter you will learn

- to express need
- to make, accept, and decline requests; to tell someone what to do
- to offer, accept, or refuse food

And you will

- listen to French-speaking people talk about the foods they like
- read recipes for African dishes
- write about your favorite and least favorite foods
- find out about the metric system of weights and measures

② Tu me rapportes des fruits?

③ Tiens, Djeneba, tu peux m'aider?

Culture Note

You might point out the CFA bills at the bottom of this page. The CFA, used throughout francophone Africa, comes in bills of 100, 500, 1,000, 2,500, 5,000, and 10,000 CFA. Coins are available in 5, 10, 25, and 100 CFA. There are actually *two* CFAs in Africa, which are more or less equal in value. The West African CFA is used in Côte d'Ivoire, Senegal, Mali, Burkina Faso, Niger, Togo, and Benin. The Central African CFA is used in Cameroon, Central African Republic, Chad, Congo, Equatorial Guinea, and Gabon.

Focusing on Outcomes

Have students think of different situations where the functions listed in the outcomes might be used. Ask them to be as specific as possible. You might write their ideas on the board or on a transparency. Ask students to match the outcomes to the photos. NOTE: You may want to use the video to support the objectives. The self-check activities in **Que sais-je?** on page 226 help students assess their achievement of the objectives.

Teaching Suggestion

Have students list all the food vocabulary they can remember from previous chapters and then check off the items they see pictured on pages 202 and 203.

Photo Flash!

② In Côte d'Ivoire, it is common to see women carrying food, firewood, a bucket of water, or various other loads on their head. If the object is heavy, two other women might lift it onto the third woman's head. High school girls will sometimes carry their books on their heads as they walk to and from school. In the market, it is not uncommon to see a woman carrying a bowl of food items on her head, a baby riding on her back, and a bag in one hand. With this arrangement, the woman still has the other hand free to carry on with her business, and the baby has a cozy place to sleep!

**VIDEO PROGRAM
OR EXPANDED VIDEO
PROGRAM,**
Videocassette 3
16:03–20:26

OR *VIDEODISC PROGRAM,*
Videodisc 4B

Search 4085, Play To 12035

Video Synopsis

In this segment of the video, Djeneba's mother (Mme Diomandé) and aunt (Aminata) are discussing what to prepare for lunch. Djeneba's mother asks her to go shopping at the market. She tells her what she needs to make lunch, specifying different quantities of items. At the market, Djeneba buys fish, tomatoes, rice, and the other things her mother asked for. When she returns home, she and her mother prepare lunch. When they are almost done, someone knocks at the door, and Djeneba realizes that she forgot to tell her mother that she invited a guest for lunch!

Motivating Activities

• Have students imagine what the climate, crops, and culture are like in Côte d'Ivoire. Ask them to find evidence in the photos to support their ideas. Ask them if they can name parts of the United States that are similar to Côte d'Ivoire with respect to climate and crops (southern Texas, California).

• Ask students what they normally eat for lunch. What would they make if a guest were coming over?

Teacher Note

Foutou and **sauce arachide** are described on page 216.

Mise en train

Djeneba   Mme Diomandé   Aminata

Une invitée pour le déjeuner

Where does Djeneba go to do the grocery shopping?
Do you recognize any of the food items she buys?

Le matin chez les Diomandé, à Abidjan. C'est l'heure du petit déjeuner.

1 kilo de riz
250 grammes de pâte d'arachide
1 poisson
7 oignons
1 douzaine de tomates
3 citrons
un paquet de beurre
du pain

① Encore du pain, Aminata?

Non, merci. Je n'ai plus faim.

Je pense faire du foutou avec de la sauce arachide pour le déjeuner.

② Tiens, te voilà, Djeneba. Tu me fais le marché?

Volontiers! Qu'est-ce qu'il te faut?

③ Il me faut des légumes, du riz, du poisson... Tu me rapportes aussi du pain... Et prends de la pâte de tomates.

Bon, d'accord.

204 *deux cent quatre*   CHAPITRE 8   Au marché

RESOURCES FOR MISE EN TRAIN

Textbook Audiocassette 4B/Audio CD 8
Practice and Activity Book, p. 85
Video Guide
    Video Program
    Expanded Video Program, Videocassette 3
Videodisc Guide
    Videodisc Program, Videodisc 4B

Djeneba va au marché…

…puis, elle rentre chez elle.

Voilà le poisson, les 250 grammes de pâte d'arachide, les oignons, les tomates et les citrons. J'ai aussi acheté un paquet de beurre, de la pâte de tomates, du pain et du riz.

Merci, chérie.

Mme Diomandé fait la cuisine.

Viens. Goûte voir. C'est bon?

Oui, très bon.

Toc toc toc!

Ah, j'ai oublié… Devine qui j'ai vu au marché.

Aucune idée… Va voir qui est à la porte.

MISE EN TRAIN

deux cent cinq 205

Presentation

Before students view the video, introduce the characters in the story. Write their names on the board and ask students to guess what their relationships are. Then, have students watch the episode to get the gist of the story. When they have finished viewing the episode for the first time, ask them to tell what they think is happening in the story. You might have students look over the questions in Activity 1 on page 206 and keep them in mind as they watch the episode again. After students have read the story, have volunteers read the dialogue aloud for the class. Ask students to name the items that Djeneba buys at the market.

Teaching Suggestion

Ask students if they are familiar with the units of measurement used in the shopping list. The metric system is presented on page 214.

Photo Flash!

(7) (9) In these photos, Djeneba is holding a pestle that she is using to make **foutou.** This dish is usually made by pounding boiled yams, **manioc** *(cassava),* or plantains in a mortar until they are the consistency of paste. They are then shaped into round balls for serving (see page 216).

Video Integration

- *EXPANDED VIDEO PROGRAM,* Videocassette 3, 20:27–24:19
- *VIDEODISC PROGRAM,* Videodisc 4B

Search 12035, Play To 19035

You may choose to continue with **Une invitée pour le déjeuner (suite)** at this time or wait until later in the chapter. When the story continues, we discover that Miss Riggs, Djeneba's English teacher, is at the door. The next scene is a flashback to the market where Miss Riggs is asking Djeneba how to make **sauce arachide.** Djeneba tells her that her mother is making it for lunch and invites Miss Riggs. Back home, Djeneba's mother tells Miss Riggs about **sauce arachide.** At the table, Djeneba's mother offers everyone **foutou** and **sauce arachide.**

Multicultural Link

Ask students if they have tried food specialties from other countries and how they liked them. You might also have them choose a country and research its food specialties. Have students list specialties of their own town or area.

Teaching Suggestions

1 You might want to have students work in pairs to answer these questions.

2 Have students identify the photo that proves or disproves each statement. Have them correct the false statements.

2–4 Have students do these activities individually or in pairs. You might want to check answers orally.

3 Bring in these food items or pictures of them and hold them up. Have students call out the number of the corresponding answer.

5 You might have students write down the expressions as they locate them in the story.

For videodisc application, see *Videodisc Guide*.

1 Tu as compris? See answers below.

1. What time of day is it?
2. What does Mme Diomandé want Djeneba to do? Why?
3. What are some of the things Djeneba buys?
4. What happens at the end of the story?
5. Judging from the title, what do you think Djeneba forgot?

2 Vrai ou faux?

1. Aminata va au marché.   faux
2. Mme Diomandé va faire du foutou avec de la sauce arachide.   vrai
3. Djeneba ne veut pas aller au marché.   faux
4. Djeneba achète des bananes au marché.   faux
5. Djeneba oublie le pain.   faux

3 Choisis la photo

Match the foods that Djeneba bought to their pictures.

1. du poisson   b   2. des tomates   d   3. des oignons   e   4. des citrons   a   5. du pain   c

a.   b.   c.   d.   e.

4 C'est qui?

1. «Non, merci. Je n'ai plus faim.»   Aminata
2. «Tu me fais le marché?»   Mme Diomandé
3. «J'ai aussi acheté un paquet de beurre, du riz, de la pâte de tomates et du pain.»   Djeneba
4. «Ah, j'ai oublié... »   Djeneba
5. «Va voir qui est à la porte.»   Mme Diomandé

5 Cherche l'expression

In **Une invitée pour le déjeuner**, how does . . .

1. Mme Diomandé offer more food to Mme Bonfils?   Encore du pain?
2. Aminata refuse the offer?   Non, merci. Je n'ai plus faim.
3. Mme Diomandé ask Djeneba to do the shopping?   Tu me fais le marché?
4. Mme Diomandé tell Djeneba what she needs?   Il me faut...
5. Djeneba agree to do what Mme Diomandé asks?   Volontiers! Bon, d'accord.

6 Et maintenant, à toi

Who does the grocery shopping in your family? Where do they do the shopping?

206   *deux cent six*   CHAPITRE 8   Au marché

Answers

1 1. morning
   2. She wants her to go to the market. Mme Diomandé needs some ingredients for a dish she is planning to make.
   3. fish, peanut butter, onions, tomatoes, lemons, rice, butter, bread, and tomato paste
   4. Someone knocks at the door.
   5. Djeneba forgot that she invited a guest for lunch.

PREMIERE ETAPE

Expressing need

VOCABULAIRE

Qu'est-ce qu'on trouve **au marché?**

Qu'est-ce qu'on vend **au supermarché?**

du beurre	butter	du gâteau	cake	des fraises (f.)	strawberries
de la confiture	jam	de la tarte	pie	du raisin	grapes
du lait	milk	des pommes (f.)	apples	des petits pois (m.)	peas
du yaourt	yogurt	des poires (f.)	pears	des carottes (f.)	carrots
du riz	rice	des pêches (f.)	peaches	des champignons (m.)	mushrooms
de la farine	flour	des citrons (m.)	lemons		

* **Poule** refers to live chickens, while **poulet** refers to cooked chicken.

Jump Start!

Have students list three things they might order in a café.

MOTIVATE

Ask students if they ever go grocery shopping, what their favorite foods are, and if they like to cook.

TEACH

Presentation

Vocabulaire Bring in real or toy food items or magazine pictures to present this vocabulary. Present the new words by food groups, holding up the object or illustration as you say the word for each one. Then, hold up the items or pictures, asking **Qu'est-ce que c'est?** Encourage students to make charts for each food group. Have them create a set of picture flashcards.

Language Notes

• Make sure students pronounce **poisson** with the *s* sound, not with a *z* sound as in **poison**.

• The final -**f** is pronounced in **œuf**, but not in the plural **œufs**. Teach students the phrase *One egg is* **un œuf** *("enough")* to help them remember to pronounce the -**f** only in the singular form.

Game

ATTRAPE-LE! Place three food items on a table (**une mangue, une tomate, un citron**). Call two students to the front. Say what you'd like to have. (**Je voudrais un citron.**) The first student to grab the item and hand it to you wins. The winner stays at the table and another player comes to the front. You might add more items to make the game more challenging.

RESOURCES FOR PREMIERE ETAPE

Textbook Audiocassette 4B/Audio CD 8
Practice and Activity Book, pp. 86–88
Video Guide
   Video Program
   Expanded Video Program, Videocassette 3
Videodisc Guide
   Videodisc Program, Videodisc 4B

Chapter Teaching Resources, Book 2
• Teaching Transparency Master 8-1, pp. 175, 178
   Teaching Transparency 8-1
• Additional Listening Activities 8-1, 8-2, p. 179
   Audiocassette 10A/Audio CD 8
• Realia 8-1, pp. 183, 185
• Situation Cards 8-1, pp. 186–187
• Student Response Forms, pp. 188–190
• Quiz 8-1, pp. 191–192
   Audiocassette 8A/Audio CD 8

For Individual Needs

7 Challenge Before playing the recording, you might have students practice categorizing the vocabulary. Distribute the flashcards (see the **Vocabulaire** presentation on page 207) randomly to students. Write *Fruit, Vegetables, Meat, Poultry, Fish,* and *Dairy* on the board at the top of five columns, and ask students to tape their flashcards in the correct category. As an alternative, number the categories 1 to 5 and have students give the number of the appropriate category as you say different vocabulary words.

Presentation

Grammaire To present the partitive article, first draw a whole pizza and a whole cake on the board. Identify them orally, using the indefinite article: **une pizza, un gâteau.** Then, divide each into pieces and shade one of the pieces. Identify the portions, using the partitive article: **de la pizza, du gâteau.** Next, bring in a food item (**une tarte, un pain, une orange**) and have students ask for some or all of it. (**Je voudrais de la tarte/du pain/une orange, s'il vous plaît.**) Remind students that they learned how to use **de** after **ne... pas** in Chapter 3.

Additional Practice

Grammaire Hold up real or toy food items or the picture side of vocabulary flashcards and ask students if they want some of the item. (**Tu veux du gâteau?**)

---

7 Ecoute!

Listen to the dialogues and decide if the people are talking about fruit, vegetables, fish, or poultry. Answers on p. 201C.

*G*rammaire   The partitive articles **du, de la, de l', and des**

Use **du, de la, de l',** or **des** to indicate *some of* or *part of* something.

> Je voudrais **du** gâteau.
> Tu veux **de la** salade?
> Elle va prendre **de l'**eau minérale.
> Il me faut **des** oranges.

- If you want to talk about a whole item, use the articles **un** and **une.**

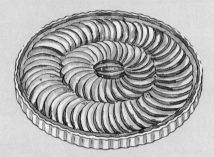

Il achète **une** tarte.   Il prend **de la** tarte.

- In a negative sentence, **du, de la, de l',** and **des** change to **de** *(none* or *any).*

  —Tu as **du** pain?   —Tu prends **de la** viande?
  —Désolée, je n'ai pas **de** pain.   —Merci, je ne prends jamais **de** viande.

- You can't leave out the article in French as you do in English.
  Elle mange **du** fromage. *She's eating cheese.*

8 Qu'est-ce qu'on prend?

Complète ce dialogue avec du, de la, de l' ou des.

ASSIKA   J'ai très faim, maman.
MAMAN   Qu'est-ce que tu veux manger?
ASSIKA   Moi, je voudrais __1__ poisson, __2__ riz et __3__ haricots.   du, du, des
MAMAN   Bon. Tu peux prendre __4__ pain aussi.   du
ASSIKA   Et comme boisson?
MAMAN   Prends __5__ eau minérale.   de l'
ASSIKA   D'accord.
MAMAN   Et comme dessert, prends __6__ bananes ou __7__ oranges.   des, des
ASSIKA   C'est tout?
MAMAN   Non, tu peux prendre __8__ yaourt aussi.   du

Teaching Suggestion

8 Have students rewrite the dialogue, substituting their favorite foods for the items mentioned and leaving the numbered blanks empty. Have them exchange papers with a partner, who fills in the blanks and then returns the paper for correction.

9 Qu'est-ce qu'elles ont acheté?

What are Prisca, Clémentine, and Adjoua buying at the market? See answers below.

1.   2.   3.

NOTE CULTURELLE

Shopping at a market in Côte d'Ivoire can be an exciting and colorful experience. Every city, town, and village has an open-air market where people come to buy and sell food, cloth, housewares, medicine, and herbal remedies. Although French is the official language in Côte d'Ivoire, more than 60 different African languages are spoken there. To make shopping easier for everyone, there is a common market language called **djoula**. Here are a few phrases in **djoula**.

í ní sɔ̀gɔ̀ma	(ee nee so*g*oma)	*Good morning.*
í ní wúla	(ee *nee* woulah)	*Good afternoon./Hello.*
í ká kɛ́nɛ wá?	(ee kah keh*neh* wah)	*How are you?/How's it going?*
n ká kɛ́nɛ kósobɛ	(nnkah keh*neh* kuh*s*ohbeh)	*I'm fine.*

10 Qu'est-ce qu'il y a dans le chariot?

Your partner has mixed his or her shopping cart with five others whose contents are listed below. Ask about the contents until you have enough information to guess which cart belongs to your partner. Then, change roles.

— Tu as acheté des tomates? — Non.
— Tu as acheté du poisson? — Oui.
— Ton chariot, c'est le numéro... ? — Oui.

1. du poisson
   des tomates
   des bananes
   du fromage
   du lait

2. du pain
   des œufs
   des oignons
   du poisson
   des haricots

3. du sucre
   des ananas
   du lait
   du maïs
   des tomates

4. des tomates
   des haricots
   des œufs
   du sucre
   du maïs

5. des ananas
   des bananes
   du fromage
   des oignons
   des haricots

6. des bananes
   des œufs
   du poisson
   du pain
   des tomates

Answers

9 1. du riz, un ananas, des citrons, des œufs, du beurre, une banane
2. des tomates, des œufs, du maïs, un oignon
3. du riz, un oignon, des pommes de terre, une tomate, une orange

Teacher Note

You might want to invite someone from West Africa or someone who has traveled there to speak to your class. Try contacting the international student office at a local college or university. Returned Peace Corps volunteers might also be classroom visitors. Write to Peace Corps, Office of World Wise Schools, 1990 K Street, Washington, D.C. 20526, or call the Peace Corps Africa desk at 1-800-424-8580, extension 2262.

Teaching Suggestion

Note Culturelle Have partners practice greeting each other in **Djoula**. They might also choose to use these greetings in activities and skits later in the chapter.

For videodisc application, see *Videodisc Guide*.

Culture Notes

• Prices in West African markets are not fixed and customers are expected to bargain. With the buyer's first inquiry, the vendor often extols the virtues of the item and quotes a high price, sometimes triple the price usually paid. The customer should never pay this price, but make a counteroffer of approximately half the usual price. The vendor and customer will usually bargain back up to a happy compromise.

• In many African countries, it is believed that a vendor who allows the first customer of the day to leave without purchasing something will have bad luck for the rest of the day.

Language Note

For *seller* or *merchant,* the words **vendeur**(-**euse**) and **commerçant**(**e**) are generally interchangeable.

For Individual Needs

10 Slower Pace/Visual Learners Hold up pictures of the foods mentioned in this activity and have students give the number of the cart that contains each one. For example, if you hold up a picture of pineapples, the class would respond **trois et cinq.**

Presentation

Comment dit-on... ?
Distribute vocabulary cards to students. Then, ask various students **De quoi est-ce que tu as besoin?** or **Qu'est-ce qu'il te faut?** and have them respond according to the item on their cards. Then, have groups of five or six play the game "**Quels ingrédients?**" To play, each student repeats all the previously mentioned ingredients and adds another. This game is explained in more detail on page 201F.

Building on Previous Skills

Re-enter previously learned vocabulary by playing the game described above, substituting activities and clothing. (**Pour jouer au basket, il me faut... des baskets, un tee-shirt,...**)

Teaching Suggestion

13 Students might want to greet each other in Djoula to begin the activity.

CLOSE

To close this **étape,** show *Teaching Transparency 8-1* and have students identify the food items shown.

ASSESS

Quiz 8-1, *Chapter Teaching Resources, Book 2,* pp. 191–192

Assessment Items, Audiocassette 8A/Audio CD 8

Performance Assessment

Have students make a shopping list of at least five items, using the partitive articles. Then, have them pair off and take turns asking what their partner needs.

COMMENT DIT-ON... ?

Expressing need

— Qu'est-ce qu'il te faut?
— **Il me faut** des bananes, du riz et de l'eau minérale.

— De quoi est-ce que tu as besoin? *What do you need?*
— **J'ai besoin de** riz pour faire du foutou. *I need . . .*

Note de Grammaire

The expression **avoir besoin de** can be followed by a noun or a verb. The partitive article is not used with this expression.

> Tu **as besoin de** tomates?
> Nous **avons besoin d'**œufs pour l'omelette.
> J'**ai besoin d'**aller au marché.

À la française

Many French expressions involve foods: **On est dans la purée** *(We're in trouble);* **C'est pas de la tarte** *(It's not easy).* Can you guess what **C'est du gâteau** means? *

Vocabulaire à la carte

Here are some additional words you may want to know:

du concombre	cucumber
des cornichons (m.)	pickles
de la moutarde	mustard
des noix (f.)	nuts
du poivre	pepper
du sel	salt

11 Que faut-il? See answers below.

Tu as besoin de quoi pour faire...

1. un bon sandwich?
2. une quiche?
3. une salade?
4. une salade de fruits?
5. un banana split?

12 Un repas entre amis

Sandrine is having a party, but she won't tell what she's cooking. Based on what she needs, try to guess what she's preparing.

1. J'ai besoin de salade, de tomates, de carottes, d'oignons... une salade
2. J'ai besoin de fromage, de pain, de jambon... un sandwich
3. J'ai besoin d'œufs, de champignons, de fromage, de lait... une omelette
4. J'ai besoin de bananes, de pommes, d'oranges... une salade de fruits

> une tarte aux pommes
> un banana split   une salade de fruits
> une salade   un sandwich
> une omelette

13 De quoi est-ce que tu as besoin?

You're going to cook a special meal for your host family. Decide what you want to make. Then, go to the market and buy what you need. Take turns with a partner playing the role of the merchant.

* It means *It's easy; it's a piece of cake.*

Teaching Suggestion

Students might also enjoy compiling a list of French cooking terms used in English, such as **sauté, julienne,** and **purée.**

Possible answers

11 1. du pain, du fromage, de la viande, des cornichons, de la moutarde
2. des œufs, du fromage, du lait, des champignons, des oignons
3. de la salade, des tomates, des carottes, des champignons, du concombre
4. des oranges, des fraises, des bananes, un ananas
5. des bananes, de la glace, des noix

PANORAMA CULTUREL

Louise • France

Angèle • Côte d'Ivoire

Micheline • Belgique

Where does your family go to shop for groceries? People in francophone countries have several options. We asked these people where they shop. Here's what they had to say.

Où est-ce que tu aimes faire des provisions?

«Je vais le plus souvent au supermarché, mais je préfère le marché, parce que le marché, c'est dehors et puis, l'ambiance est meilleure.»
—Louise

«Je préfère aller au super-marché pour aller faire des achats parce que là-bas, c'est plus sûr et bien conservé.»
—Angèle

«Je préfère aller au marché, chez les petits commerçants, parce qu'il y a le contact personnel, il y a le choix, il y a les odeurs, les couleurs, le plaisir de la promenade aussi dans le marché.»
—Micheline

Qu'en penses-tu? See answers below.

1. Where do these people shop for groceries?
2. What are the advantages and disadvantages of shopping in these different places?
3. Are there outdoor farmers' markets in your community? What can you buy there?
4. Does your family sometimes shop in small specialty stores?

Savais-tu que... ?

Many people in francophone countries grocery shop in supermarkets (**supermarchés**) or hypermarkets (**hypermarchés**) because it's convenient. Others prefer to shop in small grocery stores (**épiceries**) or outdoor markets (**marchés en plein air**). **Supermarchés** are similar to their American counterparts. **Hypermarchés** are very large stores that carry just about anything you can imagine—all under one roof! Americans may be surprised to learn, however, that stores are not open 24 hours a day or even late in the evening. **Epiceries** are usually closed between 12:30 P.M. and 4 P.M. and on Sunday and/or Monday.

Answers

1. in the supermarket and market
2. *Possible answers*
   In a supermarket, everything is conveniently under one roof and well-refrigerated, but the atmosphere can be impersonal. At the market, the atmosphere is lively, and the food is fresh, but you may have to visit several vendors to complete all of your shopping, and shopping carts aren't available.

Questions

1. **Pourquoi est-ce que Louise préfère aller au marché? (C'est dehors, l'ambiance est meilleure.)**
2. **Pourquoi est-ce qu'Angèle préfère aller au supermarché pour faire ses achats? (C'est plus sûr et bien conservé.)**
3. **Pourquoi est-ce que Micheline préfère aller au marché? (Il y a le contact personnel, le choix, les odeurs, les couleurs, le plaisir de la promenade.)**

DEUXIEME ETAPE

Making, accepting, and declining requests; telling someone what to do

Jump Start!

Draw or display pictures of several food items (a whole cake, a piece of fruit, eggs, a piece of cheese, and a slice of bread) and have students write them in French, using the indefinite or partitive article.

MOTIVATE

Ask students when or of whom they might ask a favor. When would they tell someone to do something? What might they tell someone to do?

TEACH

Presentation

Comment dit-on… ? Play the beginning of **Une invitée pour le déjeuner.** Have students identify the requests that the mother makes and how Djeneba responds. Then, have students tell what is happening in the illustration on this page and repeat the requests after you. Ask them to suggest other ways to complete **Tu peux… ?** and **Tu me rapportes… ?** Ask students to get various items for you. **(Tu me rapportes du jambon?)** If one refuses, ask another student for the same item. Have partners or small groups make and respond to requests for two things they need.

(TPR) Place pictures of food items or real food items on a table. Give various students commands **(Rapporte-moi du lait.)** and have them respond by handing you the appropriate picture or item.

Language Note

Remind students that you drop the final **-s** in the **tu** command for **-er** verbs, but not for other types of verbs.

212   **DEUXIEME ETAPE**

COMMENT DIT-ON… ?

Making, accepting, and declining requests; telling someone what to do

To make requests: *Une demande*

Tu peux aller faire les courses?
  Can you . . . ?
Tu me rapportes des œufs?
  Will you bring me . . . ?

To tell someone what to do:

Rapporte(-moi) du beurre.
  Bring (me) back . . .
Prends du lait. *Get . . .*
Achète(-moi) du riz. *Buy (me) . . .*
N'oublie pas d'acheter le lait.
  Don't forget to . . .

To accept:

Pourquoi pas?
Bon, d'accord.
Je veux bien. *Gladly.*
J'y vais tout de suite.
  I'll go right away.

To decline:

Je ne peux pas maintenant.
Je regrette, mais je n'ai pas le temps. *I'm sorry, but I don't have time.*
J'ai des trucs à faire.
J'ai des tas de choses à faire.

212 *deux cent douze*   CHAPITRE 8   Au marché

RESOURCES FOR DEUXIEME ETAPE

Textbook Audiocassette 4B/Audio CD 8
Practice and Activity Book, pp. 89–91
Videodisc Guide
  Videodisc Program, Videodisc 4B

Chapter Teaching Resources, Book 2
• Communicative Activity 8-1, pp. 171–172
• Teaching Transparency Master 8-2, pp. 176, 178
  Teaching Transparency 8-2
• Additional Listening Activities 8-3, 8-4, p. 180
  Audiocassette 10A/Audio CD 8
• Realia 8-2, pp. 184, 185
• Situation Cards 8-2, pp. 186–187
• Student Response Forms, pp. 188–190
• Quiz 8-2, pp. 193–194
  Audiocassette 8A/Audio CD 8

14 Ecoute! Answers on p. 201C.

a. Listen to these dialogues. Is the first speaker making a request or telling someone what to do?

b. Now, listen again. Does the second speaker accept or decline the request or command?

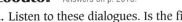

A la française

You already know that the verb **faire** means *to do*. What do you think the verb **refaire** might mean? The prefix **re-** in front of a verb means *to redo* something; *to do something again*. Use **r-** in front of a verb that begins with a vowel.

Tu dois **re**lire ce livre. *You need to reread this book.*
On va **ra**cheter du lait. *We'll buy milk again.*
Rapporte-moi du beurre! *Bring me back some butter!*

Does this same rule apply in English?

Grammaire   The verb pouvoir

Pouvoir is an irregular verb. Notice how similar it is to the verb **vouloir**, which you learned in Chapter 6.

pouvoir *(to be able to, can, may)*

Je **peux**	
Tu **peux** } faire les courses?	Nous **pouvons**
Il/Elle/On **peut**	Vous **pouvez** } promener le chien?
	Ils/Elles **peuvent**

---

15 Tu peux... ?

Ask your classmates to bring something back for you, depending on where they're going. Your classmates will accept or refuse your requests.

— Tu vas à la bibliothèque?
— Oui.
— Tu peux me rapporter un livre?
— Bien sûr!

au supermarché
à la librairie au fast-food
au marché aux magasins

16 On peut?

Find out if your classmates can do these things with or for you.

—Vous pouvez écouter de la musique après l'école?
—Non, nous ne pouvons pas.

regarder la télé après l'école
aller nager   faire des courses avec moi
me rapporter un sandwich
jouer au foot demain   sortir ce soir

DEUXIEME ETAPE   *deux cent treize* **213**

Teaching Suggestion

14 Ask students to listen to the intonation as well as to the words themselves.

Presentation

Grammaire   First, ask students to recall the forms of the verb **vouloir**. Have individuals write one form they remember on the board until the paradigm is complete. Write the forms of **pouvoir** next to the paradigm. Next, say a subject pronoun and toss a ball to a student, who says the correct verb form as he or she catches the ball. Then, that student continues by tossing the ball to another student while calling out a subject pronoun.

For Individual Needs

15 **Slower Pace**   Have the class suggest several errands that could be done at each place before they break into groups. Write their suggestions on the board for reference during the activity.

16 **Challenge**   Encourage students to offer excuses for declining their classmates' requests. Have students find at least two classmates with whom to do each activity.

Language Notes

• **A la française** Ask students to try to guess the meanings of the following verbs that are formed with the prefix **re-**: **reprendre, redonner, recommencer** *(to take back, to give back, to begin again).*

• A famous proverb says **Vouloir, c'est pouvoir.** Have students try to guess what the English equivalent is. *(Where there's a will, there's a way.)*

VOCABULAIRE

Vous en voulez combien?

un kilo(gramme) de
pommes de terre et
une livre d'oignons

une bouteille
d'eau minérale

une douzaine d'œufs

une boîte de tomates   un paquet de sucre

une tranche de jambon

un morceau de fromage   un litre de lait

Note de Grammaire

Notice that you always use **de** or **d'** after expressions of quantity.

> Une tranche **de** jambon, s'il vous plaît.
>
> Je voudrais un kilo **d'**oranges.

NOTE CULTURELLE

The metric system was created shortly after the French Revolution and has since been adopted by nearly all countries in the world except the United States. Although the United States is officially trying to convert to the metric system, many people aren't yet used to it. In the metric system, distances are measured in centimeters and meters, rather than inches and yards. Large distances are measured in kilometers. Grams and kilograms are the standard measures of weight. **Une livre** is about half a kilo. Liquids, including gasoline, are measured in liters. To convert metric measurements, use the following table:

1 centimeter = .39 inches	1 gram = .035 ounces
1 meter = 39.37 inches	1 kilogram = 2.2 pounds
1 kilometer = .62 miles	1 liter = 1.06 quarts

214 *deux cent quatorze*   CHAPITRE 8   Au marché

17 Ecoute!

Listen to Sophie as she does her shopping.
Write down the items and the quantities she asks for. Answers on p. 201C.

18 Allons au marché!

You're shopping for groceries. Make sure that you place your orders in appropriate quantities. Your partner will be the merchant. Then, change roles.

> Vous avez choisi?
>
> Et avec ça?   Voilà.
>
> Vous désirez?   C'est tout?
>
> Je voudrais... Il me faut...
>
> Je prends...

*avocats
tomates
vinaigre
oignons
oeufs
pain
huile d'olive
fromage
riz
haricots
raisin
sucre*

19 Essaie!

You're at a market in Côte d'Ivoire and you decide to try some fruits you're unfamiliar with. Ask the vendor if he or she has the fruits and how much they cost. The vendor will ask how many you would like. Act out this scene with a partner. Then, change roles. See answers below.

1.

2.

3.

4.

5.

20 Jeu de rôle

You're working as a volunteer to pick up groceries for senior citizens. Make a list of what you need to get and the quantity of each item. Take turns with your partner playing the role of the senior citizen.

DEUXIEME ETAPE   *deux cent quinze*   **215**

Possible answers
19 1. Est-ce que vous avez des mangues?
   2. ... des ananas?
   3. ... des papayes?
   4. ... des noix de coco?
   5. ... des goyaves?

Teaching Suggestions

17 You might have partners listen to the recording together, with one writing the item as the other writes the quantity.

18 Have students list the quantities they intend to buy before working with a partner.

19 Before students begin this activity, bring in a mango, a papaya, and a guava, and ask **Qu'est-ce que c'est?**

19 Students might begin their dialogues with a few phrases in Djoula.

20 Before beginning the activity, have students make a list of what they need to get. Then, after the partners have read their lists to each other, they might exchange them to check for accuracy.

Additional Practice

Show *Teaching Transparency 8-2* and have partners act out the situation.

CLOSE

To close this **étape,** hold up various food items and have students ask for a specific quantity of each one.

ASSESS

Quiz 8-2, *Chapter Teaching Resources, Book 2,* pp. 193–194

Assessment Items, Audiocassette 8A/Audio CD 8

Performance Assessment

In groups of four, students will plan a typical American dinner for a guest from Côte d'Ivoire. Have them make a grocery list **(Nous avons besoin de...).** Then, one student asks the others to go get the various items at the supermarket. The others respond appropriately.

Motivating Activity

Ask students if they've ever tried food from another country. Have them describe what the food looked like and how it tasted. Ask them if they used any special utensils or if certain customs were connected with eating the food.

Presentation

Have students look at the pictures and guess what each dish is made of. Then, have three volunteers read the descriptions. Ask for reactions in French. (**Comment tu trouves ça?**) Students might answer **C'est bon, C'est dégoûtant**, or **C'est pas mal**. Have small groups of students answer the questions in **Qu'en penses-tu?** and report back to the class.

Culture Notes

• In Ivorian villages, **foutou** is eaten without silverware and only with the right hand. It is considered rude to eat with the left hand, which is reserved for personal hygiene. To eat **foutou**, individuals break off a piece, form a small ball, and then dip it in the sauce accompanying the meal.

• Tell students that when they are guests for dinner in Africa, they should at least taste everything that they are served. When they are offered a second helping, it is polite to accept at least some, even though they may not want more.

• Since most meals are not made with prepared foods, a typical meal might take from six to seven hours, including a visit to the market and cleaning up afterwards. For this reason, the sauce that is eaten for lunch is often eaten for dinner on the same day.

RENCONTRE CULTURELLE

◀ **Le foutou**, the national dish of Côte d'Ivoire, is a paste made from boiled plantains, manioc, or yams. It is eaten with various sauces, such as peanut sauce or palm oil nut sauce.

▼ **La sauce arachide** is one of the many sauces eaten in Côte d'Ivoire. It is made from peanut butter with beef, chicken, or fish, hot peppers, peanut oil, garlic, onions, tomato paste, tomatoes, and a variety of other vegetables. It is usually served over rice.

▶ **L'aloco**, a popular snack food in Côte d'Ivoire, is a dish of fried plantain bananas. It is usually eaten with a spicy sauce (**sauce pimentée**).

Qu'en penses-tu? See answers below.

1. Do these dishes resemble any that are eaten in the United States?
2. Which ingredients in these dishes can you find in your neighborhood grocery store? Which ingredients are unfamiliar?
3. What dishes are typical of your part of the country? Why are they more common than others?

Savais-tu que... ?

Yams (**ignames**) and plantains are abundant in the Republic of Côte d'Ivoire, which explains why **foutou** is a popular dish. A typical lunch consists of one main course — often **foutou**, rice, or **attiéké** (ground manioc root) with a sauce; and a dessert — usually tropical fruits such as guavas, pineapples, or papayas. Lunch is traditionally followed by an hour-long siesta. To accommodate this custom, stores are closed from noon until 3:00 P.M., even in large cities such as Abidjan. Unlike lunch, dinner tends to be a much lighter meal. Heavy foods are rarely eaten in the evening.

Community Link

Call up the local parks and recreation association, community education program, or community college and try to find someone who teaches African cooking. Ask this person to come and speak to your students about popular recipes and ingredients or even prepare a dish.

Possible answers
1. **Le foutou** is a unique dish that has no American equivalent. **La sauce arachide** resembles a dark sauce, stew, or soup. **L'aloco** resembles banana fritters.

VOCABULAIRE

Qu'est-ce qu'on prend pour...

le petit déjeuner?

le déjeuner?

le goûter?

le dîner?

TROISIEME ETAPE

deux cent dix-sept **217**

𝒥ump Start!

Have students write two sentences for each of these food items: **eau minérale** and **fraises**. In the first sentence, students say they need the item, and in the second sentence, they ask or tell someone to get a quantity of the item.

MOTIVATE

Ask students if they have ever been served food they didn't like and what they did in that situation. Discuss how to avoid being rude in such a situation. Have students consider the consequences of being an inconsiderate guest. Ask students how they would feel if a guest refused to taste something they had prepared.

TEACH

Presentation

Vocabulaire Ask students to name the different foods shown on each table. Ask them **A quelle heure est-ce que tu manges ça?** Then, tell what you have for breakfast, lunch, a snack, and dinner. Hold up pictures of various food items and have students name the meal at which they would eat that food.

Culture Notes

• Point out that in France, **le déjeuner** is usually the main meal of the day, whereas **le dîner** is typically a light, simple meal.

• In Côte d'Ivoire, people might have popcorn (**du pop-corn**), peanuts (**des arachides**), roasted yams, or **aloco** with hot sauce (**sauce pimentée**) for an afternoon snack.

---

21 Slower Pace Before playing the recording, you might have pairs of students name the foods shown in each illustration, or you might say the items in each breakfast and have students identify the letter of the illustration you're describing.

Culture Note
Nutella® is a spread made from hazelnuts and chocolate. It is very popular in Europe and sometimes eaten at breakfast or for a snack (**le goûter**).

Thinking Critically
Comparing and Contrasting
Ask students to compare a French breakfast with what Americans normally eat for breakfast. Ask students if they generally have a light breakfast or a heavy one.

Teaching Suggestion
22 Before doing this activity, you might have students choose three or four things they would normally offer a guest for a snack. For additional food items, refer students to the Supplementary Vocabulary on page 342.

---

 21 Ecoute! 1. c 2. a 3. b
Listen to these people tell what they have for breakfast. Match each speaker with his or her breakfast.

a.

b.

c.

NOTE CULTURELLE

In the morning, most francophone people have a very light breakfast (**le petit déjeuner**). Coffee with hot steamed milk (**café au lait**) or hot chocolate is the drink of choice. It is usually served with bread or croissants, butter, and jam. Children may eat cereal for breakfast as well, sometimes with warm milk. The largest meal of the day, **le déjeuner**, has traditionally been between noon and 1:00 P.M. Dinner (**le dîner**) is eaten after 7:00 P.M.

 22 Et comme goûter?
Ton ami(e) et toi, vous rentrez chez toi après l'école.
Qu'est-ce que vous allez prendre comme goûter?

— Qu'est-ce que tu voudrais?
— Tu as une pomme?
— Non, il n'y a pas de pommes. Mais il y a des poires.
— Alors, donne-moi une poire, s'il te plaît.

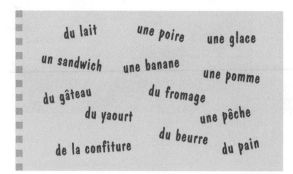

du lait   une poire   une glace
un sandwich   une banane   une pomme
du gâteau   du fromage
du yaourt   une pêche
de la confiture   du beurre   du pain

Culture Note
In Africa, as in France, people almost never drink milk with meals. Ask students if they could easily adopt French or African eating habits.

Language Note
Students might be interested to know that **jeûner** means *to fast,* so **déjeuner** is *to break a fast.* **Goûter** means *to taste,* and **dîner** is *to dine.*

23 Quel repas?

Describe one of these meals to your partner. He or she will try to guess which meal you're talking about. Take turns. See answers below.

Il y a du poulet,...

1.

2.

3.

24 Devine!

Write down what you think you'll have for your meals tomorrow, using the **Vocabulaire** on p. 207. Your partner will do the same. Take turns guessing what each of you will have.

—Au petit déjeuner, tu vas prendre... ?
—Oui, c'est ça. *or* Non, pas de...

COMMENT DIT-ON... ?
Offering, accepting, or refusing food

To offer food to someone:
Tu veux du riz?
Vous voulez de l'eau minérale?
Vous prenez du fromage?
Tu prends du fromage?
Encore du pain? *More . . . ?*

To accept:
Oui, s'il vous/te plaît.
Oui, j'en veux bien.
Yes, I'd like some.
Oui, avec plaisir.
Yes, with pleasure.

To refuse:
Non, merci.
Je n'en veux plus. *I don't want any more.*
Non, merci. Je n'ai plus faim. *No thanks. I'm not hungry anymore.*

---

25 Ecoute!

Is the speaker offering, accepting, or refusing food? Answers on p. 201D.

TROISIEME ETAPE

deux cent dix-neuf **219**

Answers
23 1. Il y a du poulet, du riz, du maïs, du pain, du fromage, une salade avec des tomates, des fraises et de l'eau minérale.
2. Il y a du poulet, du riz, des haricots, du pain, du beurre, une salade avec des tomates, des pêches et de l'eau minérale.
3. Il y a du bifteck, du riz, du maïs, du pain, du fromage, une salade avec des œufs, des fraises et du lait.

Language Note
Tell students that responding to an offer of food by saying **Merci** alone might be taken as a refusal. Another expression of acceptance is **Oui, je veux bien.**

For Individual Needs

23 Slower Pace Before having students do the activity, you might have them point out the differences among the three meals, using **Il n'y a pas de...**

Teaching Suggestion

23 This activity could also be done by having students write a description of one of the meals. Then, have them exchange papers with a partner, who will guess which meal is described.

Presentation

Comment dit-on... ? Bring in real food items or pictures of them. Offer different items to individuals, varying your expressions. (**Tu veux du poulet? Tu prends de l'eau?**) Next, have students offer you the food items, using the **vous** form. Alternately, accept and refuse the various food items, having students repeat after you.

For videodisc application, see *Videodisc Guide.*

For Individual Needs

Tactile Learners Bring in mineral water, sliced bread, or food that can be broken into pieces. Offer some to the first person in each row. After that student responds, give him or her the food. He or she then offers some to the next student, and so on.

Teaching Suggestion

25 Remind students to listen for intonation to help distinguish offering from accepting or refusing.

For Individual Needs

26 Slower Pace You might have the class orally identify the food items shown before beginning the activity.

Teaching Suggestion

26 You might have students change roles after offering several items.

Portfolio

26 Oral This activity is appropriate for students' oral portfolios. For portfolio information, see *Assessment Guide*, pages 2–13.

Presentation

Grammaire On five separate index cards, write each word and the question mark of the question **Tu veux des mangues?** Write **en** on a sixth card. Give one card, with the exception of **en,** to each of five students and have them stand side by side to form the question **Tu veux des mangues?** Then, remove the two students holding the cards for **des** and **mangues** and substitute another student holding the card for **en** in the proper position to form **Tu en veux?** Have students repeat both questions and explain what has happened. Repeat this procedure for the other examples.

Additional Practice

27 Have students tell or write about three things that Aïssata doesn't have in her basket. For example, **Du chocolat? Elle n'en a pas.**

---

26 Encore du pain?

An Ivorian exchange student is having dinner at your house. Encourage him or her to try some of the foods on the table. Your friend will accept or politely refuse.

Look for opportunities to practice your French wherever you go. Try to meet French-speaking people and talk with them. Ask your teacher to help you find a pen pal in a French-speaking country. Rent videocassettes of French films. See how many French products you can find at the grocery store and the cosmetic counter, and how many French dishes you can find on restaurant menus.

Grammaire The pronoun **en**

En takes the place of a phrase beginning with **du, de la, de l', des,** or **de** to avoid repetition. **En** usually means *some (of it/them)* or simply *it/them*.

— Tu veux **des mangues**?
— Oui, j'**en** veux bien.
— Tu manges **des légumes**?
— Oui, j'**en** mange souvent.

In a negative sentence, **en** means *any* or *none*.

— Tu veux **du beurre**?
— Merci, je n'**en** veux pas.

---

27 Elle en a combien?

What quantity of each of these items would you expect Aïssata to have in her basket?

Des haricots? Elle en a un kilo.

1. Du lait?   Elle en a un litre.
2. Du beurre?   Elle en a un paquet.
3. Des tomates?   Elle en a trois.
4. Du riz?   Elle en a un kilo.
5. Des œufs?   Elle en a six.
6. De l'eau minérale?   Elle en a une bouteille.

220   *deux cent vingt*   CHAPITRE 8   Au marché

Teacher Note

De bons conseils For information on international pen pal organizations, see page T50.

28 Tu en veux?

Take turns with a partner asking each other if you eat the foods shown in Activity 26. Use the pronoun **en** in your answers.

> — Tu manges du poulet?
> — Oui, j'en mange souvent.

PRONONCIATION

The sounds [o] and [ɔ]

The sound [o] is similar to the vowel sound in the English word *boat*. To make the sound [o], hold your mouth in a whistling position. Keep the lips and tongue steady to avoid the glide heard in *boat*. Repeat each of these words: **trop, kilo, mot.** The spellings **au, eau, ô,** and sometimes **o** represent the sound [o]. Now, repeat these words: **jaune, chaud, beau, rôle.**

The sound [ɔ] is between the vowel sounds in the English words *boat* and *bought*. Usually, this sound is followed by a consonant sound in the same syllable. The sound [ɔ] is more open, so hold your mouth in a semi-whistling position to produce it. This sound is usually spelled with the letter **o.** Now repeat these words: **bof, donne, fort, carotte.**

A. A prononcer

Repeat the following words and phrases.

1. au revoir	un stylo jaune	au restaurant
2. un gâteau	moi aussi	des haricots verts
3. des pommes	d'abord	une promenade
4. encore	dormir	l'école

B. A lire

Take turns with a partner reading each of the following sentences aloud.

1. Elle a une gomme violette et un stylo jaune.
2. Tu aimes les carottes? Moi, j'adore. J'aime bien aussi les escargots et le porc.
3. Elle est occupée aujourd'hui. Elle a informatique et biologie.
4. Il me faut un short parce qu'il fait trop chaud.
5. Tu peux sortir si tu promènes d'abord le chien.

C. A écrire

You're going to hear a short dialogue. Write down what you hear. Answers on page 201D.

Teacher Note

Prononciation Notice that in Part A, rows 1 and 2 contain examples of the [o] sound, and rows 3 and 4, the [ɔ] sound.

For Individual Needs

28 Challenge Have students extend their answers by telling how often they have each item, using **souvent, (une) fois par jour/semaine,** and **ne... jamais.** They might also give their opinion of each food item.

Teaching Suggestion

Prononciation After correcting the dictation in Part C, have students underline the letters that represent the [o] sound and circle the letters that represent [ɔ].

CLOSE

To close this **étape,** write a list of food items on a transparency and have students tell whether they would be eaten **au petit déjeuner, au déjeuner, au goûter,** or **au dîner** in a francophone country.

ASSESS

Quiz 8-3, *Chapter Teaching Resources, Book 2,* pp. 195–196

Assessment Items, Audiocassette 8A/Audio CD 8

Performance Assessment

On separate index cards, write the names of the meals in French. Have students pair off and have one partner in each pair draw a card. Partners must then offer and accept or refuse four items that would normally be served at that meal. Encourage students to bring in the food items, paper plates, and plastic eating utensils to make their skits more realistic.

LISONS!

Skim the titles and photographs. What will you be reading?

DE BONS CONSEILS
Remember to look for cognates to help you figure out what you're reading. Occasionally, you will encounter false cognates, words that look alike in two languages but have different meanings.

Context clues can sometimes help you recognize false cognates. An example of a false cognate is the French phrase **fruits de mer**. **Fruits de mer** may make you think of the English word *fruit*, but it means *seafood*.

A. You already know a few false cognates. Try to figure out the meaning of the false cognates in the sentences below.

1. Je vais à San Francisco à 11h00. Maintenant, il est 10h40, et **j'attends** le train.

   a. I'm attending
   b. I'm late for
   c. I'm waiting for

2. J'adore les sciences. Ce soir, je vais **assister** à une conférence sur l'ozone.

   a. to attend
   b. to assist
   c. to teach

la cuisine autour du monde

LA CUISINE AFRICAINE

Les desserts

Croissants au coco et au sésame
(Afrique occidentale)

Prép. : 30 mn. - Cuiss. : 10 mn.
Repos : 1 h. - 8 pers.

2 œufs
140 g de sucre
190 g de noix de coco râpée

170 g de farine
Vanille en poudre
Graines de sésame.

Mélanger la noix de coco râpée, le sucre, la vanille et les œufs entiers. Incorporer la farine. Travailler la pâte. Former une boule. Laisser reposer 1 heure au frais.
Étaler la pâte sur 1/2 cm. Découper en croissants. Les rouler dans le sésame. Cuire au four à 200 °C, (th. 6-7), 10 minutes.

222 *deux cent vingt-deux*

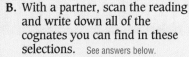
Signification des symboles accompagnant les recettes

Recettes

  ✗ élémentaire

  ✗✗ facile

  ✗✗✗ difficile

Recettes

  ◯ peu coûteuse

  ◯◯ raisonnable

  ◯◯◯ chère

Les entrées

Mousseline africaine de petits légumes
(Afrique occidentale - Bénin - Togo)

Prép. : 40 mn. - Cuiss. : 15 mn.

4 pers.

✗ ◯◯

2 petits concombres
Ail
1 lime
1 radis noir
1/2 papaye

1 avocat
1 épi de maïs
Graines de carvi
4 petites brioches
Sel.

Eplucher les concombres. Les détailler en dés. Faire la même chose avec l'avocat.
Débarrasser l'épis de maïs des feuilles et des barbes. Le faire cuire durant 15 minutes à l'eau bouillante. Saler en fin de cuisson.
Egrener le maïs. Débarrasser la papaye de ses graines. La découper en petits dés. Emincer le radis noir. Parfumer de graines de carvi et d'ail haché. Arroser la salade de jus de lime.
Retirer le chapeau des brioches. Les évider. Les garnir de la salade parfumée.

*Les brioches ne doivent pas être sucrées. Si on les fabrique, il convient d'ôter le sucre.
Ne pas saler l'épi de maïs au début de la cuisson mais à la fin afin d'éviter qu'il durcisse.*

B. With a partner, scan the reading and write down all of the cognates you can find in these selections. See answers below.

C. Did you find any false cognates? Were you able to figure out what they mean? If so, how? See answers below.

D. Where would you expect to find these reading selections? Where are these dishes from? cookbook; Africa

E. Which of the dishes would make a good dessert? croissants

F. Are these dishes easy or difficult to make? How do you know? Are they expensive or inexpensive to make? How do you know? See answers below.

G. To make **croissants,** how long do you need to chill the dough? At what temperature do you bake them? What temperature is that on the Fahrenheit scale? (To convert from Celsius to Fahrenheit, multiply by $\frac{9}{5}$ and add 32.) See answers below.

H. To make **mousseline,** how long do you have to cook the corn? Do you think this dish would taste sweet or salty? How many people does this dish serve? See answers below.

I. Now, with a partner, write the instructions for an easy recipe that you know how to make. Include the ingredients, the steps required to prepare the dish, and the cooking and preparation time required.

The background design on the two **Lisons!** pages is from a piece of cloth purchased in Côte d'Ivoire.

deux cent vingt-trois **223**

Thinking Critically

Comparing and Contrasting
After students have read the recipes carefully, ask them if the ingredients listed would be difficult to find in local stores. Ask students if the recipes sound appetizing and if they are similar to dishes that they have eaten.

(TPR) Say various cooking instructions, having students mime the actions. You might provide props such as a bowl, a spoon, and a baking pan.

POSTREADING
Activity I

Teaching Suggestion

I. Ask students to use metric measurements in their recipes. You might have students demonstrate how to prepare their dishes in front of the class, using props if they choose. Have one partner read aloud the recipe while the other acts out the instructions. You might also have students make their dishes at home and bring them in for the class to sample.

⬧ For Individual Needs

Challenge As an additional chapter project, students might compile all the recipes into a class cookbook. They might design and draw a cover and illustrate each recipe. You might have them make copies to distribute to the entire class.

Answers

B *Possible answers:* africaine, coco, sésame, vanille, symboles, raisonnable, desserts, avocat

C *Possible answers:* parfumer *(to flavor)*, former *(to make)*, détailler *(to cut separately)*, fabriquer *(to make)*

F Symbols show both recipes are very easy (**élémentaire**) and moderately priced (**raisonnable**).

G one hour; 200°C; 392°F

H 15 minutes; salty; four people

Math Link

I. If students use the oven for their recipes, have them give the oven temperature in Celsius. The formula for converting Fahrenheit to Celsius is F − 32 × 5/9.

MISE EN PRATIQUE

The **Mise en pratique** reviews and integrates all four skills and culture in preparation for the Chapter Test.

Teaching Suggestion

1 Before you play the recording, tell students that they should not expect to hear the prices given immediately after the food item. You might pause the recording after one or two items are mentioned to give students time to write.

For Individual Needs

1 Challenge As a follow-up activity, students might prepare and record similar advertisements.

Building on Previous Skills

2 Encourage students to expand their conversation by re-entering previously learned functions. One partner might ask the other if he or she has decided. **(Tu as choisi?)** The other might hesitate. **(Euh... je ne sais pas.)** The first student might make a recommendation **(Prends...).**

Portfolio

3 Written This activity is appropriate for students' written portfolios. It can also be done as an individual project. For portfolio suggestions, see *Assessment Guide,* page 21.

1 Listen to this supermarket advertisement. List four of the foods that are on sale. Then, listen again for the prices of the four items you listed.   Answers on page 201D.

2 On the plane to Abidjan, you order dinner. Discuss the menu with your partner and decide what you're both going to have.

AIR AFRIQUE

MENU

Crevettes Sauce Cocktail

Sauté d'Agneau Créole

Pomme Duchesse

Petits Pois à l'Anglaise

ou

Saumon au Gratin

Champignons Sautés aux Fines Herbes

Riz à la Créole

Fromage

Gâteau Coco et Pistache

Café

Il est possible que le plat chaud que vous avez choisi ne soit plus disponible, nous vous remercions de votre compréhension.

MY

3 Choose a food item. Pretend you're the producer of that item and you need to sell it. With a partner, write an ad that encourages people to buy your product. Tell people when they should have it and why it's good. Include pictures or logos as well. Consider your audience, the people who might be likely to buy your product.

224 *deux cent vingt-quatre*   CHAPITRE 8   Au marché

Language Note

Students might want to know the following expressions from the menu: **agneau** *(lamb);* **saumon** *(salmon);* and **au gratin** *(topped with cheese and baked).*

4

LES GROUPES D'ALIMENTS

Les aliments sont regroupés en 6 catégories selon leurs caractéristiques nutritionnelles :

- **Le lait et les produits laitiers** sont nos principaux fournisseurs de calcium.
- **Viandes, poissons et œufs** sont nos sources essentielles de protéines de bonne qualité.
- **Le groupe du pain, des féculents et des légumes secs** apporte les «glucides lents» libérant progressivement l'énergie nécessaire à notre organisme.
- **Légumes et fruits** sont nos sources de fibres, vitamines et minéraux.
- **Les matières grasses** sont les sources énergétiques les plus importantes pour notre corps.
- **Le sucre et ses dérivés** apportent les «glucides rapides» nécessaires au bon fonctionnement cérébral et musculaire.

Groupe	Lait Produits Laitiers	Viandes Poissons Œufs	Pains Féculents	Fruits Légumes	Matières Grasses	Sucre Dérivés
Intérêt Principal	Calcium	Protéines	Glucides	Fibres Vitamines A et B	Lipides	Glucides
Intérêt Secondaire	Protéines Vitamines A, B, D	Fer Vitamine B	Fibres	Glucides	Vitamines (A, E, selon mat. grasses)	

L'ensemble de ces catégories permet, au sein d'une alimentation diversifiée, de couvrir tous nos besoins.

See answers below.

1. What kind of chart is this?

2. What do the six categories listed mean?

3. According to the chart, what are some of the nutrients found in . . .
   a. produits laitiers?
   b. viandes?
   c. pain?
   d. fruits et légumes?
   e. matières grasses?
   f. sucre et ses dérivés?

4. Give some examples of foods you know in French that fall into each category.

5. Name three foods that are high in protein and three that are high in calcium.

5 What are some differences between meals in Africa, France, and the United States?
See answers below.

6

JEU DE ROLE

a. Make a list in French of everything you've eaten for the last two days. Use the food vocabulary that you've learned in this chapter.

b. Now, you go to a nutrition counselor. The counselor will evaluate your diet, telling you what you need to eat more of and what you shouldn't eat anymore. Act out this scene with a partner. Then, change roles.

Portfolio

6 Oral This activity might be included in students' oral portfolios and/or performed as a skit for the class. For portfolio suggestions, see *Assessment Guide,* page 21.

Health Link

Have students bring in the latest charts of recommended foods and of foods to avoid. If possible, have them describe the foods in French.

 Video Wrap-Up

- **VIDEO PROGRAM**
- **EXPANDED VIDEO PROGRAM,** Videocassette 3, 16:03–28:32
- **VIDEODISC PROGRAM,** Videodisc 4B

At this time, you might want to use the video resources for additional review and enrichment. See *Video Guide* or *Videodisc Guide* for suggestions regarding the following:
- **Une invitée pour le déjeuner** (Dramatic episode)
- **Panorama Culturel** (Interviews)
- **Vidéoclips** (Authentic footage)

Answers

4 1. food groups
2. milk and milk products; meats, fish, and eggs; breads (starches); fruits and vegetables; fats; sugar
3. a. calcium, protein, vitamins A, B, and D
   b. protein, iron, vitamin B
   c. glucides, fiber
   d. fiber, vitamins A and B, glucides
   e. lipids, vitamins A and E
   f. glucides

4. *Possible answers*
   Lait: lait, fromage, yaourt
   Viandes: poulet, bifteck, porc
   Pain/féculents: pain, pommes de terre, riz
   Fruits/légumes: oranges, petits pois, carottes, pommes de terre
   Matières grasses: beurre
   Sucre: gâteau, glace, confiture
5. *Answers will vary.*

5 *Possible answers:* In Africa and France, lunch is often the largest meal of the day, while in the United States, dinner is the largest meal. Dinner is eaten later in Africa and France than in the United States. In Africa, lunch is followed by an hour-long siesta and stores are generally closed from noon to 3:00 P.M.

QUE SAIS-JE?

This page is intended to help students prepare for the test. It is a brief checklist of the major points covered in the chapter. The students should be reminded that this is only a checklist and does not necessarily include everything that will appear on the test.

Additional Practice

1 Have students write a grocery list specifying quantities of these items.

Teacher Note

4 Remind students that not all measures of quantity are appropriate for all food items; however, several answers may be possible for some of the items in this activity.

Teaching Suggestion

7 Have students tell what they would have for these meals in France or Côte d'Ivoire.

Can you use what you've learned in this chapter?

Can you express need? p. 210

1 How would you tell someone that you need these things? *See answers below.*

1.   2.   3.
4.   5.

Can you make, accept, and decline requests or tell someone what to do? p. 212

2 How would you . . .
1. ask someone to go grocery shopping for you? *Tu peux aller faire les courses?*
2. tell someone to bring back some groceries for you? *Tu me rapportes... ?*

3 How would you accept the requests in number 2? How would you refuse? *Accept: Bon, d'accord. Je veux bien. J'y vais tout de suite.*
Refuse: Je ne peux pas maintenant. Je regrette, mais je n'ai pas le temps.

4 How would you ask for a specific quantity of these foods? *See answers below.*
1. œufs   4. beurre
2. lait   5. jambon
3. oranges   6. eau minérale

Can you offer, accept, or refuse food? p. 219

5 How would you offer someone these foods? *See answers below.*
1. some rice
2. some oranges
3. some milk

6 How would you accept the foods listed in number 5 if they were offered? How would you refuse them? *Accept: Oui, s'il vous/te plaît. Oui, avec plaisir.*
Refuse: Non, merci. Je n'en veux plus. Je n'ai plus faim.

7 How would you tell someone what you have for . . . *See answers below.*
1. breakfast?   3. an afternoon snack?
2. lunch?   4. dinner?

226   *deux cent vingt-six*   CHAPITRE 8   Au marché

Answers
1 1. Il me faut du poisson. J'ai besoin de poisson.
  2. Il me faut des pommes de terre. J'ai besoin de pommes de terre.
  3. Il me faut du riz. J'ai besoin de riz.
  4. Il me faut du gâteau. J'ai besoin de gâteau.
  5. Il me faut un ananas. J'ai besoin d'ananas.

4 *Possible answers*
  Je voudrais... ; Je prends... ; Il me faut...
  1. une douzaine d'œufs.
  2. un litre de lait.
  3. un kilo d'oranges.
  4. un paquet de beurre.
  5. une tranche de jambon.
  6. une bouteille d'eau minérale.

5 *Possible answers:* Tu veux... ; Vous voulez... ; Tu prends... ; Vous prenez... ; Encore...
  1. du riz?
  2. des oranges?
  3. du lait?

7 *Possible answers*
  1. Pour le petit déjeuner, je prends...
  2. Pour le déjeuner, je prends...
  3. Pour le goûter, je prends...
  4. Pour le dîner, je prends...

PREMIERE ETAPE

Expressing need

Qu'est-ce qu'il te faut? *What do you need?*
Il me faut... *I need . . .*
De quoi est-ce que tu as besoin? *What do you need?*
J'ai besoin de... *I need . . .*
du, de la, de l', des *some*

Foods; Shopping

des ananas (m.) *pineapples*
des avocats (m.) *avocados*
des bananes (f.) *bananas*
du beurre *butter*
du bifteck *steak*
des carottes (f.) *carrots*
des champignons (m.) *mushrooms*

des citrons (m.) *lemons*
de la confiture *jam*
de la farine *flour*
des fraises (f.) *strawberries*
du fromage *cheese*
des gâteaux (m.) *cakes*
des gombos (m.) *okra*
des goyaves (f.) *guavas*
des haricots (m.) *beans*
du lait *milk*
du maïs *corn*
des mangues (f.) *mangoes*
des noix de coco (f.) *coconuts*
des œufs (m.) *eggs*
des oranges (f.) *oranges*
du pain *bread*
des papayes (f.) *papayas*
des pêches (f.) *peaches*

des petits pois (m.) *peas*
des poires (f.) *pears*
du poisson *fish*
des pommes (f.) *apples*
des pommes de terre (f.) *potatoes*
du porc *pork*
des poules (f.) *live chickens*
du poulet *cooked chicken*
du raisin *grapes*
du riz *rice*
de la salade *salad, lettuce*
des tartes (f.) *pies*
des tomates (f.) *tomatoes*
de la viande *meat*
des yaourts (m.) *yogurt*
le marché *the market*
le supermarché *the supermarket*

DEUXIEME ETAPE

Making, accepting, and declining requests

Tu peux...? *Can you . . . ?*
Tu me rapportes... ? *Will you bring me . . . ?*
Bon, d'accord. *Well, OK.*
Je veux bien. *Gladly.*
J'y vais tout de suite. *I'll go right away.*
Je regrette, mais je n'ai pas le temps. *I'm sorry, but I don't have time.*

Je ne peux pas maintenant. *I can't right now.*

Telling someone what to do

Rapporte(-moi...) *Bring (me) back . . .*
Prends... *Get . . .*
Achète(-moi)... *Buy (me) . . .*
N'oublie pas de... *Don't forget . . .*
pouvoir *to be able to, can, may*

Quantities

une boîte de *a can of*
une bouteille de *a bottle of*
une douzaine de *a dozen*
un kilo(gramme) de *a kilogram of*
un litre de *a liter of*
une livre de *a pound of*
un morceau de *a piece of*
un paquet de *a carton/box of*
une tranche de *a slice of*

TROISIEME ETAPE

Offering, accepting, or refusing food

Tu veux... ? *Do you want . . . ?*
Vous voulez... ? *Do you want . . . ?*
Vous prenez... ? *Will you have . . . ?*
Tu prends... ? *Will you have . . . ?*

Encore de... ? *More . . . ?*
Oui, s'il vous/te plaît. *Yes, please.*
Oui, j'en veux bien. *Yes, I'd like some.*
Oui, avec plaisir. *Yes, with pleasure.*
Non, merci. *No, thank you.*
Je n'en veux plus. *I don't want any more.*

Non, merci. Je n'ai plus faim. *No thanks. I'm not hungry anymore.*
en *some, of it, of them, any*

Meals

le petit déjeuner *breakfast*
le déjeuner *lunch*
le goûter *afternoon snack*
le dîner *dinner*

Teaching Suggestion

To review vocabulary, you might play the game "**Quels ingrédients?**" described on page 201F.

Language Note

Point out to students that in French, unlike in English, **carotte** is spelled with one **r** and two **t**'s.

CHAPTER 8 ASSESSMENT

CHAPTER TEST

- *Chapter Teaching Resources, Book 2,* pp. 197–202
- *Assessment Guide,* Speaking Test, p. 31
- *Assessment Items,* Audiocassette 8A Audio CD 8

TEST GENERATOR, CHAPTER 8

ALTERNATIVE ASSESSMENT

Performance Assessment

You might want to use the **Jeu de rôle** (p. 225) as a cumulative performance assessment activity.

Portfolio Assessment

- **Written: Mise en pratique,** Activity 3, *Pupil's Edition,* p. 224
  Assessment Guide, p. 21
- **Oral: Mise en pratique, Jeu de rôle,** *Pupil's Edition,* p. 225
  Assessment Guide, p. 21

♜ Game

CONCOURS DE VOCABULAIRE Have students bring in pictures of the food listed on this page. Form two teams and have one member from each team go to the board. Show them one of the pictures. Writing on the board, the players must identify the item (**du lait**), give an appropriate quantity of it (**un litre de lait**), say that they need the item (**J'ai besoin de lait**), ask someone to buy it (**Tu peux acheter du lait?**), and offer it to someone (**Encore du lait?**). Give a point to the player who first writes all the information correctly.

Allez, viens en Arles! pp. 228–305

EXPANDED VIDEO PROGRAM, *Videocassette 3* 28:33–31:21

OR *VIDEODISC PROGRAM,* *Videodisc 5A*

Search 1, Play To 5060

Motivating Activity

Ask students if they can name any cities in southern France (Nice, Cannes, Marseille, Avignon). Ask them if any of the cities they mentioned are near Arles. You might have students turn to the detailed map of France on page xxi, or show them *Map Transparency 1.* Ask them what they know about this part of France concerning the climate, crops, customs, history, or any other aspect. Have students compare their impressions with the photos presented on pages 228–231.

Background information

In 46 B.C., Julius Caesar established a Roman colony in Arles, and in 306 A.D., Constantine the Great made the city one of the capitals of his empire. It became known as "the little Rome of the Gauls." In 1239, Arles became part of Provence, which, in 1481, became part of France. Between 1888 and 1890, Vincent Van Gogh painted 300 pictures in Arles, which is typical of southern French towns with its pale white, pink, and cream-colored buildings with tiled roofs.

Language Note

The preposition **en** is used instead of **à** with the town of Arles.

CHAPITRES 9, 10, 11

Allez, viens en Arles!

La ville d'Arles

Thinking Critically

Observing Have students compare the photo of the city of Arles on pages 228 and 229 with the photos of Poitiers on pages 12–15 and Paris on pages 120–123. Ask students if they notice any differences (the tiled roofs) or similarities (the window shutters and number of stories in a building). What mixture of ancient and modern times can they find? (The ancient church on this page is surrounded by television antennas and even a satellite dish.)

Geography Link

The smallest administrative division of France is a **commune,** which consists of a town and some of the surrounding area. Arles is the largest **commune** in France because of its location near the **Camargue** (see page 231). The entire area covers approximately 190,000 acres.

Arles

Population : plus de 50.000

Points d'intérêt : la place Richelme, la place du Forum, les arènes romaines, les thermes de Constantin, les Alyscamps, le théâtre antique

Aux environs d'Arles : les Baux-de-Provence, les Antiques à St-Rémy-de-Provence, le moulin d'Alphonse Daudet

Personnages célèbres : Alphonse Daudet, Vincent Van Gogh, Frédéric Mistral

Musées : le musée Réattu, le musée Lapidaire d'Art païen, le Museon Arlaten, le musée d'Art chrétien

Industries : riz, papier, industries chimiques et métalliques

deux cent vingt-neuf 229

Using the Almanac and Map

Terms in the Almanac

- **Les thermes de Constantin** once served as public baths for the Romans.
- **Les Baux-de-Provence,** the ruins of a medieval city, sits on a rock promontory in the **Alpilles** *(little Alps).* Bauxite, discovered in the area in 1821, was named after **Les Baux.**
- **Les Antiques à St.-Rémy-de-Provence** is home to two ancient monuments: the best preserved mausoleum in the world and a small **arc de triomphe.**
- **Le moulin d'Alphonse Daudet,** located in Fontvieille, is where Daudet supposedly wrote *Les lettres de mon moulin.*
- **Alphonse Daudet** (1840–1897), the author of several short stories and novels that celebrate Provence, wrote the novel *Tartarin de Tarascon* (1872) and a collection of short stories entitled *Les lettres de mon moulin* (1866).
- **Frédéric Mistral** (1830–1914) wrote a narrative poem, *Mirèio* (1859) in Provençal, a language spoken in Provence.
- **Le musée Réattu** contains Italian, French, Dutch, and Provençal paintings from the sixteenth through eighteenth centuries.
- **Le musée Lapidaire d'Art païen** is home to statues and artifacts uncovered in archeological excavations.
- **Le Museon Arlaten** is a folklore museum of Provençal life founded in 1896 by Frédéric Mistral.
- **Le musée d'Art chrétien** is a museum of sculptures and ancient marble sarcophagi.

Using the Map

Have students look at the map and suggest reasons why the Greeks and Romans were the first to colonize what is now southern France.

Geography Link

Ask students if they can name the mountain ranges in France (**les Pyrénées, les Alpes, le Jura,** and **les Vosges**).

History Link

Ask students if they can name any other areas of the world where the Romans established settlements (southern Europe, the Middle East, North Africa, Germany, Belgium, and Great Britain).

Culture Note

In addition to founding the city of Arles, the Greeks introduced grape cultivation to France.

Using the Photo Essay

① **Les arènes romaines,** when originally built in the first century, could seat approximately 25,000 spectators. After the fall of the Roman Empire, 200 houses and even a church were constructed inside the arena. Restoration began in 1825. The structure had been severely damaged throughout the centuries as stones were removed for other construction. In fact, the third level of galleries is completely gone. The view from the upper level, overlooking the Rhône River and the surrounding countryside, is magnificent.

② **Les Alyscamps** is a cemetery that was famous from Roman times through the Middle Ages. Tombs of more than 80 generations of people who were buried there were discovered in three layers. Unfortunately, in later centuries, stones and sarcophagi were taken for building projects and souvenirs. Today, a shaded pathway lined with ancient tombs offers the visitor an eerie glimpse of history.

② **Vincent Van Gogh** (1853–1890) was a postimpressionistic Dutch painter who spent most of his life in France. From 1888–1890, he lived in Arles, where he produced 300 paintings, including *Starry Night, The Bridge at Arles,* and *L'Arlésienne.* His use of bright colors and harsh brush strokes was revolutionary. In fact, one of his paintings, *Sunflowers,* sold at that time for the highest price ever paid for a painting. Van Gogh suffered from mental problems and spent time in an asylum. He cut off one of his ears after an argument with painter Paul Gauguin and finally committed suicide. Many of his works are now on display in Paris at the **musée d'Orsay.**

Arles

Founded by the Greeks in the fifth century B.C., Arles later prospered for hundreds of years under Roman rule. It was the largest city in Provence and the capital of ancient Gaul. In the Middle Ages, Arles was an important religious center. It did not became a part of France until 1481. In 1888, Vincent Van Gogh moved to Arles and painted some of his most famous works. Today, Arles still attracts artists, as well as historians and archeologists. But Arles is not only famous for its past. Festivals, the many museums, and the beautiful countryside draw thousands of visitors every year to this very special place known to some as "the soul of Provence."

① **Les arènes romaines,** one of the most ancient Roman amphitheaters, dates back to the first century B.C. Measuring 136 meters long and 107 meters wide, it is also one of the largest, holding 12,000 spectators..

② **Les Alyscamps is** well-known as an ancient Christian burial site. Both Vincent van Gogh and Paul Gauguin immortalized it in their paintings.

230   *deux cent trente*

Geography Link

Located on the Rhône River, the city of Arles is officially known as Arles-sur-Rhône to distinguish it from Arles-sur-Tech, which is located in the eastern Pyrenees Mountains.

Art Link

Van Gogh generally painted three types of subjects: still life, landscape, and figure, most of which portrayed the daily lives of the peasants, the hardships they endured, and the countryside they cultivated. During the time Van Gogh spent in Arles, he painted blossoming fruit trees, views of the town, self-portraits, portraits of Roulin the postman, his own family and friends, interiors and exteriors of houses, a series of sunflowers, and a sky full of stars.

③ The marshland known as la **Camargue**, is a stunningly beautiful nature reserve. It is particularly known for its pink flamingos and wild horses.

④ Arles is home to several festivals that feature dancers from all over Provence dressed in their traditional costumes.

⑤ **Le théâtre antique**, constructed in the first century B.C., is still in use. It is here that the Festival d'Arles, the Rencontres Internationales de la Photographie, and numerous shows are staged.

③ **La Camargue**, established as a nature preserve in 1928, is the delta of the Rhône River. The river splits into two arms: **le Grand Rhône**, which makes up nine-tenths of the volume, and **le Petit Rhône**, just upstream from Arles. In certain areas, the delta area advances from 10 to 50 meters a year because of silt deposits, but it has receded in other areas. **La Camargue** is famous for its pink flamingos, bulls, and the white horses shown in the photo. Scattered throughout the delta are **mas**, or *farms,* where the **gardians** work herding the bulls.

④ Many festivals are held in Arles every year. **Le festival d'Arles** lasts the entire month of July and consists of concerts, theatrical and dance performances, and exhibitions. **La fête des gardians**, a tame version of a rodeo, takes place on May 1. **Le Salon international des santonniers**, held every December, is famous for its Nativity scenes (**crèches**) and ornamental figures (**santons**).

⑤ **Le théâtre antique**, a Roman theater located a short distance from the **arènes**, is the site for many drama and dance performances, as well as the **festival d'Arles**, held every July. When the **théâtre antique** was built, it was able to hold approximately 7,000 spectators. After the fifth century A.D., it was used as a quarry, and all that remains today are some of the seats and two marble Corinthian columns from the original wall behind the acting area.

Culture Notes

③ The village of Saintes-Maries-de-la-Mer, the unofficial capital of the **Camargue**, is the destination of an annual pilgrimage on May 24 and 25 by European gypsies.

③ The famous bulls raised in the **Camargue** are often reluctant participants in bullfights held in southern France. Bullfights in France are different from those in Spain; the bull lives after the fight. For a lively description of a Provençal bullfight, read *Caravan to Vaccares,* a novel by Alistair Maclean. Bullfights and other events are held in the **arènes** in Arles and Nîmes, a city northwest of Arles considered to be the gateway to the Rhône Valley and Provence.

Chapitre 9 : Au téléphone
Chapter Overview

Mise en train pp. 234–236	Un week-end spécial		Practice and Activity Book, p. 97	Video Guide OR Videodisc Guide
	FUNCTIONS	**GRAMMAR**	**CULTURE**	**RE-ENTRY**
Première étape pp. 237–242	• Asking for and expressing opinions, p. 237 • Inquiring about and relating past events, p. 238	• The **passé composé** with **avoir**, p. 239 • Placement of adverbs with the **passé composé**, p. 240	**Note Culturelle,** History of Arles, p. 240	• Chores • Asking for, giving, and refusing permission
Deuxième étape pp. 243–246	Making and answering a telephone call, p. 244	The **-re** verbs: **répondre**, p. 245	• Realia: Ad for phone services, p. 243 • **Note Culturelle,** The French telephone system, p. 244 • Realia: **Télécartes** from **France Télécom**, p. 244 • **Panorama Culturel,** Telephone habits of French-speaking teenagers, p. 246	**aller** + infinitive
Troisième étape pp. 247–249	• Sharing confidences and consoling others, p. 247 • Asking for and giving advice, p. 247	The object pronouns **le, la, les, lui,** and **leur,** p. 247		

Prononciation p. 249	The vowel sounds [e] and [ɛ]	**Dictation:** Textbook Audiocassette 5A/Audio CD 9
Lisons! pp. 250–251	Minitel 2	**Reading Strategy:** Combining different reading strategies
Review pp. 252–255	Mise en pratique, pp. 252–253	Que sais-je? p. 254	Vocabulaire, p. 255

Assessment Options	**Etape Quizzes** • *Chapter Teaching Resources, Book 3* **Première étape,** Quiz 9-1, pp. 23–24 **Deuxième étape,** Quiz 9-2, pp. 25–26 **Troisième étape,** Quiz 9-3, pp. 27–28 • *Assessment Items, Audiocassette 8A/Audio CD 9*	**Chapter Test** • *Chapter Teaching Resources, Book 3,* pp. 29–34 • *Assessment Guide,* Speaking Test, p. 32 • *Assessment Items, Audiocassette 8A/Audio CD 9* **Test Generator, Chapter 9**

Video Program OR *Expanded Video Program, Videocassette 3* OR *Videodisc Program, Videodisc 5A*

Textbook Audiocassette 5A/Audio CD 9

RESOURCES: Print	RESOURCES: Audiovisual

Textbook Audiocassette 5A/Audio CD 9

Practice and Activity Book, pp. 98–100
Chapter Teaching Resources, Book 3
- Teaching Transparency Master 9-1, pp. 7, 10 . . . . *Teaching Transparency 9-1*
- Additional Listening Activities 9-1, 9-2, p. 11 . . . . *Additional Listening Activities, Audiocassette 10A/Audio CD 9*
- Realia 9-1, pp. 15, 17
- Situation Cards 9-1, pp. 18–19
- Student Response Forms, pp. 20–22
- Quiz 9-1, pp. 23–24 . . . . *Assessment Items, Audiocassette 8A/Audio CD 9*
Videodisc Guide . . . . *Videodisc Program, Videodisc 5A*

Textbook Audiocassette 5A/Audio CD 9

Practice and Activity Book, pp. 101–103
Chapter Teaching Resources, Book 3
- Communicative Activity 9-1, pp. 3–4
- Teaching Transparency Master 9-2, pp. 8, 10 . . . . *Teaching Transparency 9-2*
- Additional Listening Activities 9-3, 9-4, p. 12 . . . . *Additional Listening Activities, Audiocassette 10A/Audio CD 9*
- Realia 9-2, pp. 16, 17
- Situation Cards 9-2, pp. 18–19
- Student Response Forms, pp. 20–22
- Quiz 9-2, pp. 25–26 . . . . *Assessment Items, Audiocassette 8A/Audio CD 9*
Video Guide . . . . *Video Program* OR *Expanded Video Program, Videocassette 3*
Videodisc Guide . . . . *Videodisc Program, Videodisc 5A*

Textbook Audiocassette 5A/Audio CD 9

Practice and Activity Book, pp. 104–106
Chapter Teaching Resources, Book 3
- Communicative Activity 9-2, pp. 5–6
- Teaching Transparency Master 9-3, pp. 9, 10 . . . . *Teaching Transparency 9-3*
- Additional Listening Activities 9-5, 9-6, p. 13 . . . . *Additional Listening Activities, Audiocassette 10A/Audio CD 9*
- Realia 9-2, pp. 16, 17
- Situation Cards 9-3, pp. 18–19
- Student Response Forms, pp. 20–22
- Quiz 9-3, pp. 27–28 . . . . *Assessment Items, Audiocassette 8A/Audio CD 9*
Videodisc Guide . . . . *Videodisc Program, Videodisc 5A*

Practice and Activity Book, p. 107

Video Guide . . . . *Video Program* OR *Expanded Video Program, Videocassette 3*
Videodisc Guide . . . . *Videodisc Program, Videodisc 5A*

Alternative Assessment
- Performance Assessment
  Première étape, p. 242
  Deuxième étape, p. 245
  Troisième étape, p. 249
- Portfolio Assessment
  Written: **Mise en pratique,** Activity 5, *Pupil's Edition,* p. 253
    Assessment Guide, p. 22
  Oral: **Mise en pratique, Jeu de rôle,** *Pupil's Edition,* p. 253
    Assessment Guide, p. 22

Chapitre 9 : Au téléphone
Textbook Listening Activities Scripts

For Student Response Forms, see *Chapter Teaching Resources, Book 3,* pp. 20–22.

Première étape

7 Ecoute! p. 237

1. — Salut. Alors, tu as passé un bon week-end?
   — Oh, c'était épouvantable!

2. — Dis, tu as passé un bon week-end?
   — Ça a été.

3. — Tu as passé un bon week-end?
   — Oui, très bon.

4. — Tiens, tu as passé un bon week-end?
   — Oui, très chouette.

5. — Tu as passé un bon week-end?
   — Oh, pas mauvais.

Answers to Activity 7
1. no fun at all
2. mildly good
3. really good
4. really good
5. mildly good

10 Ecoute! p. 239

1. — Bonjour, Serge. Ça va? Tu as passé un bon week-end?
   — Ça a été. Je suis allé au cinéma avec Sandrine.

2. — Tiens, Eric! Qu'est-ce que tu vas faire ce week-end?
   — Oh, je ne sais pas. Je vais peut-être regarder un match à la télé.

3. — Dominique, ça va?
   — Oui, ça va bien. Et toi?
   — Ça va. Ecoute. On va danser samedi soir. Tu viens?
   — Bonne idée!

4. — Salut, Christine!
   — Salut!
   — Tu as passé un bon week-end?
   — Oui, très bon.
   — Qu'est-ce que tu as fait?
   — Je suis allée à la plage, et j'ai rencontré des copains.

5. — Tiens, Sylvie, tu es allée où ce week-end?
   — Je suis allée au café avec Patrick.
   — Tu as passé un bon week-end?
   — Oui, très chouette.

Answers to Activity 10
1. last weekend
2. next weekend
3. next weekend
4. last weekend
5. last weekend

Deuxième étape

19 Ecoute! p. 244

1. — Allô?
   — Bonjour. Je suis bien chez Michel Perrault?
   — Oui. Qui est à l'appareil?
   — C'est Françoise.
   — Salut, Françoise! C'est moi, Paul.
   — Ah salut, Paul. Michel est là?
   — Une seconde, s'il te plaît.
   — D'accord.

2. — Allô?
   — Salut, Suzanne! C'est Jeanne à l'appareil. Ça va?
   — Oui, ça va bien.
   — Je peux parler à Thierry?
   — Thierry n'est pas là. Tu peux rappeler plus tard?
   — D'accord.

3. — Allô?
   — Bonjour, Anne?
   — Non, c'est Brigitte.
   — Ah, Anne est là?
   — Euh, je ne sais pas. Une seconde, s'il vous plaît. Vous pouvez rappeler? Elle est occupée.
   — Je peux lui laisser un message?
   — Bien sûr.
   — Vous pouvez lui dire que Daniel a téléphoné?
   — D'accord. C'est noté.

Answers to Activity 19
1. Françoise; Michel   2. Jeanne; Thierry   3. Daniel; Anne

21 Ecoute! p. 245

1. — Allô?
   — Bonjour. Est-ce que Madame Tissot est là?
   — Non, elle n'est pas là.
   — Je peux laisser un message?
   — Bien sûr.
   — Vous pouvez lui dire que Madame Morel a téléphoné?
   — Madame Moran?
   — Non, Morel. M-O-R-E-L.
   — Ah, Morel. D'accord.
   — Merci. Au revoir.
   — Au revoir.

2. — Allô?
   — Bonjour. Je peux parler à Monsieur Tissot? C'est son frère, Roger.
   — Désolé, mais il n'est pas là.
   — Vous pouvez lui dire que je ne peux pas aller au restaurant samedi soir?
   — D'accord.
   — Merci. Allez, au revoir.
   — Au revoir.

3. — Allô?
   — Bonjour! C'est Claire Laroche à l'appareil. Anne est
   là, s'il vous plaît?
   — Non, elle n'est pas là. Vous pouvez rappeler plus
   tard?
   — Oui. Mais, est-ce que je peux laisser un message?
   — Bien sûr.
   — Vous pouvez lui dire qu'on va au cinéma à neuf
   heures moins le quart?
   — Euh, à quelle heure? Vous pouvez répéter?
   — A neuf heures moins le quart.
   — D'accord.
   — Bon, merci. Au revoir.
   — Au revoir.

4. — Allô?
   — Bonjour. Je suis bien chez Philippe?
   — Oui. Qui est à l'appareil?
   — C'est Marc. Je peux lui parler?
   — Désolé, mais il n'est pas là.
   — Alors, je peux laisser un message?
   — Bien sûr.
   — Vous pouvez lui dire qu'on va jouer au foot samedi
   après-midi?
   — D'accord.
   — Merci bien. Au revoir.
   — Au revoir.

Answers to Activity 21
Possible answers
1. Mme Tissot — Mme Morel a téléphoné.
2. M. Tissot — Votre frère Roger ne peut pas aller au restaurant samedi soir.
3. Anne — Claire Laroche a téléphoné. Vous allez au cinéma à neuf heures
   moins le quart.
4. Philippe — Marc a téléphoné. Vous allez jouer au foot samedi après-midi.

*T*roisième étape

24 Ecoute! p. 247

1. — Je veux sortir avec Jean-Luc. Tu crois que je peux
   l'inviter?

2. — Eh bien, si tu ne veux pas rater ton examen, tu
   devrais étudier.

3. — Bruno? Moi, je trouve qu'il n'est pas très gentil.
   Oublie-le!

4. — Moi, je voudrais bien aller au concert de Vanessa
   Paradis, mais ça coûte très cher! Qu'est-ce que je
   fais?

5. — Alors, si tu veux acheter une voiture, pourquoi tu ne
   travailles pas cet été?

6. — Je ne mange pas beaucoup, mais je trouve que je suis
   un peu gros quand-même. Qu'est-ce que tu me conseilles?

7. — Si elle n'a pas encore téléphoné, téléphone-lui!

Answers to Activity 24
1. asking	4. asking	7. giving
2. giving	5. giving	
3. giving	6. asking	

25 Ecoute! p. 247

   — Allô?
   — Salut, Mireille. C'est Simone. Ça va?
   — Oui, ça va. Et toi?
   — Pas terrible. Je peux te parler? Tu as une minute?
   — Oui.
   — J'ai un petit problème.
   — Je t'écoute.
   — Ben, j'ai raté mon examen de maths. Je ne sais pas
   quoi faire.
   — Ne t'en fais pas, Simone!
   — Mais, j'ai beaucoup étudié. J'ai bien préparé mes
   réponses, et j'ai quand même raté.
   — Qu'est-ce que je peux faire?
   — Je peux étudier avec toi, Mireille?
   — Bien sûr! Ne t'en fais pas. Ça va aller mieux!

Answer to Activity 25
Elle a raté son examen de maths.

*P*rononciation, p. 249

For the scripts for Parts A and B, see p. 249.

C. A écrire

   (Dictation)
   — Allô?
   — Salut, Hélène. Tu peux parler? J'ai un problème.
   — Je t'écoute.

*M*ise en pratique

1 p. 252

Salut, c'est Martin. Comment vas-tu? Tu as passé un bon
week-end? Moi, j'ai passé un week-end génial. Je suis allé
à la plage. Il a fait un temps superbe. Samedi, j'ai fait du
ski nautique et après, j'ai joué au volley-ball. Ensuite,
dimanche, j'ai fait du jogging. Et toi, qu'est-ce que tu as
fait? Appelle-moi quand tu rentres. Salut!

Answers to Mise en pratique Activity 1
1. false	3. true	5. true
2. true	4. false	6. false

La Provence
(Individual Project)

ASSIGNMENT

Have students work individually to research topics associated with the region of Provence. Projects should include a written report and an oral and visual presentation, all in English.

MATERIALS

✂ **Students may need**
• Reference books
• Posterboard
• Colored markers

PREPARATION

Ask each student to select a topic. Possible topics include:
• tourist attractions or history of Avignon, Arles, Aix-en-Provence, the Camargue, Marseilles, Cannes, or Nice
• natural resources or geography of the region
• regional dishes or products
• the Roman occupation or architecture
• the artist Vincent Van Gogh in Arles
• the poet Frédéric Mistral
• the **santons**

SUGGESTED SEQUENCE

1. Students choose a topic and begin looking for reference materials. They may use encyclopedias, almanacs, travel guides, history books, and so on.

2. Students gather information and begin organizing their papers. They should also gather or make illustrations and plan how their visuals will look.

3. Once students have a rough draft of their paper, they should ask you or other students to go over it for suggestions and feedback on language use. For their oral presentations, students should submit an outline of their presentation either to you or to other students to check for clarity and organization.

4. After making any necessary changes in their rough drafts, students should edit them again for accuracy. They should also prepare and organize their visual aids.

5. Have students give their oral presentations. You might display their posters around the classroom.

GRADING THE PROJECT

You might base students' grades on content, language use, presentation, creativity, and appearance of visuals.

Suggested Point Distribution (total = 100 points)

Correct content . . . . 20 points
Language use . . . . 20 points
Oral presentation . . . . 20 points
Creativity . . . . 20 points
Appearance of visuals . . . . 20 points

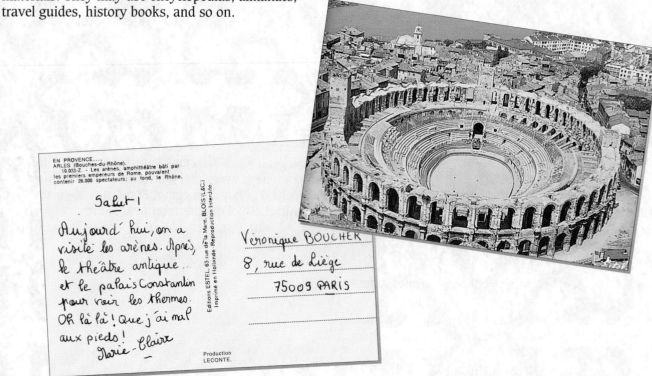

♟ *Games*

MESSAGE TELEPHONIQUE

In this game, students will practice using telephone vocabulary.

Procedure Whisper one of the short messages below only once to one student. Then, have that student whisper what you said to the next student, and so on. Once the message reaches the last student, ask that person to say the message aloud to compare it with the original. Follow the same procedure with the other messages. If the class is very large, this game might be played by two or three groups simultaneously. You might whisper the message to the first person in each group, wait for all groups to finish, and have the final student in each group say the message aloud. Try to begin each time with different students so that the same students aren't always first and last. The suggested messages here can be shortened or extended, depending on the class' success with the first few messages.

> Ne quittez pas.
> C'était épouvantable.
> Qui est à l'appareil?
> J'ai un petit problème.
> Vous pouvez rappeler plus tard?
> Qu'est-ce que tu me conseilles?
> Qu'est-ce que tu as fait vendredi soir?

VERB TENSE RACE

In this game, students will practice various verb conjugations.

Procedure This game can be played by two to five teams. Begin by saying a regular -er verb, a subject pronoun, and a tense (past, present, or future). For example, if you say **apporter, nous, passé composé**, the students should write **nous avons apporté**. Vary the subjects and tenses. You might avoid the present-tense forms of **acheter** and **répéter** due to the accent changes. To play with two teams, have one student from each team race to the board to write the correct verb form when you give a verb, a subject, and a tense. To play with three or more teams, provide each team with an overhead transparency and marker or pieces of scrap paper. Have students work together to figure out and write down the answer. The first team to hold up a correctly written answer wins. If you need a tiebreaker, give two points for correct irregular past participles. For a list of -**er** verbs and irregular past participles that students know, see the chapter vocabulary list on page 255 under **Première étape**.

Chapitre 9
Au téléphone
pp. 232–255

𝒰sing the Chapter Opener

Motivating Activity

Have students look at the objects and photos on pages 232 and 233 and guess what the teenagers might be talking about (sports, concerts, chores, friends, a picnic).

Teaching Suggestion

Ask students to describe the three photos. Then, read the captions aloud. Have students read the outcomes and relate them to what is happening in each photo. Ask students why understanding a phone conversation might be difficult in a foreign language. (There are no hints from body language or facial expressions.)

Photo Flash!

① Hélène is talking on the phone to a friend. In France, local calls are charged by the minute, just like long-distance calls in the United States. **France Télécom** is the national public phone company responsible for all local and long-distance service.

CHAPITRE 9
Au téléphone

① Allô? C'est Hélène à l'appareil.

Culture Note

In West Africa, telephone service is limited. Smaller towns and villages may not have service at all. Even in large cities, every household may not have a telephone. Public phones are scarce as well, but calls can be made from the post office. International calls can be made through hotel operators or long-distance operators in local post offices and are usually expensive. Since telephones are not always available, visits to friends and relatives often replace phone calls. In fact, it is not uncommon for visitors to drop by unannounced to catch up on the latest news of friends and family.

Teenagers in francophone countries like to talk to their friends about the good things that are happening to them, as well as their problems, just as teenagers do in the United States.

In this chapter you will learn

- to ask for and express opinions; to inquire about and relate past events
- to make and answer a telephone call
- to share confidences and console others; to ask for and give advice

And you will

- listen to French-speaking students talk about what they did during the weekend
- read letters from French teenagers
- write about what you did over the weekend
- learn about the French telephone system

② Tu as passé un bon week-end?

③ J'ai un petit problème.

Cécile Clémo
67. 64. 12. 98

Mr. et Mme Colin
rue Victor Hugo
4000 Montpellier

CD
EF
GH
IJ
KL

deux cent trente-trois 233

Video Synopsis

In this segment of the video, Magali calls her friend Hélène, and they tell each other what they did over the weekend. We see a flashback of Magali with her friends at **les arènes,** where Florent introduced her to Ahmed. Magali tells Hélène about Ahmed and how she and her friends went to **les Baux-de-Provence** on Sunday. Hélène is anxious to hear the rest, but Magali's father needs to use the telephone, so she tells Hélène she will call back.

Motivating Activity

Ask students why they call their friends on the phone. Do they discuss homework, school, parents, or friends? When is a good time to call? Do they have their friends' numbers memorized?

Presentation

Have students look at the photos for **Un week-end spécial** and answer the general questions at the top of this page. Show the video, and then have students read the dialogue aloud in pairs to help each other understand the general meaning. Ask them to answer the questions in Activity 1 on page 236 as they read.

Mise en train

Hélène

Magali

Florent   Ahmed

Un week-end spécial

What is the subject of Hélène and Magali's telephone conversation? How do you know?

Hélène et Magali sont au téléphone et racontent ce qu'elles ont fait pendant le week-end. Magali a fait beaucoup de choses. La conversation dure…

Allô?

Bof, ça a été. Je n'ai rien fait de spécial.

Hélène? C'est Magali à l'appareil. Tu as passé un bon week-end?

② Samedi, j'ai fait mes devoirs.

③ Dimanche, j'ai regardé la télévision…

④ …et j'ai lu un peu.

MISE EN TRAIN   *deux cent trente-cinq* **235**

Thinking Critically

Comparing and Contrasting
Ask students to discuss the girls' weekends in small groups or as a class. Have them compare their recent weekends with Magali's and Hélène's. Ask if they discuss their weekends on the phone with friends and if they ever have to get off the phone for another family member. Ask them what they would consider an entertaining weekend spent locally.

For Individual Needs

Visual/Tactile Learners
On a transparency, draw pictures to illustrate the activities the girls did over the weekend. For example, you might draw a book to illustrate Hélène's statement **J'ai lu un peu.** Then, write the girls' dialogue in speech bubbles on strips of transparency. Call on students to match the speech bubbles to the illustrations.

Culture Notes

• The **théâtre antique** in downtown Arles dates back to the time of the Emperor Augustus.
• **Les Baux-de-Provence** is a lively village of winding streets and small shops which is perched on a rocky promontory. A medieval castle dating from the thirteenth century offers a beautiful view of the surrounding countryside.
• **Santons** are ceramic figures that depict characters from Nativity scenes as well as people of different professions, such as shepherds or weavers, dressed in traditional **provençal** attire.

Video Integration

• *EXPANDED VIDEO PROGRAM,*
Videocassette 3, 35:05–39:04
• *VIDEODISC PROGRAM,*
Videodisc 5A

Search 11745, Play To 18905

You may choose to continue with **Un week-end spécial (suite)** at this time or wait until later in the chapter. When the story continues, Magali calls Hélène back and tells her about her trip to **les Baux-de-Provence** as we see flashbacks of Magali and her friends there. Magali tells Hélène about the sites they visited. At the end of the episode, we see a flashback of Magali opening a package. It is a gift from Ahmed, a **santon** that Magali admired at the souvenir boutique at **les Baux-de-Provence.** Magali asks Hélène for advice about getting to know Ahmed.

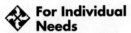
1 Tu as compris?

Answer the following questions about **Un week-end spécial.**

1. How was Hélène's weekend?   OK.
2. Did Magali have a good weekend?   Yes. Why? Why not?   She met a nice boy.
3. Do you think Magali likes Ahmed?   Yes. How can you tell?   She says he is very nice.
4. Why does Magali have to hang up?   Her father needs to make a phone call.

2 Magali ou Hélène?

Qui a fait ça, Magali ou Hélène?

1. aller aux Baux   Magali
2. faire ses devoirs   Hélène
3. lire   Hélène
4. aller au théâtre antique   Magali
5. regarder la télévision   Hélène
6. ne rien faire de spécial   Hélène

3 Mets en ordre

Put Magali's activities in order according to **Un week-end spécial.**   1, 4, 2, 3

1. Elle est allée au théâtre antique avec un copain.
2. Elle est allée aux Baux-de-Provence.
3. Elle a parlé avec Hélène au téléphone.
4. Elle a rencontré un garçon sympa.

4 C'est qui?

Match the photos of these people with the sentences that refer to them.

Magali   Hélène   Ahmed   le père de Magali

1. Cette personne veut téléphoner.   le père de Magali
2. Cette personne a passé un très bon week-end.   Magali
3. Cette personne est super gentille.   Ahmed
4. Pendant le week-end, cette personne n'a rien fait de spécial.   Hélène
5. Cette personne va téléphoner plus tard.   Magali

5 Cherche les expressions

According to **Un week-end spécial,** what do you say in French . . .   See answers below.

1. to answer the phone?
2. to identify yourself on the phone?
3. to ask if someone had a good weekend?
4. to ask what someone did?
5. to tell someone to hold?
6. to ask what happened?

6 Et maintenant, à toi

What do you think happened to Magali at les Baux?

Answers
5 1. Allô?
2. C'est... à l'appareil.
3. Tu as passé un bon week-end?
4. Qu'est-ce que tu as fait?
5. Attends une seconde.
6. Qu'est-ce qui s'est passé?

PREMIERE ETAPE

Asking for and expressing opinions; inquiring about and relating past events

COMMENT DIT-ON... ?
Asking for and expressing opinions

To ask for someone's opinion:
Tu as passé un bon week-end?
Did you have a good weekend?

To express indifference:
Oui, ça a été. *Yes, it was OK.*
Oh, pas mauvais.

To express satisfaction:
Oui, très chouette. *Yes, super.*
Oui, excellent.
Oui, très bon.

To express dissatisfaction:
Très mauvais.
C'était épouvantable.
It was horrible.

7 Ecoute!
Listen to these people talk about their weekend. Tell if they had a really good time, a mildly good time, or no fun at all. Answers on p. 231C.

8 Tu as passé un bon week-end?
Find out if some of your classmates had a good or bad weekend. Then, tell them how your weekend was.

PREMIERE ETAPE   *deux cent trente-sept* **237**

𝒥ump Start!
Have students write opinions of three of their favorite classes or activities and three of their least favorite. (**Le français, c'est génial. La biologie, c'est nul.**)

MOTIVATE
Ask students what they talk about when they see friends at school on Monday morning.

TEACH

Presentation
Comment dit-on... ? Draw three faces showing satisfaction, indifference, and dissatisfaction on the board. Read each response, making appropriate facial expressions, and have students tell which face expresses it. Then, describe weekend activities, such as **Je suis allé(e) à un concert de rock.** Have students respond with one of the new expressions. (**C'était très chouette!**) Finally, have partners ask and tell how their weekends were.

For Individual Needs

7 Visual Learners Show magazine pictures of people who are happy, indifferent, or unhappy, and ask **Il/Elle a passé un bon week-end?**

7 Kinesthetic Learners Have students respond by making the thumbs-up gesture, the **comme ci, comme ça** gesture, or the thumbs-down gesture.

Presentation

Comment dit-on... ? Tell students that you're going to talk about your weekend. Have them listen for what you did and in what order. Then, tell about your weekend activities again, writing **d'abord, ensuite, après, après ça,** and **enfin** on the board as you proceed. Next, write five of the activities you mentioned on five flashcards, and give the flashcards to five students. Have them recall in what order you recounted your activities and hold the flashcards under the appropriate sequencing expressions on the board. Have students repeat the sequencing expressions and activities. (**D'abord, j'ai fait les courses.**)

For videodisc application, see *Videodisc Guide.*

For Individual Needs

9 Slower Pace Copy these sentences randomly on a sheet of paper and give copies to pairs of students. Have students begin by finding the sentence that might start the conversation. Then, have partners underline or circle the sequencing expressions and number the sentences to show the correct order.

Additional Practice

Write each sequencing expression on a strip of transparency and distribute them to five students. Have students write an activity they did over the weekend on their strips. Then, display the strips on the overhead and have the class create a story using them. You might use this activity as a writing assignment.

COMMENT DIT-ON... ?
Inquiring about and relating past events

To inquire about past events:

Qu'est-ce qui s'est passé?
What happened?

Qu'est-ce que tu as fait vendredi soir? *What did you do . . . ?*

Et après? *And then?*

Tu es allé(e) où? *Where did you go?*

To relate past events:

Nous avons parlé. *We talked.*

D'abord, j'ai fait mes devoirs.
First, . . .

Ensuite, j'ai téléphoné à un copain.
Then, . . .

Après, je suis sorti(e).
Afterwards, I went out.

Enfin, je suis allé(e) chez Paul.
Finally, . . .

Et après ça, j'ai parlé au téléphone.
And after that, . . .

Je suis allé(e) au cinéma. *I went . . .*

9 Méli-mélo!

Remets la conversation entre Albert et Marcel dans le bon ordre.

¹ —Salut, Marcel! Ça va?

⁴ —Vendredi et samedi, rien de spécial.

³ —Et après ça?

⁹ —Pas mal. Dis, qu'est-ce que tu as fait ce week-end?

⁶ —Dimanche, j'ai téléphoné à Gisèle et nous avons décidé de sortir.

⁷ —Vous êtes allés où?

¹⁰ —Après, nous sommes allés au café et nous avons parlé jusqu'à minuit.

⁵ —Et dimanche?

⁸ —D'abord, nous avons fait un pique-nique. Ensuite, nous sommes allés au cinéma.

² —Oui, ça va bien. Et toi?

Grammaire   The passé composé with avoir

To tell what happened in the past, use the **passé composé** of the verb. The **passé composé** is composed of two parts: *(a)* a present-tense form of the helping verb **avoir** or **être**—which you've already learned—and *(b)* the past participle of the verb you want to use. You use **avoir** as the helping verb with most verbs. Only with a small number of French verbs, like **aller**, do you use **être** as the helping verb. You'll learn more about these later.

Helping Verb +	Past Participle
J' **ai**	
Tu **as**	
Il/Elle/On **a**	**parlé** au téléphone.
Nous **avons**	
Vous **avez**	
Ils/Elles **ont**	

- To form the past participle of a verb that ends in **-er**, drop the **-er** and add **-é**.
- To make a verb in the **passé composé** negative, put **ne (n')... pas** around the helping verb.

Je **n'ai pas** étudié.

- Some French verbs have irregular past participles, that is, they don't follow a regular pattern. You'll have to memorize them when you learn the verb. Here are the past participles of some irregular verbs that you've already seen.

faire	fait	J'ai **fait** mes devoirs.
prendre	pris	Ils ont **pris** un taxi.
voir	vu	Il a **vu** sa grand-mère.
lire	lu	Elle a **lu** un roman français.

10   Ecoute!

Listen to these conversations and decide whether the speakers are talking about what they did last weekend or what they're going to do next weekend.   Answers on p. 231C.

11   Une journée à la plage

Qu'est-ce que Claire et ses amis ont fait à la plage?

1.   Ils ont joué au volley.   2.   Ils ont fait un pique-nique.   3.   Claire a écouté de la musique.

Grammaire   Write the sentence **Nous avons parlé** on the board and ask students to tell what they can deduce about the past tense. Then, review the forms of **avoir** by handing students items such as a book or some pencils, asking **Qui a mon livre/mes crayons?** (**Tim a votre livre. Alicia et John ont vos crayons.**) Explain that the **passé composé** is formed with the present tense of **avoir** plus a past participle. Then, hold up pictures that demonstrate activities such as **voir un film, manger du gâteau,** and **faire du jogging** in one hand, and a card with a subject pronoun written on it in the other. Call on students to make sentences in the **passé composé**, using the card and the picture. You might occasionally shake your head to prompt students to respond in the negative.

Teaching Suggestions

10   Before starting this activity, re-enter the use of **aller** + infinitive to express future time. Write an activity on the board (**faire les devoirs**) and have one volunteer create a sentence, using that verb in the **passé composé**. Then, have a second volunteer create a second sentence with the same verb, using **aller.** You might also ask students **Qu'est-ce que tu vas faire demain?**

11   As a variation, make up several sentences about the pictures. (**Ils ont joué au volley-ball. Ils ont fait un pique-nique. Elle a écouté la radio.**) Say them at random and have students write the number of the picture each one refers to.

♟ Game

Loto!   Have each student draw a 4 × 4 grid and fill the squares with different past tense forms (**J'ai pris, Il a lu**). Write the infinitives of these verbs on slips of paper (**prendre, lire**) and put them in a box. Then, begin the "bingo" game. Select and call out an infinitive in French and have students mark the square that shows a past-tense form of the verb you called. When a student has marked four horizontally, vertically, or diagonally adjoining squares, he or she calls out **Loto!** and reads the items in French.

For Individual Needs

12 Slower Pace Have students look at the expressions in the first word box. Ask them who would use each expression, the parent or the child. You might also have students form the **passé composé** of the infinitives suggested in the second word box.

Teaching Suggestion

Note de grammaire Have one student suggest an activity (**voyager**). Then, have a second student give the **passé composé**. (**J'ai voyagé.**) Have a third student repeat the sentence, adding an adverb that relates to his or her own experience. (**J'ai beaucoup voyagé.**)

Additional Practice

Distribute the verb slips from the **Loto!** game on page 239 and have students write a sentence, using the verb in the **passé composé** and adding an appropriate adverb.

Language Notes

13 Write **Je suis allé** on the board and point out that females should add an **-e** to the past participle.

13 Students may want to know about some of the expressions on the postcard: **thermes** are *thermal baths* built by the Romans; **j'ai mal aux pieds** means *my feet hurt*.

Portfolio

13 Written This activity is appropriate for students' written portfolios. For portfolio information, see *Assessment Guide*, pages 2–13.

---

12 Jeu de rôle

You ask permission to go out. Your parent wants to know if all the chores have been done. Act out this scene with a partner. Then, change roles.

> (Est-ce que) je peux... ?
> Tu es d'accord?   C'est impossible.
> Pas question!   Est-ce que tu as... ?
> Oui, si tu... d'abord...

Note de *Grammaire*

When you are talking about what happened in the past, place short adverbs, such as **souvent, trop, beaucoup, pas encore** *(not yet)*, **bien** *(well)*, **mal** *(badly)*, and **déjà** *(already)*, before the past participle of the verb.

　　J'ai **déjà** mangé.

> faire tes devoirs   laver la voiture
> acheter le pain   sortir la poubelle
> faire la vaisselle   ranger ta chambre
> promener le chien

13 Une carte postale

Write a postcard to your classmates telling them what you did during your first weekend in Arles.

EN PROVENCE.
ARLES (Bouches-du-Rhône).
10.033-Z. – Les arènes, amphithéâtre bâti par
les premiers empereurs de Rome, pouvaient
contenir 26.000 spectateurs; au fond, le Rhône.

Salut!
Aujourd'hui, on a visité les arènes. Après, le théâtre antique et le palais Constantin pour voir les thermes. Oh là là! Que j'ai mal aux pieds!
Marie-Claire

Véronique BOUCHER
8, rue de Liège
75009 PARIS

> manger un croque-monsieur
> aller au musée   aller au café
> voir un film français   faire les vitrines
> visiter les arènes
> parler français   aller au restaurant
> faire une promenade

NOTE CULTURELLE

In the first centuries A.D., its location on the Rhône river made Arles the most important port and trading center in the Roman province of Southern Gaul, called Provincia. The Roman influence can still be seen today in Arles. You can visit the Roman amphitheater that is still in use, an ancient theater, and the largest existing thermal baths in Provence.

240   *deux cent quarante*   CHAPITRE 9   Au téléphone

History Link

The French word **Provence** comes from the latin word **Provincia,** the name the Romans gave to their province in Gaul. You might have students find out more about the Roman occupation and different Roman ruins in the area. Students might want to research how the aqueducts and baths functioned and were used. This might be done as a chapter project. (See page 231E.)

VOCABULAIRE

J'ai raté le bus.

J'ai trouvé cinquante francs.

J'ai oublié mes devoirs.

J'ai déjeuné à la cantine.

J'ai rencontré une fille sympa.

J'ai chanté dans la chorale.

J'ai acheté un CD.

J'ai travaillé au fast-food.

Here are some other activities you may have done during your day.

apporter	*to bring*	gagner	*to win, to earn*	répéter	*to rehearse, to*
chercher	*to look for*	montrer	*to show*		*practice music*
commencer	*to begin, to start*	passer un examen	*to take an exam*	retrouver	*to meet with*
dîner	*to have dinner*	rater une interro	*to fail a quiz*	visiter	*to visit (a place)*

Presentation

Vocabulaire Gather props to help present the sentences (a 50-franc bill, a fork, a CD). Act out each sentence and have students repeat it, imitating your gestures. Next, call on eight students to mime one sentence each and have the class tell what happened to them. Then, make statements using the verbs at the bottom of the page and have students respond by miming the actions.

Teaching Suggestion

Ask students if they have ever done these things. (**Qui a (déjà) raté le bus?**)

For Individual Needs

Kinesthetic Learners Write several sentences with words from the **Vocabulaire** on strips of transparency. (**Après l'école, j'ai cherché mon chat. Ensuite, Emile et Laurent ont retrouvé des amis.**) Cut the sentences into sequencing words, subjects, auxiliary verbs, past participles, and objects or complements and shuffle them. Have two students come up to the overhead and arrange the pieces to make sentences.

Teaching Suggestion

Have students write down three activities from the **Vocabulaire** that they did last week. Then, have them try to find one other student who also did the same activities by saying **J'ai déjeuné à la cantine. Et toi?** Have them report back to the class.

Language Notes

- Point out that **commencer** is followed by **à** when used with an infinitive: **J'ai commencé à comprendre.**
- Remind students that **chercher** means *to look for* and doesn't take a preposition. (**J'ai cherché mes devoirs.**)

For Individual Needs

14 Visual Learners Have students bring in magazine pictures of people engaged in different activities. As they hold up each picture, have the class tell what the people did last weekend.

Game

CE WEEK-END Have students form groups of five or six. The first person in each group begins by telling one thing he or she did last weekend. **(Ce week-end, j'ai dîné avec mes parents.)** The next person repeats the first activity and adds another. **(Ce week-end, j'ai dîné avec mes parents, et j'ai étudié.)** Groups compete to see who can go on the longest without making a mistake.

Teaching Suggestion

16 Set either a time limit or a goal of five names.

Mon journal

17 For an additional journal entry suggestion for Chapter 9, see *Practice and Activity Book,* page 153.

CLOSE

To close this **étape,** have students pair off and ask and tell each other what they did yesterday.

ASSESS

Quiz 9-1, *Chapter Teaching Resources Book 3,* pp. 23–24

Assessment Items, Audiocassette 8A/Audio CD 9

Performance Assessment

Have students imagine they are spending a weekend in Provence. Have them write a postcard home, telling what they did or didn't do. For additional activities, refer students to the word box in Activity 13 on page 240.

14 Qu'est-ce qu'ils ont fait le week-end dernier?

1. Elles ont acheté des CD.
2. Il a travaillé.
3. Il a rencontré une fille. Elle a rencontré un garçon.

15 Pierre a fait quoi?

Pierre spent a week at a sports camp. Which of the activities below do you think he did and which do you think he didn't do? See answers below.

chanter avec des copains
jouer au volley-ball
gagner un match
faire du ski nautique
rater un examen   nager
faire une promenade
manger des escargots
rater le bus   faire de l'équitation
faire les courses   acheter un CD
manger un hot-dog

> **De bons conseils**
>
> French words that look similar are often related in meaning, so you can use words you already know to guess the meanings of new words. If you already know what **chanter** means, you can probably guess the meaning of **une chanteuse.** You know what **commencer** means, so what do you think **le commencement** means? Likewise, you should be able to figure out **le visiteur** from the verb **visiter.**

voir la tour Eiffel
faire du deltaplane
étudier le japonais   manger des escargots
lire un poème français   jouer au hockey
nager dans la mer des Caraïbes
acheter une montre   travailler en été
rencontrer une fille francophone
oublier les devoirs   visiter le Louvre

16 Tu as déjà fait ça?

Try to find classmates who've already done some of the activities in the box to the right and write down their names.

> —Tu as déjà visité le Louvre?
> —Oui, j'ai visité le Louvre.
>
> *or*
>
> — Non, je n'ai jamais visité le Louvre.

17 Mon journal

Write down five things you did last weekend. Be sure to tell when you did each activity, with whom, and as many other details as you can think of.

Language Note

Remind students that **du, de la, de l', des, un,** and **une** all become **de** after a negative expression, but the definite articles **le, la,** and **les** remain the same.

Answers

15 Pierre a : joué au volley-ball, gagné un match, fait du ski nautique, nagé, fait une promenade, fait de l'équitation, chanté avec des copains.
Pierre n'a pas : raté d'examen, mangé d'escargots, raté le bus, mangé de hot-dog, acheté de CD, fait les courses.

DEUXIEME ETAPE

Making and answering a telephone call

—Allô, Anita?
—Oui. C'est moi.
—Salut. C'est François.

—Allô? C'est Michel. Véronique est là, s'il vous plaît?
—Une seconde, s'il vous plaît.
—Merci.

—Allô? Est-ce que Xuan est là, s'il vous plaît?
—Non, il est chez Robert.
—Est-ce que je peux laisser un message?
—Bien sûr.
—Vous pouvez lui dire qu'Emmanuel a téléphoné?
—D'accord.
—Merci.

18 Au téléphone

Answer the questions as you read the conversations.

1. What does each of these people say to answer the phone? *Answers vary.*
2. Who has to wait a few seconds to speak to his or her friend? *Michel*
3. Who gets to talk right away to the person he or she is calling? *François*
4. Who isn't home? *Xuan*

Allô, ☎
Les spécialistes du téléphone

Microcommutateurs • Téléphones sans fil • Téléphones de voiture • Répondeurs • Télécopieurs personnels • Interphones • Alarmes

18, rue Lafayette — **13200 ARLES** **90-96-45-75**
26, rue de la Liberté — **13200 ARLES** **90-49-54-16**

DEUXIEME ETAPE   *deux cent quarante-trois* **243**

ⱥ ump Start!

Have students write three sentences telling what they did or didn't do after school yesterday. Students might exchange and edit each other's papers.

MOTIVATE

Ask students to imagine that a French-speaking student is staying with them for the summer. As a class or in small groups, have students brainstorm English expressions the student might need to know in order to answer the phone and take messages.

TEACH

✦ For Individual Needs

18 Slower Pace Have students tell who the caller is and who is answering the phone in each conversation. Have students list the words that helped them decide.

Teaching Suggestion

18 Act out the conversations for students, using a toy phone. Then, distribute typed copies of the dialogues. Have students underline the expressions they used to answer the questions. Then, have them pair off to practice reading the conversations aloud.

Thinking Critically

Drawing Inferences Have students look at the ad and figure out what type of company placed it. Using the context and English cognates, have students guess what items are sold.

Presentation

Comment dit-on... ? Using two toy phones, act as both the caller and the person called for a simple conversation, using the expressions from **Comment dit-on... ?** Then, dial a number, make telephone ringing sounds, turn to the class, and say **Ça ne répond pas.** Dial again, making busy signal sounds, and tell the class **C'est occupé.** Then, pretend to answer the phone, pause, and say **Ne quittez pas.** Turn to the class and hand the phone to a student, saying **C'est pour toi.** Have students repeat the new expressions. Then, have them pair off and role-play calling and taking a message.

For videodisc application, see _Videodisc Guide._

Language Notes

• Other useful telephone expressions are: **composer le numéro** *(to dial the number);* **l'annuaire** *(phone book);* **décrocher** *(to pick up the receiver);* **raccrocher** *(to hang up).*

• Have students practice difficult sounds, as in **l'appareil** and **seconde** (the c is pronounced like a **g**). Point out that **lui** can mean either *(to) him* or *(to) her.*

Additional Practice

19 After doing this activity, hand out typed copies of the script and have partners read the conversations aloud. You might also delete parts of the conversations and have students supply their own substitutions.

 COMMENT DIT-ON...?
Making and answering a telephone call

To make a phone call:

Bonjour.

Je suis bien chez Véronique?
Is this . . . 's house?

C'est Michel.

(Est-ce que) Véronique **est là, s'il vous plaît?**

Je peux parler à Véronique?

Je peux laisser un message?
May I leave a message?

Vous pouvez lui dire que j'ai téléphoné?
Can you tell her/him that I called?

To answer a phone call:

Allô?

Qui est à l'appareil?
Who's calling?

Vous pouvez rappeler plus tard?
Can you call back later?

Une seconde, s'il vous plaît.

D'accord.

Bien sûr.

Here are some additional phrases you may need:

Ne quittez pas. *Hold on.*

Ça ne répond pas.
There's no answer.

C'est occupé.
It's busy.

19 Ecoute!

Ecoute ces conversations téléphoniques. Qui téléphone? A qui voudrait-il/-elle parler?
Answers on p. 231C.

NOTE CULTURELLE

The French telephone system is run by the **France Télécom** office. You can make telephone calls at the post office, where you will always find a telephone booth. Coin-operated telephones (**téléphones à pièces**) are gradually being replaced by card-operated ones (**publiphones à cartes**), which have greatly reduced vandalism. These modern phones accept "smart cards" (**télécartes**), which can be purchased at the post office and at newsstands. Each card contains credits for a specific number of units. Units are deducted according to the distance and the duration of a call. To make a call, you simply insert the card in the phone. A readout will tell you how many units you have remaining.

244 *deux cent quarante-quatre* CHAPITRE 9 Au téléphone

Culture Note

Students might be interested to know that even local calls from public phones in France have a time limit, approximately six minutes. After this, a signal shows that more money must be deposited, or the call will be cut off. One advantage of using **télécartes** to make long-distance calls is that they operate silently; otherwise, the caller's coins drop during the conversation, often causing noise on the line.

Multicultural Link

Have students compare the French public phone system to the one they're used to. You might want to assign countries to students and have them find out how public phones work there. They might ask someone who has traveled to a particular country, or call or write to the nearest tourist office. Then, have them report their findings to the class.

20 Méli-mélo!

Ecris cette conversation dans le bon ordre. See answers below.

—D'accord.
—Salut, Aurélie. Désolée, elle n'est pas là. Tu peux rappeler plus tard?
—Allô?
—Bien sûr.
—Qui est à l'appareil?

—Tu peux lui dire que j'ai téléphoné?
—Bonjour. Je peux parler à Nicole?
—Est-ce que je peux laisser un message?
—C'est Aurélie.

21 Ecoute!

During your exchange visit to France, you stay with a French family, **les Tissot.** You're the only one at home today. Several of their friends call and leave messages. Write down the messages and compare your notes with a classmate's. Answers on p. 231D.

22 On fait quoi ce week-end?

Phone a classmate and discuss three things you're planning to do this weekend. Don't forget to arrange the times and decide with whom you're going to do these things.

—Allô. Philippe?
—Oui, c'est moi.
—Dis, tu vas faire quoi ce week-end?
—Samedi, je vais...

23 Jeu de rôle

The friend you're phoning isn't home, so you leave a message. Take turns playing the role of the friend's parent.

Note de *Grammaire*

You've learned about **-er** verbs, like **aimer,** the largest group of regular French verbs. Other regular verbs, with infinitives ending in **-re,** follow a slightly different pattern.

répondre *(to answer)*

Je **réponds**
Tu **réponds**
Il/Elle/On **répond** } au téléphone.
Nous **répondons**
Vous **répondez**
Ils/Elles **répondent**

- **Réponds** and **répond** are pronounced alike. **Répondre** is followed by a form of **à.**
- Another regular **-re** verb you've seen is **attendre** *(to wait for).*
- The past participle of regular **-re** verbs ends in **-u:** j'ai répondu, tu as attendu.

Additional Practice

20 Have students give an appropriate response to each of the following questions: Allô? Qui est à l'appareil? Je peux parler à Nicole? Tu peux rappeler plus tard?

Presentation

Note de grammaire Bring in a toy phone and a bell. Place the phone on a student's desk and ring the bell. As the student picks up the phone, ask the class **Qu'est-ce qu'il/elle fait?** Then, put the phone on your desk and ring the bell. As you answer the phone, ask students what you are doing. (**Vous répondez au téléphone.**)

For Individual Needs

21 Slower Pace Stop the recording after each phone call to allow students time to jot down a few words to help them recall the message.

Teaching Suggestion

23 Have pairs sit back to back to simulate a phone call and to avoid giving visual clues.

CLOSE

Say some of the telephone expressions and have students tell whether you are the caller or the person receiving the call.

ASSESS

Quiz 9-2, *Chapter Teaching Resources Book 3,* pp. 25–26

Assessment Items, Audiocassette 8A/Audio CD 9

Performance Assessment

Have students act out a phone conversation between two friends who are asking about each other's weekends.

Answers

20 — Allô?
— Bonjour. Je peux parler à Nicole?
— Qui est à l'appareil?
— C'est Aurélie.
— Salut, Aurélie. Désolée, elle n'est pas là. Tu peux rappeler plus tard?
— Est-ce que je peux laisser un message?
— Bien sûr.
— Tu peux lui dire que j'ai téléphoné?
— D'accord.

Language Note

You might point out that **un coup de téléphone** or **un coup de fil** is an informal way of saying *a phone call.* One might give someone a call (**donner un coup de téléphone/un coup de fil à quelqu'un**) or get a call from someone (**recevoir un coup de téléphone/un coup de fil de quelqu'un**).

Search 18905, Play To 21180

Teacher Notes

- See *Video Guide, Videodisc Guide,* and *Practice and Activity Book* for activities related to the **Panorama Culturel.**
- Remind students that cultural material may be included in the Chapter Quizzes and Test.
- The interviewees' language represents informal, unrehearsed speech. Occasionally, edits have been made for clarification.

Motivating Activity

Before students view the video, you might have them answer questions 2 and 3 in **Qu'en penses-tu?**

Presentation

Play the video. Pause after each interview to ask **Il/Elle aime téléphoner?** Ask what else students understand from the first viewing. Then, write the **Questions** below on the board or on a transparency and have students answer them as they read the interviews in pairs.

Thinking Critically

Synthesizing Ask students how they would keep in touch with friends and family in a French home where phone calls are very expensive.

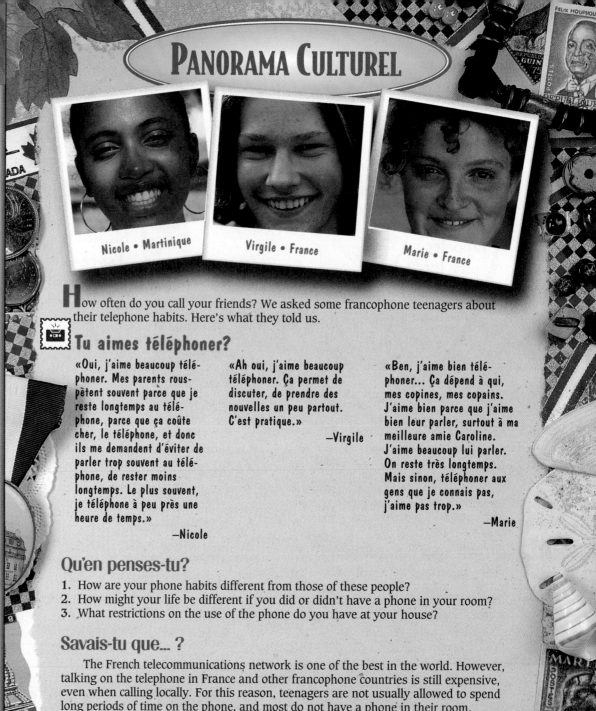

PANORAMA CULTUREL

Nicole • Martinique   Virgile • France   Marie • France

How often do you call your friends? We asked some francophone teenagers about their telephone habits. Here's what they told us.

Tu aimes téléphoner?

«Oui, j'aime beaucoup téléphoner. Mes parents rouspètent souvent parce que je reste longtemps au téléphone, parce que ça coûte cher, le téléphone, et donc ils me demandent d'éviter de parler trop souvent au téléphone, de rester moins longtemps. Le plus souvent, je téléphone à peu près une heure de temps.»

—Nicole

«Ah oui, j'aime beaucoup téléphoner. Ça permet de discuter, de prendre des nouvelles un peu partout. C'est pratique.»

—Virgile

«Ben, j'aime bien téléphoner... Ça dépend à qui, mes copines, mes copains. J'aime bien parce que j'aime bien leur parler, surtout à ma meilleure amie Caroline. J'aime beaucoup lui parler. On reste très longtemps. Mais sinon, téléphoner aux gens que je connais pas, j'aime pas trop.»

—Marie

Qu'en penses-tu?

1. How are your phone habits different from those of these people?
2. How might your life be different if you did or didn't have a phone in your room?
3. What restrictions on the use of the phone do you have at your house?

Savais-tu que... ?

The French telecommunications network is one of the best in the world. However, talking on the telephone in France and other francophone countries is still expensive, even when calling locally. For this reason, teenagers are not usually allowed to spend long periods of time on the phone, and most do not have a phone in their room.

Questions

1. Pourquoi est-ce que les parents de Nicole rouspètent? (parce qu'elle reste longtemps au téléphone)
2. Pourquoi est-ce que Virgile aime téléphoner? (Ça permet de discuter, de prendre des nouvelles. C'est pratique.)
3. A qui est-ce que Marie aime téléphoner? (à ses copines et à ses copains, à Caroline)
4. Est-ce que Marie aime téléphoner aux gens qu'elle ne connaît pas? (Non)

Thinking Critically

Drawing Inferences Have students guess what **rouspètent** means from the context of Nicole's interview *(moan, grumble, grouse).* Have students ever seen adults do this? Under what circumstances?

TROISIEME ETAPE

Sharing confidences and consoling others; asking for and giving advice

COMMENT DIT-ON... ?

Sharing confidences and consoling others; asking for and giving advice

To share a confidence:
> **J'ai un petit problème.**
> *I've got a little problem.*
>
> **Je peux te parler?**
> *Can I talk to you?*
>
> **Tu as une minute?**
> *Do you have a minute?*

To ask for advice:
> **A ton avis, qu'est-ce que je fais?**
> *In your opinion, what do I do?*
>
> **Qu'est-ce que tu me conseilles?**
> *What do you advise me to do?*

To console someone:
> **Je t'écoute.** *I'm listening.*
>
> **Qu'est-ce que je peux faire?**
> *What can I do?*
>
> **Ne t'en fais pas!** *Don't worry!*
>
> **Ça va aller mieux!**
> *It's going to get better!*

To give advice:
> **Oublie-le/-la/-les!**
> *Forget him/her/it/them!*
>
> **Téléphone-lui/-leur!**
> *Call him/her/them!*
>
> **Tu devrais lui/leur parler.**
> *You should talk to him/her/them.*
>
> **Pourquoi tu ne** téléphones **pas?**
> *Why don't you . . . ?*

Note de *Grammaire*

In the expressions above, **le, la,** and **les** are object pronouns that refer to people or things. The pronouns **lui** and **leur** only refer to people. You will learn more about these pronouns later. For now, translate them as: *him, her, them,* or *to him, to her, to them.*

> **De bons conseils**
>
> Study at regular intervals. It's best to learn language in small chunks and to review frequently. Cramming will not usually work for French. Study at least a little bit every day, whether you have an assignment or not. The more often you review words and structures, the easier it will be for you to understand and speak in class. And don't forget to talk to yourself or to a classmate in French!

24 **Ecoute!**

Are these people giving advice or asking for advice? Answers on p. 231D.

25 **Ecoute!**

Ecoute cette conversation entre Mireille et Simone. Qui a un problème? Quel est le problème? Answers on p. 231D.

TROISIEME ETAPE · *deux cent quarante-sept* **247**

RESOURCES FOR TROISIEME ETAPE

Textbook Audiocassette 5A/Audio CD 9
Practice and Activity Book, *pp. 104–106*
Videodisc Guide
  Videodisc Program, Videodisc 5A

Chapter Teaching Resources, Book 3
• Communicative Activity 9-2, pp. 5–6
• Teaching Transparency Master 9-3, pp. 9, 10
  Teaching Transparency 9-3
• Additional Listening Activities 9-5, 9-6, p. 13
  Audiocassette 10A/Audio CD 9
• Realia 9-2, pp. 16, 17
• Situation Cards 9-3, pp. 18–19
• Student Response Forms, pp. 20–22
• Quiz 9-3, pp. 27–28
  Audiocassette 8A/Audio CD 9

---

26 J'ai un petit problème

Match each of the following problems with a logical solution.

1. Mon frère ne me parle plus depuis *(for)* cinq jours.   d
2. Je veux acheter un vélo, mais je n'ai pas d'argent.   b
3. J'ai oublié mes devoirs.   c
4. Je vais rater l'interro d'anglais.   a

a. Tu devrais étudier plus souvent.
b. Pourquoi tu ne travailles pas?
c. Refais-les!
d. Parle-lui!

27 Pauvre Hervé!

Console Hervé.

Possible answers:

1. Ça va aller mieux!

2. Oublie-la!

3. Ne t'en fais pas!

28 Et à ton avis?

Your friend phones and asks to speak to you. He or she is having a lot of problems and wants to ask your advice about some of them. Console your friend and offer some advice. Then, change roles.

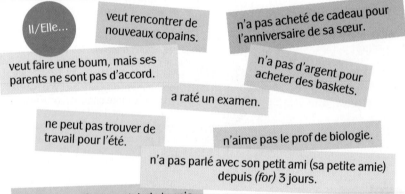

Il/Elle...

veut rencontrer de nouveaux copains.

n'a pas acheté de cadeau pour l'anniversaire de sa sœur.

veut faire une boum, mais ses parents ne sont pas d'accord.

n'a pas d'argent pour acheter des baskets.

a raté un examen.

ne peut pas trouver de travail pour l'été.

n'aime pas le prof de biologie.

n'a pas parlé avec son petit ami (sa petite amie) depuis *(for)* 3 jours.

n'a pas gagné son match de tennis.

a oublié ses devoirs.

29 Ne t'en fais pas!

Your friend asks you to listen to his or her account of a very bad day. Console your friend. Act this out with a partner. Then, change roles.

P R O N O N C I A T I O N

 ## The vowel sounds [e] and [ε]

Listen to the vowels in the word **préfère**. How are they different? The first one is pronounced [e], and the second one [ε]. To make the vowel sound [e], hold your mouth in a closed smiling position. Keep your lips and tongue steady to avoid the glide as in the English word *day*. Repeat these words.

été   désolé   occupé   répondre

Now, take a smiling position once again, but this time open your mouth wider. This will produce the vowel sound [ε]. Repeat these words.

règle   algèbre   achète   frère

In the examples, you can see that **é** represents the sound [e], while **è** represents the sound [ε] in writing. You've probably noticed that **e** with no accent and some other letter combinations can represent these sounds as well. Repeat these words.

apportez   trouver

You see that the spellings **ez** and **er** normally represent the sound [e]. This is true of all infinitives ending in **-er**. Now repeat these words.

fait	français	neige	bête
elle	cassette	examen	cherche

Some spellings of the vowel sound [ε] are **ait**, **ais**, **ei**, and **ê**. An unaccented **e** is pronounced as open [ε] when it is followed by a double consonant, such as **ll** or **tt**, when followed by **x**, and, in most cases, when followed by **r**, or by any pronounced consonant.

A. A prononcer
Repeat the following words.

1. délicieux	méchant	théâtre	vélo
2. après-midi	père	mère	très
3. février	chanter	chez	prenez
4. cette	française	treize	pêches

B. A lire
Take turns with a partner reading each of the following sentences aloud.

1. Ne quittez pas! Je vais chercher mon frère.
2. Marcel a visité Arles en mai. Il est allé au musée, à la cathédrale et aux arènes.
3. Elle n'aime pas trop l'algèbre et la géométrie, mais elle aime bien l'espagnol.
4. Tu ne peux pas aller au cinéma. Tu n'as pas fait la vaisselle.

C. A écrire
You're going to hear a short dialogue. Write down what you hear. *Answers on p. 231D.*

Teaching Suggestions

Prononciation Make sure students look over their work for accents before the dictation in Part C is corrected. Look over their sentences for common errors, and review accent and sound correlations, if necessary.

• Show *Teaching Transparency 9-3* and ask students to give the problem for each situation illustrated. Then, have volunteers role-play asking a friend or family member for advice about one of the problems.

CLOSE

To close this **étape**, copy onto a transparency some of the problems and solutions that students wrote for Group Work (Activity 26) on page 248. Have the class match the problems with the solutions.

ASSESS

Quiz 9-3, *Chapter Teaching Resources, Book 3*, pp. 27–28

Assessment Items, Audiocassette 8A/Audio CD 9

Performance Assessment

Have pairs write a phone conversation in which one person brings up a problem and the other offers consolation and advice. Have students act it out in front of the class. If last year's class videotaped their skits, you might show them to get students started on their own conversations.

Language Note

Prononciation Make sure students don't make a diphthong out of the **[e]** sound, commonly pronounced by Americans as *ay-ee*.

Teacher Note

For an additional reading, see *Practice and Activity Book,* page 107.

PREREADING
Activities A–C

Motivating Activity

Ask students if they have ever used a computerized information or library catalogue system. What kind of information was available? (titles, authors, books by subject, location of books, and so on) How is it used? What are some advantages over the card catalogue system?

Teaching Suggestion

B. Students should pick out the three main ideas of the passage from the six suggestions and match each one to the related section.

Teacher Note

Minitel is used not only to find addresses and phone numbers, but also to find employment listings, housing ads, and airport, entertainment, and weather information. Leaving messages is just one of its numerous interactive uses. Many businesses or organizations can be contacted through **Minitel**. The equipment itself is free, but calls and services have varying fees.

Teaching Suggestion

Have students look through French magazines to find ads that have 3615 and a **Minitel** code reference. Have them compile a list of the companies that offer product information through **Minitel**.

LISONS!

*H*ow will the "information superhighway" affect your life? How will you be able to use your computer and TV set in the future? As you look at the illustrations, what do you expect this reading will be about?

DE BONS CONSEILS

As you read, you use many different reading strategies at the same time. You may start by looking at illustrations, then move on to the titles and subtitles. You may need to skim the passage to get the general idea, then scan for specific details, and finally read the passage for more complete comprehension.

A. According to the illustrations, titles, and subtitles, you should be able to tell that **Minitel** is a kind of computer. It links your home computer screen and keyboard to the outside world. Using **Minitel,** you can connect to various services that allow you to shop, get entertainment information, weather reports, travel information, and so on. Do we have anything similar in the United States? See answers below.

B. Now, skim the information in the three major sections. What is the purpose of each section?

1. To explain how to disconnect Minitel
2. To explain how to hook up Minitel   Section 2
3. To introduce the reader to all of Minitel's advantages   Section 1
4. To tell how to purchase Minitel

250   *deux cent cinquante*

Minitel 2
Mode d'emploi modèle Alcatel

Présentation

Votre Minitel 2 qui appartient à la nouvelle gamme des Minitel de FRANCE TELECOM est conçu pour une utilisation tant privée que professionnelle. Bi-standard, Télétel et ASCII, compatible avec tous les autres Minitel, votre Minitel 2 est en plus :

Simple
pour obtenir un service Télétel, composez le n° d'appel directement sur le clavier de votre Minitel 2. un haut-parleur permet de suivre l'établissement de votre appel ; la présence d'un poste téléphonique associé n'est donc pas nécessaire.

Efficace
pour vous faciliter l'accès aux services fréquemment consultés, le répertoire télématique du Minitel 2 garde en mémoire jusqu'à 10 numéros d'appel avec les codes de service Télétel associés.

Sûr
le verrouillage du Minitel 2 vous protège contre les utilisations abusives ou indésirables. Détenteur du mot de passe, vous pouvez laisser libre l'utilisation des seuls services inscrits dans le répertoire ou vous réserver totalement l'utilisation de votre Minitel 2.

Disponible
à tout moment, votre Minitel 2 en état de veille est prêt à fonctionner sur votre demande ou celle d'un dispositif branché sur la prise péri-informatique (télécommande, domotique, télésurveillance, ...).

Performant
le Minitel 2 dispose de plusieurs jeux de caractères dont un téléchargeable (DRCS*) par les serveurs et qui permet des présentations graphiques précises.

*DRCS : Dynamically Redefinable Character Set (Jeu de caractères dynamiquement redéfinissable).

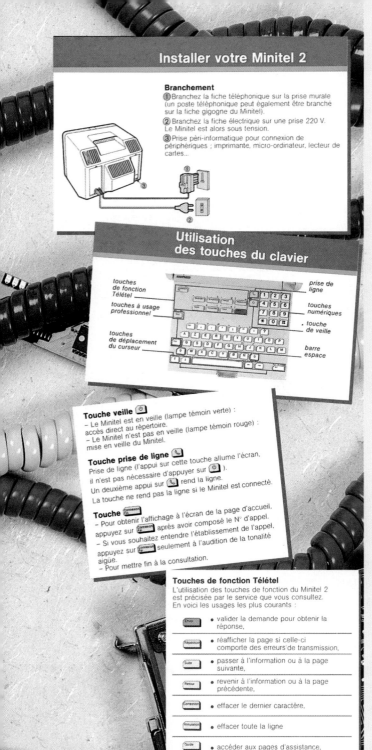

Installer votre Minitel 2

Branchement

① Branchez la fiche téléphonique sur la prise murale (un poste téléphonique peut également être branché sur la fiche gigogne du Minitel).

② Branchez la fiche électrique sur une prise 220 V. Le Minitel est alors sous tension.

③ Prise péri-informatique pour connexion de périphériques ; imprimante, micro-ordinateur, lecteur de cartes...

Utilisation des touches du clavier

touches de fonction Télétel
touches à usage professionnel
touches de déplacement du curseur
prise de ligne
touches numériques
touche de veille
barre espace

Touche veille ☺
– Le Minitel est en veille (lampe témoin verte) : accès direct au répertoire.
– Le Minitel n'est pas en veille (lampe témoin rouge) : mise en veille du Minitel.

Touche prise de ligne ☎
Prise de ligne (l'appui sur cette touche allume l'écran, il n'est pas nécessaire d'appuyer sur ☺).
Un deuxième appui sur ☎ rend la ligne.
La touche ne rend pas la ligne si le Minitel est connecté.

Touche Connexion Fin
– Pour obtenir l'affichage à l'écran de la page d'accueil, appuyez sur Connexion Fin après avoir composé le N° d'appel.
– Si vous souhaitez entendre l'établissement de l'appel, appuyez sur Connexion Fin seulement à l'audition de la tonalité aigüe.
– Pour mettre fin à la consultation.

Touches de fonction Télétel
L'utilisation des touches de fonction du Minitel 2 est précisée par le service que vous consultez.
En voici les usages les plus courants :

Envoi	• valider la demande pour obtenir la réponse,
Répétition	• réafficher la page si celle-ci comporte des erreurs de transmission,
Suite	• passer à l'information ou à la page suivante,
Retour	• revenir à l'information ou à la page précédente,
Correction	• effacer le dernier caractère,
Annulation	• effacer toute la ligne,
Guide	• accéder aux pages d'assistance,
Sommaire	• aller au début du service.

5. To explain how to use the Minitel keyboard   Section 3

6. To discourage people from using Minitel

C. Présentation

Skim the section entitled **Présentation**. Then, try to match each subtitle with its English equivalent.

d 1. **Simple**   a. *efficient*
a 2. **Efficace**   b. *always available*
c 3. **Sûr**   c. *safe*
b 4. **Disponible**   d. *easy to use*
e 5. **Performant**   e. *high performance*

D. Installer votre Minitel 2

1. What do you think **branchement** means?   hookup

2. How many steps are involved in hooking up **Minitel**?   3

E. Utilisation des touches du clavier

Match each of the following cognates with the appropriate English equivalent.

d 1. **précédante**   a. *key*
a 2. **touche**   b. *beginning screen*
f 3. **caractère**   c. *line*
e 4. **accéder**   d. *preceding*
b 5. **début**   e. *to access*
c 6. **ligne**   f. *character*

F. Which button do you press . . .

1. to get help?   guide

2. to return to the preceding page?   retour

3. to go back to the opening screen?   sommaire

4. to erase the last character that you typed?   correction

G. If **Minitel** became widely available in the United States, how would it change your life? What kinds of things would you like to be able to do through the computer?

READING
Activities D–F

Teaching Suggestions

• Have students read the documents thoroughly, individually or in pairs. Have them do Activities D through F. Encourage them to use the illustrations to help them understand unfamiliar words. Many unfamiliar words and directions should be understood if students use context clues. For example, under **Touche,** since students are familiar with the verb **appeler,** they should be able to deduce the meaning of **appel** *(call).*

• You might want to do Activities D–F orally with the whole class after all students have had a chance to read the related sections.

Terms in Lisons!

Students might want to know the following words: **écran** *(screen);* **effacer** *(to erase);* **mettre fin à** *(to end).*

POSTREADING
Activity G

Thinking Critically

Analyzing   Ask for reactions to the **Minitel** service. Ask students if they think it's useful and easy to use. Ask them how they would redesign the system to adapt it to American needs.

Computer Science Links

• Ask students if they use on-line computer services, either at school or at home. Have them describe how to access the service and the kinds of information they obtain.

• Ask students if they know of any computer-related innovations that have been made recently and if they anticipate any in the future.

MISE EN PRATIQUE

The **Mise en pratique** reviews
and integrates all four skills
and culture in preparation for
the Chapter Test.

Teaching Suggestion

1 Have students read the
statements before they listen
to the recording.

For Individual
Needs

1 Challenge Have stu-
dents correct the false statements to make them true. You
might also have them tell
whether or not they did the
activities mentioned last week-
end.

Teacher Note

3 If students have problems
with any of these questions,
tell them to read over the **Note
Culturelle** on page 244.

1 A friend has left a message on your answering machine telling you what he did
over the weekend. Listen, then decide if these sentences are true or false. *Answers on p. 231D.*

1. Martin a passé un mauvais week-end.
2. Il est allé à la plagè.
3. Il a fait beau pendant le week-end.
4. Il a joué au football samedi.
5. Il n'a pas joué au tennis.
6. Dimanche, il a fait de l'aérobic.

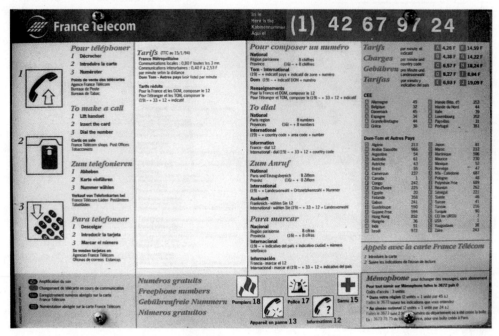

2 Answer the following questions based on the document above.

1. What kind of information is this? Where would you expect to find it? *telephone; on a public telephone*
2. What number could you call to find someone else's number in France? *12*
3. What emergency numbers are provided? *fire, police, telephone repair service, medical emergency*

3 Based on what you know about the French telephone system, tell whether the
statements below are true or false.

1. The only way to make a call from a public phone in France is to use coins. *false*
2. You can generally find a public phone at the post office. *true*
3. You can't buy phone cards at the post office. *false*
4. Card-operated phones are being replaced by coin-operated ones. *false*
5. If you make a call using a phone card, you will be charged based on the
   distance and duration of the call. *true*

252 *deux cent cinquante-deux*   CHAPITRE 9   Au téléphone

4 You're going to have a party! "Phone" your classmates and invite them to come. Be sure to tell them when and where the party will be. If you can't reach them, leave a message. Act out this scene with your group.

5 You just had the best (or worst) weekend in your life.

1. Make a list of six things that happened to you.
2. Using the list of what happened, write a note to a friend, telling about your weekend. Be sure to include details such as where you went, who was with you, in what order things happened, and so on.

6 Scan these letters first and then read them more carefully. What are they about? Who is Agnès? See answers below.

1. What is Monique's problem?
2. How does Agnès respond?
3. Who is S having difficulties with?
4. What does Agnès advise her to do?

| Chère Agnès

Agnès vous comprend. Vous pouvez lui confier tous vos problèmes. Elle trouve toujours une solution! | **Il me dit qu'il veut sortir avec moi. Est-ce vrai?**

Chère Agnès,

J'aime beaucoup un garçon, Pierre, qui me dit, dans une lettre très tendre, qu'il veut sortir avec moi. Mais il ne m'appelle jamais. Se moque-t-il de moi? Aide-moi car je suis dingue de lui!

--Monique..

Ne sois pas découragée! Tu aimes ce garçon et il t'aime également. Tu t'imagines qu'il se moque de toi, mais lui aussi doit se demander s'il a ses chances. A toi d'aller vers lui. Bonne chance! | **Toute ma famille me déteste**

Chère Agnès,

J'ai 14 ans et j'ai un problème: tout le monde dans ma famille me déteste, sauf ma mémé. Mes parents et ma sœur se moquent toujours de moi et me disent que je suis laide. Je suis très déprimée. Au secours!

--S

Ah S...! N'écoute pas ce que ta famille te dit. Et puis, il y a toujours ta mémé qui t'aime. Tu as 14 ans et tes parents ont sûrement peur de perdre leur petite fille. Parle-leur de tes sentiments et tu verras, tout ira mieux. |

7 1. Make up an imaginary problem. Describe your problem in a brief letter to Agnès, sign a fictitious name, and place your letter in a pile together with your classmates' letters.

2. Choose a letter from the pile and write a response, offering advice. Place your response together with your classmates' responses.

3. Now, find and read the response to your own letter. What do you think of the advice?

8

JEU DE ROLE

You haven't seen your friend in a while. You want to find out what he or she has been doing. Phone and ask to speak to your friend. Talk about what you both did last weekend. Find out also what your friend is planning to do next summer. Act this out with a partner.

Answers
6 1. A boy asked her out, and she doesn't know if he's serious.
2. She tells Monique not to be discouraged and to approach the boy.
3. her family
4. She tells S not to pay attention to the negative comments and to tell her family she's unhappy.

Teaching Suggestion
4 You might have one student in each group call all the others, or each group member call one or two others. It is better if students don't face each other when doing this activity.

Portfolio
5 Written This activity is appropriate for students' written portfolios.

8 Oral This activity is appropriate for students' oral portfolios. For portfolio suggestions, see *Assessment Guide,* page 22.

 Video Wrap-Up
- *VIDEO PROGRAM*
- *EXPANDED VIDEO PROGRAM,* **Videocassette 3, 31:22–43:03**
- *VIDEODISC PROGRAM,* **Videodisc 5A**

At this time, you might want to use the video resources for additional review and enrichment. See *Video Guide* or *Videodisc Guide* for suggestions regarding the following:
- **Un week-end spécial** (Dramatic episode)
- **Panorama Culturel** (Interviews)
- **Vidéoclips** (Authentic footage)

This page is intended to help students prepare for the test. It is a brief checklist of the major points covered in the chapter. The students should be reminded that this is only a checklist and does not necessarily include everything that will appear on the test.

Teacher Note

4 You might have students review other forms of the **passé composé** in addition to the **je** form as suggested in the activity.

Teaching Suggestions

- You might play the "Verb Tense Race" described on page 231F to review the verbs used in the chapter.
- You might also have students review the regular -re verbs, such as **répondre** and **attendre**.

QUE SAIS-JE?

Can you ask for and express opinions?
p. 237

Can you inquire about and relate past events?
p. 238

Can you make and answer a telephone call? p. 244

Can you share confidences, console others, and ask for and give advice? p. 247

Can you use what you've learned in this chapter?

1 How would you ask a friend how his or her weekend went?
Tu as passé un bon week-end?

2 How would you tell someone that your weekend was . . .
1. great? C'était très chouette. C'était excellent. C'était très bon.
2. OK? Ça a été. Pas mauvais.
3. horrible? C'était épouvantable. Très mauvais.

3 If you were inquiring about your friend's weekend, how would you ask . . .
1. what your friend did? Qu'est-ce que tu as fait?
2. where your friend went? Tu es allé(e) où?
3. what happened? Qu'est-ce qui s'est passé?

4 How would you tell someone that you did these things?

1. J'ai chanté.
2. J'ai gagné le match de tennis.
3. J'ai raté le bus.

5 If you were making a telephone call, how would you . . . See answers below.
1. tell who you are?
2. ask if it's the right house?
3. ask to speak to someone?
4. ask to leave a message?
5. ask someone to say you called?
6. tell someone the line's busy?

6 If you were answering a telephone call, how would you . . .
1. ask who's calling? Qui est à l'appareil?
2. ask someone to hold? Une seconde, s'il vous plaît.
3. ask someone to call back later? Vous pouvez rappeler plus tard?

7 How would you approach a friend about a problem you have?
J'ai un petit problème. Je peux te parler? Tu as une minute?

8 What would you say to console a friend?
Ne t'en fais pas! Ça va aller mieux!

9 How would you ask a friend for advice?
A ton avis, qu'est-ce que je fais? Qu'est-ce que tu me conseilles?

10 How would you tell a friend what you think he or she should do?
Tu devrais... ; Pourquoi tu ne... pas?

Answers
5 1. C'est...
2. Je suis bien chez... ?
3. (Est-ce que)... est là, s'il vous plaît? (Est-ce que) je peux parler à... ?
4. Je peux laisser un message?
5. Vous pouvez lui dire que j'ai téléphoné?
6. C'est occupé.

PREMIERE ETAPE

Asking for and expressing opinions

Tu as passé un bon week-end? *Did you have a good weekend?*
Oui, très chouette. *Yes, super.*
Oui, excellent. *Yes, excellent.*
Oui, très bon. *Yes, very good.*
Oui, ça a été. *Yes, it was OK.*
Oh, pas mauvais. *Oh, not bad.*
Très mauvais. *Very bad.*
C'était épouvantable. *It was horrible.*

Inquiring about and relating past events

Qu'est-ce qui s'est passé? *What happened?*
Nous avons parlé. *We talked.*
Qu'est-ce que tu as fait... ? *What did you do . . . ?*

D'abord,... *First, . . .*
Ensuite,... *Then, . . .*
Après, je suis sorti(e). *Afterwards, I went out.*
Enfin,... *Finally, . . .*
Et après (ça)? *And after (that)?*
Tu es allé(e) où? *Where did you go?*
Je suis allé(e)... *I went . . .*
fait (faire) *done, made*
pris (prendre) *taken*
vu (voir) *seen*
lu (lire) *read*
déjà *already*
bien *well*
mal *badly*
ne... pas encore *not yet*
acheter *to buy*
apporter *to bring*
chanter *to sing*
chercher *to look for*

commencer *to begin, to start*
déjeuner *to have lunch*
à la cantine *at the cafeteria*
dîner *to have dinner*
gagner *to win, to earn*
montrer *to show*
oublier *to forget*
rater le bus *to miss the bus*
passer un examen *to take an exam*
rater une interro *to fail a quiz*
rencontrer *to meet for the first time*
répéter *to rehearse, to practice music*
retrouver *to meet with*
travailler au fast-food *to work at a fast-food restaurant*
trouver *to find*
visiter *to visit (a place)*

DEUXIEME ETAPE

Making and answering a telephone call

Allô? *Hello?*
Je suis bien chez... ? *Is this . . . 's house?*
Qui est à l'appareil? *Who's calling?*
(Est-ce que)... est là, s'il vous plaît? *Is . . . there, please?*

Une seconde, s'il vous plaît. *One second, please.*
(Est-ce que) je peux parler à... ? *May I speak to . . . ?*
Bien sûr. *Certainly.*
Vous pouvez rappeler plus tard? *Can you call back later?*
Je peux laisser un message? *May I leave a message?*

Vous pouvez lui dire que j'ai téléphoné? *Can you tell her/him that I called?*
Ne quittez pas. *Hold on.*
Ça ne répond pas. *There's no answer.*
C'est occupé. *It's busy.*
attendre *to wait for*
répondre (à) *to answer*

TROISIEME ETAPE

Sharing confidences and consoling others

J'ai un petit problème. *I've got a little problem.*
Je peux te parler? *Can we talk?*
Tu as une minute? *Do you have a minute?*
Je t'écoute. *I'm listening.*
Qu'est-ce que je peux faire? *What can I do?*
Ne t'en fais pas! *Don't worry!*

Ça va aller mieux! *It's going to get better!*

Asking for and giving advice

A ton avis, qu'est-ce que je fais? *In your opinion, what do I do?*
Qu'est-ce que tu me conseilles? *What do you advise me to do?*
Oublie-le/-la/-les! *Forget him/her/it/them!*

Téléphone-lui/-leur! *Call him/her/them!*
Tu devrais lui/leur parler. *You should talk to him/her/them.*
Pourquoi tu ne... pas? *Why don't you . . . ?*
le *him, it*
la *her, it*
les *them*
lui *to him, to her*
leur *to them*

VOCABULAIRE   *deux cent cinquante-cinq* **255**

♜ Game

♟ RÉPONDS! For each student, write a question from one of the **Comment dit-on... ?** boxes on an index card. (**Tu as passé un bon week-end? Je peux parler à... ? Qu'est-ce que tu me conseilles?**) Have students stand in two lines facing each other. Each student reads the question on his or her card, and the student facing him or her has ten seconds to respond. At your signal, the students in each line move down one, and the person at the end moves to the front. Repeat the process until students are back in their original positions.

CHAPTER 9 ASSESSMENT

CHAPTER TEST
- *Chapter Teaching Resources, Book 3,* p. 29–34
- *Assessment Guide,* Speaking Test, p. 32
- *Assessment Items,* Audiocassette 8A Audio CD 9

TEST GENERATOR, CHAPTER 9

ALTERNATIVE ASSESSMENT

Performance Assessment
You might want to use the **Jeu de rôle** (p. 253) as a cumulative performance assessment activity.

📁 Portfolio Assessment
- **Written: Mise en pratique,** Activity 5, *Pupil's Edition,* p. 253
  Assessment Guide, p. 22
- **Oral: Mise en pratique, Jeu de rôle,** *Pupil's Edition,* p. 253
  Assessment Guide, p. 22

Chapitre 10 : Dans un magasin de vêtements
Chapter Overview

Mise en train pp. 258–260	Chacun ses goûts	Practice and Activity Book, p. 109	*Video Guide* OR *Videodisc Guide*

	FUNCTIONS	**GRAMMAR**	**CULTURE**	**RE-ENTRY**
Première étape pp. 261–264	Asking for and giving advice, p. 264	The verb **mettre**, p. 263		• The future with **aller** • Sequencing adverbs • Colors
Deuxième étape pp. 265–269	Expressing need; inquiring, p. 265	• Adjectives used as nouns, p. 265 • The **-ir** verbs: **choisir**, p. 267	• Realia: Clothing ad from **Trois Suisses**, p. 266 • Realia: French size chart, p. 267 • **Note Culturelle**, Clothing sizes, p. 267 • **Panorama Culturel**, Fashion in francophone countries, p. 269	Likes and dislikes
Troisième étape pp. 270–275	• Asking for an opinion; paying a compliment; criticizing, p. 270 • Hesitating; making a decision, p. 274	• The direct object pronouns **le**, **la**, and **les**, p. 273 • **c'est** versus **il/elle est**, p. 274	**Rencontre Culturelle**, Responding to compliments, p. 272	

Prononciation p. 275	The glides [j], [w], and [ɥ]	**Dictation:** *Textbook Audiocassette 5B/Audio CD 10*

Lisons! pp. 276–277	La mode au lycée	**Reading Strategy:** Distinguishing fact from opinion

Review pp. 278–281	**Mise en pratique**, pp. 278–279	**Que sais-je?** p. 280	**Vocabulaire**, p. 281

Assessment Options	**Etape Quizzes**
	 • *Chapter Teaching Resources, Book 3*
	   Première étape, Quiz 10-1, pp. 79–80
	   Deuxième étape, Quiz 10-2, pp. 81–82
	   Troisième étape, Quiz 10-3, pp. 83–84
	 • *Assessment Items, Audiocassette 8B/Audio CD 10*
		Chapter Test
		 • *Chapter Teaching Resources, Book 3*, pp. 85–90
		 • *Assessment Guide*, Speaking Test, p. 32
		 • *Assessment Items, Audiocassette 8B/Audio CD 10*
		
		 Test Generator, Chapter 10

Video Program OR *Expanded Video Program, Videocassette 4*
OR *Videodisc Program, Videodisc 5B*

Textbook Audiocassette 5B/Audio CD 10

RESOURCES: Print	**RESOURCES: Audiovisual**

Textbook Audiocassette 5B/Audio CD 10

Practice and Activity Book, pp. 110–112
Chapter Teaching Resources, Book 3
• Teaching Transparency Master 10-1, pp. 63, 66 . . . . *Teaching Transparency 10-1*
• Additional Listening Activities 10-1, 10-2, p. 67 . . . . *Additional Listening Activities, Audiocassette 10B/Audio CD 10*
• Realia 10-1, pp. 71, 73
• Situation Cards 10-1, pp. 74–75
• Student Response Forms, pp. 76–78
• Quiz 10-1, pp. 79–80 . . . . *Assessment Items, Audiocassette 8B/Audio CD 10*
Videodisc Guide. . . . . *Videodisc Program, Videodisc 5B*

Textbook Audiocassette 5B/Audio CD 10

Practice and Activity Book, pp. 113–115
Chapter Teaching Resources, Book 3
• Communicative Activity 10-1, pp. 59–60
• Teaching Transparency Master 10-2, pp. 64, 66 . . . . *Teaching Transparency 10-2*
• Additional Listening Activities 10-3, 10-4, p. 68 . . . . *Additional Listening Activities, Audiocassette 10B/Audio CD 10*
• Realia 10-2, pp. 72, 73
• Situation Cards 10-2, pp. 74–75
• Student Response Forms, pp. 76–78
• Quiz 10-2, pp. 81–82 . . . . *Assessment Items, Audiocassette 8B/Audio CD 10*
Video Guide. . . . . *Video Program* OR *Expanded Video Program, Videocassette 4*
Videodisc Guide. . . . . *Videodisc Program, Videodisc 5B*

Textbook Audiocassette 5B/Audio CD 10

Practice and Activity Book, pp. 116–118
Chapter Teaching Resources, Book 3
• Communicative Activity 10-2, pp. 61–62
• Teaching Transparency Master 10-3, pp. 65, 66 . . . . *Teaching Transparency 10-3*
• Additional Listening Activities 10-5, 10-6, p. 69 . . . . *Additional Listening Activities, Audiocassette 10B/Audio CD 10*
• Realia 10-2, pp. 72, 73
• Situation Cards 10-3, pp. 74–75
• Student Response Forms, pp. 76–78
• Quiz 10-3, pp. 83–84 . . . . *Assessment Items, Audiocassette 8B/Audio CD 10*
Videodisc Guide. . . . . *Videodisc Program, Videodisc 5B*

Practice and Activity Book, p. 119

Video Guide. . . . . *Video Program* OR *Expanded Video Program, Videocassette 4*
Videodisc Guide. . . . . *Videodisc Program, Videodisc 5B*

Alternative Assessment
• Performance Assessment
  Première étape, p. 264
  Deuxième étape, p. 268
  Troisième étape, p. 275
• Portfolio Assessment
  Written: **Mise en pratique,** Activity 3, *Pupil's Edition,* p. 278
    Assessment Guide, p. 23
  Oral: **Mise en pratique, Jeu de rôle,** *Pupil's Edition,* p. 279
    Assessment Guide, p. 23

For Student Response Forms, see *Chapter Teaching Resources, Book 3,* pp. 76–78.

Première étape

7 Ecoute! p. 262

ARMELLE J'ai acheté des tas de vêtements pour la rentrée. J'ai trouvé une jupe orange en coton avec la ceinture qui va avec. Elle est super, tu vas voir. Je vais la mettre demain. J'ai aussi acheté un chemisier noir avec le cardigan assorti. Très chic.

AMIE Tu n'as pas acheté de chaussures cette fois-ci? C'est ton habitude.

ARMELLE Non, il me faut des chaussures, mais c'était trop cher. Mais j'ai acheté des chaussettes en solde et aussi une paire de boucles d'oreilles pour l'anniversaire de ma sœur.

Answer to Activity 7
c

13 Ecoute! p. 264

1. — Je vais au cinéma avec Chantal ce soir. Dis, Pierre, qu'est-ce que je mets?

2. — Si tu veux être chic, Dianne, pourquoi tu ne mets pas ta nouvelle robe?

3. — Mais non! Il ne faut pas mettre ton jean! Pourquoi est-ce que tu ne mets pas un pantalon?

4. — Je ne sais pas quoi mettre pour aller à la boum. J'aimerais quelque chose de joli.

5. — Tu vas avoir trop chaud, Luc. Mets un short et des sandales!

Answers to Activity 13
1. asking   4. asking
2. giving   5. giving
3. giving

Deuxième étape

17 Ecoute! p. 265

1. — Je cherche un maillot de bain.

2. — Vous avez ça en quarante?

3. — Je peux vous aider?

4. — J'aimerais des chaussures pour aller avec ma robe.

5. — Non, mais nous l'avons en bleu.

6. — Je peux l'essayer?

7. — Vous avez choisi?

Answers to Activity 17
1. customer   5. salesperson
2. customer   6. customer
3. salesperson   7. salesperson
4. customer

18 Ecoute! p. 266

1. — Vous avez ça en quarante-quatre?

2. — Il me faut des chaussettes noires.

3. — Ça coûte cent vingt francs.

4. — Je peux essayer la jupe blanche?

5. — Le blouson en cuir, c'est huit cent quatre-vingt-quinze francs.

6. — Vous l'avez en trente-huit?

Answers to Activity 18
1. size   3. price   5. price
2. color   4. color   6. size

Troisième étape

26 Ecoute! p. 271

1. — Dis, comment tu trouves ma jupe?
   — Euh, je la trouve un peu démodée.

2. — Elle est super chic, ta robe!
   — Tu trouves?

3. — Dis, Nicole, tu sais, ces chaussures, elles ne vont pas du tout avec ta jupe!
   — Ah oui? C'est vrai?

4. — Il n'est pas trop serré, ce chemisier?
   — Euh, si, je le trouve un peu serré.

5. — Il est sensas, ton pantalon!
   — Tu crois?
   — Oui, il te va très bien!

6. — Elle me va, cette robe?
   — C'est tout à fait ton style!

7. — Elle te plaît, ma veste? Elle n'est pas trop courte?
   — Non. Je la trouve très branchée.

Answers to Activity 26

1. criticizing	5. complimenting
2. complimenting	6. complimenting
3. criticizing	7. complimenting
4. criticizing	

31 Ecoute! p. 274

1. VENDEUR Ce manteau vous va très bien, monsieur. Vous le prenez?
   CLIENT Il me plaît, mais il est beaucoup trop cher.

2. VENDEUR Alors, vous avez décidé de prendre cette casquette, monsieur?
   CLIENT Elle est super. Je la prends.

3. VENDEUR Et ces baskets? Vous les prenez?
   CLIENT Euh, j'hésite. Elles sont sensas, mais pas vraiment mon genre.

4. VENDEUR Très bien, monsieur. Et vous avez décidé pour ces bottes?
   CLIENT Pourquoi pas? Je les prends aussi.

5. VENDEUR Et cette chemise, vous la prenez, monsieur?
   CLIENT Je ne sais pas. J'aime la couleur, mais elle est chère.

6. VENDEUR C'est tout à fait votre style, ce blouson. Vous le prenez?
   CLIENT Euh, je ne sais pas. Il est un peu trop court.

Answers to Activity 31

1. doesn't take	4. takes
2. takes	5. can't decide
3. can't decide	6. can't decide

Prononciation, p. 275

For the scripts for Parts A and B, see p. 275.

C. A écrire

(Dictation)
— Je cherche un maillot de bain.
— Voilà.
— Je peux l'essayer?
— Oui, bien sûr.

Mise en pratique

1 p. 278

VENDEUSE Bonjour. Je peux vous aider?

PHILIPPE Oui, euh... je voudrais une chemise.

VENDEUSE Quel genre de chemise cherchez-vous?

PHILIPPE Bof, je ne sais pas. Quelque chose de cool, de branché. Une chemise bleue ou kaki, à carreaux peut-être.

VENDEUSE Et bien, nous avons des chemises américaines, style western. Ça vous intéresse?

PHILIPPE Ouais, ...

VENDEUSE Les voilà. Comment les trouvez-vous?

PHILIPPE Pas mal. Ouais, j'aime bien celle-ci.

VENDEUSE Vous faites quelle taille?

PHILIPPE Euh... je ne sais pas... Vous l'avez en trente-sept/trente-huit?

VENDEUSE Voici.

PHILIPPE Je peux l'essayer?

VENDEUSE Bien sûr.

Plus Tard

VENDEUSE Elle vous va très bien. C'est tout à fait votre style! Et c'est tellement à la mode!

PHILIPPE Mais moi, je la trouve un peu serrée. Vous avez ça en trente-neuf/quarante?

VENDEUSE Oui, en trente-neuf/quarante, mais en rouge.

PHILIPPE Euh... j'hésite. J'aime pas trop la rouge, j'aime mieux la bleue. Bon, alors. Ça va. C'est combien?

VENDEUSE Deux cent quarante-neuf francs.

PHILIPPE Ah? Deux cent quarante-neuf francs! Je regrette, c'est trop cher. Je ne la prends pas.

Answers to Mise en pratique Activity 1
1. a shirt
2. blue and khaki
3. The shirt suits him, it's his style, and it's in fashion.
4. It's a little tight.
5. No.

Un défilé de mode
(Group Project)

ASSIGNMENT

This project may be oral or written. Students will organize a fashion show. They may actually model clothes on a runway, accompanied by an oral commentary, or draw their designs and provide a written description on a poster.

MATERIALS

✂ Students may need

- Clothing or fabric
- Posterboard
- Colored pencils or markers
- Fashion magazines
- French-English dictionaries

SUGGESTED SEQUENCE

1. Have students form groups of three or four. Have each group decide on the general style of their fashion line: grunge, evening wear, retro, modern, and so on. They should also choose the colors and patterns they would like to feature.

2. Have students look through fashion magazines for ideas. If they plan to do a runway show, they might also list their favorite clothing items from their own closets.

3. Have students sketch or collect the items for their show. Have them write out complete descriptions of each item. They might consult a dictionary for French words to describe the fashions. Remind students that their goal is to sell the clothes, so their commentaries should include when and where they can be worn as well as a description of the overall look.

4. Have students organize their projects and decide in what order to present the items or plan the layout of their poster. Have them exchange their written descriptions with peers for editing.

5. Have students recopy or type their descriptions and finalize their visuals if they are doing a written project.

If they are making a poster, they might attach samples of fabric or jewelry to add texture to their illustrations. If they are doing a runway presentation, have them present the fashions to the class as a narrator from the group reads the description of each item. Have them change narrators after every few items.

GRADING THE PROJECT

You might want to base students' grades on completion of the assignment, creativity, accuracy of language use, and presentation.

Suggested Point Distribution (total = 100 points)

Completion of assignment	20 points
Creativity	30 points
Language use	20 points
Presentation	30 points

DESSINEZ-MOI!

In this game, students will review clothing vocabulary.

Describe an outfit to students (see examples below) and have them draw the outfit on a piece of paper as they listen to you. Say each item of clothing only once. After the outfit is complete, have students hold up their drawings and award a point for each correct one, or you might have volunteers draw their version of the outfit on the board. The outfits might be serious, humorous, or even bizarre.

Examples of outfits:

1. **un maillot de bain, un chapeau, un manteau large, une ceinture trop serrée, des bottes moches, des lunettes de soleil**

2. **un sweat-shirt court, des baskets trop grandes, une écharpe, un jean, des boucles d'oreilles longues, un cardigan large**

3. **un pantalon court, une chemise, une petite cravate, une casquette, de grandes chaussettes**

Variation Give students pieces of paper and crayons or transparencies and colored markers and have them draw colored illustrations as you describe them.

MEMOIRE

This game will test students' recognition of clothing vocabulary.

This game is played like Concentration®. First, assign sections of the **Vocabulaire** on page 281 to groups of students. Have them create two cards for each item: one with the French word or expression on it, and the other with an illustration of the item. Collect the cards, mix them thoroughly, and number them consecutively on the back. Tape them to the board or wall in numerical order so that only the numbers show. Then, have players ask to see two cards by saying the numbers in French **(trois, douze)**. Turn over the two cards. If they match, the player wins a point, keeps the cards, and the next player takes a turn. Continue until all students have had a chance to guess or until all cards have been matched. You might want to give out small prizes to the students who get the most points.

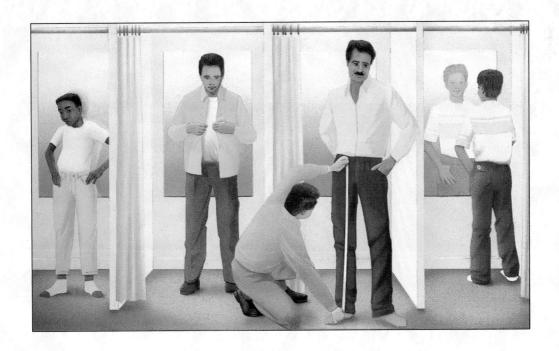

Chapitre 10
Dans un magasin de vêtements

pp. 256–281

*U*sing the Chapter Opener

Motivating Activity

Ask students how they would rate the importance of clothing in their lives on a scale of 1 to 10, with 10 being the most important. Have them explain their ratings. Ask what they consider more important than clothing.

Teaching Suggestions

• Have students read the caption for each photo and ask them to pick out words or phrases they already know. Have them use context and the photos to guess the meaning of the other words. After matching the outcomes with the photos, ask students to infer how the outcomes are portrayed in the photos.

• Assign photos to pairs of students. Have them write speech bubbles for the people in their photo. Then, collect the speech bubbles, read them aloud, and have the class guess which photo they accompany.

Photo Flash!

① This photo shows a girl shopping for an outfit to wear to a party. Point out that **faire les boutiques** or **faire les magasins** refers to *shopping,* while **faire les vitrines** or **faire du lèche-vitrines** refers to *window shopping,* or shopping without the intent to buy.

CHAPITRE

10
Dans un magasin de vêtements

① Je ne sais pas quoi mettre pour aller à la boum.

It's not easy to decide what to wear on a special occasion. It's often a welcome excuse to buy something new. But what? It depends on the statement you want to make. Chic? Casual? How do you create just the right look?

In this chapter you will learn

- to ask for and give advice
- to express need; to inquire
- to ask for an opinion; to pay a compliment; to criticize; to hesitate; to make a decision

And you will

- listen to French-speaking students talk about what they like to wear on different occasions
- read about the clothing styles French-speaking teenagers like
- write about what you wear on different occasions
- find out how francophone teenagers feel about fashion

② J'aimerais un foulard pour aller avec cette jupe.

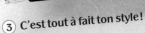

③ C'est tout à fait ton style!

x

deux cent cinquante-sept 257

Focusing on Outcomes

Ask students to tell how the outcomes could be used to discuss clothing. Then, have them suggest other situations where these outcomes could be used and how (when buying school supplies or gifts, when discussing new hairstyles). NOTE: You may want to use the video to support the objectives. The self-check activities in **Que sais-je?** on page 280 help students assess their achievement of the objectives.

Teaching Suggestion

Have students read the introductory paragraph on this page. Ask if they agree that clothing makes a statement. Find out what clothing styles students like.

Building on Previous Skills

② Ask students which colors Hélène prefers, judging from the skirt she's considering buying. Have them describe the colors in their favorite outfit.

For Individual Needs

Kinesthetic Learners Write the number 1, 2, or 3 on several cards and have each student choose a card. Students should mime the action in the photo with the corresponding number, and the class should guess which photo is being portrayed.

Family Link

Ask students to interview their family members about what they like to wear and why. Have students report their results to the class and give possible explanations for the different preferences. Students can provide results for a famous or imaginary family if they prefer.

VIDEO PROGRAM
OR EXPANDED VIDEO
PROGRAM,
Videocassette 4
01:22–06:35

OR VIDEODISC PROGRAM,
Videodisc 5B

Search 1, Play To 9405

Video Synopsis

In this segment of the video, Magali and Hélène discuss what they are going to wear to Sophie's birthday party. Later, we see Sophie leaving a clothes boutique. Magali enters the same boutique. Inside, she is helped by a saleswoman and tries on several items. When Magali finally finds something she likes, she discovers that it costs 670 F! She is reluctant to spend that much money and doesn't know what to do.

Motivating Activity

Ask students to suggest expressions that salespeople in a clothing store might say to customers. Ask students what their favorite stores are and what they wear to parties or to go out with friends.

Presentation

After viewing the video, play the recording and have students follow along in their books. Stop the recording to ask the questions in Activity 1 on page 260 to check students' comprehension: after the first scene, question 1; after the second, question 2; after the third, question 3; after the ninth, question 4; and after the tenth, question 5.

Mise en train

Chacun ses goûts

What event are Hélène and Magali discussing at the beginning of the story? Where does Magali go? Why do you think Hélène doesn't go with her?

258 *deux cent cinquante-huit*   CHAPITRE 10 Dans un magasin de vêtements

RESOURCES FOR MISE EN TRAIN

Textbook Audiocassette 5B/Audio CD 10
Practice and Activity Book, p. 109
Video Guide
   Video Program
   Expanded Video Program, Videocassette 4
Videodisc Guide
   Videodisc Program, Videodisc 5B

Language Note

The expression **Chacun ses goûts** is the French equivalent of *To each his own.*

Nous avons des jupes, si vous voulez. Tenez, celle-ci fait jeune. Comment la trouvez-vous?

Elle est jolie, n'est-ce pas? Nous l'avons en bleu, en rouge et en vert. La voilà en 38.

J'aime bien cette jupe-ci. Est-ce que vous l'avez en vert?

Magali essaie la jupe...

Très joli. Ça vous va très bien.

Oui, c'est pas mal, mais elle est un peu large, non? Est-ce que vous l'avez en 36?

Bof. C'est pas tellement mon style.

Quelques minutes plus tard...

Ah, très chic! C'est tout à fait votre style.

Nous avons ces chemisiers, si vous aimez. Taille unique. Ça va très bien avec la jupe.

Vous trouvez? Mais, je ne sais pas quoi mettre avec.

Ça fait combien, l'ensemble?

Il est en solde. La jupe fait 400 F et le chemisier 270. Ça vous fait 670 F.

670 F!!! C'est cher!

Vous savez, mademoiselle, l'originalité n'a pas de prix.

MISE EN TRAIN

deux cent cinquante-neuf 259

Thinking Critically

Analyzing Have students discuss the questions that Magali asks at the clothing store. Ask students if they ask the same questions and if there are other things to consider when buying clothes. Ask them whether they agree with the saleswoman that it's worth any price to look original.

For Individual Needs

Auditory Learners Describe each photo aloud in random order. For example, for Photo 5, you might say **Magali trouve une jupe, mais ce n'est pas son style.** Have students call out the number of the photo you're describing.

Culture Note

The outfit that Magali tries on is made of **provençal** fabric. These prints are characterized by one or more distinctive **provençal** motifs, which are recognizable by their floral designs, medallions, or paisleys.

📺 Video Integration

- **Expanded Video Program,** *Videocassette 3, 06:36–10:47*
- **Videodisc Program,** *Videodisc 5B*

Search 9405, Play To 16950

You may choose to continue with **Chacun ses goûts (suite)** at this time or wait until later in the chapter. When the story continues, Hélène enters the clothing boutique and sees Magali. Magali asks her about the outfit she has on, and Hélène compliments her on it. Magali is unsure and still can't figure out what to do. Later, at Sophie's, everything is ready for the party. Malika arrives, and then Ahmed, Charles, and Florent. When Magali arrives, she and Sophie discover they've bought the same shirt! Magali is upset at first, but then smiles. Florent takes a photo of Magali and Sophie.

For Individual Needs

2 Slower Pace/Visual Learners If students have problems with this, show the video, stopping it when you come to each of these quotes, and have students identify the speaker.

For videodisc application, see *Videodisc Guide*.

Teaching Suggestion

3 Form three groups and assign each group one of these tasks.

Group Work

5 Have students work together in small groups to do this activity. Set a time limit and have each member of the group turn in a copy of the group's findings.

Teaching Suggestions

5 Ask students what else they might say or ask at a clothing store.

6 This activity might be done orally as a class or in pairs. You might also have students write down their answers.

1 Tu as compris?

1. Why does Magali want to buy something new?   She is going to a birthday party.
2. What is Hélène going to wear? Why?   jeans and a T-shirt; They are simple and comfortable.
3. What type of clothing is Magali looking for?   something original and not too expensive
4. What outfit does Magali like?   a green skirt and a shirt
5. What does she think of the price?   She thinks it is expensive.

2 C'est qui?

Qui parle? C'est Magali, Hélène ou la vendeuse?

1. «J'aimerais quelque chose d'original et pas trop cher.»   Magali
2. «Je peux vous aider?»   la vendeuse
3. «Moi, j'aime bien être en jean et en tee-shirt. C'est simple et agréable à porter.»   Hélène
4. «Qu'est-ce que vous faites comme taille?»   la vendeuse
5. «Chacun ses goûts.»   Hélène
6. «Est-ce que vous l'avez en vert?»   Magali
7. «C'est tout à fait votre style.»   la vendeuse
8. «Ce n'est pas tellement mon style.»   Magali

3 Chacun ses goûts

What does Magali say about these things?

1. le jean et le tee-shirt d'Hélène   Pourquoi est-ce que tu ne trouves pas quelque chose d'original? De mignon?
2. la jupe verte en 38   C'est pas mal, mais elle est un peu large.
3. le prix de l'ensemble   C'est cher.

4 Qu'est-ce qu'elle répond?

Qu'est-ce que Magali répond à la vendeuse?

1. Qu'est-ce que vous faites comme taille?   b
2. Comment la trouvez-vous?   d
3. Je peux vous aider?   c
4. Ça vous fait 670 francs.   a

a. C'est cher!
b. Je fais du 38.
c. Je cherche quelque chose pour aller à une fête.
d. Bof. Ce n'est pas tellement mon style.

5 Cherche les expressions

Look back at **Chacun ses goûts** to find how you would . . .

1. express indecision.   Je ne sais pas quoi mettre.
2. express satisfaction with your clothes.   J'aime bien (être en)... ; C'est simple et agréable à porter.
3. tell a salesperson what you want.   Je cherche quelque chose pour... ; J'aimerais quelque chose de...
4. tell what size you wear.   Je fais du... (38).
5. express dissatisfaction with clothes.   Bof. C'est pas tellement mon style. Elle est un peu large.
6. ask for a certain color or size.   Est-ce que vous l'avez en... (vert/36)?
7. ask what all of your purchases cost.   Ça fait combien, l'ensemble?

6 Et maintenant, à toi

Do you prefer Magali's style or Hélène's? What sort of clothes do you like to wear?

260   *deux cent soixante*   CHAPITRE 10   Dans un magasin de vêtements

PREMIERE ETAPE

Asking for and giving advice

Vocabulaire

La mode décontractée

blouson noir **1290 F**

chaussettes noires, blanches, pêche ou bleues **9,90 F** la paire

chaussures noires **279 F**

chemise bleue ou blanche **69 F**

chemisier blanc **89 F**

maillot de bain bleu, rouge et vert **99 F**

Le style chic

bottes noires 399 F

manteau bleu ou noir 845 F

jupe grise 299 F

robe noire à fleurs 349 F

veste bleue 690 F

PRINTEMPS

Les accessoires

écharpe blanche ou noire 99,50 F

casquette blanche 159 F

cravate bleue 79 F

chapeau noir 249 F

ceinture noire ou marron 99,50 F

boucles d'oreilles 249 F

montre noire 259 F

lunettes de soleil 59,50 F

Here are some other words you may want to use to talk about what you're wearing.

des baskets (f.)	un jean	des sandales (f.)
un bracelet	un pantalon	un short
un cardigan	un pull (-over)	un sweat-shirt

PREMIERE ETAPE   *deux cent soixante et un*   **261**

RESOURCES FOR PREMIERE ETAPE

Textbook Audiocassette 5B/Audio CD 10
Practice and Activity Book, pp. 110–112
Videodisc Guide
   Videodisc Program, Videodisc 5B

Chapter Teaching Resources, Book 3
• Teaching Transparency Master 10-1, pp. 63, 66
   Teaching Transparency 10-1
• Additional Listening Activities 10-1, 10-2, p. 67
   Audiocassette 10B/Audio CD 10
• Realia 10-1, pp. 71, 73
• Situation Cards 10-1, pp. 74–75
• Student Response Forms, pp. 76–78
• Quiz 10-1, pp. 79–80
   Audiocassette 8B/Audio CD 10

---

*J*ump Start!

Have students list three colors they're wearing today.

MOTIVATE

Ask students if they shop alone or with family or friends, whether they pay for or make their own clothes, if they hunt for bargains or for a certain brand, and whether they ask for advice from friends when buying clothes.

TEACH

Presentation

Vocabulaire Present the vocabulary with real clothing items or magazine pictures. Then, ask individuals how much various items in the ads cost. **(Combien coûte la montre noire?)** Next, point to various items of clothing that students are wearing, asking **Qu'est-ce que c'est?** You might also hold up an item or illustration and ask students what other item(s) of clothing they would suggest to go with it.

Thinking Critically

Drawing Inferences Ask students what **la mode décontractée, le style chic,** and **les accessoires** mean, judging from the items listed under each *(casual style, chic,* and *accessories).*

For Individual Needs

Visual/Kinesthetic Learners With a permanent marker, draw stick figures on a transparency. Copy the items from the **Vocabulaire** onto cards and distribute them to students. Then, call on students to draw their clothing item on one of the figures on the transparency.

For Individual Needs

7 Slower Pace Before playing the recording, have students identify the items in the illustrations. Have them point out the similarities and differences among the three groups. You might want to play the recording twice.

Building on Previous Skills

8 Before students begin, you might re-enter family vocabulary from Chapter 7 by showing a transparency of a family tree or referring to the one on page 180. Ask questions about the members. **(Raymond est le père ou la mère d'Isabelle?)** Have students recall the use of **son, sa,** and **ses** as well. This activity might also be written.

9 Have students include colors for the clothing on their lists. They might want to use the phrase **en or** *(gold)*.

Reteaching

Adjective agreement Ask students what is added to most adjectives to form the feminine and the plural. Then, remind them that the last consonant may be doubled before the **-e** is added: **violet(te)**, or that the feminine form may be irregular: **blanc(blanche).** Show various clothing articles and have students describe them, including colors. You might also have students write the descriptions on the board to check adjective agreement.

Teaching Suggestion

10 Have students write out this activity. They might use this list as a point of departure for Activity 33 on page 274.

---

7 Ecoute!

Listen as Armelle tells her friend about her big shopping trip. Then, choose the illustration that represents her purchases. c

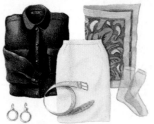

a.   b.   c.

8 Des cadeaux

Look at the picture and tell what Lise bought for her family. See answers below.

Elle a acheté... pour...

9 Pas de chance!

On your way to France, the airline lost your luggage. Fortunately, the airline is paying you $500 for new clothes. Make a list of the clothes you'll buy.

—D'abord, je vais acheter...

10 La fête

Imagine that you've been invited to a party. Of the clothes you listed in Activity 9, which would you choose to wear? What clothes would you need that aren't on your list?

262   *deux cent soixante-deux*   CHAPITRE 10   Dans un magasin de vêtements

---

Language Note

Another term for **un cardigan** is **un gilet.** A sweatsuit is called **un jogging.**

Culture Note

Teenagers and adults in France and Canada don't often wear shorts. In Martinique's warm climate, however, shorts are popular.

Answers

8 Lise a acheté une cravate pour son père, des boucles d'oreilles pour sa mère, une casquette pour son frère, des chaussettes pour sa sœur, un bracelet pour sa grand-mère et une écharpe pour son grand-père.

Grammaire The verbs mettre and porter

mettre *(to put, to put on, to wear)*

Je **mets**	Nous **mettons**
Tu **mets** } un pull.	Vous **mettez** } un pull.
Il/Elle/On **met**	Ils/Elles **mettent**

- **Mets** and **met** are pronounced alike. You don't pronounce the final consonant(s) **ts** and **t**.
- The past participle of **mettre** is **mis**: Elle **a mis** une jupe.
- You can also use the regular verb **porter** to tell what someone is wearing: Elle **porte** une robe.

11 Qu'est-ce qu'on met?

Ces gens vont sortir. Qu'est-ce qu'ils mettent?

1. Elle met une jupe, une ceinture et un pull.

2. Elles mettent une robe et des chaussures.

3. Il met un blouson.

4. Ils mettent des baskets.

12 Qu'est-ce que tu as mis hier?

Ask your partner what he or she wore yesterday and tell what you wore.

> **De bons conseils**
> Although it's common to feel a little uncomfortable when speaking a new language, the best way to overcome it is to talk and talk and talk. Whenever you answer a question or have a conversation with a partner, try to keep the conversation going as long as possible. Don't worry about making a mistake. The more you think about making mistakes, the less likely you will be to talk.

Language Note

Porter also means *to wear,* but most people prefer to use **mettre** *(to put on, to wear)* in everyday conversation. Caution your students, however, that **mettre** cannot be used to tell what someone is wearing now. **Elle met une jupe** means either *She is putting on a dress,* or *She is going to wear a dress (tonight).* To say that someone is wearing a dress now, **porter** must be used. (**Elle porte une robe aujourd'hui.**)

Teacher Note

De bons conseils Encourage students to speak French by telling them that native French speakers, just like English speakers, often make errors when they speak. Also, point out that when students speak to their friends in English, they probably concentrate on the message rather than on saying every word correctly.

Presentation

Grammaire Write the forms of **mettre** on large flashcards and mix them. Write the subject pronouns on the board. Show the cards to students and have them deduce which verb form goes with each pronoun and say each form as you tape the cards to the board. Then, bring in magazine photos of boys and girls and ask students **Qu'est-ce qu'il/elle met pour la boum ce soir?** You might also tell students there's a party tonight and ask them what they're going to wear. (**Qu'est-ce que tu mets pour la boum ce soir?**)

Additional Practice

Grammaire Describe what a student is wearing, asking the class **Qui a mis des baskets, un jean et un tee-shirt rouge aujourd'hui?** The first person to call out the correct student's name asks the next question. You might also show *Teaching Transparency 10-1* and ask students **Qu'est-ce qu'elles mettent?**

For Individual Needs

11 Auditory Learners As a variation for listening practice, tell what the people in the pictures are putting on. (**Elle met une jupe.**) Have students write the number of the appropriate illustration.

12 Kinesthetic/Visual Learners As one partner describes a classmate's outfit, the other one draws it, writing in the colors. The first student then checks the drawing for accuracy.

Teaching Suggestion

12 You might suggest that students imagine an original outfit to describe.

CHAPITRE 10

Presentation

Comment dit-on... ? Ask individuals for advice on what to wear to a party (**à une boum**), to school (**à l'école**), and to a restaurant (**au restaurant**). Write prompts for their responses on the board. Then, have them ask you for advice. Finally, have partners ask for and give advice on what to wear for these occasions.

For videodisc application, see *Videodisc Guide*.

Language Note

Remind students that the **tu** form of **mettre** retains the final **-s** in the command form since it is not an **-er** verb.

For Individual Needs

14 Visual Learners

Assign a clothing item to each student. Have them draw and color a picture of it on one side of an index card and write the French word on the other. Distribute the cards to partners and have them ask for and give advice about what to wear with the item.

Mon journal

16 For an additional journal entry suggestion for Chapter 10, see *Practice and Activity Book,* page 154.

CLOSE

To close this **étape**, list various places on the board (**à l'école, à un mariage**). Have one student ask a second student **Qu'est-ce que je mets pour... ?** The second student gives advice, and then asks a third student what to wear for another occasion. Continue until all students have asked a question.

COMMENT DIT-ON... ?
Asking for and giving advice

To ask for advice:

Je ne sais pas quoi mettre pour aller à la boum. *I don't know what to wear for (to) . . .*

Qu'est-ce que je mets? *What shall I wear?*

To give advice:

Pourquoi est-ce que tu ne mets pas ta robe? *Why don't you wear . . . ?*

Mets ton jean. *Wear . . .*

13 Ecoute!

Are these people asking for or giving advice? Answers on p. 255C.

14 Harmonie de couleurs

Ask your partner's advice on what you should wear with the following items. Take turns.

—Qu'est-ce que je mets avec ma jupe noire?
—Pourquoi tu ne mets pas ton pull gris?

1. Avec mon pantalon bleu?
2. Avec ma chemise rouge?
3. Avec mes baskets violettes?
4. Avec mon pull gris?
5. Avec mon short orange?

15 Qu'est-ce que je mets?

Tell your partner where you'll go and what you'll do during your stay as an exchange student in France. Ask for advice about what you should wear. Then, change roles.

—Je vais aller au café. Qu'est-ce que je mets?
—Pour aller au café? Mets un jean et un sweat-shirt.

pour aller à une boum

pour aller au café

pour aller à la plage

pour dîner dans un restaurant élégant

pour jouer au football

pour aller au parc

pour aller au théâtre

pour faire du patin à glace

pour aller au musée

pour faire du ski

16 Mon journal

Write about what you normally wear to school, to parties, to go out with friends, or what you wear to dress up for a special occasion.

ASSESS

Quiz 10-1, *Chapter Teaching Resources, Book 3,* pp. 79–80

Assessment Items, Audiocassette 8B Audio CD 10

Performance Assessment

Have partners write and act out a short dialogue between friends who are deciding what to wear to a school party that will include a picnic and dancing.

DEUXIEME ETAPE

Expressing need; inquiring

COMMENT DIT-ON... ?

Expressing need; inquiring

To express need:
When the salesperson asks you:

Vous désirez?

(Est-ce que) je peux vous aider?
May I help you?

BONJOUR, J'AIMERAIS UN PANTALON POUR ALLER AVEC MON TEE-SHIRT!

VOUS AVEZ CES CHAUSSURES EN 43?

You might answer:

Oui, il me faut un chemisier vert.

Oui, vous avez des chapeaux?

Je cherche quelque chose pour aller à une boum.
I'm looking for something to . . .

J'aimerais un chemisier **pour aller avec** ma jupe.
I'd like . . . to go with . . .

Non, merci, je regarde.
No, thanks, I'm just looking.

Je peux l'/les essayer?
Can I try it/them on?

Je peux essayer le/la/les bleu(e)(s)?
Can I try on the . . . ?

To inquire about prices:

C'est combien,... ?

Ça fait combien?

To ask about sizes, color, and fabric:

Vous avez ça en 36?
Do you have that in . . . ?

en bleu?

en coton? *cotton?*

en jean? *denim?*

en cuir? *leather?*

Note de Grammaire

You can use colors and other adjectives as nouns by putting **le, la,** or **les** before them. Change their spelling according to the things they refer to: **le bleu, la bleue** = *the blue one;* **les verts, les vertes** = *the green ones.*

17 Ecoute!

Listen and decide whether a customer or salesperson is speaking.
Answers on p. 255C.

RESOURCES FOR DEUXIEME ETAPE

Textbook Audiocassette 5B/Audio CD 10
Practice and Activity Book, pp. 113–115
Video Guide
   Video Program
   Expanded Video Program, Videocassette 4
Videodisc Guide
   Videodisc Program, Videodisc 5B

Chapter Teaching Resources, Book 3
• Communicative Activity 10-1, pp. 59–60
• Teaching Transparency Master 10-2, pp. 64, 66
  Teaching Transparency 10-2
• Additional Listening Activities 10-3, 10-4, p. 68
  Audiocassette 10B/Audio CD 10
• Realia 10-2, pp. 72, 73
• Situation Cards 10-2, pp. 74–75
• Student Response Forms, pp. 76–78
• Quiz 10-2, pp. 81–82
  Audiocassette 8B/Audio CD 10

Jump Start!

Display a picture of an outfit and have students write a description of it.

MOTIVATE

Ask students what they would need to say when shopping for clothes in France. Then, ask them to list appropriate expressions they already know in French. You might also ask students if they have ever worked in a clothing store and, if so, how they addressed their customers.

TEACH

Presentation

Comment dit-on... ? Begin by playing the video for **Chacun ses goûts (Mise en train)**, pausing it for students to repeat each of the expressions in **Comment dit-on... ?** as it is used. Then, act as a salesperson and ask students **Je peux vous aider?** Bring in real clothing items or pretend to show them. Criticize the fit and color to encourage students to ask for different sizes and colors. Next, practice clothing and colors by having students describe different items that you point to. (**C'est un sac en cuir. C'est une jupe en jean.**)

For videodisc application, see *Videodisc Guide.*

Teaching Suggestion

Note de grammaire Practice this structure by holding up two items, such as notebooks, which are the same except for the color. Ask individual students to choose the one they prefer. (**Tu aimes mieux le blanc ou le jaune?**)

Teaching Suggestion

18 You might have students write their answers, using C for color, S for size, and P for price.

For Individual Needs

18 Challenge Have students tell what the color, price, or size of each item is.

19 Challenge/Visual Learners Show *Teaching Transparency 10-2.* Have partners write another conversation based on what they see, cut it into strips line by line, and exchange it with another pair. Students should then reassemble the conversation and hand it back to the pair who wrote it to be checked. You might also have them act out the conversation.

For Individual Needs

20 Challenge Have students make their own clothing catalogue. Have them draw items or cut out pictures from magazines. They should label the items and give a price for each in francs. Be sure they give their store a name. You might choose to use this as a chapter project.

20 Challenge Assign an item featured in the ad to each of three groups of students. Have them read the description and tell as much as they can about the items. For example, they might give the sleeve length, the type of fabric used, the type of collar, or other features listed. If students have difficulty finding the information, you might first have them scan the ads and guess the French words for *turtleneck, long-sleeved, pockets, elastic waist band,* and *acrylic.*

18 Ecoute!

Listen and decide whether these people are talking about the color, price, or size of the items they're looking at. Answers on p. 255C.

19 Méli-mélo!

Mets cette conversation en ordre.

5 —Oui. Nous les avons en bleu, en rouge et en orange.

6 —C'est combien?

3 —Voilà, ces maillots de bain sont très chic.

8 —Oh là là! C'est trop cher, ça!

7 —C'est 450 F.

1 —Je peux vous aider?

4 —Euh, je n'aime pas trop la couleur. Vous les avez en bleu?

2 —Oui, je cherche un maillot de bain.

20 Préférences

You and a partner are looking at some clothes in the **Trois Suisses** catalogue. Talk about which items you both like and in which colors.

—J'aimerais un pull pour aller avec mon pantalon marron. J'aime bien ce polo en beige. Et toi?
—Moi, j'aime mieux le vert.

Math Link

20 You might extend this activity by having students add up the cost of their favorite items.

NOTE CULTURELLE

The French don't use the same clothing sizes as Americans. Look at this size conversion chart to find the size you'd ask for if you were shopping in France.

TABLE DE COMPARAISON DE TAILLES

Robes, chemisiers et pantalons femmes.

France	34	36	38	40	42	44
USA	3	5	7	9	11	13

Chaussures femmes.

France	36	37	38	38½	39	40
USA	5-5½	6-6½	7-7½	8	8½	9

Tricots, pull-overs, pantalons hommes.

France	36	38	40	42	44	46
USA	26	28	30	32	34	36

Chemises hommes.

France	36	37	38	39	40	41
USA	14	14½	15	15½	16	16½

Chaussures hommes.

France	39	40	41	42	43	44
USA	6½-7	7½	8	8½	9-9½	10-10½

21 Jeu de rôle

You need something to go with some of the items below. Tell the salesperson what you need and ask about prices and sizes. Act out this scene with a partner. Then, change roles.

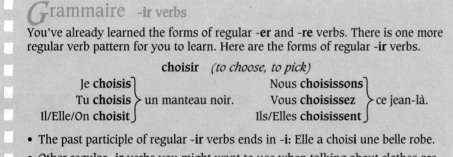

un jean   un blouson en jean
une veste en cuir noir
un pull jaune   un short noir
une chemise en coton

Vocabulaire à la carte

à rayures	*striped*	en laine	*wool*
à carreaux	*checked*	en nylon	*nylon*
à pois	*polka dot*	en lin	*linen*
à fleurs	*flowered*	en soie	*silk*
bleu clair	*light blue*	bleu foncé	*dark blue*

*G*rammaire -ir verbs

You've already learned the forms of regular -**er** and -**re** verbs. There is one more regular verb pattern for you to learn. Here are the forms of regular -**ir** verbs.

choisir *(to choose, to pick)*

Je **choisis** ⎫
Tu **choisis** ⎬ un manteau noir.
Il/Elle/On **choisit** ⎭

Nous **choisissons** ⎫
Vous **choisissez** ⎬ ce jean-là.
Ils/Elles **choisissent** ⎭

• The past participle of regular -**ir** verbs ends in -**i**: Elle a choisi une belle robe.
• Other regular -**ir** verbs you might want to use when talking about clothes are: **grandir** *(to grow)*, **maigrir** *(to lose weight)*, and **grossir** *(to gain weight)*.

Math Link

Have students figure out the pattern of conversion from American to French sizes.

Language Notes

Vocabulaire à la carte Point out that **bleu clair** and **bleu foncé** are invariable. Write **une jupe bleu foncé** on the board and have students copy it into their notebooks.

Grammaire Point out that a single **s** between vowels sounds like a *z*, while double **s** sounds like an *s*. Have students practice saying **choisissons**, pronouncing the first **s** like a *z* and the double **s** like an *s*.

Building on Previous Skills

Note Culturelle Re-enter numbers by naming a type of clothing, the gender of the wearer, and an American size. (**chemise, homme, quinze et demi.**) Have students give the corresponding French size. Then, reverse the procedure. You might also want to have students determine the French equivalents of their own sizes for shirts, shoes, dresses, and pants and write them down in their notebooks to use in later activities.

📁 Portfolio

21 Oral This activity is appropriate for students' oral portfolios. For portfolio information, see *Assessment Guide,* pages 2–13.

Presentation

Grammaire Write the subject pronouns and the stem **chois-** on the board or on a transparency and have students repeat the verb forms as you add the endings -**is**, -**is**, -**it**, -**issons**, -**issez**, -**issent**. Then, hold up pictures of two different hats. Ask a student **Quel chapeau est-ce que tu choisis?** When the student responds, ask the class **Quel chapeau est-ce que Pierre a choisi?** Continue with pictures of different clothing items.

Additional Practice

Show pictures of a baby, Santa Claus, and a stick person. Ask students **Qu'est-ce qu'ils doivent** *(should)* **faire?** (grandir, maigrir, grossir) You might write **grandir, grossir,** and **maigrir** on the board and ask students to come up and write the different verb forms.

22 Qu'est-ce qu'ils choisissent?

Qu'est-ce qu'ils choisissent pour aller avec leurs ensembles?

1. Elle choisit les chaussures rouges.

2. Ils choisissent le blouson noir.

3. Il choisit la cravate rouge.

4. Elles choisissent le chemisier bleu.

23 Ça ne me va plus!

Why can't these people wear these clothes anymore? Remember to use the **passé composé** in your answer.

1. Il a maigri.

2. Il a grandi.

3. Il a grossi.

4. Elles ont grandi.

24 En vacances!

You're going to Montreal for a winter vacation and you need some new clothes for the trip. Go shopping, tell the salesperson what you need, and inquire about prices, sizes, and colors. Act out this scene with a partner. Then, change roles.

25 Dans un grand magasin

With a partner, act out a scene in a department store between a customer and salesperson. The customer should tell what he or she is looking for, ask about size, colors, styles, fabrics, and prices, and ask to try things on. The salesperson should respond appropriately. Change roles.

PANORAMA CULTUREL

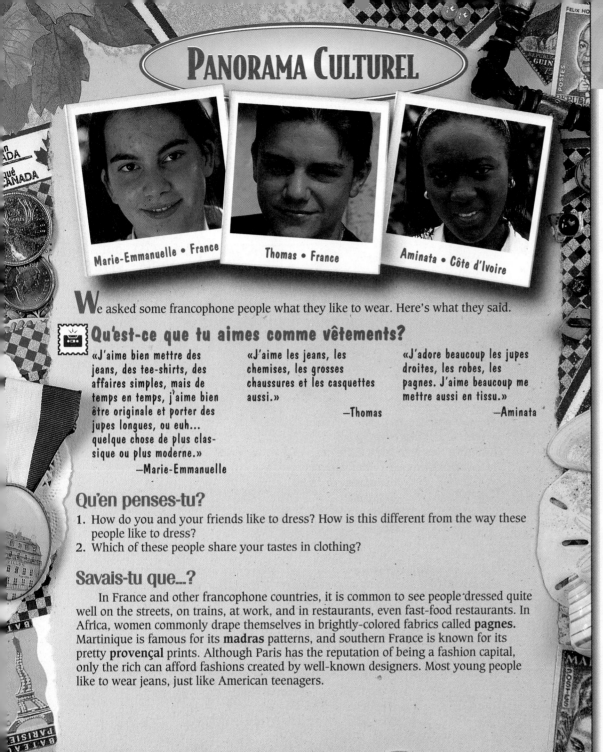

Marie-Emmanuelle • France

Thomas • France

Aminata • Côte d'Ivoire

VIDEO PROGRAM
OR EXPANDED VIDEO
PROGRAM,
Videocassette 4
10:48–13:44

OR VIDEODISC PROGRAM,
Videodisc 5B

Search 16950, Play To 18765

We asked some francophone people what they like to wear. Here's what they said.

Qu'est-ce que tu aimes comme vêtements?

«J'aime bien mettre des jeans, des tee-shirts, des affaires simples, mais de temps en temps, j'aime bien être originale et porter des jupes longues, ou euh... quelque chose de plus classique ou plus moderne.»
—Marie-Emmanuelle

«J'aime les jeans, les chemises, les grosses chaussures et les casquettes aussi.»
—Thomas

«J'adore beaucoup les jupes droites, les robes, les pagnes. J'aime beaucoup me mettre aussi en tissu.»
—Aminata

Qu'en penses-tu?

1. How do you and your friends like to dress? How is this different from the way these people like to dress?
2. Which of these people share your tastes in clothing?

Savais-tu que...?

In France and other francophone countries, it is common to see people dressed quite well on the streets, on trains, at work, and in restaurants, even fast-food restaurants. In Africa, women commonly drape themselves in brightly-colored fabrics called **pagnes**. Martinique is famous for its **madras** patterns, and southern France is known for its pretty **provençal** prints. Although Paris has the reputation of being a fashion capital, only the rich can afford fashions created by well-known designers. Most young people like to wear jeans, just like American teenagers.

♪ump Start!

Write the following questions on the board and have students write an appropriate response: **Je peux vous aider? Qu'est-ce que vous faites comme taille? Qu'est-ce que vous allez mettre avec ce pantalon vert?**

MOTIVATE

Ask students what they say to compliment their friends' clothes and what they say if they don't like their clothes but don't want to be rude.

TEACH

Presentation

Comment dit-on... ? Bring in a number of pictures from magazines that show a variety of clothing and fits (short, tight, baggy, and so on). Comment on each one and have students repeat the expressions after you. Then, hold up the pictures and ask students to compliment or criticize the clothing. You might bring in some old clothes you no longer wear and ask for opinions of them.

For videodisc application, see *Videodisc Guide.*

Teacher Note

Remind students that the gender of an item of clothing is very important for these expressions. If students made vocabulary cards for the clothing items, have them show the picture side to a partner, who will compliment or criticize it, using the subjects **il(s), elle(s)** and the object pronouns **le, la, les** correctly.

TROISIEME ETAPE

Asking for an opinion; paying a compliment; criticizing; hesitating; making a decision

⬭ COMMENT DIT-ON... ?

To ask for an opinion:
- **Comment tu trouves... ?**
- **Elle me va, cette robe?**
  Does this dress suit me?
- **Il te/vous plaît, ce jean?**
  Do you like these jeans?
- **Tu aimes mieux** le bleu **ou** le noir?

To pay a compliment:
- **C'est parfait.** *It's perfect.*
- **C'est tout à fait ton/votre style.** *It looks great on you!*
- **Elle te/vous va très bien, cette jupe.** *That skirt suits you really well.*
- **Il/Elle va très bien avec** ta chemise. *It goes very well with . . .*
  Je le/la/les trouve... *I think it's/they're . . .*
  - **à la mode.** *in style.*
  - **chic.** *chic.*
  - **mignon(mignonne)(s).** *cute.*
  - **sensas.** *fantastic.*

To criticize:
- **Il/Elle ne te/vous va pas du tout.** *That doesn't look good on you at all.*
  Il/Elle est (Ils/Elles sont) trop serré(e)(s). *It's (They're) too tight.*
  - **large(s).** *baggy.*
  - **petit(e)(s).** *small.*
  - **grand(e)(s).** *big.*
  - **court(e)(s).** *short.*
- **Il/Elle ne va pas du tout avec** tes chaussures. *That doesn't go at all with . . .*
- **Je le/la/les trouve moche(s).** *I think it's/they're tacky.*
  - **démodé(e)(s).** *old-fashioned.*
  - **horrible(s).** *terrible.*
  rétro. *the style of the Forties or Fifties.*

RESOURCES FOR **TROISIEME ETAPE**

Textbook Audiocassette 5B/Audio CD 10
Practice and Activity Book, pp. 116–118
Videodisc Guide
   Videodisc Program, Videodisc 5B

Chapter Teaching Resources, Book 3
- Communicative Activity 10-2, pp. 61–62
- Teaching Transparency Master 10-3, pp. 65, 66
  Teaching Transparency 10-3
- Additional Listening Activities 10-5, 10-6, p. 69
  Audiocassette 10B/Audio CD 10
- Realia 10-2, pp. 72, 73
- Situation Cards 10-3, pp. 74–75
- Student Response Forms, pp. 76–78
- Quiz 10-3, pp. 83–84
  Audiocassette 8B/Audio CD 10

26 Ecoute!

Listen to the following conversations and decide if the speakers are complimenting or criticizing each other's clothing.   Answers on p. 255D.

27 Un après-midi au grand magasin

You and a friend are spending the afternoon shopping at **Printemps**. If these people asked you for advice, what would you say?   See answers below.

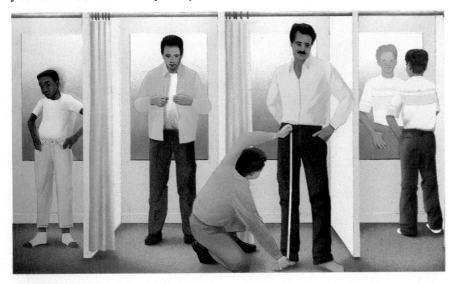

28 Sondage

Complete this survey from a French fashion magazine. How many points did you get? Which category do you fall into? Compare your answers with your partner's.

ENQUETE: LA MODE

Es-tu à la mode?

Fais notre petit test pour savoir si tu es vraiment à la dernière mode.

En général, quelle sorte de vêtements est-ce que tu portes?
a. Des vêtements super chic. (3 points)
b. Ça dépend de l'occasion. (2 points)
c. Des jeans, des tee-shirts et des baskets. (1 point)

Tu achètes de nouveaux vêtements...
a. très souvent. (3 points)
b. quelquefois. (2 points)
c. presque jamais. (1 point)

Quand tu achètes des vêtements, en général, tu...
a. achètes ce qui est à la dernière mode. (3 points)
b. achètes quelque chose que tu aimes. (2 points)
c. achètes ce qui est en solde. (1 point)

Dans un magazine de mode, tu vois que les chemises en plastique fluorescentes sont très populaires. Tu...
a. achètes 4 chemises de 4 couleurs différentes. (3 points)
b. attends patiemment pour voir si les autres en portent. (2 points)
c. tu refuses d'en acheter! Tu ne veux pas être ridicule! (1 point)

Réponses :
10 -12 points : Tu es vraiment à la mode! Attention! Tu risques de perdre ton originalité.
5 - 9 points : Parfaitement raisonnable! Tu es à la mode tout en gardant ton propre style.
0 - 4 points : Tu ne t'intéresses pas à la mode! Tu sais, il y a quelquefois des styles uniques. Essaie de les trouver.

NE PRENDS PAS CE TEST TROP AU SERIEUX!

TROISIEME ETAPE   *deux cent soixante et onze*   **271**

Teaching Suggestion
26 Have students write a plus sign to indicate a compliment and a minus sign to indicate criticism. You might also ask them to write the key words that support their answers: **démodé(e), super chic, trop serré(e),** and so on.

Group Work
27 Have groups of three students act out the scene. One is trying on the clothes, the friend offers criticism, and the salesperson offers compliments and help finding different colors and sizes.

Teaching Suggestions
28 Before students complete the survey, have them guess what the following words mean from context: **la dernière mode** *(the latest fashion),* and **en solde** *(on sale).* You might also have them read the descriptions under **Réponses** in the right-hand column and try to guess which description fits them.

28 Have students hand in their results anonymously and have a few volunteers compile them to find out which styles are most common in the class.

For Individual Needs
28 Challenge Have groups create their own three- or four-question fashion survey and administer it to the class.

Possible answers
27 Ce pantalon bleu est trop court. Cette chemise bleue est trop serrée. Ce pantalon noir est trop long. Ce pantalon rouge est trop large et trop long.

Teacher Note
27 Printemps is a major French department store. For a photo, see page 268.

Motivating Activity

Ask students when they might compliment someone and what they would say. Ask how they respond to compliments. You might have two students role-play a scene in English in which one compliments an item of clothing and the other responds.

Presentation

Have two students read each dialogue for the class. Then, ask students the first question in **Qu'en penses-tu?** Next, have partners act out one of the dialogues. You might have volunteers perform their dialogue for the class.

Additional Practice

Have partners pay compliments and respond in French.

◆ For Individual Needs

Visual Learners Have students draw their own scenes, illustrating a situation in which one person is paying a compliment and the other person is responding. Have them write the French dialogue in speech bubbles. This item would be appropriate for students' written portfolios.

Thinking Critically

Analyzing Have students read **Savais-tu que... ?** and give possible reasons why the French don't pay compliments very often. Ask them how they think the French might view people from other cultures who pay compliments frequently and why.

Read the following dialogues to find out how French people compliment one another.

—J'aime bien ta chemise.
—Ah oui?
—Oui, elle est pas mal.
—Tu trouves? Tu sais, c'est une vieille chemise.

—Il est super, ce chapeau!
—Tu crois?
—Oui, il te va très bien.
—C'est gentil.

—Tu es ravissante aujourd'hui!
—Vraiment? Je n'ai rien fait de spécial.

Qu'en penses-tu?

1. How do these people react to a compliment? They downplay the compliment.
2. How do you usually react to a compliment? How is that different from the French reactions you've just read? Answers will vary; Americans often say thank you, while the French tend to downplay compliments.

Savais-tu que...?

The French do not compliment freely and generally do so only in exceptional cases. They rarely respond to compliments with **Merci**, since that could be viewed as conceited. French people are much more likely to respond with a modest expression of disbelief, such as **Vraiment? Tu crois? Tu trouves? Ah oui?** or a comment downplaying the importance of the item complimented, such as **Oh, c'est vieux; Ce n'est rien.**

■ Multicultural Link

You might have students interview people from different cultures or people who have studied particular cultures to find out acceptable ways to pay and accept compliments in those cultures. Discuss their findings in class.

● Culture Note

In West Africa, it is wise to use caution when paying compliments. Normally, when someone compliments you on what you are wearing or on something you own, you are expected to offer it to that person. Likewise, when you compliment someone on something, he or she will often offer it to you, even if it is the last shirt a man owns or a woman's favorite earrings.

29 Fais des compliments!

Compliment two things that your partner is wearing. He or she should respond in the French way.

—Elles sont sensas, tes baskets!
—Vraiment?
—Oui, elles sont très à la mode!

Grammaire The direct object pronouns le, la, and les

The pronouns **le,** *him* or *it,* **la,** *her* or *it,* and **les,** *them,* refer to people or things. In the sentences below, what do the pronouns **le, la,** and **les** refer to?*

— Ce pull, il te plaît?   — Oui, je **le** trouve assez chic.
— Comment tu trouves cette   — Je **la** trouve démodée.
  robe?
— Vous aimez ces chaussures?   — Oui, je vais **les** prendre.

- You normally place the direct object pronouns before the conjugated verb.
  Je **le** prends.   Je **l'**ai pris.
  Je ne **la** prends pas.   Ne **les** prends pas!

- There are two exceptions to this rule. You place the direct object pronoun after the conjugated verb in a positive command and when an infinitive follows.
  Prends-**le!**
  Je vais **la** prendre.

- When **le** or **la** comes before a verb that starts with a vowel, it changes to **l'.**
  Je vais essayer **le pull.** Je vais **l'**essayer.

30 Prends-le!

Imagine you and a friend are shopping. Tell what you think of the items you see. If your friend likes something, encourage him or her to buy it. Take turns.

—Ce pantalon est très chic.
—Tu trouves?
—Oui, j'aime bien.
—Il me va?
—Oui, il te va très bien. Prends-le!

* the pullover, the dress, the shoes

Portfolio

29 Oral This item is appropriate for students' oral portfolios. For portfolio information, see *Assessment Guide,* pages 2–13.

Presentation

Grammaire Bring to class the following items or pictures of them: a sweater, a dress, and a pair of shoes. For each item, ask **Qu'est-ce que c'est?** and write the responses on the board. Then, ask the question **Ce pull (cette robe, ces chaussures), comment tu le/la/les trouves?** as you hold up the appropriate item. Model the answers **Je le/la/les trouve...** Then, ask individual students how they like each item. Continue with different items or illustrations. Read the grammar explanation. Then, repeat the questioning process with **Tu prends ce pull (cette robe, ces chaussures)?** and have students answer **Oui, je le/la/les prends** or **Non,...**

For Individual Needs

30 Slower Pace Before starting the activity, have the class name each item and give the corresponding direct object pronoun.

30 Kinesthetic Learners Have students bring in clothing items and arrange them around the classroom, simulating departments of a clothing store. Have students pair off and walk around the room to shop.

Teaching Suggestion

30 List a price for each item on a transparency. Tell students they must keep within a budget of 500 F for new clothes as they shop.

Language Note

Students are not required to use the direct object pronouns with the past tense in this chapter. The agreement of the past participle with the direct object pronoun is presented in Level 2.

Motivating Activity

Ask students if they ever have difficulty deciding whether or not to buy something and why.

Presentation

Comment dit-on... ? Write the expressions for *hesitating* and *making a decision* on a transparency. Then, hold up various clothing items or pictures of them. Give a price for each and ask students **Vous le/la/les prenez?** Make some prices outrageously high (6.000 F for a pair of socks) and some unbelievably low (2 F for a dress).

✦ For Individual Needs

Visual Learners Write **Je le/la/les prends** or **C'est trop cher** on cards for each student. Then, give a card and a picture of an item of clothing to pairs of students. Have them act out the dialogues suggested by their cards.

Additional Practice

Note de grammaire Write the following sentences on the board or on a transparency and have students complete them: ___ **est trop serrée, cette robe. On n'a pas école demain.** ___ **est génial! Tu aimes ce pantalon?** ___ **est chic, n'est-ce pas? J'aime parler au téléphone parce que** ___ **est agréable.**

31 Type the listening script with some of the words deleted. Make copies and have partners fill in the blanks.

📁 Portfolio

32 Written This activity is appropriate for students' written portfolios. For portfolio information, see *Assessment Guide*, pages 2–13.

COMMENT DIT-ON...?
Hesitating; making a decision

When the salesperson asks you:

Vous avez choisi?

Vous avez décidé de prendre ce pantalon? *Have you decided to take . . . ?*

Vous le/la/les prenez? *Are you going to take it/them?*

To hesitate, say:

Je ne sais pas.

Euh... J'hésite.
  Oh, I'm not sure.

Il/Elle me plaît, mais il/elle est cher/chère.
  I like it, but it's expensive.

To make a decision, say:

Je le/la/les prends.
  I'll take it/them.

C'est trop cher.
  It's too expensive.

Note de *Grammaire*

• Use **il/elle/ils/elles** when you are referring to a specific item.

Comment tu trouves cette robe? Elle est chouette, n'est-ce pas?

• Use **ce (ça)** when you are speaking in general.

J'aime porter des pantalons parce que c'est pratique.

In the sentence above, **ce (c'est)** refers to the general idea of wearing pants.

• Here, **c'est** refers to the idea of passing a test.

—**J'ai réussi à mon examen d'anglais!**

—**C'est super!**

---

31 Ecoute!

Listen to these exchanges between a customer and a salesperson. Tell whether the customer takes the item, doesn't take it, or can't decide.
Answers on p. 255D.

32 Qu'est-ce qu'ils disent?

Write down what you think these people are saying. Then, get together with a partner and compare what you both have written.

1.   2.   3.   4.

33 J'hésite

You're shopping for something new to wear to a party. The salesperson helps you find something. You're unsure, but your friend offers you advice. Take turns.

✦ For Individual Needs

32 Kinesthetic Learners Have partners act out their conversation. The first person to guess which illustration they're dramatizing acts out his or her conversation with a partner.

32 Auditory Learners Collect the conversations students wrote and read one scene aloud. Have students write the number of the corresponding illustration.

P R O N O N C I A T I O N

The glides [j], [w], and [ɥ]

As you listen to people speak French, you may notice a sound that reminds you of the first sound in the English word *yes*. This sound is called a *glide,* because one sound glides into another. Now, try making the sound [j] in these common French words: **mieux, chemisier, bien**. Did you notice that this gliding sound often occurs when the letter **i** is followed by **e?** The sound is also represented by the letters **ill** in words such as **maillot** and **gentille**.

There are two more glides in French. [w] sounds similar to the *w* sound you hear in *west wind.* Listen to these French words: **moi, Louis, jouer**.

The last glide sound is the one you hear in the French word **lui**. It sounds like the French vowel sounds [y] and [i] together. This sound is often written as **ui**. Listen to the glide [ɥ] in these words: **cuir, huit, juillet**.

A. A prononcer
Repeat the following words.

1. travailler	monsieur	combien	conseiller
2. pouvoir	soif	poires	moins
3. suis	minuit	suite	juillet

B. A lire
Take turns with a partner reading each of the following sentences aloud.

1. J'aime bien tes boucles d'oreilles. Elles sont géniales!
2. Il me faut des feuilles de papier, un taille-crayon et un cahier.
3. Elle a choisi un blouson en cuir et une écharpe en soie. C'est chouette!
4. Tu as quoi aujourd'hui? Moi, j'ai histoire et ensuite, je vais faire mes devoirs.
5. —Tu veux promener le chien avec moi?
   —Pourquoi pas?

C. A écrire
You're going to hear a short dialogue. Write down what you hear. *Answers on p. 255D.*

Language Note

Prononciation Make sure students don't split the glides into two separate syllables.

 For Individual Needs

Slower Pace Have students begin by breaking up the sentences in Part B into three- or four-word phrases, and work up to saying entire sentences.

Teaching Suggestion

Show *Teaching Transparency 10-3* and have students suggest what the customers and salespeople might be saying. You might have partners write a brief dialogue between a customer and a salesperson.

CLOSE

To close this **étape**, have partners ask and respond to the following questions:
1. **Comment tu trouves les jeans courts?**
2. **Qu'est-ce que tu as mis hier?**
3. **Qu'est-ce que tu mets pour aller à une fête?**

ASSESS

Quiz 10-3, *Chapter Teaching Resources, Book 3,* pp. 83–84

Assessment Items, Audiocassette 8B/Audio CD 10

Performance Assessment

Have students bring in a picture of an outfit from a magazine. Have them form groups of three, with one person acting as the salesperson and the other two as friends. The friends ask for and give their opinions of each other's outfits and compliment or criticize the outfits. The salesperson offers help and compliments. Have students take turns playing the role of the salesperson.

READING STRATEGY

Distinguishing fact from opinion

Teacher Note

For an additional reading, see *Practice and Activity Book,* page 119.

Motivating Activity

Ask students why they think fashion is important to some people and not to others. Have them look at the photos and tell what they can guess about the personalities of these people based on their clothing.

PREREADING
Activities A–C

Teaching Suggestion

A., B. Have students answer the questions in these activities in small groups.

For Individual Needs

B. Kinesthetic/Visual Learners Provide large sheets of paper and have students draw the styles pictured and write their opinions of them.

Thinking Critically

Comparing and Contrasting
Have students compare present styles with those of the past and discuss the differences.

READING
Activities D–H

Teaching Suggestion

D. Have students suggest words or phrases in French that teenagers might say if they consider fashion important and if they consider it unimportant. (**C'est cool; C'est nul.**)

LISONS!

$\mathcal{H}$ow important is fashion to you? Do you generally favor one style or do you like to vary the look of what you wear?

DE BONS CONSEILS

When you read, be careful to separate facts from opinions. A fact is something that can be proven true by observation or specific information. **Le jean est rouge** is a fact that you could prove by looking at the jeans to see if they're red or not. An opinion is someone's personal view of something. **La mode, c'est important** is an opinion. While some people may believe that to be true, it cannot be proven.

A. Think for a moment about the role fashion plays in your life.
1. Do you follow trends you see in magazines or at school?
2. How much influence do your parents have on your wardrobe?
3. Do you think clothing is a reflection of a person's personality or lifestyle?

B. How would you categorize styles that are popular at your school or in your town? What words would you use to describe them?

C. What can you tell about the people who wrote these essays? Answers will vary.

D. Which of the students consider fashion important? Which consider it unimportant? Answers will vary.

LA MODE AU LYCÉE

Mélanie
• 15 ans. En seconde au lycée Théodore Aubanel, Avignon.

Ce que je trouve dommage aujourd'hui, c'est que les filles ressemblent de plus en plus à des garçons. Au lycée, presque toutes mes copines portent des jeans ou des pantalons avec des sweat-shirts. Moi aussi, j'aime bien les jeans, mais de temps en temps, je préfère m'habiller «en fille» avec des robes ou des jupes. Je porte aussi beaucoup de bijoux, surtout des boucles d'oreilles; j'adore ça. Et puis en même temps, ça fait plaisir à mes parents quand je suis habillée comme ça; ils préfèrent ça au look garçon manqué.

Christophe
• 17 ans. En terminale au lycée Henri IV, Paris.

Moi, ce qui m'énerve avec la mode, c'est que si tu ne la suis pas, tout le monde te regarde d'un air bizarre au lycée. Moi, par exemple, le retour de la mode des années 70, les pattes d'eph et le look grunge, c'est vraiment pas mon truc. Je trouve ça horrible. Alors, je ne vois pas pourquoi je devrais m'habiller comme ça, simplement parce que c'est la mode. Je préfère porter des pantalons à pinces, des blazers et des chemises avec des cravates. Mes copains trouvent que ça fait trop sérieux, trop fils-à-papa, mais ça m'est égal. Je suis sûr que dans quelques années, quand ils travailleront, ils seront tous habillés comme moi et quand ils regarderont des photos de terminale, ils rigoleront bien en voyant les habits qu'ils portaient à 18 ans!

Terms in Lisons!

Some useful expressions that you might write on the board or on a transparency are **ce qui m'énerve** *(what annoys me);* **fabriquer** *(to make);* **un foulard** *(a decorative scarf).*

Serge

• 16 ans. En première au lycée Ampère de Lyon.

Pour moi, ce qui est vraiment important, c'est d'avoir des vêtements confortables. Je suis très sportif et j'aime pouvoir bouger dans mes habits. Mais, je veux aussi des trucs cool. Pas question de porter des vêtements très serrés ou très chers, par exemple. Je ne vois pas l'intérêt d'avoir un blouson qui coûte 4 000 F. Je préfère un blouson bon marché dans lequel je peux jouer au foot avec les copains. Comme ça, si je tombe ou si je l'abîme, c'est pas tragique. En général, je mets des jeans parce que c'est pratique et sympa. En été, je porte des tee-shirts très simples et en hiver, des sweat-shirts. Et comme chaussures, je préfère les baskets.

Emmanuelle

• 17 ans et demi. Lycée Mas de Tesse, Montpellier.

Pour moi, la façon dont quelqu'un s'habille est un reflet de sa personnalité. Au lycée, j'étudie les arts plastiques, et comme on le dit souvent, les artistes sont des gens originaux et créatifs. Je n'aime pas dépenser beaucoup pour mes vêtements. Je n'achète jamais de choses très chères, mais j'utilise mon imagination pour les rendre plus originales. Par exemple, j'ajoute toujours des accessoires sympa : bijoux fantaisie que je fabrique souvent moi-même, foulards, ceintures, sacs... Parfois, je fais même certains de mes vêtements, surtout les jupes car c'est facile. Et comme ça, je suis sûre que personne ne portera la même chose que moi!

E. Although many people consider France a fashion capital, America also influences fashion. What English words can you find in the essays? See answers below.

F. Look for the words in the box below in the essays. Then, try to match them with their English equivalents.

1. bijoux d		a. fashion
2. la mode a		b. things
3. pattes d'eph f		c. ruin
4. bouger e		d. jewelry
5. abîme c		e. to move
6. les trucs b		f. bell-bottoms

G. Which student . . .
1. likes clothes that are practical and comfortable? Serge
2. Makes some of his or her clothing and jewelry? Emmanuelle
3. doesn't buy expensive clothes? Serge, Emmanuelle
4. thinks girls should wear feminine clothes sometimes? Mélanie

H. Which of the following sentences are facts and which are opinions?
1. En été, je porte des tee-shirts.
2. Les artistes sont des gens originaux et créatifs. fact / opinion
3. Les filles ressemblent de plus en plus à des garçons. opinion
4. Je n'achète jamais de choses très chères. fact
5. La façon dont on s'habille est un reflet de sa personnalité. opinion

I. Write a short paragraph in French telling what you like to wear. Mention colors and any other details you feel are important.

Teaching Suggestions

H. Have students give their reactions to each of these statements. If they disagree, have them tell why.

H. Have students write two sentences, one fact and one opinion. You might have them form groups to compile their statements and determine whether they are labeled accurately. Then, have the groups turn in their statements.

Thinking Critically

Analyzing   Have students discuss their reactions to the reading. Would these teenagers fit in at their school? Why or why not? Do students agree or disagree with the attitudes expressed in the interviews?

POSTREADING
Activity I

📁 **Portfolio**

I. Written   Students may want to add a drawing of themselves to illustrate their paragraphs. Have them use pictures from magazines to make a collage that illustrates their sense of fashion. This activity is appropriate for students' written portfolios. For portfolio information, see *Assessment Guide,* pages 2–13.

Answers
E jeans, sweat-shirts, look grunge, blazers, cool, tee-shirts, baskets

♜ **Game**

C'EST QUI?   In small groups, one student names an item worn by one of the teenagers or quotes from one of the essays. The other students try to identify the teenager. The student who guesses correctly takes the next turn.

MISE EN PRATIQUE

The **Mise en pratique** reviews and integrates all four skills and culture in preparation for the Chapter Test.

Teaching Suggestions

1 Tell students to read the questions before they listen to the recording. Encourage them to listen to the entire conversation before they write their answers. Then, play the recording again so students can check their work or complete the activity.

2 Instead of acting out this scene, you might have students draw it as a comic strip and write their dialogues in speech bubbles.

 Portfolio

3 **Written** This activity is appropriate for students' written portfolios. For portfolio suggestions, see *Assessment Guide,* page 23.

Teaching Suggestions

3 You might have students videotape their interviews.

5 As additional items for the fashion show, have students use pictures that they bring in or the illustrations suggested for the Portfolio activity for Activity I on page 277.

Additional Practice

5 Give students cards with **chic, moche,** or **rétro** written on them. Have them draw and label an outfit that fits that description. You might have a contest to see which drawing best fits each description.

 1 Listen to this conversation between Philippe and a saleswoman at a French department store. Then, answer these questions.   Answers on p. 255D.

1. What does Philippe want to buy?
2. What colors does he prefer?
3. What does the salesperson say about the first item Philippe tries on?
4. How does Philippe feel about the way the item fits?
5. Does he end up buying it?

 2 You've been invited to a party. What should you wear? Ask your partner's advice and advise him or her what to wear.

 3 You've been hired by a French magazine to write about fashion trends among American teenagers today. Interview two or three classmates about their tastes in clothing. Find out what clothes they like to wear, what they wear to parties (**les boums**), what colors they like to wear, and their favorite article of clothing. Take notes and write a short article in French based on your interviews.

4 From what you know about French culture, are these statements true or false?

1. The French are famous for giving lots of compliments.   false
2. The French tend to downplay the compliments they receive.   true
3. If you say **merci** in response to a compliment, you could be considered conceited.   true
4. A common French way to respond to a compliment on something you're wearing is to say **Tu trouves?**   true

5 You and your friend are watching a fashion show. Ask each other how you like the clothes you see.

—Comment tu trouves ce pantalon?
—Je le trouve moche!

1.   2.   3.

NOUVELLE COLLECTION CLAUDE SAINT GENEST

FEMME : Pantalon imprimé bleu, 100 % viscose. Du 36 au 44, **199 F.** Existe en rouge. **Pull** tunique, maille brillante, sable, 50 % coton 50 % acrylique. Du 38/40 au 42/44, **189 F.** Existe en indigo. **HOMME : Chemise** à carreaux, manches longues, indigo, 100 % coton. Du 2 au 6, **139 F. Pantalon** pinces, micro-sablé, chiné beige, 50 % polyester 50 % viscose. Du 38 au 52, **239 F.** Existe en tilleul et anthracite. **Pull** maille anglaise indigo, 50 % coton 50 % acrylique. Du 2 au 6, **149 F.** Existe en lichen et beige. **ENFANT : Tee-shirt** uni rouge, broderie poitrine, 100 % coton peigné. Du 2 au 5 ans, **29 F.** Existe en 17 coloris. **Jean** western marine, 100 % coton. Du 2 au 5 ans, **79 F.** Existe en sable, bleu et blanc.

VENDUE EXCLUSIVEMENT DANS LES HYPERMARCHES GEANT CASINO ET RALLYE

6 Look over the advertisement above. Then, answer these questions.

1. Who does **Claude Saint Genest** make clothes for? men, women, and children
2. How many colors does the child's T-shirt come in? 17
3. The women's pants are available in what sizes? 36 to 44
4. What material is the men's shirt made of? cotton
5. What's the most expensive item on the page? The least expensive?
   Most expensive: men's pants, 239 F
   Least expensive: child's T-shirt, 29 F

7

J E U   D E   R O L E

Choose one of the items from the advertisement and ask the salesperson about it. Do they have it in your size? Can you try it on? The salesperson should compliment the way it looks, and you should decide whether to buy it or not. Take turns playing the role of salesperson.

Additional Practice

6 Have students give the prices and colors of each clothing item in the ad. You might assign each item to a group of students. Have them note the sizes and colors it is available in, the price, and the fabric. Since most of the colors in the ad are cognates, encourage students to guess at what the colors might be.

For Individual Needs

6 Challenge Have students create an ad for an article of clothing they're wearing or for a favorite article of clothing, using this ad as a model.

Portfolio

7 Oral This activity is appropriate for students' oral portfolios. For portfolio suggestions, see *Assessment Guide,* page 23.

Video Wrap-Up

- *VIDEO PROGRAM*
- *EXPANDED VIDEO PROGRAM,* Videocassette 4, 01:22–15:18
- *VIDEODISC PROGRAM,* Videodisc 5B

At this time, you might want to use the video resources for additional review and enrichment. See *Video Guide* or *Videodisc Guide* for suggestions regarding the following:
- **Chacun ses goûts** (Dramatic episode)
- **Panorama Culturel** (Interviews)
- **Vidéoclips** (Authentic footage)

This page is intended to help students prepare for the test. It is a brief checklist of the major points covered in the chapter. The students should be reminded that this is only a checklist and does not necessarily include everything that will appear on the test.

Teaching Suggestions

2 To practice the **passé composé,** have students say that their friend wore these clothes to a party yesterday.

6 Ask students what else they might ask a friend when they try on clothing.

9 Remind students to give examples of both positive and negative responses.

Teacher Note

You might want to have students review other forms of **mettre** and **choisir** as well. You might play the "Verb Tense Race" described on page 231F.

QUE SAIS-JE?

Can you use what you've learned in this chapter?

Can you ask for and give advice? p. 264

1 How would you ask a friend what you should wear to a party?
Qu'est-ce que je mets pour aller à la boum?

2 How would you advise a friend to wear these clothes, using the verb **mettre?** See answers below.

1.   2.

Can you express need and inquire? p. 265

1. Je peux l'/les essayer?
Je peux essayer le/la/les... ?

3 How would you tell a salesperson . . .

1. that you're just looking?
Je regarde.

2. what you would like?
J'aimerais... ; Je cherche...

4 How would you ask a salesperson . . .

1. if you can try something on?
2. if they have what you want in a different size?
Vous avez ça en... (36)?

3. if they have what you want in a particular color? Vous avez ça en... (rouge)?
4. how much something costs?
C'est combien? Ça fait combien?

5 How would you tell what these people are choosing? See answers below.

Charles   Jean-Marc et Farid   Astrid   Delphine et Camille

Can you ask for an opinion, pay a compliment, and criticize? p. 270

6 If you were shopping with a friend, how would you ask . . .

1. if your friend likes what you have on? Comment tu trouves... ? Ça te plaît?
2. if something fits? Ça me va?
3. if it's too short? Il/Elle est trop court(e)?

7 How would you compliment a friend's clothing? How would you criticize it? See answers below.

Can you hesitate and make a decision? p. 274

8 How can you express your hesitation?
J'hésite. Je ne sais pas. Ça me plaît, mais c'est cher.

9 How would you tell a salesperson what you've decided to do?
Je le/la/les prends. C'est trop cher.
pas

280   *deux cent quatre-vingts*   CHAPITRE 10   Dans un magasin de vêtements

Answers

2 1. Pourquoi est-ce que tu ne mets pas ton pantalon bleu? Mets ton pantalon bleu.
2. Pourquoi est-ce que tu ne mets pas ton pull? Mets ton pull.

5 1. Charles choisit une veste bleue et verte.
2. Jean-Marc et Farid choisissent un manteau en cuir bleu.
3. Astrid choisit des chaussures en cuir.
4. Delphine et Camille choisissent des chaussettes blanches.

7 *Possible answers*

Complimenting: C'est tout à fait ton style. Il/Elle te va très bien. Il/Elle va très bien avec... ; Je le/la/les trouve chic/à la mode/mignon(ne)(s)/sensas. C'est parfait.

Criticizing: Il/Elle ne te va pas du tout. Il/Elle ne va pas du tout avec... ; Il/Elle est (Ils/Elles sont) trop serré(e)(s)/large(s)/petit(e)(s)/grand(e)(s)/court(e)(s). Je le/la/les trouve moche(s)/démodé(e)(s)/horrible(s)/rétro.

PREMIERE ETAPE

Clothes

un blouson   *a jacket*
des bottes (f.)   *boots*
des boucles d'oreilles (f.)   *earrings*
un bracelet   *a bracelet*
un cardigan   *a cardigan*
une casquette   *a cap*
une ceinture   *a belt*
un chapeau   *a hat*
des chaussettes (f.)   *socks*
des chaussures (f.)   *shoes*
une chemise   *a shirt (men's)*

un chemisier   *a shirt (women's)*
une cravate   *a tie*
une écharpe   *a scarf*
une jupe   *a skirt*
des lunettes (f.) de soleil   *sunglasses*
un manteau   *a coat*
un pantalon   *(a pair of) pants*
une robe   *a dress*
des sandales (f.)   *sandals*
un maillot de bain   *a bathing suit*
une veste   *a suit jacket, a blazer*

Asking for and giving advice

Je ne sais pas quoi mettre pour...   *I don't know what to wear for (to) . . .*
Qu'est-ce que je mets?   *What shall I wear?*
Pourquoi est-ce que tu ne mets pas...?   *Why don't you wear . . . ?*
Mets...   *Wear . . .*
mettre   *to put, to put on, to wear*
porter   *to wear*

DEUXIEME ETAPE

Expressing need; inquiring

Vous désirez?   *What would you like?*
(Est-ce que) je peux vous aider?   *May I help you?*
Je cherche quelque chose pour...   *I'm looking for something to . . .*
J'aimerais... pour aller avec...   *I'd like . . . to go with . . .*

Non, merci, je regarde.   *No, thanks, I'm just looking.*
Je peux l'/les essayer?   *Can I try it/them on?*
Je peux essayer le/la/les... ?   *Can I try on the . . . one(s)?*
Vous avez ça... ?   *Do you have that . . . ? (size, fabric, color)*
en bleu   *in blue*

en coton   *cotton*
en jean   *denim*
en cuir   *leather*

Other useful expressions

choisir   *to choose, to pick*
grandir   *to grow*
maigrir   *to lose weight*
grossir   *to gain weight*

TROISIEME ETAPE

Asking for an opinion; paying a compliment; criticizing

Comment tu trouves... ?   *How do you like . . . ?*
Il/Elle me va?   *Does . . . suit me?*
Il/Elle te (vous) plaît?   *Do you like it?*
C'est parfait.   *It's perfect.*
C'est tout à fait ton style.   *It looks great on you!*
Il/Elle te/vous va très bien.   *It suits you really well.*
Il/Elle va très bien avec...   *It goes very well with . . .*
Je le/la/les trouve...   *I think it's/ they're . . .*
   à la mode   *in style*

chic   *chic*
mignon (mignonne)   *cute*
sensas   *fantastic*
serré(e)(s)   *tight*
large(s)   *baggy*
petit(e)(s)   *small*
grand(e)(s)   *big*
court(e)(s)   *short*
moche(s)   *tacky*
démodé(e)(s)   *old-fashioned*
horrible(s)   *terrible*
rétro   *the style of the Forties or Fifties*
Il/Elle ne te/vous va pas du tout.   *It doesn't look good on you at all.*
Il/Elle ne va pas du tout avec...   *It doesn't go at all with . . .*

Hesitating; making a decision

Vous avez choisi?   *Have you decided?*
Vous avez décidé de prendre...?   *Have you decided to take . . . ?*
Vous le/la/les prenez?   *Are you taking it/them?*
Je ne sais pas.   *I don't know.*
Euh... J'hésite.   *Well, I'm not sure.*
Il/Elle me plaît, mais il/elle est cher (chère).   *I like it, but it's expensive.*
Je le/la/les prends.   *I'll take it/ them.*
C'est trop cher.   *It's too expensive.*

CHAPITRE 10   VOCABULAIRE   **281**

♜ **Game**

♜ **CONCOURS DE FAMILLE**   This game is played like Family Feud®. First, group the chapter vocabulary into categories: what you wear every day, what you wear for special occasions, what a salesperson might say, what you might say if something doesn't fit, and so on. Then, divide the class into two or more teams and have a player from each team go to the board. Call out a category. The team whose player first gives an appropriate expression has one minute to list on the board all the words or expressions that fit into that category. Award points for correctly spelled answers. You may play up to a certain number of points or until you have exhausted all the categories.

CHAPTER 10 ASSESSMENT

CHAPTER TEST

• *Chapter Teaching Resources, Book 3,* pp. 85–90
• *Assessment Guide,* Speaking Test, p. 32
• *Assessment Items, Audiocassette 8B* *Audio CD 10*

TEST GENERATOR, CHAPTER 10

ALTERNATIVE ASSESSMENT

Performance Assessment

You might want to use the **Jeu de rôle** (p. 279) as a cumulative performance assessment activity.

📁 **Portfolio Assessment**

• **Written:** Mise en pratique, Activity 3, *Pupil's Edition,* p. 278
   Assessment Guide, p. 23
• **Oral:** Mise en pratique, Jeu de rôle, *Pupil's Edition,* p. 279
   Assessment Guide, p. 23

Chapitre 11 : Vive les vacances!
Chapter Overview

Mise en train pp. 284–286	Bientôt les vacances!		Practice and Activity Book, p. 121		Video Guide OR Videodisc Guide

	FUNCTIONS	GRAMMAR	CULTURE	RE-ENTRY
Première étape pp. 287–292	• Inquiring about and sharing future plans, p. 289 • Expressing indecision; expressing wishes, p. 289	The prepositions **à** and **en**, p. 290	• **Note Culturelle, Colonies de vacances**, p. 288 • **Panorama Culturel**, Annual vacations in France, p. 292	• **aller** + infinitive • Asking for advice • Making, accepting, and refusing suggestions
Deuxième étape pp. 293–296	• Reminding; reassuring, p. 293 • Seeing someone off, p. 296	The **-ir** verbs: **partir**, p. 294	Realia: Itinerary for **Provence**, p. 295	• Clothing • The imperative • Weather expressions
Troisième étape pp. 297–299	• Asking for and expressing opinions, p. 297 *Review* • Inquiring about and relating past events, p. 297			• The **passé composé** • The verb **vouloir**

Prononciation p. 299	Aspirated **h**; **th, ch**, and **gn**		**Dictation:** *Textbook Audiocassette 6A/Audio CD 11*

Lisons! pp. 300–301	Tourist information for Provence	**Reading Strategy:** Reading for a purpose

Review pp. 302–305	**Mise en pratique**, pp. 302–303	**Que sais-je?** p. 304	**Vocabulaire**, p. 305

Assessment Options	**Etape Quizzes** • *Chapter Teaching Resources, Book 3* **Première étape**, Quiz 11-1, pp. 135–136 **Deuxième étape**, Quiz 11-2, pp. 137–138 **Troisième étape**, Quiz 11-3, pp. 139–140 • *Assessment Items, Audiocassette 8B/Audio CD 11*	**Chapter Test** • *Chapter Teaching Resources, Book 3*, pp. 141–146 • *Assessment Guide*, Speaking Test, p. 33 • *Assessment Items, Audiocassette 8B/Audio CD 11* **Test Generator, Chapter 11**

Video Program OR Expanded Video Program, Videocassette 4
OR Videodisc Program, Videodisc 6A   Textbook Audiocassette 6A/Audio CD 11

RESOURCES: Print	RESOURCES: Audiovisual

Textbook Audiocassette 6A/Audio CD 11

Practice and Activity Book, pp. 122–124
Chapter Teaching Resources, Book 3
• Teaching Transparency Master 11-1, pp. 119, 122 . . . . Teaching Transparency 11-1
• Additional Listening Activities 11-1, 11-2, p. 123 . . . . Additional Listening Activities, Audiocassette 10B/Audio CD 11
• Realia 11-1, pp. 127, 129
• Situation Cards 11-1, pp. 130–131
• Student Response Forms, pp. 132–134
• Quiz 11-1, pp. 135–136 . . . . Assessment Items, Audiocassette 8B/Audio CD 11
Video Guide . . . . Video Program OR Expanded Video Program, Videocassette 4
Videodisc Guide . . . . Videodisc Program, Videodisc 6A

Textbook Audiocassette 6A/Audio CD 11

Practice and Activity Book, pp. 125–127
Chapter Teaching Resources, Book 3
• Communicative Activity 11-1, pp. 115–116
• Teaching Transparency Master 11-2, pp. 120, 122 . . . . Teaching Transparency 11-2
• Additional Listening Activities 11-3, 11-4, p. 124 . . . . Additional Listening Activities, Audiocassette 10B/Audio CD 11
• Realia 11-2, pp. 128, 129
• Situation Cards 11-2, pp. 130–131
• Student Response Forms, pp. 132–134
• Quiz 11-2, pp. 137–138 . . . . Assessment Items, Audiocassette 8B/Audio CD 11
Videodisc Guide . . . . Videodisc Program, Videodisc 6A

Textbook Audiocassette 6A/Audio CD 11

Practice and Activity Book, pp. 128–130
Chapter Teaching Resources, Book 3
• Communicative Activity 11-2, pp. 117–118
• Teaching Transparency Master 11-3, pp. 121, 122 . . . . Teaching Transparency 11-3
• Additional Listening Activities 11-5, 11-6, p. 125 . . . . Additional Listening Activities, Audiocassette 10B/Audio CD 11
• Realia 11-2, pp. 128, 129
• Situation Cards 11-3, pp. 130–131
• Student Response Forms, pp. 132–134
• Quiz 11-3, pp. 139–140 . . . . Assessment Items, Audiocassette 8B/Audio CD 11
Videodisc Guide . . . . Videodisc Program, Videodisc 6A

Practice and Activity Book, p. 131

Video Guide . . . . Video Program OR Expanded Video Program, Videocassette 4
Videodisc Guide . . . . Videodisc Program, Videodisc 6A

Alternative Assessment
• Performance Assessment   • Portfolio Assessment
  Première étape, p. 291   Written: **Mise en pratique,** Activity 3, Pupil's Edition, p. 303
  Deuxième étape, p. 296   Assessment Guide, p. 24
  Troisième étape, p. 299   Oral: **Mise en pratique, Jeu de rôle,** Pupil's Edition, p. 303
                                    Assessment Guide, p. 24

Chapitre 11 : Vive les vacances!
Textbook Listening Activities Scripts

For Student Response Forms, see *Chapter Teaching Resources, Book 3,* pp. 132–134.

Première étape

6 Ecoute! p. 287

1. — Bonjour, Nathalie. Qu'est-ce que tu vas faire pendant tes vacances?
   — Je ne sais pas encore, mais je voudrais aller au bord de la mer et faire du bateau.
   — Eh bien, bonnes vacances.
   — Merci beaucoup.

2. — Alors, Bruno. Qu'est-ce que tu vas faire cet été?
   — Je vais aller à Paris avec mes parents.
   — Ah, c'est génial. Tu aimes Paris, toi?
   — Je n'y suis jamais allé.
   — Tu vas voir, c'est très joli. J'espère qu'il va faire beau.
   — Moi aussi!

3. — Bonjour, Pauline. Où est-ce que tu vas aller en vacances?
   — Au mois de juillet, je vais aller chez mes cousins à La Rochelle.
   — C'est chouette, La Rochelle.
   — Je sais, mais, moi, j'aimerais mieux aller en colonie de vacances avec des copains.
   — Amuse-toi bien quand même.
   — Merci.

4. — Alors, Emile, tu as décidé? Où est-ce que tu vas aller en vacances?
   — Euh, je pense aller à la montagne.
   — Pour faire de la randonnée?
   — Oui, mais c'est cher.
   — Dommage. Tu n'y vas pas alors?
   — Si. J'y vais quand même.
   — Et bien, bonnes vacances.
   — Merci beaucoup.

Answers to Activity 6
1. Nathalie is going boating on the coast.
2. Bruno is going to Paris with his parents.
3. Pauline is going to visit her cousins in La Rochelle.
4. Emile is going hiking in the mountains.

8 Ecoute! p. 289

1. — Qu'est-ce que tu vas faire pendant les vacances, Sabine?
   — Euh, je n'ai rien de prévu. Je voudrais bien aller chez mes grands-parents, mais j'ai envie de travailler aussi.

2. — Dis, Gilbert, où est-ce que tu vas aller pendant les vacances?

— Oh, ça va être super! En juillet, je vais voir mon oncle au Canada, et en août, je vais voyager en Afrique.

3. — Qu'est-ce que tu vas faire en été, Arianne?
   — Euh, j'hésite. Je voudrais bien aller à la plage, mais je ne sais pas.

4. — Tu vas travailler cet été?
   — Euh, je me demande. Je voudrais bien si je peux trouver du travail. Est-ce qu'il y a du travail à la station-service?

5. — Qu'est-ce que tu vas faire pendant les vacances?
   — Je vais dans un camp de tennis. C'est chouette, hein? On va jouer au tennis trois heures par jour.

Answers to Activity 8
1. undecided   3. undecided   5. definite plans
2. definite plans   4. undecided

13 Ecoute! p. 291

ALAIN   Je ne sais pas où aller pendant les vacances. Tu as une idée?

VALÉRIE   Tu devrais aller à la Martinique.

ALAIN   Ah oui?

VALÉRIE   Oui, j'y suis allée plusieurs fois.

ALAIN   C'est comment?

VALÉRIE   C'est chouette. Il fait toujours beau. Les gens sont très sympa.

ALAIN   Qu'est-ce qu'on peut y faire?

VALÉRIE   Oh, plein de choses. Il y a des plages superbes. Tu peux y faire de la planche à voile, du bateau, de la plongée. Tu peux aussi visiter Fort-de-France. C'est une ville très intéressante.

ALAIN   Qu'est-ce qu'on peut voir à Fort-de-France?

VALÉRIE   Le marché aux poissons, le marché aux fruits et aux légumes ou la place de la Savane, qui est très belle.

ALAIN   Eh bien, c'est une bonne idée. J'ai envie d'y aller!

Answers to Activity 13
1. vrai   2. faux   3. vrai   4. faux

Deuxième étape

18 Ecoute! p. 294

1. — Tu as les cadeaux, Frédéric? N'oublie surtout pas les cadeaux!

2. — J'ai mon manteau, mon écharpe, ma cravate. J'ai pensé à tout!

3. — Tu as pensé à ton dictionnaire? Il ne faut pas que tu l'oublies. Il te faut absolument un dictionnaire.

4. — Eh bien, j'ai regardé ma liste deux fois. Je suis sûr, je n'ai rien oublié.

5. — Tu n'as pas oublié tes sandales? Tu sais, il va faire très chaud.

6. — Oui, j'ai mon appareil-photo. Ne t'en fais pas.

7. — Tu ne prends pas ton maillot de bain? Pourquoi? Tu vas en avoir besoin.

Anwers to Activity 18

1. reminding	3. reminding	5. reminding	7. reminding
2. reassuring	4. reassuring	6. reassuring	

25 Ecoute! p. 296

1. — Salut, Michel! Ça va? Ça fait longtemps! Qu'est-ce que tu fais?

2. — A bientôt, Nathalie! Amuse-toi bien!

3. — Eh bien, bon voyage, Luc! N'oublie pas de m'écrire! Je vais penser à toi!

4. — Salut, Amira! Tu vas mieux? On va au cinéma ce soir. Tu viens?

5. — Salut, Paul! Tu as de la chance, toi, d'aller en Italie! Passe de bonnes vacances!

6. — Salut, Albert! Ça s'est bien passé, le week-end? Qu'est-ce que tu as fait?

Answers to Activity 25

1. arrive	2. part	3. part	4. arrive	5. part	6. arrive

Troisième étape

29 Ecoute! p. 297

1. — Tu as passé un bon été?
 — Oh, pas mal. J'ai beaucoup travaillé. Mais j'ai gagné de l'argent.

2. — Ça s'est bien passé, tes vacances en Italie?
 — C'était un véritable cauchemar! Il a fait tellement chaud, et c'était trop cher!

3. — Tu t'es bien amusée en vacances, Fabienne?
 — Ah oui, c'était formidable! Il a fait très beau! On est allés à la plage tous les jours!

4. — Dis, Etienne, tu as passé un bon week-end?
 — Euh, pas vraiment. Je suis allé chez mes cousins à la montagne. C'est barbant chez eux!

5. — Tu t'es bien amusé en colonie de vacances?
 — Oh, ça a été. On a beaucoup joué au football, mais moi, j'aime mieux le tennis.

6. — Ça s'est bien passé, tes vacances à la montagne?
 — C'était épouvantable! J'y suis allé pour faire du ski, et il n'y avait pas de neige!

7. — Tu t'es bien amusé à Paris?
 — C'était formidable! On est allés au Louvre, à Notre-Dame, à la tour Eiffel et au Sacré-Cœur.

Answers to Activity 29

1. fair	3. good	5. fair	7. good
2. bad	4. bad	6. bad	

Prononciation, p. 299

For the scripts for Parts A and B, see p. 299.

C. A écrire

(Dictation)

— Salut, Michel! Qu'est-ce que tu fais cet été?
— Je vais chez mon oncle à la campagne. Il a trois chats mignons et quatre chiens méchants.

Mise en pratique

1 p. 302

Vous voulez découvrir des horizons nouveaux? Vous avez l'esprit d'aventure? Pierre et Vacances peut vous aider à partir au bout du monde! Grands voyages pour petits budgets!

Envie de soleil, de plages tranquilles, de musique exotique? Sortez votre maillot de bain et votre crème solaire. Venez passer une semaine au Maroc y faire de la planche à voile et de la plongée sous-marine.

Envie de neige et de descentes olympiques? Les montagnes de Grenoble vous attendent. Hôtel, location de skis et chaussures, forfait téléski, voyage en train compris, au départ de Paris, deux mille cinq cents francs.

Envie de sensation forte et de paysages spectaculaires? La randonnée de votre vie vous attend! Descente du Grand Canyon avec un guide. Campez au bord des eaux vertes du Colorado. Pour les amoureux du risque, rafting possible.

Pour profiter des prix hors saison, voyagez avant le quinze juin. Nous avons des prix étudiant et des prix de groupes. Si les voyages vous intéressent, venez nous voir ou téléphonez Pierre et Vacances, quarante-sept, vingt-trois, trente-deux, vingt-deux.

Answers to Mise en pratique Activity 1
1. travel agency
2. *Possible answers:* Morocco, Grenoble, the Grand Canyon, Colorado
3. windsurfing, scuba diving, skiing, hiking, camping, rafting
4. students and groups

Le monde du voyageur
(Individual or Group Project)

ASSIGNMENT
Students will create posters of travel scenes.

MATERIALS
✂ **Students may need**
- French-English dictionary
- Posterboard or construction paper
- Markers or colored pencils
- Magazines and catalogues

SUGGESTED SEQUENCE
1. Students might work alone or in small groups. Tell them that they will depict an airport, train station, or vacation scene, with labels on important items and speech bubbles for the people in the scene. Individuals might create a scene on construction paper and groups might use a piece of posterboard. You might show *Teaching Transparency 11-2* as an example of a travel scene. As preparation for their own projects, have students suggest labels for objects and speech bubbles for the people in the scene. You might write their suggestions on a transparency overlay.

2. Students choose the location for their scenes and begin gathering or drawing pictures to illustrate it. They may wish to present a story or simply show people doing different things.

3. Before creating the final draft, have students plan the layout of their pictures and look up words they don't know in the dictionary. They might cut out pictures from magazines as well. Have them label as many items as possible, such as clothes, travel items, objects in the scene, activities, and so on. Remind them to check their spelling.

4. Next, have students write speech bubbles for the people shown. They might choose to demonstrate greeting or seeing people off, giving advice, or other appropriate functions.

5. Have students edit one another's work; they should make any corrections in labels or language use. They should then add any final touches to their posters to make them look complete and attractive.

GRADING THE PROJECT
You might want to base students' grades on completion of the assignment, creativity, language use, and appearance.

Suggested Point Distribution (total = 100 points)

Completion of assignment . . . . 30 points
Creativity . . . . 30 points
Language use. . . . . 20 points
Appearance . . . . 20 points

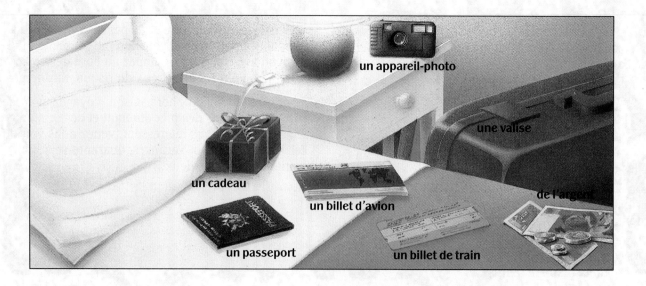

Chapitre 11 : Vive les vacances!
 Games

DESSIN ANIME

In this game, students will review vocabulary related to vacation activities.

Procedure   First, divide the class into two or more teams and have a player from the first team go to the board. Give the player the name of a vacation place or activity in French and have him or her draw a representation of that activity. If the player's team correctly guesses the activity or place within 30 seconds, that team wins a point. The turn then goes to the second team.

Variation   This game may also be played in small groups. In this case, students may choose an activity from the vocabulary list at the end of the chapter and draw their illustrations on paper or on a transparency.

JE L'AI TROUVE!

The object of this game is to have students recognize the names of francophone countries and identify their location on a map.

Procedure   Before playing this game, give students a few minutes to look over the map of the francophone world on page xxiv in their books. You might also show *Map Transparency 4.* Then, display two world maps and divide the class into two teams. Have a player from each team stand by a map. Call out a country name in French. The first player to point out the country on the map and say **Je l'ai trouvé!** wins a point. Give each team a point in case of a tie.

REPONDS VITE!

In this game, students will practice verb forms.

Procedure   Divide the class into two teams and place a bell or squeaky toy on top of a desk. Then, have one player from each team come forward. Name a subject, a verb, and a tense **(je, partir, présent)**. The first student to ring the bell responds with the correct verb form. If that student is wrong, the other player has a chance to respond. A correct answer wins a point for the team. Then, both players return to their seats, and two other players come forward. In case of confusion due to mispronunciation, have the player write the verb form on the board. In addition to verb forms, you can also ask students to give functional expressions, such as *see someone off* or *suggest that someone go to the beach.*

Chapitre 11
Vive les vacances!

pp. 282–305

*U*sing the Chapter Opener

Motivating Activity

Ask students where they would go on vacation if they had unlimited time and money. You might also have them recall popular vacation spots mentioned in previous chapters.

Teaching Suggestion

Have partners ask and answer the questions about vacations in the introduction at the top of page 283. Then, have students read the outcomes and write a short description of each photo. As a challenge, have them write their description in French.

Photo Flash!

① The beach is a popular vacation destination for the French. Many flock to the beaches of the **Côte d'Azur** in southern France or the trendy resort town of Biarritz on the Atlantic coast. The beaches of Grand-Bassam and Assinie in Côte d'Ivoire attract both African and European tourists. The teenager in this photo is relaxing on **La plage des Salines** in Martinique, a popular overseas vacation destination. Since Martinique is a **département** and officially a part of France, French citizens do not need a passport to travel there.

CHAPITRE
11
Vive les vacances!

① Pourquoi tu ne vas pas à la plage?

Multicultural Link

Ask students which holidays they have off from school. Have them suggest both national holidays, such as Martin Luther King Day or Columbus Day, and religious holidays, such as Yom Kippur, Christmas, or Ramadan. Then, have them research national and religious holidays in other countries and how they're celebrated.

Language Note

Have students guess what **Vive** in the expression **Vive les vacances!** means. You might write **Vive le roi!** or **Vive la France!** on the board as additional examples.

ow do you spend your vacation? Do you work? Do you do things in your hometown with your friends? Do you travel to other places and meet new people?

In this chapter you will learn

- to inquire about and share future plans; to express indecision; to express wishes; to ask for advice; to make, accept, and refuse suggestions
- to remind; to reassure; to see someone off
- to ask for and express opinions; to inquire about and relate past events

And you will

- listen to francophone students talk about their vacation plans
- read about tourist attractions in Provence
- write about your ideal vacation
- find out where French-speaking people go and what they do during their vacations

② Tu n'as pas oublié ton dictionnaire?

③ C'était formidable, les vacances en Provence!

deux cent quatre-vingt-trois **283**

Focusing on Outcomes

Ask students to describe a vacation they have taken or an imaginary vacation and tell why they enjoyed it. Then, have partners suggest how they would express the chapter outcomes, using vocabulary and structures they already know. Ask them to list English expressions related to the outcomes. NOTE: You may want to use the video to support the objectives. The self-check activities in **Que sais-je?** on page 304 help students assess their achievement of the objectives.

Building on Previous Skills

Ask students to recall and name in French particular sports and activities they might do on vacation.

Photo Flash!

② Florent is packing his bags for a trip. You might ask students if they can guess where he might be going, judging from what he is packing.

③ The region of Provence, known as **Provincia** by the Romans, is famous for its mild climate, which is characterized by long, warm summers and mild winters.

Teaching Suggestions

- Ask students if they like to take pictures when they visit a different city or country and what they might take pictures of. There might be an experienced photographer in your class who would be willing to explain how to take good photographs.
- Assign photos from pages 282 and 283 to groups of students and have them write new captions for them.

VIDEO PROGRAM
OR EXPANDED VIDEO
PROGRAM,
Videocassette 4
15:19–17:45

OR VIDEODISC PROGRAM,
Videodisc 6A

Search 1, Play To 4400

Video Synopsis

In this segment of the video, Ahmed and Florent are playing soccer when Magali comes up to greet them. They talk about their plans for the summer. Magali is going to a summer camp, and Ahmed plans to go camping and then work at a gas station in Arles. Florent doesn't have any vacation plans yet. Magali and Ahmed each make suggestions. Florent wants to do something interesting, but he doesn't know what!

Motivating Activity

Ask students what they did during summer vacation last year and what they would like to do this year. You might find out what vacation options are available to students. Ask students what types of jobs are available during the summer and if there are any nearby summer camps. Ask if they would like to work and what they would save for.

Presentation

As a prereading activity, have students answer the questions at the top of page 284. Then, have them scan the **Mise en train** for cognates. Play the video and then have students answer the questions in Activity 1 on page 286. Ask them to suggest advantages and disadvantages of each teenager's vacation plans.

Mise en train

Bientôt les vacances!

What are these teenagers discussing? What clues do you have? What is Florent's dilemma?

Alors, les copains, qu'est-ce que vous allez faire pendant les vacances?

C'est sympa!

Moi, je pars en colonie de vacances.

Et en août, je vais voir mes cousins à la montagne. Ils habitent à Sisteron, dans les Alpes de Haute-Provence. C'est super joli là-bas.

En août, je travaille dans une station-service. J'aimerais bien acheter une mobylette.

Et toi, Ahmed, tu vas à l'étranger?

Non. En juillet, je vais faire du camping dans les Gorges du Verdon.

C'est génial!

284   *deux cent quatre-vingt-quatre*

CHAPITRE 11   Vive les vacances!

RESOURCES FOR MISE EN TRAIN

Textbook Audiocassette 6A/Audio CD 11
Practice and Activity Book, p. 121
Video Guide
   Video Program
   Expanded Video Program, Videocassette 4
Videodisc Guide
   Videodisc Program, Videodisc 6A

Geography Link

Ask students to look in an atlas and locate **Sisteron** and **les Gorges du Verdon**. Have them find out about the attractions at these places and what the weather is like in the summer.

Teaching Suggestion

Stop the recording or video periodically to ask students where the teenagers are going on vacation. **(Il/Elle va où en vacances?)**

Thinking Critically

Comparing and Contrasting

Ask students to compare what these French teenagers are planning to do for the summer with what they usually do. Do they find any of the activities unusual? Why? What might an American teenager do that these French teenagers didn't mention?

Group Work

After students have watched the video several times, divide them into groups of three and have them role-play **Bientôt les vacances!** They might substitute other vacation activities and destinations.

For Individual Needs

Challenge Have students write a caption for each photo that summarizes the conversation or describes the scene.

 Video Integration

- **EXPANDED VIDEO PROGRAM,**
  Videocassette 4, 17:46–25:05
- **VIDEODISC PROGRAM,**
  Videodisc 6A

Search 4400, Play To 17600

You may choose to continue with **Bientôt les vacances! (suite)** at this time or wait until later in the chapter. When the story continues,

Florent's father sees an ad for a **séjour linguistique** in England and thinks Florent should participate. Florent tells Ahmed of his plans. Ahmed says that it won't be fun and that it rains all the time in England. Florent is reluctant to go to England, but his parents finally persuade him to go. At the end of the story, Florent's parents receive a package from him. He has sent back his rain gear and is having a great time after all!

1 Tu as compris? See answers below.

Answer the following questions about **Bientôt les vacances!** Don't be afraid to guess.

1. What time of year is it? How do you know?
2. Who is planning to travel during the vacation? Where?
3. Who is going to work during the vacation? Why?
4. What is Florent going to do?

2 C'est qui?

D'après **Bientôt les vacances!** qui a l'intention de (d')...

Florent   **Ahmed**   **Magali**

Magali — aller dans les Alpes?

Ahmed — travailler en Arles?

Florent — rester en Arles?

Magali — partir en colonie de vacances?

aller voir ses cousins? — Magali

aller à la montagne? — Magali

faire du camping? — Ahmed

3 Vrai ou faux?

1. Tous les jeunes restent en France pendant les vacances. vrai
2. Les cousins de Magali habitent à la montagne. vrai
3. Ahmed va faire du camping dans les Alpes. faux
4. Ahmed va travailler dans un café. faux
5. Ahmed veut aller au Festival de la photographie. faux
6. Florent part en colonie de vacances. faux

4 Cherche les expressions

According to **Bientôt les vacances!**, what can you say in French. . .

1. to ask what someone is going to do? ... qu'est-ce que vous allez faire... ?
2. to tell what a place looks like? C'est super joli...
3. to express an opinion? C'est sympa! C'est génial!
4. to express indecision? ... je n'ai rien de prévu. Je n'ai pas encore décidé.
5. to make a suggestion? Pourquoi est-ce que tu ne... pas... ? Tu peux...
6. to express a preference? ... je préfère...

5 Et maintenant, à toi

Whose vacation plans are the most interesting to you? Why?

PREMIERE ETAPE

Inquiring about and sharing future plans; expressing indecision; expressing wishes; asking for advice; making, accepting, and refusing suggestions

VOCABULAIRE

Où est-ce que tu vas aller pendant tes vacances?

à la montagne

à la campagne

au bord de la mer

en forêt

en colonie de vacances

chez les grands-parents

Qu'est-ce qu'on peut y faire?

faire du camping

faire de la randonnée

faire du bateau

faire de la plongée

faire de la planche à voile

faire de la voile

6 Ecoute!

Listen as Nathalie, Bruno, Pauline, and Emile tell about their vacation plans. What is each teenager going to do? Answers on p. 281C.

PREMIERE ETAPE   *deux cent quatre-vingt-sept* **287**

RESOURCES FOR PREMIERE ETAPE

Textbook Audiocassette 6A/Audio CD 11
Practice and Activity Book, pp. 122–124
Video Guide
  Video Program
  Expanded Video Program, Videocassette 4
Videodisc Guide
  Videodisc Program, Videodisc 6A

Chapter Teaching Resources, Book 3
• Teaching Transparency Master 11-1, pp. 119, 122
  Teaching Transparency 11-1
• Additional Listening Activities 11-1, 11-2, p. 123
  Audiocassette 10B/Audio CD 11
• Realia 11-1, pp. 127, 129
• Situation Cards 11-1, pp. 130–131
• Student Response Forms, pp. 132–134
• Quiz 11-1, pp. 135–136
  Audiocassette 8B/Audio CD 11

Jump Start!

Have students write sentences telling whether or not they do the following sports: **faire de l'aérobic, faire de la natation, faire du vélo, jouer au football, jouer au tennis, faire du ski nautique.**

MOTIVATE

Tell students to plan a summer camp for their friends and classmates. Ask them where they would have the camp and what activities they would offer.

TEACH

Presentation

Vocabulaire Use magazine illustrations to present the new vocabulary. Then, ask **On est où?** as you show pictures of the places, and **Qu'est-ce qu'on fait?** as you show pictures of activities. Next, ask if students have been to these places (**Tu es déjà allé(e) à la montagne?**) and what there is to do there. (**Qu'est-ce qu'on peut y faire?**) Finally, have pairs of students do a clustering activity. Tell them to write down one of the locations and circle it; this is the center of a flower. Then, have them write related words, expressions, and activities in French and English in the petals of the flower.

Teaching Suggestion

6 Stop the recording after each person speaks to elicit answers.

For Individual Needs

Visual/Kinesthetic Learners
To practice the vacation vocabulary, have students play the game "**Dessin animé,**" described on page 281F.

Teaching Suggestions

De bons conseils Have students look back at the vocabulary pages in previous chapters to find examples of words with these endings. Examples include **éducation, sortie, vaisselle, piscine, heure, plage, ménage, devoir, classeur,** and **manteau.** You might have groups compete to find the most words.

Tu te rappelles? You might want to review the forms of **aller** with students before doing Activity 7.

Additional Practice

7 Ask students to tell or write whether they are going to do the same activities, using **je** or **nous.**

♜ Game

♜ **VRAI OU FAUX?** Have students write three true-false statements about what Vincent and Roland are going to do on vacation. Then, form two teams. Have the first player from one team read a statement. The player from the other team tells whether the statement is true or false. If the player is correct, he or she reads a statement to the first team. If not, the second player of the first team reads another statement. Award points for correct answers.

Teaching Suggestion

Note Culturelle You might want to take a poll of how many students have ever attended a summer camp. Ask them if they enjoyed it, how long they stayed there, and what activities were offered. You might have students compare the activities they've enjoyed at summer camps or seen in movies about summer camps with the types of activities offered in the **colonies de vacances.**

Although there are few hard-and-fast rules to help you remember if a noun is masculine or feminine, you can often predict the gender of a word by its ending. Some of the endings that usually indicate a feminine word are **-tion, -sion, -ie, -ette, -elle, -ine, -ude,** and **-ure.** Endings that often signal a masculine word are **-ment, -age, -oir, -ier, -et,** and **-eau.** But be careful! There are exceptions.

Tu te rappelles?

Do you remember how to tell what is going to happen? Use a form of the verb **aller** *(to go)* plus the infinitive of another verb.
Demain, je **vais faire** du bateau.

Si tu as oublié the verb aller va à la page 154.

7 Dans une colonie de vacances

Qu'est-ce que Vincent et Roland vont faire en colonie de vacances?

Ils vont... **1.** faire de la planche à voile.　**2.** faire de la plongée.　**3.** faire du ski nautique.

4. jouer au football.　**5.** faire de l'équitation.　**6.** faire de la voile.

NOTE CULTURELLE

In francophone countries, many children and teenagers attend summer camps (**colonies de vacances**), where they learn folklore, folk dances, arts and crafts, foreign languages, and many other subjects. Of course, they also participate in sports. The camps are usually run by young adults called **animateurs.** In France alone there are hundreds of **colonies de vacances.**

288 *deux cent quatre-vingt-huit*　　　　CHAPITRE 11　Vive les vacances!

Language Notes

- The word **animateur (animatrice)** is also used to describe hosts of TV shows or anyone who plans and leads group activities.
- You might want to point out that **au bord de la mer** *(to/on the coast)* is not exactly synonymous with **à la plage,** which refers specifically to the beach.

COMMENT DIT-ON... ?

Inquiring about and sharing future plans; expressing indecision; expressing wishes

To inquire about someone's plans:
> Qu'est-ce que tu vas faire cet été?
> Où est-ce que tu vas aller pendant les vacances?

To express indecision:
> J'hésite.
> Je ne sais pas.
> Je n'en sais rien. *I have no idea.*
> Je n'ai rien de prévu. *I don't have any plans.*

To share your plans:
> En juillet, **je vais** travailler.
> En août, **j'ai l'intention d**'aller en Algérie. . . . *I intend to . . .*

To express wishes:
> **Je voudrais bien** aller chez mes cousins.
> **J'ai envie de** travailler. *I feel like . . .*

8 Ecoute!

Listen to these speakers talk about their vacations. Do they have definite plans or are they undecided? Answers on p. 281C.

9 Les vacances en France

Imagine you're going to France on vacation next summer. Your partner will ask about your vacation plans. Tell what you feel like doing or plan to do there. Then, change roles.

visiter le Louvre   faire des photos   faire du ski   rencontrer des jeunes français   voir la tour Eiffel   parler français   aller à un concert de rock français   aller au café

🏰 Game

LES VACANCES Write different answers to the question **Qu'est-ce que tu vas faire cet été?** on index cards. Write each answer on two separate cards. Include plans that your students would be likely to have, such as **Je vais travailler comme maître nageur** *(lifeguard)* **à la piscine.** Distribute one card to each student. Students circulate and ask about each other's plans until they find the person whose card matches theirs.

CHAPITRE 11   PREMIERE ETAPE   289

Presentation

Comment dit-on... ? To introduce the new expressions, prompt three students to ask you the questions. In response to one student, express indecision. In response to another student, share your plans, and in response to a third, express your wishes. Then, ask students what they would like to do tonight and what they're going to do tonight. Finally, have partners ask each other about their weekend plans. You might want to have students refer to their "cluster flowers" for activities they'd like to do. (See Presentation on page 287.)

 For videodisc application, see *Videodisc Guide.*

Teaching Suggestions

8 You might have students write down the destination(s) or activities mentioned by the speakers.

9 Have students suggest other things they'd like to do. Write their suggestions on a transparency for reference during the activity. Remind students to reverse roles.

◆ For Individual Needs

9 Visual Learners Show *Teaching Transparency 11-1.* Have students look at the posters displayed in the travel agency for additional vacation destinations and activities.

Presentation

Note de grammaire After explaining the use of **à** with cities and **en** and **au** with countries, have students practice by asking one another where they would like to go for their next vacation. You might also have small groups make suggestions and decide together on a vacation destination. Write **Pourquoi pas aller... ?** and **On peut aller... ?** on the board as prompts.

Game

Où se trouve... ? Hold a geography contest. Students on one team name a well-known city; their opponents tell in which country or state it is located. Refer students to the Supplementary Vocabulary on page 344 for additional country names.

For Individual Needs

10 Challenge Have students write one or two sentences describing what they would like to see or do on vacation and have the class guess where each student would like to go. Encourage them to use the locations already presented in the book (Poitiers, Quebec, Paris, Abidjan, Arles).

Teaching Suggestion

12 Before students do this activity, re-enter the expressions in **Tu te rappelles?** by asking students for advice on where to go for vacation.

Portfolio

12 Oral This activity is appropriate for students' oral portfolios. For portfolio information, see *Assessment Guide*, pages 2–13.

Note de *Grammaire*

- To say *to* or *in* before the names of most cities, use the preposition **à**.

  Tu vas **à** Paris pendant les vacances?

- Names of countries are either masculine or feminine. Use **au** *(to, in)* before all masculine names and **en** *(to, in)* before all feminine names. Use **en** before the names of all countries that begin with a vowel. Before any plural name, use **aux**.

  Vous allez **au** Canada?

  Hélène va **en** Allemagne.

  Nous allons **aux** Etats-Unis.

- States and provinces follow slightly different rules.

Vocabulaire *à la carte*

en Angleterre	en Floride
en Allemagne	en Italie
en Australie	au Maroc
en Belgique	au Mexique
au Brésil	en Russie
en Californie	au Sénégal
en Chine	en Suisse
en Egypte	au Texas
en Espagne	au Viêt-Nam

---

10 Où vont-ils?

Dans quel pays vont-ils passer leurs vacances?

au Canada   au Maroc
aux Etats-Unis
en Russie   en Angleterre
en Egypte   en France

1. Murielle va prendre des photos de la tour Eiffel.   en France
2. Monique va visiter le château Frontenac.   au Canada
3. Joseph va visiter la tour de Londres.   en Angleterre
4. Mathieu va voir les pyramides.   en Egypte
5. Than et Laure vont visiter le Texas.   aux Etats-Unis
6. Dominique va voir le Kremlin.   en Russie
7. Paul et Gilles vont aller à Casablanca.   au Maroc

11 On y fait quoi?

Select two of the countries from Activity 10 and discuss with your group at least three activities you would like to do on vacation in each one.

12 Un voyage gratuit

You've won a trip from an airline to anywhere you want. Where will you go? Why? What will you do there? Discuss this with a partner. Take turns.

Tu te rappelles?

Do you remember how to ask for advice? Make, accept, and refuse suggestions?

To ask for advice:
Je ne sais pas quoi faire (où aller).
Tu as une idée?
Qu'est-ce que tu me conseilles?

To make suggestions:
Je te conseille de...
Tu devrais...

To accept suggestions:
C'est une bonne idée!
Pourquoi pas?
D'accord!
Allons-y!

To refuse suggestions:
Non, ce n'est pas possible.
Non, je ne peux pas.
Ça ne me dit rien.
C'est trop cher.

290   *deux cent quatre-vingt-dix*   CHAPITRE 11   Vive les vacances!

Geography Link

To practice the country names, you might want to play the game "**Je l'ai trouvé,**" which is described on page 281F. To prepare your students for the game, divide the class into small groups and give each group a list of ten or twelve countries to locate on a world map.

Language Notes

- The preposition **en** is used instead of **à** with the town of Arles.
- Point out that the names of countries are feminine if they end in **-e**, with the exception of **le Mexique** and **le Zaïre**.

13 Ecoute!

Ecoute Alain et Valérie qui parlent de leurs vacances. Est-ce que ces phrases sont vraies ou fausses? *Answers on p. 281C.*

1. Alain ne sait pas quoi faire.
2. Valérie n'a pas d'idées.
3. Valérie est déjà allée à la Martinique.
4. Alain ne veut pas aller à la Martinique.

^A la française

Use the words **alors** *(so, then, well, in that case)* and **donc** *(so, then, therefore)* to connect your sentences.

J'adore faire de la plongée, **donc** je vais en Australie.
Tu aimes faire du bateau? **Alors,** tu devrais aller à Marseille.

14 Des conseils

Ces élèves rêvent *(are dreaming)* de ce qu'ils aiment. Ils ne savent pas où aller pendant les vacances. Tu as une idée? *Possible answers:* Tu devrais aller... ; Je te conseille d'aller...

Malika   au musée.

Marion   en forêt.

Hai   en Egypte.

Christian   au bord de la mer.

Adrienne   en Afrique.

Ali   en colonie de vacances.

15 Où aller?

Tell your partner what you like to do on vacation. Your partner will then make some suggestions about where you might want to go. Accept your partner's suggestions, or refuse them and give an excuse. Then, change roles.

16 Mon journal

Décris un voyage que tu vas faire ou que tu voudrais faire. Où veux-tu aller? Quand? Avec qui? Qu'est-ce que tu vas y faire?

For Individual Needs

13 Slower Pace Before playing the recording, read the statements aloud. Ask students what they think the conversations will be about, based on these statements.

Teaching Suggestion

A la française Write the following sentences on a transparency. Have students match and then combine them, using **donc** or **alors.**

1. J'aime faire du camping.
2. Je vais chez ma tante.
3. J'aime faire de la voile.
4. Je vais au bord de la mer.

a. Je vais au Québec.
b. Je vais au bord de la mer.
c. J'apporte un cadeau.
d. J'ai besoin de mon maillot de bain.

Mon journal

16 For an additional journal entry suggestion for Chapter 11, see *Practice and Activity Book,* page 155.

CLOSE

To close this **étape**, have students choose cards with vacation destinations written on them (**au Québec, à la montagne, en Côte d'Ivoire**) and list at least two things they plan to do there.

ASSESS

Quiz 11-1, *Chapter Teaching Resources, Book 3,* pp. 135–136

Assessment Items, Audiocassette 8B/Audio CD 11

Performance Assessment

Have students create radio commercials to promote their favorite vacation destination. They should describe the activities available as well as the weather.

VIDEO PROGRAM OR EXPANDED VIDEO PROGRAM, Videocassette 4 25:06–28:24

OR *VIDEODISC PROGRAM,* Videodisc 6A

Search 17600, Play To 20340

Teacher Notes

- See *Video Guide, Videodisc Guide,* and *Practice and Activity Book* for activities related to the **Panorama Culturel.**
- Remind students that cultural material may be included in the Chapter Quizzes and Test.
- The interviewees' language represents informal, unrehearsed speech. Occasionally, edits have been made for clarification.

Presentation

Before playing the video, ask students to listen for what the people do on vacation. Remind them that they don't need to understand every word, just the general idea. After playing the video, have students read the interviews in groups and write answers to the questions in **Qu'en penses**-tu? Then, have groups share their answers.

Thinking Critically

Drawing Inferences After reading **Savais-tu que… ?,** have groups discuss the following questions: Why do you think people in the United States aren't guaranteed five weeks of vacation a year? What would happen if everyone went on vacation at the same time? Why do you think it is different in France?

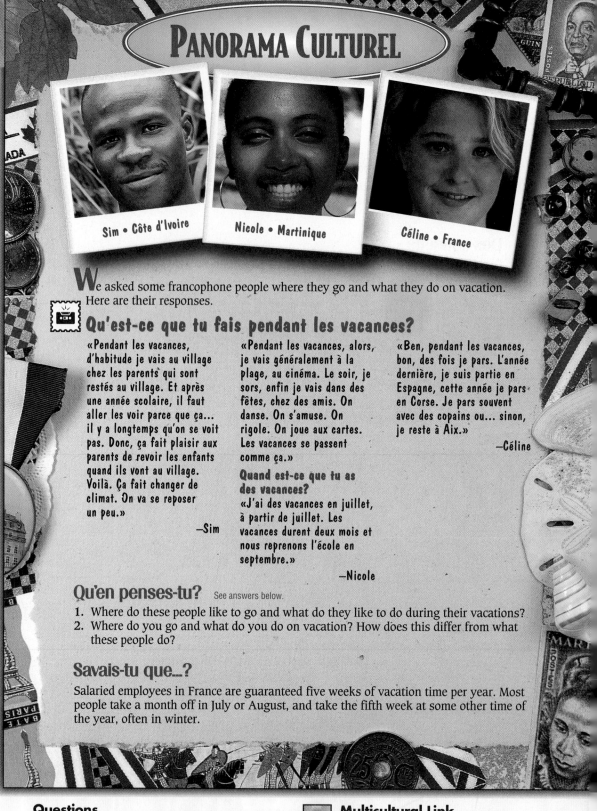

PANORAMA CULTUREL

Sim • Côte d'Ivoire

Nicole • Martinique

Céline • France

We asked some francophone people where they go and what they do on vacation. Here are their responses.

Qu'est-ce que tu fais pendant les vacances?

«Pendant les vacances, d'habitude je vais au village chez les parents qui sont restés au village. Et après une année scolaire, il faut aller les voir parce que ça... il y a longtemps qu'on se voit pas. Donc, ça fait plaisir aux parents de revoir les enfants quand ils vont au village. Voilà. Ça fait changer de climat. On va se reposer un peu.»

—Sim

«Pendant les vacances, alors, je vais généralement à la plage, au cinéma. Le soir, je sors, enfin je vais dans des fêtes, chez des amis. On danse. On s'amuse. On rigole. On joue aux cartes. Les vacances se passent comme ça.»

Quand est-ce que tu as des vacances?

«J'ai des vacances en juillet, à partir de juillet. Les vacances durent deux mois et nous reprenons l'école en septembre.»

—Nicole

«Ben, pendant les vacances, bon, des fois je pars. L'année dernière, je suis partie en Espagne, cette année je pars en Corse. Je pars souvent avec des copains ou... sinon, je reste à Aix.»

—Céline

Qu'en penses-tu? See answers below.

1. Where do these people like to go and what do they like to do during their vacations?
2. Where do you go and what do you do on vacation? How does this differ from what these people do?

Savais-tu que…?

Salaried employees in France are guaranteed five weeks of vacation time per year. Most people take a month off in July or August, and take the fifth week at some other time of the year, often in winter.

Questions

1. Pourquoi est-ce que Sim va au village? (pour voir les parents, parce que ça fait changer de climat)
2. Qu'est-ce que Nicole fait aux fêtes de ses amis? (Elle danse, s'amuse, rigole, joue aux cartes.)
3. Nicole a combien de mois de vacances? (deux)
4. Avec qui est-ce que Céline part en vacances? (avec des amis)

Multicultural Link

Have students choose a country and find out how much vacation time people usually have and when they usually take their vacations.

Answers

1. parents' village, the beach, the movies, parties, friends' homes, Spain, Corsica; dance, have fun, laugh, play cards

DEUXIEME ETAPE

Reminding; reassuring; seeing someone off

VOCABULAIRE

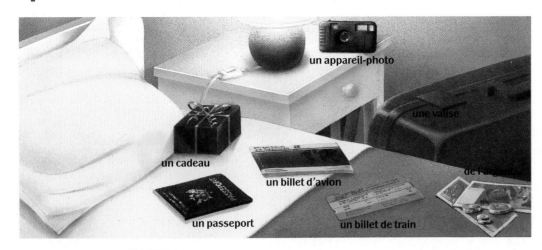

un appareil-photo
une valise
un cadeau
un billet d'avion
de l'argent
un passeport
un billet de train

17 Qu'est-ce qu'il te faut?

1. Qu'est-ce qu'il faut pour entrer dans un pays étranger?   un passeport
2. Qu'est-ce qu'il faut pour prendre le train?   un billet de train
3. Qu'est-ce qu'il faut pour acheter des souvenirs?   de l'argent
4. Qu'est-ce qu'on offre à des amis?   un cadeau

COMMENT DIT-ON... ?
Reminding; reassuring

To remind someone of something:
   N'oublie pas ton passeport!
   Tu n'as pas oublié ton billet d'avion?   *You didn't forget . . . ?*
   Tu ne peux pas partir sans ton écharpe!   *You can't leave without . . . !*
   Tu prends ton manteau?   *Are you taking . . . ?*

To reassure someone:
   Ne t'en fais pas.
   J'ai pensé à tout.   *I've thought of everything.*
   Je n'ai rien oublié.   *I didn't forget anything.*

Jump Start!

Have students write where the following people could be going on vacation: **Nous voulons voir les pyramides. Anne-Marie et Yvette aiment faire du ski. Marco veut pratiquer son espagnol.**

MOTIVATE

Have students tell in French what they would need to pack for a vacation in Martinique, France, Canada, or Côte d'Ivoire.

TEACH

Presentation

Vocabulaire   Introduce the vocabulary using real items or pictures from magazines. Then, mime actions that involve the items and have students call out the French names.

Comment dit-on... ?   After introducing the expressions, have students use them to remind you of items to pack for your trip, using the items in the **Vocabulaire** as well as clothing vocabulary. You might bring a real suitcase and various clothing items and pack according to students' instructions. Vary your destinations. (**Je vais faire du ski dans les Alpes. Je vais en colonie de vacances.**)

For videodisc application, see *Videodisc Guide.*

Culture Note
   Ask students who the gift in the **Vocabulaire** is for (the host family). In many francophone regions, it is considered polite for a guest to bring a small gift for his or her host. Have students suggest small gifts they might bring.

For Individual Needs

18 Slower Pace Before playing the recording, say random expressions from **Comment dit-on... ?** on page 293 and ask students to indicate whether you are reminding or reassuring someone.

19 Slower Pace Before students list what Jean-Paul has forgotten, have them copy his list and check off what he remembered to pack.

19 Challenge You might also want to have students make a list of things Jean-Paul may have packed that are not on his list.

Teaching Suggestion

20 Before doing this activity, have students make a short list of items they might need.

Presentation

Grammaire Walk out the door, saying **Salut! Je pars!** Then, have various students walk towards the door as you describe their actions, using the forms of **partir**. Have students repeat the forms after you, and then have them deduce the forms of **sortir** and **dormir**. Write their guesses on a transparency, correcting any mistakes. Next, have students mime sleeping or leaving and ask the class **Qu'est-ce qu'il/elle fait?**

♟ Game

TIC-TAC-TOE Draw a tic-tac-toe grid on the board. Write a subject pronoun and the infinitive **sortir, dormir,** or **partir** in each square and have students copy the grid. In order to mark an *X* or an *O* in a square, players must first write the correct verb form in that square. Have students play the game with a partner.

---

18 **Ecoute!**

Listen to these speakers. Are they reminding or reassuring someone? *Answers on p. 281D.*

19 **Qu'est-ce qu'il a oublié?**

Read the list of things Jean-Paul needs for his trip. Make a list of what he's forgotten to pack. Next, play the role of Jean-Paul's parent and remind him what to take. Then, change roles.

Si tu as oublié clothing va à la page 261.

appareil-photo
billet d'avion
billet de train
passeport
dictionnaire
magazines

casquette
baskets
shorts
chaussures
chaussettes
cadeaux

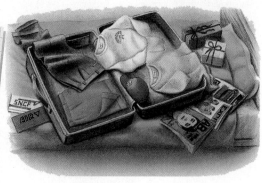

20 **Jeu de rôle**

You're going on a trip to France this summer with the French Club. Ask your friend, who went last year, what you should take. He or she will remind you of some things you'll need. Act this out with a partner and then change roles.

---

*G*rammaire   **The verb partir**

A small group of verbs whose infinitives end in **-ir** follow a pattern different than the one you learned in Chapter 10.

partir *(to leave)*

Je **pars**
Tu **pars** ⎫ à dix heures.
Il/Elle/On **part** ⎭

Nous **partons**
Vous **partez** ⎫ à dix heures.
Ils/Elles **partent** ⎭

- Don't pronounce the **s** or **t** in **pars** or **part**.
- **Sortir** *(to go out)* and **dormir** *(to sleep)* also follow this pattern.

A la française

French speakers often use the present tense to talk about the future.

Je **pars** à neuf heures. *I'm leaving (or) I'm going to/will leave . . .*
Je **vais** à la plage samedi. *I'm going (or) I'm going to/will go . . .*

---

294 *deux cent quatre-vingt-quatorze*   CHAPITRE 11   Vive les vacances!

Teacher Note

Students may want to know some additional travel-related vocabulary: **la gare** *(train station)*; **l'aéroport** *(airport)*; **des chèques de voyage** *(traveler's checks)*; **une pellicule/un film** *(roll of film)*.

Language Notes

- You might want to explain to your students that **partir** means *to leave* and is used to stress the action of going away. **Sortir,** however, implies that one is *going out* for a short period of time and will be returning soon.
- Remind students that **partir, sortir,** and **dormir** follow a different pattern than -ir verbs like **choisir** and **finir.**

21 On part à quelle heure?

Ces jeunes vont aller en vacances. Ils partent à quelle heure?

1. 18h15 Ils partent à dix-huit heures quinze.

2. 21h30 Elle part à vingt et une heures trente.

3. 22h15 Elles partent à vingt-deux heures quinze.

22 Vacances en Provence   See answers below.

Regarde l'itinéraire de Marianne. Ensuite, réponds aux questions.

1. D'où part Marianne?
2. Où est-ce qu'elle va?
3. Son voyage va durer combien de temps?
4. Qu'est-ce qu'elle a l'intention de faire?

23 Jeu de rôle

You're going to take the same trip as Marianne. Your partner will ask you questions about the trip and remind you what to take.

24 Bonjour de Provence!

Pendant ton voyage en Provence, écris une carte postale à ton ami(e), à tes camarades de classe ou à ton professeur.

Bienvenue en Provence!

SAMEDI :

départ Arles, bus de 9h35;
arrivée aux Baux-de-Provence à 10h10;
* visite de la Cathédrale d'Images;
dîner : Auberge de la Benvengudo

DIMANCHE :

départ pour Saint-Rémy de Provence, bus de 9h15;
arrivée à 9h45;
* visite du musée Van Gogh; déjeuner : pique-nique à Fontvieille;

* visite du moulin de Daudet;
retour aux Baux-de-Provence;
départ pour Avignon, bus de 18h16;
arrivée à 19h10 Hôtel le Midi; dîner

LUNDI :

* visite de la Cité des Papes, le Pont St-Bénézet, promenade du Rocher des Doms, le musée du Petit-Palais;
* spectacle folklorique;
départ pour Grasse 20h15;
arrivée à 22h10 Hôtel les Aromes

MARDI :

* visite de la Parfumerie Fragonard;
* Musée d'Art et d'Histoire de Provence; retour en Arles 17h42;
arrivée à 19h20

DEUXIEME ETAPE   *deux cent quatre-vingt-quinze*   **295**

Additional Practice

21 To practice the other forms of **partir,** you might use large flashcards with different subject pronouns written on them and a clock with moveable hands. Set the clock to a certain time and hold up a subject flashcard, asking **On part à quelle heure?**

For Individual Needs

22 Challenge Have students write a short paragraph describing what Marianne is going to do during one day of her vacation. This might also be done orally. This activity is appropriate for students' written or oral portfolios.

Portfolio

24 Written This activity might be included in students' written portfolios. For portfolio information, see *Assessment Guide,* pages 2–13.

Teaching Suggestion

24 Students might write this activity on an index card and illustrate it on the reverse side. Refer them to the Location Opener on pages 228–231 for illustration ideas.

Teacher Note

The postcard below Activity 24 features fields of lavender (**la lavande**), a flower native to the Provence region.

Answers

22 1. d'Arles

2. aux Baux-de-Provence, à Saint-Rémy de Provence, à Avignon et à Grasse
3. quatre jours
4. *Possible answers:* visiter une cathédrale, des musées et une parfumerie, assister à un spectacle folklorique

History Link

23 Before doing this activity, you might have groups of students research the historical significance of each of the places Marianne is visiting: **la Cathédrale d'Images, le musée Van Gogh, le moulin de Daudet, la Cité des Papes, le Pont Saint-Bénézet, le Rocher des Doms, le musée du Petit Palais, la Parfumerie Fragonard,** and **le Musée d'Art et d'Histoire de Provence.**

Presentation

Comment dit-on... ? Ask students what they say in English to see someone off at the airport or at the train or bus station. Have several students read the text in the speech bubbles. Then, introduce the expressions while waving goodbye and have students practice them with a partner.

Additional Practice

Ask students what they would say to a friend who was leaving on a long car trip; who was leaving on June 1; who was going to Disneyland; who was leaving for a band competition.

Teaching Suggestion

26 Encourage students to expand their goodbyes by telling the person what to do during the flight or after he or she gets home. They might use **N'oublie pas de...** or **Pense à...**

Geography Link

27 Encourage students to use atlases or other reference materials to find out more about the climate and topography of their chosen vacation spot.

CLOSE

♟ Game

N'OUBLIE PAS! Name a vacation destination and have a student remind you of one thing to take. The next student should repeat the first item and remind you of another. Continue until everyone has had a chance to add an item or until a mistake is made, in which case, you might give another destination and restart the game.

COMMENT DIT-ON... ?
Seeing someone off

To wish someone a good trip:
Bon voyage! *Have a good trip!*
Bonnes vacances! *Have a good vacation!*
Amuse-toi bien! *Have fun!*
Bonne chance! *Good luck!*

25 Ecoute!

Ecoute ces conversations. On arrive ou on part?
Answers on p. 281D.

26 Au revoir!

It's time for your French exchange student to return home. See him or her off at the airport. Act this out with your partner.

27 Un grand voyage

You and a friend have decided to take a trip together to a foreign country. Decide where you will go and what you will do there. Talk about the weather conditions and when you will go. Discuss what clothes and other items you each plan to pack and what you will wear on the plane.

28 Un petit mot

Your friend is leaving on a trip tomorrow. Write a note wishing him or her well and suggesting things he or she might like to see and do while on vacation.

Tu te rappelles?

Do you remember how to give commands? Use the **tu** or **vous** form of the verb without a subject.

Attends! Allez!

When you use an **-er** verb, remember to drop the final **s** of the **tu** form.

Ecoute!

When you use an object pronoun with a positive command, place it after the verb, separated by a hyphen in writing.

Donnez-moi votre billet, s'il vous plaît.

Si tu as oublié weather *va à la page 106.*

ASSESS

Quiz 11-2, *Chapter Teaching Resources, Book 3*, pp. 137–138

Assessment Items, Audiocassette 8B Audio CD 11

Performance Assessment

Have students write a note to a friend who is going on vacation. They should make up a destination, make suggestions about what to take and do, and say goodbye.

TROISIEME ETAPE

Asking for and expressing opinions; inquiring about and relating past events

COMMENT DIT-ON... ?
Asking for and expressing opinions

To ask someone's opinion:
Tu as passé un bon été?

Ça s'est bien passé?
Did it go well?

Tu t'es bien amusé(e)?
Did you have fun?

To express an opinion:
Oui, très chouette.
Oui, c'était formidable!
Yes, it was great!
Oui, ça a été.
Oh, pas mauvais.
C'était épouvantable.
Non, pas vraiment. *No, not really.*
C'était un véritable cauchemar!
It was a real nightmare!
C'était ennuyeux. *It was boring.*

---

29 Ecoute!
Listen to these conversations and then tell whether these people had a good, fair, or bad vacation.
Answers on p. 281D.

30 Méli-mélo!
Remets la conversation entre Thierry et Hervé dans l'ordre.

Tu te rappelles ?
Do you remember how to inquire about and relate events that happened in the past?
Tu es allé(e) où?
Qu'est-ce que tu as fait?
D'abord,... Ensuite,... Après,... Enfin,...

—Où est-ce que vous êtes allés? 5
—Qu'est-ce que tu as fait? 3
—Et ensuite? 7
—Salut, Hervé! Ça s'est bien passé, l'été? 1

—On est allés chez mon oncle à la campagne. C'est barbant chez lui. 6
—Ah non, alors! C'était ennuyeux! 2
—Après ça, on est rentrés à la maison. 8
—Je suis allé en vacances avec mes parents. 4

TROISIEME ETAPE
deux cent quatre-vingt-dix-sept **297**

Jump Start!
Have students write a note to a French friend who is coming to visit, reminding him or her of three things to pack for the trip.

MOTIVATE
Ask students in English how their weekends were. Then, have them list French expressions they've already learned for giving opinions, such as **super, barbant,** and **chouette.**

TEACH

Presentation
Comment dit-on... ? Teach these expressions using appropriate gestures or facial expressions. Then, make the same gestures or facial expressions and have students give the appropriate French expression for each. Ask students how they would respond if they had done various activities, such as **garder ma petite sœur** or **faire la connaissance de Whitney Houston.** Ask several students to tell how their weekends were, and then have partners ask and tell each other how their weekends or summers were.

For Individual Needs
29 Challenge Have students imagine they spent their vacation in a certain place and write a sentence telling how it was. Then, have them read the sentence to a partner, who will indicate whether the student had a good, fair, or bad time.

Tu te rappelles ?

Do you remember how to form the **passé composé?** Use a form of **avoir** as a helping verb with the past participle of the main verb. The past participles of regular **-er, -re,** and **-ir** verbs end in **é, u,** and **i.**

Nous **avons** beaucoup **mangé.**   J'**ai répondu** à leur lettre.   Ils **ont fini.**

You have to memorize the past participles of irregular verbs.

J'**ai fait** du camping.   Ils **ont vu** un film.

To make a verb in the **passé composé** negative, you place **ne… pas** around the helping verb.

Il **n'a pas** fait ses devoirs.

With **aller,** you use **être** as the helping verb instead of **avoir.**

31 Qu'est-ce qu'elle a fait ?

Mets ces activités en ordre d'après l'itinéraire de Marianne à la page 295.   See answers below.

D'abord, elle…

visiter le musée Van Gogh

voir un spectacle folklorique

visiter la Parfumerie Fragonard

visiter la Cité des Papes

voir le moulin de Daudet

faire la promenade du Rocher des Doms

faire un pique-nique

32 On fait la même chose ?

You and your partner took these photographs on a trip to France last year. Take turns telling where you went, what you did, and what you thought of each place or activity.

Un café sur le cours Mirabeau

Le palais des Papes, c'est formidable.

La mer Méditerrarée

Les arènes à Arles

La Côte d'Azur

298   *deux cent quatre-vingt-dix-huit*   CHAPITRE 11   Vive les vacances !

33 On est de retour

Tu reviens d'un voyage. Ton ami(e) te demande où tu es allé(e), avec qui, ce que tu as fait et comment ça s'est passé.

P R O N O N C I A T I O N

Aspirated h, th, ch, and gn

You've learned that you don't pronounce the letter **h** in French. Some words begin with an aspirated **h** (**h aspiré**). This means that you don't make elision and liaison with the word that comes before. Repeat these phrases: **le haut-parleur; le houx; les halls; les haricots.**

Haut and **houx** begin with an aspirated **h**, so you can't drop the **e** from the article **le.** **Halls** and **haricots** also begin with an aspirated **h**, so you don't pronounce the **s** in the article **les.** How will you know which words begin with an aspirated **h**? If you look the words up in the dictionary, you may find an asterisk (*) before an aspirated **h.**

How do you pronounce the combination **th**? Just ignore the letter **h** and pronounce the **t.** Repeat these words: **mathématiques, théâtre, athlète.**

What about the combination **ch**? In French, **ch** is pronounced like the English *sh,* as in the word *show.* Compare these English and French words: *change/***change,** *chocolate/***chocolat,** *chance/***chance.** In some words, **ch** is pronounced like *k.* Listen to these words and repeat them: **chorale, Christine, archéologie.**

Finally, how do you pronounce the combination **gn**? The English sound /ny/, as in the word *onion* is similar. Pronounce these words: **oignon, montagne, magnifique.**

A. A prononcer

Repeat the following words.

1. le héros	la harpe	le hippie	le hockey
2. thème	maths	mythe	bibliothèque
3. Chine	choisir	tranche	pêches
4. espagnol	champignon	montagne	magnifique

B. A lire

Take turns with a partner reading each of the following sentences aloud.

1. J'aime la Hollande, mais je veux aller à la montagne en Allemagne.
2. Je cherche une chemise, des chaussures et un chapeau.
3. Il n'a pas fait ses devoirs de maths et de chimie à la bibliothèque dimanche.
4. Charles a gagné trois hamsters. Ils sont dans ma chambre! Quel cauchemar!

C. A écrire

You're going to hear a short dialogue. Write down what you hear. *Answers on p. 281D.*

Portfolio

33 Oral This might be included in students' oral portfolios. For portfolio information, see *Assessment Guide,* pages 2–13.

Teaching Suggestion

Prononciation You might have students prepare any two of the sentences in Part B to read aloud for oral assessment.

CLOSE

To close this **étape,** show *Teaching Transparency 11-3.* Ask students what the teenagers did on vacation and how they felt about it. You might have students form groups of four and role-play the teenagers' discussion.

ASSESS

Quiz 11-3, *Chapter Teaching Resources, Book 3,* pp. 139–140

Assessment Items, Audiocassette 8B/Audio CD 11

Performance Assessment

Have students act out a phone conversation between two friends who are comparing their weekends. Be sure they mention how their weekends were and what they did.

Language Notes

• The word **le houx** means *holly.*
• Many words with the **h aspiré** are of Germanic rather than Latin origin, or were borrowed from modern German or English. You might point out that words of these origins generally do not have **l'** preceding them, with the exception of **l'héroïne.**

Teacher Note

For an additional reading, see *Practice and Activity Book,* page 131.

PREREADING
Activities A–D

Motivating Activity

Point out Provence on a map. Have students share information they have already learned about Provence through the Location Opener for Chapters 9–11, the **Notes Culturelles,** and their projects for Chapter 9. Ask students what kinds of things they would do if they were to go on a vacation to Provence. You might show a short video or some slides of Provence, or read a short passage from a book about Provence. See Peter Mayle's books: *A Year in Provence, Provence, Toujours Provence,* and *Hôtel Pastis.*

Teaching Suggestion

Before beginning the activities, have students look at travel guides for New York City, Chicago, Dallas, and so on. You might also ask them to bring in travel guides. Have groups of students go through the guides that are available and identify the general categories of information found in them. Then, do Activities A-D as a class.

LISONS!

$\mathcal{W}$hat would you like to do if you were visiting Provence?

DE BONS CONSEILS

When you read for a purpose, it's a good idea to decide beforehand what kind of information you want. If you're looking for an overview, a quick, general reading may be all that is required. If you're looking for specific details, you'll have to read more carefully.

A. The information at the top of both pages is from a book entitled *Le Guide du Routard.* Do you think this is

1. a history book?
2. <u>a travel guide?</u>
3. a geography book?

B. You usually read a book like this to gather general information about what is going on, or to find details about a certain place or event. What general categories of information can you find? Under what titles?   See answers below.

C. Where should you stay if . . .

1. you plan to visit Provence in November?
2. you want a balcony?
3. you want the least expensive room you can get?
4. you have a tent and a sleeping bag?   See answers below.

D. Which restaurant should you try if . . .   See answers below.

1. you want the most expensive meal available?
2. you love salad?
3. you want to go out on Sunday night?

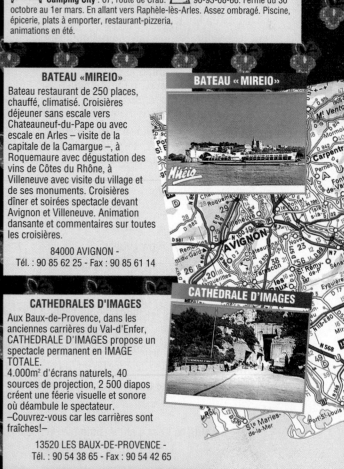

ARLES (13200)

Où dormir?

Très bon marché

Auberge de jeunesse : 20, av. Foch. ☎ 90-96-18-25. Fax : 90-96-31-26. Fermée pendant les vacances de Noël. 100 lits. 75 F la nuit, draps et petit déjeuner compris. Fait aussi restaurant. Repas à 45 F.

Prix modérés

Hôtel Gauguin : 5, place Voltaire. ☎ 90-96-14-35. Fermé du 15 novembre au 20 décembre et du 10 janvier au 15 février. De 130 à 190 F la double. Sur trois étages. Chambres simples, bien aménagées. Celles qui donnent sur la place ont un balcon. Peu de charme cependant dans ce quartier de l'après-guerre.

Plus chic

Hôtel Diderot : 5, rue Diderot. ☎ 90-96-10-30. Fermé du 6 janvier au 31 mars. 14 chambres. De 140 F la double avec cabinet de toilette, à 220 et 290 F avec douche ou bains, et w.-c. Chambres sobres et bien meublées.

Camping

Camping City : 67, route de Crau. ☎ 90-93-08-86. Fermé du 30 octobre au 1er mars. En allant vers Raphèle-lès-Arles. Assez ombragé. Piscine, épicerie, plats à emporter, restaurant-pizzeria, animations en été.

BATEAU «MIREIO»

Bateau restaurant de 250 places, chauffé, climatisé. Croisières déjeuner sans escale vers Chateauneuf-du-Pape ou avec escale en Arles – visite de la capitale de la Camargue –, à Roquemaure avec dégustation des vins de Côtes du Rhône, à Villeneuve avec visite du village et de ses monuments. Croisières dîner et soirées spectacle devant Avignon et Villeneuve. Animation dansante et commentaires sur toutes les croisières.

84000 AVIGNON -
Tél. : 90 85 62 25 - Fax : 90 85 61 14

CATHEDRALES D'IMAGES

Aux Baux-de-Provence, dans les anciennes carrières du Val-d'Enfer, CATHEDRALE D'IMAGES propose un spectacle permanent en IMAGE TOTALE.
4.000 m² d'écrans naturels, 40 sources de projection, 2 500 diapos créent une féerie visuelle et sonore où déambule le spectateur.
–Couvrez-vous car les carrières sont fraîches!–

13520 LES BAUX-DE-PROVENCE -
Tél. : 90 54 38 65 - Fax : 90 54 42 65

Science Link

You might have your students do research to find out how caves such as the **Grottes de Thouzon** are formed.

ARLES (13200)

Où manger?

Bon marché

Vitamine : 16, rue du Docteur-Fanton. ☎ 90-93-77-36. Fermé le dimanche. Une carte de 50 salades différentes, de 16 à 45 F, et 15 spécialités de pâtes de 28 à 42 F, le tout dans une salle agréablement décorée (expos photos) et avec un accueil décontracté.

Hôtel-restaurant-d'Arlaten : 7, rue de la Cavalerie. ☎ 90-96-24-85. Fermé le dimanche soir. Intérieur très simple. Menu intéressant à 68 F, avec une entrée, un plat, légumes et dessert. Trois autres menus à 88, 105 et 135 F. Réserver.

Le Poisson Banane : 6, rue du Forum. ☎ 90-96-02-58. Ouvert uniquement le soir. Fermé le mercredi. Avec sa grande terrasse couverte de verdure, ce petit resto caché derrière la place du Forum passe facilement inaperçu et c'est dommage. Il est agréable de venir y goûter une cuisine sucrée-salée inventive avec un menu à 125 F, et une spécialité antillaise : le «poisson-banane», bien sûr. Plat du jour à 70 F environ.

CHATEAU MUSEE DE L'EMPERI

CHATEAU MUSEE DE L'EMPERI

Le CHATEAU DE L'EMPERI, la plus importante forteresse médiévale en Provence, abrite une des plus somptueuses collections d'art et d'uniformes militaires qui soit en Europe. Cette collection unique illustre l'évolution des uniformes et de l'art militaire de Louis XIV à 1914. La période napoléonienne est la plus présente. Le Château de l'Emperi est situé en plein cœur de la ville ancienne.

13300 SALON DE PROVENCE - Tél : 90 56 22 36

GROTTES DE THOUZON

GROTTES DE THOUZON

Les décors de stalactites qui parent « le ciel » de ce réseau naturel forment des paysages souterrains merveilleux. (Photo : M. CROTET) Grotte réputée pour la finesse de ses stalactites (fistuleuses). Parcours aisé pour les personnes âgées et les enfants. Seule grotte naturelle aménagée pour le tourisme en Provence. Ouvert du 1/04 au 31/10. Groupe toute l'année sur rendez-vous.

84250 LE THOR - Tél. : 90 33 93 65 - Fax : 90 33 74 90

E. Do you think the descriptions of the hotels were written by the hotel management? How do you know? No; Some remarks are unfavorable.

F. At the bottom of both pages, you will find descriptions of several tourist attractions in Provence. After you've read them, match the items listed below with the sites where you would find them.

1. a dinner cruise b
2. stalactites c
3. thousands of projection screens a
4. a collection of military art and uniforms d

a. Cathédrale d'images
b. Bateau «Miréio»
c. Grottes de Thouzon
d. Château Musée de l'Emperi

G. Are there similar tourist attractions in your area? What are they?

H. If you were working at a tourist information office, what would you recommend to someone who . . . See answers below.
1. wants a comfortable cruise package?
2. would like to visit a medieval castle?
3. likes to explore caves?
4. is interested in military art?

I. You and your friend have three days to spend in Arles. You're on a very tight budget, but you still want to enjoy your trip. Where will you stay? Where will you eat your lunches and dinners? How much will you spend for these three days?

trois cent un **301**

READING
Activities E–H

Thinking Critically

Drawing Inferences Ask students to suggest reasons why the places listed under **Où dormir?** are closed during various times of the year.

Building on Previous Skills

You might assign small groups various categories, such as meals, food, months of the year, days of the week, and so on, and ask them to scan the travel information and list words they recognize that fit their category.

POSTREADING
Activity I

Teaching Suggestion

I. Using Marianne's itinerary on page 295 as an example, students might write out their final itinerary and hand it in.

For Individual Needs

Challenge Have students research lodgings and restaurants in a city they'd like to visit or in their own city. Have them create a brochure for French tourists that rates the hotels and restaurants. Price categories might include **très bon marché, bon marché, prix modérés,** and **plus chic.** They might also find out hotel rates and average menu prices and list them in francs. Current exchange rates can be obtained from the newspaper or from larger banks.

Answers

H 1. Bateau «Miréio»
2. Château Musée de l'Emperi
3. Grottes de Thouzon
4. Château Musée de l'Emperi

The **Mise en pratique** reviews and integrates all four skills and culture in preparation for the Chapter Test.

Teaching Suggestion

1 You might first have students listen to the recording, read the questions, and then listen again for the answers.

⬥ For Individual Needs

1 Slower Pace Have students write a list of the vacation words and expressions they expect to hear in this advertisement; they can look at this list while they listen to the recording. In this ad, three questions about three different types of vacations are posed and then answered. You might pause the recording after each type of vacation to assess comprehension.

2 Challenge After students have answered the questions, have them discuss or write about their reaction to the ad. You might have them design a similar ad aimed at Americans who might like to experience the culture of France or of other francophone countries.

MISE EN PRATIQUE

 1 Listen to this radio advertisement and then answer these questions. <small>Answers on p. 281D.</small>

1. What is being advertised?
2. Can you name two places that are mentioned in the advertisement?
3. What activities are mentioned in the advertisement?
4. For whom do they offer discounts?

2 Read the brochure and then answer the questions that follow.

Le rêve américain devient réalité, en séjour Immersion avec EF

Vivre à l'américaine

Qui n'a rêvé un jour de vivre une autre vie ? Ce rêve devient réalité, grâce à la formule EF Immersion : pendant quelques semaines, vous devenez totalement américain. Parce que les familles d'accueil sont soigneusement séléctionnées par EF, votre intégration est immédiate, et vos progrès linguistiques sont aussi spectaculaires que durables. C'est, sans nul doute, la formule qui vous assure la connaissance la plus directe et la plus profonde du mode de vie américain.

Vacances de Printemps

N° de séjour	Date de départ	Date de retour	Durée du séjour	Région	Frais de séjour*
550	11 avril	25 avril	2 sem.	Côte Est	7.730
551	18 avril	2 mai	2 sem.	Côte Est	7.730
552	18 avril	2 mai	2 sem.	Sud-Est	8.170

*Voyage inclus (départ Paris)

1. Where do students go if they sign up for this trip? <small>the United States</small>
2. Where do they stay? <small>with a family</small>
3. What do they learn? <small>English language, American lifestyle</small>
4. In what months can students make this trip? <small>April, May</small>
5. How long does it last? <small>2 weeks</small>
6. To what regions of the country can students go? <small>the East Coast, the Southeast</small>
7. How much does this trip cost? <small>7.730 F for the East Coast, 8.170 F for the Southeast</small>

3 Imagine that an exchange student is coming to stay with your family. Write a letter telling him or her about the weather where you live, what there is to do and see there, and what he or she should bring.

4 Using what you've learned about French culture, decide whether the statements below are true or false.

1. Only a few French children attend summer camp. *false*
2. French children can study foreign languages at summer camp. *true*
3. Most French people take a one week summer vacation. *false*
4. Small businesses may close in the summer when the owners go on vacation. *true*

5

JEU DE ROLE

a. You want to take a trip for your vacation, but you're not sure where. Tell your travel agent what you like to do and what you'd like to see. The travel agent will make some suggestions about where you might go and what there is to do there. He or she will also describe the weather conditions and tell you what clothes to take, where you can stay, and when and from where you can leave. The travel agent will also remind you of things you shouldn't forget to take. Act this out with your partner. Then, change roles.

b. You've returned from your trip and your friend wants to know how it went. Tell your friend about your trip and answer any questions he or she has about what you did. Act this out with your partner and then change roles.

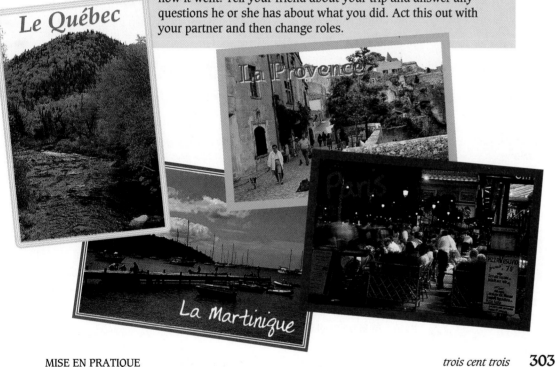

Portfolio

3 **Written** This activity is appropriate for students' written portfolios. For portfolio suggestions, see *Assessment Guide*, page 24.

Teaching Suggestion

5 For this activity, students may use information they learned about Canada and Côte d'Ivoire from previous chapters, the research they did for projects, or the activities they did in this chapter.

Portfolio

5 **Oral** This activity is appropriate for students' oral portfolios. For portfolio suggestions, see *Assessment Guide*, page 24.

 Video Wrap-Up

- *VIDEO PROGRAM*
- *EXPANDED VIDEO PROGRAM,* Videocassette 4, 15:19–30:28
- *VIDEODISC PROGRAM,* Videodisc 6A

At this time, you might want to use the video resources for additional review and enrichment. See *Video Guide* or *Videodisc Guide* for suggestions regarding the following:
- **Bientôt les vacances!** (Dramatic episode)
- **Panorama Culturel** (Interviews)
- **Vidéoclips** (Authentic footage)

QUE SAIS-JE?

This page is intended to help students prepare for the test. It is a brief checklist of the major points covered in the chapter. The students should be reminded that this is only a checklist and does not necessarily include everything that will appear on the test.

Teaching Suggestions

4 You might want to encourage students to add other activities, such as hiking or sailing, and other destinations, such as Mexico, England, or Vietnam.

5 Encourage students to offer several different ways to accept and reject the suggestions.

8 You might suggest other subjects and times for more practice with **partir.**

Can you use what you've learned in this chapter?

Can you inquire about and share future plans? Express indecision and wishes? p. 289

1 How would you ask where a friend is going on vacation and what he or she is going to do? How would you answer these questions?
See answers below.

2 How would you tell someone . . .   See answers below.

1. you're not sure what to do?   2. where you'd really like to go?

Can you ask for advice? Make, accept, and refuse suggestions? p. 290

3 How would you ask a friend for advice about your vacation?
Je ne sais pas quoi faire (où aller)... ; Tu as une idée? Qu'est-ce que tu me conseilles?

4 How would you suggest to a friend that he or she . . .   See answers below.

1. go to the country?   3. work?
2. go camping?   4. go to Canada?

5 How would you accept and refuse the suggestions in number 4?
See answers below.

Can you remind and reassure someone? p. 293

6 How would you remind a friend to take these things on a trip?
See answers below.

1.   2.   3.

7 How would you reassure someone you haven't forgotten these things?

Je n'ai pas oublié...

1. mon passeport.   2. mon billet d'avion.   3. mon billet de train.

Can you see someone off? p. 296

8 How would you tell when these people are leaving, using the verb **partir**?   See answers below.

1. Didier / 14h28   3. Nous / 11h15
2. Désirée et Annie / 20h46   4. Tu / 23h59

9 How would you wish someone a good trip?
Bon voyage! Bonnes vacances! Amuse-toi bien!

Can you ask for and express opinions? p. 297

10 How would you ask a friend how his or her vacation went?
Tu as passé un bon été? Ça s'est bien passé? Tu t'es bien amusé(e)?

11 How would you tell how your vacation went?   C'était très chouette/formidable.
Ça a été. Pas mauvais. C'était épouvantable. C'était un véritable cauchemar! C'était ennuyeux.

Can you inquire about and relate past events? p. 297

12 How would you find out what a friend did on vacation?
Qu'est-ce que tu as fait? Tu es allé(e) où?

13 How would you tell what you did on vacation?

Possible answers

1 Où est-ce que tu vas aller pendant les vacances? Qu'est-ce que tu vas faire?;
Je vais... J'ai l'intention de...

2 1. J'hésite. Je ne sais pas. Je n'en sais rien. Je n'ai rien de prévu.
  2. Je voudrais bien aller... J'ai envie d'aller...

4 Je te conseille de (d')... Tu devrais...
  1. aller à la campagne.
  2. faire du camping.
  3. travailler.

4. aller au Canada.

5 *Accept:* Tiens! C'est une bonne idée! Pourquoi pas? D'accord! Allons-y!
  Refuse: Non, ce n'est pas possible. Non, je ne peux pas. Ça ne me dit rien. C'est trop cher.

6 N'oublie pas...
Tu n'as pas oublié... ?
Tu ne peux pas partir sans...
  1. ton appareil-photo.
  2. les cadeaux.
  3. ton manteau.

8 1. Didier part à quatorze heures vingt-huit.
  2. Désirée et Annie partent à vingt heures quarante-six.
  3. Nous partons à onze heures quinze.
  4. Tu pars à vingt-trois heures cinquante-neuf.

PREMIERE ETAPE

Inquiring about and sharing future plans

Qu'est-ce que tu vas faire...?   *What are you going to do . . . ?*
Où est-ce que tu vas aller... ?   *Where are you going to go . . . ?*
Je vais...   *I'm going to . . .*
J'ai l'intention de...   *I intend to . . .*

Expressing indecision

J'hésite.   *I'm not sure.*
Je ne sais pas.   *I don't know.*
Je n'en sais rien.   *I have no idea.*
Je n'ai rien de prévu.   *I don't have any plans.*

Expressing wishes

Je voudrais bien...   *I'd really like to . . .*

J'ai envie de...   *I feel like . . .*

Vacation places and activities

à la montagne   *to/in the mountains*
en forêt   *to/in the forest*
à la campagne   *to/in the countryside*
en colonie de vacances   *to/at a summer camp*
au bord de la mer   *to/on the coast*
chez...   *to/at . . . 's house*
faire du camping   *to go camping*
faire de la randonnée   *to go hiking*
faire du bateau   *to go sailing*

faire de la plongée   *to go scuba diving*
faire de la planche à voile   *to go windsurfing*
faire de la voile   *to go sailing*
à   *to, in (a city or place)*
en   *to, in (before a feminine noun)*
au   *to, in (before a masculine noun)*
aux   *to, in (before a plural noun)*

Asking for advice; making, accepting, and refusing suggestions

See **Tu te rappelles?** on page 290.

- -

DEUXIEME ETAPE

Travel items

un passeport   *passport*
un billet de train   *train ticket*
un billet d'avion   *plane ticket*
une valise   *suitcase*
de l'argent   *money*
un appareil-photo   *camera*
un cadeau   *gift*

Reminding, reassuring

N'oublie pas...   *Don't forget . . .*

Tu n'as pas oublié... ?   *You didn't forget . . . ?*
Tu ne peux pas partir sans...   *You can't leave without . . .*
Tu prends... ?   *Are you taking . . . ?*
Ne t'en fais pas.   *Don't worry.*
J'ai pensé à tout.   *I've thought of everything.*
Je n'ai rien oublié.   *I didn't forget anything.*
partir   *to leave*

Seeing someone off

Bon voyage!   *Have a good trip!*
Bonnes vacances!   *Have a good vacation!*
Amuse-toi bien!   *Have fun!*
Bonne chance!   *Good luck!*

- -

TROISIEME ETAPE

Asking for and expressing opinions

Tu as passé un bon... ?   *Did you have a good . . . ?*
Ça s'est bien passé?   *Did it go well?*
Tu t'es bien amusé(e)?   *Did you have fun?*

Oui, très chouette.   *Yes, very cool.*
C'était formidable!   *It was great!*
Oui, ça a été.   *Yes, it was OK.*
Oh, pas mauvais.   *Oh, not bad.*
C'était épouvantable.   *It was horrible.*
Non, pas vraiment.   *No, not really.*

C'était un véritable cauchemar!   *It was a real nightmare!*
C'était ennuyeux.   *It was boring.*

Inquiring about and relating past events

See **Tu te rappelles?** on page 297.

VOCABULAIRE
trois cent cinq   **305**

Allez, viens à Fort-de-France!

pp. 306–335

EXPANDED VIDEO
PROGRAM,
Videocassette 4
30:29–32:49

OR *VIDEODISC PROGRAM,*
Videodisc 6B

Search 1, Play To 4200

Motivating Activity

Have students share what-
ever they know about the
Caribbean, specifically about
the French-speaking islands.
Ask them if they know where
French is spoken in the
Caribbean (Guadeloupe, Haiti,
and Martinique), and if they're
familiar with the climate, history, or customs of this area.
Then, have them open their
books and compare their
impressions with the photos
on pages 306–309.

Background Information

Located on the beautiful Baie
des Flamands, Fort-de-France
is the largest city and busiest
commercial center in the
French West Indies. As the
region's chief port, its exports
include sugar cane, cocoa, and
various fruits. Formerly known
as Fort-Royal, Fort-de-France
is now the **chef-lieu** *(adminis-*
trative seat or capital) of Martinique, which is a **départe-**
ment d'outre-mer *(overseas*
department) of France. Fort-
de-France became the administrative capital of Martinique
in 1902, when Saint-Pierre,
formerly the largest city of the
island, was destroyed by an
eruption of Mount Pelée that
killed approximately 38,000
people.

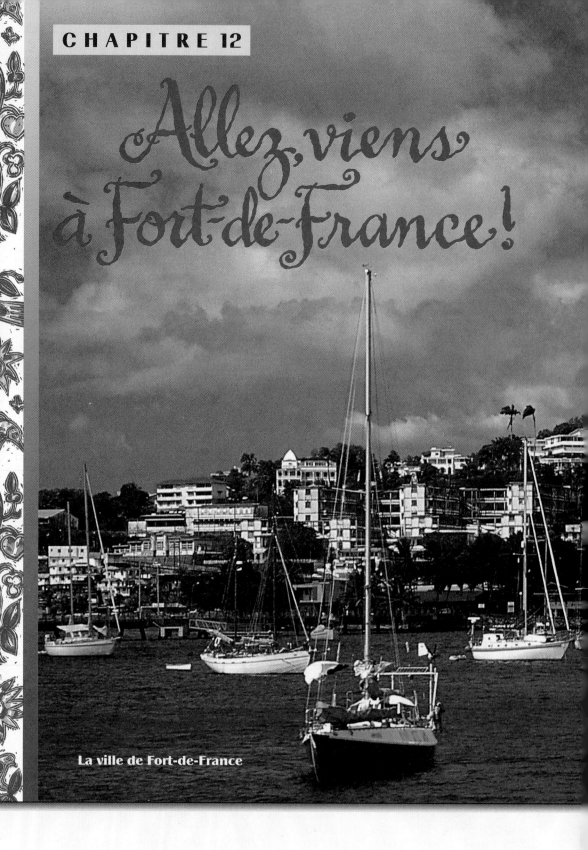

CHAPITRE 12

Allez, viens à Fort-de-France!

La ville de Fort-de-France

Fort-de-France

Ville principale de la Martinique

Population : plus de 100.000

Langues : français, créole

Points d'intérêt : la bibliothèque Schœlcher, le Musée Départemental, le fort Saint-Louis, la cathédrale Saint-Louis

Parcs et jardins : la Savane, le Parc floral et culturel

Spécialités : crabes farcis, blanc manger, boudin créole, accras de morue

Evénements : Carnaval, le Festival de Fort-de-France, les Tours des yoles rondes de la Martinique

trois cent sept **307**

Using the Almanac and Map

Terms in the Almanac

- **Créole,** one of two languages spoken in Martinique, is a blend of French, Spanish, English, and African languages. Words in Creole are usually written the way they sound.
- **Le Musée Départemental,** a museum devoted to the history of the island, includes artifacts of the Pre-Columbian Arawak and Carib civilizations, exhibits on Napoléon I and Joséphine, and information on **la Montagne Pelée** and the history of slavery on the island.
- **La cathédrale Saint-Louis,** a Romanesque cathedral built in 1671, has beautiful stained-glass windows. Many of the island's governors are interred beneath it.
- **Le Parc floral et culturel** introduces visitors to the flowers and plants of the island and also contains an aquarium with native fish.
- **crabes farcis:** deviled land crabs.
- **blanc manger:** coconut pudding.
- **boudin créole:** spicy creole sausage.
- **acras de morue:** cod fritters.

Teacher Note

Carnaval, which is mentioned below, and the **Tour des yoles rondes** are described in detail in Chapter 4 of Level 2.

Using the Map

Ask students if they know which body of water Fort-de-France is located on (the Caribbean Sea). Ask if they can identify other countries that are located near Martinique (Cuba, Haiti and the Dominican Republic, Mexico, Panama, Venezuela).

Culture Note

Several holidays and festivals take place every year in Fort-de-France and throughout Martinique. **Carnaval,** a festival of music, parades, and costumes, is celebrated for four days preceding Ash Wednesday **(le mercredi des Cendres).** Le Festival de Fort-de-France in July offers exhibits, concerts, and theatrical productions.

Using the Photo Essay

① **La bibliothèque Schœlcher** is a public library named after Victor Schœlcher, who fought to abolish slavery in the nineteenth century. Slavery was officially abolished in Martinique in 1848.

② **La Savane** Located here are statues of Pierre Belain d'Esnambuc, who led 80 settlers to Fort Saint-Pierre in 1635, and of Joséphine, the first wife of French Emperor Napoléon I. Joséphine, the daughter of a Martinique planter, was born on the island in 1763.

History Link

France began to colonize Martinique with d'Esnambuc's arrival in 1635, and the island became a domain of the French crown in 1674. The British had possession of the island three times in the eighteenth and early nineteenth centuries (1762, 1794-1802, 1809-1814). In 1815, the island was ceded by treaty to France, and in 1946, it became an overseas department. Martinique sends three deputies to the French National Assembly and is governed by a prefect appointed by the French Minister of the Interior and a general council elected by the people.

③ **Le fort Saint-Louis** was built in the seventeenth century to defend the island of Martinique. Today, special permission is needed to visit the fort.

Teacher Note

③ Call students' attention to the French flag flying atop **fort Saint-Louis.** Explain that since Martinique is a French **département,** its people are French citizens.

Fort-de-France

*Clinging to the mountains overlooking the Caribbean coast of Martinique, the city of Fort-de-France lies on the **baie des Flamands.** Nearly one-third of the population of Martinique lives in or near the city. Here you will see a blending of cultures. Although Martinique is 4,261 miles from Paris, it is a **département** of France. While its character is decidedly French, the pastel-colored buildings and wrought-iron balconies may remind you of New Orleans, and the sounds of the **créole** language and **zouk** music are purely West Indian.*

① **La bibliothèque Schœlcher** is a very elaborate building constructed in a blend of byzantine, Egyptian, and romanesque styles. Like the Eiffel Tower, it was built in 1889 for the Paris Exposition. It was later dismantled and rebuilt among the palm trees in Fort-de-France.

② **La Savane** is a 12½-acre landscaped park filled with tropical trees, fountains, benches, and gardens. This is the place to go to meet with friends, take a walk, or play a casual game of soccer.

③ Built on a rocky peninsula, **le fort Saint-Louis** overlooks the port of Fort-de-France.

History Link

The original inhabitants of Martinique were Indians from South America who gradually migrated through the islands of the Caribbean, most likely reaching Martinique and Guadeloupe in the second century A.D. Gradually, the Arawaks, another Indian people, settled there. Subsequently, a cannibalistic warrior race called the Caribs (who gave their name to the Caribbean Sea) conquered the Arawaks. In the early sixteenth century, when Columbus arrived in Martinique for the first time, he encountered the descendants of the Caribs, whose excellent fighting skills prevented the Europeans from immediately gaining possession of the island.

④ Martinique is known for its colorfully printed fabrics, called **madras.**

⑤ Fresh fruits and vegetables are sold daily in the colorful **marché.**

⑥ The steeple of **la cathédrale Saint-Louis** towers over downtown Fort-de-France.

Thinking Critically

④ **Drawing Inferences**
Have students suggest reasons why head coverings are important. (In Martinique, the intense heat and sun of the tropical climate create the need for some sort of headcovering. Scarf-like headcoverings serve to hold one's hair in place, are decorative and stylish, and often match the outfit being worn.)

⑤ **Observing** Have students try to identify the different fruits and vegetables in the photos. They might recognize the tomatoes and pineapples, but you might want to identify the other food items. Moving from left to right, you can see *yams* (**des ignames**), which students will recall from Chapter 8; *star fruit* (**des caramboles**); breadfruit (**fruit de l'arbre à pain**), sitting in front of the pineapples; and hot peppers (**piments**), in the bowl behind the star fruit and tomatoes. The flowers behind the pineapples are called *anthuriums,* known as the official flower of Martinique.

⑤ **Comparing and Contrasting** Have students recall from Chapter 8 the differences between shopping in an open-air market and in a store. How might the produce be different? What quantities might one buy? Are prices fixed? How does the shopper carry his or her purchases? In Martinique, most produce sold in open-air markets is fresh, and women will often carry their purchases on their heads, as students will notice in Photo 5. Shoppers generally bring their own shopping bags and pay in cash. They might bargain with the seller on the price of a particular item. Tasting is also common before one buys something.

Teaching Suggestion

⑤ Ask students what the advantages and disadvantages are of carrying heavy loads on one's head. If students can't think of any advantages, have them try to carry a book on their head. Although it requires some practice and balance, carrying things on one's head leaves the hands free and is probably easier on the back. It also ensures excellent posture!

Chapitre 12 : En ville
Chapter Overview

Mise en train pp. 312–314	Un petit service		Practice and Activity Book, p. 133	Video Guide OR Videodisc Guide

	FUNCTIONS	GRAMMAR	CULTURE	RE-ENTRY
Première étape pp. 315–319	Pointing out places and things, p. 317	*Review* Contractions with **à**, p. 316	• **Note Culturelle,** Store hours in France and Martinique, p. 316 • **Rencontre Culturelle,** Making "small talk" in francophone countries, p. 319	• Food items and school supplies • The **passé composé**
Deuxième étape pp. 320–324	• Making and responding to requests, p. 320 • Asking for advice and making suggestions, p. 322	• The pronoun **y**, p. 323 *Review* • The partitive, p. 320	• Realia: A French stamp, p. 321 • **Panorama Culturel,** Getting a driver's license in francophone countries, p. 324	• Expressing need • Making an excuse • Inviting
Troisième étape pp. 325–329	Asking for and giving directions, p. 327	*Review* Contractions with **de**, p. 325	• **Note Culturelle, DOMs** and **TOMs**, p. 326 • **Note Culturelle,** Public areas downtown, p. 327	• Family vocabulary • Possessive adjectives

Prononciation p. 329 Review	Dictation: *Textbook Audiocassette 6B/Audio CD 12*

Lisons! pp. 330–331 **Cheval de bois**	Reading Strategy: Combining different reading strategies

Review pp. 332–335   Mise en pratique, pp. 332–333   Que sais-je? p. 334   Vocabulaire, p. 335

Assessment Options

Etape Quizzes
• *Chapter Teaching Resources, Book 3*
  Première étape, Quiz 12-1, pp. 191–192
  Deuxième étape, Quiz 12-2, pp. 193–194
  Troisième étape, Quiz 12-3, pp. 195–196
• *Assessment Items, Audiocassette 8B/Audio CD 12*

Chapter Test
• *Chapter Teaching Resources, Book 3*, pp. 197–202
• *Assessment Guide,* Speaking Test, p. 33
• *Assessment Items, Audiocassette 8B/Audio CD 12*

Test Generator, Chapter 12

Video Program OR Expanded Video Program, Videocassette 4
OR Videodisc Program, Videodisc 6B   Textbook Audiocassette 6B/Audio CD 12

RESOURCES: Print	RESOURCES: Audiovisual

Textbook Audiocassette 6B/Audio CD 12

Practice and Activity Book, pp. 134–136
Chapter Teaching Resources, Book 3
• Teaching Transparency Master 12-1, pp. 175, 178 . . . . Teaching Transparency 12-1
• Additional Listening Activities 12-1, 12-2, p. 179 . . . . Additional Listening Activities, Audiocassette 10B/Audio CD 12
• Realia 12-1, pp. 183, 185
• Situation Cards 12-1, pp. 186–187
• Student Response Forms, pp. 188–190
• Quiz 12-1, pp. 191–192 . . . . Assessment Items, Audiocassette 8B/Audio CD 12
Videodisc Guide . . . . Videodisc Program, Videodisc 6B

Textbook Audiocassette 6B/Audio CD 12

Practice and Activity Book, pp. 137–139
Chapter Teaching Resources, Book 3
• Communicative Activity 12-1, pp. 171–172
• Teaching Transparency Master 12-2, pp. 176, 178 . . . . Teaching Transparency 12-2
• Additional Listening Activities 12-3, 12-4, p. 180 . . . . Additional Listening Activities, Audiocassette 10B/Audio CD 12
• Realia 12-2, pp. 184, 185
• Situation Cards 12-2, pp. 186–187
• Student Response Forms, pp. 188–190
• Quiz 12-2, pp. 193–194 . . . . Assessment Items, Audiocassette 8B/Audio CD 12
Video Guide . . . . Video Program OR Expanded Video Program, Videocassette 4
Videodisc Guide . . . . Videodisc Program, Videodisc 6B

Textbook Audiocassette 6B/Audio CD 12

Practice and Activity Book, pp. 140–142
Chapter Teaching Resources, Book 3
• Communicative Activity 12-2, pp. 173–174
• Teaching Transparency Master 12-3, pp. 177, 178 . . . . Teaching Transparency 12-3
• Additional Listening Activities 12-5, 12-6, p. 181 . . . . Additional Listening Activities, Audiocassette 10B/Audio CD 12
• Realia 12-2, pp. 184, 185
• Situation Cards 12-3, pp. 186–187
• Student Response Forms, pp. 188–190
• Quiz 12-3, pp. 195–196 . . . . Assessment Items, Audiocassette 8B/Audio CD 12
Videodisc Guide . . . . Videodisc Program, Videodisc 6B

Practice and Activity Book, p. 143

Video Guide . . . . Video Program OR Expanded Video Program, Videocassette 4
Videodisc Guide . . . . Videodisc Program, Videodisc 6B

Alternative Assessment
• Performance Assessment
  Première étape, p. 318
  Deuxième étape, p. 323
  Troisième étape, p. 329

• Portfolio Assessment
  Written: Activity 30, *Pupil's Edition,* p. 328
    Assessment Guide, p. 25
  Oral: **Mise en pratique, Jeu de rôle,** *Pupil's Edition,* p. 333
    Assessment Guide, p. 25

Final Exam
Assessment Guide, pp. 49–56
Assessment Items,
  Audiocassette 8B
  Audio CD 12

For Student Response Forms, see *Chapter Teaching Resources Book 3,* pp. 188–190.

Première étape

7 Ecoute! p. 316

1. — De l'aspirine, s'il vous plaît.
   — Voilà. C'est tout?

2. — Vous avez des disques compacts en espagnol?
   — Oui, bien sûr.

3. — Je voudrais déposer deux cents francs.
   — Le numéro de votre compte, s'il vous plaît?

4. — Je voudrais des timbres.
   — Vous en voulez combien?

5. — Il me faut du papier, des stylos et des enveloppes.
   — Ça fait trente-neuf francs.

6. — Mmm... il a l'air très bon, ce gâteau-là. Je vais le prendre.
   — N'oublie pas, tu es au régime!

Answers to Activity 7
1. at the drugstore
2. at the record store
3. at the bank
4. at the post office
5. at the book/stationery store
6. at the pastry shop/bakery

Deuxième étape

15 Ecoute! p. 320

1. — Marie, tu peux aller à la poste acheter des timbres?
   — Désolée, mais je n'ai pas le temps!

2. — Est-ce que tu peux aller à la pharmacie? J'ai mal à la tête, mais je n'ai plus d'aspirine.
   — Oui, d'accord. J'y vais tout de suite.

3. — Tu peux me rendre un petit service? J'ai besoin d'argent. Est-ce que tu peux aller à la banque ce matin?
   — Oui, si tu veux.

4. — Au retour, tu peux passer à la boulangerie? Prends deux baguettes, s'il te plaît.
   — Oui, maman. C'est tout?

5. — Tu pourrais passer par la bibliothèque aujourd'hui? Je veux rendre ces livres.
   — Désolé, je ne peux pas. J'ai des tas de choses à faire.

6. — Zut alors! J'ai oublié les tomates! Tu peux passer au marché pour moi?
   — Oui, je veux bien. Je pars tout de suite.

Answers to Activity 15
1. refuses   4. agrees
2. agrees   5. refuses
3. agrees   6. agrees

19 Ecoute! p. 323

1. — Comment est-ce qu'on va en ville?
   — On peut y aller à vélo, si tu veux.

2. — J'aimerais bien aller au cinéma.
   — Bonne idée. Comment veux-tu y aller?
   — On peut prendre le bus.

3. — Je vais à Paris cet été.
   — Ah oui? Comment est-ce que tu y vas?
   — J'y vais en avion.

4. — Tu veux aller à la plage ce week-end?
   — Oui, on peut y aller à pied.

5. — Comment est-ce que tu vas à Fort-de-France demain?
   — J'y vais en voiture avec mes parents.

6. — Tu ne veux pas aller au musée samedi?
   — Si. On peut prendre un taxi collectif.

Answers to Activity 19
1. to town, by bike
2. to the movies, by bus
3. to Paris, by plane
4. to the beach, on foot
5. to Fort-de-France, by car
6. to the museum, by taxi

*T*roisième étape

23 Ecoute! p. 325

1. La boulangerie est à côté du cinéma.
2. La banque est au coin de la rue.
3. La pharmacie est loin de la papeterie.
4. Le café est entre la poste et le cinéma.
5. Le cinéma est en face du lycée.
6. La poste est près du café.

Answers to Activity 23

1. false	3. false	5. true
2. true	4. true	6. true

27 Ecoute! p. 327

En sortant de la gare routière, prenez à gauche. Vous serez sur le boulevard du Général de Gaulle. Ensuite, prenez la première rue à gauche, c'est la rue Schœlcher. Continuez jusqu'à la rue Victor Sévère et tournez à gauche. Vous allez passer devant la bibliothèque. Juste après la bibliothèque, prenez à droite, rue de la Liberté. Allez tout droit jusqu'à la rue Antoine Siger. Là, tournez à droite et ce sera le premier bâtiment sur votre gauche.

Answer to Activity 27
to the post office

*P*rononciation, p. 329

For the scripts for Parts A and B, see p. 329.

C. A écrire

(Dictation)
— Tu pourrais faire des courses pour moi?
— Volontiers!
— Passe à la poste. Prends des timbres. Et n'oublie pas les enveloppes à la papeterie.
— Bon, d'accord.

*M*ise en pratique

3 p. 332

1. — La bibliothèque Schœlcher est très grande, et elle est aussi très belle, n'est-ce pas?
2. — Les plages de sable blanc de la Martinique sont magnifiques. On peut à la fois s'y baigner et y faire du bateau.
3. — Ça, c'est le marché. C'est un vrai paradis pour les yeux : on y trouve des légumes de toutes les couleurs.
4. — Là, c'est le disquaire où j'ai acheté le dernier CD de Kassav', un groupe de musique zouk, qui est très populaire ici.

Answers to Mise en pratique Activity 3
c, d, a, b

Chapitre 12 : En ville
Projects

Ma ville
(Individual or Group Project)

ASSIGNMENT

Students will create a brochure with maps of their town or neighborhood and written directions to important places for French-speaking visitors.

MATERIALS

✂ **Students may need**

- Construction paper
- Scissors
- Local maps
- Glue
- Markers or colored pens
- Telephone directories
- Brochures of local attractions

SUGGESTED SEQUENCE

1. Have students make a list of interesting and important places in their area that visitors might want or need to visit. These may include hospitals, subway or bus stops, bus depots, airports, pharmacies, restaurants, the main post office, the Chamber of Commerce, and so on.

2. Have students find out exactly where each place is located. They might call for directions. Then, have them sketch a rough map of the city with each place correctly indicated. They should also begin to gather or draw pictures to illustrate their maps.

3. Have students write directions to the points of interest from main streets or designated locations. They might want to use the following vocabulary: **l'autoroute** *(highway);* **Prenez la 35 jusqu'à...** *(Take highway 35 to . . .);* **la sortie** Main Street *(the . . . exit);* **un pont** *(bridge);* **faire demi-tour** *(to make a U-turn);* **un carrefour** *(intersection);* **une rue en sens unique** *(one-way street).*

4. Have students exchange their written directions for peer editing. Students should check the clarity and accuracy of the directions by trying to follow them on a city map. They should also check for completeness and for accuracy of language use.

5. Have students select their final illustrations and plan the final layout of their maps.

6. Have students finalize their maps. They should copy the final version of the written directions at the bottom or on the reverse side of the map.

These brochures might be displayed at school, added to portfolios, or sent to local tourist offices or Chambers of Commerce.

GRADING THE PROJECT

Suggested Point Distribution (total = 100 points)

Completion of assignment . . . . 20 points

Content/creativity . . . . 30 points

Language use. 25 points

Presentation . . . . 25 points

CHASSE L'INTRUS

In this game, students will practice new and previously learned vocabulary.

Procedure Give students index cards. Ask them to write a group of four words: three should have something in common, and the fourth should be unrelated. For example, students might write **banque, pharmacie, avion,** and **boulangerie.** Words can be related according to their meanings or their parts of speech. Collect and shuffle the cards. Divide the class into two teams. Give a card to the first player on the first team. The player says **Chasse l'in-trus!** to his or her opponent and reads aloud the four words on the card. If the opposing player correctly identifies the word that doesn't belong within a specified amount of time, his or her team wins a point. Teams alternate, asking questions until all the cards have been read. The team with the most points wins. NOTE: If pronunciation is a problem, have students show their card to the opposing player.

LES MOTS EN FAMILLE

In this game, students will review vocabulary from all twelve chapters.

Procedure Skim the French-English vocabulary list at the back of the book and make a list of general categories, such as **les vêtements, l'école, à manger,** and **les sports.** Have students pair off or form small groups. Give each pair or group a transparency and a marker. Then, announce a category and give partners or groups 2 or 3 minutes to write down as many related words as they can think of, without consulting their books or dictionaries. Then, project the transparencies and have the class verify the spelling and appropriateness of each item. Give one point for each appropriate word that is spelled correctly. The team with the most points wins. This game might be played with functional expressions as well as with vocabulary words.

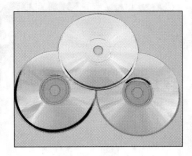

Chapitre 12
En ville

pp. 310–335

*U*sing the Chapter Opener

Motivating Activity

Ask students if they have ever been lost and how they reacted. Ask them to imagine getting lost in another country. Would they use the same strategies to find their way as they would in the United States?

Teaching Suggestion

Have students substitute local places in the caption of each photo. (**Tu pourrais passer chez Musicworld? Pardon, monsieur. Nous cherchons le Super Vidéo, s'il vous plaît.**)

Photo Flash!

① Fort-de-France is the departmental seat of Martinique as well as the island's business center. This view from the **baie des Flamands** also shows the historic, romanesque bell tower of the **cathédrale Saint-Louis.**

Teaching Suggestion

Have students tell where in town they go to run errands.

CHAPITRE

12 En ville

① Regarde, c'est la cathédrale Saint-Louis !

310 *trois cent dix*

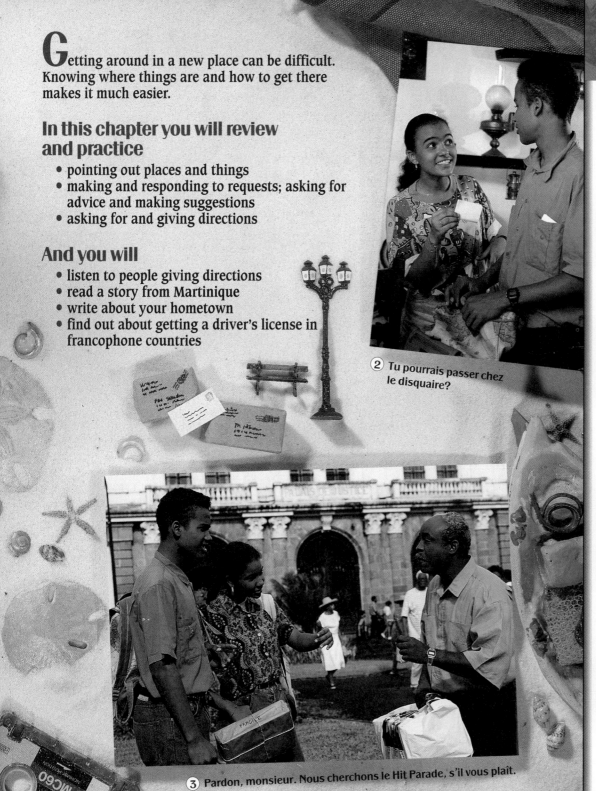

Getting around in a new place can be difficult. Knowing where things are and how to get there makes it much easier.

In this chapter you will review and practice

- pointing out places and things
- making and responding to requests; asking for advice and making suggestions
- asking for and giving directions

And you will

- listen to people giving directions
- read a story from Martinique
- write about your hometown
- find out about getting a driver's license in francophone countries

② Tu pourrais passer chez le disquaire?

③ Pardon, monsieur. Nous cherchons le Hit Parade, s'il vous plaît.

Focusing on Outcomes

Begin by having students match the photos to the outcomes. Since some of these functions were presented in earlier chapters, you might review them by asking students to recall familiar expressions for each function. NOTE: You may want to use the video to support the objectives. The self-check activities in **Que sais-je?** on page 334 help students assess their achievement of the objectives.

Photo Flash!

③ Lucien and Mireille are asking a man for directions in front of the **Palais de Justice** in Fort-de-France.

Teaching Suggestion

Have students suggest other functions involved in running errands and finding their way around town. Examples include making purchases, making excuses, and hesitating.

Building on Previous Skills

Have students describe the photos in French. You might prompt them by asking **Comment est Lucien? Qu'est-ce qu'il porte? Comment est Fort-de-France? Qu'est-ce qu'il y a à faire là-bas?**

VIDEO PROGRAM
OR EXPANDED VIDEO
PROGRAM,
Videocassette 4
32:50–36:11

OR VIDEODISC PROGRAM,
Videodisc 6B

Search 4200, Play To 10245

Video Synopsis

In this episode, Lucien plans to meet his friend Mireille in town and visit Fort Saint-Louis. As he is getting ready to leave, his mother, father, and sister all ask favors of him. Although they ask him to do a lot of errands, Lucien reluctantly agrees to everyone's requests. When a neighbor enters and asks if anyone is going to town, however, Lucien has had enough.

Motivating Activity

Have students answer the questions in the introduction at the top of this page. Ask them if they would mind doing the errands Lucien is being asked to do. Have students recall the vocabulary for household chores that they learned in Chapter 7 (**sortir la poubelle, faire la vaisselle, débarrasser la table**).

Mise en train

Un petit service

Do you ever run errands for your family? What kinds of things do you have to do? Look at the pictures below and see if you can figure out what Lucien's mother, father, and sister are asking him to do.

Lucien   Lisette   La mère

Le père   Une voisine

1. Maman, je vais en ville. J'ai rendez-vous avec Mireille. On va passer la journée à Fort-de-France. Je vais lui faire visiter le fort Saint-Louis.

2. Avant de rentrer, passe au marché et prends de l'ananas, des oranges et des caramboles.

3. Ah, tu peux rendre ces livres à la bibliothèque aussi, s'il te plaît? Et en échange, tu me prends trois autres livres. Voilà ma carte.

Est-ce que tu peux aller à la poste et envoyer ce paquet?

4. Je ne sais pas si je vais avoir le temps.

BIBLIOTHÈQUE SCHŒLCHER
NOM LAPIQUONNE   N° 1075
Prénom Lisette
Né le 17 décembre 79
Adresse 29, rue Damas
Fort - de - Faam
Profession étudiante

RESOURCES FOR MISE EN TRAIN

Textbook Audiocassette 6B/Audio CD 12
Practice and Activity Book, p. 133
Video Guide
  Video Program
  Expanded Video Program, Videocassette 4
Videodisc Guide
  Videodisc Program, Videodisc 6B

History Link

The Schœlcher Library is at the site of the old **Hôtel du Petit Gouvernement,** where Empress Joséphine of France used to live. The library did not take the name Schœlcher to commemorate Victor Schœlcher's campaign to abolish slavery, but rather to acknowledge his gift of about 10,000 volumes to further the education of the people of Martinique.

5 Je vais d'abord au fort Saint-Louis, puis je dois aller au marché et ensuite...

C'est important...

Bon.

6 Tu peux passer chez le disquaire? J'ai commandé un disque-compact.

Bien. C'est tout?

Au retour, tu peux aller à la boulangerie? Prends deux baguettes.

Tiens, voilà 5 francs. Prends-moi aussi le journal.

Merci, Lucien. C'est sympa.

Tu vas voir, c'est très intéressant, le fort Saint-Louis.

7

8 Bon, ça suffit pour aujourd'hui!

9

10 Bonjour. Est-ce que par hasard vous allez en ville aujourd'hui?

Au secours!

MISE EN TRAIN

Video Integration

- *Expanded Video Program,* Videocassette 4, 36:12–46:21
- *Videodisc Program,* Videodisc 6B

Search 10245, Play To 28545

You may choose to continue with **Un petit service (suite)** at this time or wait until later in the chapter. When the story continues, Mireille accompanies Lucien on his errands. They get lost trying to find a record store and ask a man for directions. Then, they take a ferry to deliver a package, and Lucien points out landmarks in Fort-de-France. When Lucien returns home, everyone thanks him for doing their errands. His mother asks him about the fort, and he realizes he completely forgot about visiting it!

For videodisc application, see *Videodisc Guide*.

Teaching Suggestions

3 Have students match these errands with the people in Activity 2 who requested them. Have students tell what else they could do in each place.

4 Ask students to correct any false statements. If the statements are true, have students tell why or for whom Lucien does the errand.

◆ For Individual Needs

4 Challenge Copy the sentences onto the board or a transparency, omitting several words. (**Lucien va acheter des ____, des pêches et des ____.**) Have students complete these sentences to make them true. You might have them recopy the complete sentences into their notebooks.

Thinking Critically

6 Comparing and Contrasting Have students list where they go to do each of their errands and compare

---

1 Tu as compris?

Answer the following questions about **Un petit service.**

1. What are Lucien's plans for the day? to visit fort Saint-Louis in Fort-de-France with Mireille
2. What are Lucien and his family talking about? running errands in town
3. Is Lucien happy with the situation? Why or why not? No; He's afraid he won't have time for everything.
4. What happens at the end? Lucien calls for help when a neighbor starts to ask a favor.

2 Qui dit quoi?

Lucien

Lisette

M. Lapiquonne

Mme Lapiquonne

1. «Tu peux aller à la boulangerie?»
2. «Tu peux rendre ces livres à la bibliothèque aussi, s'il te plaît?»
3. «Est-ce que tu peux aller à la poste et envoyer ce paquet?»
4. «Tu peux passer chez le disquaire?»
5. «Passe au marché et prends de l'ananas, des oranges et des caramboles.»
6. «Prends-moi aussi le journal.»

1. Mme Lapiquonne
2. Lisette
3. M. Lapiquonne
4. Lisette
5. Mme Lapiquonne
6. M. Lapiquonne

3 Où va-t-il?

Où est-ce que Lucien va aller pour...

1. acheter des caramboles?
2. envoyer le paquet?
3. rendre des livres?
4. acheter le disque compact?
5. acheter des baguettes?

1. au marché
2. à la poste
3. à la bibliothèque
4. chez le disquaire
5. à la boulangerie

> à la boulangerie
> à la poste
> chez le disquaire
> au marché
> à la bibliothèque

4 Vrai ou faux?

1. Lucien va acheter des caramboles, des pêches et des pommes. faux
2. Il va rendre des livres à la bibliothèque. vrai
3. Lucien va à la boulangerie. vrai
4. Lisette lui donne de l'argent pour acheter un livre. faux
5. Lucien va chez le disquaire pour son père.
6. Il va acheter le journal pour la voisine.
   5. faux 6. faux

5 Cherche les expressions

According to **Un petit service,** how do you . . .

1. say you're meeting someone?
2. say you don't know if you'll have time?
3. ask someone to do something for you?
4. express your annoyance?
5. call for help?

1. J'ai rendez-vous avec...
2. Je ne sais pas si je vais avoir le temps.
3. Tu peux... ? Est-ce que tu peux... ?
4. ... ça suffit!
5. Au secours!

6 Et maintenant, à toi

What errands do you do? Do you go to the same places as Lucien?

PREMIERE ETAPE

Pointing out places and things

VOCABULAIRE

Où est-ce qu'on va pour faire les courses?

à **la boulangerie** pour acheter du pain

à **la pâtisserie** pour acheter **des pâtisseries**

à **l'épicerie** pour acheter de la confiture

à **la poste** pour acheter **des timbres** et **envoyer des lettres**

à **la banque** pour **retirer** ou **déposer** de l'argent

à **la librairie-papeterie** pour acheter des livres ou **des enveloppes**

à **la pharmacie** pour acheter **des médicaments**

chez le disquaire pour acheter des disques compacts ou des cassettes

à **la bibliothèque** pour **emprunter** ou **rendre** des livres

---

RESOURCES FOR **PREMIERE ETAPE**

Textbook Audiocassette 6B/Audio CD 12
Practice and Activity Book, pp. 134–136
Videodisc Guide
   Videodisc Program, Videodisc 6B

Chapter Teaching Resources, Book 3
- Teaching Transparency Master 12-1, pp. 175, 178
  Teaching Transparency 12-1
- Additional Listening Activities 12-1, 12-2, p. 179
  Audiocassette 10B/Audio CD 12
- Realia 12-1, pp. 183, 185
- Situation Cards 12-1, pp. 186–187
- Student Response Forms, pp. 188–190
- Quiz 12-1, pp. 191–192
  Audiocassette 8B/Audio CD 12

---

*J*ump Start!

Have students make a shopping list in French of at least five things they need to buy. They might include groceries, school supplies, or clothing. Have them begin the list with **Il me faut...**

MOTIVATE

Ask students to name three or four places tourists might want to go in their town during a vacation and why.

TEACH

Presentation

Vocabulaire Bring in various items (a jar of jam, money, medicine) and have students tell where to find each item (**On va à...**). You might want to have students give local equivalents of the places mentioned (World of Music, People's Bank). Then, hold up pictures of the items that can be purchased at each store, having students repeat after you. Write the store names and the items available at each one on strips of transparency. Scatter the strips across the overhead. Then, have two students come to the projector and match the stores with the items available at each one. Have students name in French other items they might find at these places.

Additional Practice

For listening practice, you might want to create and read aloud several true-false statements based on the **Vocabulaire,** such as **On va à la bibliothèque pour acheter du pain.** Call on individual students to correct the false statements.

Additional Practice

Tu te rappelles? You might have students recall the French names of other places where they might go after school (**au café, au ciné, chez Eric**) and write them on the board. Then, have partners ask and tell where they're going after school today or this weekend.

 **For Individual Needs**

8 Slower Pace Type Frédéric's letter, omitting the places he went. Give copies to partners to complete.

8 Challenge Have students write a response to Frédéric's letter, describing a similar day that they have had recently.

 **For Individual Needs**

9 Visual Learners In pairs, one student draws a picture of a building that Yvette visited (**la pharmacie, la poste**). When his or her partner correctly identifies the place and calls out what Yvette said there, he or she then draws a different building.

9 Challenge Ask students to suggest additional quotes and have classmates guess where they might hear them.
—Je voudrais acheter le nouveau CD de Vanessa Paradis.
—Chez le disquaire.

Thinking Critically

Analyzing — Note Culturelle Have students consider how late stores usually stay open in the United States. Have them compare these hours to the hours that French stores usually keep. What are the advantages and disadvantages of French hours? Of American hours?

---

7 Ecoute!

Listen to these conversations and tell where the people are.
Answers on p. 309C.

8 Un petit mot

Read this note that Frédéric wrote to his friend. Then, list three places he went and tell what he did there. See answers below.

Tu te rappelles?

Remember, **au, à la, à l'**, and **aux** mean *to the* or *at the*. Use **au** before a masculine singular noun, **à la** before a feminine singular noun, **à l'** before any singular noun beginning with a vowel sound, and **aux** before any plural noun.

Je vais { **au** musée. / **à la** boulangerie. / **à l'** épicerie.

Je vais { **à l'** hôtel. / **aux** Etats-Unis.

> Cher Pierre,
>
> Ici, rien de bien nouveau. Hier, mes parents sont allés passer la journée chez leurs amis, alors j'étais tout seul. J'en ai profité pour faire des courses. D'abord, je suis allé à la boulangerie acheter du pain. Ensuite, je suis allé à la poste parce que je n'avais plus de timbres, et j'en ai profité pour envoyer une lettre à Jules, mon correspondant québécois. Puis, je suis allé à la bibliothèque emprunter quelques livres parce que j'ai fini de lire toute ma collection. Je n'ai pas trouvé le dernier livre de Stephen King à la bibliothèque (il paraît qu'il est super!), alors je suis allé à la librairie pour l'acheter. Finalement, je suis passé à l'épicerie acheter des légumes et du fromage pour mon déjeuner. Voilà, c'est tout. Ecris-moi vite pour me dire comment tu trouves ton nouveau lycée. Salut.
>
> Frédéric

9 1. à la pâtisserie
2. à la bibliothèque
3. à la pharmacie
4. à la poste
5. à la banque

9 Des courses en ville

Yvette fait des courses en ville. Où est-elle?

1. «Je voudrais ce gâteau au chocolat, s'il vous plaît.»
2. «Je voudrais emprunter ces trois livres, s'il vous plaît.»
3. «Eh bien, je voudrais des médicaments pour ma mère.»
4. «C'est combien pour envoyer cette lettre aux Etats-Unis?»
5. «Zut, alors! Elle est fermée. Je ne peux pas déposer de l'argent!»

NOTE CULTURELLE

Stores in France and Martinique don't stay open 24 hours a day. Between 12:30 P.M. and 3:30 P.M., very few small businesses are open; however, they usually remain open until 7 P.M. By law, businesses must close one day a week, usually Sunday. Only grocery stores, restaurants, and certain places related to culture and entertainment, such as museums and movie theaters, may stay open on Sunday.

Culture Note

Stores in Côte d'Ivoire usually follow the French system of closing for a few hours in the early afternoon. To escape the heat, people usually take a short nap (**la sieste**) at this time.

Possible answers

8 To the bakery to buy bread, to the post office to buy stamps and send a letter, to the library to borrow some books, to the bookstore to buy a book, to the grocery store to buy vegetables and cheese.

10 Il va où? See answers below.

a. Regarde la liste d'Armand. Où va-t-il?

b. Qu'est-ce qu'il peut acheter d'autre là où il va?

> **De bons conseils**
>
> You've already learned that an ending can often help you guess the gender of a word. An ending can also help you guess the meaning of a word. For example, the ending **-erie** often indicates a place where something is sold or made. Look at these words: **poissonnerie, fromagerie, chocolaterie, croissanterie.** What do you think they mean? Another common ending that carries a particular meaning is **-eur (-euse).** It indicates a person who performs a certain activity. In French, **chasser** means *to hunt.* A person who hunts is a **chasseur.** Since **chanter** means *to sing,* how do you think you would say *singer* in French? If **danser** means *to dance,* how would you say *dancer?**

11 Devine!

Think of something that you bought. Then, tell your partner where you went to buy it. Your partner will try to guess what you bought there. Take turns.

> *Si tu as oublié le passé composé va à la page 239.*

— Je suis allé(e) à la boulangerie.
— Tu as acheté des croissants?
— Non.

COMMENT DIT-ON... ?
Pointing out places and things

Voici tes timbres.
Regarde, voilà ma maison.
  Look, here/there is/are . . .
Ça, c'est la banque.
  This/That is . . .
Là, c'est mon disquaire préféré.
  There, that is . . .
Là, tu vois, c'est la maison de mes grands-parents.
  There, you see, this/that is . . .

*chanteur, danseur

Language Note

The official French term for a *Walkman®* is **un baladeur,** which translates literally as *one who walks around.* A **conteur** is *someone who narrates stories.* **Rapporter** means *to tell on* or *to tattle,* so a **rapporteur** is not a very popular person!

Teaching Suggestions

10 You might have students work in pairs to answer these questions. Have them do **10a** first and then write their answers on the board. Students can then use these place names as the basis for answering **10b.**

De bons conseils You might have students think of common suffixes in English, such as *-ly, -er,* and *-ment,* and suggest words that have these endings (*happily, buyer, punishment*).

For Individual Needs

Challenge — De bons conseils Have students guess what the ending -**ant** means from looking at the following words they're already familiar with: **barbant, intéressant, embêtant, dégoûtant.** You might have them go through the French vocabulary at the end of the book to find endings that signal adjectives (-**é,** -**eux,** -**euse,** and so on).

Teaching Suggestion

11 You might ask students to think of two or three additional things that they bought at different stores.

Presentation

Comment dit-on... ? Begin by having students identify other students or pictures of celebrities that you bring in. Then, use the expressions to identify different items in the classroom and pictures of buildings. Finally, hold up pictures of different places or things or point to various objects in the classroom and have students identify them.

For videodisc application, see *Videodisc Guide*.

Teaching Suggestions

12 You might also have students bring in photos they've taken on vacation or pictures they've cut from magazines and identify them to a partner or to the class.

A la française After reading the explanation with students, have them practice using circumlocution to identify the photos in Activity 12. You might also give students English words and ask them to explain them in French. Examples include a bank teller, an ice cream shop, a gift shop, a waiter or waitress, and a card catalogue.

Teacher Note

For more information on the **bibliothèque Schœlcher**, see page 308 of the Location Opener and the History Link on page 312.

 Portfolio

13 Written This activity might be expanded into the chapter project described on page 309E. This item is appropriate for students' written portfolios. For portfolio information, see *Assessment Guide*, pages 2–13.

CLOSE

To close this **étape,** name a local store *(Cathy's Cakes)*. Have one student name what type of store it is (**une pâtisserie**) and another student name something they could buy there (**des gâteaux**).

---

12 A la Martinique

During your trip to Martinique you took the photos below. Take turns with your partner pointing out and identifying the places and objects in the photos. Possible answers:

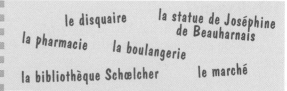

le disquaire	la statue de Joséphine de Beauharnais
la pharmacie	la boulangerie
la bibliothèque Schœlcher	le marché

1. Voici la statue de Joséphine de Beauharnais.
2. Regarde, voilà la pharmacie.
3. Ça, c'est le disquaire.

4. Là, c'est le marché.
5. Là, tu vois, c'est la bibliothèque Schœlcher.
6. Voici la boulangerie.

A la française

When you try to communicate in a foreign language, there will always be times when you can't remember or don't know the exact word you need. One way to get around this problem is to use *circumlocution*. Circumlocution means substituting words and expressions you do know to explain what you mean. For example, if you can't think of the French word for *pharmacy,* you might say **l'endroit où on peut acheter des médicaments** *(the place where you can buy medicine).* Other expressions you can use are **la personne qui/que** *(the person who/whom),* and **le truc qui/que** *(the thing that).*

13 Mon quartier

For an exchange student who is coming to stay with your family for a semester, draw a map of your neighborhood and label the school, post office, grocery store, and so on.

14 Jeu de rôle

As your exchange student asks where various places are, point them out on the map you made for Activity 13. Tell what you buy or do there. Take turns playing the role of the exchange student.

318   *trois cent dix-huit*   CHAPITRE 12   En ville

ASSESS

Quiz 12-1, *Chapter Teaching Resources, Book 3,* pp. 191–192

Assessment Items, Audiocassette 8B
Audio CD 12

Performance Assessment

Have students write a note to a friend, telling all the things they plan to do over the weekend. They should include at least three separate chores, errands, or activities.

RENCONTRE CULTURELLE

Look at the illustrations below. Where are these people? What are they talking about?

— Bonjour, Madame Perrot. Vous avez passé de bonnes vacances?
— Très bonnes. On est allés en Guadeloupe. Vous savez, ma sœur habite là-bas, et...

— Et votre père, il va bien?
— Oui, merci. Il va beaucoup mieux depuis...

— Qu'est-ce que vous allez faire avec ça?
— Ma voisine m'a donné une très bonne recette. C'est très simple. Tout ce qu'il faut faire, c'est...

Qu'en penses-tu?

1. family, vacation, recipes; For the **Martiniquais,** it is more important to spend time finding out what's going on in one another's life than to get business done quickly:

1. What are the topics of these conversations? What does this tell you about the culture of Martinique?
2. What kind of relationships do you or your family have with the people who work in your town? Do you know them? Do you often make "small talk" with them?

Savais-tu que... ?

In Martinique, as in many parts of France, people like to take the time to say hello, ask how others are doing, and find out what's going on in one another's lives. Of course, the smaller the town, the more likely this is to occur. While it may be frustrating to Americans in a hurry, especially when they are conducting business, in West Indian culture it is considered rude not to take a few minutes to engage in some polite conversation before talking business.

Culture Notes

• Even in large cities like Paris, owners of small shops often greet customers as they come into the store and say goodbye as they leave. Customers often respond with a polite **Bonjour, madame/monsieur** or **Merci, au revoir!**

• Small talk is also very common in Côte d'Ivoire and can be quite involved. When people run into a friend or acquaintance during the day, they often inquire at length about that person's health, job, and family situation. Friends will also inquire about the health, job, and general situation of that person's entire family and circle of friends.

RENCONTRE CULTURELLE
CHAPITRE 12

Motivating Activity

Ask students for examples of "small talk" in English. Ask them in what situations and with whom they might make small talk.

Presentation

Have two students read each conversation aloud. After each one, ask the class where the people are, what they are talking about, and what the other people are doing. **(On est où? De quoi est-ce qu'on parle? Que font les autres?)** Then, have students answer the questions in **Qu'en penses-tu?** as a class or with a partner.

Teaching Suggestion

You might ask students if there are places or situations in the United States where small talk is expected or discouraged.

Thinking Critically

Comparing and Contrasting Ask students how Americans behave when they have to stand in line and if their behavior is different from that shown here. Ask students if they consider themselves to be very patient.

Synthesizing Have students write and act out skits of similar situations that would normally occur in their own town. Small groups might rewrite all three situations, or you might assign them to three large groups. Have some students play the other customers waiting in line. Groups should also add dialogue for the customers as well.

DEUXIEME ETAPE

Making and responding to requests; asking for advice and making suggestions

COMMENT DIT-ON... ?
Making and responding to requests

To make a request:
  (Est-ce que) tu peux aller au marché?
Tu me rapportes des timbres?
Tu pourrais passer à la poste acheter des timbres?
  Could you go by . . . ?

To accept requests:
  D'accord.
  Je veux bien.
  J'y vais tout de suite.
  Si tu veux. *If you want.*

To decline requests:
  Je ne peux pas maintenant.
  Je suis désolé(e), mais je n'ai pas le temps.

15 Ecoute!

Listen to the following conversations and decide if the person agrees to or refuses the request.
Answers on p. 309C.

Tu te rappelles **?**

Use the partitive articles **du, de la,** and **de l'** when you mean *some* of an item. If you mean a whole item instead of a part of it, use the indefinite articles **un, une,** and **des.** Du, **de la, de l', des, un,** and **une** usually become **de/d'** in negative sentences.

16 Un petit service

What would these people say to ask you a favor? See answers below.

1. 2. 3. 4.

17 Il me faut...

Si tu as oublié expressing need va à la page 210.

Decide which of these items you need and ask your partner to go to the appropriate store. Your partner will accept or decline your request. Take turns.

  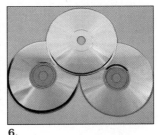

1. 2. 3.

4. 5. 6.

18 Tu pourrais me rendre un service?

Ask your classmates to do these favors for you. They will either accept or decline and make an excuse.

chercher un livre à la bibliothèque

acheter un dictionnaire de français à la librairie

acheter un CD chez le disquaire

acheter un sandwich au fast-food

acheter une règle à la papeterie

acheter des timbres à la poste

Si tu as oublié making an excuse va à la page 129.

DEUXIEME ETAPE

trois cent vingt et un 321

Possible answers

16 1. (Est-ce que) tu peux aller à la poste envoyer des lettres?
2. (Est-ce que) tu pourrais passer à la bibliothèque rendre des livres?
3. Tu me rapportes un CD?
4. (Est-ce que) tu pourrais passer à la pharmacie acheter des médicaments?

Culture Note

The second photo of Activity 17 shows a common French stamp. The stamp bears the allegorical image of **la République française**, also known as **Marianne.** This image also appears on French coins.

For Individual Needs

16 Auditory Learners
Read aloud appropriate requests and have students match them with the illustrations.

16 Challenge Encourage students to say or write other requests each person might make. Have them expand their requests by telling why the errand needs to be done.

17 Slower Pace Before students do the activity, have them write the store they would go to for each item.

Additional Practice

17 You might also show the items you used for the **Vocabulaire** presentation on page 315 (a jar of jam, money, medicine, a croissant, and a library book) and have partners make appropriate requests.

Reteaching

17 The partitive Review the use of the partitive, using **Tu te rappelles?** on page 320. You might bring in a loaf of bread to demonstrate **un pain,** and then break off a piece and offer it to students to illustrate the partitive **du pain.** Have students say each item, using the correct partitive article.

Teaching Suggestion

18 Have students vary the way they request and respond to favors.

Additional Practice

Show *Teaching Transparency 12-2.* Assign one of the people shown to each of four groups. Have them write a speech bubble on a strip of transparency for the person they were assigned. Project their transparencies on top of the original transparency and have the class match the speech bubbles to the people.

Presentation

Comment dit-on… ? Ask students if they ever have problems getting where they want to go. Have them name in French several places they might want to visit in a new town. Then, suggest local places and ask **Comment est-ce qu'on peut y aller? En voiture? En bus?**

Vocabulaire Begin by having students look at the photos and tell what means of transportation are available in their town or area. Then, mime each form of transportation, having students repeat as they imitate your actions. Ask students how to get to different places, such as **la cantine, le supermarché, New York, l'Australie, la Martinique,** and so on. Have them make picture flashcards for each item and then practice the expressions by showing the picture to a partner and asking **Comment est-ce qu'on y va?**

Teaching Suggestions

• Ask students which forms of transportation they use. **(Comment est-ce que tu vas à l'école? Au cinéma? Au centre commercial?)**
• Have pairs of students ask each other **Comment est-ce que tu vas à l'école?** and report their findings to the class.

COMMENT DIT-ON… ?

Asking for advice and making suggestions

To ask for advice on how to get somewhere:
Comment est-ce qu'on y va? *How can we get there?*

To suggest how to get somewhere:
On peut y aller en train. *We can go . . .*
On peut prendre le bus. *We can take . . .*

VOCABULAIRE

Comment est-ce qu'on y va?

en bus (m.)

à pied (m.)

à vélo (m.)

en voiture (f.)

en taxi (m.)

en bateau (m.)

en avion (m.)

en train (m.)

en métro (m.)

322 *trois cent vingt-deux* CHAPITRE 12 En ville

Language Notes

• Explain that **à** is used instead of **en** with **pied** and **vélo** because one isn't inside a vehicle.
• You might point out that either the definite article or indefinite article can be used with transportation after **prendre** (**prendre le train, prendre un taxi**).

Multicultural Link

Have students choose a foreign city or country and imagine what form of transportation is the most popular and efficient there. They may want to find out about typical bus, train, metro, and plane fares there.

19 Ecoute!

Listen to these conversations. Where are these people going and how are they going to get there? *Answers on p. 309C.*

20 Comment vont-ils voyager?

1. en bateau   2. en métro   3. en train   4. en avion

Grammaire The pronoun y

You've already seen the pronoun **y** *(there)* several times. Can you figure out how to use it?

—Je vais **à la bibliothèque**. Tu **y** vas aussi?
—Non, je n'**y** vais pas.

—Je vais **chez le disquaire**. Tu veux **y** aller?
—Non, j'**y** suis allé hier.

It can replace an entire phrase meaning *to, at,* or *in* any place that has already been mentioned. Place it before the conjugated verb, or, if there is an infinitive, place **y** before the infinitive: Je vais **y** aller demain.

21 On va en ville

How do you and your friends get to these places?

Au cinéma? Nous y allons en bus.

au cinéma	au supermarché	à la poste	à la bibliothèque
à la piscine	au centre commercial		au stade
au parc	à la librairie	au lycée	au concert

Si tu as oublié inviting va à la page 159.

22 Qu'est-ce qu'on fait vendredi soir?

You call your friend and invite him or her to do something Friday night. When you've decided where you want to go, talk about how to get there.

DEUXIEME ETAPE   *trois cent vingt-trois* **323**

CLOSE

To close this **étape,** have small groups review the forms of transportation by playing charades.

ASSESS

Quiz 12-2, *Chapter Teaching Resources, Book 3,* pp. 193–194

Assessment Items, Audiocassette 8B Audio CD 12

Performance Assessment

Write the items sold at the stores on page 315 on index cards (**du pain, de l'argent**). Have students draw a card and ask a classmate to go to the appropriate store for it. (**Tu pourrais passer à la boulangerie?**) The partner responds accordingly. (**Je veux bien.**)

◆ For Individual Needs

19 Slower Pace Before doing this activity, have students list expressions they might expect to hear.

20 Challenge You might also have students write brief explanations of what the people are going to do and why.

Presentation

Grammaire Write **Il, va, à la bibliothèque,** and **y** on strips of transparency. Arrange the first three strips to form the sentence **Il va à la bibliothèque** and have students repeat. Then, replace **à la bibliothèque** with **y** to form the sentence **Il y va.** Write the subjects, verbs, and prepositional phrases of several similar sentences and the pronoun **y** on strips, scramble them, and call on students to arrange them into sentences, first without **y,** and then forming a new sentence using **y.**

Additional Practice

Write destinations like **chez le disquaire** and **à la bibliothèque** on cards and distribute them to students. Then, have them pair off and ask questions until they find out where their partner is going.
—**Tu vas à la bibliothèque?**
—**Non, je n'y vais pas.**
—**Tu vas chez le disquaire?**
—**Oui, je vais y aller aujourd'hui.**

21 In order to practice all the forms of transportation, you might want to hold up picture flashcards as cues.

▣ Portfolio

22 Oral This activity might be recorded for students' oral portfolios. For portfolio information, see *Assessment Guide,* pages 2–13.

VIDEO PROGRAM
OR EXPANDED VIDEO
PROGRAM,
Videocassette 4
46:22–49:09

OR VIDEODISC PROGRAM,
Videodisc 6B

Search 28545, Play To 31590

Teacher Notes

- See *Video Guide, Videodisc Guide,* and *Practice and Activity Book* for activities related to the **Panorama Culturel.**
- Remind students that cultural material may be included in the Chapter Quizzes and Test.
- The interviewees' language represents informal, unrehearsed speech. Occasionally, edits have been made for clarification.

Motivating Activity

Ask students question 1 under **Qu'en penses-tu?** Ask whether they have or would like to have a driver's license and why or why not.

Presentation

After students view the video, have them scan the interviews for cognates and skim for a general idea of what each person is saying. Then, ask the **Questions** below.

Thinking Critically

Comparing and Contrasting

Have students compare the French, Canadian, and American requirements for a driver's license. Which requirements are stricter? What do students think the requirements for a license should be?

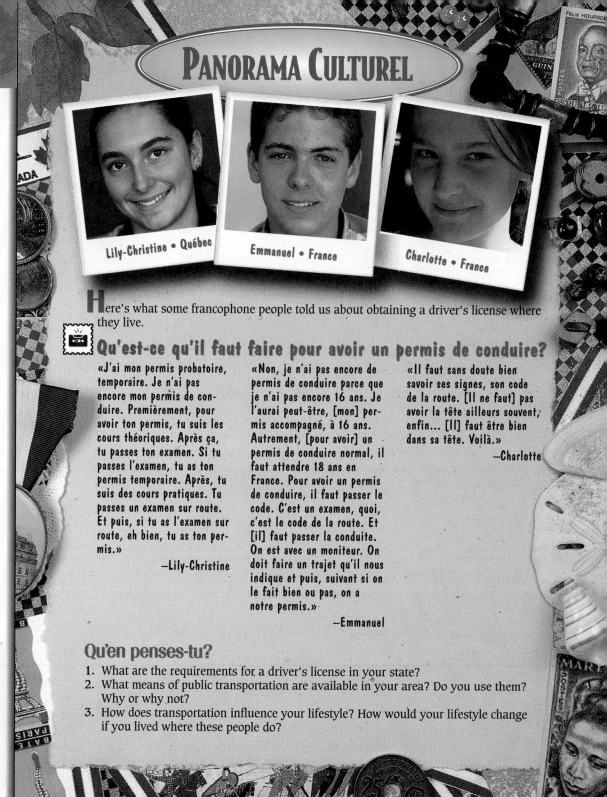

PANORAMA CULTUREL

Lily-Christine • Québec

Emmanuel • France

Charlotte • France

Here's what some francophone people told us about obtaining a driver's license where they live.

Qu'est-ce qu'il faut faire pour avoir un permis de conduire?

«J'ai mon permis probatoire, temporaire. Je n'ai pas encore mon permis de conduire. Premièrement, pour avoir ton permis, tu suis les cours théoriques. Après ça, tu passes ton examen. Si tu passes l'examen, tu as ton permis temporaire. Après, tu suis des cours pratiques. Tu passes un examen sur route. Et puis, si tu as l'examen sur route, eh bien, tu as ton permis.»

—Lily-Christine

«Non, je n'ai pas encore de permis de conduire parce que je n'ai pas encore 16 ans. Je l'aurai peut-être, [mon] permis accompagné, à 16 ans. Autrement, [pour avoir] un permis de conduire normal, il faut attendre 18 ans en France. Pour avoir un permis de conduire, il faut passer le code. C'est un examen, quoi, c'est le code de la route. Et [il] faut passer la conduite. On est avec un moniteur. On doit faire un trajet qu'il nous indique et puis, suivant si on le fait bien ou pas, on a notre permis.»

—Emmanuel

«Il faut sans doute bien savoir ses signes, son code de la route. [Il ne faut] pas avoir la tête ailleurs souvent; enfin... [Il] faut être bien dans sa tête. Voilà.»

—Charlotte

Qu'en penses-tu?

1. What are the requirements for a driver's license in your state?
2. What means of public transportation are available in your area? Do you use them? Why or why not?
3. How does transportation influence your lifestyle? How would your lifestyle change if you lived where these people do?

Language Note

You might want to define the following terms: **sur route** *(on the road);* **conduite** *(driving);* **trajet** *(route);* **ailleurs** *(elsewhere).*

Questions

1. Est-ce que Lily-Christine a son permis de conduire? (Non, elle a son permis probatoire.)
2. D'après Lily-Christine, combien d'examens est-ce qu'on passe pour avoir le permis de conduire? (deux)
3. Est-ce qu'Emmanuel a son permis de conduire? Pourquoi ou pourquoi pas? (Non; Il faut avoir 18 ans.)
4. D'après Charlotte, qu'est-ce qu'il faut bien savoir? (les signes, le code de la route)

TROISIEME ETAPE

Asking for and giving directions

VOCABULAIRE

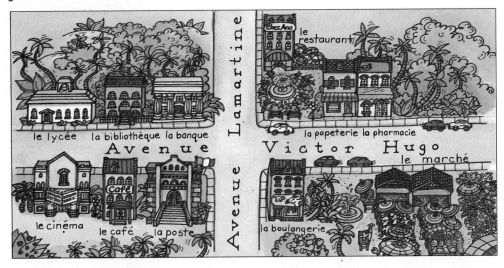

La bibliothèque est **entre** le lycée et la banque.
La poste est **à droite du** café.
Le cinéma est **à gauche du** café.

La boulangerie est **au coin de** la rue.
Le café est **en face de** la bibliothèque.

Here are some other prepositions you may want to use to give directions:

à côté de	*next to*	**loin de**	*far from*
devant	*in front of*	**près de**	*near*
derrière	*behind*		

23 Ecoute!

Listen to the following statements and tell whether they are true or false, according to the **Vocabulaire**.
Answers on p. 309D.

24 Qui est-ce?

Tell where a classmate is seated in your classroom. The others in your group will try to guess who it is.

> Cette personne est derrière
> David et à côté d'Isabelle.

Tu te rappelles ?

Do you remember how to use the preposition **de** *(of, from)*?
De and **le** become **du. De** and **les** become **des. De** doesn't change before **la** or **l'.**

C'est près **du** musée.
C'est près **des** vélos.
C'est au coin **de la** rue Mouffetard.
La bibliothèque est à côté **de l'**école.

TROISIEME ETAPE

trois cent vingt-cinq **325**

For Individual Needs

25 Challenge Have partners write one or two additional questions Hervé might ask about places in their own town. They might ask their partner these questions, or you might collect them to ask the class.

26 Challenge You might also have students draw their own family pictures like Arianne's (or pictures of a famous or imaginary family) and exchange them with a partner. The partner will ask about the people and places in the drawings and help write appropriate captions. Students might include this "photo album" in their written portfolios.

Additional Practice

26 Ask additional questions about the photos. For example, for the fifth photo, you might ask **Où est l'épicerie?** (**Elle est à côté de la maison.**)

Reteaching

Family vocabulary Draw the family tree of a TV family or of a royal family and ask students to describe the relationships between the family members. You might expand this activity by having students describe where the families live and what they like to do. You might also ask questions about familial relationships, such as **Le frère de ton père, c'est ton oncle ou ta mère?**

25 Il est perdu!

Your friend, Hervé, has a poor sense of direction. Everything is in just the <u>opposite</u> direction or location from what he thinks. Help him out by answering his questions.

> —La poste est loin de la bibliothèque?
> —Mais non, elle est près de la bibliothèque.

1. Est-ce que la papeterie est près de la pharmacie?
2. Le cinéma est devant le centre commercial?
3. La bibliothèque est à droite?
4. Est-ce que le café est derrière le stade?

1. Mais non, elle est loin de la pharmacie.
2. Mais non, il est derrière le centre commercial.
3. Mais non, elle est à gauche.
4. Mais non, il est devant le stade.

NOTE CULTURELLE

Martinique is an overseas possession of France known as a **département d'outre-mer**, or **DOM**. It has the same administrative status as a department in France, and the people of Martinique, who are citizens of France, have the same rights and responsibilities as other French citizens. Other DOMs include Guadeloupe, French Guiana, and Reunion Island. France also has overseas territories, like New Caledonia and French Polynesia. These territories are called **térritoires d'outre-mer**, or **TOMs**.

26 La visite d'Arianne

Arianne a pris des photos pendant sa visite chez son oncle et sa tante. Complète les descriptions des photos avec des prépositions.

1. *C'est mon oncle et ma tante dans le jardin _____ leur maison.*
devant

2. *Là, _____ ma tante, c'est mon cousin Daniel.*
à côté de

3. *Et voilà ma cousine Adeline, _____ mon oncle.*
derrière

4. *Il y a une boulangerie _____ leur maison. Les croissants sont délicieux le matin!*
en face de/près de

5. *Leur maison est _____ une autre maison et une épicerie.*
entre

6. *Il y a un parc au coin de la rue, _____ leur maison.*
près de

326 *trois cent vingt-six*

CHAPITRE 12   En ville

🌐 **Culture Note**

Since Martinique is a **département** of France, people in Martinique refer to continental France as **la métropole**.

COMMENT DIT-ON...?
Asking for and giving directions

To ask for directions:

Pardon, madame. La poste, **s'il vous plaît?**

Pardon, mademoiselle. Où est la banque, **s'il vous plaît?**

Pardon, monsieur. Je cherche le musée, **s'il vous plaît.** *Excuse me, sir. I'm looking for . . . please.*

To give directions:

Vous continuez jusqu'au prochain feu rouge. *You keep going until the next light.*

Vous allez tout droit jusqu'au lycée. *You go straight ahead until you get to . . .*

Vous tournez à droite. *You turn . . .*

Prenez la rue Lamartine, **puis traversez la rue** Isambert. *Take . . . Street, then cross . . . Street.*

Vous passez devant la boulangerie. *You'll pass . . .*

C'est tout de suite à gauche. *It's right there on the . . . .*

27 Ecoute!

Guy is at the bus station **(la gare routière)** in Fort-de-France. Follow M. Robinet's directions, using the map on page 328. Where does Guy want to go?   to the post office

NOTE CULTURELLE

In many French towns, intersections have a traffic circle at the center, which is often decorated with flowers, fountains, or statues. Vehicles enter and continue around the center island, turning off at the various streets that open into the circle. Most towns have at least one public square, often located in front of a public building or a church. Numerous cities have closed off some of the tiny streets in the **centre-ville** and made pedestrian areas where people can stroll freely, without having to worry about traffic.

28 Où est-ce?

Give directions from school to your favorite fast-food restaurant or record store. Your partner will try to guess the name of the place. Take turns.

Presentation

Comment dit-on... ? Have students ask you how to get to various places in town. Answer their questions, using the expressions for giving directions. Then, draw a map to a nearby building or park and ask students to give directions to it. In order to allow several students to participate, have each student give only one segment of the directions.

 For videodisc application, see *Videodisc Guide.*

For Individual Needs

Auditory Learners Give directions to several places in town and have students tell whether your directions are accurate.

27 Challenge Have students listen to the recording with their books closed and sketch the route.

Thinking Critically

Comparing and Contrasting Ask students if there is a place comparable to a town square in their own town. Are there any statues, fountains, or public gardens? Where? Are there any areas that are off-limits to cars? What are the advantages and disadvantages of having an outdoor pedestrian mall?

Community Link

You might have students look up the history of a public square, town hall, local landmark, or historical building in their town. They might go to the Chamber of Commerce or the local library to find out when the building was built, whether it's been renovated, and what happened there of historical importance.

Teaching Suggestion

28 This activity could also be done using maps of Paris or other francophone cities, or by giving directions in the classroom or school.

For Individual Needs

29 Slower Pace Before students do this activity, have them locate the two sites in the photos on the map. Then, have them locate the major landmarks and streets mentioned in the letter.

29 Challenge Have students write directions to a different location on the map and read them to a partner. The partner follows the directions and tells where they lead.

Additional Practice

29 Give directions to various locations on the map. (**De la préfecture, vous prenez à droite dans la rue Félix Eboué. Vous passez devant la bibliothèque. Enfin, vous tournez à droite rue Antoine Siger. C'est tout de suite à gauche.**) Have students tell where your directions lead (**la poste**).

Portfolio

30 Written This activity is appropriate for students' written portfolios. For portfolio suggestions, see *Assessment Guide,* page 25.

Mon journal

30 If students don't want to write about their towns or neighborhoods, have them describe an ideal city or neighborhood. For an additional journal entry suggestion for Chapter 12, see *Practice and Activity Book,* page 156.

29 Quel monument est-ce? la cathédrale Saint-Louis

Your pen pal from Martinique wrote directions for you to a site that he thinks you should visit. Follow his directions on the map of Fort-de-France to find out which of these sites it is.

la bibliothèque Schœlcher

la cathédrale Saint-Louis

Quand tu sors de la gare routière, va à droite sur le boulevard du Général de Gaulle. Prends la première à droite – c'est la rue Félix Eboué – et continue tout droit. Tu vas passer devant la préfecture. Traverse l'avenue des Caraïbes et va tout droit dans la rue de la liberté jusqu'à la poste. Ensuite, tourne à droite rue Blénac et continue tout droit. Ça sera à droite, tout de suite après la rue Schœlcher.

30 Mon journal

Write a description of your city or neighborhood. What does it look like? Where are things located? Draw a small map to accompany your description.

328 *trois cent vingt-huit* CHAPITRE 12 En ville

History Link

29 You might have students find out about the people for whom the streets on the map were named and their major accomplishments (General Charles de Gaulle, Victor Schœlcher, Alphonse de Lamartine, or Antoine Siger). They might do the same for streets in their own town.

Community Link

29 Have students create a map and brochure of their own town with directions to help French-speaking tourists get around town. They might include local points of interest, good restaurants, hotels, post offices, and so on. See the project on page 309E for an expanded version of this activity.

P R O N O N C I A T I O N

 Prononciation

Do you remember what you've learned about French pronunciation? Here is a quick pronunciation review. If you've forgotten how to produce any of these sounds, check the Pronunciation Index at the back of the book and go back to the chapters where they were introduced. Repeat these words.

[y]	du	étude	[u]	rouge		voudrais
[o]	escargots	gâteau	[ɔ]	pomme		carottes
[ø]	veut	heureux	[œ]	sœur		beurre
[e]	cinéma	trouver	[ɛ]	frère		anglaise
[ā]	anglais	il prend	[ɔ̃]	allons		poisson
[ɛ̄]	quinze	pain	[œ̃]	lundi		emprunter
[j]	papier	viande	[w]	moi		pouvoir
[ɥ]	lui	ensuite	[t]	maths		théâtre
[r]	très	roux	[ʃ]	chat		chercher
[']	le héros	le hockey	[ɲ]	montagne		Allemagne

A. A prononcer

Repeat the following words.

1. nourriture	boutique	bateau	poste
2. feu	déposer	près	derrière
3. devant	avion	timbre	emprunter
4. pied	voiture	envoyer	tout de suite
5. rue	gauche	prochain	bibliothèque

B. A lire

Take turns with a partner reading each of the following sentences aloud.

1. Quand le chat n'est pas là, les souris dansent.
2. Il est mieux de travailler que de s'amuser.
3. Beaucoup de bruit pour rien.
4. Un poisson n'est jamais trop petit pour être frit.
5. On n'attrape pas les mouches avec du vinaigre.

C. A écrire

You're going to hear a short dialogue. Write down what you hear.   Answers on p. 309D.

Teaching Suggestion

You might want to have students match the words in Part A with the corresponding sounds from the list above.

Portfolio

Oral You might want to assess students' pronunciation by having them record the list at the beginning of **Prononciation** for their oral portfolios. For portfolio information, see *Assessment Guide*, pages 2–13.

CLOSE

(TPR) To close this **étape**, play "**Jacques a dit**," using the new expressions from this **étape** as well as vocabulary students have already learned. (**Allez à gauche. Mettez le livre devant/derrière vous. Allez loin de la fenêtre.**)

ASSESS

Quiz 12-3, *Chapter Teaching Resources, Book 3*, pp. 195–196

Assessment Items, Audiocassette 8B/Audio CD 12

Performance Assessment

Distribute maps or a section of a map of your city. Have students tell a partner how to get from the school to their house or another place in the city. The partner should follow along on the map and tell where the directions lead. Have students reverse roles. As an alternative, show *Teaching Transparency 12-3* and have students give directions to a place in Fort-de-France.

Language Note

The sentences in Part B are well-known proverbs. You might want to have students quote similar English proverbs. Students might need to know **souris** *(mice)*, **bruit** *(noise, rumor)*, and **mouches** *(flies)*.

READING STRATEGY

Combining different reading strategies

Teacher Note

For an additional reading, see *Practice and Activity Book*, page 143.

PREREADING
Activity A

Motivating Activity

Have students answer the introductory questions about stories they like to read. Then, ask them what fairy tales or folk tales they remember from their childhood. Did they have a favorite? Have them describe characters or themes that are usually found in fairy tales. You might also have them discuss the purpose or moral of their favorite fairy tales.

Teaching Suggestion

A. You might want to do this activity with the entire class. Remind students just to look at the titles and pictures. Then, ask them how they arrived at their answers.

READING
Activities B–F

Teaching Suggestion

B. Remind students just to scan for the information and to skip over the other details.

For Individual Needs

C. Slower Pace First, have students use the pictures and key words to find the page of the story on which each event takes place. Then, have them look more closely at each page to finalize the order.

$\mathcal{W}$hat kinds of stories do you like to read? Stories about the past? About the future? About exotic places?

DE BONS CONSEILS

When you read stories, newspaper and magazine articles, or novels that were written for native French speakers, you're bound to come across many unfamiliar words. Just remember to use all the reading tips that you know to try to understand what you're reading.

A. a wooden horse; in Saint-Pierre, Martinique

A. Look at the title and illustrations that accompany the text. What is this story going to be about? Where does the story take place?

B. Scan the story to see if you can find the answers to these questions. See answers below.

1. Who are the main characters in the story?
2. What is going on when the story starts?
3. Why does Congo come to help the horse?
4. How does Congo help the horse?

C. Read the story carefully and then see if you can put these events in the correct order.

1. Congo burns the blue horse. 5
2. A child is frightened by the blue horse. 2
3. Congo first comes to see the blue horse. 4
4. M. Quinquina and his sons play music. 1
5. The blue bird is freed. 6
6. The mayor goes to see Congo. 3

Cheval de bois

$\mathcal{C}$ette année, la ville de Saint-Pierre accueille le manège de la famille Quinquina pour sa fête patronale. Le manège s'est

installé sur la place du marché, face à la mer. Madame Quinquina tient une buvette où elle sert des limonades multicolores.

Monsieur Quinquina et ses deux fils jouent de la flûte de bambou et du "ti-bwa". Au rythme de cette musique, le manège de chevaux de bois, poussé par de robustes jeunes gens, tourne, tourne, tourne.

Cheval bleu, bleu comme l'océan.
Cheval noir, noir comme la nuit.
Cheval blanc, blanc comme les nuages.
Cheval vert, vert comme les bambous.
Cheval rouge, rouge comme le flamboyant.
Cheval jaune, jaune comme l'allamanda.

$\mathcal{L}$es chevaux de bois tournent, tournent et, sur leur dos, tous les enfants sont heureux.

Mais quand la nuit parfumée caresse l'île, les chevaux de bois rêvent. Le cheval bleu, bleu comme l'océan, rêve de partir, partir loin, visiter les îles, visiter le monde. Il a entendu dire que la terre est ronde. Vrai ou faux? Il aimerait bien savoir ! Cela fait si longtemps qu'il porte ce rêve dans sa carcasse de bois que cette nuit-là, son rêve devient oiseau. L'oiseau bat des ailes dans le corps du cheval bleu, bleu comme l'océan.

Au matin, un enfant monte sur le cheval bleu.
Tout à coup, il commence à hurler :
— Maman, maman, il y a une bête dans le cheval. J'ai peur! Je veux descendre.

Language Note

Le flamboyant (used to describe the red horse) is a tree that is between 20 and 40 feet tall with feathery leaves and scarlet or orange flowers. You might ask students what the English word *flamboyant* means, and point out the associated word *flame*. **L'allamanda** (used to describe the yellow horse) is a shrub with large, funnel-shaped, golden flowers.

Answers

B 1. The blue horse and Congo
2. There is a fair in town.
3. The mayor asked him to help.
4. He frees him and lets his dream come true.

On arrête la musique, on arrête le manège. C'est un tollé général : les mères rassemblent leurs enfants. En quelques secondes, la place est vide. Le maire et ses conseillers décident d'aller chercher le sage Congo.

...Congo s'approche du manège et caresse les flancs du cheval bleu, bleu comme l'océan :
— Je vais te délivrer ! cheval bleu, bleu comme l'océan, car ton rêve est vivant, il s'est métamorphosé en oiseau.
Congo s'assied près du cheval bleu, bleu comme l'océan. Quand le maire voit Congo tranquillement assis, il sort de la mairie en courant et hurle :

— Que faites-vous ?
— J'attends, dit doucement Congo.
— Vous attendez quoi? demande le maire.
— J'attends que la nuit mette son manteau étoilé et ouvre son œil d'or. Je ferai alors un grand feu.

Quand la nuit met son manteau étoilé et ouvre son œil d'or, Congo prend tendrement dans ses bras le cheval bleu, bleu comme l'océan, et le dépose dans les flammes. Le feu crépite, chante, et l'or des flammes devient bleu, bleu comme l'océan. Les habitants de Saint-Pierre voient un immense oiseau bleu, bleu comme l'océan, s'élever dans la nuit étoilée et s'envoler vers l'horizon. Congo, heureux, murmure :
-Bon vent, oiseau-rêve !

RAPPEL As you read the story, you probably came across some unfamiliar words. Remember, you don't have to understand every word to get a sense of what you're reading. If you decide that the meaning of a particular word is necessary to help you understand the story, there are two techniques you've learned that can help: using the context to figure out the meaning of the word, and trying to see a cognate in the word.

D. Below are some cognates that appear in *Cheval de bois*. See if you can match them with their English equivalents.

1. habitants f   a. counselors
2. fête d   b. to descend; to get down
3. flammes e   c. island
4. conseillers a   d. festival
5. île c   e. flames
6. descendre b   f. inhabitants, people who live in a certain area

For Activities E and F, see answers below.

E. Make a list of all of the other cognates you can find in *Cheval de bois*. You should be able to find at least six more. Watch out for false cognates!

F. How can you tell this story was written for a young audience?

G. What stories, fairy tales, or myths have you read or heard that are similar to this story? In what ways are they similar? In what ways are they different?

H. Do you think there really was a bird inside the horse? What do you think the bird represents?

I. Compose a fairy tale of your own. Write it out or record it on tape in French. Keep it simple so that your teacher can use it in the future with students who are beginning to learn French! Illustrate your story to make it easier to understand.

trois cent trente et un **331**

Terms in Lisons!

Students might want to know these words: **cheval** *(horse)*; **bois** *(wood)*; **manège** *(merry-go-round)*; **rêve** *(dream)*; **oiseau** *(bird)*; **feu** *(fire)*; **devient** *(becomes)*.

POSTREADING
Activities G-I

Thinking Critically
Comparing and Contrasting
Have students compare the characters in this fairy tale to ones they're familiar with. How are they similar or different? Have them compare the ending of the story to the ending of *Cinderella* or *Beauty and the Beast*. Is there a moral to the story?

Teaching Suggestion

I. You might have students write their stories in a book they make out of construction paper and illustrate with drawings or magazine pictures. This would also be appropriate for students' written portfolios or as a chapter project.

Cooperative Learning

Have the class act out the story. In small groups, they should choose a director and a narrator, as well as actors to play the other characters. You might videotape the performance to show to other classes.

Language Arts Link

Ask students how the use of repetition affects the story. Have them also find examples of symbolic or metaphoric language (**la nuit met son manteau étoilé, les chevaux de bois rêvent, le rêve devient oiseau**).

Answers
E *Possible answers:* flûte *(flute)*, bambou *(bamboo)*, rythme *(rhythm)*, musique *(music)*, robuste *(robust, strong)*, océan *(ocean)*, parfumée *(perfumed)*, caresse *(caress)*, ronde *(round)*, carcasse *(carcass)*, commence *(commence)*, secondes *(seconds)*, sage *(sage)*, flanc *(flank)*, tranquillement *(quietly, tranquilly)*, tendrement *(tenderly)*, immense *(immense)*, horizon *(horizon)*
F It is short, relatively simple, and magical. The illustrations are colorful and simple.

Literature Link

Famous Caribbean authors are Maryse Condé, Jacques Roumain, Léon-Gontran Damas, and Simone Schwartz-Bart. Damas joined Léopold Senghor of Senegal and Aimé Césaire of Martinique in founding the **Négritude** movement, which stressed African cultural, economic, social, and political values.

MISE EN PRATIQUE

Teaching Suggestion

1 Have students do this activity orally with a partner or have all students write the answers. You might make a contest of this activity by giving students a time limit within which they must write down the answers to both **a** and **b**.

 For Individual Needs

2 Kinesthetic Learners Have groups of three act out the dialogues they write, using gestures.

3 Slower Pace Have students list words or phrases they associate with each picture before they listen to the recording.

Teaching Suggestion

3 After doing this activity, have partners identify what is in the photos.

1 a. Brigitte et Cara ont fait des courses. Qu'est-ce qu'elles ont acheté?

b. Qui a écrit le petit mot? La mère de Brigitte ou la mère de Cara?
See answers below.

Salut, chérie! Ça va aujourd'hui? Est-ce que tu pourrais faire des courses pour moi? Il me faut des timbres et des enveloppes. Tu peux passer à la poste? Le livre qu'il me faut est enfin à la bibliothèque. Tu peux aller le chercher? Tu pourrais aussi passer à la pharmacie pour prendre de l'aspirine? Merci

 2 Write the dialogue that is taking place in the situation shown here.

 3 Listen to Didier tell his family about his trip to Martinique. Put the pictures in order according to Didier's description. c, d, a, b

a. b. c. d.

332 *trois cent trente-deux* CHAPITRE 12 En ville

Answers

1 a. *Brigitte:* une baguette, du beurre, du lait, du jambon, une bouteille d'eau minérale
Cara: des enveloppes, du papier, des livres, des médicaments
b. la mère de Cara

4 You're planning a trip to Martinique and you'll need some transportation. Look at these ads. What kinds of transportation are available? *See answers below.*

LOCATION TROIS-ILETS
Anse à l'Ane - 97229 Trois-Ilets

68.40.37
Lundi à Vendredi
8 H - 13 H
et 15 H - 18 H
Week-end :
à la demande

Avec Location TROIS-ILETS, la moto que vous avez louée par téléphone, 48 heures plus tôt, vient à vous. Chez vous. Si vous vous trouvez dans la commune des Trois-Ilets. Location possible pour une semaine au moins.

TAXI FORT-DE-FRANCE
102 Rue de la République -
97200 Fort-de-France

70.44.08 Tous les jours : 5 H - 20 H

Nos taxis répondent sans délais quand vous téléphonez à Taxi Fort-de-France. Déplacement dans toute l'île.

LOCA CENTER
3 Km Route de Schœlcher -
97200 Fort-de-France

Livraison de voiture (Renault Super-cinq) à domicile (Nord Caraïbe, Schœlcher, Fort-de-France) pour une durée minimum de trois jours. Pas de frais de déplacement. Pendant la haute saison, pour une location de 10 jours au moins, réserver un mois à l'avance. Pour une location d'une durée de 3 à 7 jours, réserver 48 heures à l'avance. Pendant la basse saison, réserver la veille ou le jour même.

61.05.95
61.40.12
Lundi à
Vendredi
7 H 30 -
16 H 30
Week-end :
à la
demande

1. Where can you call if you want a taxi? When is the latest you can call?
2. Where can you call if you want to rent a Renault? What about a motorcycle?
3. What's the minimum length of time you can rent these vehicles?
4. How long in advance do you need to make a reservation?
5. Are these places open on weekends?

5

JEU DE ROLE

a. While visiting Fort-de-France, you stop at the tourist office to ask for directions to **la Savane, le Musée départemental, le Grand Marché, la cathédrale Saint-Louis,** and **le parc floral.** The employee is new, so write down the directions and ask questions if the directions aren't clear.

b. Now, pick some other sites on the island you would like to visit. Ask the employee how you can get there.

Martinique

Answers
4 motorcycle, taxi, rental car
1. Taxi Fort-de-France; 8:00 P.M.
2. Loca Center; Location Trois-Ilets
3. Renault: three days; Motorcycle: one week
4. Location Trois-Ilets: 48 hours; Taxi Fort-de-France; advance reservation not necessary;

Loca Center: high season, one month (if renting for at least 10 days) or 48 hours (if renting for 3–7 days); low season, the night before or the same day
5. Location Trois-Ilets and Loca Center: open on request; Taxi Fort-de-France: yes

Additional Practice

4 You might want to review the means of transportation by showing picture flashcards. After students identify the means of transportation, they might tell where they have gone using that form of transportation.

Teaching Suggestion

5 Have partners reread together the written directions to each site to check for comprehensibility and make any necessary corrections.

Portfolio

5 **Oral** This activity is appropriate for students' oral portfolios. For portfolio suggestions, see *Assessment Guide,* page 25.

Teacher Note

For more information on the sites in Martinique, see the Location Opener on pages 306–309 or contact the Caribbean Tourism Association, whose address and phone number are given on page T50.

Video Wrap-Up

* *VIDEO PROGRAM*
* *EXPANDED VIDEO PROGRAM,* Videocassette 4, 32:50–51:01
* *VIDEODISC PROGRAM,* Videodisc 6B

At this time, you might want to use the video resources for additional review and enrichment. See *Video Guide* or *Videodisc Guide* for suggestions regarding the following:
* **Un petit service** (Dramatic episode)
* **Panorama Culturel** (Interviews)
* **Vidéoclips** (Authentic footage)

QUE SAIS-JE?

This page is intended to help students prepare for the test. It is a brief checklist of the major points covered in the chapter. The students should be reminded that this is only a checklist and does not necessarily include everything that will appear on the test.

Teaching Suggestions

1 You might want to review different types of buildings in town by giving a local example of a place *(Prescriptions To Go)* and asking students to identify it (**C'est une pharmacie**).

2, 3 Encourage students to vary the ways they request and respond to favors.

5 You might want to review other means of transportation in addition to the ones shown.

8 Have students illustrate expressions for giving directions on the board or mime them for their classmates to guess.

Can you point out places and things? p. 317

Can you make and respond to requests? p. 320

Can you ask for advice and make suggestions? p. 322

Can you ask for and give directions? p. 327

Can you use what you've learned in this chapter?

1 How would you identify . . . *Possible answers:*
 1. a certain building? Voici...
 2. a certain store? Regarde, voilà...
 3. a certain person? Ça, c'est...

2 How would you ask someone to . . . *Possible answers:*
 1. buy some stamps? Tu peux me rapporter des timbres?
 2. go to the bookstore? Tu pourrais passer à la librairie?
 3. deposit some money? (Est-ce que) tu peux déposer de l'argent?

3 How would you agree to do the favors you asked in number 2? How would you refuse? See answers below.

4 How would you ask a friend which means of transportation you should use to get to a certain store? Comment est-ce qu'on y va?

5 How would you suggest these means of transportation? On peut y aller... On peut prendre...

1. en voiture. la voiture.
2. en bateau. un bateau.
3. en taxi. un taxi.
4. en bus. le bus.

6 How would you tell someone that you're looking for a certain place?
Pardon, monsieur/madame/mademoiselle. Je cherche... , s'il vous plaît.

7 How would you ask someone where a certain place in town is?
Pardon, monsieur/madame/mademoiselle. Où est... , s'il vous plaît?

8 How would you give someone directions to your house from . . .
 1. your school?
 2. your favorite fast-food restaurant?

334 *trois cent trente-quatre* CHAPITRE 12   En ville

♜ **Game**
♜ **Où est... ?** To practice giving directions, create a city in the classroom by labeling the aisles as streets and areas or objects in the room (your desk, the blackboard, the door) as buildings. Form two teams. A player from one team names a place, and a player from the opposing team must direct the first player there in French.

Answers
3 *Agree:* D'accord. Je veux bien. J'y vais tout de suite. Si tu veux.
 Refuse: Je ne peux pas maintenant. Je suis désolé(e), mais je n'ai pas le temps.

PREMIERE ETAPE

Pointing out places and things

Voici... *Here is/are . . .*
Regarde, voilà... *Look, here/there is/are . . .*
Ça, c'est... *This/That is . . .*
Là, c'est... *There, that is . . .*
Là, tu vois, c'est... *There, you see, this/that is . . .*

Buildings

la banque *bank*

la boulangerie *bakery*
chez le disquaire *at the record store*
l'épicerie (f.) *small grocery store*
la librairie *bookstore*
la papeterie *stationery store*
la pâtisserie *pastry shop*
la pharmacie *drugstore*
la poste *post office*

Things to do or buy in town

envoyer des lettres *to send letters*

un timbre *a stamp*
retirer de l'argent (m.) *to withdraw money*
déposer de l'argent *to deposit money*
rendre *to return something*
emprunter *to borrow*
des médicaments (m.) *medicine*
une enveloppe *envelope*
une pâtisserie *pastry*

Teaching Suggestions

- To review pronunciation and vocabulary, have students find words in the **Vocabulaire** that contain the sounds listed in the **Prononciation** on page 329.
- To review vocabulary from all twelve chapters, play the game "**Les mots en famille**" described on page 309F.

DEUXIEME ETAPE

Making and responding to requests

Tu peux... ? *Can you . . . ?*
Tu me rapportes... ? *Will you bring me . . . ?*
Tu pourrais passer à... ? *Could you go by . . . ?*
D'accord. *OK.*
Je veux bien. *Gladly.*
J'y vais tout de suite. *I'll go right away.*
Si tu veux. *If you want.*
Je ne peux pas maintenant. *I can't right now.*

Je suis désolé(e), mais je n'ai pas le temps. *I'm sorry, but I don't have time.*

Asking for advice and making suggestions

Comment est-ce qu'on y va? *How can we get there?*
On peut y aller... *We can go . . .*
On peut prendre... *We can take . . .*
y *there*

Means of transportation

en bus (m.) *by bus*
à pied (m.) *on foot*
à vélo (m.) *by bike*
en voiture (f.) *by car*
en taxi (m.) *by taxi*
en bateau (m.) *by boat*
en avion (m.) *by plane*
en train (m.) *by train*
en métro (m.) *by subway*

CHAPTER 12 ASSESSMENT

CHAPTER TEST

- *Chapter Teaching Resources, Book 3,* pp. 197–202
- *Assessment Guide,* Speaking Test, p. 33
- *Assessment Items, Audiocassette 8B Audio CD 12*

TEST GENERATOR, CHAPTER 12

ALTERNATIVE ASSESSMENT

Performance Assessment

You might want to use the **Jeu de rôle** (p. 333) as a cumulative performance assessment activity.

Portfolio Assessment

- **Written:** Activity 30, *Pupil's Edition,* p. 328
  Assessment Guide, p. 25
- **Oral:** Mise en pratique, Jeu de rôle, *Pupil's Edition,* p. 333
  Assessment Guide, p. 25

FINAL EXAM

- *Assessment Guide,* pp. 49–56
- *Assessment Items, Audiocassette 8B Audio CD 12*

TROISIEME ETAPE

Asking for and giving directions

Pardon, ..., s'il vous plaît? *Excuse me, . . . please?*
Pardon, ... Où est..., s'il vous plaît? *Excuse me, . . . Where is . . . , please?*
Pardon, ... Je cherche..., s'il vous plaît. *Excuse me, . . . I'm looking for . . . , please.*
Vous continuez jusqu'au prochain feu rouge. *You keep going until the next light.*

Vous allez tout droit jusqu'à... *You go straight ahead until you get to . . .*
Vous tournez... *You turn . . .*
Prenez la rue..., puis traversez la rue... *Take . . . Street, then cross . . . Street.*
Vous passez... *You'll pass . . .*
C'est tout de suite à... *It's right there on the . . .*

Locations

à côté de *next to*
loin de *far from*
près de *close to*
au coin de *on the corner of*
en face de *across from*
derrière *behind*
devant *in front of*
entre *between*
à droite(de) *to the right*
à gauche(de) *to the left*

VOCABULAIRE

trois cent trente-cinq 335

SUMMARY OF FUNCTIONS

Function is another word for the way in which you use language for a specific purpose. When you find yourself in specific situations, such as in a restaurant, in a grocery store, or at school, you'll want to communicate with those around you. In order to communicate in French, you have to "function" in the language.

Each chapter in this book focuses on language functions. You can easily find them in boxes labeled **Comment dit-on... ?** The other features in the chapter—grammar, vocabulary, culture notes—support the functions you're learning.

Here is a list of the functions presented in this book and their French expressions. You'll need them in order to communicate in a wide range of situations. Following each function are the numbers of the chapter and page where it was presented.

SOCIALIZING

Greeting people   Ch. 1, p. 22

> Bonjour.
> Salut.

Saying goodbye   Ch. 1, p. 22

> Salut.   A bientôt.
> Au revoir.   A demain.
> A tout à l'heure.   Tchao.

Asking how people are and telling how you are
Ch. 1, p. 23

> (Comment) ça va?   Bof.
> Ça va.   Pas mal.
> Super!   Pas terrible.
> Très bien.   Et toi?
> Comme ci, comme ça.

Extending invitations   Ch. 6, p. 159

> Allons... !
> Tu veux... ?
> Tu viens?
> On peut...

Accepting invitations   Ch. 6, p. 159

> Je veux bien.   D'accord.
> Pourquoi pas?   Bonne idée.

Refusing invitations   Ch. 6, p. 159

> Désolé(e), je suis occupé(e).
> Ça ne me dit rien.
> J'ai des trucs à faire.
> Desolé(e), je ne peux pas.

Identifying people   Ch. 7, p. 179

> C'est...
> Ce sont...
> Voici...
> Voilà...

Introducing people   Ch. 7, p. 183

> C'est...
> Je te/vous présente...
> Très heureux (heureuse).   (FORMAL)

Inquiring about past events   Ch. 9, p. 238

> Qu'est-ce que tu as fait... ?
> Tu es allé(e) où?
> Et après?
> Qu'est-ce qui s'est passé?

Relating past events   Ch. 9, p. 238

> D'abord,...
> Ensuite,...
> Après,...
> Je suis allé(e)...
> Et après ça,...
> Enfin,...

Inquiring about future plans   Ch. 11, p. 289

> Qu'est-ce que tu vas faire... ?
> Où est-ce que tu vas aller... ?

Sharing future plans   Ch. 11, p. 289

> J'ai l'intention de...
> Je vais...

Seeing someone off   Ch. 11, p. 296

> Bon voyage!
> Bonnes vacances!
> Amuse-toi bien!
> Bonne chance!

EXCHANGING INFORMATION

Asking someone's name and giving yours
Ch. 1, p. 24

> Tu t'appelles comment?
> Je m'appelle...

Asking and giving someone else's name
Ch. 1, p. 24

Il/Elle s'appelle comment?
Il/Elle s'appelle...

Asking someone's age and giving yours
Ch. 1, p. 25

Tu as quel âge?
J'ai... ans.

Asking for information Ch. 2, pp. 51, 54

Tu as quels cours... ?
Tu as quoi... ?
Vous avez... ?
Tu as... à quelle heure?

Giving information Ch. 2, pp. 51, 54

Nous avons...
J'ai...

Telling when you have class Ch. 2, p. 54

à... heures
à... heures quinze
à... heures trente
à... heures quarante-cinq

Making requests Ch. 3, p. 72

Tu as... ?
Vous avez... ?

Responding to requests Ch. 3, p. 72

Voilà.
Je regrette.
Je n'ai pas de...

Asking others what they need and telling what you need Ch. 3, p. 74

Qu'est-ce qu'il te faut pour... ?
Qu'est-ce qu'il vous faut pour... ?
Il me faut...

Expressing need Ch. 8, p. 210; Ch. 10, p. 265

Qu'est-ce qu'il te faut?
Il me faut...
De quoi est-ce que tu as besoin?
J'ai besoin de...
Oui, il me faut...
Oui, vous avez... ?
Je cherche quelque chose pour...
J'aimerais... pour aller avec...
Non, merci, je regarde.

Asking for information Ch. 3, p. 82

C'est combien?

Expressing thanks Ch. 3, p. 82

Merci.
A votre service.

Getting someone's attention
Ch. 3, p. 82; Ch. 5, p. 135

Pardon
Excusez-moi.
... , s'il vous plaît.
Monsieur!
Madame!
Mademoiselle!

Exchanging information Ch. 4, p. 104

Qu'est-ce que tu fais comme sport?
Qu'est-ce que tu fais pour t'amuser?
Je fais...
Je ne fais pas de...
Je (ne) joue (pas)...

Ordering food and beverages Ch. 5, p. 135

Vous avez choisi?
Vous prenez?
Je voudrais...
Je vais prendre... , s'il vous plaît.
... , s'il vous plaît.
Donnez-moi... , s'il vous plaît.
Apportez-moi... , s'il vous plaît.
Vous avez... ?
Qu'est-ce que vous avez comme... ?
Qu'est-ce que vous avez comme boissons?

Paying the check Ch. 5, p. 139

L'addition, s'il vous plaît.
Oui, tout de suite.
Un moment, s'il vous plaît.
Ça fait combien, s'il vous plaît?
Ça fait... francs.
C'est combien,... ?
C'est... francs.

Making plans Ch. 6, p. 153

Qu'est-ce que tu vas faire... ?
Tu vas faire quoi... ?
Je vais...
Pas grand-chose.
Rien de spécial.

Arranging to meet someone Ch. 6, p. 163

Quand (ça)?   et quart
tout de suite   moins le quart
Où (ça)?   moins cinq
devant   midi (et demi)
au métro...   minuit (et demi)
chez...   vers
dans...   Quelle heure est-il?
Avec qui?   Il est...
A quelle heure?   On se retrouve...
A cinq heures...   Rendez-vous...
et demie   Entendu.

Describing and characterizing people
Ch. 7, p. 185

Il est comment?
Elle est comment?

Ils/Elles sont comment?
Il est...
Elle est...
Ils/Elles sont...

Making a telephone call   **Ch. 9, p. 244**

Bonjour.
Je suis bien chez... ?
C'est...
(Est-ce que)... est là, s'il vous plaît?
(Est-ce que) je peux parler à... ?
Je peux laisser un message?
Vous pouvez lui dire que j'ai téléphoné?
Ça ne répond pas.
C'est occupé.

Answering a telephone call   **Ch. 9, p. 244**

Allô?
Bonjour.
Qui est à l'appareil?
Une seconde, s'il vous plaît.
D'accord.
Bien sûr.
Vous pouvez rappeler plus tard?
Ne quittez pas.

Inquiring   **Ch. 10, p. 265**

(Est-ce que) je peux vous aider?
Vous désirez?
Je peux l'(les) essayer?
Je peux essayer... ?
C'est combien,... ?
Ça fait combien?
Vous avez ça en... ?

Pointing out places and things   **Ch. 12, p. 317**

Là, tu vois, c'est...
Ça, c'est...
Regarde, voilà...
Là, c'est...
Voici...

Asking for advice   **Ch. 12, p. 322**

Comment est-ce qu'on y va?

Making suggestions   **Ch. 12, p. 322**

On peut y aller...
On peut prendre...

Asking for directions   **Ch. 12, p. 327**

Pardon, ..., s'il vous plaît?
Pardon, ... Où est..., s'il vous plaît?
Pardon, ... Je cherche..., s'il vous plaît.

Giving directions   **Ch. 12, p. 327**

Vous continuez jusqu'au prochain feu rouge.
Vous tournez...
Vous allez tout droit jusqu'à...
Prenez la rue... puis traversez la rue...
Vous passez devant...
C'est tout de suite à...

EXPRESSING FEELINGS AND EMOTIONS

Expressing likes, dislikes, and preferences about things   **Ch. 1, pp. 26; 32**

J'aime (bien)...	J'aime mieux...
Je n'aime pas...	J'adore...
Je préfère...	

Ch. 5, p. 138
C'est...
    bon!
    excellent!
    délicieux!
    pas bon!
    pas terrible!
    dégoûtant!

Telling what you'd like and what you'd like to do
Ch. 3, p. 77

Je voudrais...
Je voudrais acheter...

Telling how much you like or dislike something
Ch. 4, p. 102

Beaucoup.
Pas beaucoup.
Pas tellement.
Pas du tout.
surtout

Inquiring about likes and dislikes   **Ch. 1, p. 26**

Tu aimes... ?

Ch. 5, p. 138
Comment tu trouves ça?

Sharing confidences   **Ch. 9, p. 247**

J'ai un petit problème.
Je peux te parler?
Tu as une minute?

Consoling others   **Ch. 9, p. 247**

Je t'écoute.
Ne t'en fais pas!
Ça va aller mieux!
Qu'est-ce que je peux faire?

Making a decision   **Ch. 10, p. 274**

Vous avez décidé de prendre... ?
Vous avez choisi?
Vous le/la/les prenez?
Je le/la/les prends.
Non, c'est trop cher.

Hesitating   **Ch. 10, p. 274**

Euh... J'hésite.
Je ne sais pas.
Il/Elle me plaît, mais il/elle est...

Giving permission   Ch. 7, p. 189

Oui, si tu veux.
Pourquoi pas?
D'accord, si tu... d'abord...
Oui, bien sûr.

Refusing permission   Ch. 7, p. 189

Pas question!
Non, c'est impossible.
Non, tu dois...
Pas ce soir.

Making requests   Ch. 8, p. 212

Tu peux aller faire les courses?
Tu me rapportes... ?

Ch. 12, p. 320
Est-ce que tu peux... ?
Tu pourrais passer à... ?

Accepting requests   Ch. 8, p. 212

Pourquoi pas?
Bon, d'accord.
Je veux bien.
J'y vais tout de suite.

Ch. 12, p. 320
D'accord.
Si tu veux.

Declining requests   Ch. 8, p. 212

Je ne peux pas maintenant.
Je regrette, mais je n'ai pas le temps.
J'ai des tas de choses (trucs) à faire.

Ch. 12, p. 320
Non, je ne peux pas.
Je suis désolé(e), mais je n'ai pas le temps.

Telling someone what to do   Ch. 8, p. 212

Rapporte(-moi)...
Prends...
Achète(-moi)...
N'oublie pas de...

Offering food   Ch. 8, p. 219

Tu veux... ?
Vous voulez... ?
Vous prenez ... ?
Tu prends... ?
Encore de... ?

Accepting food   Ch. 8, p. 219

Oui, s'il vous/te plaît.
Oui, avec plaisir.
Oui, j'en veux bien.

Refusing food   Ch. 8, p. 219

Non, merci.
Non, merci. Je n'ai plus faim.
Je n'en veux plus.

Asking for advice   Ch. 9, p. 247

A ton avis, qu'est-ce que je fais?
Qu'est-ce que tu me conseilles?

Ch. 10, p. 264
Je ne sais pas quoi mettre pour...
Qu'est-ce que je mets?

Giving advice   Ch. 9, p. 247

Oublie-le/-la/-les!
Téléphone-lui/-leur!
Tu devrais...
Pourquoi tu ne... pas?

Ch. 10, p. 264
Pourquoi est-ce que tu ne mets pas... ?
Mets...

Reminding   Ch. 11, p. 293

N'oublie pas...
Tu n'as pas oublié... ?
Tu ne peux pas partir sans...
Tu prends... ?

Reassuring   Ch. 11, p. 293

Ne t'en fais pas.
J'ai pensé à tout.
Je n'ai rien oublié.

SUPPLEMENTARY VOCABULARY

This list presents additional vocabulary you may want to use when you're working on the activities in the textbook and workbook. It also includes the optional vocabulary labeled **Vocabulaire à la carte** that appears in several chapters. If you can't find the words you need here, try the English-French and French-English vocabulary lists beginning on page 352.

ADJECTIVES

absurd   *absurde*
awesome (impressive)   *impressionnant(e)*
boring   *ennuyeux (ennuyeuse)*
chilly   *froid(e), frais* (m.)/*fraîche* (f.)
colorful (thing)   *vif (vive)*
despicable   *méprisable*
eccentric   *excentrique*
incredible   *incroyable*
tasteless (flavor)   *insipide;* (remark, object)   *de mauvais goût*
tasteful (remark, object)   *de bon goût*
terrifying   *terrifiant(e)*
threatening   *menaçant(e)*
tremendous (excellent)   *formidable*
unforgettable   *inoubliable*
unique   *unique*

CLOTHING

blazer   *un blazer*
button   *un bouton*
coat   *un manteau*
collar   *le col*
eyeglasses   *des lunettes* (f.)
gloves   *des gants* (m.)
handkerchief   *un mouchoir*
high-heeled shoes   *des chaussures* (f.) *à talons*
lace   *de la dentelle*
linen   *le lin*
nylon   *le nylon*
pajamas   *un pyjama*
polyester   *le polyester*
raincoat   *un imperméable*
rayon   *la rayonne*
sale (discount)   *les soldes* (m.)
silk   *la soie*
sleeve   *une manche*
slippers   *des pantoufles* (f.)
suit (man's)   *un costume;* (woman's)   *un tailleur*
suspenders   *des bretelles* (f.)
velvet   *le velours*
vest   *un gilet*
wool   *la laine*
zipper   *une fermeture éclair*

COLORS AND PATTERNS

beige   *beige*

checked   *à carreaux*
colorful   *coloré(e), vif/vive*
dark blue   *bleu foncé*
dark-colored   *foncé*
flowered   *à fleurs*
gold (adj.)   *d'or, doré*
light blue   *bleu clair*
light-colored   *clair*
patterned   *à motifs*
polka-dotted   *à pois*
striped   *à rayures*
turquoise   *turquoise*

ENTERTAINMENT

blues   *le blues*
CD player   *un lecteur de CD*
flash   *un flash*
folk music   *la musique folklorique*
headphones   *les écouteurs*
hit (song)   *un tube*
lens   *l'objectif* (m.)
microphone   *un micro(phone)*
opera   *l'opéra* (m.)
pop music   *la musique pop*
reggae   *le reggae*
roll of film   *une pellicule (photo)*
screen   *l'écran* (m.)
speakers   *des enceintes* (f.), *des baffles* (m.)
to turn off   *éteindre*
to turn on   *allumer*
turntable   *une platine*
walkman   *un walkman*

FAMILY

adopted   *adopté(e), adoptif (adoptive)*
brother-in-law   *le beau-frère*
child   *un(e) enfant*
couple   *un couple*
daughter-in-law   *la belle-fille*
divorced   *divorcé(e)*
engaged   *fiancé(e)*
godfather   *le parrain*
godmother   *la marraine*
grandchildren   *les petits-enfants*
granddaughter   *la petite-fille*
grandson   *le petit-fils*
great-granddaughter   *l'arrière-petite-fille* (f.)

great-grandfather *l'arrière-grand-père* (m.)
great-grandmother *l'arrière-grand-mère* (f.)
great-grandson *l'arrière-petit-fils* (m.)
half-brother *un demi-frère*
half-sister *une demi-sœur*
husband *le mari*
mother-in-law *la belle-mère*
only child *un/une enfant unique*
single *célibataire*
sister-in-law *la belle-sœur*
son-in-law *le gendre; le beau-fils*
stepbrother *le demi-frère*
stepdaughter *la belle-fille*
stepfather *le beau-père*
stepmother *la belle-mère*
stepsister *une demi-sœur*
stepson *le beau-fils*
widow *une veuve*
widower *un veuf*
wife *la femme*

FOODS AND BEVERAGES

appetizer *une entrée*
apricot *un abricot*
asparagus *des asperges* (f.)
bacon *du bacon*
beef *du bœuf*
bowl *un bol*
Brussels sprouts *des choux* (m.) *de Bruxelles*
cabbage *du chou*
cauliflower *du chou-fleur*
cereal *des céréales* (f.)
chestnut *un marron*
cookie *un biscuit*
cucumber *un concombre*
cutlet *une escalope*
fried eggs *des œufs au plat;* hard-boiled egg *un œuf dur;* scrambled eggs *des œufs brouillés;* soft-boiled egg *un œuf à la coque*
eggplant *une aubergine*
French bread *une baguette*
fruit *un fruit*
garlic *de l'ail* (m.)
grapefruit *un pamplemousse*
honey *du miel*
liver *du foie*
margarine *de la margarine*
marshmallows *des guimauves* (f.)
mayonnaise *de la mayonnaise*
medium (cooked) *à point*
melon *un melon*
mustard *de la moutarde*
nuts *des noix*
onion *un oignon*
peanut butter *du beurre de cacahouètes*
popcorn *du pop-corn*
potato chips *des chips* (f.)
raspberry *une framboise*
salmon *du saumon*
salt *du sel*
pepper (spice) *du poivre;* (vegetable) *un poivron*

shellfish *des fruits* (m.) *de mer*
soup *de la soupe*
spinach *des épinards* (m.)
spoon *une cuillère*
syrup *du sirop*
veal *du veau*
watermelon *une pastèque*
zucchini *une courgette*
bland *doux (douce)*
hot (spicy) *épicé(e)*
juicy (fruit) *juteux (juteuse);* (meat) *tendre*
rare (cooked) *saignant*
medium (cooked) *à point*
spicy *épicé(e)*
well-done (cooked) *bien cuit(e)*
tasty *savoureux (savoureuse)*

HOUSEWORK

to clean *nettoyer*
to dry *faire sécher*
to dust *faire la poussière*
to fold *plier*
to hang *pendre*
to iron *repasser*
to put away *ranger*
to rake *ratisser*
to shovel *enlever à la pelle*
to sweep *balayer*

PETS

bird *un oiseau*
cow *une vache*
frog *une grenouille*
goldfish *un poisson rouge*
guinea-pig *un cochon d'Inde*
hamster *un hamster*
horse *un cheval*
kitten *un chaton*
lizard *un lézard*
mouse *une souris*
parrot *un perroquet*
pig *un cochon*
puppy *un chiot*
rabbit *un lapin*
turtle *une tortue*

PLACES AROUND TOWN

airport *un aéroport*
beauty shop *le salon de coiffure*
bridge *un pont*
church *l'église* (f.)
consulate *le consulat*
hospital *l'hôpital* (m.)
mosque *la mosquée*
police station *le commissariat de police*

synagogue   *la synagogue*
tourist office   *l'office du tourisme* (m.)
town hall   *l'hôtel* (m.) *de ville*

PROFESSIONS

Note: If only one form is given, that form is used for both men and women. Note that you can also say **une femme banquier, une femme médecin,** and so forth.

archaeologist   *un(e) archéologue*
architect   *un(e) architecte*
athlete   *un(e) athlète*
banker   *un banquier*
businessman/businesswoman   *un homme d'affaires (une femme d'affaires)*
danser   *un danseur (une danseuse)*
dentist   *un(e) dentiste*
doctor   *un médecin*
editor   *un rédacteur (une rédactrice)*
engineer   *un ingénieur*
fashion designer   *un(e) styliste de mode*
fashion model   *un mannequin*
hairdresser   *un coiffeur, une coiffeuse*
homemaker   *un homme au foyer/une femme au foyer*
lawyer   *un(e) avocat(e)*
manager   (company)   *le directeur (la directrice);* (store, restaurant)   *le gérant (la gérante)*
mechanic   *un mécanicien*
painter   (art)   *un peintre;* (buildings)   *un peintre en bâtiment*

pilot   *un pilote*
plumber   *un plombier*
scientist   *un(e) scientifique*
secretary   *un(e) secrétaire*
social worker   *un assistant social (une assistante sociale)*
taxi driver   *un chauffeur de taxi*
technician   *un technicien (une technicienne)*
truck driver   *un routier*
veterinarian   *un(e) vétérinaire*
worker   *un ouvrier (une ouvrière)*
writer   *un écrivain*

SCHOOL SUBJECTS

accounting   *la comptabilité*
business   *le commerce*
home economics   *les arts ménagers* (m.)
languages   *les langues* (f.)
marching band   *la fanfare*
orchestra   *l'orchestre* (m.)
shorthand   *la sténographie*
social studies   *les sciences sociales* (f.)
typing   *la dactylographie*
woodworking   *la menuiserie*
world history   *l'histoire mondiale* (f.)

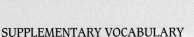

SCHOOL SUPPLIES

calendar   *un calendrier*
colored pencils   *des crayons* (m.) *de couleur*
compass   *un compas*
correction fluid   *du liquide correcteur*
glue   *de la colle*
gym suit   *une tenue de gymnastique*
marker   *un feutre*
rubber band   *un élastique*
scissors   *des ciseaux* (m.)
staple   *une agrafe*
stapler   *une agrafeuse*
transparent tape   *du ruban adhésif* (m.)

SPORTS AND INTERESTS

badminton   *le badminton*
boxing   *la boxe*
fishing rod   *une canne à pêche*
foot race   *une course à pied*
to go for a ride   (by bike, car, motorcycle, moped)   *faire une promenade, faire un tour (à bicyclette, en voiture, à moto, à vélomoteur)*
to do gymnastics   *faire de la gymnastique*
hunting   *la chasse*
to lift weights   *soulever des haltères*
mountain climbing   *l'alpinisme* (m.)
to play cards   *jouer aux cartes*
to play checkers   *jouer aux dames*
to play chess   *jouer aux échecs*
to ride a skateboard   *faire de la planche à roulettes*
to sew   *coudre; faire de la couture*
speed skating   *le patinage de vitesse*
to surf   *faire du surf*

WEATHER

barometer   *le baromètre*
blizzard   *une tempête de neige*
cloudy   *nuageux*
drizzle   *la bruine*
fog   *le brouillard*
It's sleeting.   *Il tombe de la neige fondue.*
frost   *la gelée*
hail   *la grêle* **to hail**   *grêler*
heat wave   *la canicule*
hurricane   *un ouragan*
ice   (on the road)   *le verglas*
It's pouring.   *Il pleut à verse.*
lightning bolt   *un éclair*
mist   *la brume*
shower   (rain)   *une averse*
storm   *une tempête*
sunny   *Il fait du soleil.*
thermometer   *un thermomètre*
thunder   *le tonnerre*
thunderstorm   *un orage*
tornado   *une tornade*

CITIES

Algiers *Alger*
Brussels *Bruxelles*
Cairo *Le Caire*
Geneva *Genève*
Lisbon *Lisbonne*
London *Londres*
Montreal *Montréal*
Moscow *Moscou*
New Orleans *La Nouvelle-Orléans*
Quebec City *Québec*
Tangier *Tanger*
Venice *Venise*
Vienna *Vienne*

THE CONTINENTS

Africa *l'Afrique* (f.)
Antarctica *l'Antarctique* (f.)
Asia *l'Asie* (f.)
Australia *l'Océanie* (f.)
Europe *l'Europe* (f.)
North America *l'Amérique* (f.) *(du Nord)*
South America *l'Amérique* (f.) *(du Sud)*

COUNTRIES

Algeria *l'Algérie* (f.)
Argentina *l'Argentine* (f.)
Australia *l'Australie* (f.)
Austria *l'Autriche* (f.)
Belgium *la Belgique*
Brazil *le Brésil*
Canada *le Canada*
China *la Chine*
Egypt *l'Egypte* (f.)
England *l'Angleterre* (f.)
France *la France*
Germany *l'Allemagne* (f.)
Greece *la Grèce*
Holland *la Hollande*
India *l'Inde* (f.)
Ireland *l'Irlande* (f.)
Israel *Israël* (m.) *(no article)*
Italy *l'Italie* (f.)
Ivory Coast *la République de Côte d'Ivoire*
Jamaica *la Jamaïque*
Japan *le Japon*
Jordan *la Jordanie*
Lebanon *le Liban*
Libya *la Libye*
Luxembourg *le Luxembourg*
Mexico *le Mexique*
Monaco *Monaco* (f.) *(no article)*
Morocco *le Maroc*
Netherlands *les Pays-Bas* (m.)
North Korea *la Corée du Nord*
Peru *le Pérou*
Philippines *les Philippines* (f.)

Poland *la Pologne*
Portugal *le Portugal*
Russia *la Russie*
Senegal *le Sénégal*
South Korea *la Corée du Sud*
Spain *l'Espagne* (f.)
Switzerland *la Suisse*
Syria *la Syrie*
Tunisia *la Tunisie*
Turkey *la Turquie*
United States *les Etats-Unis* (m.)
Vietnam *le Viêt-Nam*

STATES

California *la Californie*
Florida *la Floride*
Georgia *la Géorgie*
Louisiana *la Louisiane*
New Mexico *le Nouveau Mexique*
North Carolina *la Caroline du Nord*
Pennsylvania *la Pennsylvanie*
South Carolina *la Caroline du Sud*
Virginia *la Virginie*

OCEANS AND SEAS

Atlantic Ocean *l'Atlantique* (m.), *l'océan* (m.) *Atlantique*
Caribbean Sea *la mer des Caraïbes*
English Channel *la Manche*
Indian Ocean *l'océan* (m.) *Indien*
Mediterranean Sea *la mer Méditerranée*
Pacific Ocean *le Pacifique, l'océan* (m.) *Pacifique*

OTHER GEOGRAPHICAL TERMS

Alps *les Alpes* (f.)
border *la frontière*
capital *la capitale*
continent *un continent*
country *un pays*
hill *une colline*
lake *un lac*
latitude *la latitude*
longitude *la longitude*
mountain *une montagne*
North Africa *l'Afrique* (f.) *du Nord*
ocean *l'océan* (m.)
plain *une plaine*
Pyrenees *les Pyrénées* (f.)
river *une rivière, un fleuve*
sea *la mer*
state *un état*
the North Pole *le pôle Nord*
the South Pole *le pôle Sud*
valley *une vallée*

SUPPLEMENTARY VOCABULARY

GRAMMAR SUMMARY

ARTICLES

SINGULAR		PLURAL	
MASCULINE	FEMININE	MASCULINE	FEMININE
un frère un ami	une sœur une amie	des frères des amis	des sœurs des amies
le frère l'ami	la sœur l'amie	les frères les amis	les sœurs les amies
ce frère cet ami	cette sœur cette amie	ces frères ces amis	ces sœurs ces amies

ADJECTIVES: FORMATION OF FEMININE

	MASCULINE	FEMININE
Most adjectives (add -**e**)	Il est brun.	Elle est brune.
Most adjectives ending in -**é** (add -**e**)	Il est démodé.	Elle est démodée.
All adjectives ending in an unaccented -**e** (no change)	Il est jeune.	Elle est jeune.
Most adjectives ending in -**eux** (-**eux** → -**euse**)	Il est délicieux.	Elle est délicieuse.
All adjectives ending in -**ien** (-**ien** → -**ienne**)	Il est ivoirien.	Elle est ivoirienne.

ADJECTIVES AND NOUNS: FORMATION OF PLURAL

		MASCULINE	FEMININE
Most noun and adjective forms	SING. PL.	un pantalon vert des pantalons verts	une jupe verte des jupes vertes
All noun and masculine adjective forms ending in -**eau**	SING. PL.	le nouveau manteau les nouveaux manteaux	la nouvelle robe les nouvelles robes
All noun and masculine adjective forms ending in -**s**	SING. PL.	un bus gris des bus gris	une maison grise des maisons grises
All masculine adjective forms ending in -**x**	SING. PL.	un garçon heureux des garçons heureux	une fille heureuse des filles heureuses

POSSESSIVE ADJECTIVES

SINGULAR		PLURAL		SINGULAR		PLURAL	
MASCULINE	FEMININE	MASCULINE	FEMININE	MASCULINE	FEMININE	MASCULINE	FEMININE
mon frère	ma sœur	mes frères	mes sœurs	notre frère	notre sœur	nos frères	nos sœurs
mon ami	mon amie	mes amis	mes amies			nos amis	nos amies
ton frère	ta sœur	tes frères	tes sœurs	votre frère	votre sœur	vos frères	vos sœurs
ton ami	ton amie	tes amis	tes amies			vos amis	vos amies
son frère	sa sœur	ses frères	ses sœurs	leur frère	leur sœur	leurs frères	leurs sœurs
son ami	son amie	ses amis	ses amies			leurs amis	leurs amies

CONTRACTIONS WITH à AND de

à or **de** + article =	CONTRACTION
à + le =	au
à + la =	à la (no contraction)
à + l' =	à l' (no contraction)
à + les =	aux
de + le =	du
de + la =	de la (no contraction)
de + l' =	de l' (no contraction)
de + les =	des

PRONOUNS

INDEPENDENT PRONOUNS	SUBJECT PRONOUNS	DIRECT OBJECT PRONOUNS	INDIRECT OBJECT PRONOUNS	PRONOUN REPLACING **à, dans, sur...** + noun phrase	PRONOUN REPLACING **de** + noun phrase
moi toi lui elle	je (j') tu il elle on nous vous ils elles	le la les les	lui lui leur leur	y	en

REGULAR VERBS

	STEM	ENDING	STEM	ENDING	STEM	ENDING	STEM	ENDING
INFINITIVE	aim	-er	sort	-ir	chois	-ir	répond	-re
PRESENT	aim	-e -es -e -ons -ez -ent	sor sort	-s -s -t -ons -ez -ent	chois	-is -is -it -issons -issez -issent	répond	-s -s — -ons -ez -ent
REQUESTS COMMANDS SUGGESTIONS	aim	-e -ons -ez	sor sort	-s -ons -ez	chois	-is -issons -issez	répond	-s -ons -ez

Verbs like **sortir: dormir, partir**

		AUXILIARY	PAST PARTICIPLE
PASSE COMPOSE	with **avoir**	ai as a avons avez ont	**aim** -é **chois** -i **répond** -u

GRAMMAR SUMMARY   *trois cent quarante-sept*   **347**

VERB INDEX

VERBS WITH STEM AND SPELLING CHANGES

Verbs listed in this section are not irregular, but they do show some stem and spelling changes. The forms in which the changes occur are printed in boldface type.

Acheter	(to buy)
Present	**achète, achètes, achète,** achetons, achetez, **achètent**
Commands	**achète,** achetons, achetez
Passé Composé	*Auxiliary:* avoir *Past Participle:* acheté

Essayer	(to try)
Present	**essaie, essaies, essaie,** essayons, essayez, **essaient**
Commands	**essaie,** essayons, essayez
Passé Composé	*Auxiliary:* avoir *Past Participle:* essayé

Appeler	(to call)
Present	**appelle, appelles, appelle,** appelons, appelez, **appellent**
Commands	**appelle,** appelons, appelez

Manger	(to eat)
Present	mange, manges, mange, **mangeons,** mangez, mangent
Commands	mange, **mangeons,** mangez

Commencer	(to start)
Present	commence, commences, commence, **commençons,** commencez, commencent
Commands	commence, **commençons,** commencez
Passé Composé	*Auxiliary:* avoir *Past Participle:* commencé

Préférer	(to prefer)
Present	**préfère, préfères, préfère,** préférons, préférez, **préfèrent**
Commands	**préfère,** préférons, préférez
Passé Composé	*Auxiliary:* avoir *Past Participle:* préféré

VERBS WITH IRREGULAR FORMS

Verbs listed in this section are those that do not follow the pattern of verbs like **aimer,** verbs like **choisir,** verbs like **sortir,** or verbs like **répondre.**

Aller	(to go)
Present	vais, vas, va, allons, allez, vont
Commands	va, allons, allez
Passé Composé	*Auxiliary:* être *Past Participle:* allé

Devoir	(to have to)
Present	dois, dois, doit, devons, devez, doivent
Commands	dois, devons, devez
Passé Composé	*Auxiliary:* avoir *Past Participle:* dû

Avoir	(to have)
Present	ai, as, a, avons, avez, ont
Commands	aie, ayons, ayez
Passé Composé	*Auxiliary:* avoir *Past Participle:* eu

Dire	(to say, tell)
Present	dis, dis, dit, disons, dites, disent
Commands	dis, disons, dites
Passé Composé	*Auxiliary:* avoir *Past Participle:* dit

Ecrire	*(to write)*		**Pouvoir**	*(to be able, can)*
Present	écris, écris, écrit, écrivons, écrivez, écrivent		*Present*	peux, peux, peut, pouvons, pouvez, peuvent
Commands	écris, écrivons, écrivez		*Passé Composé*	*Auxiliary:* avoir
Passé Composé	*Auxiliary:* avoir			*Past Participle:* pu
	Past Participle: écrit			

Ecrire *(to write)*

Present   écris, écris, écrit, écrivons, écrivez, écrivent

Commands   écris, écrivons, écrivez

Passé Composé   *Auxiliary:* avoir

Past Participle: écrit

Etre *(to be)*

Present   suis, es, est, sommes, êtes, sont

Commands   sois, soyons, soyez

Passé Composé   *Auxiliary:* avoir

Past Participle: été

Faire *(to make, to do)*

Present   fais, fais, fait, faisons, faites, font

Commands   fais, faisons, faites

Passé Composé   *Auxiliary:* avoir

Past Participle: fait

Lire *(to read)*

Present   lis, lis, lit, lisons, lisez, lisent

Commands   lis, lisons, lisez

Passé Composé   *Auxiliary:* avoir

Past Participle: lu

Mettre *(to put, to put on)*

Present   mets, mets, met, mettons, mettez, mettent

Commands   mets, mettons, mettez

Passé Composé   *Auxiliary:* avoir

Past Participle: mis

Pouvoir *(to be able, can)*

Present   peux, peux, peut, pouvons, pouvez, peuvent

Passé Composé   *Auxiliary:* avoir

Past Participle: pu

Prendre *(to take)*

Present   prends, prends, prend, prenons, prenez, prennent

Commands   prends, prenons, prenez

Passé Composé   *Auxiliary:* avoir

Past Participle: pris

Venir *(to come)*

Present   viens, viens, vient, venons, venez, viennent

Commands   viens, venons, venez

Passé Composé   *Auxiliary:* être

Past Participle: venu

Voir *(to see)*

Present   vois, vois, voit, voyons, voyez, voient

Commands   vois, voyons, voyez

Passé Composé   *Auxiliary:* avoir

Past Participle: vu

Vouloir *(to want)*

Present   veux, veux, veut, voulons, voulez, veulent

Passé Composé   *Auxiliary:* avoir

Past Participle: voulu

PRONUNCIATION INDEX

CHAPTER	LETTER COMBINATION	IPA SYMBOL	EXAMPLE
Ch. 1, p. 35 Intonation			
Ch. 2, p. 59 Liaison			vous_avez des_amis
Ch. 3, p. 83 The **r** sound	the letter **r**	/ʀ/	rouge vert
Ch. 4, p. 113 The sounds [y] and [u]	the letter **u** the letter combination **ou**	/y/ /u/	une nous
Ch. 5, p. 141 The nasal sound [ɑ̃]	the letter combination **an** the letter combination **am** the letter combination **en** the letter combination **em**	/ɑ̃/	anglais jambon comment temps
Ch. 6, p. 167 The vowel sounds [ø] and [œ]	the letter combination **eu** the letter combination **eu**	/ø/ /œ/	deux heure
Ch. 7, p. 191 The nasal sounds [ɔ̃], [ɛ̃], and [œ̃]	the letter combination **on** the letter combination **om** the letter combination **in** the letter combination **im** the letter combination **ain** the letter combination **aim** the letter combination **(i)en** the letter combination **un** the letter combination **um**	/ɔ̃/ /ɛ̃/ /œ̃/	pardon nombre cousin impossible copain faim bien lundi humble
Ch. 8, p. 221 The sounds [o] and [ɔ]	the letter combination **au** the letter combination **eau** the letter **ô** the letter **o**	/o/ /ɔ/	jaune beau rôle carotte
Ch. 9, p. 249 The vowel sounds [e] and [ɛ]	the letter combination **ez** the letter combination **er** the letter combination **ait** the letter combination **ais** the letter combination **ei** the letter **ê**	/e/ /ɛ/	apportez trouver fait français neige bête
Ch. 10, p. 275 The glides [j], [w], and [ɥ]	the letter **i** the letter combination **ill** the letter combination **oi** the letter combination **oui** the letter combination **ui**	/j/ /w/ /ɥ/	mieux maillot moi Louis huit
Ch. 11, p. 299 **h**, **th**, **ch**, and **gn**	the letter **h** the letter combination **th** the letter combination **ch** the letter combination **gn**	/'/ /t/ /ʃ/ /ɲ/	les halls théâtre chocolat oignon
Ch. 12, p. 329 Review			

NUMBERS

0	zéro	20	vingt	80	quatre-vingts
1	un(e)	21	vingt et un(e)	81	quatre-vingt-un(e)
2	deux	22	vingt-deux	82	quatre-vingt-deux
3	trois	23	vingt-trois	90	quatre-vingt-dix
4	quatre	24	vingt-quatre	91	quatre-vingt-onze
5	cinq	25	vingt-cinq	92	quatre-vingt-douze
6	six	26	vingt-six	100	cent
7	sept	27	vingt-sept	101	cent un
8	huit	28	vingt-huit	200	deux cents
9	neuf	29	vingt-neuf	300	trois cents
10	dix	30	trente	800	huit cents
11	onze	31	trente et un(e)	900	neuf cents
12	douze	32	trente-deux	1.000	mille
13	treize	40	quarante	2.000	deux mille
14	quatorze	50	cinquante	3.000	trois mille
15	quinze	60	soixante	10.000	dix mille
16	seize	70	soixante-dix	19.000	dix-neuf mille
17	dix-sept	71	soixante et onze	40.000	quarante mille
18	dix-huit	72	soixante-douze	500.000	cinq cent mille
19	dix-neuf	73	soxiante-treize	1.000.000	un million

- The word **et** is used only in 21, 31, 41, 51, 61, and 71.
- **Vingt (trente, quarante,** and so on) **et une** is used when the number refers to a feminine noun: **trente et une cassettes.**
- The **s** is dropped from **quatre-vingts** and is not added to multiples of **cent** when these numbers are followed by another number: **quatre-vingt-cinq; deux cents,** *but* **deux cent six.** The number **mille** never takes an **s: deux mille insectes.**
- **Un million** is followed by **de** + a noun: **un million de francs.**
- In writing numbers, a period is used in French where a comma is used in English.

LES NOMBRES ORDINAUX

1er, 1ère	premier, première	9e	neuvième	17e	dix-septième
2e	deuxième	10e	dixième	18e	dix-huitième
3e	troisième	11e	onzième	19e	dix-neuvième
4e	quatrième	12e	douzième	20e	vingtième
5e	cinquième	13e	treizième	21e	vingt et unième
6e	sixième	14e	quatorzième	22e	vingt-deuxième
7e	septième	15e	quinzième	30e	trentième
8e	huitième	16e	seizième	40e	quarantième

FRENCH-ENGLISH VOCABULARY

This list includes both active and passive vocabulary in this textbook. Active words and phrases are those listed in the **Vocabulaire** section at the end of each chapter. You are expected to know and be able to use active vocabulary. All entries in black heavy type in this list are active. All other words are passive. Passive vocabulary is for recognition only.

The number after each entry refers to the chapter where the word or phrase is introduced. Verbs are given in the infinitive. Nouns are always given with an article. If it is not clear whether the noun is masculine or feminine, *m.* (masculine) or *f.* (feminine) follow the noun. Irregular plurals are also given, indicated by *pl.* An asterisk (*) before a word beginning with *h* indicates an aspirate *h.* Phrases are alphabetized by the key word(s) in the phrase.

The following abbreviations are used in this vocabulary: pl. (plural), pp. (past participle), and inv. (invariable).

A

à *to, in (a city or place),* 11; à côté de *next to,* 3; **à la** *to, at,* 6; **A bientôt.** *See you soon.* 1; **A demain.** *See you tomorrow.* 1; à la carte *pick and choose,* 3; à la française *French-style,* 1; **à la mode** *in style,* 10; **A quelle heure?** *At what time?* 6; **A tout à l'heure!** *See you later!* 1; **A votre service.** *At your service; You're welcome,* 3; de 0 à 20 *from 0 to 20,* 0; Et maintenant, à toi. *And now, it's your turn,* 1

l' **abbaye** (f.) *abbey,* 6

abîmer *to ruin,* 10

abonnez: abonnez-vous à... *subscribe to . . . ,* 3

l' **abricot** (m.) *apricot,* 5

absent *absent,* 2

accompagner *to accompany,* 4

accueille (accueillir) *to welcome*

l' accueil (m.) *reception, welcome,* 4

acheter *to buy,* 9; **Achète (-moi)...** *Buy me . . . ,* 8; Je n'achète pas... *I won't buy . . . ,* 3

l' **activité** (f.) *activity,* 4

l' **addition** (f.): **L'addition, s'il vous plaît.** *The check please.* 5

adorer *to adore,* 1; **J'adore...** *I adore . . .* 1

adorerais: J'adorerais *I would adore,* 1

l' **aérobic: faire de l'aérobic** *to do aerobics,* 4

afin de *in order to,* 7

âgé(e) *older,* 7

l' **âge** (m.): **Tu as quel âge?** *How old are you?* 1

l' agenda (m.) *planner,* 4

agit: il s'agit de *it's concerned with; it's about,* 6

agréable *pleasant,* 4

ai: J'ai... *I have . . . ,* 2

aider: (Est-ce que) je peux vous aider? *May I help you?* 10

aimé(e) (pp.) *loved,* 1

aimer *to like,* 1; **aimer mieux: J'aime mieux...** *I prefer . . .* 1; **aimerais: J'aimerais... pour aller avec...** *I'd like . . . to go with . . . ,* 10; **Je n'aime pas...** *I don't like . . .* 1; **Moi, j'aime (bien)...** *I (really) like . . .* 1; **Tu aimes... ?** *Do you like . . . ?* 1

ainsi que *as well as,* 4

l' **algèbre** (f.) *algebra,* 2

l' Algérie (f.) *Algeria,* 0

l' **alimentation** (f.) *food,* 12

les aliments (m.) *nutrients,* 8

l' **allemand** (m.) *German,* 2

aller *to go,* 6; **Ça va aller mieux!** *It's going to get better!* 9; On peut y aller... *We can go there . . . ,* 12

allez: Allez au tableau! *Go to the blackboard!* 0; Allez, viens! *Come along!* 0

allons: Allons-y! *Let's go!,* 4; **Allons...** *Let's go . . .* 6

allé(e) (pp.): **Je suis allé(e)...** *I went . . . ,* 9; **Tu es allé(e) où?** *Where did you go?* 9

l' aise (f.) *ease,* 7

Allô? *Hello?* 9

alors *well, then,* 3

l' alphabet (m.) *alphabet,* 0

aménagé(e) *newly equipped,* 6

américain(e) *American,* 0

l' **ami(e)** *friend,* 1

amical(e) (pl. amicaux) *friendly,* 2

amicalement (to close a letter) *best wishes,* 1

l' **amitié** (f.) *friendship,* 1

l' **amour** (m.) *love,* 1

amusant(e) *funny,* 7

amuser (s'amuser): Amuse-toi bien! *Have fun!* 11; Qu'est-ce que tu fais pour t'amuser? *What do you do to have fun?* 4; **Tu t'es bien amusé(e)?** *Did you have fun?* 11

les **ananas** (m.) *pineapples,* 8

ancien (ancienne): l'ancienne gare *the former train station,* 6

Andorre (no article) *Andorra,* 0

l' **anglais** (m.) *English,* 1

les annonces (f.): petites annonces *personal or business ads,* 1

ans: J'ai... ans. *I am . . . years old.* 1

les **antiquités** (f.) *antiquities, antiques,* 6

août *August,* 4

l' **appareil-photo** (m.) *camera,* 11

l' **appareil** (m.): **Qui est à l'appareil?** *Who's calling?* 9

appartient (appartenir) à *to belong to,* 9

appeler: s'appeler *to call oneself, to be called,* 1; **Il/Elle s'appelle comment?** *What's his/her name?* 1; **Il/Elle s'appelle...** *His/Her name is . . .* 1; **Je m'appelle...** *My name is . . .* 1; **Tu t'appelles comment?** *What's your name?* 1

appel: composez le numéro d'appel *dial the telephone number,* 9

apporter *to bring,* 9; **Apportez-**

moi... , s'il vous plaît. *Please bring me . . .* 5
apprendre *to learn,* 0
aprèm: cet aprèm *this afternoon,* 2
après-guerre *post-war,* 11
l' **après-midi** *in the afternoon,* 2; **l'après-midi libre** *afternoon off,* 2
après: Après, je suis sorti(e). *Afterwards, I went out.* 9; **Et après?** *And afterwards?* 9
l' ardoise (f.) *writing slate,* 3
argent: de l'argent *money,* 11
l' arrivée (f.) *arrival,* 6
arroser *to sprinkle,* 8
l' artiste (f.) *artist,* 0
les **arts** (m.) **plastiques** *art class,* 2
as: Tu as... ? *Do you have . . . ?* 3; **Tu as... à quelle heure?** *At what time do you have . . . ?* 2
l' ascenseur (m.) *elevator,* 6
l' ascension (f.): ascension en haut de la tour *ascent/climb to the top of the tower,* 6
Asseyez: Asseyez-vous! *Sit down!* 0
assez *enough, fairly,* 2
assidu *regular (punctual),* 2
l' **assiette** (f.) *plate,* 5
l' **athlétisme** (m.): **faire de l'athlétisme** *to do track and field,* 4
attachant(e) *loving,* 7
attendre *to wait for,* 9
au *to, at,* 6; *to, in (before a masculine noun),* 11; **au métro...** *at the . . . metro stop,* 6; **Au revoir!** *Goodbye!* 1
l' auberge de jeunesse *youth hostel,* 11
aucun(e) *none,* 7
aujourd'hui *today,* 2
aussi *also,* 1; **Moi aussi.** *Me too.* 2
autant *as much, equally,* 4
l' **automne** (m.) *autumn, fall,* 4; **en automne** *in the fall,* 4
autre *other,* 4
aux *to, in (before a plural noun),* 11
Av. (abbrev. of avenue) *avenue,* 6
avant *before,* 1
avec *with,* 1; **avec moi** *with me,* 6; **Avec qui?** *With whom?* 6
avez: **Qu'est-ce que vous avez comme... ?** *What kind of . . . do you have?* 5; **Vous avez... ?** *Do you have . . . ?* 2
l' **avion** (m.): *plane;* **en avion** *by plane,* 12

avis: A ton avis, qu'est-ce que je fais? *In your opinion, what do I do?* 9
les **avocats** (m.) *avocados,* 8
avons: Nous avons... *We have . . . ,* 2
avoir *to have* 2; **avoir faim** *to be hungry,* 5; **avoir soif** *to be thristy,* 5
avril *April,* 4
ayant: ayant pu donner *having been able to give,* 2

B

le baby (foot) *an arcade soccer game,* 5
le bac(alauréat) *The secondary school exam for entering a university,* 2
le bachelier *someone who has passed the bac exam,* 2
se balader *to stroll,* 6
les **bananes** (f.) *bananas,* 8
les bandes dessinées (f.) *comic strips,* 2
la **banque** *bank,* 12
barbant *boring,* 2
la barre espace *space-bar,* 9
le **base-ball** *baseball,* 4
le basilic *basil,* 5
le **basket(ball): jouer au basket** *to play basketball,* 4
les **baskets** (f.) *sneakers,* 3
le **bateau** *boat,* 11; **en bateau** *by boat,* 12; **faire du bateau** *to go sailing,* 11
Bd (abbrev. of **boulevard**) *boulevard,* 6
beau: Il fait beau. *It's nice weather,* 4
Beaucoup. *A lot.* 4; **Oui, beaucoup.** *Yes, very much.,* 2; **Pas beaucoup.** *Not very much.* 4
belge *Belgian,* 1
la Belgique *Belgium,* 0
belle maille jersey *jersey knit,* 10
le besoin *need,* 8; **De quoi est-ce que tu as besoin?** *What do you need?* 8; **J'ai besoin de...** *I need . . . ,* 8
le beurre *butter,* 8
la bibliothèque *the library,* 6
bien: Je veux bien. *Gladly.* 8; **Je veux bien.** *I'd really like to.* 6; **J'en veux bien.** *I'd like some.* 8; **Moi, j'aime (bien)...** *I (really) like . . .* 1; **Très bien.** *Very well.* 1
Bien sûr. *Of course,* 3; *Certainly,* 9; **Oui, bien sûr.** *Yes, of course.* 7

le bien-vivre *good living, the good life,* 6
bientôt: A bientôt. *See you soon.* 1
Bienvenue! *Welcome!* 0
le **bifteck** *steak,* 8
les bijoux (m.) *jewelry,* 10
le **billet** *ticket,* 11; **d'avion** *plane ticket,* 11; **billet de train** *train ticket,* 11
la biologie *biology,* 2
blanc(he) *white,* 3
bleu(e) *blue,* 3
blond(e) *blond,* 7
le blouson *jacket,* 10
Bof! *(expression of indifference),* 1
la boisson *drink, beverage* 5; **Qu'est-ce que vous avez comme boissons?** *What do you have to drink?* 5
la **boîte: une boîte de** *a can of,* 8
le bon *coupon,* 6
bon *good,* 5; **Bon courage!** *Good luck!* 2; **Bon voyage!** *Have a good trip!* 11; **Bon, d'accord.** *Well, OK.* 8; **de bons conseils** *good advice,* 1; **Oui, très bon.** *Yes, very good.* 9; **pas bon** *not very good,* 5; **bon marché** *inexpensive,* 10
Bonjour *Hello,* 1
bonne: Bonne chance! 11; **Bonne idée.** *Good idea.* 4; **Bonnes vacances!** *Have a good vacation!* 11
le bord: **au bord de la mer** *to/at the coast,* 11
les **bottes** (f.) *boots,* 10
les **boucles d'oreilles** (f.) *earrings,* 10
bouger *to move,* 10
la boulangerie *bakery,* 12
la boule *ball,* 8
la **bouteille** *bottle,* 8; **une bouteille de** *a bottle of,* 8
la boutique *store, shop,* 3; **une boutique de souvenirs** *a souvenir shop,* 3
le **bracelet** *a bracelet,* 3
branché *plugged in,* 9
le branchement *hookup,* 9
la brochure *brochure,* 4
brun(e) *brunette,* 7
le **bus** *bus,* 12; **en bus** *by bus,* 12
la buvette *refreshment stand,* 12

C

ça fait: **Ça fait combien, s'il vous plaît?** *How much is it,*

please? 5; **Ça fait... francs.** *It's . . . francs.* 5

ça: Ça boume *How's it going?* 2; **Ça va.** *Fine.* 1; **Ça va?** *How are things going?* 1; **Ça, c'est...** *This/That is . . . ,* 12; **Et après ça...** *And after that, . . . ,* 9; **Oui, ça a été.** *Yes, it was fine.* 9

le cadeau *gift,* 11

le café *coffee, café* 5

le cahier *notebook,* 0

la calculatrice *calculator,* 3; une calculatrice-traductrice *translating calculator,* 3

la **Californie** *California,* 4

le **caméscope** *a camcorder,* 4

la campagne *countryside,* 11; **à la campagne** *to/at the countryside,* 11

le camping *camping,* 11; **faire du camping** *to go camping,* 11

le **canal** *channel,* 3

le **canari** *canary,* 7

la cantine: à la cantine *at the school cafeteria,* 9

le **cardigan** *a sweater,* 10

la **carrière** *quarry,* 11

la carte *map,* 0; à la carte *pick and choose,* 3; **La carte, s'il vous plaît.** *The menu, please.* 5

la **cartouche: cartouche d'encre** *ink cartridge,* 3

carvi: graines de carvi *cumin seeds,* 8

la casquette *cap,* 10

la cassette *cassette tape,* 3

la **cassette vidéo** *videocassette,* 4

la **cathédrale** *cathedral,* 1

le cauchemar *nightmare,* 11; **C'était un véritable cauchemar!** *It was a real nightmare!* 11

ce *this; that,* 3; **Ce sont . . .** *These (those) are . . . ,* 7

C'est... *It's . . . ,* 2; **C'est...** *This is . . . ,* 7; **C'est qui?** *Who is it?* 2; **Ça, c'est...** *This/That is . . . ,* 12

la ceinture *a belt,* 10

le centre commercial *the mall,* 6

le cercle *circle, group,* 6; au cercle français *at French Club,* 4

ces *these; those,* 3

cet *this; that,* 3

cette *this; that,* 3

chacun: Chacun ses goûts! *To each his own!,* 1

chacun *each (person),* 5

la chambre *room,* 7; **ranger ta chambre** *to pick up your room,* 7

les **champignons** (m.) *mushrooms,* 8

la chance *luck,* 11; **Bonne chance!** *Good luck!* 11

chanter *to sing,* 9

chantilly: la crème Chantilly *sweetened whipped cream,* 5

le chapeau *hat,* 10

chaque *each,* 4

chargé(e) *busy,* 2

chasse: une chasse au trésor *treasure hunt,* 3

le **chat** *cat,* 7

chaud: Il fait chaud. *It's hot.* 4

chauffé(e) *heated,* 11

les **chaussettes** (f.) *socks,* 10

les **chaussures** (f.) *shoes,* 10

le **chef-d'œuvre** *masterpiece,* 6

la **chemise** *a shirt (men's),* 10

la chemise *folder,* 3

le chemisier *a shirt (women's),* 10

cher (chère) *dear,* 1 *expensive,* 3; **C'est trop cher.** *It's too expensive.* 10

chercher *to look for,* 9; **Je cherche quelque chose pour...** *I'm looking for something for . . . ,* 10

le **cheval** *horse,* 12

chez... *to/at . . . 's house,* 11; **chez le disquaire** *at the record store,* 12; **Je suis bien chez... ?** *Is this . . . 's house?* 9; chez: chez les garçons *with boys, according to boys,* 4

chic *chic,* 10

le **chien** *dog,* 7; **promener le chien** *to walk the dog,* 7

les **chiffres** (m.) *numbers,* 0

la chimie *chemistry,* 2

le **chocolat** *chocolate,* 1; **un chocolat** *hot chocolate,* 5

choisir *to choose, to pick,* 10

la chorale *choir,* 2

la chose *thing,* 4

choses: J'ai des tas de choses (trucs) à faire. *I have lots of things to do.* 5

chou: mon chou *my darling, dear,* 1

chouette: Oui, très chouette. *Yes, very cool.* 9

le **cinéma** *the movie theater,* 6; *the movies,* 1

le **clavier** *keyboard,* 9

le **classeur** *loose-leaf binder,* 3

classique *classical,* 4

climatisé(e) *air-conditioned,* 11

le **coca** *cola,* 5

le **coin: au coin de** *on the corner of,* 12

au col montant *turtleneck,* 10

le **collant** *hose,* 10

la **colle: un pot de colle** *container of glue,* 3

la colonie: en colonie de vacances *to/at a summer camp,* 11

le **coloris** *color, shade,* 3

combien *how much, how many,* 3; **C'est combien,... ?** *How much is . . . ?* 5; **C'est combien?** *How much is it?* 3; **Ça fait combien, s'il vous plaît?** *How much is it, please?* 5

comme: Comme ci, comme ça. *So-so.* 1; Qu'est-ce qu'ils aiment comme cours? *What subjects do they like?* 2; **Qu'est-ce que tu fais comme sport?** *What sports do you play?* 4; **Qu'est-ce que vous avez comme boissons?** *What do you have to drink?* 5; **Qu'est-ce que vous avez comme... ?** *What kind of . . . do you have?* 5

commencer *to begin, to start,* 9

comment *what,* 0; **(Comment) ça va?** *How's it going?* 1; Comment dit-on? *How do you say it?* 1; Comment le dire? *How should you say it?* 1; **Comment tu trouves ça?** *What do you think of that/it?,* 2; **Comment tu trouves... ?** *What do you think of . . . ?,* 2; **Elle est comment?** *What is she like?* 7; **Il est comment?** *What is he like?* 7; **Ils/Elles sont comment?** *What are they like?* 7; **Tu t'appelles comment?** *What is your name?* 0

le **compagnon** *companion,* 7

le **compas** *a compass,* 3

compétent(e) *competent,* 2

compléter *to complete,* 4

composez: composez le numéro d'appel *dial the telephone number,* 9

compris *included,* 5

compris: Tu as compris? *Did you understand?* 1

les **concerts** (m.) *concerts,* 1

conçu(e) (pp.) *conceived,* 9

la confiture *jam,* 8

connaissance: Faisons connaissance! *Let's get acquainted.* 1

connais: Tu les connais? *Do you know them?* 0

connu: le plus connu *the best-known (adj.),* 6

le **conseil** *advice,* 1; de bons conseils *good advice,* 1

conseiller: Qu'est-ce que tu me conseilles? *What do you advise me to do?* 9

conservé: ce bulletin doit être conservé *this report card must be kept,* 2

content(e), *happy, pleased,* 1

consultés: services fréquemment consultés *frequently-used services,* 9

continuer *to continue,* 12; **Vous continuez jusqu'au prochain feu rouge.** *You keep going until the next light.* 12

contre *against,* 2

cool *cool,* 2

le cordon: le cordon de serrage *drawstring,* 10

le corps *body,* 8

le correspondant (la correspondante) *pen pal,* 1

côté: à côté de *next to,* 12

le coton: en coton *cotton,* 10

la coupe *dish(ful),* 5

courir *to run,* 7

le cours *course,* 2; **cours de développement personnel et social (DPS)** *health,* 2; **Tu as quels cours...?** *What classes do you have...?,* 2

les courses *shopping, errands,* 7; **faire les courses** *to do the shopping* 7

court(e) *short* (things), 10

le cousin *male cousin,* 7

la cousine *female cousin,* 7

coûteuse *expensive,* 8

la cravate *tie,* 10

le crayon *pencil,* 3; des crayons de couleur *colored pencils,* 3

la croisère *cruise,* 11

le croque-monsieur *toasted cheese and ham sandwich,* 5

cru *uncooked,* 5

le cuir: en cuir *leather,* 10

culturel (culturelle) *cultural,* 0

D

d'abord: D'abord, ... *First, ...,* 9

D'accord. *OK.* 4; **D'accord, si tu... d'abord...** *OK, if you..., first.* 7

d'habitude *usually,* 4

dans *in,* 6

danser *to dance,* 1; **la danse** *dance,* 2

de *from,* 0; *of,* 0; **de l'** *some,* 8; **de la** *some,* 8; **Je n'ai pas de...** *I don't have...,* 3; **Je ne fais pas de...** *I don't play/do...* 4

déambuler *to stroll,* 11

débarrasser la table *to clear the table,* 7

décédé(e) *deceased,* 7

décembre *December,* 4

le décès *death,* 7

décider *to decide,* 5; **Vous avez décidé de prendre...?** *Have you decided to take...?* 10

la découverte *discovery,* 3

dedans *inside,* 3

dégoûtant *gross,* 5

dehors *outside,* 8

déjà *already,* 9

déjeuner *to have lunch,* 9; **le déjeuner** *lunch,* 2

délicieux (délicieuse) *delicious,* 5

délirer: La techno me fait délirer *I'm wild about techno.* 1

délivré: il n'en sera pas délivré de duplicata *duplicates will not be issued,* 2

demain *tomorrow,* 6

demain: A demain. *See you tomorrow.* 6

demande: sur votre demande *on your command,* 9

demi: et demi *half past (after midi and minuit),* 6; **et demie** *half past,* 6

démodé(e) *old-fashioned,* 10

dépêchez: dépêchez-vous de... *hurry up and...,* 1

déposer *to deposit,* 12

le déplacement *movement,* 9

derrière *behind,* 12

des *some,* 8

dés: découper en dés *to dice,* 8

désagréable *unpleasant,* 4

désirer: Vous désirez? *What would you like?* 10

désolé: Désolé(e), je suis occupé(e). *Sorry, I'm busy.* 6; **Désolé(e), mais je ne peux pas.** *Sorry, but I can't.* 4

le dessin *drawing,* 3

détailler *to slice,* 8

le détenteur: détenteur du mot de passe *holder of the password,* 9

devant *in front of,* 6

deviennent: Que deviennent...? *What happened to...?* 7

Devine! *Guess!* 0

les devoirs *homework,* 2; **J'ai des devoirs à faire.** *I've got homework to do,* 5

le dévouement *devotion,* 7

devrais: Tu devrais... *You should...,* 9

la dictée *dictation,* 0

le dictionnaire *dictionary,* 3

difficile *hard,* 2

dimanche *Sunday,* 2; **le dimanche** *on Sundays,* 2

dîner *to have dinner,* 9; **le dîner** *dinner,* 8

dingue: Je suis dingue de... *I'm crazy about...,* 1

dire: Comment le dire? *How should you say it?* 1; **Dis,...** *Say, ...,* 2; **Ça ne me dit rien.** *That doesn't interest me.* 4; **Comment dit-on...?** *How do you say...?* 1; **Jacques a dit...** *Simon says...,* 0; **Qu'est-ce qu'on se dit?** *What are they saying to themselves?* 2; **Vous pouvez lui dire que j'ai téléphoné?** *Can you tell her/him that I called?* 9

direct: en direct *live,* 7

discute: Ne discute pas! *Don't argue!* 3

discuter *to discuss,* 7

disponible *available,* 8

le dispositif *device,* 9

le disquaire: chez le disquaire *at the record store,* 12

le disque compact/CD, *compact disc/CD,* 3

distant *distant,* 2

la distribution: une distribution étincelante *a brilliant cast,* 1

divers *various,* 3

le domicile *place of residence,* 4

donne sur *overlooks,* 11

donner *to give,* 5; **Donnez-moi..., s'il vout plaît.** *Please give me...* 5

dormir *to sleep,* 1

dos: un sac à dos, *backpack,* 3

la douche: avec douche ou bains *with shower or bath,* 11

la douzaine: une douzaine de *a dozen,* 8

les draps (m.) *linens, sheets,* 11

dressé *pointed,* 7

droite: à droite *to the right,* 12

du *some,* 8

le duplicata: il n'en sera pas délivré de duplicata *duplicates will not be issued,* 2

E

l' eau (f.) **minérale** *mineral water,* 5

ébattre: s'ébattre *to frolic,* 7

échange: en échange de *in exchange for,* 7

l' échantillon (m.) *sample,* 2

l' écharpe (f.) *a scarf,* 10

l' école (f.) *school,* 1; **A l'école** *At school,* 0

écouter *to listen*, 1; Ecoute! *Listen!* 0; écouter de la musique *to listen to music*, 1; Ecoutez! *Listen!* 0; Je t'écoute. *I'm listening.* 9

l' écran (m.) *screen*, 11

l' écrin (m.) *case*, 6

écrire *to write*, 2; Ecris-moi. *Write me.* 1

l' édifice (m.) *edifice, building*, 6

l' éducation (f.) physique et sportive (EPS) *physical education*, 2

efficace *efficient*, 9

égrener *to shell*, 8

égyptien (égyptienne) *Egyptian*, 6

élastique *elastic* (adj.), 3

l' éléphant (m.) *elephant* 0

l' élève (m./f.) *student*, 2

embêtant(e) *annoying*, 7

l' émission (f.) *TV program*, 4

empêche (empêcher) *to prevent, to keep from doing*, 2

emploi: un emploi du temps *schedule*, 2

emprunter *to borrow*, 12

en *in*, 1; en *some, of it, of them, any, none*, 8; en *to, in (before a feminine noun)*, 11; en coton *cotton*, 10; en cuir *leather*, 10; en français *in French*, 1; en jean *denim*, 10; en retard *late*, 2; Je n'en veux plus. *I don't want anymore,* 8; Qu'en penses-tu? *What do you think (about it)?* 1; Vous avez ça en...? *Do you have that in...? (size, fabric, color)*, 10

encore: Encore de...? *More ...,?* 8

les enfants (m.) *children*, 7

enfin *finally*, 9

enjoué(e) *playful*, 7

ennuyeux: C'etait ennuyeux. *It was boring,* 5

l'enquête (f.) *survey*, 1

ensemble *together*, 4

l' ensemble (m.) *collection, emsemble*, 3

ensuite *next*, 2

ensuite: Ensuite, ... *Then, ...* 9

entendre: s'entendre avec *to get along with*, 7

Entendu. *Agreed.* 6

entendu dire que: Il a entendu dire que... *He heard that ...,* 12

l' enthousiasme (m.) *enthusiasm*, 2

entrant *entering*, 2

entre *between*, 12

l' enveloppe (f.) *envelope*, 12

envie: J'ai envie de... *I feel like ...,* 11

envoyer: envoyer des lettres *to send letters*, 12

épi: l'épi (m.) de maïs *ear of corn*, 8

l' épicerie (f.) *grocery store*, 12

éplucher *to clean, to peel*, 8

l' éponge (f.) *sponge*, 3

épouvantable: C'était épouvantable. *It was horrible.* 9

l' équitation (f.): faire de l'équitation *to go horseback riding*, 1

l' escale *docking (of a boat)*, 11

l' escalier (m.) *staircase*, 6

les escargots (m.) *snails*, 1

l' espace (m.) *space, area*, 7

espace: une barre espace *spacebar*, 9

l' espagnol (m.) *Spanish*, 2

espère: J'espère que oui. *I hope so.* 1

l' espoir (m.) *hope*, 7

essayer: Je peux essayer...? *Can I try on...? 10*; Je peux l'/les essayer? *Can I try it/them on?* 10

Est-ce que *(Introduces a yes-or-no question)*, 4; (Est-ce que) je peux...? *May I ...?* 7

et: *and*, 1; Et après ça... *And after that, ...,* 9; Et toi? *And you?* 1

l' établissement (m.): l'établissement de votre appel *the connection of your call*, 9

l' étage (m.) *floor, story (of a building)*, 6

etaler *to spread*, 8

l' étape (f.) *part*, 1; première étape *first part*, 1; deuxième étape *second part*, 1; troisième étape *third part*, 1

l' état (m.) *state* 0

les Etats-Unis (m.) *United States*, 0

l' été (f.) *summer*, 4; en été *in the summer*, 4

été (pp.) *was*, 9

être *to be*, 7; C'est... *This is ...,* 7; Ce sont ... *These (those) are ...,* 7; Elle est... *She is ...,* 7; Il est... *He is ...,* 7; Il est... *It is ...* (time), 6; Ils/Elles sont ... *They're ...,* 7; Oui, ça a été. *Yes, it was fine.* 9

l' étude (f.) *study hall*, 2

étudier *to study*, 1

l' Europe (f.) *Europe*, 0

évider *to scoop out*, 8

éviter *to avoid*, 9

les examens (m.) *exams*, 1

excellente *excellent*, 5; Oui, excellent. *Yes, excellent.* 9

excusez: Excusez-moi. *Excuse me*, 3

exemplaire *exemplary*, 7

F

face: en face de *across from*, 12

facile *easy*, 2

faim: avoir faim *to be hungry*, 5; Non, merci. Je n'ai plus faim. *No thanks. I'm not hungry anymore.* 8

faire *to do, to make, to play*, 4; Désolé(e), j'ai des devoirs à faire. *Sorry, I have homework to do.* 5; J'ai des courses à faire. *I have errands to do.* 5; J'ai des tas de choses à faire. *I have lots of things to do.* 5; J'ai des trucs à faire. *I have some things to do.* 5; Qu'est-ce que tu vas faire...? *What are you going to do ...?* 6; Tu vas faire quoi...? *What are you going to do ...?* 6; faire les courses *to do the shopping*, 7

fais: A ton avis, qu'est-ce que je fais? *In your opinion, what do I do?* 9; Fais-moi... *Make me ...,* 3; Je fais... *I play/do ...* 4; Ne t'en fais pas! *Don't worry!* 9; Qu'est-ce que tu fais comme sport? *What sports do you play?* 4; Qu'est-ce que tu fais pour t'amuser? *What do you do to have fun?* 4; Qu'est-ce que tu fais...? *What do you do ...?,* 4; Qu'est-ce que tu fais quand...? *What do you do when ...?,* 4

faisons: Faisons connaissance!. *Let's get acquainted.* 1

fait: Il fait beau. *It's nice weather.* 4; Il fait chaud. *It's hot.* 4; Il fait frais. *It's cool.* 4; Il fait froid. *It's cold.,* 4; Qu'est-ce que tu as fait...? *What did you do ...,* 9

ferai: je me ferai une joie de... *I'll gladly ...,* 1

ferais: Je ferais le bac... *I would take bac ...,* 2

faut: Il me faut... *I need ...,* 3; Qu'est-ce qu'il te faut pour...? *What do you need for ...? (informal),* 3; Qu'est-ce qu'il te faut? *What do you need?* 8; Qu'est-ce qu'il vous faut

pour... ? *What do you need for . . . ? (formal)*, 3
la farine *flour*, 8
faux *false*, 2
les féculents (m.) *starches*, 8
la fenêtre *window*, 0
fermez: Fermez la porte. *Close the door.* 0
la fête *party*, 1; faire la fête *to live it up*, 1
la feuille: une feuille de papier *a sheet of paper*, 0
le feutre *a marker*, 3
février *February*, 4
la fiche: la fiche électrique *power plug*, 9; la fiche téléphonique *telephone plug*, 9
la fidélité *loyalty*, 7
la fille *girl*, 0
le film *movie*, 6; **voir un film** *to see a movie*, 6; un film d'aventures *adventure film*, 1
la fin *end*, 4
le flipper *pinball*, 5
fois: une fois par semaine *once a week*, 4
follement *madly*, 1
fonctionner *to function*, 9
le foot *soccer*, 4
le football *soccer*, 1; **le football américain** *football*, 4
la forêt *forest*, 0; **en forêt** *to the forest*, 11
formidable: C'était formidable! *It was great!* 11
fort(e) *strong*, 7
les fournitures scolaires (f.) *school supplies*, 3
fraîche *cool, cold*, 5
frais: Il fait frais. *It's cool.* 4
les fraises (f.) *strawberries*, 8
franc (the French monetary unit) 3; **C'est... francs.** *It's . . . francs.* 5
le français *French (language)*, 1; français(e) *French (adj.)* 0; A la française *French-style*, 2
francophone *French-speaking*, 0
fréquemment *frequently*, 9
le frère *brother*, 7
les friandises (f.) *sweets*, 6
les frites (f.) *French fries*, 1
froid: Il fait froid. *It's cold.* 4
le fromage *cheese*, 5
fuit (pp.) *fled*, 1
le fun: C'est le fun! (in Canada) *It's fun!* 4

G

gagner *to win, to earn*, 9
la gamme: la nouvelle gamme de *the new line of*, 9

le garçon *boy*, 0
garde: garde en mémoire *stores in memory*, 9
garder *to look after*, 7
le gâteau *cake*, 8
gauche: à gauche *to the left*, 12
génial(e) *great*, 2
le génie *genius*, 6
genoux: une paire de genoux *pair of knees, a lap*, 7
gentil (gentille) *nice*, 7
la géographie *geography*, 2
la géométrie *geometry*, 2
la glace *ice cream*, 1
glace: faire du patin à glace *to ice skate*, 4
le golf *golf*, 4; **jouer au golf** *to play golf*, 4
les gombos (m.) *okra*, 8
la gomme *eraser*, 3
la gosse: être traité comme une gosse *to be treated like a kid*, 2
le gouache *paint*, 3
le goûter *afternoon snack*, 8
les goûts (m.) *tastes*, 4
les goyaves (m.) *guavas*, 8
les graines (f.) *seeds*, 8
la grammaire *grammar*, 1
grand(e) *tall*, 7; *big*, 10
grand-chose: Pas grand-chose. *Not much.* 6
la **grand-mère** *grandmother*, 7
le **grand-père** *grandfather*, 7
grandir *to grow*, 10
gratuit(e) *free*, 6
grec *Greek (adj.)*, 6
gris(e) *grey*, 3
gros (grosse) *fat*, 7
grossir *to gain weight*, 10
les groupes (f.) *music groups*, 2
la Guadeloupe *Guadeloupe*, 0
le guichet *ticket window*, 6
la Guyane *Guiana*, 0

H

habitant: habitant le monde entier *living all over the world*, 1
habite: J'habite à... *I live in . . .* , 1
les habitudes (f.) *habits*, 4; **d'habitude** *usually*, 4
habituellement *usually*, 2
Haïti (no article) *Haiti*, 0
***les hamburgers** (m.) *hamburgers*, 1
*la harpe *harp*, 11
*les haricots (m.) *beans*, 8; les haricots verts (m.) *green beans*, 8
*hâte: Elle a hâte de... *She can't wait to . . .* , 7
*haut(e) *tall, high*, 6
*le haut-parleur *loudspeaker*, 11

*le havre *haven*, 7
l' hébergement (m.) *lodging*, 6
*le héros *hero*, 11
hésite: Euh... J'hésite. *Oh, I'm not sure.* 10
l' heure: à l'heure de *at the time of*, 1; **A quelle heure?** *At what time?* 6; **A tout à l'heure!** *See you later!* 1; **Quelle heure est-il?** *What time is it?* 6; **Tu as . . . à quelle heure?** *At what time do you have . . . ?*, 2
heures: à... heures *at . . . o'clock*, 2; à... heures quarante-cinq *at . . . forty-five*, 2; à... heures quinze *at . . . fifteen*, 2; à... heures trente *at . . . thirty*, 2
heureusement *luckily, fortunately*, 4
heureux: Très heureux (heureuse). *Pleased to meet you.* 7
l' histoire (f.) *history*, 2
l' hiver (m.) *winter*, 4; **en hiver** *in the winter*, 4
*le hockey *hockey*, 4; **jouer au hockey** *to play hockey*, 4
l' hôpital (pl. -aux) *hospital*, 0
horrible *terrible*, 10
*le hot-dog *hot dog*, 5
l' hôtel (m.) *hotel*, 0
*le houx *holly*, 11

I

l' idée (f.) *idea*, 4; **Bonne idée.** *Good idea.* 4
l' identité: une photo d'identité *a photo ID*, 1
il y a *there is, there are*, 4; il y a du soleil/du vent *it's sunny/ windy*, 4
l' île (f.) *island*, 0
imagines: Tu imagines? *Can you imagine?* 4
l' imprimante (f.) *printer*, 9
inclus *included*, 6
incompétent *incompetent*, 2
l' informatique (f.) *computer science*, 2
inscrit(e) *written*, 9
intelligent(e) *smart*, 7
intention: J'ai l'intention de... *I intend to . . .* , 11
intéressant *interesting*, 2
l'interro (f.) *quiz*, 9
international *international*, 5
les interviewés *interviewees*, 2
intime *personal*, 1
ivoirien, -ne, *from the Republic of Côte d'Ivoire*, 1

J

jamais: ne...jamais *never*, 4
le jambon *ham*, 5
janvier *January*, 4
le jardin *garden*, 0
jaune *yellow*, 3
le jazz *jazz*, 4
je *I*, 0
le jean *(a pair of) jeans*, 3; **en jean** *denim*, 3
le jeu: un jeu de rôle *role-playing exercise*, 1; **jouer à des jeux vidéo** *to play video games*, 4
jeudi *Thursday* 2; **le jeudi** *on Thursdays*, 2
jeune *young*, 7; les jeunes *youths*, 4
le jogging: faire du jogging *to jog*, 4
joignant (joigner) *to attach*, 1
joli(e) *pretty*, 4
jouer *to play*, 4; **Je joue...** *I play . . .* 4; **jouer à . . .** *to play (a game) . . .* 4
le jour *day*, 2
le journal *journal*, 1
la journée *day*, 2
juillet *July*, 4
juin *June*, 4
la jupe *a skirt*, 10
le jus d'orange *orange juice*, 5
le jus de pomme *apple juice*, 5
jusqu'à: jusqu'à dix numéros *up to ten numbers*, 9; **Vous allez tout droit jusqu'à...** *You go straight ahead until you get to . . .*, 12
juste *just*, 4

K

le kilo: un kilo de *a kilogram of*, 8

L

la *her, it*, 9
là *there*, 3; **-là** *there (noun suffix)*, 3; **(Est-ce que) . . . est là, s'il vous plaît?** *Is . . . , there, please?* 9
laisser: Je peux laisser un message? *Can I leave a message?* 9
le lait *milk*, 8
laitiers: les produits laitiers (m.) *dairy products*, 8
large *baggy*, 10
le latin *Latin*, 2
laver: laver la voiture *to wash the car*, 7
la légèreté *lightness*, 6
le *him, it*, 9

les *them*, 9
leur *to them*, 9
leur/leur(s) *their*, 7
levez: Levez la main! *Raise your hand!* 0; **Levez-vous!** *Stand up!* 0
la librairie *bookstore*, 12
la librairie-papeterie *bookstore*, 3
liégeois: café ou chocolat liégeois *coffee or chocolate ice cream with whipped cream*, 5
la limonade *lemon soda*, 5
lire *to read*, 1
lisons: Lisons! *Let's read!* 1
la litote *understatement*, 5
litre: un litre de *a liter of*, 8
la livre: une livre de *a pound of*, 8
le livre *book*, 0
la location *rental*, 4
loin: loin de *far from*, 12
le loisir *pastime*, 4
la longeur *length*, 10
la Louisiane *Louisiana*, 0
lu (pp. of lire) *read*, 9
lui *to him, to her*, 9
lundi *Monday* 2; **le lundi** *on Mondays*, 2
les lunettes (f.) de soleil *sunglasses*, 10
le Luxembourg *Luxembourg*, 0
le lycée *high school*, 2

M

ma *my*, 7
madame (Mme) *ma'am; Mrs*, 1; **Madame!** *Waitress!* 5
mademoiselle (Mlle) *miss; Miss*, 1; **Mademoiselle!** *Waitress!* 5
les magasins (m.) *stores*, 1; **faire les magasins** *to go shopping*, 1
le magazine *magazine*, 3
le magnétoscope *videocassette recorder, VCR*, 0
mai *May*, 4
maigrir *to lose weight*, 10
le maillot de bain *a bathing suit*, 10
la main *hand*, 0
maintenant *now*, 2
mais *but*, 1
le maïs *corn*, 8
la Maison des jeunes et de la culture (MJC) *the recreation center*, 6
le maître *master, owner*, 7
mal: Pas mal. *Not bad.* 1
la malchance *misfortune*, 7
malheureusement *unfortunately*, 7

le Mali *Mali*, 0
la manche *sleeve*, 10
le manchot *penguin*, 6
le manège *carousel*, 12
manger *to eat*, 6
les mangues (f.) *mangoes*, 8
manque: Qu'est-ce qui manque? *What's missing?* 2
manqué: garçon manqué *tomboy*, 10
le manteau *coat*, 10
mardi *Tuesday* 2; **le mardi** *on Tuesdays*, 2
le Maroc *Morocco*, 0
marocain(e) *Moroccan*, 1
marron (inv.) *brown*, 3
mars *March*, 4
martiniquais(e) *from Martinique*, 1
la Martinique *Martinique*, 0
le match: regarder un match *to watch a game (on TV)*, 6; **voir un match** *to see a game (in person)*, 6
les maths (f.) *math*, 1
les matières grasses (f.) *fat*, 8
le matin *in the morning*, 2
mauvais: Oh, pas mauvais. *Oh, not bad.* 9; **Très mauvais.** *Very bad.* 9
méchant(e) *mean*, 7
mécontent(e) *unhappy*, 2
les médicaments (m.) *medicine*, 12
meilleurs: les meilleurs amis *best friends*, 7
méli-mélo! *mishmash*, 1
le ménage: faire le ménage *to do housework*, 1
méprisant *contemptuous*, 2
la mer: au bord de la mer *to/at the coast*, 11
Merci. *Thank you*, 3; **Non, merci.** *No, thank you.* 8
mercredi *Wednesday*, 2; **le mercredi** *on Wednesdays*, 2
la mère *mother*, 7
mes *my*, 7
le métro: au métro... *at the . . . metro stop*, 6; **en métro** *by subway*, 12
mets: mets en ordre *put into order*, 6
mettre *to put, to put on, to wear*, 10; **Je ne sais pas quoi mettre pour . . .** *I don't know what to wear for (to) . . .*, 10; **Mets...** *Wear . . .*, 10; **Qu'est-ce que je mets?** *What shall I wear?* 10
meublé(e) *furnished*, 11
miam, miam *yum-yum*, 5
midi *noon*, 6
mieux: Ça va aller mieux! *It's*

going to get better! 9; **J'aime
mieux... ?** *I prefer . . . ?*, 10
mignon (mignonne) *cute*, 7
mince *slender*, 7
minuit *midnight*, 6
la minute: Tu as une minute? *Do
you have a minute?* 9
mise: mise en pratique *putting
into practice*, 1; mise en train
getting started, 1
mixte *mixed*, 5
le mobilier *furniture*, 6
**moche: Je le/la/les trouve
moche(s).** *I think it's/they're
tacky.* 10
la mode: à la mode *in style*, 10
le mode d'emploi *instructions*, 9
modéré(e) *moderate*, 11
moi *me*, 2
moins (with numbers) *lower*,
0; **moins cinq** *five to*, 6;
moins le quart *quarter to*, 6
**le moment: Un moment, s'il vous
plaît.** *One moment, please.* 5
mon *my*, 7
Monaco *Monaco*, 0
le monde *world*, 0
monsieur (M.) *sir; Mr.* 1;
Monsieur! *Waiter!* 5
la montagne *mountain*, 4; **à la
montagne** *to/at the mountains*, 11
la montée *ascent*, 6
la montre *watch*, 3
montrer *to show*, 9
le monument *monument*, 6
le moral *morale*, 2
le morceau: un morceau de *a
piece of*, 8
la mousseline *chiffon*, 8
murale: la prise murale *wall outlet*, 9
le musée *museum*, 6
la musique *music*, 2; **écouter de
la musique** *to listen to music*,
1; la musique classique *classical music*, 4
le mystère *mystery*, 5

N

nager *to swim*, 1
le nain *dwarf*, 6
la natation *swimming*, 4; **faire de
la natation** *to swim*, 4
nautique: faire du ski nautique
to water ski, 4
ne: ne... pas *not*, 1; **ne... pas
encore** *not yet*, 9; **ne... jamais**
never, 4
neige: Il neige. *It's snowing.* 4
le Niger *Niger*, 0

les niveaux (m.) *levels*, 6
le nocturne *late-night opening*, 6
le Noël *Christmas*, 0
noir(e) *black*, 3
la noisette *hazelnut*, 5
les noix (f.) *nuts*, 5
les noix de coco (f.) *coconuts*, 8
le nom *(last) name*, 1
non *no*, 1; **Moi non plus.**
Neither do I. 2; **Moi, non.** *I
don't.* 2; **Non, pas trop.** *No,
not too much.* 2
nos *our*, 7
notre *our*, 7
la Nouvelle-Angleterre *New
England*, 0
novembre *November*, 4
les nuages (m.) *clouds*, 12
nul *useless*, 2
le numéro *number*, 0; un numéro
de téléphone *telephone number*, 3; les numéros *issues (for
magazines, etc.)*, 3

O

l' objet (m.) *object*, 6; objets trouvés *lost and found*, 3
occuper: C'est occupé. *It's
busy.* 9; **Désolé(e), je suis
occupé(e).** *Sorry, I'm busy.* 6;
s'occuper de *to take care of*, 7
octobre *October*, 4
les œufs (m.) *eggs*, 8
l' oiseau (m.) *bird*, 12
on *one, we, you, they, people in
general*, 1; Comment dit-on... ?
How do you say . . . ? 1; **On
fait du ski?** *How about skiing?* 5; **On joue au base-ball?**
How about playing baseball? 5;
On va au café? *Shall we go
to the café?* 5; **On... ?** *How
about . . . ?* 4
l' oncle (m.) *uncle*, 7
orange (inv.) *orange (color)*, 3
les oranges (f.) *oranges*, 8
l' ordinateur *computer*, 3
où *where*, 6; **Où ça?** *Where?*
6; **Où est-ce que tu vas
aller... ?** *Where are you going
to go . . . ?* 11; **Tu es allé(e)
où?** *Where did you go?* 9
oublier *to forget*, 9; **Je n'ai rien
oublié.** *I didn't forget anything.* 11; **Oublie-le/ -la/ -les!**
Forget him/her/them! 9; **J'ai
oublié** *I forgot*, 3; **N'oublie
pas de...** *Don't forget . . .* 8;
Tu n'as pas oublié... ? *You
didn't forget your . . . ?* 11
oui *yes*, 1
ouvert(e) *open*, 6

**ouvrez: Ouvrez vos livres à la
page...** *Open your books to
page . . . ,* 0

P

la page *page*, 0
la pagne *a piece of brightly-colored
African cloth*, 10
le pain *bread*, 8
le palais *palace*, 1; le palais de justice *court, courthouse*, 1
le pamplemousse *grapefruit*, 5
le pantalon *a pair of pants*, 10
les papayes (f.) *papayas*, 8
la papeterie *stationery store*, 12;
librairie-papeterie *bookstore/
stationery store*, 3
le papier *paper*, 0
le paquet: un paquet de *a carton/
box of*, 8
par: prix par personne *price per
person*, 6
le parc *the park*, 6
Pardon *Pardon me*, 3; **Pardon,
madame... , s'il vous plaît?**
*Excuse me, ma'am . . . ,
please?* 12; **Pardon, mademoiselle. Où est... , s'il vous
plaît?** *Excuse me, miss.
Where is . . . , please?* 12;
**Pardon, monsieur. Je
cherche... , s'il vous plaît.**
*Excuse me, sir. I'm looking for
. . . , please.* 12
parfait(e) *perfect*, 3; **C'est parfait.** *It's perfect.* 10
parfois *sometimes*, 4
parfumer *to flavor*, 8
**parler: (Est-ce que) je peux
parler à... ?** *Could I speak to
. . . ?* 9; **Je peux te parler?**
Can I talk to you? 9; **Nous
avons parlé.** *We talked.* 9;
parler au téléphone *to talk
on the phone*, 1; Parlons! *Let's
talk!* 2
partagé(e) *split, shared*, 6
partir *to leave*, 11; **Tu ne peux
pas partir sans...** *You can't
leave without . . . ,* 11
pas: Pas question! *Out of the
question!* 7; pas content du tout
not happy at all, 2; pas du
tout: Il/Elle ne va pas du tout
avec... *It doesn't go at all
with . . . ,* 10; **Pas mal.** *Not
bad.* 1; **pas mauvais** *not bad*,
9; **pas super** *not so hot*, 2;
Pas terrible. *Not so great.* 1
passe: le mot de passe *password*, 9
passé: Ça s'est bien passé? *Did*

it go well? 9; **passé: Qu'est-ce qui s'est passé?** *What happened?* 9; **Tu as passé un bon week-end?** *Did you have a good weekend?* 9

le passeport *passport,* 11

passer: Tu pourrais passer à... ? *Could you go by . . . ,* ? 12; **Vous passez...** *You'll pass . . . ,* 12; **passer un examen** *to take a test,* 9

passionnant *fascinating,* 2

la pastille *tablet,* 3

le pâté *pâté,* 0

les pâtes (f.) *pasta,* 11

le patin *ice skating,* 1; **faire du patin à glace** *to ice skate,* 4

la pâtisserie *pastry shop, pastry,* 12

les pattes d'eph (f.) *bell-bottoms,* 10

pauvre *poor,* 7

le pays *country,* 6

les pêches (f.) *peaches,* 8

la peinture *painting,* 6

pendant *during,* 1

pénible *annoying,* 7

penser: J'ai pensé à tout. *I've thought of everything.* 11; **Qu'en penses-tu?** *What do you think (about it)?* 1

le père *father,* 7

performant *high-performance,* 9

le permis de conduire *driver's license,* 12

personnel (personnelle) *personal,* 4

le petit déjeuner *breakfast,* 8

petit(e) *short (height),* 7; *small (size),* 10; **petites annonces** *classified ads,* 1

les petits pois (m.) *peas,* 8

peu *not very,* 2; **peu content** *not very happy,* 2

la pharmacie *drugstore,* 12

la philosophie *philosophy,* 2

la photo: faire des photos *to take pictures,* 4

les photographies (f.) *photographs,* 6

la phrase *sentence,* 4

la physique *physics,* 2

la pièce *play,* 6; **voir une pièce** *to see a play,* 6

le pied *foot,* 12; **à pied** *on foot,* 12

le pinceau *paintbrush,* 3

pinces: des pantalons à pinces *pleated pants,* 10

le pingouin *penguin,* 0

le pique-nique: faire un pique-nique *to have a picnic,* 6

la piscine *the swimming pool,* 6

la pizza *pizza,* 1

la plage *beach,* 1

plaît: Il/Elle me plaît, mais il/elle est cher. *I like it, but it's expensive.* 10; **Il/Elle te/vous plaît?** *Do you like it?* 10; **Ça te plaît?** *Do you like it?* 2; **s'il vous (te) plaît** *please,* 3

le plaisir *pleasure, enjoyment,* 4; **Oui, avec plaisir.** *Yes, with pleasure.* 8

la planche: faire de la planche à voile *to go windsurfing,* 11

plaque: les plaques d'immatriculation (f.) *license plates,* 0

pleut: Il pleut. *It's raining.* 4

la plongée: faire de la plongée *to go scuba diving,* 11

plus *plus (math),* 2; *(with numbers)* *higher,* 0; **Je n'en veux plus.** *I don't want any more,* 8; **Moi non plus.** *Neither do I.* 2; **Non, merci. Je n'ai plus faim.** *No thanks. I'm not hungry anymore.* 8

la poche *pocket,* 10

le poème *poem,* 0

les poires (f.) *pears,* 8

le poisson *fish,* 7

la poitrine *chest,* 10

les pommes (f.) *apples,* 8; **les pommes de terre** (f.) *potatoes,* 8

le porc *pork,* 8

la porte *door,* 0; **porter** *to wear,* 10

le portefeuille *wallet,* 3

la poste *post office,* 12

le poste: un poste téléphonique *telephone subscriber,* 9

le poster *poster,* 0

le pot: pot de colle *container of glue,* 3

la poubelle *trashcan,* 7; **sortir la poubelle** *to take out the trash,* 7

la poudre *powder,* 8

les poules *chickens,* 8

le poulet *chicken meat,* 8

pour *for,* 2; **Qu'est-ce qu'il te faut pour...** *What do you need for . . . ? (informal),* 3; **Qu'est-ce que tu fais pour t'amuser?** *What do you do to have fun?* 4

pourquoi *why,* 0; **Pourquoi est-ce que tu ne mets pas... ?** *Why don't you wear . . . ?,* 10; **Pourquoi pas?** *Why not?* 6; **Pourquoi tu ne... pas?** *Why don't you . . . ?,* 9

pouvoir *to be able to, can,* 8; **(Est-ce que) je peux... ?** *May I . . . ?,* 7; **Tu peux... ?** *Can you . . . ?,* 8; **Je ne peux pas**

maintenant. *I can't right now.* 8; **Je peux te parler?** *Can I talk to you?,* 9; **Non, je ne peux pas.** *No, I can't.* 12; **Qu'est-ce que je peux faire?** *What can I do?* 9; **(Est-ce que) tu pourrais me rendre un petit service?** *Could you do me a favor?* 12; **Tu pourrais passer à... ?** *Could you go by . . . ?,* 12

précieusement *carefully,* 2

précisant: en précisant *specifying,* 1

préféré(e) *favorite,* 4

la préférence *preference,* 3

premier (première) *first,* 1

prendre *to take or to have (food or drink),* 5; **Je vais prendre... , s'il vous plaît.** *I'm going to have . . . , please.* 5; **On peut prendre...** *We can take . . . ,* 12; **Prends...** *Get . . . ,* 8; **Prends...** *Have . . . ,* 5; **Je le/la/les prends.** *I'll take it/them.* 10; **Tu prends... ?** *Are you taking . . . ?,* 11; **Tu prends... ?** *Will you have . . . ?,* 8; **Prenez une feuille de papier.** *Take out a sheet of paper.* 0; **Vous prenez...** *Will you have . . . ?,* 8; **Prenez la rue... puis traversez la rue...** *You take . . . , Street, then cross . . . Street,* 12; **Vous prenez?** *What are you having?* 5; **Vous avez décidé de prendre... ?** *Have you decided to take . . . ?* 10; **Vous le/la/les prenez?** *Are you going to take it/them?* 10

le prénom *first name,* 1

près: près de *close to,* 12

présenter: Je te (vous) présente... *I'd like you to meet . . . ,* 7; **Présente-toi!** *Introduce yourself!* 0

prêt (prête) *ready,* 9

prévu: Je n'ai rien de prévu. *I don't have any plans.* 11

le printemps *spring,* 4; **au printemps** *in the spring,* 4

pris (pp. of prendre) *took, taken,* 9

la prise *plug, outlet,* 9; **la prise murale** *wall outlet,* 9

le prix *price,* 6

le problème: J'ai un petit problème. *I've got a problem.* 9

prochain(e): Vous continuez jusqu'au prochain feu rouge. *You go down this street to the next light.* 12

le prof(esseur) *teacher*, 0
la promenade: faire une promenade *to go for a walk*, 6
promener: promener le chien *to walk the dog*, 7
promets (promettre) *to promise*, 1
prononcer *to pronounce*, 1; **prononcent: ne se prononcent pas** *no response*, 2
la prononciation *pronunciation*, 2
protège: protège contre *protects against*, 9
puis: Prenez la rue... puis traversez la rue... *Take . . . Street, then cross . . . Street*, 12
le pull(-over) *a pullover sweater*, 3

Q

qu'est-ce que *what*, 1; **Qu'est-ce qu'il y a dans...?** *What's in the . . . ?*, 3; **Qu'est-ce qu'il y a?** *What's wrong?* 2; **Qu'est-ce qu'on fait?** *What are we/they doing?* 4; **Qu'est-ce que je peux faire?** *What can I do?* 9; **Qu'est-ce que tu as fait... ?** *What did you do . . . ?* 9; **Qu'est-ce que tu fais... ?** *What do you do . . . ?* 4; **Qu'est-ce que tu vas faire... ?** *What are you going to do . . . ?* 6; **Qu'est-ce que vous avez comme boissons?** *What do you have to drink?* 5; **Qu'est-ce que vous avez comme... ?** *What kind of . . . do you have?* 5; **Qu'est-ce qui manque?** *What's missing?* 2
Qu'est-ce qui: Qu'est-ce qui s'est passé? *What happened?* 9
quand: Quand (ça)? *When?* 6
quart: et quart *quarter past*, 6; **moins le quart** *quarter to*, 6
que: Que sais-je? *Self-check (What do I know?)*, 1
le Québec *Quebec*, 0
québécois(e) *from Quebec*, 1
quel(le) *which*, 1; **Ils ont quels cours?** *What classes do they have?* 2; **Tu as quel âge?** *How old are you?* 1; **Tu as quels cours... ?** *What classes do you have . . . ?*, 2; **Tu as... à quelle heure?** *At what time do you have . . . ?*, 2; **Quelle heure est-il?** *What time is it?* 6
quelqu'un *someone*, 1
quelque chose: Je cherche quelque chose pour... *I'm looking for something for . . .*, 10

quelquefois *sometimes*, 4
la question *question*, 0
le questionnaire *questionnaire, survey*, 4
qui *who*, 0; **Avec qui?** *With whom?* 6; **C'est qui?** *Who is it?*, 2; **Qui suis-je?** *Who am I?* 0
quittez: Ne quittez pas. *Hold on.* 9
quoi: Je ne sais pas quoi mettre pour... *I don't know what to wear for . . .*, 10; **Tu as quoi... ?** *What do you have . . . ?*, 2

R

le rabat *flap*, 3
le raccourci *short cut*, 2
la radio *radio*, 3
le radis *radish*, 8
le raisin *grapes*, 8
la randonnée: faire de la randonnée *to go hiking*, 11
ranger: ranger ta chambre *to pick up your room*, 7
rappeler: Vous pouvez rappeler plus tard? *Can you call back later?* 9; **Tu te rappelles?** *Do you remember?* 3
rapporter: rapporte: Rapporte-moi... *Bring me back . . .*, 8; **Tu me rapportes... ?** *Will you bring me . . . ,?* 8
rater: rater le bus *to miss the bus*, 9; **rater une interro**, *to fail a quiz*, 9
le rayon *department*, 3; **au rayon de musique** *in the music department*, 3
la récréation *break*, 2
recueilli (pp. of recueillir) *to take in*, 7
réfléchir: Réfléchissez. *Think about it.* 2
le refuge *animal shelter*, 7
le réfugié *refugee*, 1
les refus (m.) *refusals*, 6
le regard *look*, 7
regarder: Non, merci, je regarde. *No, thanks, I'm just looking.* 10; **Regarde, voilà...** *Look, here's (there's) (it's) . . .*, 12; **regarder la télé** *to watch TV*, 1; **regarder un match** *to watch a game (on TV)*, 6; **Regardez la carte!** *Look at the map!* 0
la règle *ruler*, 3
regroupé(e) *rearranged*, 6
rejoint (pp. of rejoindre) *to rejoin*, 7

Je regrette. *Sorry*, 3; **Je regrette, mais je n'ai pas le temps.** *I'm sorry, but I don't have time.* 8
la rencontre *encounter*, 1
rencontrer *to meet*, 9
rendre *to return something*, 12; **Rendez-vous...** *We'll meet . . .* 6
renfort: renforts aux épaules *reinforced shoulder seams*, 10
la rentrée *back to school*, 2
le répertoire *index*, 9
répéter *to rehearse, to practice*, 9; **Répétez!** *Repeat!* 0
le répondant *respondent*, 4
répondre *to answer*, 9; **Ça ne répond pas.** *There's no answer.* 9
la réponse *response, answer*, 2
reposer: laisser reposer *to let stand*, 8; **se reposer** *to relax*, 11
la République de Côte d'Ivoire *the Republic of Côte d'Ivoire*, 0
respectueux (respectueuse) *respectful*, 2
ressemblez: si vous me ressemblez *if you're like me*, 1
le restaurant *restaurant*, 6
la restauration *dining*, 6
retard: en retard *late*, 2
retirer: retirer de l'argent (m.) *withdraw money*, 12
le retour *return*, 6
rétro (inv.) *style of the Forties or Fifties*, 10
retrouve: Bon, on se retrouve... *We'll meet . . .* 6
retrouver *to find again*, 6
la Réunion *the island of Réunion*, 0
rêvait (imp. of rêver) *to dream*, 7
rien: Ça ne me dit rien. *That doesn't interest me.* 4; **Je n'ai rien oublié.** *I didn't forget anything.* 11; **Rien de spécial.** *Nothing special.* 6
le riz *rice*, 8
la robe *dress*, 10
le rock *rock (music)*, 4
le roller: faire du roller en ligne *to in-line skate*, 4
romain(e) *Roman (adj.)*, 6
le roman *novel*, 3
ronronner *to purr*, 7
le rosbif *roast beef*, 5
rose *pink*, 3; **la rose** (flower) *rose*, 0
le rôti *roast*, 5
rouge *red*, 3
le rouleau: un rouleau protège livres *a roll of plastic material to protect books*, 3

roux (rousse) *redhead,* 7
rouspètent (rouspéter) *to complain,* 9
le **ruban: ruban adhésif transparent** *transparent adhesive tape,* 3

S

sa *his, her,* 7
le **sac (à dos)** *bag; backpack,* 3
sage *wise,* 12
Je n'en sais rien. *I have no idea.* 11; **Je ne sais pas.** *I don't know.* 10; **Que sais-je?** *Self-check (What do I know?),* 1; **savais: Savais-tu que... ?** *Did you know . . . ?* 2
la **saison** *season,* 4
la **salade** *salad, lettuce,* 8
la **salle** *room,* 2; **la salle de classe** *classroom,* 2
Salut *Hi! or Goodbye!* 1
samedi *Saturday* 2; **le samedi** *on Saturdays,* 2
les **sandales** (f.) *sandals,* 10
le **sandwich** *sandwich,* 5
sans *without,* 3
le **saucisson** *salami,* 5
savoir *to know,* 1
les **sciences** (f.) **naturelles** *natural science,* 2
scolaire: la vie scolaire *school life,* 2
la **séance** *showing* (at the movies), 6
seconde: Une seconde, s'il vous plaît. *One second, please.* 9
secours: poste de secours *first-aid station,* 6
le **séjour** *stay, residence,* 7
la **semaine: une fois par semaine** *once a week,* 4
le **Sénégal** *Senegal,* 0
sensas (sensationnel) *fantastic,* 10
septembre *September,* 4
sera: ce sera *it will be,* 6
le **serpent** *snake,* 0
serré(e) *tight,* 10
service: A votre service. *At your service; You're welcome,* 3
ses *his, her,* 7
sévère *severe, harsh,* 0
le **short** *(a pair of) shorts,* 3
si: Moi, si. *I do.* 2
le **siècle** *century,* 6
s'il vous plaît *please,* 5
le **ski** *skiing,* 1; **faire du ski** *to ski,* 4; **faire du ski nautique** *to water-ski,* 4
la **sœur** *sister,* 7
soif: avoir soif *to be thirsty,* 5

soigné(e) *with attention to detail,* 10
le **soir** *evening, in the evening,* 4; **Pas ce soir.** *Not tonight.* 7
le **soleil** *sun, sunshine,* 4
son *his, her,* 7
le **sondage** *poll,* 1
la **sortie** *dismissal,* 2
sortir: sortir avec les copains *to go out with friends,* 1; **sortir la poubelle** *to take out the trash,* 7
souvent *often,* 4
spécial: Rien de spécial. *Nothing special.* 6
le **sport** *gym,* 2; *sports,* 1; **faire du sport** *to play sports,* 1; **Qu'est-ce que tu fais comme sport?** *What sports do you play?* 4
le **sportif (la sportive)** *sportsman, sportswoman,* 4
le **stade** *the stadium,* 6
le **steak-frites** *steak and French fries,* 5
le **style: C'est tout à fait ton style.** *It looks great on you!* 10
le **stylo** *pen,* 0; **un stylo plume** *fountain pen,* 3
la **subvention** *subsidy,* 7
suis: Qui suis-je? *Who am I?* 0
suisse *Swiss,* 1; **la Suisse** *Switzerland,* 0
suite: tout de suite *right away,* 6; **C'est tout de suite à...** *It's right there on the . . . ,* 12; **J'y vais tout de suite.** *I'll go right away.* 8
suivre *to follow,* 9
super *super,* 2; **Super!** *Great!* 1; **pas super** *not so hot,* 2
supportez (supporter) *to put up with,* 2
sur: sur place *on-site,* 4; **sur un total de** *out of a total of,* 4
sûr(e) *safe,* 9
surtout *especially,* 1
le **sweat-shirt** *a sweatshirt,* 3
sympa (abbrev. of **sympathique**) (inv.) *nice,* 7
sympathique *nice,* 7

T

ta *your,* 7
le **tableau** *blackboard,* 0
la **tache** *spot,* 7
la **taille elastiquée** *elastic waist,* 10
le **taille-crayon** *pencil sharpener,* 3
tant: tant privée que professionelle *more private than professional,* 9

la **tante** *aunt,* 7
la **tarte** *pie,* 8
tas: J'ai des tas de choses à faire. *I have lots of things to do.* 5
le **taux de réussite** *rate of success,* 2
le **taxi: en taxi** *by taxi,* 12
le **Tchad** *Chad,* 0
Tchao! *Bye!* 1
le **tee-shirt** *T-shirt,* 3
le **téléphone** *telephone,* 0; **téléphone: parler au téléphone** *to talk on the phone,* 1; **téléphoner: Téléphone-lui/ -leur!** *Call him/her/them!* 9
la **télévision** *television,* 0; **regarder la télé(vision)** *to watch TV,* 1
tellement: Pas tellement. *Not too much.* 4
temps: de temps en temps *from time to time,* 4; **Je suis désolé(e), mais je n'ai pas le temps.** *Sorry, but I don't have time.* 12; **Quel temps est-ce qu'il fait à... ?** *How's the weather in . . . ?* 4
le **tennis** *tennis,* 4
la **tenue: une tenue de gymnastique** *a gym suit,* 3
termine (terminer) *to finish,* 2
terrible: Pas terrible. *Not so great.* 1
tes *your,* 7
le **théâtre** *the theater,* 6; **faire du théâtre** *to do drama,* 4
le **thon** *tuna,* 5
Tiens! *Hey!* 3
tient (tenir) *to hold,* 12
le **timbre** *stamp,* 12
timide *shy,* 7
toi: Et toi? *And you?* 1
les **tomates** (f.) *tomatoes,* 8
ton *your,* 7
la **touche** *button, key,* 9
tour: tour de poitrine *chest size,* 10
tournez: Vous tournez... *You turn . . . ,* 12
le **tournoi** *tournament,* 4
tous *all,* 2
tout: A tout à l'heure! *See you later!* 1; **J'ai pensé à tout.** *I've thought of everything.* 11; **pas du tout** *not at all,* 2; **Il/Elle ne va pas du tout avec...** *It doesn't go at all with . . .* 10; **tout à fait: C'est tout à fait ton style.** *It looks great on you!* 10; **tout de suite** *right away,* 6; **C'est tout de suite à...** *It's right there on*

the . . . , 12; **Oui, tout de suite.** *Yes, right away.* 5; **tout droit: Vous allez tout droit jusqu'à...** *You go straight ahead until you get to . . .* , 12

le train: en train *by train,* 12

traité: **être traité comme une gosse** *to be treated like a kid,* 2

la tranche: une tranche de *a slice of,* 8

le travail scolaire *school work,* 2

travailler *to work,* 9; **travailler la pâte** *to knead the dough,* 8

les travaux (m.) **pratiques** *lab,* 2

très: Très bien. *Very well.* 1

le trésor *treasure,* 3; **chasse au trésor** *treasure hunt,* 3

la trompette *trumpet,* 0

trop *too (much),* 10; **Il/Elle est trop cher.** *It's too expensive.* 10; **Non, pas trop.** *No, not too much.,* 2

la trousse *pencil case,* 3

trouver *to find,* 9; **Comment tu trouves ça?** *What do you think of that/it?,* 2; **Comment tu trouves... ?** *What do you think of . . . ?,* 2; **Je le/la/ les trouve...** *I think it's/ they're . . . ,* 10

les trucs: J'ai des trucs à faire. *I have some things to do.* 5

tu *you,* 0

la Tunisie *Tunisia,* 0

U

un *a, an,* 3

une *a, an,* 3

l' utilisation (f.) *the use of,* 9

utiliser *to use,* 10

V

va: Ça va. *Fine.* 1 **(Comment) ça va?** *How's it going?* 1; **Comment est-ce qu'on y va?** *How can we get there?* 12; **Il/Elle me va?** *Does . . . suit me?* 10; **Il/Elle ne te/vous va pas du tout.** *It doesn't look good on you at all.* 10; **Il/Elle ne va pas du tout avec...** *It doesn't go at all with . . . ,* 10; **Il/Elle te/vous va très bien.**

It suits you really well. 10; **Il/Elle va très bien avec...** *It goes very well with . . . ,* 10

les vacances (f.) *vacation,* 4; **Bonnes vacances!** *Have a good vacation!* 11; **en colonie de vacances** *to/at a summer camp,* 11; **en vacances** *on vacation,* 4

vais: Je vais... *I'm going . . .* 6; *I'm going (to) . . . ,* 11

la vaisselle: faire la vaisselle *to do the dishes,* 7

valable *valid,* 6

la valise *suitcase,* 11

la vedette *celebrity,* 1

veille: en état de veille *ready,* 9

le vélo *biking,* 1; **à vélo** *by bike,* 12; **faire du vélo** *to bike,* 4

vendredi *Friday* 2; **le vendredi** *on Fridays,* 2

la vente *sales,* 6

la verdure *vegetation,* 11

véritable *veritable,* 6; **C'était un véritable cauchemar!** *It was a real nightmare!* 11

le verre *glass,* 6

viens: Tu viens? *Will you come?* 6

le verrouillage *lock,* 9

vers *about,* 6

vert(e) *green,* 3

la veste *a suit jacket, a blazer,* 10

la viande *meat,* 8

la vidéo: faire de la vidéo *to make videos,* 4; **faire des jeux vidéo** *to play video games,* 4

la vidéocassette *a videotape,* 3

viennois(e) *Viennese* (adj), 5

vietnamien(ne) *Vietnamese,* 1

vieux *old,* 4

violet(violette) *purple,* 3

la virgule *comma,* 3

visiter *to visit (a place),* 9

vite *fast, quickly,* 2

vitrines: faire les vitrines *to window-shop,* 6

vivant *living,* 7

Vive... ! *Hurray for . . . !* 3

vivre *to live,* 2

le vocabulaire *vocabulary,* 1

Voici... *Here's . . . ,* 7

Voilà. *Here,* 3; **Voilà...** *There's . . . ,* 7

la voile *sailing,* 11; **faire de la planche à voile** *to go wind-surfing,* 11; **faire de la voile** *to go sailing,* 11

voir: voir un film *to see a movie,* 6; **voir un match** *to see a game (in person),* 6; **voir une pièce** *to see a play,* 6

le voisin *neighbor,* 1

la voiture *car,* 7; **en voiture** *by car,* 12; **laver la voiture** *to wash the car,* 7

la voix *voice,* 3

le volley(-ball) *volleyball,* 4

vos *your,* 7

votre *your,* 7

vouloir *to want,* 6; **Je veux bien.** *Gladly,* 12; **Je veux bien.** *I'd really like to.* 6; **Oui, si tu veux.** *Yes, if you want to.* 7; **Tu veux... ?** *Do you want . . . ?* 6; **Je voudrais acheter...** *I'd like to buy . . . ,* 3; **Je voudrais bien...** *I'd really like to . . . ,* 11; **Je voudrais...** *I'd like . . . ,* 3; **voulez: Vous voulez... ?** *Do you want . . . ?* 8

vous *you,* 0

voyager *to travel,* 1; **un voyage** *trip,* 0; **Bon voyage!** *Have a good trip!* 11

vrai *true,* 2

vraiment: Non, pas vraiment. *No, not really.* 11

vu (voir) *seen,* 9

la vue *view,* 6

W

le week-end: **ce week-end** *this weekend,* 6

le western *western (movie),* 0

Y

y *there,* 12; **Allons-y!** *Let's go!,* 4; **Comment est-ce qu'on y va?** *How can we get there?* 12; **On peut y aller...** *We can go there . . . ,* 12

le yaourt *yogurt,* 8

Z

le zèbre *zebra,* 0

zéro *a waste of time,* 2

le zoo *the zoo,* 6

Zut! *Darn!,* 3

ENGLISH-FRENCH VOCABULARY

In this vocabulary, the English definitions of all active French words in the book have been listed, followed by the French. The number after each entry refers to the chapter in which the entry is introduced. It is important to use a French word in its correct context. The use of a word can be checked easily by referring to the chapter where it appears.

French words and phrases are presented in the same way as in the French-English vocabulary.

A

a *un, une,* 3
about *vers,* 6
across from *en face de,* 12
adore: I adore . . . *J'adore...* 1
advise: What do you advise me to do? *Qu'est-ce que tu me conseilles?* 9
aerobics: to do aerobics *faire de l'aérobic,* 4
after: And after that, . . . *Et après ça...* 9
afternoon: afternoon off *l'après-midi libre,* 2; in the afternoon *l'après-midi* (m.), 2
afterwards: Afterwards, I went out. *Après, je suis sorti(e).* 9; And afterwards? *Et après?* 9
Agreed. *Entendu.* 6
algebra *l'algèbre* (f.), 2
all: Not at all. *Pas du tout.* 4
already *déjà,* 9
also *aussi,* 1
am: I am . . . years old. *J'ai... ans.* 1
an *un, une,* 3
and *et,* 1
annoying *embêtant(e),* 7; *pénible,* 7
answer *répondre,* 9; There's no answer. *Ça ne répond pas.* 9
any (of it) *en* 8; any more: I don't want any more *Je n'en veux plus.* 8
anything: I didn't forget anything. *Je n'ai rien oublié.* 11
apple juice *le jus de pomme,* 5
apples *les pommes* (f.), 8
April *avril,* 4
are: These/those are . . . *Ce sont...*7; They're . . . *Ils/Elles sont...* 7
art class *les arts* (m.) *plastiques,* 2
at *à la,* 6; *au,* 6; at . . . fifteen *à... heure(s) quinze,* 2; at . . . forty-five *à... heure(s) quarante-cinq,* 2; at . . . thirty *à... heure(s) trente,* 2; at . . . (s) house *chez... ,* 6; at the record store *chez le disquaire,* 12; At what time? *À quelle heure?* 6

B

August *août,* 4
aunt *la tante,* 7
avocados *les avocats* (m.), 8

backpack *le sac à dos,* 3
bad: Not bad. *Pas mal.* 1; Very bad. *Tres mauvais.*
bag *le sac,* 3
baggy *large(s),* 10
bakery *la boulangerie,* 12
bananas *les bananes* (f.), 8
bank *la banque,* 12
baseball: to play baseball *jouer au base-ball,* 4
basketball: to play basketball *jouer au basket(-ball),* 4
bathing suit *le maillot de bain,* 10
be *être,* 7
be able to, can: *pouvoir,* 8; Can you . . . ? *Tu peux... ?* 12
beach *la plage,* 1
beans *les haricots* (m.), 8
begin *commencer,* 9
behind *derrière,* 12
belt *la ceinture,* 10
better: It's going to get better! *Ça va aller mieux!* 9
between *entre,* 12
big *grand(e),* 10
bike: *le vélo; faire du vélo,* 4; by bike *à vélo,* 12
biking *le vélo,* 1
binder: loose-leaf binder *le classeur,* 3
biology *la biologie,* 2
black *noir(e),* 3
blackboard *le tableau,* 0; Go to the blackboard! *Allez au tableau!* 0
blazer *la veste,* 10
blond *blond(e),* 7
blue *bleu(e),* 3
boat: by boat *en bateau,* 12
book *le livre,* 0
bookstore *la librairie,* 12
boots *les bottes* (f.), 10

boring *barbant,* 2; *C'etait ennuyeux. It was boring.* 5
borrow *emprunter,* 12
bottle: a bottle of *une bouteille de,* 8
box: a carton/box of *un paquet de,* 8
boy *le garçon,* 8
bracelet *le bracelet,* 3
bread *le pain,* 8
break *la récréation,* 2
breakfast *le petit déjeuner,* 8
bring *apporter,* 9; Bring me back . . . *Rapporte-moi...* 8; Please bring me . . . *Apportez-moi... , s'il vous plaît.* 5; Will you bring me . . . ? *Tu me rapportes... ?* 8
brother *le frère,* 7
brown *marron* (inv.), 3
brunette *brun(e),* 7
bus: by bus *en bus,* 12
busy: It's busy. *C'est occupé.* 9; Sorry, I'm busy. *Désolé(e), je suis occupé(e).* 6
but *mais,* 1
butter *le beurre,* 8
buy *acheter,* 9; Buy me . . . *Achète(-moi)...* 8
Bye! *Tchao!* 1

C

cafeteria: at the school cafeteria *à la cantine,* 9
cake *le gâteau,* 8
calculator *la calculatrice,* 3
call: Call him/her/them! *Téléphone-lui/-leur!* 9; Can you call back later? *Vous pouvez rappeler plus tard?* 9; Who's calling? *Qui est à l'appareil?,* 9
camera *l'appareil-photo* (m.), 11
camp: to/at a summer camp *en colonie de vacances,* 11
camping: to go camping *faire du camping,* 11
can: to be able to, can *pouvoir,* 8; Can you . . . ? *Est-ce que tu peux... ?* 12; Can you . . . ? *Tu*

peux aller... ? 8; **Can I try on . . . ?**
Je peux l'/les essayer... ? 10

can't: I can't right now. *Je ne peux pas maintenant.* 8

can: a can of *une boîte de,* 8

canary *le canari,* 7

cap *la casquette,* 10

car: by car *en voiture,* 12; **to wash the car** *laver la voiture,* 7

carrots *les carottes* (f.), 8

carton: a carton/box of *un paquet de,* 8

cassette tape *la cassette,* 3

cat *le chat,* 7

CD/compact disc *le disque compact/le CD,* 3

Certainly. *Bien sûr.* 9

chair *la chaise,* 0

check: The check please. *L'addition, s'il vous plaît.* 5

cheese *le fromage,* 5; **toasted cheese and ham sandwich** *le croque-monsieur,* 5

chemistry *la chimie,* 2

chic *chic,* 10

chicken: chickens *les poules,* 8; **chicken meat** *le poulet,* 8

chocolate *le chocolat,* 1

choir *la chorale,* 2

choose *choisir,* 10

class: What classes do you have . . . ? *Tu as quels cours... ?* 2

clean: to clean house *faire le ménage,* 7

clear: to clear the table *débarrasser la table,* 7

Close the door! *Fermez la porte!* 0

close to *près de,* 12

coast: to/at the coast *au bord de la mer,* 11

coat *le manteau,* 10

coconuts *les noix de coco* (f.), 8

coffee *le café,* 5

cola *le coca,* 5

cold: It's cold. *Il fait froid.* 4

come: to come: Will you come? *Tu viens?* 6

compact disc/CD *le disque compact/le CD,* 3

computer *l'ordinateur* (m.), 3

computer science *l'informatique* (f.), 2

concerts *les concerts* (m.), 1

cool *cool,* 2; **It's cool out.** *Il fait frais.* 4; **Yes, very cool.** *Oui, très chouette.* 9

corn *le maïs,* 8

corner: on the corner of *au coin de,* 12

cotton (adj.) *en coton,* 10

could: Could you go by . . . ? *Tu pourrais passer à... ?* 12

country: to/at the countryside *à la campagne,* 11

course *le cours,* 2

course: Of course. *Bien sûr.* 3

cousin *le cousin (la cousine),* 7

cute *mignon (mignonne),* 7

D

dance *danser,* 1; **dance (subject)** *la danse,* 2

Darn! *Zut!* 3

December *décembre,* 4

decide: Have you decided? *Vous avez choisi?* 5; **decide: Have you decided to take . . . ?** *Vous avez décidé de prendre... ?* 10

delicious *délicieux,* 5

denim: in denim *en jean,* 10

deposit: to deposit money *déposer de l'argent,* 12

dictionary *le dictionnaire,* 3

dinner *le dîner,* 8; **to have dinner** *dîner,* 9

dishes: to do the dishes *faire la vaisselle,* 7

dismissal (when school gets out) *la sortie,* 2

do *faire,* 4; **Do you play/do . . . ?** *Qu'est-ce que tu fais...?* 4; **I do.** *Moi, si.* 2; **to do homework** *faire les devoirs,* 7; **to do the dishes** *faire la vaisselle,* 7; **I don't play/do . . .** *Je ne fais pas de...* 4; **I have errands to do.** *J'ai des courses à faire.* 5; **I play/do . . .** *Je fais...* 4; **In your opinion, what do I do?** *A ton avis, qu'est-ce que je fais?* 9; **Sorry. I have homework to do.** *Désolé(e). J'ai des devoirs à faire.* 5; **What are you going to do . . . ?** *Qu'est-ce que tu vas faire... ?* 6; *Tu vas faire quoi... ?* 6; **What can I do?** *Qu'est-ce que je peux faire?* 9; **What did you do . . . ?** *Qu'est-ce que tu as fait... ?* 9; **What do you advise me to do?** *Qu'est-ce que tu me conseilles?* 9; **What do you do . . . ?** *Qu'est-ce que tu fais...?* 4; **What do you do when . . . ?** *Qu'est-ce que tu fais quand...?* 4

dog *le chien,* 7; **to walk the dog** *promener le chien,* 7

done, made *fait* (pp.), 9

door *la porte,* 0

down: You go down this street to the next light. *Vous continuez jusqu'au prochain feu rouge.* 12

dozen: a dozen *une douzaine de,* 8

drama: to do drama *faire du théâtre,* 4

dress *la robe,* 10

drink: What do you have to drink? *Qu'est-ce que vous avez comme boissons?* 5

drugstore *la pharmacie,* 12

E

earrings *les boucles* (f.), *d'oreilles* 10

easy *facile,* 2

eat *manger,* 6

eggs *les œufs* (m.), 8

English *l'anglais* (m.), 1

envelope *l'enveloppe* (f.) 12

eraser *la gomme,* 3

especially *surtout,* 1

everything: I've thought of everything. *J'ai pensé à tout.* 11

exam *l'examen* (m.), 1

excellent *excellent,* 5

excuse: Excuse me. *Excusez-moi.* 3; **Excuse me, ma'am . . . , please?** *Pardon,... s'il vous plaît?* 12

F

fail: to fail a test *rater un examen,* 9

fall: in the fall *en automne,* 4

fantastic *sensas (sensationnel),* 10

far from *loin de,* 12

fascinating *passionnant,* 2

fat *gros (grosse),* 7

father *le père,* 7

February *février,* 4

feel: I feel like . . . *J'ai envie de...* 11

finally *enfin,* 9

find *trouver,* 9

Fine. *Ça va.* 1

first *d'abord* 9; **OK, if you . . . first.** *D'accord, si tu... d'abord...* 7

fish *le poisson,* 7

flour *la farine,* 8

foot: on foot *à pied,* 12

football: to play football *jouer au football américain,* 4

forest: to the forest *en forêt,* 11

forget *oublier,* 9; **Don't forget.** *N'oublie pas de... ,* 8; **Forget him/her/them!** *Oublie-le/-la/-les!* 9; **I didn't forget anything.** *Je n'ai rien oublié.* 11; **You didn't forget your . . . ?** *Tu n'as pas oublié... ?* 11

franc (the French monetary unit) *le franc,* 3

French *le français,* 1; **French fries** *les frites* (f.), 1

Friday: on Fridays *le vendredi,* 2

friends *les amis* (m.), 1; **to go out with friends** *sortir avec les copains,* 1

front: in front of *devant*, 6
fun: Did you have fun? *Tu t'es bien amusé(e)?* 11; **Have fun!** *Amuse-toi bien!* 11; **What do you do to have fun?** *Qu'est-ce que tu fais pour t'amuser?* 4
funny *amusant(e)*, 7

G

gain: to gain weight *grossir*, 10
game: to watch a game (on TV) *regarder un match*, 6
geography *la géographie*, 2
geometry *la géométrie*, 2
German *l'allemand* (m.), 2
get: Get . . . *Prends...* 8; **How can we get there?** *Comment est-ce qu'on y va?* 12
gift *le cadeau*, 11
girl *la fille*, 0
give: to give: Please give me . . . *Donnez-moi... , s'il vous plaît.* 5
Gladly. *Je veux bien.* 8
go *aller*, 6; **Go to the blackboard!** *Allez au tableau!* 0; **I'm going . . .** *Je vais...* 6; **What are you going to do . . . ?** *Tu vas faire quoi... ?* 6; **It doesn't go at all with . . .** *Il/Elle ne va pas du tout avec...* 10; **It goes very well with . . .** *Il/Elle va très bien avec...* 10; **to go out with friends** *sortir avec les copains*, 1; **I'd like . . . to go with . . .** *J'aimerais... pour aller avec...* 10; **Afterwards, I went out.** *Après, je suis sorti(e).* 9; **Could you go by . . . ?** *Tu pourrais passer à... ?* 12; **Did it go well?** *Ça s'est bien passé?* 11; **I'm going to have . . . , please.** *Je vais prendre... , s'il vous plaît.* 5; **What are you going to do . . . ?** *Qu'est-ce que tu vas faire... ?* 6; **I went . . .** *Je suis allé(e)...* 9; **I'm going to . . .** *Je vais...* 11; **Let's go . . .** *Allons...* 6; **to go for a walk** *faire une promenade*, 6; **We can go there . . .** *On peut y aller...* 12; **Where are you going to go . . . ?** *Où est-ce que tu vas aller... ?* 11; **Where did you go?** *Tu es allé(e) où?* 9; **You keep going until the next light.** *Vous continuez jusqu'au prochain feu rouge.* 12; **How's it going?** *(Comment) ça va?* 1
golf: to play golf *jouer au golf*, 4
good *bon*, 5; **Did you have a good . . . ?** *Tu as passé un bon... ?* 11; **not very good** *pas bon*, 5; **Yes, very good.** *Oui, très bon.* 9

Goodbye! *Au revoir!* 1; *Salut!* 1
got: No, you've got . . . to . . . *Non, tu dois...* 7
grandfather *le grand-père*, 7
grandmother *la grand-mère*, 7
grapes *le raisin*, 8
great *génial*, 2; **Great!** *Super!* 1; **It was great!** *C'était formidable!* 11; **not so great** *pas terrible*, 2
green *vert(e)*, 3
green beans *les *haricots verts* (m.), 8
grey *gris(e)*, 3
(small) grocery store *l'épicerie* (f.), 12
gross *dégoûtant*, 5
grow *grandir*, 10
guavas *les goyaves* (m.), 8
gym *le sport*, 2

H

half: half past *et demie*, 6; **half past (after midi and minuit)** *et demi*, 6
ham *le jambon*, 5; **toasted cheese and ham sandwich** *le croque-monsieur*, 5
hamburgers *les hamburgers* (m.), 1
hand *la main*, 0
happened: What happened? *Qu'est-ce qui s'est passé?* 9
hard *difficile*, 2
hat *le chapeau*, 10
have *avoir*, 2; **At what time do you have . . . ?** *Tu as... à quelle heure?* 2; **Do you have . . . ?** *Vous avez... ?* 2; *Tu as... ?* 3; **Do you have that in . . . ?** (size, fabric, color) *Vous avez ça en... ?* 10; **Have . . .** *Prends/Prenez...* 5; **What are you having?** *Vous prenez?* 5; **I don't have . . .** *Je n'ai pas de...* 3; **I have some things to do.** *J'ai des trucs à faire.* 5; **I have . . .** *J'ai...* 2; **I'll have . . . , please.** *Je vais prendre... , s'il vous plaît.* 5; **to take or to have (food or drink)** *prendre*, 5; **We have . . .** *Nous avons...* 2; **What classes do you have . . . ?** *Tu as quels cours... ?* 2; **What do you have . . . ?** *Tu as quoi... ?* 2; **What kind of . . . do you have?** *Qu'est-ce que vous avez comme... ?* 5; **Will you have . . . ?** *Tu prends... ?* 8; **Will you have . . . ?** *Vous prenez... ?* 8
health *le cours de développement personnel et social (DPS)*, 2
Hello *Bonjour*, 1; **Hello?** (on the phone) *Allô?* 9
help: May I help you? *(Est-ce que) je peux vous aider?* 10

her *la*, 9; *son/sa/ses*, 7
Here. *Voilà.* 3
Hi! *Salut!* 1
hiking: to go hiking *faire de la randonnée*, 11
him *le*, 9
his *son/sa/ses*, 7
history *l'histoire* (f.), 2
hockey: to play hockey *jouer au hockey*, 4
Hold on. *Ne quittez pas.* 9
homework *les devoirs*, 2; **to do homework** *faire les devoirs*, 7
horrible: It was horrible. *C'était épouvantable.* 9
horse: to go horseback riding *faire de l'équitation*, 1
hose *le collant*, 10
hot chocolate *le chocolat*, 5
hot dog *le hot-dog*, 5
hot: It's hot. *Il fait chaud.* 4; **not so hot** *pas super*, 2
house: at my house *chez moi*, 6; **Is this . . . 's house?** *Je suis bien chez... ?* 9; **to/at . . . 's house** *chez...* 11;
housework: to do housework *faire le ménage*, 7
how much: How much is . . . ? *C'est combien,... ?* 3; **How much is it?** (total) *Ça fait combien, s'il vous plaît?* 5
how: How old are you? *Tu as quel âge?* 1; **How about . . . ?** *On . . . ?* 4; **How do you like it?** *Comment tu trouves ça?* 5; **How much is . . . ?** *C'est combien... ?* 5; **How much is it, please?** (total) *Ça fait combien, s'il vous plaît?* 5; **How's it going?** *(Comment) ça va?* 1
hungry: to be hungry *avoir faim*, 5; **No thanks. I'm not hungry anymore.** *Non, merci. Je n'ai plus faim.* 8

I

I *je*, 1; **I do.** *Moi, si.* 2; **I don't.** *Moi, non.* 2
ice cream *la glace*, 1
ice-skate *faire du patin à glace*, 4
idea: Good idea. *Bonne idée.* 4; **I have no idea.** *Je n'en sais rien.* 11
if: OK, if you . . . first. *D'accord, si tu... d'abord...* 7
in *dans*, 6; **in (a city or place)** *à*, 11; **in (before a feminine country)** *en*, 11; **in (before a masculine country)** *au*, 11; **in (before a plural country)** *aux*, 11; **in front of** *devant*, 6; **in the afternoon**

l'après-midi, 2; **in the evening**
le soir, 4; **in the morning** *le
matin,* 2

**indifference: (expression of indiffer-
ence)** *Bof!* 1

intend: I intend to . . . *J'ai l'intention de. . .* 11

interest: That doesn't interest me.
Ça ne me dit rien. 4

interesting *intéressant,* 2

is: He is . . . *Il est... ,* 7; **It's . . .**
C'est... , 2; **She is . . .** *Elle est... ,* 7;
There's . . . *Voilà... ,* 7; **This is . . .**
C'est... ; Voici... , 7

it *le, la,* 9

It's . . . *C'est...* 2; **It's . . .** *Il est...*
(time), 6; **It's . . . francs.** *Ça fait...
francs.* 5; **No, it's . . .** *Non, c'est...*
4; **Yes, it's . . .** *Oui, c'est...* 4

J

jacket *le blouson,* 10
jam *la confiture,* 8
January *janvier,* 4
jeans *le jean,* 3
jog *faire du jogging,* 4
July *juillet,* 4
June *juin,* 4

K

kilogram: a kilogram of *un kilo
de,* 8

**kind: What kind of . . . do you
have?** *Qu'est-ce que vous avez
comme... ?* 5

know: I don't know. *Je ne sais
pas.* 10

L

lab *les travaux* (m.) *pratiques,* 2
later: Can you call back later? *Vous
pouvez rappeler plus tard?* 9; **See
you later!** *A tout à l'heure!* 1
Latin *le latin,* 2
leather: in leather *en cuir,* 10
leave *partir,* 11; **Can I leave a message?** *Je peux laisser un message?*
9; **You can't leave without . . .** *Tu
ne peux pas partir sans...* 11
left: to the left *à gauche,* 12
lemon soda *la limonade,* 5
let's: Let's go . . . *Allons...* 6; **Let's
go!** *Allons-y!* 4
letter: to send letters *envoyer des
lettres,* 12
library *la bibliothèque,* 6

like *aimer,* 1; **I'd really like . . .** *Je
voudrais bien...* 11; **Do you
like . . . ?** *Tu aimes... ?* 1; **Do you
like it?** *Il/Elle te (vous) plaît?* 10;
How do you like . . . ? *Comment
tu trouves... ?* 10; **How do you like
it?** *Comment tu trouves ça?* 5; **I
(really) like . . .** *Moi, j'aime
(bien)...* 1; **I don't like . . .** *Je
n'aime pas...* 1; **I like it, but it's
expensive.** *Il/Elle me plaît, mais
il/elle est cher (chère).* 10; **I'd like
. . .** *Je voudrais...* 3; **I'd like . . . go
with . . .** *J'aimerais... pour aller
avec...* 10; **I'd really like to.** *Je
veux bien.* 6; **I'd like to buy . . .** *Je
voudrais acheter...* 3; **What would
you like?** *Vous désirez?* 10;

like: What are they like? *Ils/Elles
sont comment?* 7; **What is he like?**
Il est comment? 7; **What is she
like?** *Elle est comment?* 7

Listen! *Écoutez!* 0; **I'm listening.**
Je t'écoute. 9; **to listen to music**
écouter de la musique, 1

liter: a liter of *un litre de,* 8

look after: to look after . . .
garder... , 7

look: Look at the map! *Regardez la
carte!* 0; **That doesn't look good on
you.** *Il/Elle ne te vous va pas du
tout.* 10; **I'm looking for something
for . . .** *Je cherche quelque chose
pour...* 10; **It looks great on you!**
C'est tout à fait ton style. 10; **Look,
here's (there's) (it's) . . .** *Regarde,
voilà...* 12; **No, thanks, I'm just
looking.** *Non, merci, je regarde.*
10; **to look for** *chercher,* 9;

looks: It looks great on you! *C'est
tout à fait ton style.* 10

lose: to lose weight *maigrir,* 10

lot: A lot. *Beaucoup.* 4

lots: I have lots of things to do. *J'ai
des tas de choses à faire.* 5; **I have
lots of things to do.** *J'ai des trucs
à faire.* 6

luck: Good luck! *Bonne chance!* 11

lunch *le déjeuner,* 2; **to have lunch**
déjeuner, 9

M

ma'am *madame (Mme),* 1
made *fait (faire),* 9
magazine *le magazine,* 3
make *faire,* 4
mall *le centre commercial,* 6
mangoes *les mangues* (f.), 8
map *la carte,* 0
March *mars,* 4

math *les maths* (f.), *les mathématiques,* 1

May *mai,* 4

may: May I . . . ? *(Est-ce que) je
peux... ?* 7; **May I help you?** *(Est-
ce que) je peux vous aider?* 10

mean *méchant(e),* 7

meat *la viande,* 8

medicine *les médicaments* (m.), 12

meet *rencontrer,* 9; **I'd like you to
meet . . .** *Je te (vous) présente...*
7; **Pleased to meet you.** *Très
heureux (heureuse).* 7; **OK, we'll
meet . . .** *Bon, se retrouve...* 6;
We'll meet. . . *Rendez-vous...* 6

menu: The menu, please. *La carte,
s'il vous plaît.* 5

message: Can I leave a message? *Je
peux laisser un message?* 9

metro: at the . . . metro stop *au
métro ... ,* 6

midnight *minuit,* 6

milk *le lait,* 8

mineral water *l'eau minérale* (f.), 5

minute: Do you have a minute? *Tu
as une minute?* 9

miss, Miss *mademoiselle (Mlle),* 1

miss: to miss the bus *rater le bus,* 9

moment: One moment, please. *Un
moment, s'il vous plaît.* 5

Monday: on Mondays *le lundi,* 2

money *l'argent* (m.), 11

More . . . ? *Encore de... ?* 8

morning: in the morning *le matin,* 2

mother *la mère,* 7

mountain: to/at the mountains *à la
montagne,* 11

movie theater *le cinéma,* 6; **the
movies** *le cinéma,* 1

Mr. *monsieur (M.),* 1

Mrs. *madame (Mme),* 1

much: How much is . . . ? *C'est
combien,... ?* 5; **How much is it,
please?** *Ça fait combien, s'il vous
plaît?* 5; **How much is it?** *C'est
combien?* 3; **No, not too much.**
Non, pas trop. 2; **Not much.** *Pas
grand-chose.* 6; **Not too much.**
Pas tellement. 4; **Not very much.**
Pas beaucoup. 4; **Yes, very much.**
Oui, beaucoup. 2

museum *le musée,* 6

mushrooms *les champignons* (m.), 8

music *la musique,* 2

my *mon/ma/mes,* 7

N

name: His/Her name is . . . *Il/Elle
s'appelle...* 1; **My name is . . .** *Je
m'appelle...* 0; **What is your name?**

Tu t'appelles comment? 0

natural science *les sciences* (f.) *naturelles,* 2

need: I need . . . *Il me faut...* 3; **I need . . .** *J'ai besoin de...* 8; **What do you need for . . . ? (formal)** *Qu'est-ce qu'il vous faut pour... 3*; **What do you need for . . . ? (informal)** *Qu'est-ce qu'il te faut pour ... ?* 3; **What do you need?** *De quoi est-ce que tu as besoin?* 8

neither: Neither do I. *Moi non plus.* 2

never *ne... jamais,* 4

next to *à côté de,* 12

nice *gentil, gentille,* 7: **It's nice weather.** *Il fait beau.* 4

nightmare: It was a real nightmare! *C'était un véritable cauchemar!* 11

no *non,* 1

none (of it) *en,* 8

noon *midi,* 6

not: Oh, not bad. *Oh, pas mauvais.* 9; **not yet** *ne... pas encore,* 9; **Not at all.** *Pas du tout.* 4; **Not me.** *Pas moi.* 2; **not so great** *pas terrible,* 5; **not very good** *pas bon,* 5;

notebook *le cahier,* 0

nothing: Nothing special. *Rien de spécial.* 6

novel *le roman,* 3

November *novembre,* 4

O

o'clock: at . . . o'clock *à... heure(s),* 2

October *octobre,* 4

of *de,* 0; **of it** *en,* 8; **of them** *en,* 8

off: afternoon off *l'après-midi libre,* 2

often *souvent,* 4

OK. *D'accord.* 4; **Is that OK with you?** *Tu es d'accord?* 7; **Well, OK.** *Bon, d'accord.* 8; **Yes it was OK.** *Oui, ça a été.*

okra *les gombos* (m.), 8

old: old-fashioned *démodé(e)(s),* 10; **How old are you?** *Tu as quel âge?* 1; **I am . . . years old.** *J'ai... ans.* 1; **older** *âgé(e),* 7

on: Can I try on . . . ? *Je peux essayer le/la/les... ?* 10; **on foot** *à pied,* 12; **on Fridays** *le vendredi,* 2; **on Mondays** *le lundi,* 2; **on Saturdays** *le samedi,* 2; **on Sundays** *le dimanche,* 2; **on Thursdays** *le jeudi,* 2; **on Tuesdays** *le mardi,* 2; **on Wednesdays** *le mercredi,* 2; **once: once a week** *une fois par semaine,* 4

open: Open your books to page . . . *Ouvrez vos livres à la page...,* 0

opinion: In your opinion, what do I do? *A ton avis, qu'est-ce que je fais?* 9

orange *orange,* (inv.), 3; **orange juice** *le jus d'orange,* 5; **oranges** *les oranges* (f.), 8

our *notre/nos,* 7

out: Out of the question! *Pas question!* 7

P

page *la page,* 0

pair: pair of pants *le pantalon,* 10; **(a pair of) jeans** *le jean,* 3; **(a pair of) shorts** *le short,* 3

papayas *les papayes* (f.), 8

paper *le papier,* 0; **sheets of paper** *les feuilles* (f.) *de papier,* 3

pardon: Pardon me. *Pardon,* 3

park *le parc,* 6

pass: You'll pass . . . *Vous passez devant...* 12

passport *le passeport,* 11

pastry *la pâtisserie,* 12; **pastry shop** *la pâtisserie,* 12

peaches *les pêches* (f.), 8

pears *les poires* (f.), 8

peas *les petits pois* (m.), 8

pen *le stylo,* 0

pencil *le crayon,* 3; **pencil case** *la trousse,* 3; **pencil sharpener** *le taille-crayon,* 3

perfect: It's perfect. *C'est parfait.* 10

phone: to talk on the phone *parler au téléphone,* 1

physical education *l'éducation* (f.) *physique et sportive (EPS),* 2

physics *la physique,* 2

pick *choisir,* 10; **to pick up your room** *ranger ta chambre,* 7

picnic: to have a picnic *faire un pique-nique,* 6

picture: to take pictures *faire des photos,* 4

pie *la tarte,* 8

piece: a piece of *un morceau de,* 8

pineapple *les ananas* (m.), 8

pink *rose,* 3

pizza *la pizza,* 1

plane ticket *le billet d'avion,* 11

plane: by plane *en avion,* 12

plans: I don't have any plans. *Je n'ai rien de prévu.* 11

play *jouer,* 4; *faire,* 4; **I don't play/do . . .** *Je ne fais pas de...* 4; **I play . . .** *Je joue...* , 4; **I play/do . . .** *Je fais...,* 4; **to play baseball** *jouer au base-ball,* 4; **to play bas-**

ketball *jouer au basket(-ball),* 4; **to play football** *jouer au football américain,* 4; **to play golf** *jouer au golf,* 4; **to play hockey** *jouer au hockey,* 4; **to play soccer** *jouer au foot(ball),* 4; **to play sports** *faire du sport,* 1; **to play tennis** *jouer au tennis,* 4; **to play volleyball** *jouer au volley(-ball),* 4; **What sports do you play?** *Qu'est-ce que tu fais comme sport?* 4; **What do you do to have fun?** *Qu'est-ce que tu fais pour t'amuser?* 4

please *s'il vous/te plaît,* 3

pleased: Pleased to meet you. *Très heureux (heureuse).* 7

pleasure: Yes, with pleasure. *Oui, avec plaisir.* 8

pork *le porc,* 8

post office *la poste,* 12

poster *le poster,* 0

potatoes *les pommes de terre* (f.), 8

pound: a pound of *une livre de,* 8

practice *répéter,* 9

prefer: I prefer . . . *Je préfère...* 1; *J'aime mieux...* 1

problem: I've got a problem. *J'ai un petit problème.* 9

pullover (sweater) *le pull-over,* 3

purple *violet(te),* 3

put *mettre,* 10; **to put on** *mettre,* 10

Q

quarter: quarter past *et quart,* 6; **quarter to** *moins le quart,* 6

question: Out of the question! *Pas question!* 7

quiz *l'interro* (f.), 9

R

radio *la radio,* 3

rain: It's raining. *Il pleut.* 4

Raise your hand! *Levez la main!* 0

read *lire,* 1; **read (p. p.)** *lu (lire),* 9

really: I (really) like . . . *Moi, j'aime (bien)...* 1; **I'd really like to . . .** *Je voudrais bien...* 11; **I'd really like to.** *Je veux bien.* 6; **No, not really.** *Non, pas vraiment.* 11

record: at the record store *chez le disquaire,* 12

recreation center *la Maison des jeunes et de la culture (MJC),* 6

red *rouge,* 3; **redhead** *roux (rousse),* 7

rehearse *répéter,* 9

Repeat! *Répétez!* 0

restaurant *le restaurant,* 6
return: to return something *rendre,* 12
rice *le riz,* 8
ride: to ride: to go horseback riding *faire de l'équitation,* 1
right: to the right *à droite,* 12
right away: *Oui, tout de suite.* Yes, right away. 5; I'll go right away. *J'y vais tout de suite.* 8
right now: I can't right now. *Je ne peux pas maintenant.* 8
right there: It's right there on the . . . *C'est tout de suite à...* 12
room: to pick up your room *ranger ta chambre,* 7
ruler *la règle,* 3

S

sailing: to go sailing *faire de la voile,* 11; *faire du bateau,* 11
salad, lettuce *la salade,* 8
salami *le saucisson,* 5
sandals *les sandales (f.),* 10
sandwich *le sandwich,* 5
Saturday: on Saturdays *le samedi,* 2
scarf *l'écharpe (f.),* 10
school *l'école (f.),* 1
scuba diving: to go scuba diving *faire de la plongée,* 11
second: One second, please. *Une seconde, s'il vous plaît.* 9
see: See you later! *A tout à l'heure!* 1; See you soon. *A bientôt.* 1; See you tomorrow. *A demain.* 1; to see a game (in person) *voir un match,* 6; to see a movie *voir un film,* 6; to see a play *voir une pièce,* 6
seen *vu (pp.),* 9
send: to send letters *envoyer des lettres,* 12
study *étudier,* 1
September *septembre,* 4
service: At your service; You're welcome. *A votre service.* 3
shall: Shall we go to the café? *On va au café?* 5
sheet: a sheet of paper *la feuille de papier,* 0
shirt (men's) *la chemise,* 10; (women's) *le chemisier,* 10
shoes *les chaussures (f.),* 10
shop: to go shopping *faire les magasins,* 1; to window-shop *faire les vitrines,* 6; Can you do the shopping? *Tu peux aller faire les courses?* 8
short (height) *petit(e),* 7; (length) *court(e),* 10

shorts: (a pair of) shorts *le short,* 3
should: You should talk to him/her/them. *Tu devrais lui/leur parler.* 9
show *montrer,* 9
shy *timide,* 7
sing *chanter,* 9
sir *monsieur (M.),* 1
sister *la sœur,* 7
Sit down! *Asseyez-vous!* 0
skate: ice-skate *faire du patin à glace,* 4; to in-line skate *faire du roller en ligne,* 4
ski *faire du ski,* 4; to water-ski *faire du ski nautique,* 4; skiing *le ski,* 1
skirt *la jupe,* 10
sleep *dormir,* 1
slender *mince,* 7
slice: a slice of *une tranche de,* 8
small *petit(e)(s),* 10
smart *intelligent(e),* 7
snack: afternoon snack *le goûter,* 8
snails *les escargots (m.),* 1
sneakers *les baskets (f.),* 3
snow: It's snowing. *Il neige.* 4
so: not so great *pas terrible,* 5; So-so. *Comme ci, comme ça.* 1
soccer *le football,* 1; to play soccer *jouer au foot(ball),* 4
socks *les chaussettes (f.),* 10
some *des,* 3; some *du, de la, de l', des,* 8; some (of it) *en,* 8
sometimes *quelquefois,* 4
soon: See you soon. *A bientôt.* 1
Sorry. *Je regrette.* 3; *Désolé(e).* 5
Spanish *l'espagnol (m.),* 2
speak: Could I speak to . . . ? *(Est-ce que) je peux parler à... ?* 9
special: Nothing special. *Rien de spécial.* 6
sports *le sport,* 1; to play sports *faire du sport,* 1; What sports do you play? *Qu'est-ce que tu fais comme sport?* 4
spring: in the spring *au printemps,* 4
stadium *le stade,* 6
stamp *le timbre,* 12
Stand up! *Levez-vous!* 0
start *commencer,* 9
stationery store *la papeterie,* 12
steak *le bifteck,* 8; steak and French fries *le steak-frites,* 5
stop: at the . . . metro stop *au métro ... ,* 6
stores *les magasins (m.),* 1
straight ahead: You go straight ahead until you get to . . . *Vous allez tout droit jusqu'à... ,* 12
strawberries *les fraises (f.),* 8
street: You keep going until the next light. *Vous continuez jusqu'au*

prochain feu rouge. 12; Take . . . Street, then cross . . . Street. *Prenez la rue... , puis traversez la rue...* 12
strong *fort(e),* 7
student *l'élève (m./f.),* 2
study hall *l'étude (f.),* 2
style: in style *à la mode,* 10; style of the Forties or Fifties *rétro (inv.)* 10
subway: by subway *en métro,* 12
suit jacket *la veste,* 10
suit: Does it suit me? *Il/Elle me va?* 10; It suits you really well. *Il/Elle te/vous va très bien.* 10
suitcase *la valise,* 11
summer: in the summer *en été,* 4
Sunday: on Sundays *le dimanche,* 2
sunglasses *les lunettes (f.) de soleil,* 10
super *super,* 2
sure: I'm not sure. *J'hésite.* 10
sweater *le cardigan,* 10
sweatshirt *le sweat-shirt,* 3
swim *nager,* 1; *faire de la natation,* 4
swimming pool *la piscine,* 6

T

T-shirt *le tee-shirt,* 3
table: to clear the table *débarrasser la table,* 7
tacky: I think it's (they're) really tacky. *Je le/la/les trouve moche(s).* 10
take out: Take out a sheet of paper. *Prenez une feuille de papier.* 0; to take out the trash *sortir la poubelle,* 7
take or have (food or drink) *prendre,* 5; Are you going to take it/them? *Vous le/la/les prenez?* 10; Are you taking . . . ? *Tu prends...?* 11; Have you decided to take . . . ? *Vous avez décidé de prendre... ?* 10; I'll take it/them. *Je le/la/les prends.* 10; to take a test *passer un examen* (9); to take pictures *faire des photos,* 4; We can take . . . *On peut prendre...* 12; Take . . . Street, then . . . Street. *Prenez la rue... , puis la rue...* 12
taken *pris (prendre),* 9
talk: Can I talk to you? *Je peux te parler?* 9; to talk on the phone *parler au téléphone,* 1; We talked. *Nous avons parlé.* 9;
tall *grand(e),* 7
taxi: by taxi *en taxi,* 12
teacher *le professeur,* 0

television   *la télévision*, 0

tell: to tell: Can you tell her/him that I called?   *Vous pouvez lui dire que j'ai téléphoné?* 9

tennis: to play tennis   *jouer au tennis*, 4

terrible   *horrible(s)*, 10

tests   *les examens* (m.), 1

Thank you.   *Merci.* 3; No thanks. I'm not hungry anymore.   *Non, merci. Je n'ai plus faim.* 8

that   *ce, cet, cette,* 3; This/That is . . .   *Ça, c'est...* 12

theater   *le théâtre,* 6

their   *leur/leurs,* 7

them   *les,* 9

then   *ensuite* 9

there: there   *-là (noun suffix),* 3; there   *y,* 12; Is. . . there, please?   *(Est-ce que)... est là, s'il vous plaît?* 9; There's . . .   *Voilà...* 7

these   *ces,* 3; These/those are . . .   *Ce sont...* 7

things: I have lots of things to do.   *J'ai des tas de choses à faire.* 5; I have some things to do.   *J'ai des trucs à faire.* 5

think: I think it's/they're . . .   *Je le/la/les trouve...* 10; I've thought of everything.   *J'ai pensé à tout.* 11; What do you think of . . . ?   *Comment tu trouves... ?* 2; What do you think of that/it?   *Comment tu trouves ça?* 2

thirsty: to be thirsty   *avoir soif,* 5

this   *ce, cet, cette,* 3; This is . . .   *C'est...* 7; This is . . .   *Voici...* 7; This/That is . . .   *Ça, c'est...* 12

those   *ces,* 3; These (those) are . . .   *Ce sont...* 7

Thursday: on Thursdays   *le jeudi,* 2

ticket: plane ticket   *le billet d'avion,* 11; train ticket   *le billet de train,* 11

tie   *la cravate,* 10

tight   *serré(e)(s),* 10

time: a waste of time   *zéro,* 2; At what time do you have . . . ?   *Tu as... à quelle heure?* 2; At what time?   *A quelle heure?* 6; from time to time   *de temps en temps,* 4; I'm sorry, but I don't have time.   *Je regrette, mais je n'ai pas le temps.* 8; I'm sorry, but I don't have time.   *Je suis désolé(e), mais je n'ai pas le temps.* 12; What time is it?   *Quelle heure est-il?* 6

to   *à la,* 6; *au,* 6; to (a city or place)   *à,* 11; to (before a feminine noun)   *en,* 11; to (before a masculine noun)   *au,* 11; to (before a plural noun)   *aux,* 11; to her   *lui,* 9; to him   *lui,* 9; to them   *leur,* 9; five

to   *moins cinq,* 6

today   *aujourd'hui,* 2

tomatoes   *les tomates* (f.), 8

tomorrow   *demain,* 2; See you tomorrow.   *A demain.* 1

tonight: Not tonight.   *Pas ce soir.* 7

too: It's/They're too . . .   *Il/Elle est (Ils/Elles sont) trop...* 10; Me too.   *Moi aussi.* 2; No, it's too expensive.   *Non, c'est trop cher.* 10; No, not too much.   *Non, pas trop.* 2; Not too much.   *Pas tellement.* 4

track: to do track and field   *faire de l'athlétisme,* 4

train: by train   *en train,* 12; train ticket   *le billet de train,* 11

trash: to take out the trash   *sortir la poubelle,* 7

travel   *voyager,* 1

trip: Have a good trip!   *Bon voyage!* 11

try: Can I try it (them) on ?   *Je peux l'(les) essayer?* 10

Tuesday: on Tuesdays   *le mardi,* 2

turn: You turn . . .   *Vous tournez...* 12

TV: to watch TV   *regarder la télé(vision),* 1

U

uncle   *l'oncle* (m.), 7

useless   *nul,* 2

usually   *d'habitude,* 4

V

vacation   *les vacances* (f.), 1; Have a good vacation!   *Bonnes vacances!* 11; on vacation   *en vacances,* 4

VCR (videocassette recorder)   *le magnétoscope,* 0

very: not very good   *pas bon,* 5; Yes, very much.   *Oui, beaucoup.* 2

video: to make videos   *faire de la vidéo,* 4; video games   *des jeux vidéo,* 4

videocassette recorder, VCR   *le magnétoscope,* 0

videotape   *la vidéocassette,* 3

visit (a place)   *visiter,* 9

volleyball: to play volleyball   *jouer au volley (-ball),* 4

W

wait for   *attendre,* 9

Waiter!   *Monsieur!* 5

Waitress!   *Madame!* 5; *Mademoiselle!* 5

walk: to go for a walk   *faire une*

promenade, 6; to walk the dog   *promener le chien,* 7

wallet   *le portefeuille,* 3

want   *vouloir,* 6; Do you want . . . ?   *Tu veux... ?* 6; Do you want . . . ?   *Vous voulez... ?* 8; Yes, if you want too.   *Oui, si tu veux.* 7

wash: to wash the car   *laver la voiture,* 7

waste: a waste of time   *zéro,* 2

watch   *la montre,* 3

watch: to watch a game (on TV)   *regarder un match,* 6; to watch TV   *regarder la télé(vision),* 1

water: to water ski   *faire du ski nautique,* 4

wear   *mettre, porter,* 10; I don't know what to wear for . . .   *Je ne sais pas quoi mettre pour...* 10; Wear . . .   *Mets...* 10; What shall I wear?   *Qu'est-ce que je mets?* 10; Why don't you wear . . . ?   *Pourquoi est-ce que tu ne mets pas... ?* 10

Wednesday: on Wednesdays   *le mercredi,* 2

weekend: Did you have a good weekend?   *Tu as passé un bon week-end?* 9; on weekends   *le week-end,* 4; this weekend   *ce week-end,* 6

welcome: At your service; You're welcome.   *A votre service.* 3

well: Did it go well?   *Ça s'est bien passé?* 11; Very well.   *Très bien.* 1

went: Afterwards, I went out.   *Après, je suis sorti(e).* 9; I went . . .   *Je suis allé(e)...* 9

what   *comment,* 0; What is your name?   *Tu t'appelles comment?* 0; What are you going to do . . . ?   *Qu'est-ce que tu vas faire... ?* 6; What are you going to do . . . ?   *Tu vas faire quoi... ?* 6; What do you have to drink?   *Qu'est-ce que vous avez comme boissons?* 5; What do you need for . . . ? (formal)   *Qu'est-ce qu'il vous faut pour... ?* 3; What do you think of . . . ?   *Comment tu trouves... ?* 2; What do you think of that/it?   *Comment tu trouves ça?* 2; What kind of . . . do you have?   *Qu'est-ce que vous avez comme... ?* 5; What's his/her name?   *Il/Elle s'appelle comment?* 1

When?   *Quand (ça) ?* 6

where: Where?   *Où (ça) ?* 6; Where did you go?   *Tu es allé(e) où?* 9

white   *blanc(he)(s),* 3

who: Who's calling? *Qui est à l'appareil?* 9

whom: With whom? *Avec qui?* 6

why: Why don't you . . . ? *Pourquoi tu ne... pas?* 9; Why not? *Pourquoi pas?* 6

win *gagner,* 9

window *la fenêtre,* 0; to window-shop *faire les vitrines,* 6

windsurfing: to go windsurfing *faire de la planche à voile,* 11

winter: in the winter *en hiver,* 4

with: with me *avec moi,* 6; With whom? *Avec qui?* 6

withdraw: withdraw money *retirer de l'argent* (m.), 12

without: You can't leave without . . . *Tu ne peux pas partir sans...* 11

work *travailler,* 9

worry: Don't worry! *Ne t'en fais pas!* 9

would like: I'd like to buy . . . *Je voudrais acheter...* 3

Y

yellow *jaune,* 3

yes *oui,* 1

yet: not yet *ne... pas encore,* 9

yogurt *le yaourt,* 8

you *tu, vous,* 0

young *jeune,* 7

your *ton/ta/tes,* 7; *vos,* 0; *votre* 7

Z

zoo *le zoo,* 6

GRAMMAR INDEX

A

à: contractions with **à** and **de**, p. 101; the prepositions **à** and **en**, p. 290

adjectives: adjective agreement and placement, p. 79; adjective agreement, p. 186; adjectives used as nouns, p. 265; demonstrative adjectives **ce, cet, cette,** and **ces**, p. 77; possessive adjectives, p. 181

adverbs: adverbs of frequency, p. 110; placement of adverbs with the **passé composé**, p. 240

agreement: adjective agreement and placement, p. 79; adjective agreement, p. 186

aimer, p. 33 (regular)

aller, p. 154 (irregular)

articles: the definite articles **le, la, l', les** and the gender of nouns, p. 28; the indefinite articles **un, une, des**, p. 73; the partitive articles **du, de la, de l',** and **des**, p. 208

avoir, p. 51 (irregular); **passé composé** with **avoir**, p. 239

avoir besoin de, p. 210

C

ce, cet, cette, ces: demonstrative adjectives, p. 77

c'est versus **il/elle est**, p. 274

choisir, p. 267 (regular)

contractions with **à** and **de**, p. 101

D

days of the week: using **le** with days of the week, p. 153

de: **de** after a negative verb, p. 104; **de** with expressions of quantity, p. 214; contractions with **à** and **de**, p. 101; possession with **de**, p. 180

de la, de l': partitive articles, p. 208

definite articles: the definite articles **le, la, l', les** and the gender of nouns, p. 28

demonstrative adjectives: **ce, cet, cette,** and **ces**, p. 77

des: indefinite articles, p. 73; partitive articles, p. 208

direct object pronouns **le, la,** and **les**, p. 247, p. 273

du: partitive articles, p. 208

E

en: the prepositions **à** and **en** p. 290; the pronoun **en**, p. 220

-er verbs, p. 33, 107

être, p. 187 (irregular)

F

faire, p. 104 (irregular)

frequency: adverbs of frequency, p. 110

G

gender: the definite articles **le, la, l', les** and the gender of nouns, p. 28

I

il est: **c'est** versus **il/elle est**, p. 274

imperatives, p. 136

indefinite articles: **un, une,** and **des**, p. 73

information questions, p. 165

-ir verbs: **choisir**, p. 267 (regular)

L

l': definite articles, p. 28

la: definite articles, p. 28; object pronouns, p. 247, p. 273

le: definite articles, p. 28; object pronouns, p. 247, p. 273; using **le** with days of the week, p. 153

les: definite articles, p. 28; object pronouns, p. 247, p. 273

leur, leurs: possessive adjectives, p. 181; object pronouns, p. 247

lui: object pronouns, p. 247

M

ma: possessive adjectives, p. 181

mes: possessive adjectives, p. 181

mettre, p. 263 (irregular)

mon: possessive adjectives, p. 181

N

ne... pas, p. 26
negative: **de** after a negative verb, p. 104
notre, nos: possessive adjectives, p. 181

O

object pronouns: **le, la, les, lui**, and **leur**, p. 247
oui: using **si** instead of **oui** to contradict a negative statement, p. 50

P

partir, p. 294 (regular)
partitive articles: **du, de la, de l'**, and **des**, p. 208
passé composé: **passé composé** with **avoir**, p. 239; placement of adverbs with the **passé composé**, p. 240
possession with **de**, p. 180
possessive adjectives, p. 181
pouvoir, p. 213 (irregular)
prendre, p. 133 (irregular)
prepositions: the prepositions **à** and **en**, p. 290
pronouns: the object pronouns **le, la, les, lui**, and **leur**, p. 247, p. 273; the pronoun **en**, p. 220; the pronoun **y**, p. 323

Q

question formation, p. 103
questions: Information questions, p. 165

R

-re verbs, p. 245
répondre, p. 245 (regular)

S

son, sa, ses: possessive adjectives, p. 181
si: using **si** instead of **oui** to contradict a negative statement, p. 50
subject pronouns and **-er** verbs, p. 33

T

ton, ta, tes: possessive adjectives, p. 181

U

un, une: indefinite articles, p. 73

V

votre, vos: possessive adjectives, p. 181
vouloir, p. 160 (irregular)

Y

y: the pronoun **y**, p. 323

ACKNOWLEDGMENTS (continued from page ii)

EF Ecole Européenne de Vacances S.A.R.L.: From "Le rêve américain devient réalité, en séjour Immersion avec EF," photograph, and "Vacances de Printemps" "from" "Les U.S.A. en cours Principal: le séjour EF idéal" from *1993: EF Voyage: Hiver, Printemps, et Eté.*

Établissement public du Grand Louvre: Photograph, "Palais du Louvre," from *Les 34 Musées Nationaux,* 1992 edition.

Femme Actuelle: Text from "En direct des refuges: Poupette, 3 ans" by Nicole Lauroy from *Femme Actuelle,* #414, August 31-September 6, 1992. Copyright © 1992 by Femme Actuelle. Text from "En direct des refuges: Jupiter, 7 ans" by Nicole Lauroy from *Femme Actuelle,* #436, February 1993. Copyright © 1993 by Femme Actuelle. Text from "En direct des refuges: Flora, 3 ans" by Nicole Lauroy from *Femme Actuelle,* #457, July, 1993. Copyright © 1993 by *Femme Actuelle.* Text from "En direct des refuges: Dady, 2 ans; Mayo a trouvé une famille" by Nicole Lauroy from *Femme Actuelle,* #466, August 30-September 5, 1993. Copyright © 1993 by Femme Actuelle. Text from "En direct des refuges: Camel, 5 ans" by Nicole Lauroy from *Femme Actuelle,* #472, October 11-17, 1993. Copyright © 1993 by Femme Actuelle.

France Miniature: Illustration, phototgraph, and excerpt from *Le Pays France Miniature.*

France Télécom: Cover and excerpts from Minitel 2 : *Mode d'emploi modèle Alcatel.* Illustration from page 2048 from *Paris Annuaire Officiel des Abonnées au Téléphone,* Volume 2, f/m, April 1988.

Galeries Lafayette: Two photographs with captions of Naf-Naf products and four photographs with captions of Cacharel products from *RENTREE TRES CLASSE A PRIX PETITS: Nouvelles Galeries Lafayette.*

Grands Bateaux de Provence: Advertisement, "Bateau 'Mireio'," from *Évasion Plus.*

Grottes de Thouzon: Advertisement, "Grottes de Thouzon," from *Évasion Plus.* Photograph by M. Crotet, *Évasion Plus.* Provence, Imprimerie Vincent, 1994.

Groupe Filipacchi: Advertisement, "Casablanca," from *7 à Paris,* page 43, no. 534, February 2-18, 1992.

Hachette Livre: Title and descriptions from pages 67,68,77, and 78 from *Le guide du Routard-Provence Côte d'Azur 1994-1995.* Copyright © 1994 by Hachette Livre (Littérature générale: Guides de Voyages.)

L'Harmattan: Excerpts from French text and photographs from *Cheval de bois/Chouval bwa* by Isabelle et Henri Cadoré, illustrations by Bernadette Coléno. Copyright © 1993 by L'Harmattan.

Larousse: "Les monuments les plus visités" and "Les musées les plus visités" from *Francoscopie: 1993* by Gérard Mermet. Copyright © 1992 by Larousse.

Loca Center: Advertisement, "Loca Center," from *Guide des Services: La Martinique à domicile.*

Michelin Travel Publications: From Map #989: France/Francia. Copyright © 1994 by Michelin Travel Publications.

Ministère de la Culture et de la Francophonie: ticket, "Ministère de la Culture: C.N.M.H.S.: droit d'entrée."

Ministère de l'Education Nationale: Direction de l'Évaluation et de la Prospective (DEP): Table, "Bac 1991: 75% de reçus" from *Francoscopie 1993* by Gérard Mermet.

Musée du Louvre: Front of entry ticket for the Louvre.

NAF-NAF: Two photographs from *RENTREE TRES CLASSE A PRIX PETITS. Nouvelles Galeries Lafayette.*

Office Départmental du Tourisme de la Martinique: Map of Fort-de-France from *Martinique: Plan de Fort-de-France/Carte de la Martinique.*

OUI FM: Logo from OUI FM, 102.3 MHz (Paris).

Parc Astérix S.A.: Cover of *Parc Astérix,* 1992 edition. Advertisement for Parc Astérix from *Paris Vision,* 1993 edition, page 29.

Parc du Mont-Sainte-Anne: Cover of *Parc du Mont-Sainte-Anne: A Mountain of Summer Fun, 1993 Season.* Photograph by Jean Sylvain.

Parc Zoologique de Paris: Cover and map from *Parc Zoologique de Paris.*

Paris Midnight: French text and photograph from "Musée d'Orsay," text from "Notre-Dame de Paris," and text from "La Tour Eiffel" from *Paris Midnight,* no. 31, June 1993. Copyright © 1993 by Paris Midnight.

Paris Promotion: Map of Paris from *Paris: Mode d'emploi 93/94,* edited by Paris Promotion.

Paristoric: Advertisement, "Paristoric: Le Film."

Pomme de pain: Menu, "La carte pomme de pain."

Printemps: Illustration and Printemps logo from *Invitation.* From map of Paris from *Printemps: Plan de Paris/Map of Paris.*

PROSUMA: Société Ivoirienne de Promotion de Supermarchés: Illustration from *3 éléphants prennent votre défense!*

RATP: ticket, "Section Urbaine."

RCV: La Radio Rock: Logo from RCV: La Radio Rock, 99 MHz (Lille).

Réunion des Musées Nationaux: Text from "Palais du Louvre" from *Les 34 Musées Nationaux,* 1992 edition.

Réunion des Musées Nationaux, Agence photographique: Photograph, "Palais du Louvre" from *Les 34 Musées Nationaux,* 1992 edition.

Editions S.A.E.P.: Recipe and photograph for "Croissants au coco et au sésame," recipe and photograph for "Mousseline africaine de petits légumes," and "Signification des symboles accompagnant les recettes" from *La cuisine Africaine* by Pierrette Chalendar. Copyright © 1993 by S.A.E.P.

Société Anonyme Montparnasse 56: Cover of *La Vue Parisienne.*

Télé 7 Jours: From "Sport: La semaine en direct" from *Télé 7 Jours,* September 26-October 2, 1992. Copyright © 1992 by Télé 7 Jours.

Tourisme Québec: "Le Climat" from *Destination Québec: Guide Pratique de voyage,* Edition 92-93, page 11.

Trois Suisses: Text and photographs from "Le pull col montant," "Le pantalon de jogging," and "Les polos" from 3 Suisses le Chouchou, Autumn-Winter 92-93.

L'Union des écrivaines et écrivains québécois: Text and illustrations from "Les jeunes au micro" by F. Gagnon from *Vidéo-Presse,* vol. XX, no. 9, May 1991. Copyright © 1991 by UNEQ. From "Résultats de l'enquête VIP" from *Vidéo-Presse,* December 1993. Copyright © 1993 by UNEQ.

Village des Sports: Advertisement, "Village des Sports: c'est l'fun, fun, fun!" from *Région de Québec.*

CHAPTER OPENER Background Photographs: Scott Van Osdol

TABLE OF CONTENTS: Page v HRW Photo by Sam Dudgeon, vi(tl), vi(bl), HRW Photo by Marty Granger/Edge Productions, vi(all remaining), HRW Photo by Scott Van Osdol; vii(tl), vii(tc), HRW Photo by Marty Granger/Edge Productions; vii(all remaining), HRW Photo by Scott Van Osdol; viii(inset), viii(tl), viii(br), HRW Photo by Marty Granger/Edge Productions; viii(bl), HRW Photo by Sam Dudgeon; viii(all remaining), HRW Photo by Scott Van Osdol; ix(tr), ix(bl), HRW Photo by Marty Granger/Edge Productions; ix(cr), ix(bc), ix(br), HRW Photo by Scott Van Osdol; ix(all remaining), HRW Photo by Sam Dudgeon; x(tl), x(br), HRW Photo by Marty Granger/Edge Productions; x(tr), HRW Photo; x(cr), x(bl), HRW Photo by Sam Dudgeon; x(all remaining), HRW Photo by Scott Van Osdol; xi(tc), xi(tr), HRW Photo by Marty Granger/Edge Productions; xi(cr), HRW Photo by Sam Dudgeon; xi(all remaining), HRW Photo by Scott Van Osdol; xii(tr), xii(bl), HRW Photo by Marty Granger/Edge Productions; xii(all remaining), HRW Photo by Scott Van Osdol; xiii(tr), xiii(br), HRW Photo by Louis Boireau/Edge Productions; xiii(all remaining), HRW Photo by Scott Van Osdol; xiv(tl), xiv(bl), HRW Photo by Marty Granger/Edge Productions; xiv(all remaining), HRW Photo by Scott Van Osdol; xv(tc), xv(br), HRW Photo by Marty Granger/Edge Productions; xv(all remaining), HRW Photo by Scott Van Osdol; xvi(tl), xvi(br), HRW Photo by Marty Granger/Edge Productions; xvi(all remaining), HRW Photo by Scott Van Osdol; xvii(tr), xvii(cl), HRW Photo by Marty Granger/Edge Productions; xvii(bc), HRW Photo by Sam Dudgeon; xvii(all remaining), HRW Photo by Scott Van Osdol.

Preliminary Chapter: Page v-1(tc), HRW Photo by Mark Antman; 1 (bc), HRW Photo by Marty Granger/Edge Productions; 1(tr), HRW Photo by Marty Granger/Edge Productions; (br), SuperStock; 2(tl), Sipa Press; 2(tr), Reuters/Bettmann; 2(c), Archive photos; 2(b), Vedat Acickalin/Sipa Press; 3(cl), J. M. Jimenez/Keystone/-Shooting Star; 3(cr), Kathy Willens/Wide World photos, Inc.; 3(b), Archive photos; 4(tl), HRW Photo by Sam Dudgeon; 4(tc), Barthelemy/Sipa Press; 4(tr), Arianespace/Sipa Press; 4(cl), 4(c), 4(cr), HRW Photo by Marty Granger/Edge Productions; 4(bl), Robert Frerck/Odyssey Productions; 4(bc), David R. Frazier/David R. Frazier photolibrary; 4(br), Derek Berwin/The Image Bank; 5(both), HRW Photo by Marty Granger/Edge Productions; 7(tl), Clay Myers/The Wildlife Collection; 7(tc), Leonard Lee Rue/FPG International; 7(tr), 7(bc), Tim Laman/The Wildlife Collection; 7(bl), Jack Swenson/The Wildlife Collection; 7(br), Martin Harvey/The Wildlife Collection; 10(tl), HRW Photo by Daniel Aubry; 10(tr), HRW Photo by Ken Lax; 10(br), HRW Photo by Louis Boireau/Edge Productions; 10(all remaining), HRW Photo by Marty Granger/Edge Productions.

UNIT ONE: Page 12-13, HRW Photo by Marty Granger/Edge Productions; 14-15(bckgd), Terry Qing/FPG International; 14 (tr), Tom Craig/FPG International; 14(cl), 14(br) HRW Photo by Marty Granger/Edge Productions. 15(all)/HRW Photo by Marty Granger/Edge Productions. Chapter One: Page 16-17(all), HRW Photo by Marty Granger/Edge Productions; 18(tr-both) HRW Photo by Louis Boireau/Edge Productions; 18(all remaining) HRW Photo by Marty Granger/Edge Productions. 19(all) HRW Photo by Marty Granger/Edge Productions. 21(tc), HRW Photo by Sam Dudgeon; 21(br), HRW Photo by Alan Oddie; 21(all remaining), HRW Photo by Marty Granger/Edge Productions; 22(l), HRW Photo by John Langford; 22(r), HRW Photo by Marty Granger/Edge Productions; 22(cl), HBJ photo by Mark Antman; 22(c), HRW Photo; 22(cr), IPA/The Image Works; 23-24(all), HRW Photo by Marty Granger/Edge Productions; 25(tr), Toussaint/Sipa Press; 30(all), HRW Photo by Marty

Granger/Edge Productions; 34(tl), HRW Photo by Sam Dudgeon; 34(tc), HRW Photo by Marty Granger/Edge Productions; 34(tr), Robert Brenner/PhotoEdit; 34(cl), HRW Photo by David Frazier; 34(c), Capretz/Harbrace photo; 34(cr), M. Antman/The Image Works; 34(bl), Lawrence Migdale/Stock Boston; 34(bc), HRW Photo by Ken Karp; 34(br), HBJ photo by Mark Antman; 34(b), R. Lucas/The Image Works; 36(t), The Picture Cube; 36(tl), Richard Hutchings/PhotoEdit; 36(c), David C. Bitters/The Picture Cube; 37(t), 37(b), HRW Photo by Russell Dian; 37(tl), HRW Photo by May Polycarpe; 37(c), R. Lucas/The Image Works; 38(cl), David Young-Wolff/PhotoEdit; 38(all remaining), HRW Photo by Marty Granger/Edge Productions. Chapter Two: Page 42-45(all), HRW photo by Marty Granger/Edge Productions; 56(l), HRW Photo by Louis Boireau/Edge Productions; 56(both), HRW Photo by Marty Granger/Edge Productions; Chapter Three: Page 66-69(all), HRW Photo by Marty Granger/Edge Productions; 71(t), HRW Photo; 71(all remaining), HRW Photo by Sam Dudgeon; 72-73(all), HRW Photo by Sam Dudgeon.; 75(l), HRW Photo by Louis Boireau/Edge Productions; 75(c), 75(r), HRW Photo by Marty Granger/Edge Productions; 78(all), HRW photo by Sam Dudgeon; 80-81(all), HRW Photo by Sam Dudgeon; 88(both), HRW Photo by Sam Dudgeon.

UNIT TWO: Page (90-91), J. A. Kraulis/Masterfile; 92(all), HRW Photo by Marty Granger/Edge Productions; 93(t), 93(b), HRW Photo by Marty Granger/Edge Productions; 93(cl), Wolfgang Kaehler; 93(cr), Jean-Guy Kerouac/Hervey Smyth, Vue de la Prise de Quebec, le septembre 1759, 35.9 x 47.8cm, Musée du Quebec, 78,375. Chapter Four: Page 94-95(all), HRW Photo by Marty Granger/Edge Productions; 96(tr) HRW Photo by Edge Productions; 97(all) HRW Photo by Marty Granger/Edge Productions; 99(all), HRW Photo by Marty Granger/Edge Productions; 100(tc), David Young-Wolff/PhotoEdit; 100(tr), HRW Photo by Sam Dudgeon; 100(cl), PhotoEdit; 100(bl), David Lissy/Leo de Wys; 100(bc), 100(br), HRW photo; 100(all remaining), HRW Photo by Marty Granger/Edge Productions; 103(l), 103(r), M. Jacob/The Image Works; 103(cl), Robert Fried/Robert Fried photography; 103(c), R. Lucas/The Image Works; 103(cr), Mat Jacob/The Image Works; 105(l), Robert Fried photography; 105(r), 105(cl), HRW Photo by Sam Dudgeon; 105(c), HBJ photo by May Polycarpe; 105(cr), HRW Photo by Marty Granger/Edge Productions; 109(l), HRW Photo/by Louis Boireau Edge Productions; 109(r), 109(c), HRW Photo by Marty Granger/Edge Productions.

UNIT THREE: Page 120-121(bckgd), Paul Steel/The Stock Market; 122(all), HRW Photo by Marty Granger/Edge Productions; 123(bl), Peter Menzel/Stock Boston; 123(all remaining), HRW Photo by Marty Granger/Edge Productions. Chapter Five: Page 124-127(all), HRW Photo by Marty Granger/Edge Productions; 134(l), 134(c), HRW Photo by Marty Granger/Edge Productions; 134(r), HRW Photo by Louis Boireau/Edge Productions; 138(l), 138(cl), HRW Photo by Russell Dian; 138(r), HRW Photo by Sam Dudgeon; 138(cr), HRW Photo by Robert Haynes; 142(t), HRW Photo by Stuart Cohen; 143(t), HRW Photo by Helena Kolda; 143(c), 143(b), Pomme de Pain; 143(br), Steven Mark Needham/Envision. Chapter Six: Page 148-149(all), HRW Photo by Marty Granger/Edge Productions; 150(tr), Sebastien Raymond/Sipa Press; 150-151(all remaining) HRW Photo by Marty Granger/Edge Productions; 154(bl), HRW Photo by Sam Dudgeon; 154(bc), Owen Franken/Stock Boston; 154(all remaining) HRW Photo by Marty Granger/Edge Productions; 156(top row), (1-3) HRW Photo by Marty Granger/Edge Productions; (4) Tabuteau/The Image Works; (center row) (1) Jean Paul Nacivet/Leo de Wys; (2) Greg Meadors/Stock Boston; (3-4) HRW Photo by Marty Granger/Edge Productions; (bottom row) (1) Robert Fried/Stock

Boston; (2) HRW Photo by Marty Granger/Edge Productions; (3) HBJ photo by Mark Antman; (4) R. Lucas/The Image Works; 158(l) HRW Photo by Louis Boireau/Edge Productions, 158(c), 158(r)/HRW Photo by Marty Granger/Edge Productions; 162(tl), Ulrike Welsch/PhotoEdit; 162(tr), HBJ photo by Mark Antman; 162(cr), HRW Photo by Marty Granger/Edge Productions; 170, HRW Photo by Capretz; 171, HRW Photo by Dianne Schrader. **Chapter Seven:** Page 174-175(all), HRW Photo by Marty Granger/Edge Productions; 176(cl), 176(cr), HRW photo by Edge Productions; 176(top), HRW Photo by Marty Granger/Edge Productions; 176(b), HRW Photo by Russell Dian; 177(b), HRW photo by Marty Granger/Edge Productions; 177(all remaining), HRW Photo by Edge productions; 178(tl), 178(bc) HRW Photo by Russell Dian; 178(all remaining), HRW Photo; 179(b), HRW Photo by Russell Dian; 180(Rows 1-2), HRW Photos; 180 (Row 3), (l) HRW Photo by Edge Productions, (2) HRW Photo by Marty Granger/Edge Productions, (3-5) HRW Photo by Russell Dian; 180 (Row 4), (l) HRW Photo by Cherie Mitschke; (2) HRW Photo by Marion Bermondy, (3) David Austen/Stock Boston; (4) John Lei/Stock Boston; 181(l), HRW Photo by Daniel Aubry; 181(r), HRW Photo by Sam Dudgeon; 181(cl), David Young-Wolff/PhotoEdit; 181(c), HRW Photo by May Polycarpe; 181(cr), Tony Freeman/PhotoEdit; 185(bc), Firooz Zahedi/The Kobal Collection; 185(br), TM © 20th Century Fox Film Corp/ 1992; 188(all), HRW Photo by Marty Granger/Edge Productions; 192(t), 192(b), Walter Chandoha; 192(c), HRW Photo; 193(t), 193(c), Walter Chandoha; 193(b), Gerard Lacz/Peter Arnold, Inc.

UNIT FOUR: Page 198-199, Nabil Zorkot/Pro Foto; 200(l), John Elk III/Bruce Coleman, Inc.; 200(tr), Nabil Zorkot/Pro Foto; 200(c), M. & E. Bernheim/Woodfin Camp & Associates; 201(all), Nabil Zorkot/Pro Foto. **Chapter Eight:** Page 202-205(all), HRW Photo by Louis Boireau/Edge Productions; 206(l), HRW Photo; 206(all remaining), HRW Photo by Louis Boireau/Edge Productions; 211(l), 211(r), HRW Photo by Marty Granger/Edge Productions 211(c) HRW Photo by Louis Boireau/Edge Productions; 215-216(all), HRW Photo by Louis Boireau/Edge Productions; 217(tl), HRW Photo by Lance Shriner; 217(tr), HRW Photo by Louis Boireau/Edge Productions; 217(bl), HRW Photo by Sam Dudgeon; 217(br), HRW Photo by Eric Beggs.

UNIT FIVE: Page 228-229, HRW Photo by Marty Granger/Edge Productions; 230(tr), HRW Photo by Cherie Mitschke; 230(cr), Erich Lessing/Art Resource; 230(bl), HRW Photo by Marty Granger/Edge Productions. **Chapter Nine:** Page 231(t), W. Gontscharoff/SuperStock; 231(cl), G. Carde/SuperStock; 231(b), HRW Photo by Marty Granger/Edge Productions; 232-235(all), HRW Photo by Marty Granger/Edge Productions; 236(r), Ermakoff/The Image Works; 236(all remaining), HRW Photo by Marty Granger/Edge Productions; 242(l), 242(r), HRW Photo by Marty Granger/Edge Productions; 242(c), Owen Franken/Stock Boston; 246(all), HRW Photo by Marty Granger/Edge Productions; 252(c), HRW Photo. **Chapter Ten:** Page 256-259(all), HRW Photo by Marty Granger/Edge Productions; 261(all), HRW Photo by Sam Dudgeon; 268(b), Paul Conselin/PhotoEdit; 269(c), 269(l), HRW Photo by Marty Granger/Edge Productions, 269(r), HRW Photo by Louis Boireau/Edge Productions; 273, HRW Photo by Sam Dudgeon; 276-277(all), HRW Photo by Sam Dudgeon; 278(l), 278(r), Don Iron/Sipa Press; 278(c), Barthelemy/Sipa Press; 280(l), 280(r), HRW Photo by Sam Dudgeon. **Chapter Eleven:** Page 282-283(all), HRW Photo by Marty Granger/Edge Productions; 284(tl), HRW Photo by May Polycarpe; 284(cl), David Florenz/Option Photo; 284 (all remaining), HRW

Photo by Marty Granger/Edge Productions; 285-286(all), HRW Photo by Marty Granger/Edge Productions; 292(c), 292(r) HRW Photo by Marty Granger/Edge Productions; 292(l) HRW Photo by Louis Boireau/Edge Productions; 295(l), 295(c), 295(r), HRW Photo by Marty Granger/Edge Productions; 295(b), Pierre Jaques/FOC photo; 297(both), HRW Photo by Marty Granger/Edge Productions; 298(cl) HRW Photo by Marty Granger/Edge Productions; 298(cr), Robert Fried/Stock Boston; 298(br), J. Messerschmidt/Leo de Wys; 298(bl), DeRichemond/The Image Works; 298(bc), Joachim Messer/Leo de Wys; 303(all), HRW Photo by Marty Granger/Edge Productions.

UNIT SIX: Page 306-309(all), HRW Photo by Marty Granger/Edge Productions. **Chapter Twelve:** Page 310-314(all), HRW Photo by Marty Granger/Edge Productions; 315(tl), Tony Freeman/PhotoEdit; 315(cl), HBJ photo by Patrick Courtault; 315(c), HBJ photo by Capretz; 315(cr), IPA/The Image Works; 315(bc), Robert Fried/Stock Boston; 315(all remaining), HRW Photo by Marty Granger/Edge Productions; 318(tl), 318(br), Chris Huxley/Leo deWys; 318(all remaining), HRW Photo by Marty Granger/Edge Productions; 321(cl), Helen Kolda/HRW Photo; 321(cr), HRW Photo by Sam Dudgeon/Duly authorized by CASTER-MAN, Belgium; 321(bc), HRW Photo by Russell Dian; 321(all remaining), HRW Photo by Sam Dudgeon; 322(tl), Elizabeth Zuckerman/PhotoEdit; 322(tr), Amy Etra/PhotoEdit; 322(c), HRW Photo by Louis Boreau/Edge Productions; 322(bl), Robert Rathe/Stock Boston; 322(bc), Dean Abramson/Stock Boston; 322(br), Antman/The Image Works; 322(all remaining), HRW Photo by Marty Granger/Edge Productions; 324(all), HRW Photo by Marty Granger/Edge Productions; 328(c), Chris Huxley/Leo deWys; 330(bckgd), HRW Photo by Mark Antman; 332(l), 332(cl), 332(cr) HRW Photo by Marty Granger/Edge Productions; 332(r), Chris Huxley/Leo de Wys.

ILLUSTRATION AND CARTOGRAPHY CREDITS

Beier, Ellen: 9
Bouchard, Jocelyne: 11, 23, 26, 102, 118, 155, 164, 180, 182, 220, 254
Bylo, Andrew: 47, 129, 131, 207, 212, 245
Cooper, Holly: i, vi, ix, xiii, xvii
de Masson, Anne: 317, 319, 320, 326, 327, 332, 334
Foissy, Jean-Pierre: 82, 140, 159, 161, 163, 186, 237, 238, 264, 265, 270, 274, 296, 321
Garnier, Pascal: 52, 184, 189, 190, 196
Kimani, George: 209, 220
Krone, Mike: 192-193
Larvor, Yves: 27, 31, 146, 157, 214, 226, 262, 280, 294, 304
Loppé, Michel: 73, 81, 83, 101, 108, 218, 219, 243, 262, 271, 293
Maestracci, Guy: 55, 139, 157, 182, 189, 241, 272, 288
Meyer, Camille: 28, 133, 208, 239, 289
Moore, Russell: 287
Petrus, Keith: 54
Rio, Vincent: 22, 33, 72, 79, 130, 132, 179, 183, 187, 190, 263
Roberts, Bruce: 6, 48, 50, 64, 105, 291
Stanley, Anne: 325, 328
Stevens, Brian: 48, 58, 74, 76, 106, 160, 185, 248, 268, 287, 323